PERSPECTIVES ON 42

EDITED BY **BILL NOWLIN** AND **GLEN SPARKS**
ASSOCIATE EDITORS: **LEN LEVIN** AND **CARL RIECHERS**

Society for American Baseball Research, Inc.
Phoenix, AZ

Jackie
Perspectives on 42
Edited by Bill Nowlin and Glen Sparks
Associate editors: Len Levin and Carl Riechers
Society for American Baseball Research, Inc.
Phoenix, AZ

> Note on usage: In April 1947, when Jackie Robinson took the field with the Brooklyn Dodgers, his debut in the National League was considered by the newspapers of the day, by those in the game, and by Robinson himself as breaking the "color line" in what was then defined as major-league baseball. In the year 2020, the definition of what constitutes a major league was expanded by today's Major League Baseball to include a number of leagues that operated as what have been known as the "Negro Leagues." Racial discrimination prevented many of the Negro Leagues' players from joining the National and American Leagues on the basis of their merit. In the various articles in this book, the words "major league" or "major leagues" often appear. The usage will almost always reflect the understanding of Robinson's day. As we read through these articles, we are confident that all will appreciate the significance of Robinson's role in desegregation.

ISBN 978-1-970159-50-9 ebook
ISBN 978-1-970159-51-6 paperback
Library of Congress Control Number (LCCN): 2021902531

Copyright © 2021 Society for American Baseball Research, Inc.
All rights reserved. Reproduction in whole or in part without permission is prohibited.
Book design: Rachael E. Sullivan
Society for American Baseball Research
Cronkite School at ASU
555 N. Central Ave. #416
Phoenix, AZ 85004
Phone: (602) 496-1460
Web: www.sabr.org
Facebook: Society for American Baseball Research
Twitter: @SABR

CONTENTS

1. INTRODUCTION 7

2. JACKIE ROBINSON 9
   By Rick Swaine

3. MY HERO - JACKIE ROBINSON 16
   by Larry Lester

4. RACHEL ROBINSON 17
   by Ralph Carhart

5. BEFORE JACKIE ROBINSON: BASEBALL'S CIVIL RIGHTS MOVEMENT 27
   by Peter Dreier

6. JACKIE ROBINSON: THE BEST ATHLETE ON THE WEST COAST 38
   by Vince Guerrieri

7. PACIFIC COAST CONFERENCE FOOTBALL TITLE GAME 42
   DECEMBER 9, 1939: UCLA 0, USC 0, AT THE LOS ANGELES COLISEUM
   by Bryan Steverson

8. "A DISCIPLINARIAN COACH": JACKIE ROBINSON'S LITTLE-KNOWN STINT COACHING COLLEGE BASKETBALL 46
   by Eric Enders

9. THERE BUT FOR THE GRACE OF GOD 49
   by Bryan Steverson

10. LIEUTENANT JACKIE ROBINSON, MORALE OFFICER, UNITED STATES ARMY 51
    by J.M. Casper

11. JACKIE ROBINSON IN 1945: FROM BOSTON "TRYOUT" TO A NEGRO LEAGUES STAR 61
    by Bob LeMoine

12. HAPPY HELPING? INSIDE COMMISSIONER CHANDLER'S ROLE IN JACKIE ROBINSON'S GREAT QUEST 68
    by Joe Cox

13. JACKIE ROBINSON, JERSEY CITY, AND HIS FIRST GAME IN ORGANIZED BASEBALL 73
    by John Burbridge

14. A GREAT LEAP FORWARD: THE VIEW FROM MONTREAL OF JACKIE ROBINSON AND THE MONTREAL ROYALS 75
    by Jack Anderson

15. JACKIE ROBINSON - HISTORY MADE IN 1946 AT THE JUNIOR WORLD SERIES 86
    by Marc J. Steiner

16. THE JACKIE ROBINSON BARNSTORMING TOUR OF 1946 90
    by Alan Cohen

17. JACKIE ROBINSON'S 1947 BREAKTHROUGH BEGAN IN HAVANA 95
    by César Brioso

18. I MET JACKIE ROBINSON'S FIRST MAJOR-LEAGUE MANAGER 100
    by Wayne Soini

19. THE "STRIKE" AGAINST JACKIE ROBINSON: TRUTH OR MYTH? 103
    by Warren Corbett

20. JACKIE ROBINSON AND THE *KANSAS CITY CALL* 108
    by William A. Young

21. FORD FRICK AND JACKIE ROBINSON: THE ENABLER 114
by Dave Bohmer

22. JACKIE ROBINSON PLAYS HIS FIRST EXHIBITION GAME FOR THE MONTREAL ROYALS 122
MARCH 17, 1946: BROOKLYN DODGERS 7, MONTREAL ROYALS 2, AT CITY ISLAND BALLPARK, DAYTONA BEACH, FLORIDA
by Bob Webster

23. ROBINSON LEADS ROYALS ROMP IN 1946 REGULAR-SEASON DEBUT 125
APRIL 18, 1946: MONTREAL ROYALS 14, JERSEY CITY GIANTS 1, AT ROOSEVELT STADIUM, JERSEY CITY
by Frederick C. Bush

24. JACKIE ROBINSON LEADS MONTREAL TO THRILLING 10-INNING VICTORY OVER LOUISVILLE 129
OCTOBER 2, 1946: MONTREAL ROYALS 6, LOUISVILLE COLONELS 5, AT DE LORIMIER STADIUM, MONTREAL
by Gary Belleville

25. ROBINSON'S HEROICS PUT MONTREAL ON VERGE OF FIRST JUNIOR WORLD SERIES TITLE 132
OCTOBER 3, 1946: MONTREAL ROYALS 5, LOUISVILLE COLONELS 3, AT DE LORIMIER STADIUM, MONTREAL
by Gary Belleville

26. JACKIE ROBINSON, ROYAL AT EBBETS FIELD 135
APRIL 10, 1947: MONTREAL ROYALS 4, BROOKLYN DODGERS 3, AT EBBETS FIELD, BROOKLYN, NEW YORK
by Steven C. Weiner

27. JACKIE ROBINSON DEBUTS FOR DODGERS AT EBBETS FIELD 138
APRIL 11, 1947: BROOKLYN DODGERS 14, NEW YORK YANKEES 6, AT EBBETS FIELD, BROOKLYN
by Steven C. Weiner

28. JACKIE ROBINSON'S MAJOR-LEAGUE DEBUT 141
APRIL 15, 1947: BROOKLYN DODGERS 5, BOSTON BRAVES 3, AT EBBETS FIELD, BROOKLYN
by Lyle Spatz

29. THE FIRST OF 1,518: JACKIE ROBINSON GETS HIS FIRST MAJOR-LEAGUE HIT 144
APRIL 17, 1947: BROOKLYN DODGERS 12, BOSTON BRAVES 6, AT EBBETS FIELD, BROOKLYN
By Kevin Larkin

30. ROBINSON TALLIES FIRST CAREER HOMER AND FIRST RBI AGAINST RIVAL GIANTS 146
APRIL 18, 1947: NEW YORK GIANTS 10, BROOKLYN DODGERS 4, AT THE POLO GROUNDS, NEW YORK
by Brian Wright

31. JACKIE ROBINSON'S FIRST MEETING WITH BEN CHAPMAN 149
APRIL 22, 1947: BROOKLYN DODGERS 1, PHILADELPHIA PHILLIES 0, AT EBBETS FIELD, BROOKLYN
by Alan Cohen

32. RACIAL SLURS WON'T STOP JACKIE ROBINSON 152
MAY 9, 1947: PHILADELPHIA PHILLIES 6, BROOKLYN DODGERS 5 (11 INNINGS), AT SHIBE PARK, PHILADELPHIA
by Alan Cohen

33. ROBINSON'S BASERUNNING AND HODGES' HOMER LIFT DODGERS 155
JUNE 18, 1947: BROOKLYN DODGERS 5, CHICAGO CUBS 3, AT WRIGLEY FIELD, CHICAGO
by Paul Hofmann

34. JACKIE ROBINSON STEALS HOME FOR THE FIRST TIME 157
JUNE 24, 1947: BROOKLYN DODGERS 4, PITTSBURGH PIRATES 2, AT FORBES FIELD, PITTSBURGH
by Steven Kuehl

35. ROOKIE ROBINSON'S HIT STREAK REACHES 20 GAMES 160
JULY 3, 1947: NEW YORK GIANTS 19, BROOKLYN DODGERS 2, AT EBBETS FIELD, BROOKLYN
by Mike Huber

36. CARDINALS BEAT DODGERS IN EXTRA INNINGS; ENOS SLAUGHTER SPIKES JACKIE ROBINSON 163
AUGUST 20, 1947: ST. LOUIS CARDINALS 3, BROOKLYN DODGERS 2 (12 INNINGS), AT EBBETS FIELD, BROOKLYN
by Thomas J. Brown Jr.

37. ROBINSON'S FIRST GRAND SLAM WINS IN A WALKOFF 166
JUNE 24, 1948: BROOKLYN DODGERS 6, PITTSBURGH PIRATES 2, AT EBBETS FIELD, BROOKLYN
by Bill Nowlin

38. JACKIE ROBINSON HITS REVERSE NATURAL CYCLE AS DODGERS BEAT CARDINALS 168
AUGUST 29, 1948: BROOKLYN DODGERS 12, ST. LOUIS CARDINALS 7, AT SPORTSMAN'S PARK III, ST. LOUIS
by Michael Huber

39. JACKIE ROBINSON HAS THREE HITS WITH A HOME RUN ON OPENING DAY 170

APRIL 19, 1949: BROOKLYN DODGERS 10, NEW YORK GIANTS 3, AT EBBETS FIELD, BROOKLYN

by Nathan Bierma

40. JACKIE GETS CAREER-HIGH SIX RBIS IN DODGERS' LAMBASTING OF CARDINALS ... 173

MAY 21, 1949: BROOKLYN DODGERS 15, ST. LOUIS CARDINALS 6, AT SPORTSMAN'S PARK, ST. LOUIS

by Richard Cuicchi

41. JACKIE ROBINSON RIPS TWO HOME RUNS VS. PITTSBURGH 175

MAY 24, 1949: BROOKLYN DODGERS 6, PITTSBURGH PIRATES 1, AT FORBES FIELD, PITTSBURGH

by Blake W. Sherry

42. A "WEIRD AFFAIR" AND SLUGFEST IN FLATBUSH 177

JUNE 24, 1950: BROOKLYN DODGERS 21, PITTSBURGH PIRATES 12, AT EBBETS FIELD, BROOKLYN

by Glen Sparks

43. JACKIE'S PERFECT DAY SENDS DODGERS ON WIN STREAK 180

JULY 21, 1951: BROOKLYN DODGERS 3, ST. LOUIS CARDINALS 2, AT EBBETS FIELD, BROOKLYN

by Richard Cuicchi

44. JACKIE ROBINSON SAVES THE DAY AND THE SEASON 182

SEPTEMBER 30, 1951: BROOKLYN DODGERS 9, PHILADELPHIA PHILLIES 8 (14 INNINGS), AT SHIBE PARK, PHILADELPHIA

by C. Paul Rogers III **PLAYOFF FOR NL PENNANT KNOTTED AT ONE GAME APIECE   185**

OCTOBER 2, 1951: BROOKLYN DODGERS 10, NEW YORK GIANTS 0, AT THE POLO GROUNDS, NEW YORK

by Alan Cohen

45. A WET ALL-STAR GAME AT SHIBE 188

JULY 8, 1952: NATIONAL LEAGUE 3, AMERICAN LEAGUE 2, AT SHIBE PARK, PHILADELPHIA

by Paul E. Doutrich

46. JACKIE AND DODGERS END SLUMP IN HOME-RUN BARRAGE 191
47. SEPTEMBER 15, 1952: BROOKLYN DODGERS 11, CINCINNATI REDS 5, AT EBBETS FIELD, BROOKLYN

by Gregory H. Wolf

48. ROBINSON, ERSKINE LEAD DODGERS TO VICTORY 194

SEPTEMBER 20, 1952: BROOKLYN DODGERS 1, BOSTON BRAVES 0, AT BRAVES FIELD, BOSTON

by Glen Sparks

49. JOE BLACK AND TREMENDOUS DEFENSE BEAT YANKEES IN GAME ONE OF 1952 WORLD SERIES 197

OCTOBER 1, 1952: BROOKLYN DODGERS 4, NEW YORK YANKEES 2, AT EBBETS FIELD, BROOKLYN

by Brian M. Frank

50. ROBINSON'S BIG DAY HELPS DODGERS COMPLETE HOME SWEEP OF CARDINALS .. 200

SEPTEMBER 1, 1953: BROOKLYN DODGERS 12, ST. LOUIS CARDINALS 5, AT EBBETS FIELD, BROOKLYN

by Mark Simon

51. JACKIE ROBINSON STEALS HOME VS PITTSBURGH 202

APRIL 23, 1954: BROOKLYN DODGERS 6, PITTSBURGH PIRATES 5, AT FORBES FIELD, PITTSBURGH

by Blake W. Sherry

52. JACKIE ROBINSON STEALS HOME: THE CALL, THE MEANING 204

SEPTEMBER 28, 1955: NEW YORK YANKEES 6, BROOKLYN DODGERS 5, WORLD SERIES GAME ONE, YANKEE STADIUM, NEW YORK

by Steven C. Weiner

53. BROOKLYN DODGERS WIN NL PENNANT ON FINAL DAY OF SEASON 207

SEPTEMBER 30, 1956: BROOKLYN DODGERS 8, PITTSBURGH PIRATES 6, AT EBBETS FIELD, BROOKLYN

by Thomas J. Brown Jr.

54. **LABINE HURLS EXTRA-INNING SHUTOUT TO FORCE GAME SEVEN** 209
    OCTOBER 9, 1956: BROOKLYN DODGERS 1, NEW YORK YANKEES 0 (10 INNINGS), AT EBBETS FIELD, BROOKLYN GAME SIX OF THE WORLD SERIES
    by Brian M. Frank

55. **SAYONARA JACKIE ROBINSON:** 213
    HOW AN AMERICAN HERO FINISHED HIS CAREER IN JAPAN
    by Robert K. Fitts

56. **JACKIE ROBINSON CALLS IT QUITS** 219
    by Robert Nash

57. **JACKIE ROBINSON, ALL-STAR** 223
    by Mark S. Sternman

58. **JACKIE ROBINSON AND THE WORLD SERIES** 225
    by Steven C. Weiner

59. **JACKIE ROBINSON'S STEALS OF HOME** 230
    by Bill Nowlin

---

60. **ANALYZING JACKIE ROBINSON AS A SECOND BASEMAN** 239
    by Mike Huber

61. **JACKIE ROBINSON AND OWNERS** 243
    by Andy McCue

62. **MANAGING HISTORY: JACKIE ROBINSON AND MANAGERS** 246
    by Joe Cox

63. **JACKIE ROBINSON'S FAITH SUSTAINED HIM DURING UNRELENTING TURMOIL** 250
    by Chris Lamb

64. **JACKIE ROBINSON AND THE DECLINE OF THE NEGRO LEAGUES** 254
    by Nathan Bierma

65. **JACKIE ROBINSON AND CIVIL RIGHTS: FROM 1947 UNTIL HIS DEATH** 257
    by Leslie Heaphy

66. **THE BLACK KNIGHT: A POLITICAL PORTRAIT OF JACKIE ROBINSON** 263
    by Steven K. Wisensale

67. **JACKIE ROBINSON, REPUBLICAN** 270
    by Jeff English

68. **JOURNEY TO JUSTICE** 278
    THE CONVERGING PATHS OF JACK ROOSEVELT ROBINSON AND DR. MARTIN LUTHER KING JR.
    by Bryan Steverson

69. **JACKIE'S LAST STAND: JACKIE ROBINSON'S LAST PUBLIC APPEARANCE AND HIS APPEAL FOR THE INTEGRATION OF MAJOR-LEAGUE BASEBALL MANAGEMENT** 281
    by Richard J. Puerzer

70. **"THE NECESSITIES" AL CAMPANIS'S MOMENT OF TRUTH** 285
    by Warren Corbett

71. **OF MEMORY AND MYSTERY GUESTS: JACKIE ROBINSON, SOUPY SALES, AND *WHAT'S MY LINE*?** 289
    by David Krell

72. **JACKIE ROBINSON AND JOURNAL SQUARE** 291
    by David Krell

73. **NOT AN EASY TALE TO TELL: JACKIE ROBINSON ON STAGE AND SCREEN** 293
    by Ralph Carhart

74. **REACHING THE NEXT GENERATION: JACKIE ROBINSON'S STORY IN CHILDREN'S AND YOUNG ADULT LITERATURE** 302
    by Mary E. Corey

75. **THE JACKIE ROBINSON FOUNDATION:** 309
    A Legacy of Excellence and Impact by Mark Harnischfeger

76. **CONTRIBUTORS** 315

INTRODUCTION

No one can doubt the immense courage shown by Jackie Robinson when he took his position at first base at Ebbets Field on Tuesday afternoon, April 15, 1947. The first play of the game was a groundball to third base, a throw across the diamond to Robinson at first base, and the first putout of the game.

It wasn't just the one moment, of course, but the ongoing import of what his presence on the field meant. Robinson was the first Black American to play what was then defined as major-league baseball at a time when baseball was dominant in American culture – truly the national pastime, but an institution that had been segregated by race.

Challenges to racism have always been fraught with peril. A generation later, Rev. Martin Luther King was shot and killed as he stood on a hotel-room balcony in Memphis. He was one among many who have lost their lives in the struggle for civil rights. More than 50 years later, and nearly 75 years after Robinson's debut, Black citizens of the United States still suffer discrimination and obstacles and still find their very lives more in danger than do many of their fellow Americans.

To be a pioneer in 1947 required bravery. In some respects, baseball led the way to a more integrated society. Even after Jackie Robinson's debut, however, it took 12 more years before every one of the 16 teams in the American and National Leagues integrated. Robinson had by then completed his 10-year Hall of Fame playing career. The six-time All-Star with a lifetime batting average of .309 and an on-base percentage of .409 has baseball statistics that rightly place him in Cooperstown. He won the first Rookie of the Year Award and, two years later, the National League Most Valuable Player honor. Robinson played on six pennant winners and in the World Series in 1955.

Perhaps it is true that celebrating Jackie Robinson's courageous role in integration can sometimes reduce him to a symbol, and oversimplify his grappling with the complex racial issues of his day, allowing him to become a convenient and self-congratulatory icon celebrated by Major League Baseball today. But, in fact, he was – and remains – an important symbol, and a very meaningful and inspirational one. Certainly, there are myths related to Jackie Robinson. That comes with legend.

There is no question that there was another side to his breaking the color barrier, to be followed by Larry Doby and others. There was gain, but there was loss as well: the vibrant Negro Leagues lasted only a very few more years after that.

Our thought in assembling this book was not to take a particular tack, or drive any narrative, but simply to collect a number of articles and essays that appreciate various aspects of the life and accomplishments of Jackie Robinson.

Almost all of the articles in this book were written for the book. Some 54 members of the Society for American Baseball Research (SABR) took time out as SABR begins to turn 50 and contributed their work as authors and editors to bring together a book appreciating the career and the life of this exceptional man.

Jackie Robinson with his Hall of Fame plaque.

JACKIE ROBINSON

By Rick Swaine

Jackie Robinson is perhaps the most historically significant baseball player ever, ranking with Babe Ruth in terms of his impact on the national pastime. Ruth changed the way baseball was played; Jackie Robinson changed the way Americans thought. When Robinson took the field for the Brooklyn Dodgers on April 15, 1947, more than 60 years of racial segregation in major-league baseball came to an end. He was the first acknowledged Black player to perform in the major leagues in the twentieth century and went on to be the first to win a batting title, the first to win the Most Valuable Player award, and the first to be inducted into the Baseball Hall of Fame. He won major-league baseball's first official Rookie of the Year award and was the first baseball player, Black or White, to be featured on a United States postage stamp.

The raw statistics only scratch the surface in evaluating Jackie Robinson as a ballplayer. Because of institutionalized racism and World War II, he did not play his first big-league game until he was 28 years old, and therefore his major-league career spanned only 10 seasons. His lifetime batting average was a solid .311, but because of the brevity of his career, his cumulative statistics are relatively unimpressive by Hall of Fame standards.

But in what would be considered his prime years, ages 28 to 34, Robinson hit .319 and averaged more than 110 runs scored per season. He drove in an average of 85 runs, and his average of nearly 15 home runs per season was outstanding for a middle infielder of that era. And he averaged 24 stolen bases a season for a power-laden team that didn't need him to run very often.

Colorfully described as a tiger in the field and a lion at bat, the right-handed-hitting Robinson crowded the plate and dared opposing hurlers to dust him off — a challenge they frequently accepted. He was an excellent bunter, good at the sacrifice and always a threat to lay one down for a hit. Not known as a home-run hitter, he displayed line-drive power to all fields, had a good eye for the strike zone, and rarely struck out. For his entire big-league career, he drew 740 walks and struck out only 291 times — an extremely impressive ratio.

Second base was Robinson's best position. In a 1987 "Player's Choice" survey, he was voted the greatest second baseman of his era despite having played there regularly for only five seasons. Though not a smooth glove man in the classic sense, he was sure-handed and possessed good range and instincts. He made up for an average arm by standing his ground on double plays and getting rid of the ball quickly. Robinson also displayed his versatility by playing regularly at first base, at third base, and in left field when the needs of the team dictated it.

It was running the bases, however, where Robinson's star shined brightest. He was a dynamo on the basepaths — fast, clever, daring, and rough. He was the most dangerous base runner since Ty Cobb, embarrassing and intimidating the opposition into beating themselves with mental and physical errors. Former teammate and big-league manager Bobby Bragan, who initially objected to Jackie's presence on the Dodgers, called him the best he ever saw at getting called safe after being caught in rundown situations. He created havoc by taking impossibly long leads, jockeying back and forth, and threatening to steal on every pitch. His mere presence on base was enough to upset the most steely-nerved veteran hurlers.

Robinson revived the art of stealing home, successfully making it 19 times in his career — tied with Frankie Frisch for the most since World War I. At the age of 35 in 1954, he became the first National Leaguer to steal his way around the bases in 26 years, and a year later he became one of only 12 men to steal home in the World Series.

Throughout his career, Jackie Robinson was a fearless competitor. As Leo Durocher, first his manager and later an archrival, so elegantly phrased it, "You want a guy that comes to play. But (Robinson) didn't just come to play. He came to beat you. He came to stuff the damn bat right up your ass."[1]

Jack Roosevelt Robinson was born on January 31, 1919, in Cairo, Georgia, a sleepy Southern town near the Florida border. Jackie was the youngest of five children, four boys and a girl, born to impoverished sharecroppers Jerry and Mallie Robinson. Jerry Robinson deserted the family six months after Jackie

Jackie

was born. Mallie Robinson, a strong, devoutly religious woman, moved the struggling family across the country by rail to Pasadena, California, in 1920 when Jackie was 14 months old. She worked as a domestic to support her family; leftovers from the kitchens of families she worked for often constituted their daily diet.

With the help of a welfare agency, the Robinson family purchased a home in a predominantly White Pasadena neighborhood, where neighbors immediately petitioned to get rid of the newcomers and even offered to buy them out. When those ploys failed the family was harassed for several years. The Robinson boys often had to fight to defend themselves, and young Jackie was involved in his share of scrapes with White youths and had some run-ins with authorities.

Jackie's athletic talent became evident at an early age. But he wasn't the only gifted athlete in the family. His older brother Mack became a world-class track star, finishing second in the 200-yard dash to Jesse Owens in the 1936 Olympics. But after Olympic stardom and college, the only job Mack Robinson could find was janitorial work for the City of Pasadena. It was a position he soon lost. As in most of the country at that time, Jim Crow rules prevailed in Pasadena. Black citizens were permitted to use the city's public swimming pool only one day a week. When a judge ordered full access to the pool for Black citizens, the city fathers responded by firing Black employees, including Mack Robinson.

After starring in baseball, football, basketball, and track at Muir Technical High School and Pasadena Junior College, Jackie declined many other offers to enroll at the University of California at Los Angeles, near his Pasadena home. Robinson gained national fame at UCLA in 1940 and 1941. He became the school's first four-letter man and was called the "Jim Thorpe of his race" for his multisport skills.[2] Sharing rushing duties with Kenny Washington, who later became one of the first Black men to play in the National Football League, Jackie averaged 11-plus yards per carry as a junior. *Sports Weekly* called him "the greatest ball carrier on the gridiron today."[3] On the basketball court Jackie led the Pacific Coast Conference in scoring as a junior and as a senior.

Although he wasn't named to the first, second, or third all-conference teams, one coach called him "the best basketball player in the United States."[4] Already the holder of the national junior college long-jump record, he captured the NCAA long-jump title and probably would have gone to the 1940 Olympics had they not been canceled by the war in Europe. In addition, he won swimming championships, reached the semifinals of the national Negro tennis tournament, and was the UCLA Bruins' regular shortstop. Baseball was probably Robinson's weakest sport at the university, although he'd been voted the most valuable player in Southern California junior college baseball.

Financial problems at home forced Robinson to drop out of college in his senior year a few credits short of graduation. He took a job as an athletic coach for the National Youth Administration and played semipro football for the Los Angeles Bulldogs. In the fall of 1941, he signed on to play professional football with the Honolulu Bears. Already a gate attraction and a hero in the Black community, he got top billing as "the sensational all-American halfback."

Upon returning home from Hawaii shortly after Pearl Harbor, Robinson was drafted into the Army in 1942. Stationed at Fort Riley, Kansas, he was originally denied entry into Officer Candidate School despite his college background. Intervention by a fellow soldier, boxing great Joe Louis, who was also stationed at the base, managed to get the decision reversed. Yet, Jackie was not allowed to play on the segregated camp baseball team, which infuriated him so much that he refused to play on the football team even when superior officers pressured him to do so. After OCS, Robinson was appointed morale officer for the Black troops at Fort Riley and won concessions for them that predictably angered a few higher-ups in command.

Reassigned to Ford Hood, Texas, Jackie continued to be controversial. On July 6, 1944 he defied a White bus driver's orders to move to the back of the bus "where the coloreds belonged." When the base provost marshal and military police supported the driver, Robinson objected vehemently and was subject to court-martial. Facing a dishonorable discharge, Jackie prevailed at the hearing. But the Army had had enough of the controversial young Black lieutenant and quickly mustered him out with an honorable discharge.

It's ironic that Jackie Robinson's difficulties with White authority in the military led directly to his rise to the top of Branch Rickey's list of candidates to break baseball's color barrier. Rickey, the orchestrator of Organized Baseball's desegregation, was the president, general manager, and a part-owner of the Brooklyn Dodgers. Rickey's scouts had been surreptitiously scouring the Negro Leagues for major-league talent for some time before tapping Robinson to break the unwritten, and diligently enforced, gentlemen's agreement that banned Blacks from participating in Organized Baseball.

Rickey was looking for a Black pioneer who — in addition to possessing the requisite talent — was educated, sober, and accustomed to competing with and against White athletes. Robinson met those conditions. He grew up in a racially mixed environment, attended school with White classmates, and matriculated at UCLA. He'd been an officer in the military. He was well-spoken, personable, and comfortable in front of crowds. He had experienced the glare of the spotlight and reveled in it. Also extremely important to the pious Rickey was the fact that Robinson was a nonsmoker and nondrinker. Nor was he a womanizer; he was planning to marry his college sweetheart, Rachel Annetta Isum. In addition, Jackie was a Methodist, as was Rickey, and he coincidentally shared a birthday with Branch Rickey Jr. Jackie and Rachel were married in Los Angeles on February 10, 1946.

Certainly there were other Black ballplayers who possessed the qualifications Rickey sought. Monte Irvin and Larry Doby were two obvious candidates. But when Rickey sent his scouts to scour the nation for the best Black player, Irvin and Doby were overseas, still in the armed forces. Robinson, though he was far from being considered the best player in Negro baseball, was available due to the early termination of his own military obligation.

After his discharge, Robinson had joined the Kansas City Monarchs of the Negro American League for the 1945 season. The Monarchs, one of the most successful franchises in the Negro Leagues, had been ravaged by the manpower demands of the war, but their roster still included veteran stars Ted "Double Duty" Radcliffe, Hilton Smith, and Satchel Paige. Flashy-fielding veteran Jesse Williams moved over to second base to make room for Jackie at shortstop. Though Robinson hit well over .300 and showed speed and power as a rookie, he disliked the nomadic and often boisterous barnstorming life and was incensed by the Jim Crow laws that the Monarchs often encountered on the road.

On October 23, 1945, it was announced to the world that Robinson had signed a contract to play baseball for the Montreal Royals of the International League, the top minor-league team in the Dodgers organization. Robinson had actually signed a few months earlier. In that now-legendary meeting, Rickey extracted a promise that Jackie would hold his sharp tongue and quick fists in exchange for the opportunity to break Organized Baseball's color barrier.

The integration movement in general had picked up steam during World War II as Black American soldiers fought and died beside Whites. In fact, the decade leading up to Robinson's signing had been marked by significant progress in efforts to gain equal rights for minorities in all facets of life. Yet the moguls running major-league baseball stubbornly resisted efforts to integrate the sport, refusing to consider Black players even as the talent pool was depleted by the war and one-armed and one-legged players could be found among the old-timers, teenagers, and 4-Fs gracing big-league rosters.

But in November 1944, longtime Baseball Commissioner Kenesaw Mountain Landis, who was generally thought to be against integration, died of a heart attack. Landis's passing was the break Branch Rickey needed to begin implementing his plan to integrate the Dodgers.

When Robinson's signing was announced, the news was heralded in Black newspapers and generally received positive reviews in national publications despite objections and attacks from predictable quarters. But Rickey and the Dodgers faced near-unanimous disapproval from the Organized Baseball establishment. After the initial furor died down, a campaign to downplay Robinson's talent and the import of the event began. The *New York Daily News* rated Robinson's chances of making the grade as 1,000 to 1. An editorial in *The Sporting News* deemed Robinson a player of Class C ability and predicted, "The waters of competition in the International League will flood far over his head."[5] Star pitcher Bob Feller of the Cleveland Indians said that Robinson had "football shoulders and couldn't hit an inside pitch to save his neck."[6]

Muscularly built with a thick neck and wide shoulders, Robinson did look more like a halfback than an infielder. He suffered from rickets as a child and walked with a pigeon-toed gait, but on the diamond he moved with amazing quickness. He stood 5-feet-11 and weighed 190 to 195 pounds in his prime, although he thickened noticeably in the latter stages of his career. In the decades prior to Robinson's entry into Organized Baseball, there were several major leaguers whose skin tone caused doubts about their racial background. There could be no doubt about ebony-skinned Jackie Robinson. Columnist John Crosby called him "the blackest black man, as well as one of the handsomest, I ever saw."[7]

Plagued by a sore arm during the Royals' 1946 spring training camp, Jackie performed poorly, generating numerous "I told you so" claims. But when Montreal opened the season on April 18, 1946, against the Jersey City Giants at Roosevelt Stadium in Jersey City, Robinson was playing second base and hitting second in the batting order.

The first twentieth-century appearance by an acknowledged Black player in Organized Baseball was a preview of things to come. In front of a packed house, Jackie lashed out four hits and scored four times to lead Montreal to a 14–1 victory. After grounding out in his first at-bat, he blasted a three-run homer over the left-field wall in the third inning. In the fifth inning he bunted for a hit, stole second, and made a daring play to take third on a grounder to the third baseman. From third base he danced far off the bag, darting back and forth and bluffing a steal until the harried pitcher balked him home. Two innings later, he singled sharply to right field and stole second base again before scoring on a triple. In the eighth Jackie again bunted safely. He once again took an extra base, advancing from first to third on an infield single, and again scored by provoking a balk by the Jersey City hurler.

The next day, the headline in the *Pittsburgh Courier* read: "Jackie Stole the Show."[8] According to Joe Bostic of New York City's *Amsterdam News*, "He did everything but help the ushers seat the crowd."[9]

Baseball's defense for keeping the game segregated hinged primarily on two points. The first was the contention that there just weren't any Black players good enough to merit a shot at the majors at the time. The second centered on financial concerns — the fear that White fans wouldn't pay to watch Negro players and didn't want to sit in the stands beside Black fans. There was also much feigned concern about the financial impact on the established Negro Leagues.

But Jackie Robinson's first year in Organized Baseball emphatically dispelled those tired excuses. He was a sensation on the field, the Royals dominated the International League, and the turnstiles hummed. Thanks to Jackie, the Royals established a new attendance record in Montreal, and his impact on the road was even greater, as attendance at Royals games in other International League cities almost tripled over the previous year. More than a million people came to watch Robinson and the Royals perform that year, an amazing figure for the minor leagues at the time.

For the season Robinson led the International League with a .349 batting average and scored 113 runs in 124 games to pace the circuit in that department as well. His 40 stolen bases were the second highest total in the league and he led the league's second basemen in fielding. Jackie led the Royals to the International League pennant, by a 19 1/2-game margin, and to victory in the Little World Series. After the Series, ecstatic fans wanted to hoist Jackie on their shoulders in celebration, but Jackie had a plane to catch. They chased him for three blocks, prompting a journalist to observe, "It was probably the only day in history that a black man ran from a white mob with love instead of hate on its mind."[10]

In preparation for the 1947 campaign the Brooklyn Dodgers and their top farm clubs set up spring training camp in Havana, Cuba. Based on his performance at Montreal it seemed a foregone conclusion that Robinson would get a chance with the parent team, but he was still listed on the Royals' roster when the workouts started. Rickey chose Havana to avoid the racial attitudes of the spring training sites in the South. His plan was to allow the Dodgers' veterans to gradually get used to having Jackie around and to see for themselves what an asset he would be to their pennant prospects. Three other Black players, Roy Campanella, Don Newcombe, and Roy Partlow, were also on hand. Rickey scheduled a seven-game exhibition series between the Dodgers and the Royals to showcase Robinson's skills, and Jackie dominated the contests with a .625 batting average.

One problem that Rickey and Robinson had to overcome was that the Dodgers had Eddie Stanky playing second base. Therefore it was determined that Robinson would make his major-league debut at first base, a strange position for a man who had always been involved in the action in the middle of the diamond.

During training camp, a crisis arose when a core of Southerners on the team began to circulate a petition against Robinson. The dissenters were reportedly led by outfielder Dixie Walker, who initially dismissed the news of Robinson's signing with the comment, "As long as he isn't with the Dodgers, I'm not worried."[11] Rickey and manager Leo Durocher promptly quashed the mini-rebellion. Shortly thereafter, Durocher, an avid Robinson supporter, received a one-year suspension from the commissioner's office for associating with gamblers and other "unsavory" characters. Rickey deftly took advantage of the cover provided by the resulting clamor to quietly transfer Robinson to the Brooklyn roster.

Contrary to dire predictions, Robinson's first season in the major leagues went fairly smoothly as the rookie steadfastly stuck by his promise to Rickey to turn the other cheek. Tension surrounding his first game was defused by a series of preseason exhibition contests against the Yankees in New York, and Jackie's

Opening Day debut against the Braves was actually somewhat anticlimactic.

He received death threats when the club visited Cincinnati, but, in an oft-told but undocumented story, Dodgers shortstop Pee Wee Reese, a native son of Kentucky, draped an arm over the shoulders of the nervous rookie infielder in a courageous public show of support. Later, a threatened strike by the St. Louis Cardinals was short-circuited by a show of force by league president Ford Frick.

Jackie's worst experience came at the hands of the Philadelphia Phillies. Led by manager Ben Chapman, the Phils baited Robinson so cruelly that he later admitted, "It brought me nearer to cracking up than I had ever been."[12] But the Chapman episode actually served to strengthen support for Robinson and even converted some of his detractors. Stanky, who originally had opposed playing with Robinson, challenged the Phillies to pick on someone who could fight back. Public reaction against Chapman was so severe that he had to ask Robinson to pose for a photo with him to save his job. Jackie graciously complied.

For his rookie campaign, Robinson hit .297, led the league with 29 stolen bases, and finished second in the National League with 125 runs scored. In 151 games he lashed out 175 hits, including 12 home runs. Usually hitting second in the batting order, he walked 74 times and led the league in sacrifice hits. On defense, his 16 errors at first base were the second-highest total in the league, but his fielding was generally considered adequate.

With Robinson the biggest addition to the lineup, the Dodgers captured the National League pennant. In the World Series, Jackie and his teammates lost to the powerful Yankees in a thrilling seven-game classic. The 1947 season was the first in which the full membership of the Baseball Writers Association of America selected a Rookie of the Year, and Robinson beat out 21-game winner Larry Jansen of the New York Giants for the award. In the National League Most Valuable Player voting, he finished fifth. At season's end, Dixie Walker admitted that "(Robinson) is everything Branch Rickey said he was when he came up from Montreal."[13]

The integration of major-league baseball proceeded without critical incident. Though Robinson was scorned by some of his teammates, was harassed by enemy bench jockeys, and received a steady diet of fastballs close to his head; he faithfully abided by his promise to Rickey to turn the other cheek. Even when veteran outfielder Enos "Country" Slaughter of the Cardinals appeared to deliberately try to maim him with his spikes in an August 20 game at Ebbets Field, Jackie didn't retaliate.

In fact, baseball's "Great Experiment" was a huge success. Despite the concerns of the owners, integration proved to be a financial windfall for major-league baseball. Robinson and the Dodgers eclipsed the home attendance record they had set the previous year. They also broke single-game attendance records in every National League ballpark they played in during the 1947 season, with the exception of Cincinnati's Crosley Field, where the attendance record for the first major-league night game held up. Near the end of the season, Jackie was feted by fans with a day in his honor. At year's end, he finished runner-up to crooner Bing Crosby in a national popularity poll.

Before the 1948 season, Eddie Stanky was swapped to the Boston Braves to open up the Dodgers' second-base slot for Robinson. Jackie reported to camp out of shape and got off to a poor start. He was shifted back to first base for 30 games while utilityman Eddie Miksis manned second for the Dodgers. Eventually, Gil Hodges emerged as the club's regular first baseman, and Robinson returned to second. He finished strong at the plate, ending the year with a .296 batting mark and leading the league's regular second basemen in fielding percentage. Spending more time in the power spots in the batting order, he drove in 85 runs, tops on the disappointing third-place squad.

In 1949, Robinson enjoyed the best season of his career, establishing career highs in games played, hits, batting average, slugging, runs batted in, and stolen bases as the Dodgers captured the National League pennant by a single game. He won the batting title with a .342 mark and his major-league-leading 37 steals were the highest total in the National League in 19 years. He finished second in the league in runs batted in (124), hits (203), and on-base percentage (.432), and third in slugging average (.528), runs scored (122), doubles (38), and triples (12). His efforts were rewarded with his selection as the National League Most Valuable Player.

Robinson enjoyed two more superb seasons in 1950 and 1951, batting .328 and .338 and finishing second and third respectively in the batting race. Both years the Dodgers lost the pennant on the last day of the season, although Jackie's heroics kept them in the hunt until the bitter end. In 1951, his spectacular play forced the playoff with the Giants that would be decided by Bobby Thomson's momentous home run. In the final regular-season contest against the Phillies, Robinson

Jackie

prevented the winning run from scoring in the ninth inning with a sensational diving catch, and blasted a game-winning homer in the 14th inning.

The Dodgers returned to the top of the National League standings in 1952 as Robinson hit .308, scored 104 runs, stole 24 bases, and belted 19 homers. During the 1953 season, Jackie Robinson may have had his finest moment. He had worked hard to develop into a fine defensive second baseman. In 1951 he led National League second sackers in fielding and double plays, and had repeated as the double-play leader in 1952. But the Dodgers had a young Black second baseman in their system, Jim Gilliam, who was ready for the big time.

Jackie graciously agreed to move to another position to make room for the rookie. The 34-year-old veteran played 76 games in the outfield, and appeared 44 times at third base, nine times at second, and six times at first base during the 1953 campaign. He even filled in at shortstop in one game, the only time he played his original position as a major leaguer. He hit .329, drove in 95 runs, and scored 109 times. Gilliam expertly filled the Dodgers' leadoff spot and was selected the National League Rookie of the Year.

The 1954 campaign was Robinson's last good season. Again shuttling between left field and third base, he batted .311, but age and accumulated injuries were starting to catch up with him. He stole only seven bases and missed 30 games.

In 1955, the year the Brooklyn Dodgers captured their first world championship, Robinson had the worst season statistically of his outstanding career. Sharing third base with light-hitting Don Hoak, he appeared in the field in fewer than 100 games and batted only .256. In the Dodgers' epic World Series victory, Robinson was at third base for six of the seven contests and though he hit poorly, he scored five times, including his shocking Game One steal of home.

Jackie rallied to hit .275 in 1956, his final season, while sharing third base with newly acquired Randy Jackson and occasionally filling in at second. Though a mere shadow of his former self, the 37-year-old veteran was still a force at the plate and on the basepaths. In the Dodgers' seven-game World Series loss to the Yankees, Jackie drew five walks, scored five times, and blasted a home run. He struck out in his last professional at-bat, but fittingly he went down fighting. Yankees catcher Yogi Berra had to throw him out at first base after dropping the third strike.

Jackie's last years with the Dodgers had not been harmonious. He disliked both manager Walt Alston and owner Walter O'Malley, whose power play forced Branch Rickey out of the Brooklyn front office in 1950. Though the Dodgers had captured the 1956 pennant, the once dominating nucleus was growing old. Robinson himself was no longer a top performer on the field and had become increasingly outspoken on racial issues both inside and outside of baseball. The Dodgers brass was hoping he'd step down gracefully, but Jackie refused to announce his retirement. Finally the club forced his hand by swapping him to the New York Giants on December 13, 1956, for journeyman hurler Dick Littlefield and $30,000 in cash.

On January 22, 1957 Robinson's retirement from baseball was announced in an exclusive article in *Look* magazine, in which he took a few parting shots at the remaining segregated teams in the majors. Jackie had actually decided to retire before he was dealt to the Giants, but couldn't say anything earlier because of his deal with *Look*. The Giants reportedly offered him $60,000 to stay, and the prospect of playing alongside Willie Mays definitely had some appeal. But when Brooklyn general manager Buzzie Bavasi publicly implied that Robinson was just trying to use the magazine article to get a better contract, he decided to prove the Dodgers wrong and declined the Giants' offer.

Though Robinson's career as a major-league baseball player was over, he wasn't about to retire from the spotlight. He joined the Chock Full o'Nuts coffee company as a vice president and served as the chairman of the Board of Freedom National Bank, founded to provide loans and banking services for minority members who were largely being ignored by establishment banks. He authored several autobiographical works, wrote a weekly newspaper column, and hosted a radio show. Earlier he even tried his hand at acting, starring in the movie *The Jackie Robinson Story*.

Robinson remained an unofficial spokesman for African Americans and a relentless crusader for civil rights. He became embroiled in politics. Though a strong supporter of Martin Luther King and the NAACP, he endorsed Richard Nixon over John F. Kennedy for president in 1960 because he felt Kennedy had not made it "his business to know colored people." Reportedly it was an action that he later came to regret.

In 1962 Robinson was elected to the National Baseball Hall of Fame. He was inducted along with former Cleveland pitching great Bob Feller, who had once predicted that Jackie's "football shoulders" would keep him from hitting big-league pitching. A few years after his retirement from baseball, Robinson acknowledged that he suffered from diabetes. His health declined under the ravages of the disease and at the age of 53 he suffered a fatal heart attack at his home in Stamford, Connecticut. He died on October 24, 1972, only months after his number 42 was officially retired by the Dodgers.

Although he always denied it, there's evidence that Robinson may have been the first insulin-dependent diabetic to play major-league baseball, despite his claim that it hadn't been diagnosed while he was an active player. But former tennis great Bill Talbert, a close friend of Robinson's and the first famous athlete known to perform with diabetes, believed that Jackie became insulin-dependent in midcareer. "I think Jackie felt it was a weakness. With all the publicity about blacks in baseball, he didn't want another thing to talk about," Talbert said after Robinson's death.[14]

More than two thousand people packed Riverside Church on Manhattan's Upper West Side to hear the young Rev. Jesse Jackson deliver Jackie Robinson's eulogy. Tens of thousands lined the streets of Harlem and Bedford-Stuyvesant to watch the passage of his mile-long funeral procession. Robinson is buried in Cyprus Hill Cemetery in Brooklyn, along with his mother-in-law Zellee Isum and his son Jack Roosevelt, Jr. He was survived by his wife Rachel, son David and daughter Sharon.

Shortly after his death Robinson's ordeals and accomplishments were the subject of a Broadway musical, *The First*. In 1987, on the 40th anniversary of his breaking of color barrier, the Rookie of the Year Award was redesignated as the Jackie Robinson Award in honor of its first recipient. On the 50th anniversary of his debut, his number 42 was permanently retired by all major-league teams, although current major leaguers already wearing the number were allowed to keep it for the remainder of their careers.

Among the adjectives often used to describe Robinson's personal makeup are fearless, courageous, dynamic, defiant, and proud. But the most frequently used descriptor is probably aggressive. It's a word that defines his public life as a tireless campaigner against discrimination as well as his history making athletic career. Jackie, who was not known for self-deprecation, made the greatest understatement of his life in 1945 at the announcement of his signing. "Maybe I'm doing something for my race," he ventured.[15]

Former teammate Joe Black, speaking for generations of Black ballplayers, later said, "When I look at my house. I say 'Thank God for Jackie Robinson.'"[16]

This biography is an adaptation from "The Black Stars Who Made Baseball Whole: The Jackie Robinson Generation in the Major Leagues" by Rick Swaine (McFarland, 2006). It also appears in SABR's "The Team That Forever Changed Baseball and America: The 1947 Brooklyn Dodgers" (University of Nebraska Press, 2012), edited by Lyle Spatz.

SOURCES

In addition to the sources cited in the Notes, the author also consulted:

Frommer, Harvey. *Rickey & Robinson: The Men Who Broke Baseball's Color Barrier* (New York: Macmillan, 1982).

Marshall, William. *Baseball's Pivotal Era 1945-51* (Lexington: University Press of Kentucky, 1999).

Moffi, Larry, and Jonathan Kronstadt. *Crossing the Line: Black Major Leaguers 1947-1959* (Jefferson, North Carolina: McFarland, 1994).

Polner, Murray. *Branch Rickey: A Biography* (New York: Atheneum, 1982).

Rosenthal, Harold. *The 10 Best Years of Baseball: An Informal History of the Fifties* (Chicago: Contemporary Books, 1979).

Shatzkin, Mike, and Jim Charlton. *The Ballplayers: Baseball's Ultimate Biographical Reference* (New York: Arbor House, William Morrow, 1990).

Tygiel, Jules. *Extra Bases: Reflections on Jackie Robinson, Race, & Baseball History* (Lincoln: University of Nebraska Press, 2002).

_____. *The Jackie Robinson Reader: Perspectives of an American Hero* (New York: Penguin Books, 1997).

Wilber, Cynthia J. *For the Love of the Game: Baseball Memories From the Men Who Were There* (New York: William Morrow and Company, 1992).

Ardolino, Frank, "Jackie Robinson and the 1941 Honolulu Bears," *The National Pastime*, SABR, 1995.

Jacobs, Bruce, *Baseball Stars of 1953* (New York: Timely Comics, 1953).

Kirk, Al and Robert Bradley. "Jackie Robinson and the L.A. Red Devils." http://www.apbr.org/reddevils.html

NOTES

1. Roger Kahn, *The Boys of Summer*, p. 358.
2. Vincent X. Flaherty - Jackie Robinson Scrapbooks per Jules Tygiel, *Baseball's Great Experiment: Jackie Robinson and His Legacy* (New York: Oxford University Press, 1997), 60.
3. Jackie Robinson Scrapbooks, 60
4. Unattributed - Jackie Robinson Scrapbooks, 60.
5. *The Sporting News*, November 1, 1945.
6. *Pittsburgh Courier*, November 3, 1945.
7. John Crosby, *Syracuse Herald*, November 12, 1972.
8. *Pittsburgh Courier*, April 27, 1946.
9. Joe Bostic, *Amsterdam News*, April 27, 1946.
10. Sam Maltin, *Pittsburgh Courier*, October 12, 1946.
11. *Brooklyn Eagle*, October 24, 1945.
12. Jackie Robinson and Alfred Duckett. *I Never Had It Made* (New York: G.P. Putnam's Sons, 1972), 64.
13. Peter Golenbock, *Bums: An Oral History of the Brooklyn Dodgers* (New York: G.P. Putnam's Sons, 1984), 165.
14. Arnold Schechter, *Sports Illustrated*, April 22, 1985.
15. *The Sporting News*, November 1, 1945.
16. *New York Daily News*, July 20, 1972.

MY HERO - JACKIE ROBINSON

by Larry Lester

The summer of 1960 was a special season for me. As a young lad I got my first glimpse of the legendary Jackie Robinson during a political tour. He was campaigning for Republican presidential candidate Richard Milhous Nixon. As a brash, up-and-coming little league player, I knew everything about this icon and the impact that the now-retired Jackie Robinson had had on breaking baseball's color barrier back in 1947. I copied his pigeon-toed style of running and tried holding my bat high above my big head, with my potato-chip-flat chest to emulate his batting stance. And now #42 was coming to my town to give a campaign speech on behalf of a presidential candidate.

Lucky for me, Municipal Stadium, home of the Kansas City A's, was only five blocks from where I sorted and traded baseball cards and stuffed them in my Roi-Tan cigar box, under the bed. I attended a lot of ball games, but I never got to see this great athlete play in person. Unfortunately, teams in the American League, like the A's, never hosted National League clubs like the Brooklyn Dodgers. To take this opportunity and to see Robinson in the flesh would be the ultimate, ever-lasting thrill for me.

I asked my father to take me downtown to see Mr. Robinson speak on behalf of tricky Dicky. My pleading request was met with a puzzled and concerned look from my father. Years later I discovered that my father was a Democrat. Reluctantly he took me to the Music Hall auditorium, fulfilling my Robinson fantasy. With the exception of Mr. Robinson, my father and I appeared to be the only Black folks in the Hall. We overcame the uninvited stares - nothing would keep me for seeing this man among men, whom I had read so much about.

As my father and I sat in the balcony and it seemed like an eternity, as each speaker strolled to the podium to deliver promises that even a 10-year kid knew they would not keep. Needless to say, each speaker struck out with me.

Finally, the man of the hour appeared. Sitting on the edge of my seat, I took in his high-pitched voice, his salty gray hair, his chubby belly, his eloquent delivery and his professional demeanor, as I stared in awe. I remember little of what Robinson said, but recalled how professional and sincere his presentation seemed.

It took a lot of prodding to get my Democratic father to chauffeur me to the event, but he knew, like many of us, the impact this Barrier Breaker has had towards the socialization of races through the integration of our National Pastime. I knew from that day forth Mr. Jackie Robinson would become my role model for sports and beyond. For these reasons, and many others, I chose to honor number 42, Jackie Robinson, as part of my website, www.LarryLester42.com.

RACHEL ROBINSON

by Ralph Carhart

Rachel Robinson.

It is easy to imagine that at the end of her final day of filming with acclaimed director Ken Burns, Rachel Robinson must have felt some sense of relief. When Jack died, she was only 50 years old. Since then, she had been blessed with a long life and had spent almost as many years shepherding her husband's story, safeguarding it from those who would twist, misrepresent, or abuse his legacy. The sweeping documentary by Burns, made in 2016 and titled simply *Jackie Robinson*, would be the most comprehensive, multifaceted look at Jack's tale – the crown jewel in that important aspect of her life's work. Yet, her role as guardian was just one of her many accomplishments. Rachel was also a distinguished professor at Yale, a psychiatric nurse, a vocal civil rights activist, a cunning businesswoman, and a generous philanthropist.

Hers is a stunning résumé for anyone, but most especially a Black woman born nearly a century ago.

Rachel Annetta Isum took her first breath on July 19, 1922, in Los Angeles, to parents Zellee and Charles Raymond Isum. Zellee Jones was born in Texas, and after moving to California became a gourmet cook and self-employed caterer with elite clientele in Beverly Hills and Hollywood. Charles was a second-generation Californian, and an Army veteran who'd fought in World War I and was gassed by the German army in France. After the war he got a job as a bookbinder for the *Los Angeles Times*, though he never fully recovered from the gas attack and was forced to retire while still a relatively young man.[1] Believing in the importance of exposing her children to art and culture, Zellee took Rachel to violin lessons, the museum, and the Exposition Park Rose Garden, not far from the family home at 1588 36th Place.[2] Rachel attended the acclaimed Manual Arts High School, which counted among its notable alumni filmmaker Frank Capra and California Governor Goodwin Knight. Her parents provided her with opportunities that few Black families could give their children.

When it was time for college, Rachel went to UCLA. She longed to be a doctor, but Zellee convinced her that nursing was a more appropriate career path for a woman who was destined to have a family.[3] Rachel lived at home, and drove her old, beat-up Ford V-8 to school. It was a largely isolated existence, living off-campus.[4] That changed when she met Jack Roosevelt Robinson. Prior to their introduction, she had seen Jack play for Pasadena Junior College, a rival of her own beloved Los Angeles, and had instantly disliked him. She found the popular athlete to be "cocky, conceited and self-centered." She even found the way he stood in the backfield during football games, with his hands on his hips, to give off an air of arrogance. In truth, Jack was rather shy around women. When the two, now both attending UCLA, were introduced by Jack's more outgoing friend Ray Bartlett, she found her earlier prejudices challenged.[5]

There was an instant spark between the two. Jack was attracted to her "looks and charm," she found him "impressive – a handsome, proud, and serious man with a warm smile and a pigeon-toed walk."[6] When she brought Jack home to meet her family, her mother and brothers were impressed. Her father was a harsher critic, and Rachel sensed that he harbored some jealousy of the successful athlete who was wooing his daughter. For their first formal date, Jack took her to the Bruins football homecoming dinner, an affair at the Biltmore Hotel. Rachel later remembered her anxiety about stepping out into such glamorous surroundings. The racism she faced in Los Angeles was often "unexpected and inexplicable," and an event at a place like the Biltmore was rife for a surprise reminder. There was also an underlying sexual tension that was new to the innocent Rachel. Still, despite the occasional awkwardness, the night went off seamlessly, as she and Jack danced the fox-trot and flirted, two kids in love. The road ahead for Rachel and Jack would not always be so smooth.[7]

Charles Isum died on March 6, 1941. His death deeply affected Rachel, who thought of herself as her father's guardian angel. One of the roles assigned to her by Zellee, even when she was a young child, had been to serve as a caretaker to her often-ill father. Her grief brought Rachel and Jack even closer together, as he was a loving salve for her during that difficult time. Just three days before Charles's death, Jack had dropped out of UCLA, only a few credits shy of graduation. He always claimed that it was financial hardships that forced him to leave school. He had to find work to help his mother, Mallie, with the bills. However, Rachel would note years later that she always believed that the real reason was not a financial one. Rather, by that spring he had used up his athletic eligibility. With no sports, school no longer held his interest.[8] He found work, first with the National Youth Administration in Atascadero. He was hired as an assistant athletic director, a position he enjoyed, but the approaching war cut the job short in July. After a brief tenure playing for the Los Angeles Bulldogs of the Pacific Coast Professional Football League, he quickly signed with the Honolulu Bears of the Hawaii Senior Football League, a position that came with an attached construction job.[9] Rachel supported his decision, even though it meant they would be separated. Before he left, Jack gave her a charm bracelet, a symbol that they were committed to one another.[10]

They were not separated for long. While he had some success on the gridiron in Hawaii, Jack was often hampered by injuries and he left Honolulu just two days before the attack at Pearl Harbor. Upon his return, he and Rachel immediately began spending as much time together as work and school allowed. Their reunion was short-lived. On March 23, 1942, Jack received notification that he was to report for induction into the US Army.[11] Rachel suddenly had three important men in her life serving – her brothers, Chuck and Raymond, both saw active combat. Chuck, a pilot, was even missing in action for a time, after his plane was shot down over Yugoslavia. It was while Jack was on leave from the Army in March 1943 that they formalized their engagement when he presented Rachel with a diamond ring. They promised to wed once she finished school, though in truth she was in no hurry. While she loved Jack, she had come to realize that much of her life had been lived to fulfill the goals her family had for her. She understood that with marriage, she was likely surrendering another piece of her autonomy, a reality she was happy to delay.[12]

Rachel did her part toward the war effort by taking a job as a riveter at Lockheed Aircraft, working nights while she went to school during the day. In September 1943 she transferred to the U.C. San Francisco School of Nursing, where she then worked eight-hour shifts in hospital wards, all while juggling her studies.[13] Jack wrote Rachel weekly, and arranged for a box of chocolates to appear at her dorm room every Friday. The distance was difficult for them both, especially Rachel, who was now living over six hours away from home. She watched all of her new friends go on adventures with their romantic interests, while Jack was 1,700 miles away at Fort Riley, Kansas. Worse, he and Rachel clashed when she wrote to him and informed him that she had decided to join the Cadet Nurse Corps. Jack mistakenly believed she had actually enlisted in the Army, and wrote her back, insisting she withdraw. He was certain that were she to be surrounded by enlisted men, she would quickly be seduced by them. Rachel, not one to be told what to do, returned the ring and bracelet. She joined the Corps, glad for the extra $20 a month it provided and for the chance to serve her country.[14] The two remained estranged until Jack was discharged from the Army in November 1944. At first, he hesitated to contact Rachel, but after some convincing by his mother, Mallie, he called her. Rachel was eager to rekindle their romance and he rapidly drove to San Francisco. The two reconciled, and reaffirmed their engagement when he gave her back the ring.[15]

Jack was again on the road at the beginning of 1945, playing shortstop for the Kansas City Monarchs, while Rachel was completing her studies. She graduated in June, with honors, from UCLA, receiving a B.S. in

Nursing. She also won the Florence Nightingale Award for clinical excellence, a superlative for which she was chosen by her peers. After graduation, she took a job working in the nursery of Los Angeles General Hospital.[16] Two months later, Jack was contacted by the Dodgers. It was at his August 28, 1945, meeting with Branch Rickey that the Mahatma famously asked Jack, "You got a girl?" and told him to marry her right away. In truth, Jack and Rachel had already set the date for their wedding, but before she settled into the role of wife, she wanted an adventure of her own. Rachel and her college roommate, Janice Brooks, moved to Harlem in October. There, she found work as a hostess in a restaurant, a job she left when she learned the establishment was segregated. She then found a position at the Hospital for Joint Diseases in Manhattan. Growing up in her largely White world in Los Angeles, her experience in Harlem was revelatory and it brought herself and Jack, who had spent considerably more time with fellow BIPOC, closer together. At the beginning of January, her adventure complete, Rachel and Jack returned to California to prepare for their wedding.[17] They married on February 10, 1946, an affair that was largely planned by Zellee. Jack, who adored his mother-in-law, was happy to join Rachel in indulging Zellee's flower-drenched whims.[18]

The two took an abbreviated honeymoon in San Jose, California, staying at the home of Rachel's aunt. But the future was calling and barely three weeks after the wedding, armed with a basket of fried chicken and boiled eggs given to them by Jack's mother Mallie, Rachel and Jack were on their way to Daytona Beach, Florida, for spring training with the Montreal Royals. While Rachel had experienced "unexpected" racism in California, the journey through the American South was eye-opening. Inexplicably booted from their connecting flight in New Orleans, they were forced to stay in a second-rate, grimy hotel. Unable to find a restaurant that would serve them, the only food they had was Mallie's chicken. Bumped from another flight the next day, they had to take a bus from Pensacola, where they suffered the additional indignity of being sent to the back to make room for White passengers. Jack, who had suffered court-martial rather than be forced to the back of a military bus, moved without a word. Throughout the 16-hour ride, Rachel wept at the pain she knew it caused her proud husband to stay silent.[19]

They were largely welcomed in Daytona, where they met influential community leaders and stayed with a prominent Black family, the Harrises. The city was fairly progressive for the time and place, though even there they witnessed reminders of the Jim Crow South. While it was acceptable in Daytona for Black shoppers to try on shoes, it was against the law to try on clothing in the local stores.[20] Their experiences around the rest of Florida were even more challenging, and Rachel felt Jack's nightly struggles to withstand the hatred and still manage the rather difficult task of hitting a baseball. Recognizing that Rachel would be integral in helping Jack weather the storm ahead, Rickey allowed her to join the other players in camp – the only wife allowed to do so. She quickly realized that her role in the important work that Jack was doing was to lend support, to "be a consistent presence to witness and validate the realities, love him without reservation, share his thoughts and miseries, discover with him the humor in the ridiculous behavior against us, and, most of all, help maintain our fighting spirit."[21]

Jack's first season in Organized Baseball brought them to Montreal, where Rachel was pleasantly surprised to learn that the housing discrimination she had been anticipating was not as prevalent north of the US border. After a month in a guest house, they found a home in a French-speaking neighborhood, a modest apartment at 8232 de Gaspé Avenue not far from Jarry Park. In May, she and Jack were delighted to learn that she was pregnant with their first child. She enjoyed their stay in Montreal, and would later remember that time as "blissful."[22] Still, within all the joy, the year had its obstacles. The psychological pressure was physically grueling on Jack, who by midseason was suffering from exhaustion. Rachel helped him bear the burden, while simultaneously remaining quiet about the unexpected complications she was having with her pregnancy, a struggle Jack did not learn about until much later.[23] Occasionally she traveled with him, but often she stayed at home, sewing, shopping, and generally living the domesticated home life she anticipated would come with marriage.[24] Despite his physical woes, Jack excelled on the field that season, leading the Royals to the Little World Series championship on October 4, 1946. Eight months pregnant, Rachel was on the field with her husband when he celebrated with his teammates.[25]

After the season, the family returned to Los Angeles, living in Rachel's childhood home. Their first child, Jackie Jr., was born on November 18, 1946, at Good Samaritan Hospital. Jack and Rachel had the luxury of the early support of their families, but challenges awaited them. Needing money, Jack signed on with a local basketball team, the Los Angeles Red Devils, for $50 a game, an experiment that lasted only a few weeks.[26] In late February, Jack left for spring training in Cuba, and this time Rachel (and Jackie Jr.) were not allowed to accompany the team. When they reunited it was in New York, where they established a temporary life at the McAlpin Hotel, on Broadway near Herald Square, a frequent Dodgers haunt. It was from this space, too cramped for the blossoming family, that they changed the world on April 15, 1947. Rachel was at Ebbets Field that day with Jackie Jr., and she watched her husband make history. Sitting between Ruth Campanella, whom she had befriended when Jack and Roy had been teammates in Montreal, and Roy's mother-in-law, she left her seat only to warm up the baby's bottles at the hot-dog stand. A California girl, she underestimated how cold an April day in Brooklyn could be, and by game's end Jackie Jr., who was also suffering from an upset stomach, was stuffed inside the fur coat of Ruth's mother to stay warm.[27] Minor inconveniences aside, she watched the game before her and contemplated the possibilities of social change. She understood, even in that moment, how much Jack's elevation meant to "Black America, and how much we symbolized its hunger for opportunity and its determination to make dreams long deferred possible."[28]

While Jack continued to make headlines, Rachel established their lives at home. After two weeks at the McAlpin, they received an offer from a woman to share an apartment at 526 MacDonough Street, in the Bedford-Stuyvesant neighborhood of Brooklyn. The apartment was a roach-infested tenement, but it had a small room for Jackie Jr., a separate bedroom for them, and access to a kitchen, none of which the McAlpin provided.[29] Still, it was too small and dreary, and the uninspiring quarters led to increased tensions between the couple, a situation exacerbated by Rachel's unwillingness to give voice to her own trials as part of her mission to support Jack. In an effort to fill the need for there to be more to her life than just domesticity, she took a course in interior decoration. She also began to slowly make friends with some of the other Dodgers wives, including Joan Hodges and Dottie Reese.[30]

Before the end of the playing season, the Robinsons moved again, to 407 Stuyvesant Street. Rachel oversaw all these moves while caring for an infant, and still managed to attend every home game. She embraced the role of Jack's protector, including oftentimes intercepting the mail before her beleaguered husband could read it. At first, she threw away the threatening letters that came to their home, but when they grew in ferocity, including threats to the life of Jackie Jr., she started sharing them with the Dodgers.[31] The couple grew to love Brooklyn, and thought of it as a haven. The real test to their fortitude came when Jack went on the road, where the racial taunts would be most vile. At times, Rachel went with him. She remained silent on these occasions, but sat upright in her seat, imagining herself a shield that could keep the invectives from reaching the ears of Jack on the field.[32]

Even in Brooklyn, there was the occasional reminder that they were Black citizens trying to integrate a White world, not just in baseball, but on the streets of their own home. They moved again, this time to the top-floor apartment of a two-family home at 5224 Tilden Avenue in the largely White and Jewish neighborhood of Flatbush, in April 1948.[33] Although Jack was immensely popular in Brooklyn (he had, in fact, been elected the second most popular person in America in a nationwide contest, trailing only Bing Crosby), there were still rumors of a petition being circulated in the neighborhood to prevent their Black landlady from buying the house. Some of their neighbors came to their defense, including the Satlows – Arch and Sarah – and their three children. The two families grew close. Rachel helped Sarah learn how to bake, and Jack hired her to prepare the massive amounts of fan mail he answered. The Satlows ultimately became lifelong friends; but even amid all the national adulation, the family remained isolated with few close companions.[34]

For the first time in their brief married life, they did not return to California after the season. By 1948 the family had come to think of New York as home, and with that decision, Rachel prepared for another move, this time to a house of their own. The timing was fortuitous – not long after she found a place, she learned that she was again pregnant. Their new home in the St. Albans section of Queens, near Idlewild Airport,[35] was just the right size for their burgeoning family. It was there, at 112-40 177th Street, that they finally found a place that most resembled their California childhoods, with a big backyard, a play area, and old oak trees. The house itself needed some work, but the open space, after the continually close quarters of their first two years in New York City, was a literal breath of fresh air. They purchased the house for $100 and "other good and valuable considerations."[36] Their racially mixed neighborhood included the Campanellas, who had moved there just before the Robinsons, as well as musicians like diva Leontyne Price and Count Basie. Groundbreaking education innovators Gus and Jeanne Heningburg were their neighbors, and played a role in devising the school system that the Robinson children would learn by during their stay in Queens.[37]

Sharon Robinson was born on January 13, 1950. Rachel was overjoyed that she had had a girl, as she had long harbored secret fantasies that she would have a family like her own as a child – a willful girl born between two boys. After the birth of Sharon, Jack and Jackie Jr. flew to California in February 1950 so that Jack could film the motion picture *The Jackie Robinson Story*. Rachel was to stay home with the baby and Mallie, but Jack struggled with the unfamiliar world of a film set. After two weeks, Rachel and Sharon joined him in Los Angeles, where they once again lived at her childhood home. Her arrival allowed Jack to relax and enjoy the remainder of the experience. By this point in their relationship, it was clear to both of them that her influence extended far beyond how well he handled his struggles on the diamond. Jack not only looked to her succor in private, but he recognized how his wife's brilliant mind and beautiful looks could help relieve the tremendous pressure he felt in a different way. Rachel eased Jack's suffering by simply being charming enough to occasionally direct the spotlight away from him.[38]

Despite the high drama that Jack experienced on the baseball diamond, playing an integral role in the storied battle between the Dodgers and their crosstown rival New York Yankees, for the children and Rachel the early 1950s marked an extended period of peace. Rachel delighted in being a mother, and the birth of their youngest child, David, in May 1952 finalized the picture-perfect family for which they longed. There was just one ultimate, vital piece that the Robinsons needed to achieve their familial dreams. Not only did the latest addition make the house start to feel crowded again, but Jack and Rachel had grown tired of the attention they were receiving from unwanted guests, who would show up on the front lawn of their St. Albans home and take pictures at all hours.[39] Rachel began the process of finding her dream home, a place where she and her family could finally settle, long-term. She could not have anticipated that her hunt would put her on the pages of the newspapers.

She was stymied in her searches, in both Westchester County and Connecticut, by realtors who, upon meeting her, told her that her family wasn't "the right fit" for the neighborhood. By this point, Jack was no longer under any restraints regarding how he conducted himself on the field and, on a larger scale, in his personal and political life. He started to become more vocal in his politics, and Rachel joined him. As the civil rights movement blossomed, they recognized the weight that came with their voices and they used their influence. When a reporter with the *Bridgeport Herald*, who was doing an exposé on racist housing practices, contacted the Robinsons about their struggles, she willingly spoke to him. The Robinsons became central characters in the subsequent article. When residents of North Stamford, Connecticut, read the story, they came to the family's aid.[40]

One family in particular, Andrea and Richard Simon (founder of the publishing house Simon and Schuster, and parents of future music star Carly Simon) were particularly kind. Andrea went far beyond emotional support, and used her influence with local realtors, who had been dismissive to Rachel, to help acquire the land where the Robinsons built their dream home, in North Stamford. The exotic Andrea had a Swiss father and a Cuban mother, and was 13 years Rachel's senior. Still, the two formed a lifelong friendship that "crossed all boundaries of age, race, and culture."[41] With Andrea's aid, as well as that of a pair of local Jewish bankers, the Spelke brothers, who provided the loan, the family purchased land at 103 Cascade Road in Stamford from contractor Ben Gunnar.[42] They then hired Gunnar to build them their dream home. When the house wasn't ready in time for the 1954 school year, the Simons offered the Robinsons use of their summer home so that the children could start school in Connecticut and Rachel could oversee the build.[43]

In many ways, the move was all the family longed for, but it came at a price. While they had the space and luxuries that country living provided, the largely White community of Stamford increased the feelings of isolation in the children, especially in Jackie Jr., who more than the others struggled to thrive in his father's very long shadow. Eventually, the Robinsons formed relationships with the families around them, and the kids found friends to play with them, both Black children and White. But they never stopped being reminded of their race, and the increasingly important and complex struggle of the civil rights movement. At the same time that Jack, perhaps the most famous Black man in America, was denied membership at a Connecticut country club, Emmett Till was lynched in Mississippi. Rachel recalled weeping when nine Black children were escorted into Central High School in Little Rock.[44] The news was a daily reminder of how far there was left to go, and how important a role Jack, Rachel, and the Robinson family played in that narrative.

Jackie

Only a week after Rachel and Jack returned from a December 1956 series of exhibition games in Japan, where he had appeared alongside some of his fellow Dodgers, Jack announced his retirement from baseball on the pages of *Look* magazine. It was again Rachel who provided him counsel and respite at the outset of this new stage in his life, but she also found herself in a unique position. She completely sympathized with her husband's need to move on to his new business ventures and quit the physical toil he suffered playing ball. Certainly she was overjoyed that her husband was going to be spending more time at home with the family, a coexistence she had long longed for.[45] But she also felt the keen loss that, as a fan, came with the end of his career. Jack had been an athlete for the entire length of their relationship. They had faced many challenges in the 16 years they had been together, but what came next was truly uncharted territory.[46]

Jack embroiled himself in the affairs of his new business life, as a vice president of Chock Full O' Nuts Coffee and as an activist for the NAACP and the civil rights movement. Rachel enjoyed the first real opportunity to focus on herself since her college days. She yearned for self-improvement and independence. Jack, who had witnessed his own mother work long, tiring hours, was troubled by the thought of Rachel finding work.[47] Undeterred, she applied to the Graduate School of Nursing at New York University. She was admitted to the psychiatric nursing program in 1959 and reentered college life at the age of 37. Her initial concerns, of being "a helpless and befuddled 'old lady,'" were quickly replaced by the confidence she gained when she realized that her real-life experiences had prepared her quite well for academia. Throughout her studies, she attempted to keep her connection to Jack a secret. It was important to her that she succeed on her own merits, and not because of her famous husband.[48]

Jackie Jr. shared this particular desire with his mother, perhaps most keenly of all of the children. Part of the challenge for Rachel, in her pursuit of her degree, was that this time marked the first in which she was not consistently present for her children's needs. Jackie Jr. had started to struggle in school, particularly with reading. Sharon was studious and reserved, and she kept many of the personal struggles she felt as a Black child surrounded by White playmates buried deep inside. David, who unlike his siblings was sent to a private school, found strength in isolation in a way that few children do. Rachel and Jack believed it was best if the harshness of the world was absent from the dinner-table discussions, instead choosing to encourage their children's natural inclinations toward fairness and honor. As well-intentioned as the choice was, it was one that Rachel would later come to regret.[49]

Rachel graduated from NYU in 1961, and after a brief tenure as a clinical nurse at the First Day Hospital in the Bronx, got a job as a psychiatric nurse at Albert Einstein College of Medicine, in its Department of Social and Community Psychiatry, of which she soon became the head.[50] For the next five years, she was part of a study that was dedicated to proving that family assistance was the key to a more independent, and safe, life for the mentally ill. The program statistically proved their point, but the funding never materialized to create the housing that would be necessary to enact such a program. Days at the college, spent searching for a better world for her patients, were followed by nights at home with the family, including her mother. Zellee had moved in with the family when Rachel went to school, and her steady presence led to a feeling of solidarity in a family filled with individuals who were now largely each going their own way. Jack was proud of what his wife was accomplishing in her new career, but he also struggled to adapt to their new dynamic. It was now Rachel who was absent for long stretches of time, embroiled in her important work.[51]

As Jack played a larger and larger role in the NAACP and the children were growing older, politics become a more frequent topic at home. Rachel and Jack found themselves on opposite sides of the aisle when he famously gave his support to Richard Nixon in the 1960 presidential election, a decision he later regretted. Rachel, a third-generation Democrat whose entire adolescence was spent under FDR, was troubled to see her husband side with conservatives.[52] Despite this rift, they remained a unified force for civil rights. One of the most enduring memories for the whole family was the uplifting day in August 1963 when they attended the March on Washington for Jobs and Freedom, and witnessed Martin Luther King Jr.'s "I Have a Dream" speech on the steps of the Washington Monument. Rachel listened to King's words with tears in her eyes, and left that day "filled with hope and pride."[5]

Jack and Martin Luther King were frequent collaborators, especially when it came to fundraising. In 1963, when the Robinsons learned that King needed bail money for those who were arrested on the marches, they put together a fundraiser on their six-acre homestead. They staged "An Afternoon of Jazz," featuring some of the most legendary names in the industry, including Dave Brubeck and Dizzy Gillespie, both of whom donated their union minimum salaries.[54] The festival was a hit, with over 500 attendees raising $15,000 for the cause. It became an annual event, raising money for various charities over the years. Even after Jack died, Rachel (and later, Sharon) kept it going until 2001, a nearly 50-year tradition in Connecticut.

Professionally, Rachel continued to make quite a name for herself. After leaving Albert Einstein, she took jobs as the director of nursing for the Connecticut Mental Health Center in New Haven, and as an assistant professor of nursing at Yale University. At CMHC, she applied the research she had done at Einstein, and found a whole new level of reward in her work. At the same time, as Jack went deeper and deeper into politics, taking a pay cut to do so, he began to appreciate the salary that Rachel was bringing home in a whole new way.[55] Just five years after moving past the phase of her life that was dedicated solely to her husband and her children, Rachel was a respected educator and nurse. She was enjoying the well-deserved benefits of her hard work, her keen mind, and her intense compassion.

This period of fulfillment, for her and for Jack, was not destined to last. Always in his father's shadow, Jackie Jr. led a troubled life, one that took him to Vietnam. There, he suffered an injury that led to drug addiction. After returning home, he was arrested in March 1968, on both drugs and weapons charges. His tabloid-fodder struggles dragged their private family pain into the light. Rachel was able to arrange for him to be given a room at Yale New Haven Hospital, but the family quickly learned that this was a poor choice. Surrounded by patients who were mentally unwell, but not addicts like himself, Jackie Jr. resented the setting and quickly persuaded doctors to release him. Once freed, he returned to his addiction.[56] Jackie Jr.'s troubles were just the beginning of the nightmare that was the spring of 1968. Within the next three months, the Robinsons witnessed the murders of Martin Luther King Jr. and Robert Kennedy, and the death of Mallie.

Jackie Jr. gave the family some hope when, faced with a choice between prison and rehab, he chose to enter the Daytop drug rehabilitation program. Jackie thrived at Daytop, not only successfully fighting his addiction, but later serving as a counselor to others in need.[57] The success of his heroic struggle made his untimely death from a car crash on June 17, 1971, all the more tragic. Rachel was out of town when he died, attending a conference in Massachusetts. Jack and Sharon quickly drove to her, desperate to give her the news before it hit the press. Rachel collapsed under the weight of the emotional devastation, and Jack and Sharon had to help her to the car. When they returned home, she ran through the fields surrounding their home, mad with grief. Her tears did not stop for days.[58]

In the aftermath of Jackie Jr.'s funeral, Rachel and Jack decided to stage that year's jazz concert, scheduled for just two weeks after the death of their son, and make it a tribute to their lost child. That year's event was already intended to be a fundraiser for Daytop, and Jackie Jr. had played an active role in securing the acts. That event was the culmination of his final work, and the day was poignant and cathartic. Rachel remembered walking around "in a daze, on the edge of madness."[59] The weeks that followed were tense in the Robinson household, as Jack failed to address his own grief over Jackie Jr.'s death. Instead, he transferred his pain into an increasing frustration with the amount of time Rachel dedicated to work. It all came to a head when Sharon came home one night to find her father crying, alone in the living room. Uncertain how to ease her father's suffering, she told her mother, who was reading upstairs in the bedroom. Once more, Rachel went to her husband and provided him comfort. From that point, they would slowly begin to heal from the wound of their lost son.[60] Sadly, there was even still more pain that awaited her.

Jack had been struggling with medical issues caused by his diabetes for years. He was losing his eyesight and he suffered tremendous pain in his legs. By the summer of 1972, his sight was failing enough that Rachel needed to hire a chauffeur for him.[61] That year also marked the 25th anniversary of Jack's integration of the Dodgers. Commissioner Bowie Kuhn recognized the date by presenting him with an award dedicated to his philanthropic efforts helping young people learn about the dangers of drugs, a cause he embraced after Jackie Jr.'s troubles. In a ceremony prior to Game Two of the 1972 World Series, Bowie Kuhn presented Jack with the award. His family by his side, it was Rachel who took him by the arm and led him to Kuhn when it was time for him to accept the honor. The NBC cameras respectfully cut away from his labored journey to a shot of the crowd on their feet, honoring this aged hero.

One week later, on the morning of October 24, while Rachel was making breakfast, Jack came rushing from the bedroom and into her arms. He collapsed to the floor, and quickly fell unconscious. She attempted to do what she could while she waited for help to arrive, but it was too late. Jack Robinson died of a heart attack, at the tragically young age of 53. The final words he spoke before he lost consciousness in Rachel's arms were, "I love you."[62] At his funeral four days later, over 2,500 mourners joined Rachel in saying goodbye to her husband at Riverside Church in Harlem. Even in her pain, she understood the role that Jack had played in the lives of so many, and she insisted that two-thirds of the pews be set aside for anyone who wished to join them, including a special section for the kids who played hooky from school that day to attend. "Jack loved children, so," she told the press.[63]

Her journey would have to carry on without him by her side, but Rachel was far from finished being Mrs. Jack Robinson. Just as her guidance helped shape his baseball career, her stewardship of his legacy is largely responsible for how the public thinks of him today. Within weeks of his death, she resigned from Yale and took over as the head of Jack's various financial interests. It had long been his dream to start a construction company that built affordable housing for underserved families. She quickly realized that they didn't have the resources for such a venture but, as a long-time veteran of fundraising, she did see how they were well-equipped to be real-estate developers. With the help of some of Jack's partners, she founded the Jack Robinson Development Corporation. Working with the Halpern Building Corporation, the JRDC built and managed over 1,300 units of low- and moderate-income housing in New York City and Yonkers. Rachel herself oversaw the training of the various property managers who were the caretakers of Jack's dream.[64]

Once the Jack Robinson Development Corporation was on stable footing, she turned her eyes toward honoring the rest of Jack's activism. In 1973 Rachel, along with her brother Charles Williams, lawyer and ambassador Frank Williams (no relation to Charles), and family friend Marty Edelman, formed the Jackie Robinson Foundation. The foundation's mission was to further the education and leadership development opportunities of minority children with few economic resources at their disposal. Beginning in 1975, the foundation became the sole beneficiary of the Afternoon of Jazz annual fundraiser. In 1978 the first recipient of a foundation scholarship, Debora Young, graduated from Boston College. Rachel was on hand to give Debora her diploma. Since then, more than 1,500 students have received financial support from the foundation, which as of 2020 had an annual operating budget of $9 million.[65]

Jack was the recipient of numerous posthumous accolades, and Rachel was frequently on hand to accept them. The first was just a few months after his death, when in March of 1973 the New York Urban League awarded him its annual Frederick Douglass tribute, presented by Jack's old ally, New York Governor Nelson Rockefeller.[66] In 1984 she accepted Jack's Presidential Medal of Freedom, the highest civilian award in the United States, from President Ronald Reagan. In a strange twist of fate, also honored at that event was Maria Shriver, founder of the Special Olympics and sister of Jack's earlier political foil, John F. Kennedy. Rachel returned to Washington in 2003 when he was awarded the Congressional Gold Medal, this one the highest honor a civilian can receive from Congress, turning a rare double play.[67]

Rachel received numerous superlatives of her own, including the Candace Award for Distinguished Service from the National Coalition of 100 Black Women, given to a "Black role model of uncommon distinction who ha[s] set a standard of excellence for young people of all races."[68] She also won the Equitable Life Black Achievers Award and the Associated Black Charities Black History Makers Award. She received 12 honorary doctorates, including one from her alma mater, New York University.[69] Her other alma mater presented her with the UCLA Medal in 2009, the University's highest honor. In 2017 she was given the Buck O'Neil Lifetime Achievement Award by the Baseball Hall of Fame and Museum, presented every three years to a person who enhances baseball's positive image on society.

Rachel also played an integral role in securing Jack's legacy within major-league baseball. She was a living connection to baseball's finest moment, and she understood the magnitude of that reality. Even when baseball disappointed her, she persevered and made them do better. When Dodgers vice president Al Campanis appeared on *Nightline* in 1987 and questioned the mental fitness of potential Black managers, Rachel did not shy away from her criticisms of both Campanis and the systemic racism that still existed in baseball's front office. Embarrassingly for baseball, Campanis's comments came as they were celebrating the 40th anniversary of Jack's integration of the Dodgers. Speaking to the importance of that moment, Rachel acknowledged the achievement, but quickly followed that by saying that "until there's a change in all aspects of the game – the executive structure, front offices and ownership – I don't feel any real change had occurred at all."[70] Her words moved

Commissioner Peter Ueberroth to bring her into his inner circle as he attempted to confront baseball's ongoing race issues.

The culmination of her efforts came in 1997 when, with the assistance of National League President and Jackie Robinson Foundation Chairman Len Coleman, it was announced that baseball would celebrate the league-wide retirement of Robinson's number 42. While Commissioner Bud Selig spoke of the "considerable progress" that baseball had made since Ueberroth began his initiatives, Rachel remained undeterred. When the retirement was announced, she was grateful, but even while still basking in the glow of that unprecedented honor, she made sure to let the world know that "racism is still with us and the struggle is still on. We need to have a vision and we need to have a plan."[71] Rachel was able to check another US commander-in-chief off the list, when President Bill Clinton was on hand at Shea Stadium to speak at the April 15 ceremony that prefaced the contest between the New York Mets and the Los Angeles Dodgers.

Intermingled with the host of other responsibilities she took upon herself, Rachel also played an occasional role in the dramatic interpretations of Jack, serving as a creative consultant on multiple TV, stage and book projects. Despite the vast quantity of fictionalizations, including the commercially successful 2013 film *42: The True Story of an American Legend*, starring Chadwick Boseman as Jack and Nicole Beharie as Rachel, none of those works could truly capture the full depth and breadth of his expansive life. It was her desire to see the whole of Jack's story told, which led Rachel to reach out to Ken Burns in hopes that the creator of the 10-volume omnibus, *Baseball*, might be willing to be the one to tell the tale. At first Burns hesitated, but as Rachel passed her 90th birthday, the documentarian became concerned that he was going to lose the opportunity to speak to the best firsthand witness to the life of Jack Robinson.[72] Rachel appears throughout the four-hour film; her memories, both joyful and painful, are crystal clear and told with the wisdom and humor of a woman who had seen much in her long life. And still she was not done.

On July 19, 2020, Rachel, along with three generations of Robinsons, celebrated her 98th birthday. It was, in the bizarre world of that pandemic-shortened season, Opening Day for the Los Angeles Dodgers. She looked resplendent in a bright red dress, surrounded by an array of floral arrangements in her New York City apartment. The family enjoyed the well-wishes that flooded in from social media, as well as a compilation of tributes that had been put together by the Jackie Robinson Foundation.[73] Rachel sold the house in Stamford in the 1990s, and split her time between her home in North Salem, Connecticut, and New York City. In September 2020 she moved to Delray Beach, Florida, with Sharon, into a home they designed together.[74]

The 2020 season marked the 75th anniversary of Jack's first meeting with Branch Rickey, and this time it was Sharon who handled the bulk of the publicity when Major League Baseball celebrated the event. The festivities were particularly poignant, as America was once again gripped by racial justice protests, sparked by repeated police violence against BIPOC citizens, a familiar refrain for Rachel. There will be more anniversaries in the years to come, as Jack's legacy, one that Rachel assured, will likely be celebrated for all time. Maybe one day, those celebrations can take place in a world that Rachel and Jack sacrificed so much for – a world of true equality for all.

NOTES

1. Arnold Rampersad, *Jackie Robinson: A Biography* (New York: Ballantine Books, 1997), 76. See also 1940 US Census, accessed through Ancestry.com.
2. Gary Libman, "Rachel Robinson's Homecoming: She Recalls a Legend and Her Days in L.A.," *Los Angeles Times*, September 2, 1987.
3. Rampersad, 78.
4. Rachel Robinson and Lee Daniels, *Jackie Robinson: An Intimate Portrait* (New York: Abrams, 1996), 20.
5. Jackie Robinson, *I Never Had It Made* (New York: Harper Collins, 1995), 11.
6. *I Never Had It Made*, 10
7. *Intimate Portrait*, 22-24; Rampersad, 79.
8. Ken Burns, director, *Jackie Robinson*. Florentine Films, 2016.
9. Rampersad, 84-86.
10. Author email exchange with Jennifer Jensen, curator of Jackie Robinson Foundation, October 26, 2020.
11. Rampersad, 89.
12. Rampersad, 94.
13. *Intimate Portrait*, 27-28.
14. Rampersad, 99.
15. Rampersad, 111.
16. Jensen email exchange, October 26, 2020.
17. Rampersad, 131-132.
18. *Intimate Portrait*, 40.
19. Rampersad, 137-139.
20. Rampersad, 140.
21. *Intimate Portrait*, 50-52.
22. Ingrid Peritz, "Jackie Robinson's Wife Remembers a Welcoming Montreal," *Globe and Mail* (Toronto), April 28, 2013. theglobeandmail.com/news/national/Jack-robinsons-wife-remembers-a-welcoming-montreal/article11602715/.

23. *I Never Had It Made*, 53.
24. Rampersad, 152.
25. *Intimate Portrait*, 54-58.
26. Rampersad, 158-159.
27. *I Never Had It Made*, 66.
28. *Intimate Portrait*, 66.
29. *I Never Had It Made*, 66.
30. Rampersad, 180-182.
31. *Intimate Portrait*, 72.
32. *Intimate Portrait*, 75.
33. Jensen email exchange.
34. *Intimate Portrait*, 88; Rampersad, 195, 196.
35. Idlewild Airport was later renamed for the slain President John F. Kennedy.
36. Nicholas Hirshon, "Jackie Robinson's House Not Safe," *New York Daily News*, April 7, 2008. nydailynews.com/new-york/queens/jackie-robinson-house-not-safe-article-1.280057.
37. *Intimate Portrait*, 94-96.
38. Rampersad, 198.
39. Hirshon.
40. Susan Muaddi Darraj, *Jackie Robinson* (New York: Chelsea House, 2008), 71.
41. *Intimate Portrait*, 130-132.
42. Rampersad, 274.
43. Jensen email exchange.
44. *Intimate Portrait*, 133.
45. Rampersad, 310.
46. *Intimate Portrait*, 139.
47. *Intimate Portrait*, 144.
48. *Intimate Portrait*, 161.
49. *Intimate Portrait*, 160-161.
50. Rampersad, 360.
51. Ramersad, 361.
52. *Intimate Portrait*, 175.
53. *Intimate Portrait*, 174.
54. "Jazz Festival Earns Funds for Rev. King," *Record* (Hackensack, New Jersey), June 24, 1963: 5.
55. *Intimate Portrait*, 176.
56. *I Never Had It Made*, 219.
57. *Intimate Portrait*, 201.
58. *I Never Had It Made*, 247.
59. *Intimate Portrait*, 202.
60. Rampersad, 449-450.
61. Rampersad, 210.
62. Rampersad, 216.
63. "The Plain and Poor Remember Jack Robinson," *Democrat and Chronicle* (Rochester, New York), October 28, 1972: 3D.
64. *Intimate Portrait*. 220.
65. "History." *Jackie Robinson Foundation* website. Jackierobinson.org/timeline/#/home. Accessed October 23, 2020; Jensen email exchange.
66. "Urban League Gives Posthumous Award to Jack Robinson." *New York Times*, May 4, 1973.
67. "History," *Jackie Robinson Foundation* website.
68. *National Coalition of 100 Black Women, Inc.* ncbw.org/.
69. "Rachel Robinson Bio," *Jack Robinson Foundation* website. Jackierobinson.org/people/rachel-robinson/. Accessed October 24, 2020.
70. "After Campanis: What About Blacks' Chances," *Bismarck* (North Dakota) *Tribune*, April 12, 1987: 19.
71. Ronald Blum, "Baseball to Honor Jack Robinson in '97," *News-Press* (Fort Myers, Florida), February 27, 1997: C1.
72. Author interview with Sharon Robinson, September 18, 2020.
73. Author email exchange with Sharon Robinson, October 26, 2020.
74. Author interview with Sharon Robinson, September 18, 2020.

BEFORE JACKIE ROBINSON: BASEBALL'S CIVIL RIGHTS MOVEMENT

by Peter Dreier

In February 1933 – when Jackie Robinson was 14 years old – Heywood Broun, a syndicated columnist at the *New York World-Telegram*, addressed the annual dinner of the all-White New York Baseball Writers Association. If Black athletes were good enough to represent the United States at the 1932 Olympic Games, Broun said, "it seems a little silly that they cannot participate in a game between the Chicago White Sox and St. Louis Browns." There was no formal rule prohibiting Blacks from playing in the major leagues, he said, but instead a "tacit agreement" among owners. "Why, in the name of fair play and gate receipts should professional baseball be so exclusive?"[1]

That same month, Jimmy Powers, a popular columnist for the *New York Daily News*, the nation's largest-circulation newspaper, interviewed baseball executives and players, asking if they'd object to having Black players on their teams. NL President John Heydler, Yankees owner Jacob Ruppert, and star players Herb Pennock, Lou Gehrig, and Frankie Frisch, told Powers they didn't object. Only New York Giants manager John McGraw – who, ironically, had tried to hire a Black player (posing as a Cherokee Indian) when he managed the Baltimore Orioles in 1901 – told Powers he'd opposed the idea. In his February 8, 1933, column, Powers predicted that Blacks would eventually play major-league baseball. "I base this upon the fact that the ball player of today is more liberal than yesterday's leather-necked, tobacco-chewing sharpshooter from the cross roads."[2]

Later that month, Chester Washington, sports editor of the influential Black newspaper the *Pittsburgh Courier*, coordinated a four-month series reporting the views of major-league owners, managers, and players about baseball segregation. It began with an interview with Heydler, who said, "I do not recall one instance where baseball has allowed either race, creed, or color to enter into the question of the selection of its players."[3] The paper quoted Philadelphia Phillies President Gerry Nugent: "Baseball caters to all races and creeds. … It is the national game and is played by all groups. Therefore, I see no objections to negro players in the big leagues." Commissioner Kenesaw Mountain Landis refused to respond to the *Courier*, but his assistant Leslie O'Connor said there was no rule against Black players. Hiring decisions were made by owners, not the commissioner, he said.

The saga of how Robinson broke baseball's color line in 1947 has been told many times in books, newspaper and magazine articles, and Hollywood films. It is typically told as the tale of two trailblazers – Robinson, the combative athlete, and Dodgers President and general manager Branch Rickey, the shrewd strategist – battling baseball's, and society's, bigotry.

The Jackie Robinson Story, released in 1950 at the height of the Cold War, five years before the Montgomery bus boycott, celebrated Robinson's feat as evidence that America was a land of opportunity where anyone could succeed if he had the talent and will. The movie opens with the narrator saying, "This is a story of a boy and his dream. But more than that, it's a story of an American boy and a dream that is truly American." Rickey is portrayed as a benevolent do-gooder who, for moral and religious reasons, believes he has a responsibility to break baseball's color barrier. The 2013 film *42* spun a similar story. It depicts *Pittsburgh Courier* reporter Wendell Smith as Robinson's traveling companion and the ghostwriter for his newspaper column during his rookie season, but ignores Smith's key role as a leader of the long crusade to integrate baseball before Robinson became a household name.

Most books and articles about this saga ignore or downplay the true story of how baseball's apartheid system was dismantled. Rickey's plan came to fruition only after more than a decade of protest to desegregate the national pastime. It was a political victory brought about by a progressive movement.

Throughout the Great Depression – from 1929 to 1941 — millions of workers, consumers, students, and farmers engaged in massive protests over economic hardship. This reflected the nation's mood, a combination of anger and fear. Franklin Roosevelt's 1932 election as president, with 57 percent of the vote, added an element of hope. For most Americans, New Deal reforms – including Social Security, the minimum wage, workers' right to unionize, subsidies to troubled farmers, a massive government-funded jobs program, and stronger regulation of banks and other businesses – offered welcome relief to the suffering. In 1936, they re-elected FDR with 61 percent of the vote.

But some viewed FDR's program as halfway measures that didn't challenge the problem's root causes. The collapse of America's economy radicalized millions of Americans. Because the Depression imposed even greater hardships on Blacks than Whites, Black Americans were more open than most Whites to radical ideas.

At the time, America was deeply segregated. Black Americans, 10 percent of America's population, were relegated to second-class status and denied basic civil and political rights in the South and elsewhere. The subjugation of Negroes, wrote sociologist Gunnar Myrdal, was "the most glaring conflict in the American conscience and greatest unsolved task for American democracy."[4]

In the 1930s and 1940s, civil-rights activists fought against discrimination in housing and jobs, mobilized for a federal anti-lynching law, protested against segregation within the military, marched to open up defense jobs to Blacks during World War II, challenged police brutality and restrictive covenants that barred Blacks from certain neighborhoods, and boycotted stores that refused to hire African-Americans. The movement accelerated after the war, when returning Black veterans expected that America would open up opportunities for Black citizens.

As part of that movement, the Negro press, civil-rights groups, progressive White activists and unions, the Communist Party, and radical politicians waged a sustained campaign to integrate baseball. The coalition included unlikely allies who disagreed about political ideology but found common ground in challenging baseball's Jim Crow system. They believed that if they could push the nation's most popular sport to dismantle its color line, they could make inroads in other facets of American society.[5]

A few White journalists for mainstream papers, including Broun (a socialist) and Powers, joined the crusade. They reminded readers that two Black athletes – Jesse Owens and Mack Robinson (Jackie's older brother) – had embarrassed Hitler in the 1936 Olympics in Berlin by defeating Germany's White track stars, and that White and Black Americans alike cheered Joe Louis after he knocked out German Max Schmeling (whom Hitler touted as evidence of White Aryan superiority) in the first round at Yankee Stadium before a crowd of 70,043 in 1938.

With a few exceptions, during the 1930s and 1940s sportswriters for White-owned newspapers ignored the Negro Leagues and the burgeoning protest movement against baseball's color line. In contrast, readers of the nation's Black papers were well-informed about these players and the protests. These papers did more than report; they were advocates for civil rights in society and baseball.

Their reporters – especially Smith and Washington of the *Pittsburgh Courier*, Fay Young of the *Chicago Defender*, Joe Bostic of the *People's Voice* in New York, Sam Lacy and Art Carter of the *Baltimore Afro-American*, Mabray "Doc" Kountze of Cleveland's *Call and Post*, and Dan Burley of New York's *Amsterdam News* – took the lead in pushing baseball's establishment to hire Black players. They were joined by Lester Rodney, sports editor of the Communist *Daily Worker*. They published open letters to owners, polled White managers and players, brought Black players to unscheduled tryouts at spring-training centers, and kept the issue before the public.

For Smith, the matter was personal. In 1933, as a 19-year-old, he pitched his American Legion club in Detroit to a 1-0 victory in the playoffs. A scout for the Detroit Tigers told him, "I wish I could sign you, too, but I can't," because of his race. Those words "broke me up," Smith recalled. "It was then I made a vow that I would dedicate myself to do something on behalf of the Negro ballplayers. That was one of the reasons I became a sportswriter."[6]

Thanks to Smith, the *Courier* – with the largest circulation of any Black newspaper, growing from 46,000 readers in 1933 to over 250,000 in 1945 – became the leading voice against baseball's racial divide. Smith expanded the *Courier*'s efforts to protest segregation in baseball and other sports. In his first column on the issue, on May 14, 1938, Smith criticized Black Americans for spending their hard-earned money on teams that prohibited Black players. "We know they don't want us, but we keep giving them our money." He also criticized Black Americans for not patronizing the Negro League teams, putting them in constant financial jeopardy.[7] Smith was echoing the civil-rights movement's demand to boycott businesses that refused to hire or show respect for Black Americans.

In 1939 Smith interviewed National League President Ford Frick, who claimed that major-league teams didn't employ Black athletes because White fans would not accept them. He also noted that Black players wouldn't be allowed to travel with their teams during spring training or in certain major-league cities because Southern hotels, restaurants, and trains would not accept them – a reality that, Frick said, would undermine team spirit.

Frick's comments inspired Smith to interview eight managers and 40 National League players, which he published in a series entitled "What Big Leaguers Think of Negro League Baseball Players" between July and September 1939. Among the managers, only the Giants' Bill Terry said Blacks should be barred from major-league teams. Dodgers manager Leo Durocher told Smith: "I've seen plenty of colored boys who could make the grade in the majors. Hell, I've seen a million. I've played against SOME colored boys out on the coast who could play in any big league that ever existed." He added: "I certainly would use a Negro ball player if the bosses said it was all right."[8] Other managers and players agreed with Durocher's view, expressing hope that Black players would one day play in the majors.[9]

The Negro papers extolled the talents of Black players as equal to their White counterparts. As evidence, they pointed to the outcomes of exhibition games between Negro teams and White players. On October 20, 1934, for example, the Negro Leagues' Kansas City Monarchs beat a team of major leaguers, which included the St. Louis Cardinals' ace pitcher Dizzy Dean. A week later, Satchel Paige and the Pittsburgh Crawfords defeated the same contingent of major leaguers. In 1938 Dean told the *Courier* that Paige was "the pitcher with the greatest stuff I ever see."[10] In 1939 Dean – who grew up in rural Arkansas – told Smith that Paige, Josh Gibson, and Oscar Charleston were among the best players he'd ever seen. "I have played against a Negro all-star team that was so good we didn't think we had a chance," he said.[11]

During the 1930s and 1940s, the Communist Party – although never approaching 100,000 members – had a disproportionate influence in progressive and liberal circles. The CP took strong stands for unions and women's equality and against racism, anti-Semitism, and emerging fascism in Europe. It sent organizers to the South to organize sharecroppers and tenant farmers and was active in campaigns against lynching, police brutality, and Jim Crow laws. The CP led campaigns to stop landlords from evicting tenants and to push for unemployment benefits. In Harlem, it helped launch the "Don't Buy Where You Can't Work" campaign, urging consumers to boycott stores that refused to hire Black employees.[12] Prominent Black Americans, including Paul Robeson, Richard Wright, and Langston Hughes, were attracted to the CP.

In 1938 the American Youth Congress, a group led by CP activists, passed a resolution censuring baseball for excluding Black players. In 1939 New York State Senator Charles Perry, who represented Harlem, introduced a resolution that condemned baseball for discriminating against Black ballplayers. In 1940 sports editors from New York area college newspapers, many of them influenced by radical ideas, adopted a similar resolution. A story in the *Daily Worker* in 1940 proclaimed: "The campaign for the admission of Negro players to the major leagues has now become a national issue, drawing support from tens of thousands of fans and fair-minded Americans who have the best interest of the game at heart. … There is now the Committee to End Jim Crow in Baseball, which is growing rapidly and which has just launched a campaign to end this evil. … The magnificent talents of the Negro would be a tonic to the game, enriching it beyond measure."[13]

Unions played an important part in this crusade. The New York Trade Union Athletic Association, a coalition of progressive unions, organized an "end Jim Crow in baseball" day of protest at the 1940 World's Fair.[14] Unions and civil-rights groups picketed outside Yankee Stadium, the Polo Grounds, and Ebbets Field in New York, and Comiskey Park and Wrigley Field in Chicago. The speakers included Congressman Vito Marcantonio of New York and Richard Moore of the left-wing National Negro Congress. Over several years, these activists gathered more than a million signatures on petitions, demanding that baseball tear down the color barrier. In 1943 similar pickets occurred outside Wrigley Field in Los Angeles, where the minor-league Angels played.[15] Angels President Pants Rowland wanted to give tryouts to several Black players. He and Philip Wrigley, owner of the Chicago Cubs, the parent team, met with William Patterson, a civil-rights lawyer and Communist Party member. But Wrigley nixed the tryout idea, saying he favored integration but "I don't think the time is now."[16]

No White journalist played a more central role in baseball's civil-rights movement than the *Daily Worker's* Lester Rodney. Born in 1911, he was radicalized by his family's own hardships and by the enormous suffering he witnessed during the Depression.

He first encountered the *Daily Worker* while attending New York University. He agreed with its political perspective but was appalled by its failure to take sports seriously. The paper occasionally wrote about union-sponsored and industrial baseball leagues, but not professional sports. He wrote a letter to the paper's editor, criticizing its sports coverage. "You guys are focusing on the things that are wrong in sports. And there's plenty that's wrong. But you wind up painting a picture of professional athletes being wage slaves with no joy, no elan – and that's just wrong. Of course there's exploitation, but ... the professional baseball player still swells with joy when his team wins. ... (T)hat's not fake." The paper hired him and soon made him its first sports editor. He served in the capacity from 1936 to 1958, when he quit the Communist Party.

Durocher once told Rodney: "For a fucking Communist, you sure know your baseball."[17] For a dozen years, Rodney was one of the few White sportswriters to cover the Negro Leagues and to protest baseball segregation. One of his editorials attacked "every rotten Jim Crow excuse offered by the magnates for this flagrant discrimination."[18] "Paige Beats Big Leaguers: Negro Team Wins 3-1 Before 30,000 Fans in Chicago," declared a 1942 headline, typical of the *Daily Worker*'s advocacy journalism.[19]

According to Rodney, the paper "had an influence far in excess of its circulation, partly because a lot of our readership was trade union people" and because it was "on the desk of every other newspaper" in New York.[20]

In a 1936 interview with Rodney, Frick insisted that there was no prohibition against Black players in the majors and, echoing Landis, said that owners had the responsibility for signing players. Some baseball executives told Rodney that there were no Black players good enough to play in the majors. Others blamed the fans, insisting that they wouldn't stand for having Black players on their favorite teams. Or they'd blame the players, insisting that they'd rebel if the owners hired Black players to be their teammates.

Like Smith and other sympathetic reporters, Rodney shot down the argument that most players and managers opposed baseball integration. A typical *Daily Worker* story, from July 19, 1939, was headlined: "Big Leaguers Rip Jim Crow." It quoted Cincinnati Reds manager Bill McKechnie, who said that "I'd use Negroes if I were given permission." Reds star pitcher Bucky Walters declared them "some of the best players I've ever seen." Johnny Van der Meer, another pitching ace, said: "I don't see why they're banned." Yankee slugger Joe DiMaggio told Rodney that Satchel Paige was the best pitcher he ever faced.[21]

Rodney had great rapport with the players. Between 1937 and 1939, he even recruited two progressive players – Yankees third baseman Red Rolfe and Cubs first baseman Ripper Collins – to write for the *Daily Worker*. They wrote about baseball, not politics, but, according to Irwin Silber, Rodney's biographer, "the fact that a major-league ballplayer would be willing to write for the *Daily Worker* signified a degree of legitimacy for the Communist Party – or at least its newspaper – that could hardly have been imagined a few years earlier."[22]

According to Rodney, "Readers loved it, of course, but the really fascinating thing was the next day after a story would come out. I'd go into the dressing room before the game – and just picture this – there are the Yankees – *the New York Yankees* – sitting around the dressing room reading the *Daily Worker*. If Colonel Ruppert [the Yankees owner] had walked in, he would have had a heart attack." And there was "not a word of red-baiting" of Rolfe or Collins by their teammates.[23]

Rodney interviewed Negro players to challenge the myth that they preferred playing in the Negro Leagues to breaking into the majors. In an interview with Rodney, Paige observed: "We've been playing a team of major-league all stars after the regular season in California for four years and they haven't beaten us yet. … Must be a few men who don't want us to play big league ball. The players are okay and the crowds are with us."[24]

For Rodney, reporting and advocacy were intertwined. In 1941 he and sportswriters for Negro newspapers, including Smith, sent telegrams to team owners asking them to give tryouts to Black players. In 1942 the Chicago White Sox reluctantly invited the Negro League pitcher Nate Moreland and UCLA's All-American football star Jackie Robinson to attend a tryout camp in Pasadena. Manager Jimmy Dykes raved about Robinson: "He's worth $50,000 of anybody's money. He stole everything but my infielders' gloves." But the two ballplayers never heard from the White Sox again.

In response to Rodney's telegram, the Pittsburgh Pirates invited Negro League players Roy Campanella, Sammy Hughes, and David Barnhill to a tryout. But as Campanella, later a Hall of Fame catcher with the Dodgers, recalled in his 1959 autobiography *It's Good to Be Alive,* the invitation letter from Pirates owner William Benswanger "contained so many buts that

I was discouraged even before I finished reading the letter."[25] Benswanger canceled the tryout.

Despite his strong opposition to communism, Smith acknowledged Rodney's role on behalf of baseball integration. In an August 20, 1939, letter to Rodney in the *Daily Worker*, Smith wrote that he wanted to "congratulate you and the *Daily Worker* for the way you have joined with us in the current series concerning Negro Players in the major leagues, as well as all your past great efforts in this aspect." He expressed the hope of further collaboration.[26]

After the United States entered World War II in December 1941, this coalition escalated its campaign to integrate baseball.

Some African-Americans had mixed feelings about supporting the war effort when they faced such blatant discrimination at home. When he was drafted, Nate Moreland, a Negro League pitcher, complained: "I can play in Mexico, but I have to fight for America, where I can't play." Activists carried picket signs at Yankee Stadium, asking, "If we are able to stop bullets, why not balls?"[27] An editorial in the *New Negro World* in May 1942 reflected similar frustrations:

"If my nation cannot outlaw lynching, if the uniform [of the Army] will not bring me the respect of the people that I serve, if the freedom of America will not protect me as a human being when I cry in the wilderness of ingratitude; then I declare before both God and man ... TO HELL WITH PEARL HARBOR."[28]

A month after the Japanese bombed Pearl Harbor on December 7, 1941, and the United States entered the war, James Thompson, a cafeteria worker in Kansas, coined the phrase "Double Victory" in a letter to the *Pittsburgh Courier*.

> "The V for victory sign is being displayed prominently in so-called democratic countries which are fighting for victory over aggression, slavery and tyranny," Thompson wrote. "If this V sign means that to those now engaged in this great conflict, then let we colored Americans adopt the double VV for a double victory. The first V for victory over our enemies from without, the second V for victory over our enemies from within. For surely those who perpetrate these ugly prejudices here are seeking to destroy our democratic form of government just as surely as the Axis forces."[29]

Black leaders and newspapers enthusiastically supported the "Double V" campaign. Cumberland "Cum" Posey, owner of the Negro League's Homestead Grays, suggested, in his weekly *Courier* column "Posey's Points," that every Negro League player wear a Double V symbol on its uniform.

Throughout the war years, Smith, Rodney, and other progressive sportswriters voiced their outrage about the hypocrisy of baseball's establishment.[30]

In an open letter to Landis published in the *Daily Worker* in May 1942, Rodney wrote: "Negro soldiers and sailors are among those beloved heroes of the American people who have already died for the preservation of this country and everything this country stands for – yes, including the great game of baseball. You, the self-proclaimed 'Czar' of baseball, are the man responsible for keeping Jim Crow in our National Pastime. You are the one refusing to say the word which would do more to justify baseball's existence in this year of war than any other single thing."

In a July 1942 column, Smith wrote that "big league baseball is perpetuating the very things thousands of Americans are overseas fighting to end, namely, racial discrimination and segregation." The next year, he called on President Roosevelt to adopt a "Fair Employment Practice Policy" for major-league baseball similar to the one he'd adopted in war industries and governmental agencies.

In June 1942, large locals of several major unions – including the United Auto Workers and the National Maritime Union, as well as the New York Industrial Union Council of the Congress of Industrial Organizations (CIO) – sent resolutions to Landis demanding an end to baseball segregation. The union leaders told Landis's secretary, Leslie O'Connor, that unless he let them address the owners' meeting, they would take the issue to the Fair Employment Practices Committee (FEPC), the federal agency created by FDR in 1941 to investigate discrimination in the defense industry and other sectors.[31] Landis and the owners refused to meet with them.

The unions' protest made headlines in both Negro and White newspapers across the country. The stories mostly focused on Landis's refusal to meet with them, but just getting the issue in the news helped them build public support for their cause.[32] The movement gained an important ally when Chicago's Catholic bishop, Bernard Shiel, announced he would urge Landis to support integration.[33] In July 1942, Landis summoned Durocher to a meeting in Chicago, and rebuked him for his comments claiming that baseball banned Black players. Landis issued a statement claiming that "there is no baseball rule – formal, informal, or otherwise – that says a ball player must be white."[34] Most newspapers took Landis at his word, but the Black papers and the *Daily Worker* called him a hypocrite.

That December, 10 CIO leaders went to the baseball executives' winter meetings in Chicago to demand that major-league teams recruit Black players, but Landis again refused to meet with them.[35] Only Chicago Cubs owner Phil Wrigley broke ranks. After the official meeting ended, he invited union leaders to his office and told them he favored integration and revealed that, contrary to his fellow owners' claims, there was, in fact, a "gentlemen's agreement" among them to keep Blacks out of major-league baseball. "There are men in high places," he told them, "who don't want to see it."[36] Frustrated by the lack of progress, in February 1943 a broad coalition of unions, left-wing groups, religious and civil-rights organizations, including the Urban League and the NAACP, met in Chicago and adopted a resolution demanding the integration of baseball, to send to Landis, team owners, and President Roosevelt.[37]

Smith spent much of 1943 lambasting Washington Senators owner Clark Griffith for his outspoken opposition to allowing Blacks in the majors. Griffith insisted that Blacks should focus on improving their own leagues. Smith recognized that Griffith was profiting handsomely by renting his ballpark to Negro League teams. He was also angered that during World War II Griffith signed foreign-born ballplayers, including many Latin Americans, instead of Black athletes to replace White players. Griffith "has so many foreigners on his team it is necessary to have an interpreter," Smith wrote.[38]

In December 1943 Smith asked Landis to meet with the publishers of leading Black newspapers at the owners' December meeting. Landis agreed, pressured in part by a resolution sponsored by a New York City Council member demanding that the major leagues recruit Black players. This was the first time that representatives of the Black community met directly with baseball's establishment.

Smith brought seven newspapermen along, as well as Paul Robeson, the Black actor, singer, activist, and former All-American athlete at Rutgers. Landis began the meeting by insisting that he wanted it "clearly understood that there is no rule, nor to my knowledge, has there ever been, formal or informal, or any understanding, written or unwritten, subterranean or sub-anything, against the hiring of Negroes in the major leagues."[39]

Then Landis introduced Robeson, who gave an impassioned 20-minute appeal, referencing his experience in college and professional football and his current work as an actor, dispelling the idea that desegregation creates chaos. "They said that America never would stand for my playing Othello with a white cast, but it is the triumph of my life," he declared. "The time has come when you must change your attitude toward Negroes. ... Because baseball is a national game, it is up to baseball to see that discrimination does not become an American pattern. And it should do this this year."[40]

The owners gave him a rousing applause, but Landis had instructed them to ask him no questions.

Landis next introduced John Sengstacke, president of the Negro Newspaper Publishers Association and the publisher of the *Chicago Defender*. Sengstacke called the ban against Black players "un-American" and "undemocratic." Then Ira Lewis, president of the *Courier*, told the owners it was simply untrue that major-league players would refuse to play against Black athletes, based on Smith's many interviews. He also noted that Black players could compete with White players at the same level, reminding the owners that Black teams had defeated teams of major leaguers in various exhibition games.[41]

None of the baseball owners and executives asked the Black publishers any questions. After the meeting ended, they issued an official statement repeating Landis's claims.

In 1944 Smith wrote several sympathetic stories to help publicize the court-martial of a Black soldier at Fort Hood, Texas – a former UCLA four-sport athlete – for refusing to go to the back of a military bus. The soldier was Jackie Robinson, who befriended Smith and was grateful for his support.

In early 1945, a few months after Landis died, baseball's owners selected Albert "Happy" Chandler as the next baseball commissioner. As governor and then senator from Kentucky, Chandler echoed the segregationist views of most White Kentuckians. So when *Pittsburgh Courier* reporter Ric Roberts asked Chandler about allowing Blacks in the big leagues, he was surprised to hear Chandler say that he didn't think it was fair to perpetuate the ban and that teams should hire players to win ballgames "whatever their origin or race."[42] Baseball's integration crusaders felt that even if Chandler wasn't an ally, he wouldn't be an implacable obstacle as Landis had been.

On April 6, 1945, as the war was winding down, Black sportswriter Joe Bostic of the *People's Voice* appeared unannounced at the Dodgers' Bear Mountain, New York, training camp with Negro League stars

Terris McDuffie and Dave Thomas and pressured Rickey into giving them tryouts. The next day, Rickey and manager Durocher watched the two athletes perform, but determined that they were not major-league caliber. Moreover, Rickey was furious. He wanted to bring Black players into major-league baseball, but he wanted to do it on his terms and his timetable. He didn't want the public to think that he was being pressured into it. "I am more for your cause than anybody else you know," he told Bostic, "but you are making a mistake using force. You are defeating your own aims." But the ploy made the news. The *New York Times* ran a story headlined: "Two Negroes Are Tried Out by Dodgers but They Fail to Impress President Rickey."[43]

With many progressive unions and civil-rights groups, a large Black population, and three major-league teams, New York City was the center of the movement to end Jim Crow in baseball. On Opening Day of 1944, for example, the Congress of Racial Equality (CORE) organized a demonstration outside Yankee Stadium to enlighten fans and castigate the owners of the game's most powerful franchise. Several New York politicians were allies of the campaign to integrate baseball. Running for re-election as a Communist to the New York City Council in 1945, Ben Davis – an African-American who starred on the football field for Amherst College before earning a law degree at Harvard – distributed a leaflet with the photos of two Blacks, a dead soldier and a baseball player. "Good enough to die for his country," it said, "but not good enough for organized baseball."[44]

In March of 1945, the New York State Legislature passed, and Republican Gov. Thomas E. Dewey signed, the Quinn-Ives Act, which banned discrimination in hiring, and soon formed a committee to investigate discriminatory hiring practices, including one that focused on baseball.

In short order, New York City Mayor Fiorello LaGuardia established a Committee on Baseball to push the Yankees, Giants, and Dodgers to sign Black players. Rickey met with LaGuardia but didn't reveal his plan. Left-wing Congressman Vito Marcantonio, who represented Harlem, called for the US Commerce Department to investigate baseball's racist practices.

The baseball establishment was feeling the heat. Sam Lacy, a reporter for the *Afro-American*, wrote to all of the owners suggesting that they set up an integration committee. To deflect the problem and avoid bad publicity, the owners reluctantly agreed to study the issue of discrimination. Rickey (representing the NL) agreed to serve on the committee along with Yankees President Larry MacPhail (representing the AL), Lacy, and Philadelphia Judge Joseph H. Rainey, an African-American. But, according to Lacy, "MacPhail always found a way to be too busy for us," and the full committee never met. Rickey told Lacy that he would work to integrate baseball on his own.[45]

Rickey wasn't pleased with this pressure, which he knew was partly orchestrated by Communists and other radicals.

Rickey's White scouts, unfamiliar with the Negro Leagues, couldn't help him find the Black player he wanted to be baseball's trailblazer. Instead, Rickey had subscriptions to the major Negro newspapers, which published Negro League box scores, statistics, and schedules, and whose sportswriters gave accounts of its best players. In 1945 Rickey gave his scouts a list of players to follow, pretending that he was interested in starting his own all-Black baseball league to compete with the existing Negro Leagues.

Rickey's search for the right player was inadvertently aided by Isadore Muchnick, a progressive Jewish member of the Boston City Council. In 1945 Muchnick was determined to push the Boston Red Sox to hire Black players. But owner Tom Yawkey was among baseball's strongest opponents of integration. Muchnick threatened to deny the Red Sox a permit needed to play on Sundays unless the team considered hiring Black players. Working with Smith and White sportswriter Dave Egan of the *Boston Record*, Muchnick persuaded reluctant general manager Eddie Collins to give three Negro League players – Robinson, Sam Jethroe, and Marvin Williams – a tryout at Fenway Park on April 16.

Robinson had already endured the earlier bogus tryout with the White Sox four years earlier in Pasadena. He was skeptical about the Red Sox' motives now, He and the other two players performed well. Robinson, the most impressive of the three, hit line drives to all fields. "Bang, bang, bang; he rattled it," Muchnick recalled. "Jackie hit balls over the fence and against the wall," echoed Jethroe. "What a ballplayer," said Hugh Duffy, the Red Sox' chief scout and onetime outstanding hitter. "Too bad he's the wrong color."[46]

The Red Sox, Pirates, and White Sox had no intention of signing any of the Black players from the tryouts. But the public pressure and media publicity helped raise awareness and furthered the cause. And it helped give Rickey, who *did* want to hire Black players, a sense of urgency that if he wanted to be baseball's racial pioneer, he needed to act quickly.

After the phony Fenway Park tryout, Smith headed to Brooklyn to tell Rickey about Robinson's superlative performance. Smith was convinced that among major-league owners, Rickey was the desegregation campaign's strongest ally. The meeting cemented the relationship between the two men. Smith kept offering Rickey the names of Black ballplayers, but gave Robinson his strongest endorsement.

If Bill Veeck – who voted several times for Norman Thomas, the Socialist Party candidate for president – had his way, major-league baseball would have integrated five years before Robinson signed with the Dodgers. In 1942, when he owned the minor-league Milwaukee Brewers, the 28-year old Veeck learned that the Philadelphia Phillies were bankrupt and for sale. He quietly found investors, including CIO unions, then made a deal with the Phillies' owner, Gerry Nugent, to buy the team.[47] As he left for Philadelphia to seal the deal, he ran into John Carmichael, a *Chicago Daily News* sports columnist. He told Carmichael, "I'm going to Philadelphia. I'm going to buy the Phillies. And do you know what I'm going to do? I'm going to put a whole Black team on the field."[48]

Veeck believed that recruiting Negro Leagues stars could turn the lowly Phillies into a winning team and demonstrate that Black players were of major-league caliber. But hours before leaving for Philadelphia, Veeck made the mistake of informing Landis about his intentions. Veeck later recounted: "I got on the train feeling I had not only a Major League ball club but I was almost a virtual cinch to win the pennant next year." Before he had even reached Nugent's office the next day, Veeck learned that the NL had taken over the Phillies the night before and was seeking a new owner. Veeck was not on their list. As Veeck recounted in his 1962 autobiography, Landis and Frick had orchestrated a quick sale of the Phillies to another buyer.[49]

Despite this setback, Veeck continued to participate in baseball's civil-rights movement. In the early 1940s, as owner of the minor-league Milwaukee Brewers, Veeck sat in the "colored" section of the stands during the team's spring training in Ocala, Florida. The local sheriff and mayor showed up, ordered him to move, and threatened to arrest him for violating Florida's Jim Crow laws. Veeck refused and threatened to pull the team's lucrative spring-training program. The local officials left him alone after that.[50] In 1947, shortly after Robinson joined the Dodgers, Veeck, who then owned the Cleveland Indians, hired Larry Doby as the AL's first Black player and moved the team's spring-training venue from Florida to Arizona.

A little-known episode in the battle to integrate baseball took place in the US military in Europe, led by Sam Nahem, a right-handed pitcher who embraced left-wing politics.[51] Nahem pitched for Brooklyn College's baseball team and played fullback on its football team. At the time, Brooklyn College was a center of political activism, and Nahem began participating in Communist Party activities there. Between 1938 and 1941, Nahem pitched for the Brooklyn Dodgers, St. Louis Cardinals, and Philadelphia Phillies and earned a law degree at St. John's University in the offseasons.

Like most radicals of that era, Nahem believed that baseball should be racially integrated. He talked to some of his teammates to encourage them to be more open-minded. "I did my political work there," he told an interviewer years later. "I would take one guy aside if I thought he was amiable in that respect and talk to him, man to man, about the subject. I felt that was the way I could be most effective."[52]

During World War II, many professional players were in the military, so the quality of play on military bases was excellent. After Germany surrendered in May 1945, the military expanded its baseball program. That year, over 200,000 troops played on military teams in France, Germany, Belgium, Austria, Italy, and Britain.

Many top Negro League ballplayers were in the military, but they faced segregation, discrimination, and humiliation. Monte Irvin, a Negro League standout who later starred for the New York Giants, recalled: "When I was in the Army I took basic training in the South. I'd been asked to give up everything, including my life, to defend democracy. Yet when I went to town I had to ride in the back of a bus, or not at all on some buses."[53] Most Black soldiers with baseball talent were confined to playing on all-Black teams.

Nahem entered the military in November 1942. He volunteered for the infantry and hoped to see combat in Europe to help defeat Nazism. But he spent his first two years at Fort Totten in New York. There, he pitched for the Anti-Aircraft Redlegs of the Eastern Defense Command. In 1943 he set a league record with a 0.85 earned-run average. He also finished second in hitting with a .400 batting average and played every defensive position except catcher. In September 1944, his Fort Totten team beat the Philadelphia Athletics 9-5 in an exhibition game. Nahem pitched six innings, gave up only two runs and five hits, and slugged two homers, accounting for seven of his team's runs.

Sent overseas in late 1944, Nahem served with an antiaircraft artillery division. From his base in Rheims, he was assigned to run two baseball leagues in France, while also managing and playing for his own team, the Overseas Invasion Service Expedition (OISE) All-Stars, which represented the army command in charge of communication and logistics. The team was made up mainly of semipro, college, and ex-minor-league players. Besides Nahem, only one other OISE player, Russ Bauers, who had compiled a 29-29 won-loss record with the Pirates between 1936 and 1941, had major-league experience.

Defying the military establishment and baseball tradition, Nahem insisted on having African-Americans on his team. He recruited Willard Brown, a slugging outfielder for the Kansas City Monarchs and Leon Day, a star pitcher for the Newark Eagles.

Nahem's OISE team won 17 games and lost only one, attracting as many as 10,000 fans to its games, reaching the finals against the 71st Infantry Red Circlers, representing General George Patton's Third Army. One of Patton's top officers assigned St. Louis Cardinals All-Star outfielder Harry Walker to assemble a team. Besides Walker, the Red Circlers included seven other major leaguers, including the Cincinnati Reds' 6-foot-6 inch side-arm pitcher Ewell "The Whip" Blackwell.

Few people gave Nahem's OISE All-Stars much chance to win the European Theater of Operations (ETO) championship, known as the GI World Series. It took place in September, a few months after the defeat of Germany.

They played the first two games in Nuremberg, Germany, in the same stadium where Hitler had addressed Nazi Party rallies. Allied bombing had destroyed the city but somehow spared the stadium. The US Army laid out a baseball diamond and renamed the stadium Soldiers Field.

On September 2, 1945, Blackwell pitched the Red Circlers to a 9-2 victory in the first game of the best-of-five series in front of 50,000 fans, most of them American soldiers. In the second game, Day held the Red Circlers to one run. Brown drove in the OISE's team first run, and then Nahem (who was playing first base) doubled in the seventh inning to knock in the go-ahead run. OISE won the game, 2-1. Day struck out 10 batters, allowed four hits, and walked only two hitters.

The teams flew to OISE's home field in Rheims for the next two games. The OISE team won the third game, as the *Times* reported, "behind the brilliant pitching of S/Sgt Sam Nahem," who outdueled Blackwell to win 2-1, scattering four hits and striking out six batters.[54] In the fourth game, the Third Army's Bill Ayers, who had pitched in the minor leagues since 1937, shut out the OISE squad, beating Day, 5-0.

The teams returned to Nuremberg for the deciding game on September 8, 1945. Nahem started for the OISE team in front of over 50,000 spectators. After the Red Circlers scored a run and then loaded the bases with one out in the fourth inning, Nahem took himself out and brought in Bob Keane, who got out of the inning without allowing any more runs and completed the game. The OISE team won the game, 2-1. *The Sporting News* adorned its report on the final game with a photo of Nahem.[55]

Back in France, Brig. Gen. Charles Thrasher organized a parade and a banquet dinner, with steaks and champagne, for the OISE All-Stars. As historian Robert Weintraub has noted: "Day and Brown, who would not be allowed to eat with their teammates in many major-league towns, celebrated alongside their fellow soldiers."[56]

One of the intriguing aspects of this episode is that, despite the fact that both major-league baseball and the American military were racially segregated, no major newspaper even mentioned the historic presence of two African-Americans on the OISE roster. If there were any protests among the White players, or among the fans – or if any of the 71st Division's officers raised objections to having African-American players on the opposing team – they were ignored by reporters. For example, an Associated Press story about the fourth game simply referred to "pitcher Leon Day of Newark."

Although Rickey knew Nahem when he played for the St. Louis Cardinals, it isn't known if Rickey was aware of Nahem's triumph over baseball segregation in the military. But in October 1945, a month after Nahem pitched his integrated team to victory in the European military championship, Rickey announced that Robinson had signed a contract with the Dodgers.

The protest movement for baseball integration had set the stage for Robinson's entrance into the major leagues.

NOTES

1 Broun repeated his remarks in his syndicated column. Heywood Broun, "It Seems to Me," *Pittsburgh Press*, February 9, 1933.

2. Chris Lamb, *Conspiracy of Silence: Sportswriters and the Long Campaign to Desegregate Baseball* (Lincoln: University of Nebraska Press, 2012), 5.

3. Robert Ruck, "Crossing the Color Line," in Lawrence D. Hogan, editor, *Shades of Glory: The Negro Leagues and the Story of African-American Baseball* (Washington: National Geographic, 2006), 327.

4. Gunnar Myrdal, *An American Dilemma: The Negro Problem and Modern Democracy* (New York: Harper & Brothers, 1944), 21.

5. The protest movement to integrate major-league baseball is discussed in Jules Tygiel, *Baseball's Great Experiment: Jackie Robinson and His Legacy* (New York: Oxford University Press, 1983); Lamb, *Conspiracy of Silence*; Irwin Silber, *Press Box Red: The Story of Lester Rodney, the Communist Who Helped Break the Color Line in American Sports* (Philadelphia: Temple University Press, 2003); Lee Lowenfish, *Branch Rickey: Baseball's Ferocious Gentleman* (Lincoln: University of Nebraska Press, 2009); Arnold Rampersad, *Jackie Robinson: A Biography* (New York: Alfred Knopf, 1997); Kelly Rusinack, "Baseball on the Radical Agenda: The Daily Worker and Sunday Worker Journalistic Campaign to Desegregate Major League Baseball, 1933-1947," in Joseph Dorinson and Joram Warmund, eds., *Jackie Robinson: Race, Sports, and the American Dream* (Armonk, New York: M.E. Sharpe, 1998); David K. Wiggins, "Wendell Smith, The Pittsburgh Courier-Journal and the Campaign to Include Blacks in Organized Baseball 1933-1945," *Journal of Sport History*, Vol. 10, No. 2 (Summer 1983): 5-29; Henry Fetter, "The Party Line and the Color Line: The American Communist Party, the 'Daily Worker,' and Jackie Robinson," *Journal of Sport History*, Vol. 28, No. 3 (Fall 2001): 375-402.

6. This discussion of Wendell Smith relies on the following sources: Brian Carroll, "A Crusading Journalist's Last Campaign: Wendell Smith and the Desegregation of Baseball's Spring Training," *Communication and Social Change* 1 (2007): 38-54; Brian Carroll, "'It Couldn't Be Any Other Way': The Great Dilemma for the Black Press and Negro League Baseball," in *Black Ball: A Negro Leagues Journal* 5 (2012): 5-23; Lamb, *Conspiracy of Silence*; Chris Lamb, "'What's Wrong With Baseball': The *Pittsburgh Courier* and the Beginning of its Campaign to Integrate the National Pastime," *The Western Journal of Black Studies* 26 (2002): 189-203; Ursula McTaggart, "Writing Baseball into History: The *Pittsburgh Courier*, Integration, and Baseball in a War of Position," *American Studies*: 47 (2006): 113-132; Andrew Schall, "Wendell Smith: The Pittsburgh Journalist Who Made Jackie Robinson Mainstream," *Pittsburgh Post-Gazette*, June 5, 2011; "Wendell Smith, Sportswriter, Jackie Robinson Booster, Dies," *New York Times*, November 27, 1972; and Wiggins, "Wendell Smith."

7. Wendell Smith, "Smitty's Sport Spurts: A Strange Tribe," *Pittsburgh Courier*, May 14, 1938: 17.

8. Wendell Smith, "'I've Seen a Million!' – Leo Durocher," *Pittsburgh Courier*, August 5, 1939: 16.

9. See, for example, Wendell Smith, "'No Need for Color Ban in Big Leagues' – Pie Traynor: These Pirates Rate Negro Players with Best in Major Leagues," *Pittsburgh Courier*, September 2, 1939: 16.

10. "Dizzy Dean Rates 'Satch' Greatest Pitcher," *Pittsburgh Courier*, September 24, 1938: 17.

11. Wendell Smith, "'Would Be a Mad Scramble for Negro Players if Okayed' – Hartnett: Discrimination Has No Place in Baseball – These Cubs Agree," *Pittsburgh Courier*, August 12, 1939: 16; Chris Lamb, "Baseball's Whitewash: Sportswriter Wendell Smith Exposes Major League Baseball's Big Lie," *NINE*, Volume 18, Number 1 (Fall 2009): 1-20.

12. The Communist Party's involvement in the civil-rights and labor movements, particularly during the Depression, is discussed in Hosea Hudson and Nell Irvin Painter, *The Narrative of Hosea Hudson, His Life As a Negro Communist in the South* (Cambridge: Harvard University Press, 1979); Robin Kelley, *Hammer and Hoe: Alabama Communists During the Great Depression* (Chapel Hill: University of North Carolina Press, 1990); Robert Korstad, *Civil Rights Unionism: Tobacco Workers and the Struggle for Democracy in the Mid-Twentieth-Century South* (Chapel Hill: University of North Caroline Press, 2003); August Meier and Elliott Rudwick, *Black Detroit and the Rise of the UAW* (New York: Oxford University Press, 1981); Mark Naison, *Communists in Harlem During the Depression* (Champaign: University of Illinois Press, 2004); and Mark Solomon, *The Cry Was Unity: Communists and African Americans, 1917-36* (Jackson: University Press of Mississippi, 1998).

13. "Batter Up," *Daily Worker*, April 18, 1940.

14. "Labor Union to Protest Major League Color Ban at New York World Fair," *Pittsburgh Courier*, May 25, 1940: 16: "10,000 at Fair Petition to End Baseball Jim Crow," *Daily Worker*, July 25, 1940.

15. John McReynolds, "Nate Moreland: A Mystery to Historians," *The National Pastime*, No. 19 (1999): 55-64.

16. Amy Essington, *The Integration of the Pacific Coast League* (Lincoln: University of Nebraska Press, 2018), 36-37

17. Silber, *Press Box Red*, 151.

18. Tygiel, *Baseball's Great Experiment*, 37.

19. "'Paige Beats Big Leaguers," *Daily Worker*, May 25, 1942.

20. Dave Zirin, "An Interview with 'Red' Rodney," *Counterpunch*, April 3, 2004. counterpunch.org/2004/04/03/an-interview-with-quot-red-quot-rodney.

21. "Dimaggio Calls Negro Greatest Pitcher," *Daily Worker*, September 13, 1937.

22. Silber, *Press Box Red*, 144.

23. Silber, *Press Box Red*, 144.

24. Silber, *Press Box Red*, 62.

25. Roy Campanella, *It's Good to Be Alive* (Boston: Little Brown and Company, 1959), 97-98.

26. Cited in Lester Rodney, "On the Scoreboard," *Daily Worker*, April 3, 1950.

27. Jules Tygiel, *Extra Bases* (Lincoln, University of Nebraska Press, 2002), 69.

28. Cited in Ethan Mitchell, *The Defender: How the Legendary Black Newspaper Changed America* (New York: Houghton Mifflin Harcourt, 2016), 244.

29. James G. Thompson, "Should I Sacrifice to Live 'Half-American?'" *Pittsburgh Courier*, January 31, 1942: 3; Doron Goldman, "The Double Victory Campaign and the Campaign to Integrate Baseball," in Marc Z Aaron and Bill Nowlin, eds., *Who's On First? Replacement Players in World War II* **(Phoenix: SABR, 2015), 405-8.** sabr.org/research/article/goldman-double-victory-campaign-and-campaign-integrate-baseball.

30. For example: Fay Young, "Challenge to the Big Leagues: Barring of Negro Players in Major Leagues Flouts Democratic Ideals of War," *Chicago Defender*, September 26, 1942.

31. "Labor Calls On Landis to Remove Color Ban in Major Leagues," *Pittsburgh Courier*, June 13, 1942: 15; "Seamen Demand Landis Lift Ban," *Daily Worker*, June 5, 1942; "Removal of Baseball Jim-Crow Against Negroes Sought by Strong White Forces," *Atlanta Daily World*, June 7, 1942; "Organized Labor Joins Fight on Major League Bias: Judge Landis Petitioned by Unions 2,000 Maritime Workers, Wholesalers Ask for Justice," *New York Amsterdam News*, June 13, 1942; "Color Ban In Baseball Hit by Packinghouse Men," *Chicago Defender*, July 11, 1942.

32. "Czar Landis Denies Rule Against Negroes in Majors," *Austin Statesman*, July 17, 1942; "You May Hire All Negro Players, No Ban Exists, Landis Tells Durocher," *New York Herald Tribune*, July 17, 1942.

33. "Drive on Jim Crow Gains Momentum," *Sunday Worker*, June 28, 1942.

34. "No Baseball Rule Against Hiring Negroes – Landis," *Elmira* (New York) *Star-Gazette*, July 17, 1942; Henry D. Fetter, "The Party Line and the Color Line: The American Communist Party, the *Daily Worker* and Jackie Robinson," *Journal of Sport History*, 28 (Fall 2001): 375-402; Henry D. Fetter, "From 'Stooge' to 'Czar': Judge Landis, the Daily Worker and the Integration of Baseball," *American Communist History*, 6:1 (2007): 29-63.

35. "Landis Denies Audience to Negro Group," *Detroit Free Press*, December 4, 1942; "CIO's Request to Ask Majors to Hire Negroes Turned Down," *Hartford Courant*, December 4, 1942; "Landis Rebuffs Plea for Negro Play in Majors: Asks Fair Play for Ball Stars/Bob Considine, Famous White Sports Writer, Urges Negro Players Be Given Their Chance," *New York Amsterdam Star-News*, December 12, 1942.

36. "Wrigley Sees 'Negroes in Big Leagues Soon': Cubs' Owner Says It Has 'Got To Come'/Would Put Negro Player on His Team if Fans Demanded Same," *Chicago Defender*, December 26, 1942; Lamb, *Conspiracy of Silence*, 218-221.

37. "Send Resolution on Negroes in Major Baseball To FDR," *Chicago Defender*, February 20, 1943; Lamb, *Conspiracy of Silence*, 221.

38. Wiggins, "Wendell Smith," 21.

39. Lamb, *Conspiracy of Silence*, 235.

40. Silber, *Press Box Red*, 83; Martin Duberman, *Paul Robeson* (New York: The New Press, 1995), 282-283.

41. Wendell Smith, "Publishers Place Case of Negro Players Before Big League Owners: Judge Landis Says No Official Race Ban Exists in Majors," *Pittsburgh Courier*, December 11, 1943: 1; "Robeson Sees Labor as Salvation of Negro Race: Praises CIO Plan to Better Racial Conditions Here," *Pittsburgh Courier*, December 25, 1943: 11.

42. Ric Roberts, "Chandler's Views on Player Ban Sought: New Czar Must Face Bias Issue," *Pittsburgh Courier*, May 5, 1945: 12.

43. "Two Negroes Are Tried Out by the Dodgers but They Fail to Impress President Rickey," *New York Times*, April 8, 1945.

44. Tygiel, *Baseball's Great Experiment*, 69.

45. Ron Fimrite, "Sam Lacy: Black Crusader a Resolute Writer Helped Bring Change To Sports," *Sports Illustrated*, October 29, 1990.

46. Bill Nowlin, *Tom Yawkey: Patriarch of the Boston Red Sox* (Lincoln: University of Nebraska Press, 2018); Bill Nowlin, ed., *Pumpsie & Progress: The Red Sox, Race, and Redemption* (Burlington, Massachusetts: Rounder Books, 2010).

47. There is some dispute about this. Veeck wrote about his plans, and Landis's and Frick's efforts to thwart them, in his biography, *Veeck as in Wreck*. A 1998 article claimed that Veeck's intention to buy the Phillies in order to integrate baseball is simply not true. See Larry Gerlach, David Jordan, and John Rossi, "A Baseball Myth Exploded: Bill Veeck and the 1943 Sale of the Phillies," *The National Pastime*, Vol. 18 (1998). sabr.org/research/article/a-baseball-myth-exploded-bill-veeck-and-the-1943-sale-of-the-phillies/. The eminent baseball historian Jules Tygiel rejected Gerlach, Jordan, and Rossi's claims. See Jules Tygiel, "Revisiting Bill Veeck and the 1943 Phillies," *Baseball Research Journal*, Volume 35 (2007): 109-114. research.sabr.org/journals/files/SABR-Baseball_Research_Journal-35.pdf. In his biography of Veeck, Paul Dickson makes the case that Veeck's version of the story is true. Paul Dickson, *Bill Veeck: Baseball's Greatest Maverick* (New York: Walker & Company, 2012), 79-83, 356-366.

48. Dickson, *Bill Veeck*, 79.

49. Bill Veeck with Ed Linn, *Veeck – As In Wreck* (New York: G.P. Putnam's Sons, 1962); Dickson, *Bill Veeck*, 80.

50. Bill Veeck with Ed Linn, *Veeck – As In Wreck*; Peggy Beck, "Working in the Shadows of Rickey and Robinson: Bill Veeck, Larry Doby, and the Advancement of Black Players in Baseball," in Peter M. Rutkoff, ed., *The Cooperstown Symposium on Baseball and American Culture, 1997* (Jefferson, North Carolina: McFarland and Company, 2000).

51. This draws on my profile of Sam Nahem: Peter Dreier, "Sam Nahem," *Society for American Baseball Research*, n.d., sabr.org/bioproj/person/focoboef; and Peter Dreier, "Sam Nahem: The Right-Handed Lefty Who Integrated Military Baseball in World War II," in William M. Simons, ed., *The Cooperstown Symposium on Baseball and American Culture, 2017-2018* (Jefferson, North Carolina: McFarland & Company, 2019).

52. Joe Eskenazi, "Artful Dodger: Baseball's 'Subway' Sam Strikes Out Batters, and With the Ladies Too," *J Weekly*, October 23, 2003. jweekly.com/article/full/20827/artful-dodger.

53. Quoted in Jackie Robinson, *Baseball Has Done It* (Philadelphia: Lippincott, 1964), 105.

54. "Oise Nine Beats Third Army," *New York Times*, September 6, 1945.

55. All Stars Win European Title in GI Playoff," *The Sporting News*, September 13, 1945: 12.

56. Robert Weintraub, *The Victory Season: The End of World War II and the Birth of Baseball's Golden Age* (New York: Little Brown & Co., 2013).

JACKIE ROBINSON: THE BEST ATHLETE ON THE WEST COAST

by Vince Guerrieri

Once he got to the major leagues, it didn't take long for Jackie Robinson to establish his credentials as a Hall of Fame baseball player.

He was named Rookie of the Year in 1947, and MVP two years later. His skill at baseball belied a tremendous athleticism. In fact, in the years leading up to American involvement in World War II, he had distinguished himself in several sports.

Thousands had filled stadiums to watch Robinson's athletic prowess as an amateur in Southern California – not in baseball, though. Although Robinson lettered in baseball at UCLA, it was probably the weakest of the *four* sports in which he excelled. Rather, they'd file into the Rose Bowl or the Coliseum to watch him play football. Robinson was also a national champion long jumper, and played basketball in college as well.

But he went on to be a trailblazer for the Brooklyn Dodgers, the year after two college teammates integrated pro football. When it came to pro sports, major-league baseball was king. The NBA didn't exist, and the NFL at the time was still regarded in many ways as a fly-by-night, pass-the-hat league, dwarfed in popularity by the college game. Race aside, Robinson could have gone professional in any sport. He was, as Newspaper Enterprise Association sportswriter Don Sanders called him, "the best all-around athlete on the coast."[1]

Robinson was born in Cairo, Georgia, in 1919, but his family moved to Southern California a little more than a year later. He attended John Muir Technical High School in Pasadena, where he participated in the glee club in addition to four sports: football, baseball, basketball, and track, competing in what was then called the broad jump but is more frequently called the long jump.

In baseball, Robinson played shortstop at Muir – except for one year when he played catcher to fill a need – and, largely on the strength of his skills, in 1935 the team received an invitation to the celebrated Pomona Tournament, an enormous event, with an appearance by Governor Frank Merriam, comedian Joe E. Brown as the banquet speaker, and Mickey Rooney throwing out the first pitch of the championship game. It was the first time a team with African-American players was allowed to participate. (However, while his White teammates were able to find lodging, Robinson had to return home to Pasadena nightly.) Robinson stole a tournament-high 11 bases.[2]

Muir returned to the tournament the following year and ended up facing another future Hall of Famer: Ted Williams and San Diego Hoover High School. In that game, Robinson had three hits and stole home, but Hoover won 8-7, as Williams hit a 450-foot home run.[3] Robinson received additional accolades in the fall of 1936, when he won the junior singles title of the Pacific Coast Negro Tennis Tournament.[4]

When Robinson came to Pasadena Junior College, after graduating from Muir, he might have been best known as the younger brother of Mack Robinson, who'd won the Silver Medal in the 200-meter dash,

Jackie Robinson in his UCLA track uniform.

Jackie Robinson playing football in 1939.

finishing second to Jesse Owens, at the 1936 Olympics in Berlin.

Jackie Robinson would soon prove himself in his own right. In his autobiography *I Never Had It Made,* Robinson recalled competing in the broad jump in Pomona one morning, setting a record, and then driving to Glendale for an afternoon baseball game, where he played shortstop as Pasadena won the championship.[5] Duke Snider, who grew up in Compton (among his high-school friends was future NFL Commissioner Pete Rozelle), recalled watching Robinson play a game in Pasadena, leave the field during a game to go to the nearby track, compete in the broad jump – still in his baseball uniform – and return to the ballgame.[6]

In his second year at Pasadena, Robinson scored 131 points on the gridiron and gained more than 1,500 yards – drawing thousands of fans to junior-college games – and set a juco record in the broad jump and was all-conference in basketball. His baseball performance was almost an afterthought, but he batted .417.[7]

Robinson had his pick of colleges to attend after Pasadena, but he ended up staying close to home, going to UCLA. (No doubt a factor was the Bruins hiring a new coach, longtime assistant Babe Horrell, a Pasadena native.) Upon Robinson's arrival at UCLA, it was treated as almost a sure thing that he'd start on the football team. "Pasadena and Westwood faithfuls pin great hopes on Jackie and predict great things on his passing and elusive running that have made him the greatest open field runner in junior college circles," the UCLA *Daily Bruin* wrote in its 1939 registration edition.[8] Running backs Robinson, Woody Strode, and Kenny Washington were referred to as the Gold Dust Trio.[9]

It didn't take long for Robinson to live up to his reputation. After just four games, the *Daily Bruin* touted him as "the toe-dancing tornado!" and said he was better than the old Galloping Ghost himself, Red Grange.[10] And that was before Robinson led the Bruins to a 16-6 win over Oregon, catching a 66-yard touchdown pass from Washington and running 83 yards for another score, prompting Ducks coach Tex Oliver to say, "You need mechanized cavalry to stop him. He runs as fast at three-quarter speed as the average player does at top speed, and he still has that extra quarter to draw upon."[11]

The season culminated in a game against Southern California that drew more than 103,000 fans – then a record for a college football game – to the Coliseum. With a bid to the Rose Bowl on the line, the teams battled to a scoreless tie, as a late drive by the Bruins stalled, leaving them, as the campus paper said, "Two yards from the Rose Bowl!"[12] USC got the bowl bid, but the Bruins still finished 6-0-4 – their first undefeated season – and were voted seventh in the Associated Press poll.

Originally, it was thought Robinson would concentrate on baseball in the spring, forgoing basketball and track (his Olympic aspirations came to a halt with the onset of World War II, leading to the cancellation of the 1940 Games), but it was announced shortly after the basketball team started practice that Robinson would be part of it.[13] Robinson scored 148 points in 12 games, good enough to lead the Southern Division of the Pacific Coast Conference. However, he opted not to participate in track at UCLA in 1940, a move that coach Harry Trotter said altered the balance of power in the league.[14]

A week after the basketball season ended, Robinson was playing in an exhibition for the baseball team, where he got four straight hits and stole four bases, including home. "The game had marked the first time Robinson has stepped on a diamond since last August," Johnny Beckler wrote in the *Daily Bruin*. "And the amazing rapidity at which he got his batting and fielding eye speaks well enough for his ability as a baseballer."[15]

In Robinson's first varsity game with UCLA, he demonstrated his talent as well as his competitive nature. In a marathon against Cal that was tied, 13-13, going into the ninth, Robinson was called to pitch as darkness started to settle in Westwood. He threw strikes – and then threw a pitch over the backstop, saying he couldn't see. Chaos ensued, with the umpire finally calling "no game."[16] (The Bears won the next day.)

Robinson's lone season on the Bruins varsity baseball team was an unspectacular one, with a .097 batting average. His defense and baserunning, however, kept him in the lineup. Once the baseball season was over, he competed with the track team – while continuing to participate in spring practice for the football team – winning the broad jump at the Pacific Coast Conference (now the PAC-12) and NCAA tournaments. His win at the NCAA tournament in Minnesota made him and his brother the first siblings to each win NCAA titles, and were it not for the fact that the Olympics were canceled in 1940 (and then again in 1944), Jackie might have followed brother Mack as a medalist. With his track participation, Robinson became the first athlete to letter in four sports at UCLA – and he'd done it all in the same academic year!

Hopes were high going into the 1940 football season. Robinson was a bright spot, leading the team in passing (444 yards), rushing (383), and scoring (36 points; in addition to being used in the backfield, he also kicked extra points). But the Bruins lost their first seven games before beating Washington State at the Coliseum in what turned out to be their only win of the season.

He played basketball again, and again won the league scoring title, this time with 133 points. But in spring 1941, Robinson left UCLA before graduating, believing "no amount of education would help a black man get a job."[17] He went to work for the National Youth Administration before that New Deal program was shuttered as war loomed. Robinson played on a variety of all-star teams, from a baseball game of California all-stars (including future major-league pitcher Ewell Blackwell) as a USO benefit[18] to the College East-West All-Star Game in Chicago against the NFL champion Chicago Bears. In that game, another brainchild of *Chicago Tribune* sports editor Arch Ward, who also organized the first major-league baseball All-Star Game, Robinson caught a touchdown pass from Charley O'Rourke of Boston College, but the Bears rolled to a 37-13 victory behind the passing of Sid Luckman, under the lights at Soldier Field.

Shortly thereafter, Robinson made his first foray into professional sports – the Honolulu Bears of the Pacific Coast Professional Football League. After the 1941 football season, Robinson, who had a construction job for a company near the US naval base at Pearl Harbor, returned to California. He departed Hawaii on December 5, 1941. While he was on the ship home, he received news that Pearl Harbor had been attacked and that war was declared. The Army beckoned, and after that, professional baseball, first with the Kansas

City Monarchs of the Negro Leagues and then with the Dodgers.

Among the qualifications Dodgers general manager Branch Rickey sought in the first player to integrate the White major leagues was that he had to be a college man, who had played for and against integrated teams, and Robinson fit the bill because of his time in Pasadena and UCLA. Robinson made his debut in the Dodgers organization in 1946 – the same year his former teammates Washington and Strode integrated the National Football League, for the new Los Angeles Rams. (The Rams, relocated from Cleveland, had to integrate to be able to play at the Coliseum; they were quarterbacked by Bob Waterfield, who arrived at UCLA from Van Nuys High School in the fall of 1941, just missing Robinson.) Robinson made his debut with the Dodgers in 1947, and became a key part to some of the best baseball teams ever, the famed Boys of Summer.

Robinson retired after the 1956 season. The next season would be the Dodgers' last in Brooklyn. The West Coast loomed, and the Los Angeles Dodgers would debut in 1958 at the Coliseum – the site of Robinson's greatest exploits as a college athlete.

NOTES

1. Don Sanders, "Towering Oregon Team Is Coast Court Choice," *Santa Cruz* (California) *Evening News*, January 6, 1941: 5.
2. cifss.org/wp-content/uploads/2018/10/CIFSS-History-111-20-30-Pomoma-Tournament.pdf.
3. Jim McConnell, "Pomona Tourney Was Historic," insidesocal.com/tribpreps/2009/03/03/mcconnell-pomon/.
4. Jason Lewis, "Black History: Jackie Robinson Excelled at a Higher Level in Other Sports," *Los Angeles Sentinel*, July 14, 2011. lasentinel.net/black-history-jackie-robinson-excelled-at-a-higher-level-in-other-sports.html.
5. Jackie Robinson, *I Never Had It Made* (New York: G.P. Putnam's Sons, 1972), 22.
6. Shav Glick, "Legend of the Fall," *Los Angeles Times*, April 14, 2005. latimes.com/archives/la-xpm-2005-apr-14-sp-robinson14-story.html.
7. Hank Shatford, "Jack Robinson – Better Than Grange," *Daily Bruin*, October 27, 1939: 3.
8. "Transfers Bolster Varsity," *Daily Bruin*, registration edition, fall 1939: 5.
9. Sometimes called Goal Dust. In fact, when Strode – who went on to fame as an actor – wrote his autobiography, he titled it *Goal Dust*.
10. Shatford, "Jack Robinson – Better Than Grange."
11. Glick, "Legend of the Fall."
12. Milt Cohen, "Bruins, Trojans Battle to Scoreless Tie," *Daily Bruin*, December 11, 1939: 1
13. "Robinson Slated as Quintet Hope," *Daily Bruin*, October 9, 1939: 3.
14. Hank Shatford, "Loss of Robinson, Strode shatters '40 track hopes," *Daily Bruin*, registration edition: 4.
15. Johnny Beckler, "UCLA, Cal in Conference Opener Today," *Daily Bruin*, March 11, 1940: 3.
16. Hank Shatford, "League Opener Ends in Near-Riot," *Daily Bruin*, March 12, 1940: 1.
17. *I Never Had It Made*, 23.
18. "All-Star Teams Tangle Tonight," *San Pedro* (California) *News-Pilot*, August 9, 1941: 7.

PACIFIC COAST CONFERENCE FOOTBALL TITLE GAME

DECEMBER 9, 1939: UCLA 0, USC 0,
AT THE LOS ANGELES COLISEUM

by Bryan Steverson

Organized Baseball's euphemistic "gentlemen's agreement" struck out on April 15, 1947, when 28-year-old African-American Jack Roosevelt Robinson took up a position at first base for the Dodgers at Ebbets Field in Brooklyn. Although much has been written about this milestone, another nearly as eventful event could have preceded it on January 1, 1940, at the Rose Bowl in Pasadena, California.

Before the 1950s, college football had its own whispered but understood "gentlemen's agreement." Although no published policy existed, segregation was regionally enforced. Football programs at Northern schools knew they could not use Black players in games with Southern schools. With few exceptions, the agreement was honored.[1]

A clear challenge to this racial-exclusion policy nearly made headlines based upon a game on December 9, 1939, in Los Angeles involving Robinson. The winner of this Pacific Coast Conference title football game between UCLA and the University of Southern California would be expected to play the second-ranked Tennessee Volunteers of the Southeastern Conference in the Rose Bowl. During the 1939 regular season, Tennessee became the last team in NCAA history to go undefeated, untied, and unscored upon.[2]

If UCLA could beat USC and earn a trip to the Rose Bowl, a star participant against Tennessee would be Robinson. The shredding of college football's "gentlemen's agreement" would precede the subsequent historic major-league baseball game in Brooklyn by more than seven years.

Jackie Robinson was UCLA's first four-sport letterman (football, basketball, track, and baseball).[3] In addition to these achievements, Robinson also excelled in tennis, handball, golf, rifle, badminton, and table tennis.[4] It would be in football, however, that his name gained early national recognition. He was college football's top ground gainer in average yards per carry in 1939. In addition, the speedy back averaged 20 yards per punt return. Sportswriters referred to him as "the Jim Thorpe of his race."[5]

THE SEASON:

After the 1938 football season, Edwin "Babe" Horrell was named UCLA's head football coach. The team Horrell inherited included senior star running back Kenny Washington and end Woody Strode. Two Pasadena Junior College All-American transfers, right halfback Jackie Robinson and end Ray Bartlett, made the team. All four were African-American.

Jackie Robinson college yearbook page, 1939.

The 1939 gridiron season went well for both the UCLA Bruins and their crosstown rivals, the all-White Trojans of Southern California. UCLA used a version of single-wing football. Halfback Washington received the snap from center and Robinson, the other halfback positioned near the line of scrimmage, would shift into the backfield. This motion-based formation provided Washington with many options, including a handoff to the swift Robinson.[6]

The senior/junior backfield combo proved successful as Washington became the first UCLA player to be named an All-American (second team). The star would end up sixth in the voting for the Heisman Trophy. In the 1939 season, Washington led the nation in total rushing and passing yards with 1,370.[7] His 1,915 career rushing yards remained a UCLA record for more than 30 years. The talented Robinson made a name for himself as an elusive runner.

UCLA entered the December 9 game against USC with a 6-0-3 record, having played to a tie against Stanford, Santa Clara, and Oregon State. Southern Cal at the time had a 7-0-1 record with a tie in their opening game against Oregon. While the Bruins had the nationally recognized Washington and Robinson, the Trojans squad included guard Harry "Blackjack" Smith, a first-team All-American, and third-team All-Americans in triple-threat quarterback Grenville Lansdell and right tackle Phil Gaspar.

THE GAME, DECEMBER 9, 1939:

The game between the two undefeated rivals was played in the Los Angeles Coliseum before 103,303 fans and a national audience tuning in to hear radio announcer Bill Stern. The contest proved to be a low scoring, defensive battle as the final game log would indicate.[8]

	UCLA	USC
Total plays from scrimmage	64	62
Net total yardage	161	222
First downs	10	11
Net rushing yardage	89	183
Net passing yardage	72	39
Passes completed/attempted	7/18	5/11
Interceptions	1	1
Fumbles recovered	2	2
Avg. punt yardage	8 for 34.3	7 for 33.0
Kick & punt return yardage	68	50
Penalty yardage	0	20

Although USC entered the game having the second most potent offense in the land, three good scoring opportunities were stymied by the stiff Bruins defense. USC even recovered a UCLA fumble at the UCLA 23-yard line only to have star quarterback Lansdell, on his way for a touchdown, fumble three yards from the goal line after a bruising hit by Bruin defensive back Robinson. As the *Los Angeles Times* wrote, "No man's arm could have withstood that blow from Robinson's body."[9] The fumbled ball bounced into the end zone where UCLA's Strode recovered it for a touchback.

The outcome of the game would be decided on a nailbiting length-of-the-field drive by UCLA late in the fourth quarter. The Bruins were faced with a fourth down on the USC 4-yard line. The team huddled, and without input from coach Horrell, became indecisive on what to do next. Quarterback Ned Mathews made the critical decision. Mathews told his teammates, "Let's go for it." After receiving the snap, Washington rolled out for a scoring pass thrown into the corner of the end zone. A Trojan defensive back batted the ball away. The game ended minutes later in a 0-0 deadlock.

Robinson finished the contest with 23 yards gained in four carries and 48 yards on four punt returns. In a postgame report, Robert Wagoner of the United Press wrote that Robinson "turned in four runs of more than 15 yards each." This included his pass receptions.[10]

ROSE BOWL:

In the final regular season 1939 College Football poll, Texas A&M was voted number 1. The undefeated University of Tennessee was named number 2 and Southern Cal, with a 7-0-2 final record, was the number-3 team. The Bruins of UCLA at 6-0-4 were ranked number 7.[11] Based upon these records, Rose Bowl invitations were extended to the Pacific Coast Conference's University of Southern California and the Southeast Conference's University of Tennessee.

WHAT IF?

What if Washington's pass had been complete and the Bruins went on to win the December 9 game? The Rose Bowl invitation would have been offered to Tennessee as the preferred opponent to face the PCC champion Bruins. Would the all-White Volunteers have accepted knowing they would face a team with four African-American stars?

Clinton "Butch" McCord was a former Negro Leaguer who would reach the highest level in Organized Baseball's minor leagues in the mid-1950s. He was a World War II Navy veteran and Tennessee native. According to McCord, Tennessee coach Robert Neyland had told the Rose Bowl officials that if UCLA won, Tennessee would not play.[12] This stance was based upon the presence of Blacks, including Jackie Robinson, on the Bruins team.

In large print in the December 9 issue of the *Tennessean* was the headline:

U.T. MAY NOT ACCEPT BID IF UCLANS GET COAST HONOR

William J. Tucker's article stated, "UCLA has two Negro stars and customarily meetings between Southern teams and those that play Negroes are politely avoided.

"However, if Tennessee and UCLA should win tomorrow, the latter could hardly help inviting the Vols, because all the other standout Eastern bowl candidates had committed themselves to other post-season classics or not to play any."[13]

Sportswriter and later Tennessee Sports Hall Of Fame inductee Raymond Johnson wrote prior to the game, "If UCLA whips Southern Cal, Tennessee will not visit Pasadena on New Year's Day. That's definite."[14]

The *Pasadena Star-News wrote that* "an embarrassing" position could result. "The University of Tennessee Volunteers were unlikely to step on the field with black players as foes."[15]

An African-American newspaper, the *California Eagle*, believed a UCLA-Tennessee game would have a transcending impact and "prove to this nation that its people can play together in the most approved manner as sportsmen, upholding as they do the democratic principles as outlined by the signing of the Declaration of Independence."[16]

Robert Neyland, Tennessee's coach, was a West Point graduate, World War I veteran, and retired brigadier general. Neyland had coached at Tennessee since being hired as an assistant in 1925. In a follow-up to what McCord had said, the author contacted the University of Tennessee's longtime (1961-2000) sports information director Haywood Harris, a historian of University of Tennessee athletics. Of a possible Rose Bowl boycott by Tennessee, Harris said he was unaware of what McCord had stated earlier. He knew Coach Neyland and doubted the veracity of the threat.[17] It was also rumored that Tennessee All-American running back George Cafego and his teammates had been polled about a Rose Bowl invitation and were "eager to meet the Far West Champions."[18]

SHATTERING THE "GENTLEMAN'S AGREEMENT":

It is arguable, but also reasonable, to assume Tennessee would have played in the January 1, 1940, Rose Bowl against UCLA.

- Their long-standing SID, Haywood Harris, knew of no boycott intention. The players were rumored to want to play. In the opinion of venerable sportswriter Sam Lacy, "Tennessee ... would have jumped at the opportunity to play the Bruins." Monetarily, over $85,000 was at stake.[19]

- The opportunity to play in the most prestigious bowl at the time, "The Granddaddy of Them All," with national coverage, would have been hard to resist, especially for an undefeated team with multiple All-Americans.

- "By any measurable criteria, Tennessee was the best team in the land the year prior, but they wound up number 2 in the AP poll."[20] They had something to prove in 1939 and could not easily "run away" from UCLA if the Bruins were the Pacific Coast Conference champs.

- The Rose Bowl was described as the "ultimate proving-ground of gridiron giants."[21] It would be an offer the "giant" UT could hardly refuse.

- Other bowls had already selected their teams so limited good alternatives existed.

- Influential coach Bob Neyland was aware of the sacrifices of Black soldiers during World War I and would have been on the side of accepting the bid.

Southern Cal beat Tennessee in the Rose Bowl, 14-0, marring the Volunteers' great season.

Had Tennessee played against UCLA, the existing Southern ban would have been broken. Just as Robinson had been a key factor during the season and in the December 9 game, he undoubtedly would have played a major role in the outcome of the Rose Bowl. The UCLA-UT game would have produced sports page headlines and photographs across the country with the probability of Robinson and three other Black athletes excelling.

Jackie Robinson's groundbreaking actions in 1947 would then have become Act II.[22]

ACKNOWLEDGEMENT

The author would like to express appreciation to fellow SABR members Larry Lester and Skip Nipper for their input.

PERSPECTIVES ON 42

NOTES

1. C.J. Schexnayder, "The 1953 Orange Bowl: Alabama Football's Racial Dilemma," SEC Football, College Football History, November 11, 2013. UCLA had played certain Southern schools earlier but they had been played in Los Angeles to avoid Jim Crow laws and never with four African-American stars. See James W. Johnson, *The Black Bruins* (Lincoln: University of Nebraska Press, 2017).

2. "Big Orange Football 1939," bigorangefootball.com/?s=1939.

3. "Jackie Robinson Was Inducted into the College Baseball Foundation's Hall of Fame Yesterday in Lubbock, Texas," *New York Post*, July 4, 2008.

4. At age 15, Robinson won the Pasadena City Ping-Pong championship. The first time he played in the Negro National Tennis Tournament, he reached the semifinals. Robinson shot a 90 early in golf. He was able to beat the Pasadena Junior College handball champion in a game. He was competitive in badminton and fired so well he was asked to join the UCLA rifle team.

5. Harvey Frommer, *Rickey and Robinson, The Men Who Broke Baseball's Color Barrier* (Lanham, Maryland: Taylor Trade, 2015), 30.

6. Gretchen Atwood, *Lost Champions, Four Men, Two Teams, and the Breaking of Pro Football's Color Line* (New York: Bloomsbury, 2016), 140.

7. Atwood, 36. In spite of his gridiron prowess at UCLA, Washington was not drafted by any NFL team.

8. "Classic UCLA Bruins Rediscovered," January 4, 2015, lvironpigs.wordpress.com/2015/01/04/1939-ucla-vs-usc/.

9. Johnson, 97.

10. "Classic UCLA Bruins Rediscovered."

11. College Football Reference, "1939 College Football Polls." https://www.sports-reference.com/cfb/years/1939-polls.html

12. Author Steverson interview with Clinton "Butch" McCord, 2005.

13. William J. Tucker, "Definitely Out for Tilt Today," *Tennessean* (Nashville, Tennessee) December 9, 1939.

14. Raymond Johnson, "One Man's Opinion," *Tennessean*, December 9, 1939.

15. Johnson, 96.

16. Johnson, 96-97.

17. Author phone interview with Haywood Harris, February 8, 2006. Coach Robert Neyland was inducted into the College Football Hall of Fame in 1956.

18. Sam Lacy, "Looking 'Em Over," *Baltimore Afro-American,"* December 30, 1939: 18.

19. Lacy.

20. 1938 College Football National Championship," tiptop25.com/champ1938.html.

21. Joe R. Osherenko, "The Good Neighbor Policy," "The Goal Post, U.C.L.A. vs. Southern California, December 9, 1939," football program: 4.

22. On September 14, 1968, sophomore end Lester McLain suited up and played for the University of Tennessee in a football game against the University of Georgia at Neyland Stadium in Knoxville. McLain became the first African-American to play for Tennessee. It would thus be nearly 20 years since the historic December 9 game.

"A DISCIPLINARIAN COACH": JACKIE ROBINSON'S LITTLE-KNOWN STINT COACHING COLLEGE BASKETBALL

by Eric Enders

In the fall of 1944, Jackie Robinson's life was at a crossroads. A few days after Thanksgiving, he was honorably discharged from the US Army, where he'd made headlines for refusing to move to the back of a military bus. Dismissed from his barracks at Fort Hood, Texas, he found himself with no job, no prospects, and no particular plans for the future. So he decided to pay a visit to an old friend – and before he knew it, Robinson stumbled into a new job as head coach of a college basketball team.

Robinson spent the winter of 1944-45 as the basketball coach of Samuel Huston College, a tiny Historically Black College (HBCU) in Austin, Texas. In a life where seemingly every moment was assiduously documented, Robinson's stint as a college coach is perhaps the least known aspect of his biography. For one thing, basketball ranks a clear fourth on the list of sports in which Robinson achieved fame, after baseball, football, and track. For another, the tiny school where he coached, Sam Huston, no longer exists in that form, having been absorbed into another Austin HBCU, Tillotson College, as part of a 1952 merger. (The resulting school, Huston-Tillotson University, occupies the former campus of Tillotson College.) Whatever scant records once existed were lost in the merger, and Austin newspapers in 1945 pointedly ignored athletic contests involving the tiny Black school with a shoestring budget. Few important people in Robinson's life were around to remember the time – his fiancée, Rachel Isum, was then living in California – and Jackie himself rarely discussed the experience. As far as this author can determine, no substantive quotes or reminiscences by Robinson about his time as a basketball coach have survived. All in all, these circumstances combine to make the first half of 1945 the most recondite and difficult-to-research period of Jackie Robinson's life.

One thing is for certain: Robinson owed his position at Sam Huston to Karl Downs, his childhood pastor and the closest thing to a father figure Robinson had in his life. The two had first met in 1938, when Downs, a tall, wiry young Texan, became the pastor at Scott United Methodist Church, which the Robinson family attended. At 25, Downs was just six years older than Robinson, and he enacted a number of programs intended to make the church more appealing to young people. "Those of us who had been indifferent church members began to feel an excitement in belonging," Robinson later wrote.[1]

Downs appears to have viewed Robinson, then a young ne'er-do-well and budding gang member, as someone who could achieve great things with the proper mentorship, and he endeavored to take the teenager under his wing. "Karl Downs had the ability to communicate with you spiritually, and at the same time he was fun to be with," Robinson wrote. "Most important, he knew how to listen. Often when I was deeply concerned about personal crises, I went to him." Before long, Robinson was teaching Sunday school at the church, and he and Downs became close friends, spending time playing golf and other sports together.[2] "He was a quiet, sweet man, someone you could talk to," Rachel Robinson said of Downs. "Karl was the father that Jack didn't have. Jack was so close to him. He kept saying that Karl changed his life."[3]

By 1944, six years later, both men had come a long way from their days at the church in Pasadena. Robinson was now an Army veteran and a famous former athlete. Downs was now the president of Sam Huston College, a tiny Black college in Austin from which he himself had graduated a decade earlier. During his time as a soldier at Fort Hood, Robinson was a frequent presence at Downs's Austin home, making the 90-minute trip to visit almost every weekend.[4] "He'd just come down and have dinner with the president," Harold "Pea Vine" Adanandus, the college's athletic trainer, recalled. "And we didn't know it at the time, but the president was also recruiting Jackie to coach the basketball team."[5]

Samuel Huston College, founded in 1876, was not named after the famous Texan hero Sam Houston, but rather after an Iowa farmer who had once donated $9,000 to the school. Since being named school president in 1943, Downs had set about modernizing and expanding the struggling college, which always seemed to be teetering on the brink of bankruptcy.[6] Downs enlarged its campus, tripled enrollment from 222 to 659, and brought in a series of prominent speakers and performers including Langston Hughes, W.E.B. Du Bois, and Duke Ellington.[7]

Downs didn't have a lot of money to funnel into improving the athletic department, but he did have one thing: a close friendship with one of the greatest college athletes of all time. Robinson, of course, had famously starred in four sports at UCLA, including basketball, in which he twice led the conference in scoring.[8] Downs persuaded him to become Sam Huston's director of athletics, a job that also included coaching the basketball team. "There was very little money involved, but I knew that Karl would have done anything for me, so I couldn't turn him down," Robinson wrote in his memoir, *I Never Had It Made*.[9] Recalled one of Downs's associates: "Bringing Jackie Robinson to campus was vintage Karl Downs. Nothing like that ever happened before Karl came."[10]

The players and staff of the Sam Huston Dragons were thrilled with the last-minute news. "We didn't know who our basketball coach was going to be," Adanandus, the athletic trainer, said. "Just before the season started, he came in and went right to work." Robinson took the job more seriously than any of his predecessors had. He instituted a physical fitness program (the school's first) and put his own impressive collection of athletic medals on display to serve as an inspiration of sorts. "We were one of the few teams that ran at that time," said one of the players, Roland Harden. "He got out there with us and actually showed us what to do and was a better player than anybody on our team. Or anybody we played, really. And he was a gentleman. He required us to wear suits and ties when we got off the bus."[11] Another player, D.C. Clements, recalled that Robinson "was a disciplinarian coach. He believed we should be students first and athletes second. If you cut a class or anything like that, he would put you off the team or give you some laps. He was a great coach and a great teacher."[12]

With the hands-on Robinson playing in the team's practices himself, it was obvious to everyone that the 26-year-old coach was a far better player than any of his students. "He liked to play around the basket, rebounding and all that," Adanandus recalled. "He was tough around the basket. He was just an exceptional athlete, and you could tell he still wanted to play. He wanted to play, but he'd have to sit on the bench when we were playing those college teams." However, Robinson was free to play as a member of the team in non-intercollegiate games – mainly scrimmages and exhibitions against nearby military teams. "We won all of [the games] when Jackie played," Adanandus said. "We were undefeated with Jackie. Any time the team seemed to be getting behind, Jackie would have to go in."[13]

The Dragons, as members of the Southwestern Athletic Conference, played an official schedule that mostly featured other HBCUs, including Prairie View College in Texas and Southern University in Baton Rouge, Louisiana. Their exact won-lost record has been lost to history. Observers remember the Dragons winning relatively few games, but they did manage one memorable highlight: a 61-59 upset of the defending league champion, Bishop College. Robinson, with his intense competitiveness and famously fiery temper, proved to be an intimidating force when dealing with referees. "I saw him go after officials when we were playing," Harden said. "He didn't get ejected, but he would go to the breaking point."[14]

Late in the season, the Dragons embarked on an extended road trip, spending a month playing games across Texas, Louisiana, and Arkansas. ("He would write to Rachel every day," Harden remembered.[15]) When the team got home, an intriguing offer was waiting for Robinson. "Upon our return from the tour, we met up in Jackie's office, and he was sorting his mail," Adanandus said. "He had received a letter from the Kansas City Monarchs. He showed me the letter, and they wanted him to play ball. They offered him a $500 bonus and $250 a month. He asked me, 'Vine, what would you do?' I said, 'Well, Jackie, I didn't even know you played any baseball.' And he said, 'Yeah, I play a little.'"[16]

He was about to play a lot more. Robinson submitted his resignation to Downs, and at the end of March he reported to the Monarchs' training camp in Houston. He performed impeccably during his brief stint in the Negro Leagues, and on August 28, he had his now-legendary meeting with Branch Rickey at Ebbets Field. In a mere six months, Robinson had gone from coaching basketball at an obscure Southern college to signing a contract with the Brooklyn Dodgers.[17]

After leaving Austin, Robinson made a point of keeping in touch with his former players. "We used to hear from him a lot after he left," Clements said. "He was always sending us a letter or a card, advising us and encouraging us to continue in school."[18] Although in his later years Robinson rarely mentioned his time as a coach, he never forgot the little college that had given him his first paying job in sports. In 1968 he was named to Huston-Tillotson's board of directors, a position he would hold until his death.[19] The school buildings where he worked in 1945 are now long gone, demolished to make room for Interstate 35 and its frontage roads. The former site of Sam Huston College is currently occupied by the Lucky Lady Bingo Parlor.[20]

The Rev. Karl Downs, meanwhile, continued to be a vital presence in Robinson's life after Jackie left his employ. When Jackie and Rachel got married in 1946, Downs traveled to California to perform the ceremony. When the Dodgers held a Jackie Robinson Day at Ebbets Field during their next to last home game of 1947, Downs was there to help pay tribute to his friend.[21]

A few months later, however, tragedy struck. Suffering from an unknown stomach ailment, Downs was rushed into emergency surgery at Austin's segregated Brackenridge Hospital on February 26, 1948. "Rather than returning his Black patient to the operating room or to a recovery room to be closely watched, the doctor in charge let him go to the segregated ward, where he died," Robinson wrote. "We believe Karl would not have died if he had received proper care." Downs's death at the shockingly young age of 35 affected Robinson enormously, and he still seemed devastated by the tragedy decades later. "It was hard to believe that God had taken the life of a man with such a promising future," he wrote in his 1972 memoir. "Karl Downs ranked with Roy Wilkins, Whitney Young, and Dr. Martin Luther King, Jr., in ability and dedication, and had he lived he would have developed into one of the front line leaders on the national scene."[22]

NOTES

1. Jackie Robinson and Alfred Duckett, *I Never Had It Made* (New York: HarperCollins, 2003), 8.
2. Robinson and Duckett, 8-9.
3. John Maher, "Huston College President Guided Jackie Robinson Down Historic Path," *Austin American-Statesman*, August 24, 2013. statesman.com/article/20130824/SPORTS/308249735.
4. Eric Enders, "A Legacy Remembered: 50 Years After Jackie Robinson Shattered Baseball's Color Barrier, Central Texans Recall His Time Here as a Basketball Coach," *Austin American-Statesman*, April 15, 1997.
5. Harold "Pea Vine" Adanandus, telephone interview, March 1997.
6. Arnold Rampersad, *Jackie Robinson: A Life* (New York: Random House, 2011), 114.
7. Garner Roberts, "Abilene Man Mentor to Jackie Robinson," *Abilene Reporter-News*, February 25, 2008. web.archive.org/web/20100316221705/http://www.reporternews.com/news/2008/feb/25/no-headline---jackie_robinson-karl_downs/.
8. "UCLA Celebrates Jackie Robinson Day," uclabruins.com, April 15, 2014. uclabruins.com/news/2014/4/15/209467368.aspx.
9. Robinson and Duckett, 69.
10. Rampersad, 114.
11. Jeff Miller, "Jackie Robinson's Forgotten Season as a College Basketball Coach," *Bleacher Report*, April 15, 2014. bleacherreport.com/articles/2004424-jackie-robinsons-forgotten-season-as-a-college-basketball-coach.
12. D.C. Clements, telephone interview, March 1997.
13. Harold "Pea Vine" Adanandus, telephone interview, March 1997.
14. "Jackie Robinson's Forgotten Season as a College Basketball Coach."
15. Ken Herman, "What It Was Like Playing Basketball for Jackie Robinson," *Austin American-Statesman*, September 3, 2016. statesman.com/news/20160903/herman-what-it-was-like-playing-basketball-for-jackie-robinson.
16. Enders.
17. Rampersad, 114.
18. D.C. Clements, telephone interview, March 1997.
19. Maher.
20. "Jackie Robinson's Forgotten Season as a College Basketball Coach."
21. Maher.
22. Robinson and Duckett, 69.

THERE BUT FOR THE GRACE OF GOD

by Bryan Steverson

"There but for the grace of God" is an expression used when someone avoids a very serious situation, possibly life-threatening, and gives credit to the Almighty.[1] In the life of Jack Roosevelt Robinson, this thankfulness applied on December 7, 1941.

After a disappointing 1940 football season in which the UCLA Bruins won only one game, and against the advice of coaches and family, the 22-year-old Robinson withdrew from the university in the spring of 1941. One semester short of graduating, he was given an "honorable dismissal."[2]

Upon leaving UCLA, Robinson, after also starring for the Bruins in basketball, track, and baseball, became the subject of high praise from the press. As UCLA's first four-sport letterman, a columnist labeled him as "the greatest colored athlete of all time," comparing him to such great Black athletes "as Jesse Owens, Paul Robeson, Jack Johnson, and Joe Lewis." Some even compared him to Red Grange, football's famous "Galloping Ghost," and the outstanding Native American athlete Jim Thorpe.[3]

After UCLA, Robinson went to work for the National Youth Administration as an assistant athletic director.[4] The camp was in Atascadero, California, halfway between Los Angeles and San Francisco. He played baseball and counseled troubled youths. The youngsters craved attention and the understanding and discipline Robinson could instill. For Robinson, it was a satisfying experience.[5] The NYA was a New Deal program that closed in 1943.[6]

On August 28 Robinson played in the eighth annual College All-Star Game, against the NFL champion Chicago Bears at Soldier Field in Chicago. In addition to a national television audience, the game was witnessed by more than 98,000 spectators. Halfback Tom Harmon from the University of Michigan (father of future UCLA quarterback and actor Tom Harmon) received the most votes, over 1.4 million, in a nationwide poll with fellow halfback Robinson receiving more than 750,000 votes.[7] As the All-Stars lost to the Bears, 37-13, Robinson caught a 36-yard pass from Boston College's Charlie O'Rourke for a touchdown[8] and Robinson became the first Black to score a touchdown in the annual game. Bears' defensive end Dick Plasman gave the former UCLA running back high praise, describing Robinson as "the fastest man I've ever seen in uniform, and further, the only time I was worried about the game was when Robinson was in there."[9]

During this time, Robinson's mother, Mallie, was facing financial difficult times, and he felt a need to help. The youngest of five children, Jackie was especially close to his mother. He joined the professional Los Angeles Bulldogs of the Pacific Coast Professional Football League. The Bulldogs were an integrated team as were the league's Hollywood Bears, who had Robinson's former UCLA Black teammates, All-American halfback Kenny Washington and end Woody Strode, on their roster. Soon Robinson was signed by the Honolulu Bears of the semipro Hawaii Senior Football League. Joining him on the island team was his close friend and Pasadena Junior College and UCLA teammate Ray Bartlett. Both men worked

All-Star Football Game program, 1941.

construction jobs during the day and earned $100 a game playing for the Bears.[10]

By early December, Robinson was homesick and wanted to leave Hawaii. On Friday, December 5, the star halfback said farewell to Bartlett and others as he boarded the passenger liner *Lurline* for the trip back home. Two days later, on Sunday, December 7, while the ship was en route to San Francisco, the Japanese attacked the Pearl Harbor military base. Robinson was playing cards with other men on the ship at the time. To their surprise, the ship's crew had been directed to paint all of its windows black. Very soon thereafter, the captain ordered everyone up on deck, giving them the news of the attack. The United States became enmeshed in World War II.

The *Lurline* moved carefully and stealthily through the night of December 7, sailing in and out of what would have been its regular sea lane. Robinson remained on emotional edge until the California coastline came into view.[11]

Homesick and realizing semipro football and construction jobs had a limited future, Robinson sought another job.[12] He found employment at Lockheed Aircraft in Los Angeles, then on March 23, 1943, was drafted into the US Army.[13]

Regarding his return, Robinson said he, in fact, had two bookings to leave Hawaii. One was the early December booking, which he accepted, and the other was on January 2. Homesickness prompted his selection of the December 5 date. He could arrive in California in time to sign up to play once again with the Bulldogs.[14]

What would have happened had Robinson chosen the January 2 departure from Hawaii? The December attack on Pearl Harbor took more than 2,400 American military and civilian lives. Another 1,000 were wounded.[15] What would Robinson's fate have been on that horrific Sunday? Is it possible he could have been one of the casualties?

As for his December 5 departure, what if Japanese submarines lurking off the coast had sunk the *Lurline* thinking it was a troop transport? What would baseball and the nation have lost?

Some, including sports journalist and author, Howard Cosell, consider Robinson the greatest American athlete of all time.[16] Some historians, among them Doris Kearns Goodwin,[17] George Will,[18] David Halberstam,[19] Tom Brokaw,[20] and Ken Burns,[21] have called Robinson one of the greatest Americans of the twentieth century.

In an interview with television host Larry King, Dr. Martin Luther King described Robinson, not himself, as "the founder of the modern civil rights movement."[22]

Jackie Robinson was a change agent in American history.

There but for the Grace of God, the nation on December 7, 1941, almost lost a role model and true national hero.

NOTES

1. "The Free Dictionary by Farlex," idioms.thefreedictionary.com/There+but+for+the+grace+of+God.

2. Arnold Rampersad, *Jackie Robinson, A Biography* (New York: Alfred A. Knopf, Inc., 1997), 82.

3. Manfred Wiedhorn, *Jackie Robinson* (New York: Atheneum, Macmillan Publishing Co., 1993), 24.

4. Gene Schoor, *Jackie Robinson, Baseball Hero* (New York: G.P. Putnam's Sons, 1958), 37-38.

5. Jackie Robinson and Alfred Duckett, *Breakthrough to the Big League, the Story of Jackie Robinson* (New York: Harper & Row, 1965), 34-35.

6. Glenn Stout and Dick Jones, *Jackie Robinson, Between the Lines* (San Francisco: Woodford Press, 1997), 30.

7. "Final Returns in the Nation-Wide Poll to Select College All-American Team of 1941," Official Program, 8th Annual All-Star Football Game, College All-Americans vs. Chicago Bears, Soldier Field, August 28, 1941: 5.

8. John R.M. Wilson, *Jackie Robinson and the American Dilemma* (New York: Longman, an imprint of Pearson Education, Inc., 2010), 26-27.

9. Danny Peary, *Jackie Robinson in Quotes: The Remarkable Life of Baseball's Most Significant Player* (Salem, Massachusetts: Page Street Publishing, 2016), 57.

10. Peary, 57.

11. Rampersad, 87.

12. Wiedhorn.

13. Michael G. Long and Chris Lamb, *Jackie Robinson, A Spiritual Biography* (Louisville, Kentucky: Westminster John Knox Press, 2017), 40, 42.

14. Lawrence F. LaMar, *Baltimore Afro American*, December 20, 1941.

15. history.com/topics/world-war-ii/pearl-harbor#:

16. Bryan Steverson, *Amazing Baseball Heroes, Inspirational Negro League Stories* (Knoxville: Tennessee Valley Publishing, 2011), 181-194.

17. Doris Kearns Goodwin, C-Span2 interview, November 6, 2005, televised subsequently on *Book TV*.

18. George Will, *Bunts, Curt Flood, Camden Yards, Pete Rose and Other Reflections on Baseball* (New York: Scribner, 1998), 87.

19. Wilson, xiv.

20. Tom Brokaw, film, *Baseball's Golden Age*, produced in 2008, shown on FSSOUTH April 15, 2012.

21. Kenny Mayne interview with Ken Burns, April 2016, prior to the premiere of the PBS documentary Burns produced on Jackie Robinson. kenburns.com/films/jackie-robinson/.

22. *Larry King Now*, interview with "Jackie Robinson's Pen Pal: Ron Rabinovitz," aired December 2013.

LIEUTENANT JACKIE ROBINSON, MORALE OFFICER, UNITED STATES ARMY

by J.M. Casper

The course of history can flip on a dime, the course of one's life often defined by a series of watershed flashpoints. Some we control; others are thrust upon us.

On December 7, 1941, Jackie Robinson was two days into his journey from a sleepy American naval port in Honolulu called Pearl Harbor. As a flume of smoke bellowed in the distance, the Second World War had come to America and found Jackie Robinson. Almost.

Jackie Robinson's World War II experience tells us a lot about the man Branch Rickey chose to wear the aspirations of an entire race on his broad shoulders. Jack Roosevelt Robinson brought his unique leadership qualities to the service where he displayed an aversion to intolerance and willingness to confront it. Robinson's experience in the military portends his ability to rouse change. He was at the center of a battle on two fronts, the fight to win a war, and the fight for first-class citizenship. The racism he encountered in the service displayed, prepared, and ushered Jackie Robinson to Brooklyn for a larger calling.

Black Panther logo 761st.

Uncle Sam called upon Robinson for his ability to galvanize morale; Jim Crow then thwarted the notion. Instead, Robinson etched his name into the American storybook as the protagonist in Rickey's audacious beta test in equal opportunity.

Robinson was a national sensation on the football field at UCLA as part of the Gold Dust Trio at UCLA and wanted to follow in his brother Mack's footsteps on the track before war canceled the 1940 Olympics. The top scorer on the basketball team played a little baseball too. Exhausted, Robinson hit .097.

Said Robinson in his 1972 autobiography: "I was convinced that no amount of education would help a black man get a job. ... I was living in an academic and athletic dream world."[1]

The trepidation that led him to leave UCLA was well-founded.[2]

In August 1941, Robinson starred in the College All-Star game and scored a touchdown against the NFL champion Chicago Bears in front of 98,200 fans at Soldier Field. Fay Young of the *Chicago Defender* couldn't help but see connection between the gridiron and the prospect of impending war:

> The game ought to make the United States Army and Navy wake up. Every time a Negro is qualified to join a particular branch of service there is a cry that Negro and whites can't do this or that together. ... [T]he Bears played against Robinson and marveled at his ability.[3]

He found himself in Hawaii because the only offer he could find was to play semipro football in Honolulu on Wednesdays and Saturdays for a $100 stipend and a job, blocks from Pearl Harbor. An ankle injury may have saved his life.[4]

"I arranged for ship passage and left Honolulu on December 5, 1941," recalled Robinson, "two days before the Japanese bombed Pearl Harbor. The day of the bombing we were on the ship playing poker, and we saw the members of the crew painting all the ship windows black. The captain summoned everyone on deck. He told us that Pearl Harbor had been bombed and that our country had declared war on Japan."[5]

He first bristled when the captain told everyone to put on a life jacket. Then reality set in. His hands trembled in disbelief. A lone target for Japanese bombers, the *Lurline* juked and jived on the vast waters of the Pacific with the desperation of a running back. Relieved, Jackie Robinson stepped ashore in California.[6]

"When we arrived home," remembered Robinson, "I knew realistically that I wouldn't be there long. Being drafted was an immediate possibility, and like all men in those days I was willing to do my part."[7]

On April 3, 1942, Robinson was inducted into the United States Army. His personnel file tells a lot about who Jackie Robinson was as a man. Asked if he had ever been convicted of a crime, Robinson stated "yes," in his own hand:[8]

> Pasadena, California. Blocking sidewalk 1939 fight was on the corner where a group of colored were watching fight between a white a colored fellow. I was arrested along with some others but was the only on[e] taken in. Case never came before court because of nature of offense.[9]

Rather than omit the arrest, he chose to disclose the incident. Even a 23-year-old Robinson had a clear sense of moral fortitude. It tells a lot about being Black in America. He was among the lucky ones, recalling that only his notoriety prevented him from becoming a statistic.

On April 10, Pvt. Robinson found himself on the vast steppes of Fort Riley, Kansas, at the Cavalry Replacement Training Center, though his wife, Rachel, said Jack was never comfortable in the saddle or with a gun.[10] Robinson, ever the dogged competitor, grabbed an M1 rifle and qualified as an "expert marksman" on the rifle range, a demonstration of his remarkable athletic talent.

Robinson spent the better part of a year distinguishing himself while training with the segregated cavalry and was promoted to corporal in March. Military brass, however, had no intention of sending Black troops into combat in 1942.

A college man, Robinson was obviously more than qualified to be an officer. Three months after applying to Officer Candidate School, he had heard nothing. Later, he called the slight his first lesson on the fate of a Black man in a Jim Crow army.[11]

JACKIE ROBINSON. Baseball great Jackie Robinson, the first African-American player to play major league baseball, served at Fort Riley during the early years of World War II. Here, Robinson is pictured on his mount in the stable area of Fort Riley's main post.

Courtesy of Fort Riley.

Jackie Robinson in cavalry.

"It seems to me," wrote Charles Hamilton Houston in a memo to the War Department," that the Army would wake up to the fact that it cannot keep on treating trained intelligent Negroes as if they were zombies."[12]

The racism that permeated every aspect of American society was rampant in the service. Secretary of War Henry L. Stinson opined that Blacks weren't fit for leadership roles and integration would be detrimental to morale.[13] The most egregious problems of race came across the desk of Judge William Hastie, civilian aide for Negro affairs at the War Department, and his deputy, Truman K. Gibson. It was often an academic exercise in futility. Military hierarchy was more concerned with damage control than enacting meaningful change. Black troops were largely consigned to segregated bases and relegated to support roles. In 1943 Hastie resigned in frustration.[14]

Said Gibson in 2001:

> … [W]e constantly just put out the fires. … It was frustrating, at the time because these instances were happening every day, somewhere. … [Y]ou put out the brush fires, but you don't put out the fire.[15]

Robinson reflected on his experience in the service thus: "I was in two wars, one against the foreign enemy, the other against prejudice at home." His sentiment evoked the *Pittsburgh Courier*'s Double-V campaign started in 1942.[16]

"The 'four freedoms' cannot be enjoyed under Jim-Crow influences," wrote Brigadier General Benjamin O. Davis Sr., alluding to President Roosevelt's famous declaration. The Double-V campaign said a fifth, beside speech, worship, want, and fear should include freedom from racism.[17]

Luckily for Robinson, Joe Louis – who had the ear of Gibson – also found himself stationed at Fort Riley. The man who passed the baton to Robinson as the torch bearer for Black America also helped pave the way. Robinson and Louis bonded over a mutual love for sport. The Brown Bomber even gave Jack boxing lessons.

It was a fortuitous association.

Now friends, Robinson aired his frustration to Louis about not being commissioned as an officer. Louis placed a call to Gibson, who applied pressure in Washington. In January of 1942, Robinson and a handful of Black candidates were accepted into OCS.[18]

While quieter than Robinson, Louis was not naïve to the injustices perpetrated on men of color. He just had a different countenance. Louis noted that the Army had problems, but "Hitler was not going to fix them." He went about things in a more diplomatic fashion than Robinson, who even at the tender age of 24 had an inner fire that was especially fueled by matters of injustice. "Jackie didn't bite his tongue for nothing," said Louis of Robinson. "I just don't have guts, you might call it, to say what he says. … But you need a lot of different types to make the world better."[19]

Wrote Robinson in his first autobiography, published with Wendell Smith in 1948:

I sincerely believe it was his worth and understanding, plus his conduct in the ring, that paved the way for the black man in professional sports. My love for Joe Louis goes much beyond what he did in the ring, even his desire to right an injustice. …[20]

"His arrival," noted Rachel Robinson, "brought some much-needed power to the Black soldiers and gave Jack an opportunity to form an alliance and work with his longtime hero."[21] Shortly after becoming an officer, Robinson directed his men in a variety show for Black troops as part of the Brown Bomber War Bond Rally that raised over $500,000.[22]

An apocryphal story by many accounts has Louis saving Robinson from "court-martial, prison and given the lawless nature of race relations in those days, possibly even death," according to Gibson, after he knocked out the teeth of an officer who called him a n----r.[23]

Wendell Smith had a different recollection in the *Pittsburgh Courier*:

Controversy followed him there. He became embroiled with some MP's because according to Robinson, they had roughed up a Negro woman passenger on a bus trip while trying to force her to sit in the back. Jack was almost court martialed. … Only the intervention of Joe Louis saved Jackie from a long sentence. Louis appealed to Washington on Jackie's behalf.[24]

Jackie Robinson, Cavalryman, #14.

Apparently a case of champagne showed up in the provost marshal's office along with some shiny new uniforms from Louis and all was forgiven.

Second Lieutenant Jack Robinson was given a commission as an officer in the United States Army on January 28, 1943, after completing the first integrated 13-week OCS course.[25] About one in 10 of the 78 commissioned officers were Black. Robinson wasn't the only athlete of note in his class. Pete Bostwick, six-time winner of the US Open Polo Championship, was one of the country's leading steeplechasers.[26]

The integrated OCS class was an anomaly at segregated Fort Riley. Fears of racial unrest pervaded the military. Black men could not directly preside over White troops. Troops of color were still relegated to supply lines and logistics. Robinson, now a cavalry officer, was put in charge of a truck battalion.

The morale of servicemen was a tactical priority all too often tested by the indignities of Jim Crow. "The colored man in uniform," wrote General Davis, "is expected by the War Department to develop a high morale in a community that offers him nothing but humiliation and mistreatment."[27]

Singled out for his leadership skills, when the need for a morale officer was pointed out to Army brass, they called on Lt. Robinson.[28] He took his solemn duty as morale officer seriously and demanded that his men be treated with respect. Immediately he took to setting an example for his unit, foreshadowing the torch he would bear for all Black America by the end of the decade.

When Robinson went to the segregated Postal Exchange, the social center of any military installation, only a small cadre of seats was cordoned off for colored servicemen. Black troops stood and endured the monotony of waiting in line while White troops cavorted in comfort. Robinson was incensed. He promised his troops he would see to it that Army brass enacted change.

Robinson's own company was skeptical. They were dubious that their brash morale officer would or could successfully lobby the wholly White chain of command at Fort Riley to get just a tinge of respite and comfort while serving their nation. "Colored" men, as it were, didn't confront White men with such frivolities and find a sympathetic ear. Many lived in a world where one wrong move could cost them their life. Recalled Robinson:

> My statement was met with scorn. I realized that not only did these soldiers feel nothing could be done, but they did not believe any black officer would have the guts to protest. Their pessimism only served to challenge me more.[29]

Robinson was determined to both incite change and ennoble his men. He picked up the phone and called the provost marshal, whose reaction was reflective of the time. Having never met Robinson, he affably listened to his concern and casually replied: "What if it was your wife sitting next to a n----r?"

Robinson popped his cork, the shrill nasality of his piercing voice unmistakable to the entire barracks.[30] Robinson vividly recalled:

> Typewriters in headquarters stopped. The clerks were frozen in disbelief at the way I ripped into the major.
>
> Colonel Longley's office was in the same headquarters, and it was impossible for him not to hear me. The major couldn't get a word in edgewise, and finally he hung up. I was sitting there, still fuming, when Warrant Officer Chambers advised me to go to Colonel Longley immediately and tell him what had happened. "I know that the colonel heard every word you said," Chambers said. "But you ought to tell him how you were provoked into blowing your top.[31]

Robinson appealed to Longley, who wrote a sizzling letter, as Robinson describes it, to the commanding general.

Robinson's men got their seats in the PX.[32]

Jackie Robinson had his first civil-rights victory. Small though it was, Robinson was able to see what moral courage on behalf of his race could potentially accomplish.

> My protest about the post exchange seating bore some results. More seats were allocated for blacks, but there were still separate sections for blacks and for whites. At least, I had made my men realize that something could be accomplished by speaking out, and I hoped they would be less resigned to unjust conditions.[33]

Robinson later opined: "[Longley] proved to me that when people in authority take a stand, good can come out of it."[34]

Attorney William Cline's son recalled that Robinson also took issue with the quality of food that his men received in comparison to their White counterparts, which made him none too popular with the Fort Riley brass.[35] Cline Jr. recalls his father opining: "He was a fine officer, he took care of his men."[36]

One place where everyone always loved Robinson was on the field. Fort Riley was eager to have one of the best football players in the country on their side in 1943. Then Jim Crow stepped in. The Centaurs opened the season against the University of Missouri, who refused to take the field with an integrated team.[37]

Put on leave to mollify Robinson without challenging the status quo, he found out the ruse and refused to play on a team that endorsed segregation. He resented the deceit – either he was part of the team or not.[38]

Recalled Robinson:

The colonel, whose son was on the team, reminded me that he could order me to play. I replied that, of course, he could. However, I pointed out that ordering me to play would not make me do my best. "You wouldn't want me playing on your team, knowing that my heart wasn't in it," I said. They dropped the matter, but I had no illusions. I would never win a popularity contest with the ranking hierarchy of that post.[39]

Point taken. Robinson would not participate.[40]

Fay Young of the *Defender* took note of Robinson's conspicuous exclusion from the East-West Army football game:

All out for victory they shout, but football fans are at a loss to understand why Jackie Robinson … is not included with the top-notch white gridiron performers who make up the West Army Squad. Robinson played with the 1941 All-Stars in Chicago and came close to being MVP. Today, Jackie is at the Cavalry Replacement Center. … Victory will have no meaning for whites, Negroes or anybody unless it is a victory for all peoples of the allied nations.[41]

While Robinson could have compromised his ideals and played football, Fort Riley's baseball team, which resembled a major-league lineup, was also segregated. Pete Reiser, later Robinson's teammate in Brooklyn, played at Fort Riley and recalled:[42]

One day we were out at the field practicing "when a Negro lieutenant came out for the team. An officer told him, 'You have to play with the colored team.'" That was a joke. There was no colored team. The black lieutenant didn't speak. He stood there for a while, watched us work out, and then he turned and walked away. … That was the first time I saw Jackie Robinson. I can still see him slowly walking away.[43]

In fact, there was a "colored" team, the Golden Mustangs. There is no mention of Robinson taking part.[44]

During his tenure in the service, Robinson did make his mark in one sport – ping-pong. He won the base tournament. No matter the game, Robinson was a competitive wunderkind. He was an avid tennis player, a sport, along with golf, he continued to enjoy throughout his adult life.

After the court-martial was over, the USO cordially invited Robinson, then stationed at Camp Breckenridge, back to Fort Riley for a ping-pong exhibition against champion Jini Boyd-O'Conner. No reply was given.[45]

Robinson's penchant for stepping to the fore was a double-edged sword. He was lauded for his leadership until his principles ran afoul of expectations. Whether the impetus was his brashness or the gravity of impending war, Robinson was transferred and assigned to the 761st Tank Battalion, whose motto was inspired by Louis: "Come Out Fighting." For three years no one heeded their battle cry, as was the case for all Black combat troops.[46]

Camp Hood, named for Confederate General John Bell Hood, was in a community overtly hostile to troops of color.[47] That enmity often extended to White officers charged with training "colored" units.[48] Even Joe Louis was arrested by military police for wearing the wrong uniform in Camp Meade.[49]

Most White officers viewed being assigned a Black unit as a demotion and treated their men with open contempt. In that respect Colonel Paul Bates was an anomaly. He turned down a promotion to stay with the 761st Tank Battalion, the "Black Panthers." Rachel Robinson later said her husband was lucky to be commanded by a proponent of fairness in an unjust system.[50]

Colonel Bates earned the trust of his men by according them respect seldom seen from White officers. Trust often made all the difference when White

Jackie Robinson, United States Army.

Courtesy National Baseball Hall of Fame Library.

officers were put in charge of Black troops.[51] Bates was a bulwark against the simmering cauldron of bigotry at Camp Claiborne in Louisiana, so bad a race riot broke out shortly after the 761st left for Camp Hood.[52] As battalion commander, the colonel let his men know they had to outperform racist presumptions. His is a lesson in leadership in many ways evocative of Branch Rickey.

Robinson, who knew nothing of artillery, was supposed to lead a highly skilled company of tankers. "I decided there was only one way to solve my problem and that was to be very honest about it. I was in charge of men who were training to go overseas."[53]

He confessed his ignorance: "Men, I know nothing about tanks." Robinson asked for their help and learned as he went along. He told his company that as their morale officer he had their back and would see to it that they had all they needed to excel.[54] "I never regretted telling them the truth. The first sergeant and the men knocked themselves out to get the job done. They gave that little extra which cannot be forced from men. They worked harder than any outfit on the post, and our unit received the highest rating."[55]

Despite his naïveté, Robinson managed to ingratiate himself. Those who didn't know Robinson from his Gold Dust days at UCLA, were swiftly informed of his athletic prowess when the company played softball. They had to move back 50 feet when he stepped to the plate.[56]

Robinson's virtuosity as a leader, an attribute the Army manual emphasizes, was patently obvious to Colonel Bates, who recognized the same inimitable qualities in Robinson as Branch Rickey.

Bates asked Robinson to join his battalion overseas as morale officer and made clear it was for his leadership abilities. He recalled: "[Bates] said that obviously no matter how much or how little I knew technically I was able to get the best out of the men I worked with."[57]

When Robinson tried to deflect credit onto his men, Bates told him: "The fact of the matter is you have still have the best outfit of all down here. That's all that counts."[58]

It was not politics or race, but Robinson's gifted legs, the very thing responsible for his fame that initially stood in the way. For almost his entire time in the service, Robinson was on limited duty, the Army's version of the disabled list.[59]

Sadly, fans never saw peak Jackie Robinson on a baseball diamond. Army medical reports are staggering when one considers that Robinson stole home 19 times as a Brooklyn Dodger and wreaked havoc with his legs on the basepaths all the way to Cooperstown.

The ankle he injured in Hawaii, which he first broke in 1937, never had a chance to recover. Every time he ran, it blew up like a balloon. Miraculously, he skipped only a few days of basic training after running the obstacle course. Then he aggravated it while playing softball and became a regular visitor to the infirmary. It might very well be the reason that Bates, also a former college football star, beat Robinson in a race while at Camp Hood.[60]

While at Fort Hood he had a rather more perilous encounter with the fog of war. A hand grenade exploded close enough to Robinson to give him a concussion, but it was his chronically arthritic right ankle that kept him from active duty.[61]

The orthopedic consult from Brooke Hospital paints a harrowing picture – traumatic arthritis in the right ankle, secondary to a nonunion fracture of medial malleolus – he fractured the bone of his inner ankle and they never fused. Loose bodies and bone chips were clearly visible with a simple X-ray. In layman's terms his ankle was so severely broken it never healed. Later, Sharon Robinson remembered him struggling with his painfully battered legs every day.[62]

As later, when Branch Rickey came calling, Robinson was eager to embrace the challenge despite the potential perils he knew lay ahead. He traveled to McCloskey Hospital to be cleared for overseas duty. Even a country at war was reluctant to assume the risk.[63]

Beseeched by Bates, Robinson signed a waiver releasing the Army from any liability should he be injured, just get to the green light from Army brass to join the 761st battalion, who were about to be called into action.[64] Given Robinson's practical nature and devotion to his family, one can deduce the patriotic sacrifice he was prepared to make when he found a dedicated partner.

He wrote, "I might've gone but for an incident which indicated that Texas, was in some respects, as hostile to Negro-Americans as Germany or Japan."[65]

On the night of July 6, 1944, Colonel Bates received a phone call to rush to the stockade. On his way home from the Officers Club, Jackie Robinson had run afoul of Jim Crow. His arms and legs shackled to a chair, Robinson was livid, his jaw clenched so tightly it was quivering.[66]

A decade before NAACP activist Rosa Parks' famous stand, Jackie Robinson was arrested for not moving to the back of the bus. Robinson had not broken any rules, yet there he was about to be court-martialed. Colonel Bates refused to sign the orders. Robinson was summarily transferred.

Robinson said the whole thing might have gone away had he been the "yessah boss" type.[67] He showed the same indignance and sense of pride he tried to imbue in his men at Fort Riley when they scoffed at the notion of challenging the status quo.

When Rickey and Robinson engaged in their famous dialectic on bravery, neither man was speaking in hypotheticals. Branch Rickey did his homework. Rickey knew all about his time in the Army and understood Jackie Robinson was no stranger to conflict.

Robinson told the NAACP: "I refused to move because I recalled a letter from Washington which states there is to be no segregation on army posts. The driver insisted I move."[68]

"The sight of a Negro sitting beside a woman who might well be white infuriated him," Robinson later recalled. "I was convinced it was Southern tradition versus Negro."

"I don't mind trouble, but I do believe in fair play and justice," he wrote Gibson. "I will tell people about it unless the trial is fair."[69]

Gibson made clear this was a powder keg portending disaster for all parties involved if not handled correctly. California Senators Sheridan Downey and Hiram Johnson were in the loop.[70]

Without causing a spectacle that might bait the military into making an example of him, Robinson made sure his case wasn't handled like those of many Black soldiers before. He lobbied behind the scenes. There was no press coverage until *after* the trial.

Meanwhile, Bates, who deftly told Robinson to go home on leave and forget his problems, had boarded a troopship for Europe with the Black Panthers.

Robinson was provided with an Army lawyer, William Cline, a third-generation country lawyer from Wharton, Texas. Both men initially thought this might not be the best match. White men with deep drawls hardly inspired confidence in men of color.

Cline's son just happened to be visiting his father at Camp Hood in the summer of 1944. On trial for his life, Robinson was kind enough to meet a young fan. "We had a friendly level of short conversation – as an 11-year-old kid I was thrilled to meet him," recalled William Jr.[71]

The starstruck child knew nothing of Robinson's plight. Robinson had, in fact, told the elder Cline he intended to procure another lawyer. Though the NAACP wanted to be kept in the loop as it were, it didn't send one.[72]

Cline recalled: "… [H]e talked about his life. He was a fine man."

The next day Robinson called and asked Cline to represent him. At trial, Cline poked holes in the racist-tinged lies by many of the witnesses and induced the bus driver to admit calling Jack a "n-----r," then lying about it. The word was used so much during the war that the Army had to issue a specific directive on how to address people of color.

It took just three hours. On August 3, 1944, Robinson was acquitted.[73] By the time it was front-page news in the *Baltimore Afro-American*[74] and the *Pittsburgh Courier*[75], the ordeal was over.[76]

Robinson called it a small victory, keenly aware that his relative notoriety had again rendered him a lucky man.[77]

Jackie Robinson never made it into combat. Bigotry had changed his fate. The call of duty that Bates cultivated was no longer there. Robinson sensed that the Army was anxious, in his judgment, to be rid of an "uppity" Black man who had challenged the hierarchy – and won.[78]

Robinson was put on light duty as a recreation officer at Camp Breckenridge. There he met a friend who played for the Kansas City Monarchs of the Negro National League, who mentioned that baseball might be an avenue to pursue.[79]

When the big push was on into Germany that Spring, I signed with the Kansas City Monarchs for $400 a month. The staggering schedule in the Negro League, the long bus trips, low pay and above all, the humiliating segregation might have depressed me if I hadn't played hard, driven myself hard to forget the indignities I suffered at Camp Hood.[80]

The highly decorated Black Panthers spent 183 straight days in combat and were among those to liberate Holocaust survivors, once reconciled to Mauthausen because of their race.[81]

In November 1944, after applying to the retirement board, Robinson was given his honorable discharge. Before the ink was dry, he was home in California on the football field, mangled ankle and all, playing at Wrigley Field with the Los Angeles Bulldogs of the Pacific Coast Football League.[82]

Lieutenant Robinson's leadership qualities epitomize everything the United States armed forces endeavor officers will impart onto their men. Robinson the officer also mirrored the man who donned number 42 for 10 years. Only his race prevented him from being the quintessential military officer:

I had served in the Armed Forces and had been badly mistreated. When I couldn't defend my country for the injustice I suffered, I was still proud to have been in uniform. I felt that there were two wars raging at once – one against foreign enemies and one against domestic foes – and the black man was forced to fight both. I felt we must not back down on either front. This land belongs to us as much as it belongs to any immigrant or any descendant of the American colonists, and slavery in this country – in whatever sophisticated form – must end.[83]

Wrote Wendell Smith in 1972 upon Robinson's passing: "Jackie Robinson was always himself. He never backed down from a fight, never quit agitating for equality. He demanded respect, too. Those who tangled with him always admitted that he was a man's man, a person who would not compromise his convictions."[84]

Jackie Robinson's career in the service underscored why America needed Jackie Robinson the baseball player. Called upon by Branch Rickey, Jack Roosevelt Robinson was prepared for what lay ahead. He arrived at their famous meeting already a man who had stood up for first-class citizenship and paid the price. Rickey, like Colonel Bates, chose Robinson for who he was as a man to end segregation in baseball. Again, Robinson answered the call to serve his nation and uplift his race. This time he would not be denied.

ACKNOWLEDGEMENTS

Thank you to Bill Nowlin for the opportunity, patience, and guidance. Special thanks to John Vernon; Pete Kessel; Ivan Harrison Jr.; Carla Crow; Cline family; Jenn Jenson; Mrs. Sharon Robinson; Branch Barrett Rickey; Dr. Robert Smith, CIV Historian Fort Riley; Cassidy Lent, National Baseball Hall of Fame; Jeffrey Flannery, Library of Congress.

NOTES

1 Jackie Robinson and Alfred Duckett. *I Never Had It Made* (New York: Putnam, HarperCollins, 1972), 34.

2 "Robinson Wuz Robbed," *Pittsburgh Courier*, March 22, 1941, notes that Robinson, an All-Southern League selection by the coaches of the Pacific Coast Conference in 1940, was left off the 1941 team despite being the basketball conference's leading scorer for the second season in a row.

3 Fay Young, "The Stuff Is Here!," *Chicago Defender*, September 6, 1941: 24.

4 Robinson, *I Never Had It Made*, 34; Red McQueen, "The Boys Are Going Pure Again," *Honolulu Advertiser*, March 11, 1941: 12; *Honolulu Star-Bulletin*, December 1, 1941, December 3, 1941. Having left on Friday, it appears Robinson sat out the Saturday game before coming home, after he was slated to return and deem questionable during the week. He had also been injured the week before and missed a Wednesday tilt.

5 Robinson, *I Never Had It Made*, 35.

6 Harvey Frommer, *Jackie Robinson* (Guilford, Connecticut: Lyons Press 1984). Location 243. Kindle. Also see Roger Kahn, *Rickey & Robinson* (New York: Rowan and Littlefield, 1982).

7 Robinson, *I Never Had It Made*, 35.

8 "Robinson Signs With Bulldogs," *Los Angeles Citizen*, December 13, 1941.

9 Robinson Military File, Service Record, 39234232.

10 Rachel Robinson and Lee Daniels, *Jackie Robinson: An Intimate Portrait* (New York: Abrams, 1997), 28

11 Robinson, *I Never Had It Made*, 36.

12 Letter from Charles Hamilton Houston to Assistant Secretary John McCloy, War Department. Letter in Papers of Hon. Wm. H, Hastie, Hollis Library,

13. Arnold Rampersad, *Jackie Robinson: A Biography* (New York: Ballantine Books), 92, 93. Stimson says this even though troops of color fought in every American war with valor. September 20, 1944. Addressed to "Mac" from "Charlie Houston," the NAACP and lawyer mentor to Thurgood Marshall. Houston seems to have found a more sympathetic ear in Assistant Secretary McCloy than Secretary Stimson, whom he bypasses. Marshall, then NAACP counsel, defended one of the mass courts-martial to which this article briefly alludes.

13. Arnold Rampersad, *Jackie Robinson: A Biography* (New York: Ballantine Books), 92, 93. Stimson says this even though troops of color fought in every American war with valor.

14. Research Division Special Service Branch, "Some New Statistics on the Negro Enlisted Man," Confidential Military Report. Washington, DC: Special Service Branch War Department, 1942. This was a study about Black soldiers that pointed out the demographic shifts from World War I. Northern Black troops had the same level of education as Southern whites. Only 3 percent of World War I Black troops went to high school; 33 percent in World War II. The differences were starker in the North, yet little consideration was given to this, a conclusion realized in 1942.

15. Truman K. Gibson, Oral History, Truman Library. Gibson gives full account of his relationship with Louis, the Robinson affair that is apocryphal, and race relations during World War II.

16. Jackie Robinson, *Baseball Has Done It* (Brooklyn: IG Publishing, 1964). Anthology that offers comprehensive oral histories of those who followed Robinson and a brief account of his life in the context of the civil-rights movement. It was republished in 2005 by Rachel Robinson, with a foreword by Spike Lee; Double V logo ad, *Pittsburgh Courier*, February 7, 1942: 1. In this issue a logo of interlocking V's appeared in the *Pittsburgh Courier* below the word Democracy with a simple statement: "Double Victory. At Home – Abroad." Black America's paper of record began the Double-V campaign, victory over the tyranny of racism at home and victory over tyranny of fascism abroad.

17. General Benjamin O. Davis Memorandum for General Peterson, Washington: War Department Office of the Inspector General, November 9, 1943, archives.gov, "A People at War." Davis and Gibson traveled the country to document racism; Edgar T. Rouzeau, "Black America War on Double Front for High Stakes," *Pittsburgh Courier*, February 14, 1942. This gives the first explanation of the "Double-V" campaign as part of an editorial.

18. Robinson Military Records, Commission Order, Serial Number 01031586, "Special Order No.19," January 20, 1943. Robinson had two serial numbers in the Army, one as a private, and the above, 01031586. When Robinson endeavored to retrieve his records in 1958 and confirm his honorable discharge, something that was important to him when he entered the corporate world and began his civil-rights work, this apparently caused some confusion. Another explanation is suspicion of Black civil-rights leaders.

19. Randy Roberts, *Joe Louis* (New Haven: Yale University Press, 2010), contradicts Mead and Joe Louis Barrow Jr., *Joe Louis: 50 Years an American Hero* (New York: McGraw-Hill, 1988). 206; Jules Tygiel, "The Court-Martial of Jackie Robinson," in *The Jackie Robinson Reader* (Middlesex, UK: Penguin Books, 1997).

20. Jackie Robinson and Wendell Smith, *My Own Story* (New York: Scribner, 1948).

21. Rachel Robinson and Lee Daniels, *Jackie Robinson, An Intimate Portrait* (New York: Harry N. Abrams, 2014), 28.

22. Emma Brady, "Covering Kansas City," *Pittsburgh Courier*, October 2, 1943: 15.

23. Truman Gibson Oral History. Truman Library 2005.

24. Wendell Smith, "The Jackie Robinson I Knew," *Pittsburgh Courier*, November 4, 1972: 9. Eulogy for Jackie Robinson from Smith, a close associate and friend during his early career, on his passing. Smith was hired by Rickey as Robinson's friend and confidant on the road during the lonely and arduous summers of 1946 and 1947, and wrote the already cited autobiography with Robinson in 1948.

25. Michael Lee Lanning, *The Court Martial of Jackie Robinson* (Mechanicsburg, Pennsylvania: Stackpole Books, 2020), Kindle Edition, 2020.

26. Robinson Military Records, Roster, 1 of 371, as collated. January 20, 1943, Special Order 19; Horace Laffaye, *Polo in the United States* (Jefferson, North Carolina: McFarland, 2011). Before the war, Bostwick Field on Long Island helped make polo a spectator sport for the masses by charging low admission. Not mentioned above are Charles Von Stade, and Louis Stoddard, also polo players. There were two polo charity matches in 1940 before the war. Von Stade also fought in Germany and was killed in 1945 in a Jeep accident. Army polo began at Fort Riley in 1896. To read about the history of Army polo see Laffaye.

27. Brigadier General Benjamin O. Davis, "Memorandum for General Peterson."

28. Rachel Robinson and Daniels, *Jackie Robinson, An Intimate Portrait*, 28.

29. Robinson and Duckett, 1. The fact that this opens his memoir shows the import he gave it and its impact on his life.

30. Robinson and Duckett, 38. No one can mistake Jackie Robinson's high-pitched voice as some call it. But his intonation is nasal, not high-pitched as some mischaracterize. Neither a blind nor deaf individual could mistake Robbie.

31. Robinson and Duckett, 39.

32. Robinson and Duckett, 39.

33. Robinson and Duckett, 41.

34. Robinson and Duckett, 39.

35. Author telephone interview with William Cline Jr., December 2020. Cline's father was Robinson's judge advocate at the court-martial hearing as briefly outlined herein. For a comprehensive look at Robinson's court-martial, read John Vernon, "Jim Crow Meet Lieutenant Robinson," *Prologue*, Summer 2008, NARA. [What is NARA? This is the first time it is mentioned.] National Archives Records Administration

36. Cline interview.

37. "Fort Riley Smothered by Missouri," *Minneapolis Star*, September 20, 1942: 35. Missouri beat Fort Riley 31-6 without Robinson. The situation foreshadowed Robinson's first season in the Dodgers organization when the town sheriff of Sanford, Florida, padlocked the stadium lest they countermand the edict of apartheid and endorse voluntary fraternization between the races.

38. Robinson and Duckett, 40; Jules Tygiel, "The Court-Martial of Jackie Robinson."

39. Robinson and Duckett. 2

40. An integrated Fort Knox team played the NFL Pittsburgh Steelers. Wendell Smith, "Smitty's Sports Shorts: Fort Knox Proves Democracy Still Lives in America," *Pittsburgh Courier*, November 21 1942. Smith wrote: "Its roster is a conglomeration of personalities and nationalities, the like of which has never been approached in the history of the Army. It's a mixed unit, which is something a lot of folks been shouting for since the war started. What is more important is the fact that the soldiers from Kentucky are going around the country playing together and living together."

41. Fay Young, "Through the Years, Past, Present, Future," *Chicago Defender*, September 26, 1942.

42. Pete Reiser's biography on the SABR BioProject notes other players with whom Reiser played, including Joe Garagiola, Harry "The Hat" Walker, and Rex Barney.

43. Rampersad, 97.

44. That well-chronicled story told by Reiser led many to believe there was no Black baseball at Fort Riley. The *Manhattan* (Kansas) *Morning Chronicle* noted the Golden Mustangs of the "colored" Cavalry School Detachment playing baseball and there are references going back to 1917. "Golden Mustangs v. Fort Riley Here," *Manhattan Chronicle*, April 26, 1942: 5.

45 Robinson Military papers, Letter to Robinson at Camp Breckenridge from USO.

46 Kareem Abdul-Jabbar and Anthony Walton, *Brothers in Arms The Epic Story of the 761st Tank Battalion* (New York, Crown Publishers, 2005), 19-23 Interviews with Pete Kessel and Ivan Harrison Jr. through the 761st Battalion Alumni Society.

47 Confederate General John Bell Hood led the Texas Brigade during the Civil War.

48 General Davis Memo to General Peterson.

49 "Bomber Louis Freed After MP Arrest," *Chicago Defender*, September 4, 1943, National edition.

50 Rachel Robinson and Daniels, 29.

51 General Davis Memorandum. Memo lists nine points of contention regarding race, all of which apply to Robinson. Davis Sr. should not be confused with Benjamin O. Davis Jr. of the Army Air Corps and Air Force.

52 Abdul-Jabbar, 20.

53 Robinson and Duckett, *I Never Had It Made*, 41.

54 Abdul-Jabbar, 20.

55 Robinson and Duckett, 41.

56 56 Abdul-Jabbar, 51.

57 Robinson and Duckett.

58 Abdul-Jabbar, 21.

59 Robinson Military Medical Records, 1942-1945. Fort Riley, McCloskey Hospital, Breckinridge. The entirety of his time as an officer was on limited duty.

60 David Williams, *Hit Hard* (New York: Bantam, 1983), 132.

61 Robinson Military Medical Records Progress Notes, Medical Reports. Final Summary.

62 Robinson Military Records, June 29, 1943, Brooke Hospital Notes, McCloskey Hospital, Progress Notes, Reports, Final Summary, Discharge. Limited Duty; interview, Sharon Robinson, October 1, 2020.

63 Robinson Military Medical Records, Transfer, intake progress notes.

64 Robinson Military Papers cleared for limited duty but able to go overseas. Letter, June 21, 1944.

65 Robinson, *Baseball Has Done It*, 48.

66 David Williams, *Hit Hard* 127. Williams's book is a memoir of his time with the 761st Tank Battalion.

67 Robinson, *Baseball Has Done It*, 48.

68 "Letter to NAACP." McCloskey Hospital, Temple, Texas: Library of Congress, Robinson File, Legal Trouble, 16 July 1944.

69 Robinson to Gibson, July 16, 1944. NARA.

70 Robinson Military Papers.

71 Author interview with William Cline Jr., December 2020.

72 Carla Crow, "My Visit with Jackie Robinson's Court-Martial Attorney," https://artsistuhcrow.blogspot.com/.

73 Robinson Military Records; Charley Cherokee, "National Grapevine," *Chicago Defender*, August 5, 1944: 13. The *Defender* said the War Department was investigating the matter. This is the first mention of the trial, in the Black press, every paper notes the Court-Martial occurring for the first time on 5 August. It already had been adjudicated, but there is no mention. These are, however, all weekly newspapers. No mention is made after.

74 "Grid Star Faces Court-Martial," *Baltimore Afro-American*, August 5, 1944.

75 "Lt. Robinson Faces Court-Martial, "*Pittsburgh Courier*, August 5, 1944: 1.

76 It is often mentioned that a big deal was made in the Black press about the Robinson case. Rampersad notes it. That is not so. While political pressure was present through the NAACP and others, there was no mention until after the trial. The first mention in the press is on August 5. The case was adjudicated on August 5.

77 Robinson says his win was a small victory, then notes his battle on two fronts. *Baseball Has Done It*, 49.

78 Robinson, *Baseball Has Done It*, 49.

79 Rampersad, *Jackie Robinson: A Biography*, 113. There is a minor inaccuracy in Rampersad's biography. He omits Robinson's second time the PCFL and seems to confuse the Honolulu Bears with the Hollywood Bears and Los Angeles Bulldogs of the PCFL, a professional league that was integrated. The latter was 1944, while the former is outlined in this story. Robinson signed his PCFL contract while at Camp Breckenridge and played football before playing baseball.

80 Robinson, *Baseball Has Done It*, 40.

81 It was a subcamp of Mauthausen, Gunskirken Interview, Kessel, Paul confirmed by Hervieux. Other sources have it simply as Mauthausen and earlier sources mistakenly cite Buchenwald; Williams, *Hit Hard*, 291. Presidential Citation given in 1978 by Jimmy Carter.

82 Robinson's discharge and potential signing is noted in "Bulldogs Sign Jackie Robinson," *Los Angeles Times*, November 8, 1944; "Robinson Makes Local Pro Debut," *Los Angeles Evening Citizen News*, November 11, 1944.

83 Robinson, *Baseball Has Done It*, 117. These comments were made in the context of Paul Robeson and the House Un-American Activities Committee, in front of whom Robinson testified at the urging of Rickey, the only man from whom he took such advice. Robinson was, until the end, staunchly anti-communist, and even in 1972 explains why he detested Robeson. He also quoted Jesse Jackson: "It might not be our country but it's our flag."

84 Wendell Smith, "The Jackie I Knew," 9.

JACKIE ROBINSON IN 1945: FROM BOSTON "TRYOUT" TO A NEGRO LEAGUES STAR

by Bob LeMoine

A brief and often forgotten chapter in the legendary life of Jackie Robinson was the five months he spent as the Negro Leagues batting star for the Kansas City Monarchs in 1945. This era is nestled between his discharge from the US Army in late 1944 and his signing with the Brooklyn Dodgers in August of 1945.

With Robinson's breaking of baseball's color barrier, inaugurating a new era in the history of sports in America, there followed the perhaps inevitable but also unfortunate demise of the Negro Leagues. An institution since 1920, the Negro Leagues became a shell of their former selves after Robinson and other African-Americans began to receive new opportunities in the major leagues. Robinson bridged the gap between the old and the new, embodying the hopes and dreams African-Americans had since the infancy of the game itself. While major-league baseball talent became more based on skill without the disqualifying element of skin color excluding many, not every player of color would have a new opportunity. However, the landmark event of desegregation, celebrated yearly in the major leagues, may not have happened if not for this brief time when Robinson was propelled to national fame by the Negro Leagues.

"That's the side of the story that's not often told," said Bob Kendrick, president of the Negro Leagues Baseball Museum. "We don't get Jackie Robinson if not for the Negro Leagues and the Kansas City Monarchs. And that story really has never been expounded on."[1] This article is an attempt to highlight that forgotten story, although for a game-by-game account of that year, see Aaron Stilley's excellent blog, "Jackie with the Monarchs: Reliving the 1945 Kansas City Monarchs Season."[2] This article will focus on the growing media coverage of Jackie from the ex-UCLA star to a disgruntled player at a Boston "tryout" to a Negro League phenom.

Robinson had been a standout athlete at UCLA in basketball, football, track, and baseball before enlisting in the US Army in 1942. Robinson was "one of thousands of Blacks thrust into the Jim Crow South during World War II," wrote Jules Tygiel.[3] In July of 1944, Robinson was a second lieutenant in the 761st Tank Battalion at Fort Hood, Texas. When he refused to move to the back of the bus (the "colored" area), he was brought before a court-martial. Robinson was exonerated, but the trial itself revealed deep-seated racism, even by those who were representing him. Robinson was honorably discharged in November 1944. "It was a small victory," Robinson wrote of the trial, "for I had learned that I was in two wars, one against the foreign enemy, the other against prejudice at home."[4]

"Had the court-martial of Jackie Robinson been an isolated incident," wrote Tygiel, "it would be little more than a curious episode in the life of a great athlete. His humiliating confrontations with discrimination, however, were typical of the experience of the Black soldier; and his rebellion against Jim Crow attitudes was just one of the many instances in which

Jackie Robinson with the Kansas City Monarchs, October 23, 1945

Courtesy of Rachel Robinson and the Estate of Jackie Robinson.

Blacks, recruited to fight a war against racism in Europe, began to resist the dictates of segregation in America."⁵ That rebellion against segregation was just beginning, however, and Robinson became a chief figure in the growing calls for civil rights. At this point, though, Robinson was "a man still moving largely in the dark," in the words of Arnold Rampersad, and "was still drifting, drifting, still largely at the mercy of fate and the whims and wishes of whites."⁶

He would not drift for long. "While waiting for discharge," Robinson remembered at Camp Breckinridge in Kentucky, "I ran into a brother named [Ted] Alexander who, before going into uniform, had been a member of the Kansas City Monarchs."⁷ The pair struck up a conversation, and Robinson learned that the Monarchs were looking for players. He wrote to the Monarchs and was invited for a tryout at their spring-training facility in Houston, Texas. In the meantime, Robinson used his blazing speed as a running back for the Los Angeles Bulldogs, an independent professional football team, and a short stint coaching basketball at Samuel Huston College⁸ in Austin, Texas.

The *Kansas City Call,* a Black newspaper, hailed Robinson as the "prize freshman" on the 1945 Monarchs.⁹ Robinson made the team and a long season awaited. The Monarchs were known for playing anybody anywhere at any time, even bringing their own portable lighting system with them to take advantage of the evenings. The exhibition season began in Houston on Easter Sunday, April 1, against a group of minor-league all-stars. Robinson went 1-for-7 in his professional baseball debut and "starred afield," contributing to "three snappy double plays."¹⁰ The game ended in a 4-4 tie after 14 innings. The team traveled to Birmingham, Alabama, on April 8 to take on the Black Barons in a Sunday doubleheader. Robinson went 2-for-4 in the opener and drove in the first two Monarchs runs as they won the first game, 7-0. They were shut out, 2-0, in the nightcap. The Monarchs played Birmingham twice more before both moved on to Atlanta on April 11.¹¹

"Players have to make the jump between cities in uncomfortable buses," Robinson remembered about the hardships of the Negro Leagues, "and then play in games while half asleep and very tired. When players are able to get a night's sleep, the hotels are usually of the cheapest kind. The rooms are dingy and dirty, and the rest rooms in such bad condition that the players are unable to use them."¹²

The *Atlanta Journal Constitution* previewed the event with the headline, "Ex-UCLA Gridder to Play

Courtesy of the National Baseball Hall of Fame Library.

Jackie Robinson in the uniform of the Negro League Kansas City Royals, photographed on October 7, 1945, by Maurice Terrell for LOOK *Magazine.*

Here." "(The Monarchs) feel that Robinson will plug the open gap they need to win the American League Pennant," the paper reported.¹³ There was a special seating section for White fans who wished to attend and all wounded veterans, no matter their skin color, were admitted free.¹⁴ The game was played at Ponce De Leon Park, famous for two trees that were in play in center field. Birmingham won, 5-2, and the Monarchs went on to play the Memphis Red Sox in Memphis and then Little Rock, Arkansas.¹⁵

However, Robinson was not with the team. Instead, he was in Boston for a scheduled "tryout" with the Boston Red Sox at Fenway Park on April 12. Robinson was joined by fellow Negro Leaguers Sam Jethroe and Marvin Williams under the supervision of Red Sox scouts and manager Joe Cronin.¹⁶ Wendell Smith, sports editor of the African-American *Pittsburgh Courier*, was responsible for setting up the tryout, although behind the scenes was Boston City Councilman Isadore H.Y. Muchnick. Muchnick pressured both the Red Sox and the Boston Braves to sign a Black player, threatening to challenge the city ordinance allowing games on Sunday if they did not do so. He had received a promise in writing from both John Quinn and Eddie Collins, general managers of the Braves and Red Sox respectively, confirming that they were receptive to a tryout of Negro League players.

The scheduled tryout on April 12 was canceled, however, for unknown reasons. It seems it would have been the perfect time to hold such a trial, given that the Red Sox and Braves were to play that afternoon at 3 P.M. in their annual spring City Series.[17] By late afternoon, news had already spread of the sudden death of President Franklin D. Roosevelt. The Red Sox-Braves games were called off for both Friday and Saturday (April 13-14).[18] Some sources have claimed the traumatic event caused the canceling of the tryout, but that doesn't explain April 12, as Roosevelt died around 4:35 P.M.[19] Even with the cancellation on Friday, the Braves and Red Sox still held practice at their own parks as they prepared for the start of the season on April 17.[20] As newspaper space was devoted to articles about the late president and the new one, Harry S. Truman, the tryout became something of an afterthought.

The Red Sox and Braves resumed on Sunday, April 15, and 13,000 turned out to see the final exhibition game. *Boston Globe* writer Melville Webb wrote, "The Negro players did not have their tryout at Fenway yesterday. They will have a session at the Yawkey yard this morning."[21] This was the first mention of the trio in that paper.

The White councilman Muchnick and the Black sportswriter Wendell Smith both sounded off in the *Courier* about the delays. "They are not fooling me," Muchnick griped. "Collins and Quinn are giving us the run-around. They promised me that they had no desire to bar Negro players and yet they 'run out' every time every time I try to pin them down. These boys came here for a tryout and if they don't get one it will simply be another mark against the undemocratic practices of major league owners and officials. We are not going to stop fighting, no matter how much they duck and hide and try to evade the facts."[22]

Smith set the scenario in historical context and compared himself and Muchnick to the White and Black American Revolutionary heroes Paul Revere and Crispus Attucks. "I am here in the cradle of democracy," Smith wrote, "here in staid old Boston, where Revere rode and Attucks died, trying to break down some of the barriers and wipe out some of the intolerance they fought to obliterate more than 170 years ago. ... We have been here almost a week now, but all our appeals for fair consideration and an opportunity have been in vain. Neither John Quinn of the Braves, nor Eddie Collins of the Red Sox, have displayed so much as a semblance of that indomitable spirit we anticipated here in the shadow of Bunker Hill. ... Our fight has not gone unnoticed. We have won compatriots here in Boston who assure us that the 'Spirit of '76' still lives."[23]

"We can consider ourselves pioneers," Robinson told Smith. "Even if they don't accept us, we are at least doing our part and, if possible, making the way easier for those who follow. Some day some Negro player or players will get a break."[24] Writing later in his autobiography, Robinson said, "Not for one minute did we believe the tryout was sincere."[25]

Robinson and others impressed in the tryout, but none of them received a major-league opportunity with the Red Sox. Cronin claimed years later that it was out of fear of sending the players to their minor-league affiliate in Louisville, where they would face harsh treatment. It was better, he thought, to keep separate White and Black leagues. Clif Keane of the *Boston Globe* was also there that day and over 30 years later claimed he heard someone yell from the stands, "Get those niggers off the field!" Keane believed the culprit was Red Sox owner Tom Yawkey, Collins, or Cronin. Others who were there said they didn't even hear the slur. If it was said, neither Robinson nor any of the players or Wendell Smith ever mentioned it.

Willie Bea Harmon in the April 27 edition of the African-American *Kansas City Call* said the tryout was "a little sweat, a train ride at the expense of the *Courier* and a lot of mumbo-jumbo about how good they looked. That statement might lead one to believe that nothing was gained from the three donning Red Sox suits and working out." Harmon felt otherwise, however, when the long-term goal was taken into consideration. "Every time a colored player dons a suit in one of the major league camps he breaks down one of the bars that keeps him from playing on major league teams."[26] The *Pittsburgh Courier* on April 21 allowed space on its front page for both the tryout at Fenway Park and President Roosevelt's funeral. It hailed Roosevelt as "the best friend the Negro has had in the White House since Abraham Lincoln."[27] There would be no "friends" for them in the Red Sox front office, however.

Robinson's rise was not going to be in Boston. While the supposed racial slur was probably a fabrication, the Red Sox were the last major-league team to integrate, 12 years after Robinson joined the Dodgers. "No different than the curved streets in its city," wrote Howard Bryant, "the Red Sox lacked a clear-cut moral direction on race; against this, the combined pioneering spirit of Isadore Muchnick and Jackie Robinson never stood a chance."[28]

Robinson's time had not yet come, and baseball's unofficial color barrier would continue for a few more months. World War II was over even sooner, and the US Army, which had once brought Robinson to a court-martial over his refusal to move to the back of a bus, began returning its GIs home into a new postwar America.

The next known spring game Robinson appeared in was played on April 22 at Pelican Stadium in New Orleans against the Cincinnati-Indianapolis Clowns. The Monarchs shut down the Clowns, 4-0, as Robinson "clouted an inside-the-park homer in the second inning and rapped out another single as well as showing up well afield and base running," wrote the *New Orleans Times-Picayune*. "The former UCLA grid star retired in the seventh inning with an injured finger."[29] The Monarchs continued to play the Clowns for the rest of the month.

"We were fortunate in getting a player of Robinson's ability," Monarchs manager Frank Duncan told Oklahoma City's *Daily Oklahoman*. "This boy can do everything expecting of an outstanding player. He is a polished, all-around performer and takes a good cut at the ball at the plate."[30] While in Houston, the human side of Robinson and other Monarchs were visible as they visited two area high schools. "The Kansas City Monarch players are always ready to oblige youngsters of today," the *New York Amsterdam News* wrote, "and will do everything possible to influence high school boys to play the diamond game. There's a real spirit in the club this year and it's mainly due to Jackie Robinson, former grid great at UCLA who is doing a grand job of shortstopping for the Monarchs."[31]

The Monarchs concluded their spring training with the Clowns in Houston, Waco, Fort Worth, Dallas, and Oklahoma City. They defeated the Chicago American Giants, 6-2, on the Negro American League's Opening Day, May 6. Robinson, batting third, knocked in one of those runs with a double. Attendance estimates at Ruppert Stadium (at other times known as Blues Stadium, Muehlebach, and Municipal Stadium) were between 12,000 and 15,000. Probably a bigger story, however, was Robinson's new "flame," described by the *Pittsburgh Courier*: "Jack (The Rabbit) Robinson is carrying a flaming torch for a young lady now attending a California college."[32] No doubt, this was the future Rachel Robinson.

The Monarchs played a Memorial Day doubleheader vs. Chicago on May 30. They rallied for a 4-2 win in the opener, which featured Satchel Paige on the mound. The Monarchs were shut out in the second game, but Robinson had a perfect day at bat in the twin bill. He "doubled, singled and tripled in the second [game]. In the first, he walked three times and on his fourth trip to the plate singled," wrote the *Kansas City Call*.[33]

As June rolled around, Robinson was receiving more attention from the press around the country. He was hailed as the "newest rookie sensation in Negro baseball," wrote the *Evening Star* in Washington, where the Monarchs played the Homestead Grays. Robinson "presently is taking his place with colored baseball's top shortstops and is a spectacular distance hitter."[34] He was batting .326 in early June, according to some accounts, and was labeled a "sensational shortstop."[35]

"Right now," manager Duncan said, "Robinson is just about the best infielder in Negro baseball and should improve with more games under his belt."[36] As the Monarchs came east for a long road trip, mainstream news was naturally highlighting Paige's arrival, but young Robinson was also mentioned by the *New York Amsterdam News*. "The colorful Monarchs, rated one of baseball's great clubs, are bringing besides Paige, the game's No. 1 attraction, one of the sport's most valuable additions in years, in the person of Jackie Robinson, stellar shortstop. ... On his showing to date with the Monarchs, he appears headed for stardom, and at the rate he is developing, may become one of the all-time great Race shortstops."[37] The *Washington Post* highlighted Robinson's talents in a preview of a doubleheader at Griffith Stadium on June 24 against the Homestead Grays: "Robinson is not only shaping up as a consistent hitter with tremendous power, but also is fitting neatly into the shortfield despite his big game. The big fellow is amazingly agile, is a smooth and graceful defensive man and has one of the best throwing arms in baseball."[38] Robinson doubled and scored in the first inning to give the Monarchs an early lead in the opener and finished the contest 4-for-4. However, Paige was rocked by the Grays and the game turned into a laugher, 11-3. The Grays kept up their hitting in the second game, winning 10-6, but Robinson finished 7-for-7 in the twin bill, reportedly tying a record by Showboat Thomas in 1943. Monarchs third baseman Herb Souell went 7-for-9 and the duo accounted for 14 of the team's 21 hits. Perhaps even more impressive was the crowd of 18,000 or more who turned out in their Sunday best.[39]

The summer was heating up but the first half of the season was cooling down. The upstart Cleveland Buckeyes and their star hitter Sam Jethroe, who was with Robinson at the Boston tryout, clinched the league's first-half championship. They were in Kansas City for doubleheaders on July 1 and 4, after which the first half concluded. The Monarchs lost both sets of doubleheaders.[40] Robinson launched two home runs in Muskogee, Oklahoma, on July 7 to beat Birmingham.[41]

Wendell Smith of the *Courier* compared the best shortstops in the Negro American League: Jud Wilson of Birmingham, batting .359 with two home runs; Avelino Cañizares, the "Cuban Wonder," of Cleveland (.344, 3); and Robinson (.350, 2). "So, there you are," Smith concluded, "three young shortstops in Negro baseball who certainly should be given a chance to play in the major leagues."[42] Bill Burk of the *Chester (Pennsylvania) Times* wrote that the Monarchs with Robinson had "a drawing card that someday may compare to that of the immortal Satchel. The sensational infielder of the Monarchs is a colored boy. If he were white the Lloyd Park (of the local Lloyd A.C. team) would be filled two hours before game time with major league scouts, managers, and owners, all trying to sign him up to a contract. As it is he is rapidly assuming his spot among the greats of his own race – Paige, Josh Gibson, Buck Leonard."[43]

The Monarchs were in Detroit on July 22 to take on Memphis in a doubleheader. The first game was scoreless until the sixth, when Robinson knocked in a run with a perfect squeeze bunt. He then stole second and third and scored on a dropped throw to the plate. Over 25,000 fans packed Briggs Stadium to see the Monarchs sweep the doubleheader.[44]

The annual East-West Game, filled with all-star talent of the Negro Leagues, was held in Chicago on July 29. Robinson batted second for the West behind teammate Jesse Williams and went 0-for-5 in a forgettable performance. The West won, 9-6, and Robinson ended the game with a slick defensive play on a grounder.[45]

In early August the Monarchs went on a road trip to Philadelphia, Pittsburgh, Washington, Boston, and New York City. In New York, 19,000 came out to Yankee Stadium to see Paige strike out eight and beat the Black Yankees, 4-1. Robinson went 2-for-3 in the dominating outing by Paige.[46] The Monarchs brought their portable lights to Boston for a game against a naval team on August 13. The much-hyped Paige failed to show due to car issues, but William "Sheep" Johnson of the African-American *Boston Chronicle* noted the fine work of Robinson in the 11-1 win, even emphasizing in caps the failure of the Red Sox not to have signed the phenom.[47]

> Jackie gave the fans thrill after thrill by his brilliant fielding, base running and hitting. His drag bunt, his delayed steal of third, and his stealing home with the opposing pitcher, looking right down his throat, unable to do anything about it, were his three sensational plays. Jackie proved why he is the talk of the country. He acts like a Big Leaguer, hits like a big leaguer, thinks like a big leaguer, throws like a big leaguer, and he fields like a big leaguer at shortstop. In fact HE IS A BIG LEAGUER AND AS THE COLONEL FROM THE BOSTON RECORD (Dave Egan) SAYS 'THE RED SOX COULD USE HIM RIGHT NOW AND PERHAPS GIVE THE BOSTON FANS A REAL BIG LEAGUE CLUB.[48]

Not that the game would have received a lot of press coverage anyway, but people were closely following news reports on the imminent surrender of Japan and the end of World War II. The *Boston Globe*'s headline in the evening edition on August 14 finalized it: "JAPS SURRENDER." The Monarchs stayed a few more days on the East Coast before settling for a tie in a game in Washington on August 16 before rushing to catch a train for Ohio.[49] The Monarchs had games against the Clowns in Indianapolis, Cincinnati, and Memphis. Robinson injured his shoulder and saw only limited action, or maybe none at all. The team then traveled to Chicago for a series August 24-27 against the Giants. The Monarchs were swept in the four-game series, but that matters little from the perspective of history. The baseball world was forever changed on August 24, 1945.

Clyde Sukeforth was a baseball lifer, having caught for Brooklyn in the 1920s and '30s, then managing in the minor leagues before being promoted in 1943 to the Dodgers major-league coaching staff. In 1945 his main job was finding players for the Brooklyn Brown Dodgers team in the new United States League that Dodgers President Branch Rickey was establishing for Black players. Jules Tygiel wrote, "The Dodger president's true design for this new entity remains unclear. Its primary function was to allow the Dodgers to search for Black players, but Rickey also attempted to create a viable league that would compete with the

Negro National and American circuits. Through the United States League, Ricky played both ends against the middle, attempting to gain a slice of the profits from Jim Crow baseball, while simultaneously spearheading the cause of integration."[50]

Sukeforth met Robinson at Comiskey Park on August 24, informing him of Rickey's interest. This led to the duo traveling to Brooklyn to meet Rickey in his office. At that momentous session the color barrier of the national pastime was forever ripped apart. Robinson returned briefly to the Monarchs, being asked by Rickey to remain silent of their historic agreement until November. "I went to the management of the Kansas City club to get permission to play up until September 21 in exhibition games and then go home, as I was tired," Robinson remembered. "I was told I would have to play all the games or none. I was left with no other alternative than to leave the ball club."[51] Robinson would spend 1946 with the Dodgers' Triple-A affiliate in Montreal before making his way to the major leagues with Brooklyn.

Negro League statistics are often problematic. Seamheads lists Robinson batting .384 with the Monarchs, while Baseball-Reference credits him at .414. The Center for Negro League Baseball Research records him batting .345 in 41 games. Nevertheless, no matter what the actual statistics were, we see a picture of the rising star who would one day change the game forever. The Monarchs finished a disappointing third in the standings, but Jackie Robinson's road to transforming the game went through Kansas City.

SOURCES

In addition to the sources listed in the Notes, the author depended on contributions from the following persons and sources:

Baseball-Reference.com

Bill Nowlin

Seamheads.com

Stout, Glenn. "Tryout and Fallout: Race, Jackie Robinson, and the Red Sox," *Massachusetts Historical Review* Vol 6 (2004): 11-37.

NOTES

1. Gregorian Vahe, "Before Changing History, Jackie Robinson's Path Was Paved by Time with KC Monarchs," *Kansas City Star*, January 31, 2019.

2. The blog can be found at jwtm1945.blogspot.com.

3. Jules Tygiel, "The Court-Martial of Jackie Robinson," *American Heritage* 35, No. 5 (1984). Retrieved November 2, 2019. americanheritage.com/court-martial-jackie-robinson.

4. Jackie Robinson, *Baseball Has Done It* (Brooklyn, New York: lg Pub, 2005), 49.

5. Tygiel.

6. Arnold Rampersad, *Jackie Robinson: A Biography*, (New York: Ballantine Books, 1997), 112.

7. Jackie Robinson, *I Never Had it Made* (New York: Harper Collins, 1995), 23; Other sources list Hilton Smith, not Alexander, as the person Robinson met, suggesting that Robinson's memory of the meeting was incorrect.

8. Samuel Huston College, now known as Huston-Tillotson University, is a historically back private institution, not to be confused with Texas's Sam Houston State University.

9. "Monarchs Ready for Training," *Kansas City Call*, March 16, 1945.

10. "Kansas City Battles All-Stars to Tie in 14-Inning Tilt," *Pittsburgh Courier*, April 7, 1945: 12.

11. "Birmingham, Monarchs, Split Two Sunday Tilts," *Pittsburgh Courier*, April 14, 1945: 12.

12. Jackie Robinson, "What's Wrong with Negro Baseball?" *Ebony* 3 No 8 (1948): 17.

13. *Atlanta Journal Constitution*, April 10, 1945: 12.

14. "Black Barons Play Monarchs," *Atlanta Journal Constitution*, April 11, 1945: 9.

15. Aaron Stilley, "A Loss to the Black Barons in Atlanta," an entry in his blog "Jackie with the Monarchs: Reliving the 1945 Kansas City Monarchs Season." Retrieved November 3, 2019. jwtm1945.blogspot.com/2010/04/loss-to-Black-barons-in-atlanta.html.

16. Though the Red Sox had also failed to sign Jethroe at the tryout, he later became National League Rookie of the Year for the Boston Braves in 1950. See Bill Nowlin, "Sam Jethroe," SABR BioProject, sabr.org/bioproj/person/5f1c7cf9.

17. *Boston Globe*, April 12, 1945: 19.

18. "School Sports, Baseball, Road Race Are Off," *Boston Globe*, April 13, 1945: 7.

19. "Suffers Fatal Stroke at Palm Springs," *Boston Globe*, April 13, 1945: 1.

20. Melville Webb, "Boston Ball Clubs Call Off Two Games," *Boston Globe*, April 14, 1945: 4.

21. Melville Webb, "13,000 See Red Sox Top Braves in Charity Game," *Boston Globe*, April 16, 1945: 13.

22. Wendell Smith, "Quinn and Collins 'Hide'; Councilman Continues Fight," *Pittsburgh Courier*, April 21, 1945: 12.

23. Wendell Smith, "'Smitty's' Sports Spurts," *Pittsburgh Courier*, April 21, 1945: 12.

24. Smith, "Quinn and Collins 'Hide.'"

25. Robinson, *I Never Had It Made*, 29.

26. The article is quoted by Aaron Stilley in his April 16, 2010, blog entry "Tryout with the Red Sox." Retrieved December 1, 2019. jwtm1945.blogspot.com/2010/04/tryout-with-boston-red-sox.html.

27. "Roosevelt Mourned as Best Friend of Race Since Lincoln and Willkie," *Pittsburgh Courier*, April 21, 1945: 1.

28. Howard Bryant, *Shut Out: A Story of Race and Baseball in Boston* (Boston: Beacon Press, 2002), 40.

29. "Monarchs Defeat Clowns in Negro Baseball, 4-0," *New Orleans Times-Picayune*, April 23, 1945: 12.

30. "Monarchs Bring UCLA Ace Here," *Daily Oklahoman* (Oklahoma City), May 1, 1945: 12.

31. The article is quoted by Aaron Stilley in his April 29, 2010, blog entry, "Exhibition Tour with Clowns Continues with Win in Houston." Retrieved December 4, 2019. jwtm1945.blogspot.com/2010/04/exhibition-tour-with-clowns-continues.html.

32 "Negro League President to Pitch First Ball Tuesday," *Journal Times* (Racine, Wisconsin), May 28, 1945: 12; Wendell Smith, "The Sports Beat," *Pittsburgh Courier*, May 19, 1945: 12.

33 Cited in Stilley's blog entry on May 30, 2010, "Satchel Makes First '45 Appearance & Jackie Is Perfect at the Plate."

34 "Newest Negro Diamond Star Makes D.C. Debut," *Washington Evening Star*, June 20, 1945: 17.

35 Hitting vs. Pitching at Dell Thursday, *The Tennessean* (Nashville), June 6, 1945: 11.

36 "Monarchs Boast New Star in Jackie Robinson," *Rochester Democrat and Chronicle*, June 12, 1945: 18.

37 *New York Amsterdam News*, June 16, 1945. Cited in Stilley's blog entry June 17, 2010, "Monarchs Invade Yankee Stadium, Take On Philly Stars." Jwtm1945.blogspot.com/2010/06/monarchs-invade-yankee-stadium-take-on.html.

38 "Monarchs Feature Paige, Robinson in Double-Header," *Washington Post*, June 23, 1945: 8.

39 "18,000 Watch Grays Blast Satchel Paige," *Washington Post*, June 25, 1945: 9; "Grays Beat Kansas City in Twin Bill," *Pittsburgh Courier*, June 30, 1945: 12. The *Courier* said the crowd was over 20,000 and that game one was a 12-3 final.

40 "Monarchs in 4 Losses," *Kansas City Call*, July 6, 1945. Cited in Stilley's blog entry July 4, 2010, "First Half Ends With Two More Losses to Buckeyes." jwtm1945.blogspot.com/2010/07/first-half-ends-with-two-more-losses-to.html.

41 "Monarchs Win Saturday Tilt," *Kansas City Call*, July 13, 1945.

42 Wendell Smith, "The Sports Beat," *Pittsburgh Courier*, July 14, 1945: 12.

43 Bill Burk, "Sports Shorts," *Delaware County Times* (Chester, Pennsylvania), July 14, 1945: 9.

44 "Kansas City Wins Two Games in Detroit Before 25,286 Fans," *Pittsburgh Courier*, July 28, 1945: 12.

45 Edward Prell, "West's Negro All-Stars Win 3d in Row, 9-6," *Chicago Tribune*, July 30, 1945: 17.

46 Haskell Cohen, "Satchel Sparkles as Kansas City Triumphs," *Pittsburgh Courier*, August 18, 1945: 12.

47 "Monarchs Win, 11-1, Without 'Satchel' Paige," *Boston Globe*, August 14, 1945: 4.

48 William "Sheep" Johnson, "Sports Shots," *Boston Chronicle*, August 25, 1945. Cited in Stilley blog entry "Monarchs Triumph in First Ever Night Game at Braves Field," August 13, 2010. jwtm1945.blogspot.com/2010/08/monarchs-triumph-in-first-ever-night.html.

49 "Memphis and Monarchs Win in Capitol," *Pittsburgh Courier*, August 25, 1945: 12.

50 Jules Tygiel, *Baseball's Great Experiment: Jackie Robinson and His Legacy* (New York: Oxford University Press, 1997), 57.

51 Robinson, "What's Wrong with Negro Baseball?" *22*.

HAPPY HELPING? INSIDE COMMISSIONER CHANDLER'S ROLE IN JACKIE ROBINSON'S GREAT QUEST

by Joe Cox

Anyone unfortunate enough to attend a seminar or professional meeting is likely familiar with the game "Two Truths and a Lie." The premise of the game is that in a roomful of more or less strangers, each person will make three statements about himself or herself, and that only two of those statements will be true. The person playing or the group of other invitees then engage in trying to guess which two of the statements are true and which is the lie.

A politician might make an unlikely choice for "Two Truths and a Lie." But in regard to Jackie Robinson's relationship with Commissioner Albert "Happy" Chandler, the subject of our hypothetical game is indeed a politician. A US senator, a state governor, and an oft-frustrated presidential hopeful, Chandler spent many more years representing political constituents than serving the game of baseball. His career planted him exactly at the turning of racial eras, in both baseball and American society at large. As such, his subsequent statements and assertions are particularly charged, and determining which are (more or less) true and which are of his own invention gives a unique window into Jackie Robinson's courageous work in integrating baseball, and to the role of the game's power brokers in assisting or hindering his work.

But here are three key statements Chandler made again and again in discussing his relationship with Robinson and his role in integrating baseball:

1. Chandler and Branch Rickey attended a meeting of major-league owners at which integration was discussed and voted down 15 to 1.
2. Rickey sought Chandler's approval and support before deciding to call up Robinson – which Chandler unequivocally granted.
3. Chandler lost his job as the commissioner because of his support of Robinson and integration.

Two were more or less accurate. One was not.

*****

Understanding Chandler's role in the promotion of Robinson and the integration of baseball does require some backward review. Chandler was the second commissioner of baseball, after Judge Kenesaw Mountain Landis died. Landis was widely revered for saving the sport in the wake of the Black Sox gambling scandal, and he ruled the game with an iron fist.[1]

It was a very poorly kept secret that the color barrier of the era was being protected by Commissioner Landis. Indeed, it was such a badly kept secret that Dodgers manager Leo Durocher talked to journalists about wanting to sign Black players in 1942, but being stopped by the unwritten rule of segregation. Landis immediately called Durocher to his office, privately dressed him down, and then publicly advised that there was not, nor had there ever been any rule against signing Black players, and that owners were free to sign whomever they pleased.[2]

Bill Veeck often told the story of trying to purchase the Phillies in 1944, with full intention of stocking the team with Black players, only for Landis to lead an effort to rebuff him.[3] While that story may or may not have been true, a fair number of disinterested observers indicated that Landis was indeed keeping the color barrier intact in baseball.

Landis died in November 1944, and Chandler was elected as his successor at the owners' meeting of April 24, 1945. Chandler had been the governor of Kentucky, where Jim Crow laws regulated intermarriage, public education, railroad cars, railroad waiting rooms, streetcars, circuses and shows, and residence in apartment buildings, among other areas. There was not a great deal of optimism in regard to the potential that Chandler would go against baseball's longstanding policy of segregation.

A group of African-American journalists went to see the newly selected commissioner, who surprised them all by declaiming, "If a Black boy can make it on Okinawa and Guadalcanal, hell, he can make it in baseball."4 Of course, even a new politician would be slick enough to tell people what they wanted to hear. But Chandler affirmed his statement again, saying, "Once I tell you something, brother, I never change. You can count on me."5

Chandler's words would soon be tested.

*****

The way Chandler told the story, in January of 1947 baseball owners met at the Waldorf Astoria in New York. A steering committee report of AL and NL owners had been commissioned in 1946 and that report was distributed and reviewed. The report was anti-integration. Chandler told a reporter in the mid-1980s, "I presided over the meeting. They discussed the Robinson situation expressly for a couple hours and then took a vote. They voted 15 to 1 not to let him play. Rickey was the only fella that cast a vote in favor of bringing Robinson to the major leagues. Well, that was advice to me and advice to Mr. Rickey. But I didn't ask for it, and I didn't feel like I had to take it."6

Rickey had talked about the meeting back in 1948. He told an audience at Wilberforce University in Ohio that the meeting (which he dated to August 1946 and placed in Chicago) had followed soon after the authorship of a secret report from Yankees owner Larry MacPhail on integration. Rickey said the copies of the report were gathered up after the 15-to-1 vote, but added, "I'd like to see the color of the man's eyes who would deny [the report]."7

Plenty did deny it in 1948, including MacPhail, Phillies owner Bob Carpenter, and Senators owner Clark Griffith.8 Given Rickey's reputation for needing a moral windmill against which he could tilt, it was presumed that he had invented the story. Chandler didn't tell it himself for years, although he included an account of the meeting in a February 1970 letter to *The Sporting News* publisher C.C. Johnson Spink.9 He discussed it at greater length in both the 1987 interview cited above and his 1989 autobiography.10

Funny enough, though, the paper trail, which Rickey had discounted as a source of confirmation, ended up supporting Chandler's story. A copy of the report ended up in Chandler's own papers, and the document, borrowing heavily from a report Larry MacPhail had presented to Mayor Fiorello LaGuardia in New York City, did indeed come from the direction indicated by Chandler and Rickey.

"The individual action of any one club may exert tremendous pressures upon the whole structure of professional baseball," the report warned, "and could conceivably result in lessening the value of several major league franchises."11

Warning for Rickey and Chandler indeed.

While there is no indication that a vote was ever taken or that any vote taken had any purpose beyond indicating to Rickey (and perhaps Chandler) exactly how contrary to the majority view their own sentiments stood, the rest of the story holds up. And at this point, the issues surrounding a vote should be considered in light of the rest of the story. Two National Baseball Hall of Fame members, in separate accounts made decades apart, confirmed the existence of the report and its contents (and in the case of Rickey's 1948 discussion, he even quoted from the report), and even explained why copies of the report apparently hadn't survived, only for Chandler's papers to end up including the report itself. In 1948 they were essentially publicly called liars by other interested parties, who denied the existence of the report.

We now know that the report existed, that Rickey and Chandler were both right about what it said, and that the report itself was ultimately produced to bear them out. If there was even an advisory vote in support of the report or in opposition to integration, considering that Robinson had already been signed by Rickey and would soon be transferred from Montreal to Brooklyn, the real purpose was clearly to try to intimidate or impose a "majority" viewpoint on Rickey and/or Chandler.

*****

The second of the three events is far less certain to have occurred, as there is no "smoking gun" document, and Rickey apparently didn't feel burdened to discuss it in public. But a close examination of Rickey's own behavior and modus operandi in springing the decision to integrate baseball gives the episode at least the ring of truth.

In numerous occasions from 1965 to 1989, Chandler discussed a meeting with Rickey at the cabin behind his home in Woodford County, Kentucky, shortly after the meeting with the 15-to-1 vote. This cabin was Chandler's de-facto office and would indeed have been a reasonable spot for such a meeting.

The details varied from story to story. The 1965 recounting lacked many details, as Chandler told *The Sporting News*, "Branch Rickey came to me in 1946 and told me he had a Negro ball player. I told Branch I didn't care what color the boy was so long as (Branch) thought the boy could play ball. I was 100 percent behind Jackie."12 It is worth noting that Rickey was still very much alive in early 1965 and remained a cantankerous force who could easily have disputed the account, which was published in the so-called Bible of Baseball.

In 1970 Chandler wrote, "I made the decision for Rickey to bring Robinson from Montreal to Brooklyn ... at my cabin on the backside of my country place at Versailles and I told Rickey that I would protect Robinson in every possible way."[13]

By Chandler's telling in 1972, Rickey had come to see him and told him he knew that he could not proceed with integration without Chandler's support. Chandler asked if Robinson could play and that was then affirmed, and he explained, "[T]hen and there I decided that I didn't want it on my conscience that I had deprived anyone of a chance to play."[14]

As the years passed, the story grew. In 1987 Chandler again reiterated that Rickey had come to the cabin, that they talked for about an hour, that Rickey stated that he would proceed only with Chandler's support. Chandler then recalled telling Rickey, "I've made up my mind that I'm going to have to meet my maker someday. If he asks me why I didn't let this boy play and I say it's because he's Black, that might not be a satisfactory answer. So you bring him in and I'll approve the transfer."[15]

That is essentially the same version Chandler told in his 1989 autobiography, albeit with yet a few more self-serving details. While the exact conversation differs from account to account, the common threads were that Rickey came to see Chandler at the cabin in Versailles, Kentucky, that they discussed Robinson's impending promotion, that Chandler assured Rickey of his cooperation and thus supported his direction.

All of this said, as one historian notes, "[T]here is no evidence that the 1947 meeting between Chandler and Rickey ever occurred."[16] The same author notes, "Moreover, the meeting as described by Chandler would not have fit Rickey's behavior pattern."[17] On this point, the otherwise thorough scholar could be mistaken.

The story of Rickey's decision to integrate baseball is full of meetings in which Rickey revealed some element of his plan to integrate the game, sought outside cooperation, and left the individual with the sincere belief that he had made some great contribution. Dodgers financier George V. McLaughlin experienced such a meeting.[18] Red Barber famously shared his own story of such a meeting.[19] Dodgers reliever Clyde King had yet another story of such a meeting.[20]

Rickey's daughter Jane Jones told one author, "Dad would say to someone, 'You're the only person I've told this to, and I don't want you to repeat it to another soul,' and then he'd proceed to say the same thing three different times on the same day to three different people – and they'd all wind up thinking that they were the only one."[21]

The meeting with Chandler feels like another Rickey production. This time, though, the timeline was set forth by Chandler himself, Rickey had signed Robinson, and he had played successfully for the Montreal farm team. Rickey didn't meet with Chandler for assurance of his path with Robinson. He met with Chandler to seek his approval and support, understanding that he could have gotten along at loggerheads with Chandler just as he could have with McLaughlin or Barber or King. But if Rickey, the man known as "The Mahatma" for his extreme gift of gab and flattery, could appeal to the better angels of Chandler's nature, he could win another supporter of the Jackie Robinson experiment.

That support was far from meaningless. Chandler did back Robinson in many small ways – from sending word to minor-league opponents to curb racist behavior to working to curb racist banter from Phillies manager Ben Chapman to condemning the Cardinals' alleged strike[22] to assigning a friend to shadow and protect Robinson,[23] Chandler was firmly in Robinson's corner. Some have discounted some of these acts, accusing Chandler of enhancing his own credentials in an act of mythology. Robinson himself wrote the former commissioner in 1956, "I will never forget your part in the so-called Rickey experiment."[24]

While there is no proof of a late 1946/early 1947 meeting at Chandler's cabin, there's plenty of context in Rickey's behavior and in Chandler's discussions of the meeting to believe that something very like what Rickey depicted did indeed occur, and was significant in securing Chandler's support.

*****

That said, not all of Chandler's stories hold up to scrutiny. Chandler loved to tell the story of how supporting Robinson cost him his job as the commissioner of baseball. "I never regretted my decision to let Robinson play, but it probably cost me my job," Chandler told *The Sporting News* in 1972.[25] The vast majority of evidence, contemporary and otherwise, shows this to be something between and embellishment and an outright fiction.

Granted, in late 1950, when Chandler was essentially maneuvered out of his job as commissioner, baseball still was very much in a conservative place on racial integration. Only a dozen African American players had seen major-league action in the four seasons of integration, and just five teams had integrated.[26] But integration was far from the only way that Chandler conflicted with many team owners.

Chandler's handling of a gambling scandal with Durocher ended up shocking the baseball world. Chandler also had Cardinals owner Fred Saigh investigated during his tenure.[27] While Saigh ended up going to prison for tax evasion, he undoubtedly did not appreciate Chandler's attention. On several other occasions, Chandler made unpopular decisions involving bonus signees or transactions, including voiding the sale of Yankees first baseman Dick Wakefield. Chandler said months after his resignation, "I would still be commissioner today if I had not ruled against the Yankees in the Dick Wakefield case in 1950."[28]

Perhaps more important than individual scandals was that Chandler was fully determined to be his own conscience as baseball's grand ruler. He negotiated the first deal to televise the All-Star Game and the World Series. He established a players pension fund, and he angered the owners by discussing the potential impact of the Korean War on baseball without consulting them. The final word might belong to Red Sox owner Tom Yawkey, who noted that Happy Chandler was "the players' commissioner, the fans' commissioner, the press and radio commissioner – everybody's commissioner but the men who pay him."[29]

For his part, Chandler always blamed baseball's rule change to a requirement of a three-quarters vote to maintain the job. In the winter of 1950, owners actually voted 9 to 7 to approve a new contract for Chandler, but being shy of three-quarters, Chandler doubtlessly saw the writing on the wall and resigned soon thereafter. "If Jesus Christ were baseball commissioner, I'm not sure he could carry twelve votes," he bitterly noted.[30]

Perhaps not. Chandler was certainly far from perfect,[31] but his political acumen and raconteur's tendency to embellish shouldn't hurt the acceptance of his role in the Robinson drama. Certainly, every detail of his supposed adventures doesn't hold up, but in the case of the secret report and vote, the cabin meeting, and the mythical loss of his job due to Robinson, as singer Meat Loaf famously observed, two out of three ain't bad.

NOTES

1. Landis's rise to power and government of baseball are discussed in many places, including Jerome Holtzman, *The Commissioners: Baseball's Midlife Crisis* (New York: Total Sports, 1998), 24-45.
2. The public aspects of the story are well-documented, including "Majors Can Sign Negroes – Landis," *Brooklyn Daily Eagle*, July 17, 1942: 9.
3. Bill Veeck with Ed Linn, *Veeck as in Wreck: The Autobiography of Bill Veeck* (New York: G.P. Putnam's Sons, 1962), 170-71.
4. Murray Polner, *Branch Rickey: A Biography* (Jefferson, North Carolina: McFarland & Company, Inc., 2007), 174.
5. Jules Tygiel, *Baseball's Great Experiment: Jackie Robinson and His Legacy* (New York: Oxford University Press, 1997), 43.
6. Jeffrey Marx, "Happy's Vote of Confidence" *Sports Heritage*, May-June 1987: 23-24.
7. Lee Lowenfish, *Branch Rickey: Baseball's Ferocious Gentleman* (Lincoln: University of Nebraska Press, 2009), 449-50.
8. Lowenfish, 451.
9. The letter to Spink, dated February 13, 1970, is included in the National Baseball Hall of Fame's file on Happy Chandler. It states in relevant part, "In fact, in the Winter before Rickey brought Robinson from Montreal to Brooklyn at an informal meeting of the owners held in New York, the vote was 15-1 not to allow Robinson to play."
10. Happy Chandler with Vance H. Trimble, *Heroes, Plain Folks, and Skunks: The Life and Times of Happy Chandler* (Chicago: Bonus Books, 1989), 226-27.
11. The author viewed the report within the National Baseball Hall of Fame's integration file and the quotes are taken verbatim from the document itself.
12. Bob Addie, "Happy Pessimistic Over Game, Proud of Its Strides Under Him," *The Sporting News*, February 6, 1965: 22.
13. The Spink letter discussed in Note 9.
14. Associated Press, "Chandler Recalls Historic Step" *Syracuse Post-Standard*, October 25, 1972: 31.
15. Marx, 24.
16. John Paul Hill, "Commissioner A.B. 'Happy' Chandler and the Integration of Major League Baseball: A Reassessment," *NINE: A Journal of Baseball History and Culture* 19.1 (Fall 2010): 38.
17. Hill: 38.
18. As recounted by Rickey himself in Jackie Robinson, *Baseball Has Done It* (Brooklyn: IG Publishing, 2005), 52.
19. Red Barber and Robert Creamer, *Rhubarb in the Catbird Seat* (Lincoln: University of Nebraska Press, 1997), 266-70.
20. David Falkner, *Great Time Coming: The Life of Jackie Robinson from Baseball to Birmingham* (New York: Simon & Schuster, 1995), 151.
21. Falkner, 151.
22. Hill: 39-41.
23. Chandler, 230.
24. Marx, 25, includes an image of the copy of the letter.
25. "Black Pioneer Jackie Robinson Dead," *The Sporting News*, November 11, 1972: 35.
26. In addition to the Dodgers, the other teams were the Indians, Browns, Giants, and Braves.
27. Hill: 43-44.
28. "Wakefield Ruling Cost Job, Chandler Declares," *The Sporting News*, August 15, 1951: 7.
29. Harold Kaese, "Chandler's Dismissal Defeat for Old Guard; Closed Ballot Decisive," *Boston Globe*, March 13, 1951: 18.
30. Chandler, 238.

31 Despite his work with Robinson, Chandler's final legacy is complicated by an embarrassing racist statement he rendered in a meeting of the trustees of the University of Kentucky near the end of his long life. For more details on the Robinson/Chandler connection, see Chapter 3 of my book: Joe Cox, *A Fine Team Man: Jackie Robinson and the Lives He Touched* (Guilford, Connecticut: Lyons Press, 2019).

JACKIE ROBINSON, JERSEY CITY, AND HIS FIRST GAME IN ORGANIZED BASEBALL

by John Burbridge

INTRODUCTION

In 1946 as a member of the Montreal Royals, Jackie Robinson played his first game in Organized Baseball at Jersey City's Roosevelt Stadium. It was a memorable occasion as Jersey City gave him a hero's welcome. Mayor Frank Hague choreographed the pregame ceremony while Jackie did his bit during the game. In 1956 Jackie returned to Jersey City, but now he was a member of the Brooklyn Dodgers and not the fans' favorite. As a result, he was jeered.

JERSEY CITY

Jersey City, New Jersey's second largest city, is directly across the river from lower Manhattan. In 1917 Frank Hague became the mayor. Like most big-city bosses, Hague exerted considerable control over most matters pertinent to the city. He also played a major role in the Democratic Party at both the state and national levels. As a major supporter of Franklin Delano Roosevelt, Hague had over 120,000 Jersey residents support a Roosevelt visit to the Jersey shore in the 1932 presidential campaign.[1]

Hague also created a kickback scheme for municipal workers which was termed "Rice Pudding Day."[2] He also received illegal funds from the city's numbers racket.[3] As a result, Hague accumulated significant wealth, allowing him to have penthouse apartments in both Jersey City and Manhattan and homes on the Jersey Shore and Florida, all on a salary that never exceeded $8,500 a year.[4]

While corrupt, Hague maintained a certain degree of popularity with the citizenry by providing basic services. For example, free medical care was provided for Jersey City residents at the Jersey City Medical Center.[5] He also promoted public education, aligned himself with the Roman Catholic Church, and supported law enforcement. As a result, new schools were built, women couldn't frequent bars, Norman Thomas, a prominent socialist, was not allowed to speak, and New York gangsters were not welcome.[6]

Hague also realized the need to provide Jersey City with baseball. He was able to secure federal funding in the 1930s to build Roosevelt Stadium, naming it after the president.[7] With a seating capacity of 24,500, Jersey City was able in 1937 to attract an International League franchise, the Jersey City Giants, a farm team of the New York Giants. Under Hague's regime, Opening Day became a holiday for municipal workers and schoolchildren.

JACKIE ROBINSON AND THE MONTREAL ROYALS

Jackie Robinson was a superb athlete who starred in several sports at UCLA. Robinson attracted the attention of Branch Rickey while playing for the Kansas City Monarchs in baseball's Negro Leagues. Rickey was on a mission to break the color barrier in Organized Baseball and sent Dodgers scout Clyde Sukeforth to observe Robinson playing for Kansas City in Chicago. Sukeforth brought Robinson back to Brooklyn to meet with Rickey, On August 28, 1945, Rickey informed Jackie he would be playing for the Montreal Royals of the International League, a Dodgers farm team, in 1946 and then with the Dodgers.[8] With that agreement, Rickey and Robinson made history. The Royals' first game in the 1946 season was scheduled against the Jersey City Giants in Jersey City's Roosevelt Stadium.

OPENING DAY, 1946

As usual, Mayor Hague went all out, printing 52,000 tickets for Robinson's debut on April 18. Obviously, not everyone who bought a ticket came to the game given the seating capacity of Roosevelt Stadium but many stood. Schools were closed to celebrate the occasion. The official paid attendance was 51,873.

Hague also orchestrated the pregame festivities, which are best described by Jimmy Breslin:

> At 2:30 the fans were thrilled by a marching band that came in from a right-field gate

and played *Take Me Out to the Ball Game*. Everyone bellowed in song.

Next, a gate in centerfield opened to reveal what appeared to be the mayor being burned at the stake. The hot sunlight exploding on the diamond stickpin in his tie enveloped Hague in a champagne-colored flame. He was a magnificent sight. Blue-gray eyes sparkled under a spanking new hat atop his bald head. He had on a dark blue double-breasted suit that was just out of the hands of a fine tailor. The crowd stilled for the national anthem. Then Hague marched across the new sod to his box seat behind first base. He greeted Branch Rickey and other notables and then sat in glory.[9]

When Robinson was announced playing second base, the crowd cheered mightily. Were they thrilled to see the debut of the first Black player in Organized Baseball? Probably not. They realized Hague wanted them to give Jackie a rousing welcome.

Jackie certainly did his part to make the day memorable. Nervous, he grounded out in his first at-bat. His three-run home run in his second at-bat set the stage for the memorable photo of George Shuba shaking his hand as he crossed home plate.[10] Robinson also hit three singles, two of them bunts, and stole two bases. In this first game, he displayed his speed and his prowess at bunting that was to mark his career. Jackie had gone 4-for-5 with four RBIs and four runs scored. He had exceeded all expectations, leading the Royals to a 14-1 win. The headline of the *Brooklyn Daily Eagle* summed up his performance: "Robinson's Debut a Roaring Success."[11]

RETURN TO JERSEY CITY

Jackie returned to Jersey City in 1956. Walter O'Malley, now the owner and president of the Dodgers, wanted a new stadium in Brooklyn. To put pressure on New York City politicians, O'Malley negotiated a contract with Jersey City to play each National League team once in Roosevelt Stadium during both the 1956 and 1957 seasons.[12] The first game, in 1956, was against the Philadelphia Phillies on a chilly April afternoon. As his baseball career neared an end, Robinson had become known as a fierce competitor with Dodgers fans loving him – and others not so much. The New York Giants had many fans in Jersey City, given its history as the site of a Giants farm team. Therefore, it was no surprise that on the occasion of this first game in Jersey City, Robinson was jeered along with some other Dodgers. Robinson also contributed an error during the game. After the game, Robinson got into a verbal tirade with a *Jersey Journal* reporter.[13]

If Frank Hague were still the mayor, the response would have probably been different: He would have probably orchestrated the first Dodgers game in 1956 as a city holiday extolling the return of Jackie to his city. Hague had retired in 1947 and died in 1956.

AFTERMATH

The fact that Jackie Robinson played and excelled in his first game in Jersey City is a significant event in his career. To commemorate that event, a statue of Jackie has been placed in Journal Square, the major hub for commuter transportation and shopping in the city.[14] It is a reminder of Jackie's legacy in Jersey City.

NOTES

1. Frank Hague 1876-1956, NJCU Jersey City Past and Present, njcu.libguides.com/jerseycitypastandpresent/frankhague.
2. Lawrence Vernon, *The Life & Times of Jersey City Mayor "I Am the Law"* (Charleston, South Carolina: History Press, 2011), 12.
3. Frank Hague.
4. "Hague's End," *Time,* May 23, 1949.
5. Vernon, 93.
6. Frank Hague.
7. David Krell, "Roosevelt Stadium The Forgotten Ballpark," *The National Pastime* (2017): 76-79.
8. James Lincoln Ray, "Clyde Sukeforth," SABR BioProject, sabr.org/bioproj/person/ecod0bd1.
9. Jimmy Breslin, *Branch Rickey* (New York: Penguin Group, 2017), 82-83.
10. Richard Goldstein, "George Shuba, 89, Dies: Handshake Heralded Racial Tolerance in Baseball," *New York Times*, September 30, 2014, nytimes.com/2014/10/01/sports/baseball/george-shuba-whose-handshake-heralded-racial-tolerance-in-baseball-dies-at-89.html.
11. "Robinson's Debut a Roaring Success," *Brooklyn Daily Eagle*, April 19, 1956, bklyn.newspapers.com/image/52904350.
12. John Burbridge, "The Brooklyn Dodgers in Jersey City," *Baseball Research Journal*, Volume 39 (Summer 2010 Number 1): 18-26.
13. Ed Brennan, "Jackie Robinson Blows Cork at Jersey City Fans," *Jersey Journal and Jersey Observer,* April 20, 1956: 22.
14. Josh Jackson, "In Jersey City, Statue Marks Jackie's Triumph," milb.com/gen/articles/printer_friendly/milb/y2009/m01/d25/c500300.jsp, February 2, 2009.

A GREAT LEAP FORWARD: THE VIEW FROM MONTREAL OF JACKIE ROBINSON AND THE MONTREAL ROYALS

by Jack Anderson

On Tuesday, October 23, 1945, 15 of Montreal's sportswriters and broadcasters were invited to a press conference at the home of the Montreal Royals, Delorimier Stadium, and were promised "a major announcement." The Triple-A International League regular-season champions had recently been eliminated in the playoffs by the second-place Newark Bears, but had a great record of 95-58 with tremendous support of up to 22,000 fans a game.

None of the sportswriters had any inkling of what the Royals were about to announce, so there was much speculation and rumor that either Babe Ruth was about to be introduced as the new Royals manager or that as reported by Harold Adkins of the *Montreal Star*, Montreal was about to be awarded a major-league franchise, rumored to be the Philadelphia Phillies.[1] The Royals needed a new manager as incumbent Bruno Betzel, in a salary dispute with the Royals, had left for the Jersey City Giants. Dink Carroll, longtime *Montreal Gazette* sports editor, said: "We'd heard that the Royals were going to announce they'd hired Babe Ruth to manage. That would have been one helluva story. What awaited us was one helluva different story."[2]

Montreal was Canada's largest city in 1945, its metropolis and industrial heartland, and Montrealers were proud of their country's great effort during the long War of 1939-45, the city's NHL Montreal Canadiens, and their baseball team. With a population of around one million, almost 80 percent of French background, Montreal was the world's second largest French-speaking city after only Paris. The Royals had actually outdrawn several major-league clubs in 1945 including the Boston Braves, Cincinnati Reds, and Philadelphia Phillies, the last two teams by over 100,000 fans, so the citizens and its sportswriters were of the opinion that a major-league team would see every success. As Royals general managers for many years would experience with their ballplayers, Montreal had an incredible and varied nightlife, with all-night speak-easies, casinos, and nightclubs, which at the time was rivaled in North America only by New York.

It was not to be either a major-league franchise, nor to name Babe Ruth as the new manager, but rather Royals club President Hector Racine, Vice President Romeo Gauvreau, and Dodgers farm system director Branch Rickey Jr. escorted in a muscular dark gentleman whom they introduced to the writers as Jack Roosevelt Robinson, the newest player to sign with the Royals. Racine announced, "Here is the newest member of the Brooklyn Dodger organization. Last year, he was the star shortstop for the Kansas City Monarchs. He will have every opportunity to make the Royals for the upcoming season, 1946."[3]

"There was no applause, and neither were there hostile outbursts. I'd sum up the reporters' approach in two words: belligerent neutrality," said *Montreal Herald* sportswriter Al Parsley.[4]

A stunned silence, then the reporters surged to the phones to call in the headline to their papers and radio

Early days with the Montreal Royals. March 6, 1946.

Courtesy of Rachel Robinson and the Estate of Jackie Robinson.

stations. Robinson and the Royals' directors posed as the ceremonial signing was photographed for posterity. Robinson stated: "Of course, I can't begin to tell you how happy I am that I am the first member of my race in Organized Baseball. I can only say that I'll do my best to come through in every manner."[5]

Dink Carroll added: "I wouldn't say he turned all the pagans into Christians then and there."[6] Lloyd McGowan of the *Star* said there was no need for Jackie Robinson in baseball, "but Robinson made a more than decent start. I know some were impressed just by the clarity of his diction."[6]

Branch Rickey had planned to keep the signing of Jackie Robinson quiet until he could complete the signings of other Negro League players, among them catcher Roy Campanella and pitchers Don Newcombe, Roy Partlow, and John Wright. Mayor Fiorello La Guardia of New York City, in an election battle, came out with the proposal that the major leagues become integrated. La Guardia urged that New York teams announce they would indeed begin to sign Negro players. Rickey immediately contacted Robinson and arranged for him to fly to Montreal for the Royals team announcement.[7]

As could have been expected, reaction was mixed, with International League President Frank "Shag" Shaughnessy stating: "As long as any fellow's the right type and can make good and get along with other players, he can play ball."[8] Shag, although born in Illinois, was a Montreal resident from soon after his playing days in major-league ball (1905-1908), and had managed the Royals from 1932 to 1934.

Others were not so supportive. Herb Pennock, general manager of the Phillies, said he would accept integration as long as Jackie didn't come play in Philadelphia.[9] It would appear the expression "Not in my back yard" was as prevalent back in the 1940s.

T.Y. Baird, president of the Negro Leagues' Kansas City Monarchs, claimed that Robinson was the property of the Monarchs, but Rickey countered by stating that the Negro leagues weren't a part of Organized Baseball and did not offer legal contracts to its players.[10] Rickey was diligent in insisting that in all his contracts with former Negro Leagues players, there was a clause indicating that the player was not under a legal contract with another team.

Cleveland Indians ace pitcher Bob Feller opined that Robinson wasn't good enough to play in the major leagues because his upper body was too muscular and would tie up his swing.[11] In a twist of fate, Feller and

Jackie Robinson rounding third base during spring training, April 20, 1946.

Robinson would be inducted into the Baseball Hall of Fame together in 1962.

The *New York Daily News* stated that although it was in favor of the integration of baseball, it felt Robinson had just a 1,000-to-1 chance of his making it.[12] *The Sporting News* added, "If Jackie Robinson was white, the best he would be offered would be a tryout in B level in the minors if he was 6 years younger."[13]

Racine said that Jackie came very highly recommended by Dodgers management, and that was enough for him. He added that the signing of Robinson was "a point of fairness."[14] Branch Rickey Jr. told reporters, "Undoubtedly, we will be criticized in some sections where racial prejudice is rampant," and added that the Dodgers were "not inviting trouble, but they won't avoid it if it comes." He then said that "some players might want to quit" than play with Black players, but suggested, "They'll be back in baseball after they work a year or two in a cotton mill." He added, "Jackie Robinson is a fine type of young man – intelligent and college-bred, and I think he can take it too."[15]

In Robinson's autobiography *I Never Had It Made*, he remembered Rickey Jr.'s comment as "I think he can make it, too." He continued: "I realize how much it means to me, to my race, and to baseball. I can only say I'll do my very best to come through in every manner."[16]

The reaction in Canada to the Robinson signing was generally positive. Paul Parizeau of the newspaper *Le Canada* wrote that he felt proud that Rickey believed Robinson would be better received in Montreal than in the United States, and that this showed that Montreal was the most democratic city in the world.[17]

Robinson didn't stay long in Montreal on his first visit. He flew to New York the next day to join a barnstorming tour.

In December 1945 Rickey announced that the Royals' new manager would be Clay Hopper, a 44-year-old Mississippian. *Gazette* writer Baz O'Meara reported, "Hopper is a gent with a drawl from the deep South, and he is going to have to handle Jackie Robinson."[18] Hopper later pleaded with Rickey to send Robinson elsewhere, saying that managing Robinson would force him to move his family and home out of Mississippi. On a later occasion, when Rickey described a Robinson catch as a "superhuman play," Hopper reportedly replied, "Mr. Rickey, do you really think a ni**er's a human being?"[19]

One would think that Hopper would be a strange choice for the meticulous Rickey to make, but events would show that Rickey had chosen wisely. Rickey had first offered a managerial position to Hopper in 1929, when Clay was only 27, and had appreciated Hopper's leadership qualities. These qualities were to be tested in 1946.

One of the first questions Branch Rickey asked Robinson at their historic meeting on August 28, 1945, was "You got a girl?" Robinson told Rickey of his engagement to the lovely and intelligent Rachel Isum, a graduate nurse back in Los Angeles. Branch replied: "You know you have a girl. When we get through today you may want to call her up because there are times when a man needs a woman by his side."[20] Rickey could not have been more right in his judgment. Rachel later said that Rickey had warned of trials to come, and that Branch was shrewd in business and thoughtful in personal relationships.

Jack Roosevelt Robinson and Rachel Isum were married on February 10, 1946, in Los Angeles. Two weeks later, they set out on a cross-country trip to the Royals' spring-training site in Daytona Beach, Florida. Rachel said they were particularly concerned about arriving on time and ready for work, and that they "were all too familiar with the racial stereotype widely believed by whites and too often acted out by blacks."[21]

Their troubles began almost as soon as their plane landed in New Orleans, where they were informed that they had been bumped from the next leg of their flight, and that there were no more flights that night. After a night in a seedy hotel, they flew on to Pensacola, Florida, where they were bumped once more. Forced to continue in a segregated bus, they finally arrived 16 hours later, days late, and were met by *Pittsburgh Courier* sportswriter Wendell Smith and photographer Billy Rowe, who had been hired by Rickey to escort them around during spring training. Rickey had arranged lodging in the local Negro community, apart from the other Royals.

When spring-training games began, the Royals were locked out in Jacksonville and Deland, and run out of the ballpark in Sanford solely due to the presence of Robinson and his Black teammate, pitcher John Wright. Rachel Robinson said, "… these events took their toll on Jack and that he began to try too hard to win a permanent place on the team as rookies could be cut before the end of training camp. He was over-swinging and having difficulty sleeping and concentrating." His arm troubles had necessitated a change of position from shortstop, which he had played for the Kansas City Monarchs, to second base and then first. She added, "He went into a slump, that mysterious ailment that plagues even the best ballplayers, but towards the end of camp Jackie broke out, began hitting and made the team."[22]

There was a way to go yet as *New York World Telegram* writer Dan Daniel wrote as early as March 6, two days after Robinson's arrival, that he wasn't of International League caliber. *La Presse* added on March 7: "It is perhaps too early to tell, but we are of the impression that Robinson won't be with the Royals this season."[23] This was before Robinson and Wright had even played a game; they weren't inserted into the lineup until March 17. The Royals management had had enough of the Florida municipalities' feeble excuses for canceling games, Racine announced: "This will be all or nothing for us. Robinson and Wright will play, or there will be no games"; in this he was backed up by Hopper. General manager Mel Jones went even further: "We don't care if we fail to play another single exhibition game. If they don't want to play us with our full team, they can pull out of the games."[24] The Royals backed up their tough talk by moving a game from Deland to Daytona Beach, and the four games the Royals were to play on their way north to start the season were all canceled.

On April 5 the Royals played the Indianapolis Indians and their experienced longtime major-league pitcher, Paul Derringer. Derringer proceeded to give Robinson the star-player treatment, by throwing hard inside and knocking Robinson down twice, with the batter responding each time with first a single, then a triple. Derringer spoke to Hopper after the game and told him that Robinson had passed the test: "Clay, your colored boy is going to do all right."[25]

Wendell Smith wrote in the *Pittsburgh Courier* on April 6 that both Wright and Robinson had made the team, despite no official confirmation. The Royals game in Sanford the next day was interrupted by the police chief, who insisted that Robinson be removed from the field, citing a municipal law prohibiting mixed sports. Robinson had already singled, stolen a base, and scored a run. Robinson was back in the lineup the next day and hit a triple, walked, and scored two runs against Jersey City.

On April 8 the Royals assigned Lou Rochelli, the other presumptive second baseman, to the St. Paul (Minnesota) Saints of the American Association. Of Rochelli, Robinson wrote in his biography: "The generosity and friendship of a white team-mate in the early days with Montreal is a fond memory," and added that Rochelli, despite competing with Robinson for the second-sacker spot, "spent a lot of time helping me, and teaching the techniques needed to be a competent second baseman."[26] Royals shortstop Stan Breard, a popular native Montrealer, was also a great supporter of Robinson. When a groundball took a bad hop and struck Robinson in the face, Breard ran over to make sure his teammate was uninjured.

As for Hopper, all agreed that he treated both Robinson and Wright fairly. He never spoke out against Rickey's great experiment and supported the Royals' stance when visiting other Florida cities. When the Royals returned to Montreal, Hopper was speaking glowingly of Robinson, calling him "a regular fella and a regular member of my baseball club"[27] and regaled the sportswriters with tales of Robinson's fielding and baserunning prowess. When the *Star* ran an Opening Day layout picturing Abraham Lincoln surrounded by Rickey, Racine, Robinson, and Hopper, the Southerner asked for an original for his home in Mississippi.[28]

At the end of spring training, the *Montreal-Matin* announced that Robinson had made the Royals and a starting spot at second base after "his truly sensational record in spring training."[29] This was clearly hyperbole, as his arm injury, sleepless nights and constant harassment from the stands would easily explain his rather mundane statistics: a .280 batting average, including two doubles and two triples, seven walks, and five stolen bases.

Wright's pitching statistics were worse, but he had thrown only 10 innings, compared with several other Royals pitchers who had over 30 innings under their belt. According to Robinson, "[E]very time he stepped out there he seemed to lose that fineness and he tried a little bit harder than he was capable of playing."[30] After Wright's last appearance in spring training, Wendell Smith reported that "he was wilder than an Egyptian Zebra"[31] Years later, superscout Clyde Sukeforth said the Dodgers did not expect great things from Wright, but were of the opinion he would be a good companion for Robinson.[32]

On Opening Day there was great anticipation in the stands as 52,000 raucous fans filled the over-capacity Roosevelt Stadium in Jersey City. Rachel was so nervous that she couldn't sit down. In Jackie's second at-bat, in the third inning, the Giants were expecting a bunt with two runners on base, but Robinson hit a three-run homer over the left-field wall for a 5-0 Royals lead. Robinson was welcomed as he crossed home plate by the next hitter, outfielder George "Shotgun" Shuba. Shotgun reached out and shook Jackie's hand to congratulate him, and the crowd roared. As he made his way back to the dugout, his teammates showed their appreciation. Jackie said, "this was the day that the dam broke between my teammates and myself. Southerners or Northerners, they let me know they appreciated what I did."[33]

La Patrie said it all in a banner headline in the sports section: "Robinson Plays the Role of Hero."[34] That was echoed by the *Courier,* whose headline was "Jackie Stole the Show."[35] Robinson had a 4-for-5 day with the home run, three singles, four RBIs, four runs scored and a fielding error. At the end of the game, fans swarmed the field to congratulate Robinson, shaking his hand and getting his autograph.

It was not an easy schedule for the Royals. After the Jersey City series, which they won two games to one, they moved on to Newark, Syracuse, and Baltimore. With the exception of Baltimore, Syracuse proved to be the most inhospitable to Robinson and Wright. In Syracuse, while Jackie was in the on-deck circle, a Syracuse player pushed a black cat on the field and yelled at Robinson: "Hey, Jackie, here's your cousin clowning on the field." The umpire ordered the Syracuse bench to behave.[36]

Baltimore was to be the real test for the great experiment. International League President Shag Shaughnessy had beseeched Rickey: "Don't let that colored boy go to Baltimore. There's a lot of trouble brewing there." Rickey replied: "We solve nothing by backing away."[37]

On a freezing cold Saturday night in late April, the few fans who showed up in Baltimore hurled awful racial abuse, so much that Rachel Robinson later commented that the Baltimore fans "engaged in the worst kind of name-calling and attacks on Jackie that I had to sit through."[38] Robinson was nervous and tentative the first three games in Baltimore, with only two hits in 10 at-bats and two errors in the field. On Monday night, he made up for his earlier performance with three hits in three at-bats and four runs scored. Baltimore pitcher Paul Calvert, a Montreal native and a former Royal, plunked Robinson on the wrist after his hitting performance.

Although the Royals had only a 6-6 record after this grueling road trip to start the season, Robinson was batting .372 with 17 runs scored and 8 stolen bases.

May 1, 1946, was a bright and sunny home opener at Delorimier Stadium for the Royals against Jersey City. Jackie Robinson was the center of attention. The *Star* noted: "The fans appreciated what they saw: One of the great athletes of our time, of any time, had all the tools to be a very good baseball player."[39] Sam Lacy wrote that the "applause for Robinson made the fences shake"[40] and Charles Mayer of the *Petit-Journal* stated that the ovation for Robinson was the greatest ever given to a Royals player.[41]

Still bandaged on his wrist and sore from the hit-by-pitch in Baltimore, Robinson did not have as explosive a game as in his debut against Jersey City. He had a single, a walk, and a run scored in a 12-9 victory for the Royals. The fans mobbed him after the game, and he had to be escorted out of the ballpark by two policemen through a side door. Rachel Robinson returned the affection by sitting at a table and signing autographs in front of the main gate.

There were still skeptics as recounted by Phil Seguin of *La Patrie*: "Jackie Robinson didn't impress yesterday. In the field he looked weak on balls hit to his right and at bat he hit the ball out of the infield only once, and was caught stealing second base."[42] Baz O'Meara of the *Star* wrote on May 16: "Most observers believe that, in a month or so, Robinson will not be hitting with any degree of consistency."[43]

In the meantime, the Robinsons had to find a place to live in Montreal. Rachel was provided with a list of rental apartments by the Royals but worried that they would have a hard time renting an apartment in the city. But she was warmly greeted by the landlady at 8232 De Gaspe Street, her first choice, and was invited inside for tea, where they agreed on renting the apartment. When it became known in the French-speaking neighborhood that the Robinsons were expecting their first child, neighbors carried Rachel's groceries for her while the women helped her make maternity clothes and gave her ration cards, exhorting her to eat more meat. The experience in Montreal was "almost blissful," Rachel later remarked. Speaking of Rachel Robinson being a rock to her husband, Lula Jones Garrett, a reporter for the *Baltimore African-American*, said: "The only person I know who can equal her is that first citizen of the world, Mrs. Eleanor Roosevelt."[44]

Rachel Robinson's fortitude was to be tested as her husband began to show signs of exhaustion in midseason. The constant pressure caused him to have insomnia and limited his appetite. A doctor advised rest away from the ballpark, and Clay Hopper tried to give him more time off as the season progressed. Rachel had her own challenges as she was pregnant with Jackie Jr. and had to visit doctors regularly, even experiencing old-time medicine as a doctor refused to perform a procedure on her without her husband's permission.

By the end of May, the Royals had improved to 27-11 and had climbed into first place in the International League. Robinson was leading the league in hitting at .356, in hits with 47, and in runs scored with 38.

Robinson missed a week of games due to a leg injury, returning on June 7 in a victory over the Baltimore Orioles. He then missed games against Baltimore and the entire series against Jersey City. He tried to play on June 12 against Jersey City, but withdrew after five innings. On Sunday, June 16, after 19 straight days on the road, the Royals drew 20,086 fans and split a doubleheader against the Syracuse Chiefs with Robinson still absent. He returned to action on June 21, in the first game of yet another doubleheader against Newark. On June 24, the holiday of Quebec's patron saint, John the Baptist, Roy Partlow threw a five-hitter against the Jersey Giants in a Royals victory, becoming the first Black pitcher to officially record a win in White Organized Baseball in the twentieth century. Robinson chipped in with two hits, one RBI, and five assists from second base.

Al Parsley of the *Herald* reported that the Royals now had a second Black star, a "dark wizard" who threw lefty with great velocity.[45] On Tuesday, June 25, Robinson had a double and two singles in a win over Jersey City, and the Royals now counted nine players hitting .300 or higher. Bruno Betzel, the manager of the Jersey City Giants, was on hand at Delorimier Stadium to see the Royals raise the 1945 pennant, when he had been the Montreal manager. He took the opportunity to state that as a manager he would have liked to have nine Jackie Robinsons on his team.[46] Another positive for the Royals was the return of star local pitcher Jean-Pierre Roy, who had won 25 games for the Royals in 1945, and picked up his first win on Thursday, June 27.

In ending June, the Royals split a doubleheader against Rochester with Robinson having three hits and three runs scored amid a great show of support from the fans. Danny Murtaugh of the Red Wings, later a major-league player and manager, tripped up Robinson in the first game, and was soundly booed the rest of the day. For the month, in which he was injured more than half the time, Jackie hit .319 with 12 runs scored, 7 RBIs, and 2 stolen bases.

The Royals had played their first 30 home games before 214,352 spectators, already 55,000 more than the previous year. Montreal, with Robinson the star attraction, was also drawing record crowds on the road. Rochester had 14,140 fans for the first two games against the Montrealers, compared with only 2,478 the previous year, and in Syracuse the first visit of the Royals drew an all-time record attendance for a weeknight game.

Sam Maltin of the *Montreal Herald*, who also reported for the *Courier*, said there was no doubt that Robinson's popularity was the main reason for the increase in ticket sales: "Jackie was regularly surrounded by admirers on this streetcar ride back home, some fans even following him to the door to get an autograph." Maltin continued: "In restaurants, Jackie's meal became cold as he was so busy signing autographs"[47] Quebec actor Marcel Sabourin, who crossed paths on the streetcar with Robinson, stated: "Instantly he became our idol. His photos filled our scrapbooks, and in the alleys all the youngsters playing ball wanted to be Jackie Robinson."[48]

Due to rainouts, the Royals had a demanding start to July with 11 games in seven days in three cities. They won nine, stretching their lead to 10½ games atop the standings. After this marathon, the parent Dodgers came to Quebec for two games over the major-league All-Star break against their Quebec farm teams. The Dodgers pounded the Class-C Trois Rivieres Royals, 6-2 on July 8, before facing the Montrealers the next day. *Le Canada*'s Paul Parizeau wondered if this wasn't a good opportunity for the Rickey-Durocher tandem to evaluate the Royals players with late-season call-ups in mind. In 1945, despite a promise by Rickey, the Dodgers had called up two of the Royals' best players, and many fans and reporters thought that this had deprived the Royals of a possible Little World Series berth. Parizeau wrote that they had taken Montreal fans for "suckers" and this should not happen again in 1946.[49] After the Dodgers broke out to a 4-0 lead, the Royals fought back to tie the game at 5-5, but the game was called so that the Dodgers could catch a night train to Chicago. Many of the 16,168 spectators booed the decision and threw seat cushions onto the field.

In mid-July the Royals headed out on a three-week road trip and visited all the other seven teams in the league. They also sent the disappointing Roy Partlow back down to the Trois Rivieres Royals. Unlike John Wright before him, Partlow did not take the demotion well. Wendell Smith said: "Partlow is acting like a spoiled child, he should think less of himself and more about the 14 million African-Americans from one ocean to the other who wanted him to succeed in white baseball."[50]

On Wednesday, July 17, the Royals swept two from Rochester, swatting 28 hits. On Sunday the 21st, they swept the Syracuse Chiefs in yet another doubleheader. Robinson knocked four hits in eight at-bats, including his second homer of the campaign. On the 24th, Jackie bunted for a hit and scored after the throw to first base rolled down the right-field line. Robinson also made an error in this game, his first in 58 games.

While the Royals were on this long road trip, the Montreal (formerly Pittsburgh) Crawfords of the United States Negro Baseball League split a doubleheader at Delorimier Stadium with the Brooklyn Black Dodgers.[51]

During the Syracuse doubleheader, *La Presse* reported, Robinson had the 10,000 fans laughing as he bunted for a hit, running so swiftly that he lost his cap and a shoe while running to first base. He quickly put the shoe back on and promptly stole second base.[52] On Friday, July 26, Robinson was the star for the Royals with three hits, including a homer, as Montreal edged Baltimore, 10-9.

The Royals continued to draw well on the road, and while splitting a doubleheader with Baltimore on July 28, the Orioles drew 26,038 to run their season total to 378,336 fans, an all-time league record. The Royals, wracked by a flu bug that caused five players to miss the last game, moved on to Newark. Although it did not show in his on-field performance, *The Sporting News* noted that "the stress continued to mount on Robinson."[53]

Nevertheless, Robinson dived to rob Newark's Yogi Berra of a bases-loaded two-out hit in the first game.

On August 9 *La Presse* eulogized the ballplayer: "Jackie Robinson will possibly move on to the Brooklyn Dodgers next year to create a precedent in the history of baseball. Yesterday, once again, Robinson showed his value to the team by smashing a hard-hit double to right field in the 10th inning to drive in the winning run in a 3-2 Royals victory."[54]

August began with a loss in Jersey City, in which Robinson had two hits. The teams split a doubleheader the next day with Robinson going 1-for-3 in the first game before sitting out the later game.

Returning home for another doubleheader on August 4 before 16,556 fans, the Royals swept two games from second-place Syracuse. *La Presse* noted that one couldn't ignore the contribution of Robinson. In the first game he hit a sharp single, knocking in a run, and made a beautiful play in the field, and also pilfered his 32nd base. In the second game, he was even more brilliant, leaping two or three feet into the air to snare a hard-hit ball by Syracuse catcher Joe Just, and then driving in the winning run.[55]

On Monday the 5th, the Royals took the train north to Trois Rivieres for an exhibition match against the Class-C Royals, defeating the home squad, 8-1. Waiting with a warm welcome at the train station for Robinson were his former roommates, Partlow and Wright.[56]

Back in Montreal to face Syracuse, poor pitching and defense led to an 18-17 defeat at foggy Delorimier Stadium on Tuesday. *La Patrie* described the game as a poor imitation of the game of baseball. Robinson had five hits but it wasn't enough for the Royals. They struck back against the Chiefs on Wednesday, 9-4, with Robinson again going 3-for-4, raising his season average to .367.

Robinson continued his hot streak against Jersey City on Thursday and *La Presse*'s headline said it all: "Jackie Robinson Gives Another Victory to Montreal." The newspaper observed: "How to vaunt the merits and to highlight the real value of the popular colored player Jackie Robinson is actually an impossible task for a sportswriter without inventing a new dictionary."[57] Robinson added another three hits, including a triple, then daringly made a mad dash home on a shallow fly ball for the winning run. The *Gazette*'s Dink Carroll, who had been previously reserved in his praise of Jackie, added "There doesn't seem to be anything he can't do."[58]

On August 9, the Royals defeated Jersey City, with Robinson again leading the way with a triple, double, single, and four RBIs. His hot streak now extended to 14 hits in his last 19 at-bats.

The Royals downed the Orioles 9-1 on Tuesday the 13th to improve their home record to 44-13, putting them 15 games ahead of the now second-place Buffalo Bisons. Robinson had two walks and two runs scored but was injured by a pitch to his biceps by Orioles hurler Stan West. Royals trainer Ernie Cook wrapped Robinson's arm in ice between innings to limit swelling.

Robinson returned to play on Wednesday the 14th as the Royals won 2-1 against Baltimore's Johnny Podgajny. After the game, Baltimore manager Alphonse Thomas told *La Presse* he was glad to be leaving Montreal, noting that the Orioles, despite being the highest paid team in the League, lacked fighting spirit and the desire to win against the first-place Royals.[59]

Fans at Delorimier Stadium certainly had their money's worth on August 15 as the Royals and Newark Bears put on an unprecedented hitting display in a doubleheader, the Royals winning the first game, 21-6, and Newark taking the nightcap, 12-2. In the first game Robinson, who was leading the league in batting, went 3-for-3 with four runs scored. He added another single and run scored in the second game. He kept pace with Newark's top entry for the batting championship, Al Clark, who had five hits in the twin bill.

After a rainout on Friday the 16th, the Royals and Bears split a doubleheader Saturday at Delorimier. Robinson went only 1-for-8 with two RBIs, dropping his average below .370.

The Royals hosted Toronto on Tuesday, August 20, downing the visitors 6-5 with Robinson chipping in a single, triple, and two RBIs. On the 21st, in a 6-2 win, Jackie had two hits and two stolen bases, and went from first to third on a sacrifice bunt. Lloyd McGowan of the *Star* commented: "All pitchers, whether right-handed or south-paws, have looked pretty much alike to Robby in recent games. He can hit the curve, and while a natural right-handed pull-hitter, he can powder the ball to all fields, and has proved he can hit behind the runner."[60] *La Presse* added: "Jackie demonstrated once again his speed in stealing two bases to run his season total to 35."[61]

Of the Royals' next series, against the Bisons in Buffalo, *The Sporting News* commented: "Robinson earned several ovations from Buffalo fandom, especially after pilfering home, and then turning an unassisted double play the following night."[62]

On Sunday, August 25, against the Rochester Red Wings, the Royals won the nightcap, 4-2, behind Curt Davis to clinch the league regular-season title with 90 wins and a 19-game lead. Robinson went 1-for-9 in the doubleheader. He desperately needed some time off to mend from injuries and the tremendous stress he had been under during this breakthrough season. Clay Hopper obliged, granting a few days off. *Newsweek* quoted him as saying, "Robinson is a player who must go to the majors. He's a big-league ballplayer, a good team hustler, and a real gentleman."[63] This was quite the turnaround of opinion from before spring training.

Robinson was listed by *La Presse* as out with a leg injury on August 26 as the Royals lost to the Red Wings.

Montreal moved on to Toronto for a doubleheader on Thursday, August 29. Reporters quizzed Montreal general manager Mel Jones, who had to quash rumors that Robinson would be heading to the Dodgers before season's end: "He's passed the test here, and he shouldn't have to go through that again in the big leagues," Jones told the *Gazette's* Lloyd McGowan.[64] Montreal swept the doubleheader against the Maple Leafs, and while Robinson was hitless in the first game, he rebounded with a single and a double and two runs scored in the second game.

The Royals split a doubleheader against Toronto on Friday. *The Sporting News* reported, "In the second game, Jackie Robinson, Negro infield star, was shifted to the hot corner, a station he is said to be ticketed for to play for Brooklyn next season."[65] On Saturday, August 31, the Royals downed the Maple Leafs, with Robinson contributing two hits, a run scored, and an RBI.

In August, he hit .366 with 10 doubles and 5 triples, had 6 stolen bases, and scored 33 runs as the Royals won 24 of 35 games.

Back on home turf at Delorimier Stadium at last on Sunday, September 1, the Royals swept Buffalo in a twin bill. The following day, Labor Day, over 27,000 fans were disappointed as their heroes were swept in yet another twin bill, the Bisons handing the Royals their first home doubleheader loss of the season. Robinson was 3-for-9 with two RBIs in the losses.

After an offday on Tuesday, the Royals returned to action at home against the Red Wings on Wednesday, September 4, splitting the doubleheader, with Robinson 2-for-7 with two stolen bases and a run scored in the two games.

On that day the headline in *La Presse* read: "Brilliant Debut for Jackie Robinson at Third Base." The article said, "The days of Cookie Lavagetto at third base for the Dodgers are numbered, as Jackie Robinson will certainly replace him next spring."[66]

After two games at third base in which Robinson started a crisp double play, made a nice catch, stopped several grounders, and made accurate throws, Hopper told reporters, "He does everything well that we ask of him."[67]

On Thursday, September 5, Robinson returned to second base in a loss to Rochester, then rested for a couple of games. On Sunday, September 8, the Royals played their 37th doubleheader of the season, accounting for not quite half of a full season's 154 games.

The Royals attained their regular-season objective of 100 victories in the second game against the Maple Leafs. Robinson went 1-for-5 in the first game and 1-for 3 in the second game to clinch the batting title at .349, scoring a league-leading 113 runs (tied with Soup Campbell of Baltimore) with 40 stolen bases. He struck out only 27 times. He finished runner-up to Rackley in stolen bases.

Newark traveled to Delorimier Stadium for the playoff semifinal series, which commenced on Wednesday, September 11. Steve Nagy, Montreal's ace with a season record of 17-4, started for the Royals and took a shutout into the ninth inning before fading as the Royals won 7-5. Robinson was the hitting star for the home team, going 3-for-4 with a double, a run, and three RBIs.

The next day the Royals needed a suicide squeeze bunt in the bottom of the ninth by Al Campanis to edge the Bears, 2-1. Robinson went 0-for-3 as Royals' Glen Moulder and Duane Pillette of the Bears each allowed only five hits.

The series moved to Newark on Saturday and Sunday the 14th and 15th, and the Bears roared back with great pitching performances to twice edge the Royals. Robinson managed only a double in the latter game, knocking in Montreal's sole run.

Branch Rickey was in the stands in Newark on Monday the 16th as Moulder again excelled in a 2-1

Royals win. Robinson drove in the winning run and went 1-for-4 as Montreal took a lead of three games to two in the series.

On Wednesday, September 18, back again in Delorimier Stadium, with the Bears leading 4-3 in the bottom of the ninth inning, Newark manager George Selkirk vehemently objected to a noncalled third strike on Royals first baseman Les Burge and was ejected along with three of his players. Given another life, Burge belted a full-count pitch for a homer to tie the game. Speedy outfielder Tom Tatum then singled, and catcher Herman Franks swatted a long double off the scoreboard as Tatum scurried around the bases and scored on a close play at home, just evading the tag by Berra. The walk-off win gave Montreal the series.

La Presse called the finale a "frenetic end of the game" and a reporter quoted a streetcar rider afterward as saying "A game like this one only happens every 25 years."

After his 2-for-4 day with two runs scored, Robinson said, "George Selkirk came over and shook my hand and those of the other players and demonstrated complete class as a gentleman despite the tough loss and elimination of his team."[68] Robinson hit .273 in the series.

Starting the next day, September 19, Montreal faced Syracuse in the Governor's Cup series, for the International League championship.

The Royals came out flat at home and lost the first game, 5-0. The next day, they roared back to win 14-12 with the winning runs scoring on an inside-the-park three-run homer by reliever Chet Kehn in the eighth inning. Old-timer Curt Davis came on in the ninth for the save as Robinson contributed with a 2-for-4 day, a double, and two runs scored.

After a travel day on Saturday, at Syracuse on Sunday, September 22, the Royals dominated the Chiefs 11-1, behind a great pitching performance by Davis. Robinson went 1-for-5 in the win.

After two rainouts in Syracuse, the Royals triumphed 7-4 on September 25. Robinson went 1-for-3 with a run scored. The next day the Royals closed out the series at MacArthur Stadium four games to one with another 7-4 victory. Robinson was instrumental in the clinching win, with four hits in five at-bats, a run scored, two RBIs, and a stolen base. After the first-game shutout, he went 8-for-17 to help the Royals clinch their second Governor's Cup final, with Robinson hitting .400 for the series.

Montreal then traveled south to Louisville, Kentucky, to face the American Association champion Colonels in the Junior World Series. Robinson had managed to withstand abuse throughout the season, but Louisville promised to raise the attacks to a higher level. Louisville outfielder John Welaj said of the Colonels fans: "They called him everything under the sun."[69] *La Presse* noted that while the Royals stayed at the Brown Hotel, Robinson had to stay in the home of a Black lawyer.

Louisville fans booed Robinson at every possible occasion, at bat or in the field. Colonels pitcher Otey Clark recalled, "I remember our pitcher Jim Wilson knocked him down, and the fans cheered. Robinson didn't seem to pay attention to any of it."[70]

Jackie struggled at bat with an 0-for-5 day in the first game on Saturday, September 28, the only time he was held hitless in five at-bats all season. The Royals struggled to a 7-5 win in the first game. The Colonels responded with a great two-hit shutout by right-hander Harry Dorish. Jackie went 0-for-2 with an error.

On Monday, September 30, the Colonels exploded for 19 hits in a 15-6 home-team win as Nagy was wild, and the relievers weren't able to stem Louisville's attack. Motorcycle policemen escorted the visitors in their taxis to the train station for the long train ride home to Montreal, with the Royals now down two games to one in the series.

Speaking of the treatment of Robinson by the local fans, Louisville outfielder George Bennington told a *La Presse* reporter on the trip to Montreal: "If I was in his place, I would have thrown my glove into the field and walked away from both the game and baseball. Robinson is truly extraordinary!"[71] Campanis added, "Robinson hasn't played well down here, but just wait until you see him in Montreal where the fans are his friends."[72]

Only 14,685 fans showed up at Delorimier Stadium on a freezing and damp Wednesday night, as the Royals evened the series at two games. *La Presse* described the situation: "As much as Jackie Robinson was booed by Louisville fans during the previous three games, he was cheered last night as he hit a Texas-leaguer to drive in the winning run in the 10th inning."[73]

In his autobiography *My Own Story,* Robinson described the home fans' response: "We discovered the Canadians were up in arms over the way I had been treated. Greeting us warmly, the let us know how they felt. ... All through that first game at home they booed every time a Louisville player came out of the dugout. I didn't approve of this kind of retaliation, but I felt a jubilant sense of gratitude for the way Canadians expressed their feelings."[74]

Montreal was trailing 5-3 going into the bottom of the ninth inning, but the Royals loaded the bases and then tied the game to set the stage for Robinson in the 10th. He went 2-for-5, with a run scored and the game-winning RBI in the victory. Louisville had intentionally walked Marv Rackley, preferring to face Robinson with the winning run on third base.

The Royals were again led by Jackie on October 3, as he doubled and scored in the first inning, tripled and scored the eventual winning run in the seventh, and bunted for a single to score Campanis with an insurance run in the eighth in a 5-3 Royals victory before 17,758 fans.

On Friday, October 4, the Royals sent wily veteran Curt Davis to the mound in search of the championship. The 43-year-old Davis was masterful as he scattered nine hits in a tight 2-0 shutout. In the ninth inning he induced a double play started by Robinson, his second of the day, to preserve the shutout. Robinson also singled twice, the only player in the game with more than one hit.

After the final out, the Royals raced to the clubhouse as thousands of fans covered the field. Stadium staff and police could do nothing against the crowd of over 19,000 fans. *Courier* and *Herald* reporter Sam Maltin, who was also a great friend, described it thus: "Ushers and police couldn't keep the crowd from the field. They refused to move and sang 'Il a gagne ses epaulettes' (He won his bars) and 'We want Robinson.' … Clay Hopper came out of the clubhouse and they … carried him around the field. … Curt Davis, who hurled the final victory, made his appearance and they carted him around. But there was no Robinson and they refused to move until he showed himself.

> A delegation of ushers went to see Jackie and asked him to step out, so they could close the park and call it a season. Jackie came out and the crowd surged on him. Men and women of all ages threw their arms around him, kissed him, and tore at his clothes, and then carried him around the infield on their shoulders, shouting themselves hoarse.
>
> Jackie, tears streaming down his face, tried to beg off further honors.[75]

In *My Own Story*, Robinson wrote, "When I at last got ready to leave the dressing room, the passageway was blocked with at least three hundred people. I couldn't get out, and the ushers and police couldn't break through and come to my rescue. Finally, I had to take a chance. I passed my bag to a friend, hunched my shoulders, and plunged smack into that throng."[76]

Maltin carried on the story: "It was a demonstration seldom seen here. Again, the crowd started hugging and kissing him. He tried to explain that he had to catch a plane, but they wouldn't listen, refused to hear him. They held on to him but – as he had done in his football days at UCLA – Robbie gently fought off his admirers and pushed his way through until he found an opening. Then he started running. The mob was running after him. Down the street he went, chased by five hundred fans. People opened windows and came pouring out of their houses to see what the commotion was about. For three blocks they chased him until a car drew up and someone shouted: 'Jump in, Jackie,' and they brought him safely to his hotel. It was probably the only day in history that a black man ran from a white mob with love instead of lynching on its mind."[77]

At the airport the next morning, Robinson boarded a flight for Detroit to join a barnstorming tour and on the newsstand was the *Le Canada* newspaper with the headline "Royals Are Champions of the World" with a team photo, and individual photos of winning pitcher, and the fans' favorite, Jackie Robinson.[78]

Robinson confided to reporter Wendell Smith, "As my plane roared skyward and the lights of Montreal twinkled and winkled in the distance, I took one last look at this great city where I had found so much happiness. I don't care if I never get to the majors," I told myself. "This is the city for me. This is paradise."[79]

Rachel Robinson said, "In Jack's book, he said he owes more to Canadians than they'll ever know. We were passionately in love and brimming with the anticipation of starting a family. I will always feel a deep sense of gratitude and appreciation for the attitudes of the people in Montreal. It had a lot to do with our future success."[80]

SOURCES

In addition to the sources cited in the Notes, the author consulted the following:

Tygiel, Jules. *Baseball's Great Experiment* (New York: Oxford, 1983).

Heaphy, Leslie. *The Negro Leagues* (Jefferson North Carolina: McFarland & Co., 2003).

Simon, Scott. *Jackie Robinson and the Integration of Baseball* (Hoboken New Jersey: Wiley & Sons, 2002).

Lowenfish, Lee. *Branch Rickey: Baseball's Ferocious Gentleman* (Lincoln: University of Nebraska Press, 2007).

Eig, Jonathan. *Opening Day* (New York: Simon & Schuster, 2007).

PERSPECTIVES ON 42

NOTES

1. Harold Adkins, *Montreal Star*, October 24, 1945.
2. Dink Carroll, *Montreal Gazette*, October 24, 1945.
3. *La Presse*, October 24, 1945.
4. Al Parsley, *Montreal Herald*, October 24, 1945.
5. *La Presse*, October 24, 1945.
6. *Montreal Star*, October 24, 1945.
7. John Thorn and Jules Tygiel, *Jackie Robinson Reader, Jackie Robinson's Signing* (New York: Dutton, 1997), 90-92.
8. *La Presse*, October 24, 1945.
9. Marcel Dugas, *Jackie Robinson, Un Été à Montréal* (Montreal: Hurtubise, 2019), 48.
10. *Daytona Beach Evening News*, October 24, 1945.
11. "Bob Feller's opinion," in William Brown, *Baseball's Fabulous Montreal Royals* (Montreal: Robert Davies, 1996), 95.
12. "A 1,000-to-1 chance," *New York Daily News*, October 24, 1945.
13. "A tryout in B level," *The Sporting News*, November 1, 1945.
14. *La Presse*, October 24, 1945.
15. *Montreal Gazette*, October 24, 1945.
16. Jackie Robinson and Alfred Duckett, *I Never Had It Made* (New York: Putnam, 1972), 35.
17. Paul Parizeau, *Le Canada*, October 24, 1945.
18. Baz O'Meara, *Montreal Star*, December 10, 1945.
19. Carl T. Rowan and Jackie Robinson, *Wait Till Next Year* (New York: Random House 1960), 145.
20. Rachel Robinson, *Jackie Robinson: An Intimate Portrait* (New York: Harry Abrams Inc., 1996), 37.
21. Rachel Robinson, 46.
22. Rachel Robinson, 52.
23. *La Presse*, March 7, 1946.
24. Lee Lowenfish, *The Imperfect Diamond: A History of Baseball's Labor Wars* (New York: Da Capo Press, 1991), 147-152.
25. *New York World Telegram and Sun*, February 2, 1957.
26. *I Never Had It Made*, 50–51.
27. *Montreal Gazette*, April 20, 1946.
28. *Montreal Star*, April 19, 1946.
29. *Montreal Matin*, April 20, 1946.
30. Robert Peterson, *Only the Ball Was White* (Oxford: Oxford University Press, 1992), 196.
31. Wendell Smith, *Pittsburgh Courier*, April 13, 1946.
32. Clyde Sukeforth, *Montreal Gazette*, March 6, 1946.
33. *La Presse*, April 20, 1946.
34. *La Patrie*, April 20, 1946.
35. *Pittsburgh Courier*, April 19, 1946.
36. *Wait Till Next Year*, 60.
37. *Wait Till Next Year*, 155-56.
38. *Wait Till Next Year*, 156.
39. *Montreal Star*, May 2, 1946.
40. Sam Lacy, *Baltimore African-American*, May 11, 1946.
41. Charles Mayer, *Le Petit Journal*, May 2, 1946.
42. Phil Seguin, *La Patrie*, May 2, 1946.
43. Baz O'Meara, *Montreal Star*, May 16, 1946.
44. *Baltimore African-American*, May 11, 1946.
45. Al Parsley, *Montreal Herald*, June 25, 1946.
46. Bruno Betzel, *The Sporting News*, September 11, 1946.
47. Sam Maltin, *Montreal Herald; Jackie Robinson Reader*, 117.
48. Marcel Sabourin, *Un Été à Montréal*, 110
49. Paul Parizeau, *Le Canada*, July 9, 1946.
50. Wendell Smith, *Pittsburgh Courier*, July 20, 1946.
51. *La Presse*, July 22, 1946.
52. *La Presse*, July 23, 1946.
53. *The Sporting News*, October 16, 1946.
54. *La Presse*, August 9, 1946.
55. *La Presse*, August 5, 1946.
56. *La Presse*, August 6, 1946.
57. *La Presse*, August 8, 1946.
58. Dink Carroll, *Montreal Gazette*, August 8, 1946.
59. Alphonse Thomas, *La Presse*, August 15, 1946.
60. Lloyd McGowan, *Montreal Star*, August 22, 1946.
61. *La Presse*, August 22, 1946.
62. *The Sporting News*, August 28, 1946.
63. *Newsweek*, August 26, 1946.
64. Lloyd McGowan and Mel Jones, *Montreal Star*, August 29, 1946.
65. *The Sporting News*, September 4, 1946.
66. *La Presse*, September 4, 1946.
67. Clay Hopper, *La Presse*, September 4, 1946.
68. *La Presse*, September 19, 1946.
69. *Montreal Gazette*, October 7, 1946.
70. Roger Kahn, *Rickey & Robinson* (New York: Rodale Inc., 2014), 218.
71. *La Presse*, October 3, 1946.
72. Al Campanis, *Montreal Star*, October 5, 1946.
73. *La Presse*, October 3, 1946.
74. Jackie Robinson and Wendell Smith, *My Own Story* (New York: Greenberg, 1948), 110.
75. Sam Maltin, *Pittsburgh Courier*, October 12, 1946.
76. *My Own Story*, 109.
77. Sam Maltin, *Pittsburgh Courier*, October 12, 1946.
78. *Le Canada*, October 5, 1946.
79. *My Own Story*, 110
80. Rachel Robinson to Patrick Sauer in Sauer, "The Year of Jackie Robinson's Mutual Love Affair with Montreal," *Smithsonian*, April 6, 2015. smithsonianmag.com/history/year-jackie.

JACKIE ROBINSON - HISTORY MADE IN 1946 AT THE JUNIOR WORLD SERIES

by Marc J. Steiner

Jackie Robinson's time in Montreal was fleeting, but he still made an impact on baseball and the world in 1946. Before the 27-year-old Robinson began to wear the famous Brooklyn Dodger blue with number 42 on his back, he wore uniform number 9 and led the International League in batting with a .349 average (a Royals record) and a league-best 113 runs scored (tied with Soup Campbell of Baltimore.) He stole 40 stolen bases and drove home 66 runs.

When the opening pitch was thrown at the 1946 Junior World Series, it was the first time a Black man had appeared on the field in such a significant game below the Mason-Dixon line. After a season in which the Montreal Royals finished with a spectacular 100-54 win-loss record, 18½ games ahead of their International League competition, they were set to meet the Louisville Colonels, who finished at 92-61 and bested their competition in the American Association. The 1946 Junior World Series was the first time in nine years that the two teams with the best regular-season records were facing off in the best-of-seven series.

GAME ONE

SEPTEMBER 28, 1946:
MONTREAL ROYALS 7,
LOUISVILLE COLONELS 5,
AT PARKWAY FIELD, LOUISVILLE, KENTUCKY

Robinson started off the series sluggishly, producing an 0-for-5 at the plate in front of an animated crowd of Southerners not accustomed to seeing a Black man on a professional baseball diamond. It was the first time all season that Robinson had gone 0-for-5.

Louisville did not exactly roll out the welcome mat for Robinson. He was not allowed to stay in the team hotel and Colonels ownership placed quotas on how many African American fans would be allowed into the ballpark for each series game. Everything he did,

"They booed him," said Colonels pitcher Otey Clark. "I remember our pitcher Jim Wilson knocked him down, and the fans cheered. Robinson didn't seem to pay attention to any of it."[1]

Despite Robinson's struggles at the plate, Game One was a success for the Royals, a 7-5 victory in front of the crowd of 13,716 at Parkway Field in Louisville.

Many years later, Louisville infielder Al Brancato recalled, "It was a very exciting time, because of all the controversy surrounding Jackie being the first Black player. He didn't even have a place to stay. There were no hotels that would take him, so they didn't even know whether or not they were even going to play."[2]

Jim Wilson got the start the on the mound for the Colonels but after yielding 11 hits and all seven Royals runs over his 7⅔ innings, he was not around to finish the affair. Tom Tatum clubbed two doubles and a triple for the Royals, while first baseman Les Burge blasted Wilson for two home runs. The Royals took a 7-2 lead into the final inning, but a walk and two triples quickly produced two runs for Louisville. Manager Clay Hopper had the bullpen close the door and ensure the Royals their victory.

GAME TWO

SEPTEMBER 29, 1946:
LOUISVILLE COLONELS 3,
MONTREAL ROYALS 0,
AT PARKWAY FIELD, LOUISVILLE, KENTUCKY

Robinson's mental strain was seemingly still in place, with the Royals dropping the game 3-0. Robinson went 0-for-2 at the plate, with an uncharacteristic error at second base.

Right-hander Curt Davis started on the hill for the Royals, and the Colonels wasted no time getting on the board with two runs in the first frame. The Royals made concerted efforts in the fourth and the sixth innings to get something going but were stifled on both attempts by Fritz Dorish, who dominated all day with a steady diet of sinkers and curves. The 6-foot-4-inch right-hander held Montreal to just two hits, both by Montreal right fielder Marv Rackley.[3] Dorish starred at the plate as well, adding two hits and a run batted in to help the cause.

The visiting Royals were able to muster only six baserunners, including a walk to Robinson, and found themselves in an intensely competitive series tied one game apiece.

GAME THREE

SEPTEMBER 30, 1946:
LOUISVILLE COLONELS 15,
MONTREAL ROYALS 6,
AT PARKWAY FIELD, LOUISVILLE, KENTUCKY

With Branch Rickey in attendance in Louisville, Robinson fared better at the plate and put up a solid 1-for-3 performance with two runs scored, but the Royals were ultimately thumped by Louisville, 15-6. The Royals took the lead in the first inning after Rackley tripled down the right-field line and Robinson drew a walk. Tom Tatum chimed in with the first of his three hits, driving in Rackley and moving Robinson to second base. Louisville third baseman Al Brancato fumbled Les Burge's sacrifice bunt to load the bases. The next Montreal hitter, catcher Herman Franks, flipped a single to right field, scoring Robinson.

In the bottom of the inning, the Colonels put three runs across the plate. Center fielder George Bennington started things off with an infield hit. Pitcher Steve Nagy then threw wildly to first base on left fielder John Welaj's dribbler toward third, permitting Bennington to score and allowing Welaj to amble down to second base. Right fielder Jim Gleason then singled to drive in Welaj; Nagy walked the next two hitters, forcing the third run of the inning home.

In the third inning a wild Nagy was driven from the game. After allowing a double to second baseman Chuck Koney, Nagy gave up two more walks and the bases were loaded. George Bennington's single to left drove in Koney. Frank Laga was summoned from the bullpen to relieve Nagy and served up a single to pinch-hitter Strick Shofner, driving in two more runs for the Colonels. The Royals were now heading home to Canada down two games to one in the series.

Robinson later noted that the trip to Louisville was one of the worst road trips during his time in baseball due to the hostile Louisville crowds in the Jim Crow South.

GAME FOUR

OCTOBER 2, 1946:
MONTREAL ROYALS 6,
LOUISVILLE COLONELS 5 (10 INNINGS),
AT DELORIMIER STADIUM, MONTREAL

Returning to Montreal, the Royals were greeted by a joyful crowd of 14,685 at Delorimier Stadium.

Robinson recalled, "We discovered that the Canadians were up in arms over the way I had been treated. Greeting us warmly, they let us know how they felt. All through that first game (at home) they booed every time a Louisville player came out of the dugout."[4]

It had snowed the night before, and the temperature was hovering around 8 degrees with some spotty snow still on the ground when the first pitch was thrown. The Royals had to battle all game to draw themselves even in the series. Glen Moulder got the call to toe the rubber for the Royals and surrendered eight hits over five innings before being lifted for Frank Laga in the sixth inning.

The Colonels started to build their lead in the first frame, scoring two runs, and added another in the third. The Royals broke through in the fifth inning when Al Campanis started off with a ringing double off the right-field fence, moved to third on a groundout by Moulder, and scored when second baseman Chuck Koney threw out Rackley at first base.

Frank Laga was summoned to the mound in the top of the sixth when Moulder walked the first three batters. Laga and the Royals were able to escape the inning unharmed. In the Royals half of the sixth, Dixie Howell homered and cut the Colonels' lead to two runs.

As the game moved into the later innings, Louisville scored again in the top of the eighth. The Royals were able to match them in the bottom half to keep the game within two runs.

In the bottom of the ninth the Royals rallied to tie the game with the help of some Louisville defensive blunders. Pinch-hitter Franks started things off with a walk. With two outs, Otey Clark walked Robinson and Tom Tatum to load the bases for lefty Les Burge. Louisville manager Nemo Leibold countered with lefty Joe Ostrowski. Ostrowski walked Burge, forcing in a run and putting the Royals within a single tally of tying the game. Colonels catcher Fred Walters then noticed that baserunner Tom Tatum was straying too far from second and threw down to try to nab him. His throw went wild and, on a heads-up play, the speedy Robinson scampered home to tie the game.

Hopper called on pitcher Chet Kehn to start the 10th inning and he made quick work of the Colonels. In the bottom of the inning, the Royals' blessings continued. Howell reached on an error by Ostrowski and moved to second on the next play when Ostrowski, fielding a bunt by center fielder Earl Naylor, tried to cut down the lead runner at second with no reward. Mel Deutsch was quickly called upon to stop the bleeding. Campanis sacrificed the runners to second and third. The Royals then tried to squeeze Howell home for the win. Kehn's attempt fell short when Colonels catcher Walters blocked the plate while applying the tag for the out. Rackley was then intentionally walked to set up a force-play situation. The strategy set up Jackie Robinson to be the hero. Robinson wasted no time, shooting a line drive over the shortstop's head to drive in Naylor and seal the 6-5 victory for the Royals. Robinson's single made him 2-for-5 with the game-winning RBI.

GAME FIVE

OCTOBER 3, 1946:
MONTREAL ROYALS 5,
LOUISVILLE COLONELS 3,
AT DELORIMIER STADIUM, MONTREAL

Hopper was awarded a victory and a contract extension for his 45th birthday. Montreal scored a single run in each of the first three innings. The Colonels got to Nagy for one run in the fifth inning and added two in the seventh to tie the score.

Kehn was called upon again in the eighth after Nagy walked the leadoff batter. In the bottom of the seventh, the Royals had charged ahead when Robinson slashed a triple into the left-center-field gap to start the noise. Tatum and Burge popped out and the Colonels seemed to be out of the woods. But Lew Riggs had other things in mind: He lined a double deep down the right-field line, scoring Robinson and vaulting the Royals back into the lead.

In the bottom of the eighth, the Royals added an insurance run on a bunt by Robinson that scored Campanis from third. Robinson easily beat the throw to first for an infield hit.

Robinson's woes at the plate seemed to be behind him for good. He collected three hits, scored twice, and drove home a run.

GAME SIX

OCTOBER 4, 1946:
MONTREAL ROYALS 2,
LOUISVILLE COLONELS 0,
AT DELORIMIER STADIUM, MONTREAL

The home crowd of 19,171 was ready to crown Robinson and the Royals as champions. All the scoring came in the second inning. After 10 previous innings pitched in the series, the Royals were finally able to score some runs off right-hander Fritz Dorish. He walked Riggs to lead off the second. Catcher Howell drove a ball down the left-field line, scoring Riggs with what would be the series-winning run. Montreal added an insurance run on Campanis's single that sent Riggs home.

Robinson ended the series with a .333 batting average, even after managing only a 1-for-11 line in the first three games in Louisville. After the series-clinching victory, Hopper – a Mississippi native who did not welcome Robinson to the Royals – made his way over to the second baseman, shook his hand and said, "You're a real ballplayer and a gentleman. It's been wonderful having you on the team."[5]

The faithful Royals fans refused to leave the ballpark for a full 30 minutes. They screamed for Hopper and refused to leave until Robinson appeared from the clubhouse. Robinson emerged in street clothes, and the mob of fans gathered around him, cheerfully trying to catch a glimpse or possibly even touch their hero. Tears flowed from Robinson's eyes when the masses lifted him up onto their shoulders chanting and singing, "*Il a gagne ses epaulettes*" ("He won his bars").[6]

Robinson commented on the occasion, "When I at last got ready to leave the dressing room, the passageway was blocked with at least three hundred people. Every time I opened the door, they'd start yelling and pushing. I couldn't get out, and the ushers and police couldn't break through and come to my rescue. Finally, I had to take a chance. I passed my bag to a friend, hunched my shoulders, and plunged smack into that throng."[7]

Minutes later, Robinson got away from the crowd and sprinted to catch a waiting airplane. Sam Maltin, a reporter from the *Pittsburgh Courier*, famously wrote that it was "probably the only day in history that a black man ran from a white mob with love instead of lynching on the mind."[8]

NOTES

1. Benjamin Hill, "Robinson Led Royals to Triple-A Title," MILB.com, September 19, 2006. Robinson led Royals to Triple-A title (milb.com).

2. Hill.

3. The *Montreal Gazette* identified the pitcher as Mel Deutsch, not Dorish, but Deutsch had just pitched in relief in the previous game and all other sources name Dorish as the Game Two pitcher.

4. Jackie Robinson with Alfred Duckett, *I Never Had It Made: An Autobiography of Jackie Robinson* (New York: Putnam, 1972), 51.

5. William C. Kashatus, *Jackie and Campy: The Untold Story of Their Rocky Relationship and the Breaking of Baseball's Color Line* (Lincoln: University of Nebraska Press, 2014), 85.

6. Jackie Robinson and Wendell Smith, *My Own Story* (New York: Greenberg Corporation, 1948), 108-109.

7. Robinson and Smith, 108-109.

8. Tabitha Marshall, "Jackie Robinson and the Montreal Royals (1946)," *The Canadian Encyclopedia*, April 7, 2017. thecanadianencyclopedia.ca/en/article/jackie-robinson-and-the-montreal-royals.

THE JACKIE ROBINSON BARNSTORMING TOUR OF 1946

by Alan Cohen

"Do you feel they'll make the big-league grade?" This question (referring to Black ballplayers) was posed to Bob Feller in October 1946. As reported in *The Sporting News* on October 30, 1946, Feller said without hesitation, "I have seen none who combine the qualities of a big-league ballplayer – Not even Jackie Robinson."[1]

Induction Day at Cooperstown in 1962 saw two new inductees voted in by the Baseball Writers Association of America. Jackie Robinson and Feller had each finished their playing careers in 1956 and their paths first crossed after the 1946 season.

In the autumn of 1946, after leading the Montreal Royals of the International League to a win in the Junior World Series, which concluded on October 4, Robinson was showcased in a barnstorming tour, which started with six games in the Midwest and concluded with several games in California. The tour was coordinated by Mickey McConnell, the Brooklyn Dodgers' director of promotions. The Dodgers organization was eager to let America meet the first Black player to enter Organized Baseball in the twentieth century. The "Robinson All-Stars" included several players from the Dodgers organization as well as players from the Negro Leagues.

That same autumn, Feller also put together a tour that was deemed to be the best organized and financed and most successful tour of its kind. Indeed, Feller's take from the barnstorming trip eclipsed his annual salary with the Indians. After facing Satchel Paige's Negro League All-Stars in the early part of his tour and Robinson's team in four games in California, Feller made the prediction that was, within a very short time, negated by Robinson and other great Black ballplayers, including several members of his 1946 barnstorming squad.

Robinson's tour was slated to begin at the Polo Grounds on October 1, but when the Royals played into October, there were cancellations and schedule changes. Plagued by poor promotion, a lack of big-name players, the late start, and poor weather, the Robinson tour did not enjoy great success. Several barnstorming tours crisscrossed the United States in the autumn of 1946. Tours led by Feller and Satchel Paige garnered the most media coverage and had the most success.

A revised schedule had Robinson's tour beginning in Detroit on October 5, and Jackie flew to Detroit after the Junior World Series ended. There is no evidence that the game scheduled for Detroit ever took place.

On October 6, two days after the Royals won the JWS, the Robinson All-Stars opened their tour at Crosley Field in Cincinnati, losing to the "Major League All-Stars," managed by Honus Wagner, 10-4. Robinson's team, which included three White ballplayers, was one of the first integrated professional squads ever to take the field at a big-league park. Bob Malloy of Cincinnati and Stan Ferens of the St. Louis Browns pitched for the winning team. A full accounting of the game is not available.

The next day, the tour stopped at Youngstown, Ohio. The Robinson team lost 6-5 to the Major League All-Stars. Robinson went 4-for-5 with a homer. Marv Rackley also homered for the Robinson All-Stars. Rackley, one of the White players on the team and a teammate of Robinson's at Montreal (the two combined for 105 stolen bases), had signed with Brooklyn prior to the 1941 season. After spending two seasons in the low minors, Rackley entered the US Army Air Force for the duration of World War II. In 1946 with Montreal, the speedster led the International League with triples (14) and stolen bases (65). He played in parts of four major-league seasons, appeared in 185 games, and batted .317.

Wagner's team included Hank Sauer. Sauer was, at the time, relatively unknown. He had played in only 47 major-league games over a three-year span. Fans of the International League were aware of him. He had hit 21 homers with 90 RBIs in 1946. The following year, in his eighth minor-league season, his 50 homers for Syracuse punched his ticket to the big leagues. In 15 major-league seasons, he hit 288 homers. In 1952 he was selected the National League MVP after hitting 37 homers with 121 RBIs for the Cubs.

Sauer's two run homer put Wagner's team ahead 2-0 in the second inning, and Eddie Miller extended the lead to 5-0 with a three-run blast in the fifth inning. With two out in the seventh inning, Robinson's squad rallied to tie the game on the back-to-back homers by Robinson and Rackley. Wagner's squad pushed across the winning run in the bottom of the ninth on a single by Pittsburgh's Lee Handley.[2]

On October 8 the caravan arrived at Pittsburgh's Forbes Field for a 4 P.M. contest. A glimpse of a scorecard from the game shows the players on the teams, along with some changes.[3] Some of Robinson's teammates in the 6-4 win are well known to this day. Others, however, have seen time pass them by.

Robinson played shortstop, because the team's regular shortstop, Al Campanis, was injured. Robinson had three hits, scored two runs, and stole a base. The White players who played for the Robinson All-Stars at Pittsburgh were outfielder Rackley and relief pitcher Richard Mlady.

The starting pitcher for the Robinson squad, Willie Pope, had spent the season with the Pittsburgh Crawfords. He played in Organized Baseball from 1950 through 1955, but never advanced beyond Triple A.

Pope was relieved during a four-run fifth-inning rally by Mlady, who had been in the Dodgers organization since 1940. Mlady never made it to the majors, posting a 40-44 record in six minor-league seasons. In 1946 he had been with Nashua of the Class-B New England League, teaming with two players who were on the Robinson All-Stars and would go on to great success with Brooklyn.

The first of the Nashua players was catcher Roy Campanella. The Dodgers signed him in 1946 and he spent the season at Nashua, batting .290 in 113 games. He arrived in Brooklyn in 1948. The other Nashua player was pitcher Don Newcombe, who was on the caravan but did not pitch at Forbes Field.

At first base for Robinson's squad was Lennie Pearson of the Negro League champion Newark Eagles. He was 28 years old, but by the time he was noticed by Organized Baseball in 1950, he was already 32. Pearson was signed by the Braves and played at Milwaukee in the Triple-A American Association in 1950, batting .305. The following season, the Braves promoted George Crowe. Pearson was sent down to the Hartford Chiefs of the Class-A Eastern League. He batted .272 in his last season in the Braves organization.

Robinson's second baseman was Larry Doby, who also had spent 1946 with the Eagles, for whom he had begun his professional career in 1942. During the 1947 season, the Cleveland Indians acquired him from Newark, and Doby went on to a Hall of Fame career. He was the first Black player signed by a team other than the Brooklyn Dodgers.

Robinson's third baseman was Herb Souell of the Kansas City Monarchs. He was 33 years old. By the time Organized Baseball signed him, he was 39 years old. He played only one minor-league season, 1952.

Robinson's outfielders included Rackley, Monte Irvin, and John Scott. Irvin was destined to be a star in the majors as he had been in the Negro Leagues. In 1946 he had played with the Newark Eagles, and remained with them through 1948. In 1949, at age 30, he was acquired by the New York Giants and was with them for seven seasons. In 1951 he led the National League in RBIs with 121 and finished third in MVP balloting. He was inducted into the Hall of Fame in 1973. Scott, a member of the Monarchs and a 1945 teammate of Robinson's, never played in Organized Baseball, finishing up his Negro League career at Kansas City in 1948.

Most of the members of the "major-league all-stars" had done little to distinguish themselves. Only a couple are remembered to this day. Al Gionfriddo started in center field. He is remembered for his catch of a long fly ball by Joe DiMaggio in the 1947 World Series. Sauer was stationed in left field, and Eddie Lukon of Cincinnati started the game in right. Batting second for the majors was Frankie Gustine, who spent the first 10 of his 12 major-league seasons with Pittsburgh. Lukon batted third, and the cleanup batter was Sauer.

Batting fifth was shortstop Pete Suder, who spent his entire 13-year major-league career with the Athletics, first in Philadelphia, then in Kansas City. In 1946 he had batted .281 in 128 games. Next up was first baseman Eddie Miller, who had homered at Youngstown. Miller was a shortstop for the Cincinnati Reds. Lee Handley, who had driven in the winning run at Youngstown, was at third base. He spent eight of his 10 major-league seasons with Pittsburgh and after his playing days stayed active, along with Gustine, in youth baseball in the Pittsburgh area.

The catcher was George Susce, who had been a backup retriever for eight seasons, playing his last major-league game in 1944. In 1946 he had been a coach with the Indians. The pitcher on October 8 was Joe Beggs, who was tagged with the loss, going the route and allowing 10 hits. Beggs, who pitched in the majors for nine seasons, was coming off a 12-10 season with Cincinnati.

Robinson's team drew first blood, scoring three runs on four hits in the third inning. With one out, Scott and Pope singled. A double by Rackley brought Scott home. Robinson singled Pope home and Rackley scored on an infield error.

Pope, who had allowed only a second-inning single to Suder and a fourth-inning double to Lukon, was victimized by a wild streak in the fifth when Wagner's team scored four runs on only two hits. Handley walked to lead off the inning and Susce singled. Beggs struck out and Gionfriddo was hit by a pitch, loading the bases. He left the game for a pinch-runner. Gustine walked, forcing in Handley, and Lukon singled in a pair of runs. After Sauer walked to load the bases again, Suder hit into a force play that scored Gustine with his team's final run.

Robinson's team tied the game in the sixth. Doby led off with a triple and came home on a two-out single by Pearson. Robinson ignited a game-winning two-run rally in the eighth inning. He doubled and, after Irvin was walked, Pearson's triple cleared the bases. After Souell was hit by a pitch, Pearson was picked off third base, ending the inning. Mlady limited Wagner's team to two hits over the last two innings to get credit for the win.

On October 11 Cleveland welcomed the barnstormers, but the game was rained out and rescheduled for Monday, October 14. The rain continued and the next day's game at Dayton was canceled.

On October 13 the Robinson entourage was at Chicago's Comiskey Park and defeated the Wagner All-Stars 10-5. By this time, Robinson had added another White player to his troupe. Mike Nozinski, who had played for Nashua with Campanella and Newcombe, augmented the pitching staff. Nozinski played 10 games at the Double-A level in 1947, but that was as high as he got.

The starting pitcher for Robinson's squad was one-time Montreal teammate Johnny Wright, who had originally pitched in the Negro Leagues with Newark in 1937 and had been with the Homestead Grays at the time he was signed by the Dodgers. Wright pitched the first five innings and left the game with a big lead.

Jackie's team went out in front in the first inning. With two out, Robinson walked and scored from first on a double by Irvin. Wright singled in the third inning, moved to second on an error, and scored on a single by Robinson. A double by Campanella ignited a two-run rally in the fourth inning that drove starting pitcher Stan Ferens from the mound. A three-run sixth for the Robinson team was topped off when Jackie executed a perfect suicide squeeze play, bunting Rackley home from third. Jackie's team took a 7-1 lead into the bottom of the sixth.

Wagner's team narrowed the gap to 7-4 with three runs in the bottom half of the inning. Ross "Satchel" Davis replaced Wright on the mound. The once and future Cleveland Buckeyes hurler walked two batters and was replaced by Nozinski, who, after filling the bases and allowing the three runners to score, calmed down and finished the game for the winners.

Robinson's squad extended its lead in the late innings. In the eighth, off reliever Bob Malloy, Robinson tripled down the right-field line, scoring Johnny Scott. Jackie scored on a fly ball by Doby. In the ninth, Dave Pope tripled home Joe Atkins but was thwarted in his attempt for an inside-the-park homer when Gionfriddo's throw was relayed by Handley and Susce applied the tag. Wagner's team scored a run in the last inning, as an errant throw to first by Nozinski allowed a runner to score from third.[4]

The teams played at Cleveland Stadium the next day and Robinson's team won 8-0. The hitting star was Irvin with a single, a double, and a triple. Jackie's team broke the game open with a five-run second inning. Atkins, who had spent the 1946 season with the Pittsburgh Crawfords, belted a sixth-inning inside-the-park-homer. At age 32 in 1954, he got to play Triple-A ball with Ottawa in the International League, but he never made it to the majors. The pitching chores were handled by Mlady, who went the first five innings, and Negro League veteran Alonzo Boone, who finished up. Between them, they allowed only two hits.[5] Boone first played professionally in 1929 for Memphis in the Negro National League. In 1946 he was with the Cleveland Buckeyes. He returned to the Buckeyes for his final competitive season in 1947.

On Tuesday, October 15, in Council Bluffs, Iowa, Robinson's team faced the Omaha Firemen at Legion Park. There was a chill in the air and attendance was only 469. In the top of the eighth, Robinson's team took a 7-5 lead when Atkins tripled in two runs. However, when he tried to make it an inside-the-park-homer, he was thrown out at the plate. Omaha's Jim "Westy" Basso retrieved the ball and threw it home by way of shortstop Frank Mancuso. Basso, who hailed from Omaha, played 13 minor-league seasons, but never got higher than Triple A. Mancuso, who also stole home in the game, played for the St. Louis Browns from 1944 through 1946 and finished up his career with Washington the following season. The smallish crowd saw the Firemen win 8-7 when they scored three runs in the ninth inning.[6]

At San Francisco's Seals Stadium on October 18, 9,813 fans watched the first matchup of the Robinson All-Stars and the Bob Feller All-Stars. Before the game, there was a home-run hitting contest featuring Stan Musial, Mickey Vernon, Charlie Keller, Sam Chapman, and Jeff Heath. Feller's team won the game, 6-0. Robinson got a hit and stole a base off the Cleveland fireballer, but his infield single, which bounced over Feller, was one of only two hits given up by the pitcher in five innings. Dutch Leonard and Spud Chandler completed the pitching chores for Feller's squad. Their offense was led by Heath, who tripled and homered. Musial had a pair of hits and scored two runs.[7]

On October 20, it was on to Oakland for Robinson's squad. They took on the Sherry Liquor team, which included several big-league players, including Bill Rigney of the Giants. The teams played to an 8-8 tie in a game halted by darkness after 10 innings.

On October 23, at Bakersfield, there was a miscommunication as barnstorming teams led by both Satchel Paige and Robinson appeared to face Feller's squad with 3,500 fans looking on. After a settlement was reached, Jackie looked on as teams led by Feller and Paige played. Feller's team won.[8] The following afternoon, at El Centro, 114 miles east of San Diego, Feller's team beat the Robinson All-Stars in front of 1,800 spectators.[9]

On the evening of October 24 at San Diego's Lane Field, with 4,414 fans looking on, Feller pitched five innings, striking out 11, as his team won 4-2. In the fourth inning, Robinson walked and scored the game's first run, flying home on a short double by Souell. Feller's team quickly tied the game when Chapman singled home Ken Keltner. When Feller left the game, his team trailed 2-1, after to a go-ahead homer by the Robinson squad's Earl "Mickey" Taborn. Taborn, who had spent the 1946 season with the Monarchs, signed with the New York Yankees and was with their Triple-A Newark affiliate in 1949. It was his only year in Organized Baseball, but he continued to play and was in the Mexican League from 1951 through 1961.

Feller's squad rallied for three eighth-inning runs to win the game. Musial led off with a single and Keller's long double put runners on second and third. Keltner singled in the runners. He advanced to second on a single by Heath and came around to score his team's final run on a single by shortstop Bob Lemon. Chandler, who entered the game in the sixth inning, was the winning pitcher.[10]

The following night, Feller took the mound again and was again outstanding at Wrigley Field in Los Angeles. He pitched five perfect innings, striking out 10, as his team won, 4-3. During the seventh and eighth innings of the game, Robinson took issue with the ball-strike calls by home-plate umpire Gordon Ford. The temper displayed by Robinson was in stark contrast to the unusual restraint he showed during his first years in the Dodgers organization.

The Oakland Larks of the West Coast Association, a Negro minor league, hosted the Robinson All-Stars on October 31, the Robinson All-Stars winning 13-7. The key blow was a three-run homer by Souell. On November 3 in San Bernardino, the Larks won, 8-5. Robinson went 3-for-4 with a double.

While he was in Southern California, Robinson began practicing with the Los Angeles Red Devils, a minor-league basketball team. He was a force on the hardwood and scored 18 points in a 39-38 win over Sheboygan on November 9.[11] The team played into January, and Robinson's teammates included two future major-league baseball players – Irv Noren and George Crowe. Robinson's last game with the team was on January 3.

Robinson and Doby advanced to the majors in 1947. They were joined in subsequent years by Campanella, Newcombe, and Irvin. The Negro Leagues would diminish in size after 1948 and although Robinson led successful barnstorming trips in the early years of his major-league career, the advent of television and the westward migration of franchises would make barnstorming by big leaguers vanish. The four remaining Negro League teams played the last Negro League East-West All-Star Game on August 26, 1962. After the 1962 season, the final big-league barnstorming tour, led by Willie Mays, visited five small towns.

SOURCES

In addition to Baseball-Reference.com, the author used:

"Robinson's Stars Split in Openers," *The Sporting News*, October 16, 1946: 23.

"Robinson Stars as Team Wins," *Pittsburgh Press*, October 9, 1946: 26.

"Robinson Stars Triumph, 6-4," *Pittsburgh Sun-Telegraph*, October 9, 1946: 25.

"West Coast Baseball Fans Pay Tribute to Jackie Robinson: Durocher Roots for Jackie's Team in Tilt Against Feller's," *Pittsburgh Courier* (National Edition), November 2, 1946: 16.

Abrams, Al. "Robinson Impresses Big League Players: Cracks Out Three Hits as His Team Defeats Major League Stars, 6-4," *Pittsburgh Post-Gazette*, October 9, 1946: 15.

Adams, Caswell. "Feller Earns $175,000 to Crack Ruth's Record," *Evening World Herald* (Omaha, Nebraska), November 8, 1946: 27.

Barthel, Thomas. *Baseball Barnstorming and Exhibition Games – 1901-1962: A History of Off-Season Major League Play* (Jefferson, North Carolina: McFarland Publishers, 2007).

Bojens, Ken. "Off the Main Line," *San Diego Union*, October 24, 1946: A-16.

Old, John B. "Jackie's Blasts at Umpire Mar Game in Los Angeles," *The Sporting News*, November 6, 1946: 2.

Stann, Francis E., "Win, Lose, or Draw," *Washington Evening Star*, November 7, 1946: C-1.

Young, Fay. "Through the Years," *Chicago Defender*, October 19, 1946: 11.

NOTES

1. Steve George, "250,000 See Feller-Paige Teams Play," *The Sporting News*, October 30, 1946: 9.
2. "Wagner's All-Stars Beat Robbie's, 6-5," *Chicago Times*, October 8, 1946: 48.
3. On August 23, 2010, PBS aired an episode of the *History Detectives*. During a segment of the broadcast, a scorecard from the October 8, 1946, game in Pittsburgh was shown. Articles from contemporary issues of the *Pittsburgh Courier* (local edition) and the *Chicago Defender* also were shown. The article by Fay Young in the *Chicago Defender* is listed in the sources. The article from the *Pittsburgh Courier* is shown in Note 4. The scorecard was completed and presents the most complete record of what transpired on October 8, 1946.
4. "Jackie Robinson's Team Beats Major leaguers, 10-5," *Chicago Defender*, October 19, 1946: 16.
5. "Robinson All-Stars Bag 8-0 Decision," *Cleveland Plain Dealer*, October 15, 1946: 16; "Robinson's All-Stars Blank Dressen's, 8-0," *Cleveland Call and Post*, October 19, 1946: 9B; "Robinson's All-Stars Win 3 Out of 5 Games," *Pittsburgh Courier* (Local Edition), October 19, 1946: 24.
6. "Omahans Rally in Last Frame," *Council Bluffs* (Iowa) *Nonpareil*, October 16, 1946: 8; Maurice Shadle, "Omaha's Stars Win in Ninth, 8-7," *Morning World Herald* (Omaha, Nebraska), October 16, 1948: 13.
7. "Feller Shuts Out Robinson's Stars," *San Francisco Examiner*, October 19, 1946: 15.
8. "Jackie Robinson Here for Contest; Could Not Compete," *Bakersfield Californian*, October 25, 1946: 15.
9. "Feller in One-Day Hops in Coast Cities," *The Sporting News*, October 30, 1946: 10.
10. "Feller Whiffs 11 in 4-2 Win: Major Leaguers Triumph Behind Four-Hit Pitching," *San Diego Union*, October 25, 1946: B-4.
11. "Red Devils Nab Cage Tilt," *Los Angeles Times*, November 10, 1946: II-7; J. Cullen Fentress, "Jackie Robinson Scores 18 Points as L.A. Tops Sheboygan," *Pittsburgh Courier* (National Edition), November 16, 1946: 13.

JACKIE ROBINSON'S 1947 BREAKTHROUGH BEGAN IN HAVANA

by César Brioso

Separated by fewer than three miles, the Hotel Los Angeles near *la Habana Vieja* (Old Havana) and the Hotel Nacional in the city's Vedado district were worlds apart.

Sitting on a bluff overlooking El Malecón, Havana's famed coastal roadway, the Nacional exuded opulence with its Andalusian-Moorish architecture, elegant bars and splendid swimming pool. And in March of 1947, the Havana landmark housed the Brooklyn Dodgers as they held spring training in Cuba. The Los Angeles was – in the words of Herbert Goren of the *New York Sun* – a "musty, third-rate hotel" that "looked like a movie version of a waterfront hostelry in Singapore."[1] That was where Jackie Robinson – along with Montreal Royals teammates Roy Campanella, Don Newcombe, and Roy Partlow – was staying.

And Robinson was not happy.

"I thought," Robinson protested, "we left Florida to train in Cuba to get away from Jim Crow."[2]

As part of Branch Rickey's grand plan for integrating major-league baseball, the Dodgers president had opted to move the organization's spring-training headquarters from Daytona Beach to Havana. He wanted Robinson's audition for breaking baseball's color barrier to take place far from fields of Jim Crow Florida. And Havana seemed like the perfect choice.

Cuba's professional winter league had been integrated since 1900, and the Dodgers were well familiar with the Cuban capital, having held spring training there in 1941 and 1942. Several days after arriving in Havana in 1947, players from the Dodgers and Royals attended the decisive game of the Cuban League season between Almendares and Havana at El Gran Stadium. After Robinson was introduced over the public-address system, "he took bows to the wild

Jackie Robinson playing in a spring training game vs. Havana Cubans.

shouting of 38,000 jabbering fans," wrote *Baltimore Afro-American* columnist Sam Lacy.³ Despite Cuba's more tolerant racial climate, Robinson and the Royals' three other African-American players found themselves in separate and unequal accommodations from the Dodgers.

"That damn hotel," Newcombe said of the Los Angeles years later. "It was full of cockroaches. It was so hot, you couldn't sleep." Robinson "hated it with a passion, as did all of us," Newcombe added. "Jackie was more outspoken about it, but he knew there wasn't anything he could do about it. He was trying to get to the big club. He had to keep his cool and be quiet."⁴

Lacy and *Pittsburgh Courier* columnist Wendell Smith were two members of the Black press who were embedded with Robinson during spring training, chronicling what they hoped would be his eventual ascension to the majors. Lacy described the Los Angeles as "a fleabag hotel where we slept on heavy spreads that we used for mattresses. The springs were coming up – pressing into our bodies – which shows you just the type of hotel we were in. That was where we had to stay during that period. ... The conditions were actually miserable."⁵

And Cuba's relative racial tolerance wasn't enough to prevent Newcombe from being removed from the lobby of the Nacional one day as he tried to meet with Rickey. "I had to get permission from the bellhop," he said. "In fact, one [white] bellhop put me out of the lobby. I told him I had to see Mr. Rickey with the Dodgers. I was allowed to go to the house telephone and call Mr. Rickey to get permission to go up to his room to see him."⁶

Newcombe, Robinson, Campanella, and Partlow were even segregated from their white teammates on the Royals, the Dodgers' Triple-A affiliate. While the Dodgers stayed at the Nacional and trained at Havana's El Gran Stadium, the Royals lived and trained at the Havana Military Academy, a fancy school for the sons of rich Cubans located about 15 miles outside the capital. Every day, Robinson and the other Black players had to be shuttled to that campus before returning to the Los Angeles after each day's workouts.

Wanting to avoid even the possibility of any disruptive racial incidents in the Royals' camp, Rickey chose to house Robinson, Campanella, Newcombe, and Partlow separately from the Royals.⁷ Rickey's abundance of caution was probably unnecessary. After all, Robinson had spent the entire 1946 season at Montreal, where he led the league in batting with a .349 average.

- *Leo Durocher and Jackie Robinson at El Gran Stadium.*

Montreal was a progressive city, and Robinson normally encountered resistance only when the Royals traveled around the International League, most notably when a riot broke out during an August series in Baltimore as fans swarmed the field after a disputed play at home plate during one game.⁸

There would be no such problems in Cuba, especially at the Royals' camp, where Robinson received a surprise visit one day from heavyweight boxing champion Joe Louis. Robinson's teammates, Black and White, looked on like giddy teenagers as Robinson and the Brown Bomber compared golf swings and talked about Robinson's prospects for making the big club. Before leaving, Louis told Robinson: "See you opening day at Ebbets Field with the Dodgers."⁹ The visit was a much-needed morale boost for Robinson, who had to deal with several issues during spring training that made his impending historic breakthrough into the majors appear unlikely:

- Minor foot surgery early in spring training.
- Learning a new position at first base.
- An injury late in camp.
- Resistance among Dodgers players.
- The periodic absence of Dodgers manager Leo Durocher.

Robinson missed only a few days after Dr. July Sanguily, a renowned Cuban physician who was one of the owners of the Almendares team in the Cuban League, removed an irritating callus on Robinson's toe. His new position, however, caused more stress.

96

Robinson had played shortstop with the Kansas City Monarchs before switching to second base with Montreal after Brooklyn signed him in 1945. The Dodgers were set at three-fourths of the infield with second baseman Eddie Stanky, shortstop Pee Wee Reese, and third baseman Spider Jorgensen. Ed Stevens and Howie Schultz had shared time at first base for Brooklyn in 1946. So Robinson's most likely path to the majors would be through first base.

Robinson started learning the new position from Hall of Famer George Sisler, who was in camp as a coach. Handed a first baseman's mitt, Robinson was asked how the new glove felt. "I honestly don't know," he responded. "I never had one on before."[10] But Robinson said he was willing to try another position switch: "I'll play where they want me to play. I never played first, but I'll try anything."[11] Privately, however, Robinson wasn't nearly as open to the change. "He didn't like it at all, but Rickey convinced him that this was his way of getting up to the majors," Lacy recalled years later. "It was just a case where he had enough problems. He had enough things to be concerned about [than] to give him this additional concern of changing positions and possibly doing poorly."[12]

After opening spring training in Havana, the Dodgers and Royals took a 12-day side trip for games in Panama, against local teams and each other. Opposition to Robinson – in the form of a petition among certain, mostly Southern Dodgers players – came to light during that trip. Dodgers pitcher Kirby Higbe spilled the beans to the team's traveling secretary, Harold Parrott while out one night at a Canal Zone watering hole. "Ol' Hig just won't do it," a drunken Higbe told Parrott. "The ol' man [Rickey] has been fair to Ol' Hig. So Ol' Hig ain't going to join any petition to keep anybody off the club."[13]

Parrott immediately informed Rickey and Durocher. Unable to sleep after hearing the news, Durocher rousted the players from their beds at the US Army barracks at Fort Gillick, where the team was quartered. Gathered for the impromptu meeting in a huge empty kitchen behind the mess hall, Durocher ripped into his players. "You know what you can do with that petition? You can wipe your ass with it. … I'm the manager of this ballclub, and I'm interested in one thing. Winning. I'll play an elephant if he can do the job, and to make room for him, I'll send my own brother home. … So I don't want to see your petition, and I don't want to hear anything more about it. The meeting is over; go back to bed."[14]

Rickey had hoped the Dodgers players themselves would call for Robinson's promotion to the majors once they had a chance to play against him, declaring in January: "The players could decide Robinson's fate. It's what I prefer – that the Dodgers players make their own decision after seeing him in action."[15] Instead the Dodgers president had to move quickly to quell a rebellion, summoning the mutineers individually to his room at the Hotel Tivoli. The most heated exchange came with catcher and Alabama native Bobby Bragan.

Rickey: "Not you nor anybody else is going to tell me who to play. It doesn't make any difference whether a guy's skin is purple, white, green, black, or blue, he is going to play if he's going to do more than the other guy. Do you understand that?"

Bragan: "Yes, sir."

Rickey: "Would you rather be traded, or would you rather play with him?"

Bragan: "I'd rather be traded."

Rickey: "Are you going to play any differently because he's here?"

Bragan: "No, I'm not."[16]

Bragan wasn't traded, finished his playing career with the Dodgers in 1948, and went on to manage integrated teams in the Cuban League. Playing with Robinson "was the greatest thing that ever happened to me," Bragan said years later. "Those people, like myself, who might have been a little slow joining Robinson at the breakfast table, we were fighting to see who would eat with him. It was a real transition. He sold everybody."[17]

Outfielder Dixie Walker, one of the purported ringleaders of the players revolt, wasn't summoned to Rickey's hotel in Panama. He had left the isthmus on March 18, flying to Miami to meet with his family on "personal business."[18] Walker's confrontation with Rickey would wait until he rejoined the Dodgers after the team returned to Havana on March 22. The Georgia native did not react well. A few days after the meeting, Walker – popular among Dodgers fans and known as the People's Choice – requested a trade in writing. Handwritten and dated March 26, 1947, Walker's letter read:

"Dear Mr. Rickey, Recently, the thought has occurred to me that a change of ball clubs would benefit both the Brooklyn Dodgers and myself. Therefore, I would like to be traded as soon as a deal could be arranged. ... For reasons I don't care to go into, I feel my decision is best for all concerned."[19]

Unlike Bragan, Walker eventually was granted his request, traded before the 1948 season to the Pittsburgh Pirates, where he finished his playing career after two seasons.

Durocher missed much of the post-petition fireworks, having left for California the morning after his late-night tirade to deal with legal issues surrounding his scandalous marriage to actress Laraine Day. (The divorce from her previous marriage was still pending when she and Durocher wed.) So Durocher didn't get to see Robinson in action against the Dodgers in Panama. That trend continued even after the Dodgers and Royals returned to Havana to finish out spring training. When he wasn't making himself the subject of gossip columns, Durocher found himself summoned to a hearing before Commissioner Happy Chandler over his ongoing feud with New York Yankees President Larry MacPhail. The two had sparred verbally over the Yankees' offseason managerial opening with Durocher penning ghostwritten columns in the *Brooklyn Eagle* to take swipes at MacPhail.

But their mutual acrimony had come to a head during a game at Havana's El Gran Stadium on March 8, when gamblers Memphis Engelberg and Connie Immerman were observed sitting in or next to MacPhail's box – depending on the person telling the story. Durocher, who had been warned by Chandler to stay away from gamblers, and Rickey wondered out loud about MacPhail's apparent guests. "Did you see those two men out there today, those two gamblers sitting in MacPhail's box?" Rickey asked the team's beat reporters.[20] "Are there two sets of rules, one applying to the managers and one applying to the club owners?" Durocher said. "Where does MacPhail come off, flaunting his company with known gamblers right in front of the players' faces? If I ever said hello to one of those guys, I'd be called before Commissioner Chandler and probably barred."[21]

An enraged MacPhail denied that Engelberg and Immerman were his guests and filed a grievance with Chandler, arguing that comments made by Dodgers officials "constitute slander and libel" and "represent ... conduct detrimental to baseball." It didn't help Durocher's cause that his marriage was creating fallout back in New York, where the Catholic Youth Organization of Brooklyn denounced his conduct on and off the field as "undermining the moral and spiritual training of our young boys."[22]

With all the swirling controversies, Durocher finally saw Robinson play for the first time on March 28 in Havana. Robinson, back in the lineup despite ongoing stomach problems, went 1-for-3, but booted two plays at first base that led to four of the Dodgers' runs as Brooklyn beat the Royals, 5-2. The next day, Robinson played seven innings at first base and went 0-for-2, drew a walk, and stole second base on a pickoff play as Higbe blanked the Royals, 7-0.

In the March 29 edition of the *Pittsburgh Courier*, Wendell Smith, citing "an unimpeachable source," reported that Robinson would be promoted to the Dodgers on April 10 and would play first base when the team opened the season on the 15th against the Boston Braves.[23] But developments on the field appeared to contradict the certitude of Smith's reporting. Robinson did not play in the March 30 game won by the Royals, 6-5, and then played second base in games on March 31, April 1, and April 3. Before the March 31 game, Rickey reversed course on the idea of letting the Dodgers players decide Robinson's fate. "No player on this club will have anything to say about who plays or who does not play on it," Rickey said. "I will decide who is on it and Durocher will decide who of those who are on it does the playing."[24]

Another potential setback came during the game on April 5. Robinson was back at first base, but injured his right arm and back after getting bowled over by Dodgers catcher Bruce Edwards, who was sliding back to the bag. Robinson sat in the stands the next day as the Dodgers beat the Royals, 6-0, in the final exhibition game at El Gran Stadium. Having left Havana after what had been the most expensive spring-training camp in history, with a $50,000 price tag,[25] the Dodgers began working their way up the US East Coast in a series of exhibition games before the regular-season opener at Ebbets Field.

What of the Royals' Black players? Campanella was promoted to Montreal, Newcombe returned for another season at Class-B Nashua, and Partlow had already been released in March. All that remained was a decision on Robinson. The plan was for Durocher to publicly ask Rickey to elevate Robinson, but as the Dodgers brain trust met on April 9 in Rickey's office on Montague Street in Brooklyn, a call came from the commissioner's office notifying the Dodgers of Chandler's decision in regard to MacPhail's grievance. Aside from fining Parrott and the Dodgers, Chandler suspended Durocher for a year for conduct detrimental to baseball.[26] The Dodgers manager would not be present when on April 10 – as Robinson played in his final exhibition game against the Dodgers – Rickey's assistant Arthur Mann posted a terse release in the press box at Ebbets Field: "The Brooklyn Dodgers today purchased the contract of Jackie Roosevelt Robinson from the Montreal Royals. He will report immediately."[27]

SOURCES

This article is adapted from *Havana Hardball: Spring Training, Jackie Robinson, and the Cuban League* by César Brioso (Gainesville, Florida: University Press of Florida, 2015), updates by the author.

NOTES

1. Herbert Goren, "Dodgers Split on Robinson," *The Sporting News*, March 12, 1947: 17.
2. Jules Tygiel, *Baseball's Great Experiment: Jackie Robinson and His Legacy* (New York: Oxford University Press, 1997), 165.
3. Sam Lacy, "Looking 'Em Over," *Baltimore Afro-American*, March 8, 1947: 12.
4. Author interview with Don Newcombe, January 1997.
5. Author interview with Sam Lacy, January 1997.
6. Author interview with Newcombe, January 1997.
7. Tygiel, *Baseball's Great Experiment*, 165.
8. Tygiel, 129.
9. Wendell Smith, "A Pair of Kings … of 'Sock.'" *Pittsburgh Courier*, March 22, 1947: 14.
10. Tygiel, 168.
11. Goren.
12. Interview with Lacy.
13. Tygiel, 168.
14. Leo Durocher with Ed Linn, *Nice Guys Finish Last* (Chicago: University of Chicago Press, 1975), 205.
15. Harold C. Burr, "Dodgers Players to Have Voice on Jackie's Climb," *The Sporting News*, January 22, 1947: 16.
16. Interview with Bobby Bragan, January 1997.
17. Interview with Bragan.
18. Roscoe McGowen, "Dodgers Play Tie with Royals, 1-1." *New York Times*, March 18, 1947: 37.
19. Maury Allen and Susan Walker, *Dixie Walker of the Dodgers: The People's Choice* (Tuscaloosa, Alabama: University of Alabama Press, 2010), 3.
20. Red Barber, *1947: When All Hell Broke Loose in Baseball* (New York: Doubleday, 1982), 106-7.
21. Barber, 107-8.
22. Jack Lang, "CYO Raps Lip, Quits Knothole Club," *The Sporting News*, March 12, 1947: 8.
23. Wendell Smith, "Jackie Robinson Will Play First Base for Brooklyn Dodgers." *Pittsburgh Courier*, March 28, 1947: 1.
24. Roscoe McGowen, "Dodgers to Drop 10 Men by Sunday." *New York Times*, April 1, 1947: 35.
25. Michael Gavin, "Jackie Robinson Gets Chance with Flatbush Troupe," *The Sporting News*, April 16, 1947: 18.
26. Durocher, 257.
27. Louis Effrat, "Dodgers Purchase Robinson, First Negro in Modern Major League Baseball," *New York Times*, April 11, 1947: 20.

I MET JACKIE ROBINSON'S FIRST MAJOR-LEAGUE MANAGER

by Wayne Soini

I met Clyde Sukeforth three times altogether.

On the first occasion, Howard V. Doyle, an old Mainer, friend, and former boss who knew I'd be interested, invited me to join him on a trip to Waldoboro, Maine, specifically to meet Clyde, with whom he'd been on a first-name basis for decades. The story is that Howard had made part of his living from sports during the Depression. Also known back then as Dizzy Doyle, he formed a semipro basketball team to round a circuit of small towns in Maine. They played games against local teams for paid admissions, which were split differently depending on which team won; that guaranteed a hard-fought contest worth seeing. He was also good as a pitcher in semipro baseball. Such a man naturally found much in common with Clyde, a catcher with the Cincinnati Reds. They kept in touch after Howard moved to Massachusetts, where he had a long, even legendary career as a union leader, while Clyde worked for a succession of major-league teams when he was not hunting or fishing in Maine.

I met Clyde in about 1985 or '86. Then as now, Waldoboro was a small town on Route 1, population about 5,000. When Howard stopped at a diner for directions, I noticed that the natives asked him questions before giving any answers. They were protective of their baseball hero's privacy. Only after you passed the test as being somebody Clyde would likely welcome did you receive more than, "Yes, he lives here in Waldoboro somewhere, over down toward the shore." Howard had the answers and the Maine accent to pass their tests.

(At the diner, I recall how we ate a quick meal, after which I selected one of the peanut-butter-frosted vanilla cupcakes under a glass case that just melted in your mouth. As we left, I asked for six of them in a box to go. There were only seven left.

("I can't sell you six, sir," the hostess said. "Then, others would come here and be disappointed." I settled for three in a stiff white bag to go.)

Clyde's modest but neat and comfortably furnished home turned out to be located not very far from the diner. He welcomed us, quickly brought us inside, offered refreshments, and had us sit on a sofa in his spacious living room. On the wall was a framed *Saturday Evening Post* cover by Norman Rockwell.[1] When we met, Clyde was in his mid-80s but still active and spry, a short and compact man, neither plump nor scrawny, of a sturdy build. He took a seat in an armchair beside us and chatted in succinct sentences and occasional dry humor.

By the way, it was not obvious to me that he was blind in one eye, although he had suffered such a devastating injury in a hunting accident in the 1930s. Clyde, who had batted .354 with the Reds in 1929 (84 hits in 84 games played), thereby lost most of his value as a player. (Only the manpower shortage at the end of World War II brought him back into play in earnest, over 18 games in the spring of 1945, during which he batted .294.)[2] He had baseball value, however, as he had off-the-field talents that surfaced. It was as a scout and even (in two games) as manager of the Brooklyn Dodgers that Clyde had made his most lasting marks.

Clyde Sukeforth as Dodgers manager, 1947.

He talked about those days with us. First, Clyde said he thought that he was assigned to be a scout because of his years as a catcher.

"A catcher sees players closer up than anybody else. And we are not looking for the better points, we are looking for a batter's weaknesses."

Even with one good eye, his trained eye was of use to Branch Rickey.

"Jackie Robinson was just burning up the charts after the war," Clyde said, a good degree of excitement still in his voice. As he described it, Branch Rickey sent him west to observe Robinson, then a star with the Kansas City Monarchs. Rickey instructed him to "pay particular attention to his arm" but, as Clyde summarized for us that day, not otherwise making his intentions explicit. Clyde said he saw a gifted player and after the game spoke with Jackie, telling him that he was there at Branch Rickey's request and asking Jackie to come to Brooklyn.

"Why does he want to see me? Why is he interested?" Clyde said, reprising the emphatic and very persistent curiosity that Jackie showed, without Clyde's being able to satisfy it.

Without more than that to say specifically, Clyde managed to get Jackie to agree to join him on a trip by train back to New York. (I think in fact this actually took a couple of efforts or talks, but Clyde did not address this point with us.) At some point, questions surfaced again and Clyde said Jackie said, "I have some questions."

"I'm sure you do," Clyde recalled saying (he smiled in reliving the moment), "and Mr. Rickey will have a lot of questions for you."

This last remark suggested to me that Clyde had been better briefed by Branch Rickey than he let on to Robinson. However, by his account he maintained confidentiality about the topics of any future grilling in Brooklyn (as did take place). With this deflection of Jackie's intense curiosity, Clyde had reached the climax and the end of his account. I think it was in that moment that Clyde experienced his greatest pride, persuading Jackie Robinson to trek to Brooklyn without revealing any more than he did – that "Mr. Rickey will have a lot of questions for" him. As soon as Clyde reached the door of the Montague Street meeting – of which he was the last living witness at this point – he stopped reminiscing and said, precisely, "And the rest you know."

(Parenthetically, I do not remember whether Clyde promised me to write up a sketch of his role in the selection of Ralph Branca to pitch in what led to Bobby Thomson's "shot heard round the world" home run of 1951. If not, then at home I promptly wrote him requesting such a note. Either way, Clyde obliged. He sent me a two-page handwritten note on small-sized stationery that explained what he did. I've given that to a nephew who collects baseball memorabilia, but I remember he commented in beginning the letter, "I hope this is the last time I have to give an account of this," or some wording very close to that. He was sensitive about the event, not as to himself but in behalf of Ralph Branca, who he told us in his living room he thought had been unfairly criticized or maligned thereafter.)

A year or two later, Howard drove up to see Clyde again, one fine summer day, and I was gladly with him. I don't recall if we were expected, or just dropped by. In any case, it was a short visit of a few minutes. We met outdoors, in Clyde's front yard, and then walked around in back of his home, where his property limit was a tidal cove in which he kept an outboard motorboat.

During this meeting, I don't think we discussed baseball at all. I remember Howard asking Clyde if neighbors complained, when he said that he usually rode out at high tides in the early morning, just at dawn, 5:30 or 6 A.M.

"I received no complaint," Clyde said, standing at a sort of proud attention, "but I felt entitled to them."

Howard told to me later that this passed as humor in Maine.

The final occasion I saw Clyde, he was well into his 90s. The local library of Waldoboro had arranged for a Clyde Sukeforth Day. When Howard and I arrived, Clyde was already seated in a sunny room surrounded by uniformed Boy Scouts and their leader, who interviewed Clyde on his career. Clyde mentioned having weighed finishing college (Georgetown University) or getting more into sports. His explanation was interesting. As he enjoyed athletic competition and liked the idea of time off during the hunting season that pursuing baseball would allow him, he became a player. When the leader quizzed Clyde about his brief manager stint – he replaced Leo Durocher at the beginning of the 1947 season, when that controversial Dodgers manager was suddenly suspended by Baseball Commissioner Happy Chandler – Clyde deflected celebrating his moment in the sun lightly with good humor.

With Clyde at the stern, the Dodgers won both games (against the Boston Braves) in Ebbets Field.

Jackie

It is in the record books. His record was 1.000 as a manager, as the Scout leader put it.

"No manager has ever done better," the leader said.

"None have done better," Clyde agreed, while drily adding, "Some have done more, but none have done better."

His heavy emphasis on the word "more" brought out the big laugh of the day.

In his living room and later in the library on his Day, Clyde chose to show a modest perspective. He had not only scouted Jackie Robinson. Historically, he took part in erasing baseball's color line as a manager. Clyde was entitled to bring it out loud and clear but he didn't. He left off each opportunity when I was present without boasting that on Opening Day of the 1947 season, April 15, 1947, as the acting manager of the Dodgers, he was the one who wrote "Jackie Robinson" into the batting order, making that game Jackie Robinson's first game in the major leagues. Others have done more. But none have done better, indeed.

NOTES

1 *Saturday Evening Post*, April 23, 1949 cover. It is known by several titles, "Tough Call," "Game Called on Account of Rain, Bottom of the Sixth Inning," and "The Three Umpires." The Brooklyn manager arguing in the background is plainly Clyde. Rockwell visited Ebbets Field during the 1948 season, along with a photographer. Clyde was not the manager in 1948 or 1949, but Rockwell was likely aware of Clyde's history. If so, transparently, he wanted to memorialize as manager the man who had been the team's temporary manager on the day Jackie Robinson began to play in the major leagues, Opening Day 1947. Rockwell used his artist's license to elevate Clyde on a rainy day and perhaps, very subtly, to evoke baseball's earlier moment in the sun.

2 In 486 major-league games over 10 seasons, Sukeforth hit for a .264 batting average (with a .319 on-base percentage). In the 399 games in which he caught, he committed 33 errors in 1,264 chances for a .974 fielding percentage.

THE "STRIKE" AGAINST JACKIE ROBINSON: TRUTH OR MYTH?

by Warren Corbett

A National League players' strike, instigated by some of the St. Louis Cardinals, against the presence in the league of Jackie Robinson, Negro first baseman, has been averted temporarily and perhaps permanently quashed.

That's the lede of Stanley Woodward's story in the *New York Herald Tribune* on May 9, 1947, four weeks after Robinson's debut.[1] The strike story has become part of the Robinson canon, a vivid illustration of the racist resistance he faced. It won the E.P. Dutton Award for best sports reporting of the year, and the writer Roger Kahn called it "the sports scoop of the century." The Cardinals' Enos Slaughter said of Woodward, "That son of a bitch kept me out of the Hall of Fame for twenty years."[2]

Yet hard evidence of a strike plot is lacking. Woodward's story was flawed, but his disciples — most prominently Kahn, author of *The Boys of Summer* — have defended his reporting for seven decades. Critics — led by St. Louis sportswriter Bob Broeg, who called the *Tribune* story "a barnyard vulgarism" — believe the "plot" was the product of some empty rants by players, plus a paranoid owner and a headline-seeking sportswriter.[3] Jules Tygiel, in his landmark book *Baseball's Great Experiment*, concluded that it was "an extremely elusive topic."[4] This review will explore the maze of conflicting evidence and try to arrive at the truth.

WOODWARD'S SCOOP

Woodward's indictment went like this: Some of the Cardinals had schemed to organize other teams to refuse to take the field against Robinson in the hope of driving him out of the league and preserving major-league baseball for White men only. But National League president Ford Frick confronted the ringleaders and forced them to back down.

Woodward wrote, "Frick addressed the players, in effect, as follows: 'If you do this, you will be suspended from the league. You will find that the friends you think you have in the press box will not support you, that you will be outcasts. I do not care if half the league strikes. Those who do will encounter swift retribution. And will be suspended, and I don't care if it wrecks the National League for five years. This is the United States of America, and one citizen has as much right to play as another.'"

Dodgers broadcaster Red Barber called the speech Frick's "finest hour."[5] Other writers have quoted it ever since.

It never happened. Frick never spoke to any Cardinals players. Woodward acknowledged that the day after he broke his big story, and Frick said so, too.[6]

Woodward cited no sources, not even anonymous ones. He wrote, "It is understood...", "it is believed...", and "we can report..." He named no conspirators, probably because the paper's lawyers wouldn't let him. Robinson is the only player mentioned by name. The story resembled the "blind items" usually confined to gossip columns: *Which married Broadway chanteuse was spotted canoodling with her co-star at Sardi's?* That may explain why the explosive report appeared in the sports pages, not on the front page, although Woodward blamed a racist editor.

DISSECTING THE SCOOP

As best events can be reconstructed so long afterward, here's how it happened, based on published accounts: The Cardinals owner, Sam Breadon, picked up rumors that some of his players were talking about striking in protest against Robinson. Breadon's source may have been Dr. Robert Hyland, the team physician. At the least, Hyland was the man responsible for letting the story out.

Sam Breadon was born poor and started his business career peddling popcorn at the 1904 St. Louis World's Fair. He got rich selling cars — Pierce-Arrows — but never escaped his origins; he was tight with a dollar and always worried about where his next one was coming from. In his anxious mind, even the whisper of a strike sounded like the roar of a crisis.

According to both Frick and Breadon, the Cardinals owner had rushed to New York to report the rumors to the NL president. Frick told him that any strikers would be punished and the league would stand behind Robinson. Breadon met with the team leaders, shortstop Marty Marion and captain and center fielder Terry Moore, who assured him that the strike talk was only talk, a few players venting. In his memoir, Frick said Breadon reported back that it was "a tempest in a teapot."[7]

Exactly when Breadon talked to Frick has never been established. Woodward said the strike threat was the reason Breadon went to New York just before the Cardinals played in Brooklyn on May 6, but Frick said they had spoken two or three weeks earlier.[8] Breadon went to New York in May because his club had lost nine straight games and he was in a panic, not unusual for him. The day before Woodward's story was published, the Cardinals finished winning two out of three from the Dodgers without incident.

The rumors had begun to leak out a few days before that series when the Yankees went to St. Louis to play the Browns. Dr. Hyland had dinner with Rud Rennie, who covered the Yankees for the *Herald Tribune*, and confided that Breadon feared a possible strike that could destroy his ball club.

Rennie knew a hot story when he heard one, but he couldn't write it without burning his friend Hyland. He passed the information to his boss, sports editor Woodward.

Stanley Woodward was a titan of the New York sportswriting fraternity. A massive former football tackle at Amherst College, Woodward liked to be called "Coach." He was too old and too nearsighted for military service in World War II, so he volunteered as a war correspondent and landed in the Nazi-occupied Netherlands aboard a glider. Woodward was tough and blunt, and was fired in 1948 after he told the *Tribune*'s owner that her society golf tournament wasn't worth covering.

How the alleged strike threat morphed from dinner-table chat to *Herald Tribune* headline is transparent. Although Woodward didn't identify his source, he later told Roger Kahn that he had talked to Frick.[9] The NL president, a former New York sportswriter and Babe Ruth's ghostwriter, knew how to plant a story without leaving fingerprints. And he was the hero of Woodward's account. But Woodward misunderstood what Frick told him and mistakenly reported that Frick had spoken to the players.

After writing that the strike was "instigated by some of the St. Louis Cardinals," Woodward switched targets two paragraphs later and said it had been "instigated by a member of the Brooklyn Dodgers, who has since recanted." That is an unmistakable reference to Dixie Walker. The star right fielder, who came from Alabama, had circulated a petition against Robinson among his teammates during spring training and had written a letter to Dodgers president Branch Rickey asking to be traded rather than play with a Black man. Walker was a Brooklyn favorite known as "The People's Choice," but when he appeared at Ebbets Field for the first time in 1947, Robinson's partisans booed him.[10]

While Woodward didn't name names, he laid blame on White southerners — "boys from the Hookworm Belt," as he contemptuously called them. The Cardinals roster could have filled out a platoon in the Confederate Army. Terry Moore, born in Alabama, grew up in Memphis and St. Louis. Marty Marion's South Carolina pedigree was said to trace back to the Revolutionary War "Swamp Fox," Francis Marion. Manager Eddie Dyer and pitcher Howie Pollet came from Louisiana, Enos Slaughter from North Carolina, Harry Walker from Alabama. And Harry was Dixie Walker's younger brother.

THE BACKLASH

Woodward's blockbuster sent other reporters scurrying to catch up. Of course, all the Cardinals denied it. "That's an out and out lie," Breadon shouted to St. Louis writer Sid Keener. "It's New York again trying to stir trouble in our organization."[11]

"Absurd," manager Dyer said. "Nobody on the Cardinals ever thought of such a thing." Then he added a key point: "I'd have known about it."[12] Dyer had managed many of the Cardinals coming up through the farm system. Several worked for him in his Houston insurance business, and his wife, Geraldine, was the godmother of their children. Someone would have tipped him off if a strike was percolating in his clubhouse.

Frick, however, confirmed that Breadon had come to him with the rumors. "I didn't have to talk to the players myself," Frick said. "Breadon did the talking. From what he told me afterward, the trouble was smoothed over."[13]

The Cardinals players did not deny that there was bitter opposition to Robinson. They did deny that it amounted to anything more than noise. Terry Moore dismissed it as "some high-sounding strike talk that meant nothing."[14] Stan Musial said, "I thought the racial talk was just hot air."[15]

Years later, Frick told writer Jerome Holtzman, "I thought very little of it until the story broke. The way

Woodward wrote it, you would have thought all the St. Louis players were against Robinson."[16]

As exaggerated as it was, the story reset the conversation about Robinson after he had played just 15 games. Most of the White press, while routinely referring to him as the "Negro first baseman," had been tiptoeing around the racial angle. Sportswriters wanted to write about baseball, not social change.

Phillies manager Ben Chapman had already been widely condemned for his vicious bench jockeying of Robinson, the ugliest public incident of the year. (Chapman and Dixie Walker were close friends and had been roommates with the Yankees.) Now big-name sports columnists rallied to Robinson's side, repeating Woodward's accusations and defending Robinson's right to play. Jimmy Cannon of the *New York Post* wrote, "There is a great lynch mob among us and they go unhooded and work without rope."[17] *The Sporting News*, a longtime apologist for segregated baseball, editorialized that "the presence of a Negro player in the majors is an accomplished fact, which no amount of ill-advised strike talk can affect."[18]

The African American sportswriter Sam Lacy thought the tide of support from Frick and the White press was a turning point signaling acceptance not just of Robinson, but of integration. "[A]t long last, it looks as though we have the wind at our backs," Lacy wrote.[19]

THE FALLOUT

The story quickly faded from the newspapers, but it has reverberated down through the decades as the Robinson saga was told and retold. Generations of writers have recycled Woodward's version, quoting the speech Frick never delivered. The sportswriter Jerry Izenberg, another Woodward acolyte, said, "All Stanley did was change history."[20] That is not so. Even if there was a scheme to strike, it was dead by the time Woodward made it public.

Over the past 70 years, just a few players have recalled conversations or activities that seemed connected to a strike plot. Those memories were dredged up decades after the fact, long after the story had been embedded in baseball history. One of the Cardinals, backup first baseman Dick Sisler, told the historian Jules Tygiel, "Very definitely, there was something going on at the time whereby they weren't going to play."[21]

In 1997, the 50th anniversary of Robinson's debut, ESPN's *Outside the Lines* reported that it had interviewed 93 of the 107 surviving players on other National League teams. Only three of them — all members of the Cubs — claimed that their club had voted to strike as part of a league-wide boycott on Opening Day. Five players — one Cub, two Pirates, and two Phillies — said their teams had voted against a strike. The other 85 either denied knowing anything or wouldn't comment.[22]

The Cardinals could never escape the stain on their reputations. After a 1990 book, *The Ballplayers*, named him and Slaughter as leaders of the strike plot, 82-year-old Terry Moore had his lawyer write to the publisher demanding a retraction.[23]

THE PLOT THINS

Overlooked in the he-said, he-said is one incontrovertible fact: a team that refused to play against Robinson would forfeit the game. The Cardinals and Dodgers had tied for first place in 1946, when St. Louis won the pennant in the majors' first playoff, and the teams were favored to fight it out again in 1947. A pennant meant a lucrative payday, a World Series share worth $5,000 or more for players, many of whom made less than $10,000 a year. It's hard to imagine the level-headed Moore and Marion agreeing to give away games and endanger their Series checks. Marion said, "I never heard such a stupid thing in my life."[24]

The Cardinals would not strike without Moore and Marion's approval. Moore, the captain since 1941, was nearing the end of his career, but he still ruled the clubhouse as the enforcer of the Cardinals code: take the extra base, break up the double play, don't even say hello to opposing players. Marion, a quieter figure, was the team's player representative and had been the primary architect in creating the players pension plan the year before.

Who would stand against them? The 26-year-old Musial was the biggest star in the National League, but he described himself as a follower of his veteran teammates, not a leader.[25] Slaughter, a roughneck throwback to the Gashouse Gang of the 1930s, was close to Moore — they remained lifelong friends — and would never oppose the captain.[26] No doubt Harry Walker was doing a lot of talking, parroting his big brother. Unlike Dixie, Harry, an annoying individual who ran his mouth *all the time*, was no leader. He was traded just before the Cardinals' first series in Brooklyn because manager Dyer wanted a more powerful bat in the outfield.

Besides Moore, Marion, and possibly Musial, no Cardinal had the clout to organize a strike. And the idea that a strike by one team would spread to the other seven sounds, frankly, crazy. Dixie Walker of the Dodgers was a respected leader who was elected National League player representative, but he had not led his own club out on strike. (Walker changed his tune about playing with Robinson. He gave the rookie batting tips and told Rickey he didn't want to be traded. Rickey traded him anyway, after the 1947 season.)

Woodward's scoop won't die because it dramatizes the terrible burden Robinson had to carry in the face of opposition even from his peers. Robinson did endure indignities that no human should have to bear. On the day Woodward's story appeared, Robinson was turned away from the Benjamin Franklin Hotel in Philadelphia, where the Dodgers had reservations. That same day he posed, with gritted teeth, for a photo with Ben Chapman, who had been ordered to make peace. Around the same time Rickey revealed that letters threatening Robinson's life had been forwarded to the FBI.

ALL TALK, NO ACTION

What is true, and what is "barnyard vulgarism"? Did Sam Breadon believe a strike by the Cardinals was a genuine threat? Yes, but he always believed doom was lurking around every corner. Did Moore and Marion convince him there was nothing to it? Yes. Were Moore and Marion lying? Circumstantial evidence says they were telling the truth.

Of course, many players didn't want Robinson in their midst, and they weren't all Cardinals or southerners. Carl Furillo of Pennsylvania later acknowledged his opposition (and regretted it) and Ewell Blackwell of California was openly hostile, to name just two.[27] But it's a giant leap from saying "we gotta do something" to organizing a league-wide strike

If there was a conspiracy, the sparse evidence indicates it most likely originated with Dixie Walker during spring training. As NL player rep, he had a network of contacts around the league. But the most specific claim of Walker's involvement is suspect. Eighty-year-old former Cub Dewey Williams told ESPN that Walker planned to trigger the strike with phone calls to other teams as soon as Robinson took the field on Opening Day: "Everybody was in the clubhouse sitting around and waiting for Dixie to call, which we thought sure he was gonna do."[28] He didn't. No one has corroborated Williams's version.

If there was such a plot, Walker either ran into opposition, changed his mind, or got cold feet. A strike faced an insurmountable hurdle. All the Dodgers and all the players on all seven other teams would have to go along — at the risk of suspension without pay, at the risk of forfeiting games, at the risk of public condemnation. As Terry Moore said when the story first surfaced, "I think I know enough to realize there is no such thing as a partial strike."[29]

Pittsburgh Courier writer Wendell Smith, Robinson's traveling companion in 1947 and the ghostwriter of his first autobiography, had no motive to play down the incident, but he did. He said it "was greatly exaggerated and made a better newspaper story than anything else."[30]

Ford Frick probably came closest to the truth. "You know baseball players," he told Jerome Holtzman. "They're like anybody else. They pop off. Sitting around a table with a drink or two they commit many acts of great courage but they don't follow through."[31]

NOTES

1. Stanley Woodward, "Views of Sport," *New York Herald Tribune*, May 9, 1947, reprinted in *The Sporting News*, May 21, 1947: 4.
2. Roger Kahn, *The Era, 1947-1957: When the Yankees, the Giants, and the Dodgers Ruled the World* (New York: Houghton Mifflin, 1993), locations 855 and 4929.
3. Bob Broeg, "Remembrance of Summers Past," in John Thorn, ed., *The National Pastime* (SABR, 1982), 22.
4. Jules Tygiel, *Baseball's Great Experiment: Jackie Robinson and His Legacy* (New York: Vintage, 1984), 186.
5. Red Barber, *1947: When All Hell Broke Loose in Baseball* (Garden City, New York: Doubleday, 1982), 175.
6. Woodward's May 10 follow-up story was also reprinted in *The Sporting News*, May 21, 1947: 4.
7. Ford Frick, *Games, Asterisks, and People* (New York: Crown, 1973), 97.
8. Jerome Holtzman, *The Commissioners* (Kingston, New York: Total Sports, 1998), 101.
9. Kahn, *Rickey and Robinson* (New York: Rodale, 2014), 259.
10. "Unfortunate Booing of Walker," *Brooklyn Eagle*, April 13, 1947: 20.
11. Sid Keener, "Breadon Flatly Denies Cards Wanted To Bar Robinson In Brooklyn Series With Birds," *St. Louis Star-Times*, May 9, 1947: 25.
12. "Strike Threat Over Robby Ended—Frick," *Brooklyn Eagle*, May 9, 1947: 17.
13. Ibid.
14. Broeg, "Cardinal Players Deny They Planned Protest Strike Against Robinson," *St. Louis Post-Dispatch*, May 9, 1947: 9C.
15. Kahn, *The Era*, 57.
16. Holtzman, 101.
17. Quoted in Kahn, *Rickey and Robinson*, 264.
18. "The Negro Player Steps on the Scales," *The Sporting News*, May 21, 1947: 14.
19. Sam Lacy, "Strike Against Jackie Spiked," *Afro-American* (Baltimore), May 17, 1947: 1.

20 "A Conversation with Jerry Izenberg, Part III," https://edodevenreporting.wordpress.com/2015/10/19/a-conversation-with-jerry-izenberg-part-iii-influences-and-more-memories/, accessed January 31, 2016.

21 Tygiel, 187.

22 *Outside the Lines: Jackie Robinson's Legacy*, ESPN, February 28, 1997. Hank Wyse, Dewey Williams, and one unidentified player said the Cubs voted to strike. Phil Cavaretta of the Cubs, Al Gionfriddo of the Pirates, and Andy Seminick of the Phillies said their clubs voted to play; the other two players were not named.

23 W. Ray Raleigh letter to William Morrow and Company, June 23, 1994, in Moore's file at the National Baseball Hall of Fame library, Cooperstown, New York.

24 Peter Golenbock, *The Spirit of St. Louis* (New York: Harper Entertainment, 2000), 384.

25 Kahn, *The Era*, 56.

26 Later in 1947 *Collier's* magazine published its own scoop, alleging that Musial and Slaughter had fought over the strike, and Slaughter had put Musial in a hospital. Musial did go to a hospital just as Woodward's story was breaking, because he was sick with appendicitis. People who saw him shirtless said he showed no sign of a beating.

27 Kahn, *Rickey and Robinson*, 120; Arnold Rampersad, *Jackie Robinson: A Biography* (New York: Random House, 1997), 183.

28 *Outside the Lines*. Williams died in 2000.

29 Broeg, "Cardinal Players Deny."

30 Tygiel, 188.

31 Jonathan Eig, *Opening Day: The Story of Jackie Robinson's First Season* (New York: Simon & Schuster, 2007), 94. Eig found Frick's unpublished comment in Jerome Holtzman's notes of the interview.

JACKIE ROBINSON AND THE *KANSAS CITY CALL*

by William A. Young

By the spring of 1945, Jackie Robinson was well known to readers of the *Kansas City Call,* the Black-owned and -operated weekly newspaper that had covered the Kansas City Monarchs thoroughly since the team's origin in 1920. The *Call* had reported on Robinson's exploits as a UCLA football star,[1] and even his winning a ping-pong tournament while he was in the US Army stationed at Fort Riley, Kansas.[2]

Robinson's joining the Monarchs was reported in the March 2, 1945, edition of the *Call,* with the headline "Monarchs Add Jackie Robinson. All-American Footballer Joins Club." The article read in full: "Leading the list of well-known players added to the Monarch roster for the coming season is none other than Jackie Robinson, nationally known letterman at the University of California at Los Angeles and former lieutenant in the army. Although Robinson is better known as an All-American football player out California way, his prowess as a baseball player is known by several clubs in both leagues. Robinson has recently received a medical discharge from the army and decided to cast his lot with the Monarchs. He is present coach at Sam Huston college in Austin, Texas. He will play in the infield in the Monarch lineup."

Two weeks later, the *Call* had this to say about the rookie: "The 'prize freshman' at the Monarchs training camp [in Houston] will be Jackie Robinson, who most likely will not report until the first week of April. He has to finish up his responsibilities at Sam Houston [sic] college where he is a coach."[3]

The first mention in the *Call* of Robinson playing in a Monarchs game described him as having "a big day afield and at bat" against the Black Barons in Birmingham on April 8. "In the game," the *Call* continued, "he drove in the first pair of Monarch runs with a line drive to left center." He had two hits in four plate appearances.[4]

The April 20, 1945, edition of the *Call* reported on the tryout of Robinson, Sam Jethroe, and Marvin Williams for the Boston Red Sox held on April 16. The team had been pressured by Boston Councilman Isadore Muchnick to grant the evaluation. Responding to the tryout, in her "Sportorial" column *Call* sports editor Willa Bea Harmon commented that "if baseball is any one thing, that thing is big business. Robinson's name means big business if he can play ball." Harmon also noted that "Robinson's name is still magic in Sportdom, since he set such a great record at UCLA sometime back in football." She also reminded *Call* readers that Monarchs manager Frank Duncan had already labeled the Monarchs rookie "a great one."

Robinson's next appearance in the *Call* was in the April 27, 1945, description of a game in New Orleans against the Indianapolis Clowns, a team about which Jackie undoubtedly had conflicted feelings. He recognized excellent athletes when he saw them, but the antics of the Clowns players likely offended him. According to the *Call,* Robinson hit an inside-the-park home run after the Clowns center fielder misplayed a fly, and was 2-for-3 in the game. It was one in a series of preseason exhibition games between the Monarchs and Clowns in which Robinson participated.

Also in the April 27 edition, Harmon sarcastically reported that all Robinson and the other players got for their efforts in what turned out to be a sham tryout with the Red Sox was "a little sweat, a train ride at the expense of the [*Pittsburgh*] *Courier* and a lot of mumbo-jumbo about how good they looked."

On May 4, 1945, the *Call* ran its first picture of Robinson and quoted manager Duncan as saying the rookie was playing very well both defensively and offensively and that the Monarchs management considered Jackie one of the best rookies in recent years. With Jackie in the lineup, according to the *Call,* the Monarchs infield was a wall and their offense was strong. The record shows that Robinson was indeed contributing on the field, and at the box office as well. At the Monarchs' 1945 home and season opener on May 6, 1945, a record-breaking crowd of 13,314 saw Robinson go 1-for-4 in his first appearance at Kansas City's Ruppert Stadium.[5] On May 27 Robinson was perfect at the plate in both games of a doubleheader against the American Giants in Chicago. In the first game he walked three times and singled. In the second contest he doubled, singled, and tripled.[6] The next week he was 2-for-5 when the Monarchs took on the Black Barons in Birmingham.[7] On Monday night, June

11, 8,100 saw Robinson hit a 350-foot-homer and go 2-for-3 in a game against the Indianapolis Clowns.[8]

On Sunday, June 17, 16,000 enthusiastic fans greeted the Monarchs rookie at Yankee Stadium, where he singled and scored in a 3-1 win over the Philadelphia Stars. After 27 games, he was batting .345.[9]

The next Sunday, 20,000 were on hand at Griffith Stadium to see Jackie tie the park record with seven consecutive hits in a doubleheader with the Homestead Grays. On July 4 Robinson moved to first base when the regular first sacker, Lee Moody, was injured.[10] On Sunday, July 8, he had two doubles in a game against Birmingham at Ruppert Stadium.[11]

At times Robinson struggled defensively. Before 30,000 at Briggs Stadium in Detroit on July 22, with Satchel Paige pitching, the Monarchs rookie's error allowed the Memphis Red Sox to beat the Monarchs, 3-2.[12]

At an exhibition game against the Sherman Field Flyers of Fort Leavenworth, Kansas, on August 5, with Paige pitching, Robinson drove in two runs.[13]

Commenting on a Monarchs tour of the East in August 1945, the *Call* reported that "Jackie Robinson is still the rage everywhere he plays. He is one of the best infielders in the league as well as in Negro baseball. Jackie has keen spirit and is one of the best competitors. He enjoys every minute of every game and performs in a scintillating manner." Duncan called him "a vital cog in the inner works," adding, "He scoops up everything that comes his way and his bat has also been a big help to the club."[14]

Noting that Robinson was tied with Ted "Double Duty" Radcliffe for most home runs in the Negro American League with 5, the *Call* on August 10 also reported that the "jim-crow" railroad cars the Monarchs were forced to take in the South, were like "the heavily loaded Nazi slave trains which carried men and women to detention camps." For Robinson, they were just one of many examples of the deplorable travel conditions in the Negro Leagues.

The *Call* did not report on the signing of Robinson by Branch Rickey for the Brooklyn Dodgers organization in New York on August 28, 1945. Robinson had been sworn to secrecy by Rickey and did not tell the Monarchs he had signed. However, Monarchs co-owners J.L. Wilkinson and Tom Baird knew their star rookie had left the team and traveled to New York without telling them the reason for the trip.

The circumstances of Robinson's departure from the Monarchs after his meeting with Rickey are somewhat unclear. He apparently asked that he be

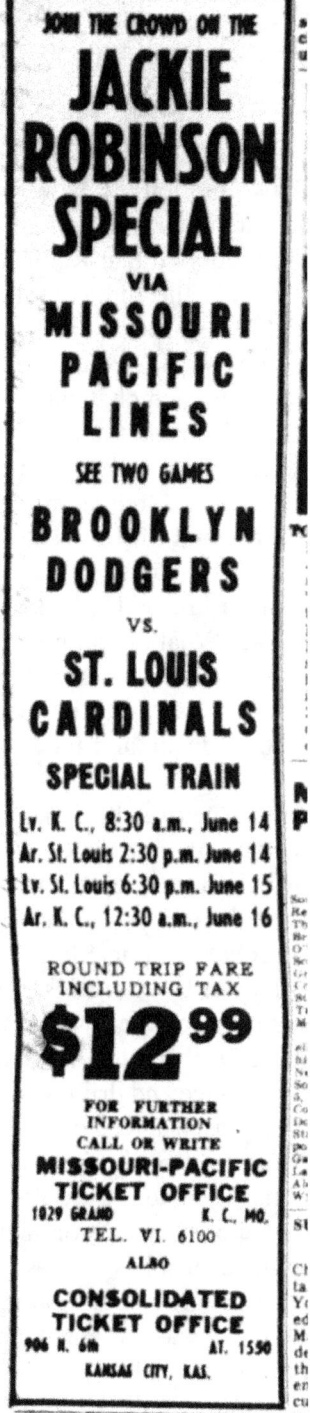

Kansas City Call, May 16, 1947.

Branch Rickey's prediction that black fans would flock to see him proved accurate. For an appearance of the Brooklyn Dodgers' rookie in St. Louis for games against the Cardinals on June 14-15, 1947, Missouri Pacific Railroad organized a "Jackie Robinson Special" to take fans from Kansas City. Needless to say, many who made the trip were Monarchs supporters, whose enthusiasm was now focused more on the former Monarchs player than the team from which Branch Rickey had raided him.

allowed to leave the Monarchs and return to California on September 21. According to Robinson, J.L. Wilkinson's son, Dick, chastised him for leaving the team to go to New York without permission and told him he would have to play out the 1945 Monarchs schedule or leave the team immediately. Robinson said he took offense and left the Monarchs.[15] Without mentioning that encounter, the September 14, 1945, edition of the *Call* reported that Robinson would not play in games against the Indianapolis Clowns on September 18 and 19 because he had been suspended. However, in the next week's edition the *Call* quoted J.L. Wilkinson as saying emphatically that Robinson had not been suspended from the Monarchs. "He was away from the team for a few days near the end of the season," Wilkinson stated, "but he was still a member of the team until the end of the season." According to Wilkinson, Robinson had not played the last few games because of an injury. He had returned to his home in California. "What his future plans are is not known," the Monarchs owner wanted it understood, "[b]ut the Monarch fans would be glad to see him again next season. ... Jackie left the team with clean hands."

According to the October 12, 1945, edition of the *Call*, Robinson was playing in California for the Kansas City Royals of Los Angeles. A crowd of 9,000 had seen him score the winning run in a game against Butch Moran's Coast League Stars on September 30 at Wrigley Field in Los Angeles. On October 5, before a standing-room-only crowd at Wrigley Field, the Royals beat the Bob Feller All-Stars, 4-2, with Robinson doubling twice and driving in a run.

When Jackie Robinson agreed on October 23, 1945, to play for the Montreal Royals, the Brooklyn affiliate in the International League, in the 1946 season, the *Call* noted in its October 26 edition that history was made at the signing, as Robinson "may be considered as the spearhead of Negro integration into baseball." Branch Rickey Jr., who was present at the signing representing his father, described Robinson as "intelligent and college bred, and I think he can take it too." In the same edition, the reactions of J.L. Wilkinson and Tom Baird to the signing of Robinson by the Dodgers organization were cited. From the outset, the two Monarchs owners were publicly supportive, although they felt they had not been fairly treated by Rickey. Tom Baird was quoted as saying, "I am happy to know that Jackie Robinson has been signed to play in the big leagues. It is a well-deserved advancement for the Negro race. He has my best wishes for his success.

The Monarchs management stands behind the idea of any man's advancement. We have no [intent] to hold any player down. I do think, however, that we should have been consulted in the matter. That would have been the proper way, but we shall do nothing to impede Jackie's progress. He played great ball for our team this season, fielding consistently and hitting .345. Of course, we would be happy to know that he would be with us again next season."

Two days before, on the basis of an Associated Press report, the *New York Times* claimed Baird planned to lodge a formal complaint with Commissioner Happy Chandler, telling him: "We won't take this lying down. Robinson signed a contract with us last year and I feel that he is our property."[16] What seems likely is that the more circumspect Wilkinson convinced his co-owner to change his tone. Wilkinson's first public statement on Robinson's signing clearly backed away from his partner's contention that an appeal to Commissioner Chandler was in order. "Although I feel the Brooklyn club or the Montreal club owes us some kind of consideration for Robinson," Wilkinson said, "we will not protest to Commissioner Chandler. I am very glad to see Jackie get this chance, and I'm sure he'll make good. He's a wonderful ballplayer. If and when he gets into the major leagues he will have a wonderful career."[17]

In the October 26 *Call* article, Baird claimed, "I was misquoted by the Associated Press story, if there was an implication that we are going to start a fight to keep Robinson out of the league, or we're going to cause him any trouble. We are glad of his advancement and hope more Negro players get the same opportunity. We are not in Negro baseball just to make money; we want to see the Negro race advance to full participation in American activities."

Also in the October 26 edition of the *Call*, the reactions of others to the signing of Robinson were outlined. Monarchs secretary Dizzy Dismukes said he had faith in Jackie and believed he would make good on any ball team. Manager Frank Duncan said he supported the selection of Robinson. Walter White, secretary of the NAACP, said, "I am delighted that big league baseball has grown up to its name." Fans along 18th Street in Kansas City were greeting each other by mentioning the advancement Robinson's signing represented. The *Call* then quoted what Robinson had said at the signing: "Of course, I can't begin to tell how happy I am to be the first of my race in organized baseball. I realize how much it means to me, to my race and to baseball. I can only say I'll do my best to come through in every way."

Call editor C.A. Franklin's editorial on the Robinson signing appeared on November 2, 1945. "Negroes like Robinson who are products of the better colleges in the U.S. know how to get along with their mates," Franklin commented. "They have no inferiority complex and therefore no chip-on-the-shoulder attitude. Negro players have already proven themselves capable in competition with white major leaguers that goes back to Rube Foster's Chicago team playing the world champion Cubs."

Then Franklin directed his comments to the African-American fans. "The Negro player's success will depend," he wrote, "on the Negro public. How will they deport themselves under the excitement of the game? Negro fans will have to maintain a brand of public conduct, not merely as good, but far better than the average. Otherwise, White fans would stay away and, forced to choose between old patrons and new, management would get rid of Negro players."

"Some conduct by Negro fans did not pass muster," Franklin wanted his readers to understand. He complained about "the chip-on-the-shoulder of those who push throughout the crowd on the street car, and by the thoughtless ones who make noise in the city as though they were all alone in the country."

Also in the October 26, 1945, edition, the *Call's* new sports editor, John L. Johnson, commended Wilkinson and Baird for their support of the signing of Robinson by Rickey, but had a caution. "There should be, however, a lesson in Robinson's going for owners of Negro clubs," Johnson wrote. "It is estimated that Negro baseball drew better than $2,000,000 through the turnstiles this year. This is not peanut money. There is considerable cost in training players until they become capable of playing jam-up baseball. If the owners of Negro baseball clubs are not organized sufficiently to prevent any Tom, Dick or Harry from plucking out of their team any desirable player they want, they should so organize, and the sooner the better. If a baseball magnate wants a player, let him pay the price. This is the American way. And any organization that can't prevent the plucking of its club's players is a shoddy one and should be reorganized … altogether."

In his "Sport-Light" column on November 2, Johnson reacted to Branch Rickey's claim that "Negro baseball is in the zone of a racket" and "I have not signed a player from what I regard as an organized league." Johnson responded by asking readers, "Isn't Negro baseball organized? Doesn't it have rules and regulations to go by; hasn't Negro baseball an organization with officials empowered to see that players and teams abide by their signed contracts?"

In the November 9, 1945, edition of the *Call* Johnson had a challenge for fans. He said that Jackie Robinson would likely face his first test with the Royals at spring training in Daytona Beach, Florida. Millions of American Negroes will be pulling for him as their "pathfinder, pioneering in organized baseball, making a way for future Negro ballplayers not yet toddling," Johnson predicted. "But 'pulling for him' is not enough."

"We should," Johnson wanted fans to understand, "write letters of congratulations when we approve and letters of strong protest when we do not. Letter writing is second only to voting in advancing our people. Branch Rickey would appreciate thousands of letters approving his stand. He undoubtedly received many disapproving letters. Blues singers used to sing: 'I can read your letters, but I can't read your mind.' … Letters have power. Letters will help Jackie Robinson."

Of all the reactions to the signing of Robinson, the comment of one anonymous African-American fan, cited in the October 26, 1945, edition of the *Call,* perhaps said it best: "Yes, sir, democracy means much more to me today than it did yesterday!"

The *Call* devoted extensive ink to the 1946 season Robinson spent with the Royals. In the April 12 edition of the *Call*, John L. Johnson claimed that "(w)hatever the future holds for Jackie Robinson and Jim Wright [another African American player Branch Rickey signed], currently playing with the Montreal Royals, no one who admires courage, stamina and the will to win can help but applaud these boys for the job they have done and are doing – for the race and for democracy."

In the April 26 edition of the *Call,* a banner headline stated that in Montreal's opening game in the 1946 International League season, "Robinson's Homer Helps Royals Top Jersey 14-1." Johnson exulted that "(m)illions of persons in America heard with pleasure the news telling of Jackie Robinson's thrilling debut in the league opener against the Jersey Giants." Then Johnson prophetically predicted that "Robinson's success in this interracial affair won not only for his team, but also won potential opportunity for many Negro boys who someday will find the route smoother by his performance."

In virtually every one of its editions during the 1946 season, the *Call* covered Robinson's performances in Montreal Royals games. For example, on June 7, 1946,

Jackie

the *Call* said Robinson was on his way to becoming the champion base stealer in the International League and was batting .347. However, the *Call's* editors knew that Robinson's successes had not magically opened the door for Blacks in other areas of American life. In the same edition, the failure of the Universities of Missouri and Oklahoma to admit African-American students was condemned.

In the midst of its coverage of Monarchs games against the Indianapolis Clowns in its July 26 edition, the *Call* noted that Robinson had homered in the first game of a doubleheader the Royals played against Syracuse and had four hits in the second game. It also reported that the Monarchs had established the Jackie Robinson Youth League in Kansas City and that Robinson was expected to be on hand to present the championship trophy at the end of the season.

In the August 9, 1946, edition of the *Call*, Robinson's role as a "crowd magnet" for the Royals both at home and on the road was featured. In a three-game series at Baltimore, more than 68,000 were in attendance. The next week, the *Call* quoted Robinson's Royals manager, Clay Hopper, a Southerner, praising Jackie for the way he "kept his head" during the "intense testing" he had faced and predicting that his prospects in baseball were "unlimited" because he had "the speed, the brains and the ability to play the game."

In the *Call's* September 20, 1946, edition, John Johnson heralded Robinson's winning of the International League's batting crown with a .349 average and 155 hits and claimed "(i)t is doubtful any other player could have done so well with the crushing odds that faced him." In the October 11 edition, the *Call's* report on the Montreal Royals winning of the Little World Series climaxed with the shout from the crowd after the clinching game: "We want Robinson!"

Despite his stunning performance in the 1946 season, Robinson was not immune from racial prejudice even among major-league players who knew how good he was. In his November 15 "Sport-Light" column, *Call* sports editor John L. Johnson quoted Cleveland Indians ace Bob Feller's claim that no Negro ballplayers, not even Robinson, were of "big league timber." Johnson responded: Feller has a right to "chomp his chinas" but "methinks that Bobbie's got a little color phobia in his peepers."

By the time Robinson joined Brooklyn for the 1947 season, the *Call's* coverage of how Jackie was faring with the Dodgers overwhelmed the paper's reporting on the Monarchs. The imbalance continued throughout the season. For example, an April 18 banner headline exulted, "Robinson Wins Friends Fast on Brooklyn Team." His first game at Ebbets Field had drawn over 24,000 fans, many Black, the *Call* noted. In its June 13 edition, the *Call* gave a banner headline to Robinson's "perfect day" (two singles, a double, and a triple) against the Cincinnati Reds, while a smaller headline read "Monarchs Drub Clowns." Jackie's first spat with an umpire drew comment in the July 4 edition of the *Call*, alongside the note that the Brooklyn rookie had hit in 18 games in a row and led the National League in steals. When Robinson wrenched his back and had to sit out a game, the September 12 *Call* took note. Alongside was an ad with Robinson's endorsement of Homogenized Bond Bread.

When the Monarchs sold the contracts of Willard Brown and Hank Thompson to the St. Louis Browns, John Johnson in his August 1, 1947, "Sport-Light" column in the *Call* noted that the Monarchs were becoming known as "foremost Negro preparatory school for the major leagues."

As the 1947 season drew to a close, there was relatively little mention of Monarchs games and players in the *Call*. The focus was on Robinson and the Dodgers reaching the World Series. For example, the October 3 edition proudly proclaimed that Jackie Robinson was "the first member of his race to play in a World Series game."

The decline of interest in the Negro Leagues after Jackie Robinson joined the Brooklyn Dodgers and the acquisition of other Black players was not unexpected and has been thoroughly documented. It is well illustrated by an ad in the *Call* on May 16, 1947, for a "Jackie Robinson Special" on June 14 that featured (for only $12.00) a train ride from Kansas City to St. Louis and back for two games between Robinson and the Brooklyn Dodgers and the St. Louis Cardinals.

SOURCES

In addition to the *Call*, portions of this essay are drawn from William A. Young, *J.L. Wilkinson and the Kansas City Monarchs: Trailblazers in Black Baseball* (Jefferson, North Carolina: McFarland & Company, 2016).

NOTES

1. *Kansas City Call*, December 29, 1939; November 22, 1940; August 8, 1941; September 5, 1941; September 19, 1941.
2. *Call*, October 27, 1944.
3. *Call*, March 16, 1945.
4. *Call*, April 13, 1945.
5. *Call*, May 11, 1945.

6 *Call*, June 1, 1945.
7 *Call*, June 8, 1945.
8 *Call*, June 15, 1945.
9 *Call*, June 22, 1945.
10 *Call*, July 6, 1945.
11 *Call*, July 13, 1945.
12 *Call*, July 27, 1945.

13 *Call*, August 10, 1945.
14 *Call*, July 27, 1945.
15 Arnold Rampersad, *Jackie Robinson: A Biography* (New York: Alfred A. Knopf, 1997), 128.
16 *New York Times*, October 24, 1945.
17 Cited in Janet Bruce, *The Kansas City Monarchs: Champions of Black Baseball* (Lawrence: University of Kansas, 1985), 112.

FORD FRICK AND JACKIE ROBINSON: THE ENABLER

by Dave Bohmer

Ford Frick, president of the National League in 1947, is not the first person who comes to mind concerning Jackie Robinson and the integration of baseball, though he deserves more consideration than he has been given. While no other individual rivals the role played by Branch Rickey in breaking the game's color barrier, other than Robinson himself, many others were certainly important. Some of Robinson's teammates stand out, particularly Pee Wee Reese, who was from a Southern state and yet demonstrated early support for Jackie. Manager Leo Durocher played a major role until he was banned from the game for a year, just before the start of the 1947 season. His strong backing helped overcome resistance on the part of some of the Dodgers' Southern players during spring training in 1947. The relatively new commissioner, Happy Chandler, also has received recognition, though his role may have been far less important than once thought.[1] In actuality, Frick was the only individual who had a formal role to play other than Rickey in integrating baseball. All major-league players had to be approved by the respective league president before they were allowed on the club roster. The only person other than the Dodgers who could formally block Robinson, except, perhaps, under the "best interests of baseball" clause, was the National League president – Frick.

The personal history of Ford Frick does not appear to have been one that would shape a progressive mindset on the issue of baseball integration. He was born in 1894 in Wawaka, Indiana, a small railroad town in the northeastern part of the state, and grew up in a similar community, Brimfield, five miles to the east. There were no Blacks in either town or any in his public schools. At 15, he spent a year in Fort Wayne, Indiana, where he briefly attended a business school and worked as a copyboy for a local newspaper. Again, any contact in the city with African Americans would have been very limited at best. His four years as a student at DePauw University would not have broadened his horizons either. The only African-American student in attendance was there part-time in the School of Music, a distinct entity separate from the College of Liberal Arts, where most students like Frick studied.[2] After graduation from DePauw in 1915, Frick moved to Colorado, where he spent most of his seven years in the state working for a newspaper in Colorado Springs. Again, his interaction with Blacks would have been limited, at best. Even his move to the far more cosmopolitan New York City to work as a sportswriter for the Hearst papers would not have expanded his horizons. His coverage focused on baseball, which was, of course, fully segregated at the time, and he lived in Bronxville, New York, an almost exclusively hite suburb of the city. His fellow sportswriters were all Caucasian. None of these experiences or exWposures would have broadened his horizons on race.

In fact, one experience would have seemed to foster the opposite perspective. During his time as a sportswriter from 1922 to 1933, Frick became one of the founders of the New York Base Ball Writers Association of America, an organization of men in the city who covered the sport. It was, reflecting the era, an all-White organization. The association quickly expanded to other cities, but the New York group became notorious for putting on the major baseball social event of the year, held in early February in conjunction with the annual scheduling meetings for the two major leagues. Consequently, the event drew all the top brass of the sport and quickly evolved into a roast of the game's elite, performed by some of the writers. During the first decades, that roast was always done in the form of a minstrel show.[3] The writers would dress up in blackface to look the stereotypical part of minstrel singers. For as long as he was a sportswriter in New York, Frick was one of the key participants in the show. In essence, like many Americans during this period, Frick unquestionably participated in helping to perpetuate racial stereotypes.

Frick's performances in the Association's annual event ended in March 1934 when he was hired as head of the National League Service Bureau, the promotional arm of the league offices. He would remain a regular attendee during his long baseball career. At year's end,

114

when John Heydler retired as National League president, Frick was named to replace him, beginning what would become a 17-year tenure in that capacity, ending only when he was elected commissioner in 1951. The new position still would not have had any meaningful impact on Frick's interaction with or perception of minorities. While he no longer dressed in blackface, his daily interactions saw little change, as the game he presided over remained a White man's game. The only on-field interaction between Black and White players occurred in offseason barnstorming and exhibition games. There is no evidence that Frick attended such games, which might have broadened his horizons had he done so.

During this period, in the thick of the Great Depression, interest in integrating the game began to grow, though much of the advocacy came from African-American or Communist newspapers. Reflecting that interest, Wendell Smith, assistant sports editor of the *Pittsburgh Courier*, a Black newspaper, was able to arrange an interview with Frick in February of 1939, in the lobby of a Pittsburgh hotel, to ascertain his thoughts on the possibility of integration. Why Frick was chosen is unclear, although his being a relative newcomer to the front office compared with AL President William Harridge and Commissioner Kenesaw Mountain Landis, combined with the fact that Pittsburgh was a National League city, may have made him seem more accessible. Frick's comments, however, certainly did not give Smith any hope that the NL president would have any inclination to be a crusader for change.

In answering Smith's questions, Frick contended that the largest obstacles to bringing a Black man into baseball were the players and the fans. Frick said many in both groups were not ready to accept integration and would create problems both on the field and in the stands. He also pointed out that spring training in the South would present major difficulties due to Jim Crow and that travel to many major-league cities would also offer challenges since many hotels and restaurants did not accept Black guests. Frick further stressed that such separation of players could impact a team's cohesiveness. In addition, he emphasized that the owners and executives of baseball were not the barriers to ending segregation and even pointed out that the sport had no formal policy barring Blacks.[4] Smith published the interview and then followed it up with numerous additional sessions during the season with National League players and managers. His articles on those interviews revealed that there was less opposition to integration, at least on the part of those whom Smith questioned, than what Frick had suggested.[5] The clear implication of the interviews, when Smith presented them in his articles, was that the barrier was exactly where Frick said it wasn't – with the owners and other executives. While the various articles by Smith never appeared in the White press, taken in context with the comments of the players and managers questioned, Frick's assertions implied, at least to later historians of the game, that the NL president may himself have been one of the major barriers to integration.

Interestingly, Smith's interview with Frick was not the first time the league president had been quoted in the African-American press. In August of 1936, the *Chicago Defender* ran a story, originally printed in the Communist *Daily Worker*, that quoted Frick on the status of Blacks playing in the major leagues. Less than two years into his job as NL president, Frick claimed he did "not recall one instance where baseball had allowed either race, creed or color to enter into the question of the selection of its players." He quickly added that the issue involved all clubs in the league and was ... "not within the province or the authority of the league president to express an official opinion in the matter." As he did later in the Smith interview, he mentioned the problem in Southern states with spring training, and then stated what would be a position he held throughout his baseball career, that "(t)he whole subject is a 'sociological problem,' something society, not the big leagues, must solve."[6] Consistent with the Smith story, Frick would deny any formal barrier and then offer other reasons as to why there were no Blacks playing in the majors or minors.

In fairness, the perception of Frick being a major barrier may not be totally appropriate. Given his regular interaction with NL owners, he clearly understood in 1939, after almost five years in the job, and even as far back as 1936, that none of the magnates had expressed any interest in signing Black players. He also was well aware that it was those same owners who had hired him, would renew his contract and, in between, pay his salary. Even if the likelihood was limited that his comments to a Black or communist newspaper journalist would ever be known by any of his club owners, he wasn't inclined to take that risk. Further, not all of his comments were off the mark. Robinson in 1947 did have problems with players, managers, and fans. There were also difficulties during spring training in Florida and on being allowed in hotels and restaurants on Dodgers road trips during the season.

His perception that a Black player would have difficulties was certainly proved accurate during Robinson's rookie season. Nonetheless, Frick's comments left the impression in later years, thanks in large part to Chris Lamb's article about the Smith interview, that the National League president was one of the barriers to baseball integration.

That perception had actually been created well before Lamb's article, thanks to allegations made by Bill Veeck in his classic 1962 book *Veeck as in Wreck*. Veeck claimed that Frick had blocked him from acquiring the Philadelphia Phillies in 1942-43 because he had planned to field a team of Black players. The maverick former owner also claimed in the book that the NL president subsequently bragged to others that he had stopped Veeck from buying the team and thus "contaminating the league."[7] Frick, still commissioner at the time, never denied the claims, but he also never commented on numerous other criticisms of him that Veeck leveled in the book. Interestingly, the topic of the Phillies story has in recent years become an ongoing debate among baseball scholars as to the extent of veracity of Veeck's allegations. Jules Tygiel, in his classic study of Robinson and integration, reaffirmed Veeck's story, including the claim about Frick. Other than citing Veeck's book, however, his only further evidence was an interview he did with the maverick executive in 1980, when he still owned the White Sox for a second time. As the definitive study of the Robinson story, Tygiel's book furthered the perception of Frick as an ardent opponent of integrating the game before 1947.[8] In essence, his study strengthened Veeck's earlier claims.

In spite of all the research that's been done since, with some authors questioning and others supporting Veeck's claim, the actual facts in the attempt to purchase the Phillies are quite limited and rather elusive.[9] The most salient details come from a special meeting of the National League's board of directors held at Frick's offices on November 4, 1942. The meeting was called by the NL president due to the extremely precarious financial situation of the Phillies as well as the extent to which the league was involved financially because of its extensive loans to the club. Phillies owner Gerald Nugent claimed during the meeting that Veeck had approached him about buying the club, indicating that the owner of the minor-league Milwaukee Brewers had some local money behind him. However, Nugent added that he hadn't "heard back from him and that was three weeks ago."[10] Later in the meeting, Frick indicated that he, too, had been approached by Veeck, even before the prospective buyer had met with Nugent. Frick claimed Veeck had indicated being able to meet the minimum amount expected by the shareholders, estimated at $154,000, but added that it was unclear if the total figure the prospective buyer had in mind was $200,000 or $400,000, further acknowledging that either number was unacceptable to Nugent. He too had heard nothing further from Veeck since. No mention was made of any plans he might have had for the club.[11] In subsequent meetings of the board, on November 30 and at the annual meeting of the owners over the next two days, a potential buyer was mentioned, but no name was offered in the minutes. The tenor of the discussion suggested it wasn't Veeck, because he had specifically been discussed at the earlier meeting. By the next meeting of the National League, on February 9 in New York, a deal had been reached to sell the club to a partnership headed by William Cox. After the November 4 meeting, Veeck was never mentioned again as a potential buyer in any league records.

Other than the acknowledgement of Veeck's interest by Frick and Nugent in early November and also a small piece in *The Sporting News* in October of 1942, there is no evidence that a formal offer was ever made. None of the primary sources suggest that a Veeck offer was rejected either directly or behind the scenes. There is also no evidence that Veeck ever had a formal meeting with Landis. There is also no historical record that Frick ever bragged to others that he had blocked Veeck from buying the team, or any indication of how Veeck would have heard that the league president had done so. All assertions that this happened are based upon interviews with various parties that took place well after the Phillies were sold, in some cases many years later. Beyond the fact that Veeck had expressed interest and then did not appear to follow through on it, there is nothing in any primary sources to verify the rest of his allegations. Whatever Frick's views and regardless of what he knew of Veeck's intent, he did not appear from the sources to have blocked any effort to purchase the woebegone Phillies, a club both Frick and the NL owners were desperate to see someone buy to get the financial burden off their backs.

While Frick may not have had much of a relationship with Veeck in 1943, he did have a friendship with Branch Rickey, the man who would ultimately integrate the game. It became even closer around the time the Phillies were sold, when Rickey left the Cardinals to replace Larry MacPhail as president of the Brooklyn Dodgers. Both men now resided in the New York area. Frick and Rickey also shared many commonalities in their backgrounds. They both grew up in small Midwestern communities. Both were products of deeply religious families. Both went to small Methodist liberal-arts colleges in the Midwest. Before moving to Brooklyn, the two had also interacted on many matters after Frick became NL president, including the suspension of Dizzy Dean and the threats Commissioner Landis presented to the Cardinals farm system that Rickey had so carefully developed. The two had also interacted regularly for almost a decade at the various league meetings and obviously had even more opportunities to cross paths when Rickey moved to Brooklyn. There is no formal record of when and how often the two might have discussed the issue of integration before or after Rickey signed Robinson to a minor-league contract in late 1945, but it is difficult to imagine there weren't conversations between them, especially given Frick's role in approving all players in the National League.

That relationship may have been of considerable importance in August of 1946 when the MacPhail Commission report was presented to a joint meeting of the two leagues. The report, so named because Larry MacPhail, part-owner of the Yankees, chaired the committee that drafted it, was largely meant to address problems of labor unrest in the majors and well as players jumping to the Mexican League. During its numerous meetings in the summer of 1946, the committee, which included the two league presidents, Tom Yawkey of the Red Sox, Sam Breadon of the Cardinals, and Phil Wrigley of the Cubs, was well aware that Jackie Robinson was playing for the Montreal Royals, the Dodgers' Triple-A club. In fact, it spent close to three pages of its 25-page report addressing the "Race Question." In the end, the report made no formal recommendations as it had on numerous other issues, though it did suggest that "(t)he individual action of any one Club may exert tremendous pressures upon the whole structure of Professional Baseball, and could conceivably result in lessening the value of several Major League franchises." It added: "Your Committee does not desire to question the motives of any organization or individual who is sincerely opposed to segregation or who believes that such a policy is detrimental in the best interests of Professional Baseball."[12]

All six committee participants, including Frick and William Harridge, the American League president, signed off on the report. At the joint meeting of the two leagues, the report's recommendations were adopted unanimously by both leagues, at which the Dodgers were represented by Branch Rickey.[13] However, the segment of the report concerning integration was never formally brought up at the meeting in any fashion, even though Rickey claimed a year and a half later, in a speech at Wilberforce College in Ohio, that owners had voted 15 to 0 against integration, with Rickey abstaining.[14] There was no such vote in the recorded meeting. Only issues like the creation of an executive committee with player representation, a minimum wage, spring-training money, and research to start a pension plan were actually enacted. Since there was no segment of the meeting that was off the record, it is fair to conclude that the discussion and vote may never have taken place that day.[15] Knowing the potential controversy it would generate, and likely aware of Rickey's plans with Robinson, it is possible that Frick, the committee member most inclined to have been supportive of Robinson, helped to persuade the other committee members and owners to exclude that segment of the report from any action. If so, Frick helped to avoid a potential controversy from coming to a head.[16]

What did remain clear was that Frick was the only person, other than the Dodgers ownership, who could have blocked Jackie Robinson from joining the club's roster. Any major-league ballplayer in each league could not be added to the roster of their club until he was approved by the president of the respective league. In essence, Frick had to sign off on Robinson's contract before he could become a Dodger. In theory, the commissioner, Happy Chandler, could have weighed in on the matter, but only by blocking Robinson under the "best interests of baseball" clause. That wasn't likely, given the aftermath of World War II, even though most owners still appeared to oppose integration. Rickey himself declared the issue of Robinson to be solely "a league matter,"[17] thus not involving Chandler. The general manager's decision to bring Robinson up from Montreal to the Dodgers and Frick's signature on the contract were all that were necessary to make baseball and national history.

It would not be the last time, though, that Frick would play an important role in the Robinson saga. From the time Robinson was brought into what had been "White" baseball, there were suggestions that some ballplayers would refuse to play on the same team. When Robinson was placed on the Triple-A Montreal Royals, their manager, Clay Hopper, who was from Mississippi, questioned having a Black man on his club.[18] There was major opposition from Southern ballplayers in the 1947 Dodger spring-training camp, precipitating concern that there would be a player rebellion. Leo Durocher's efforts helped to stop that threat.[19] By the time the season started, the Dodgers players seemed ready to accept Robinson as a teammate. It was less clear, however, whether players on other teams would be willing to play against him. That issue came to a head in early May when the St. Louis Cardinals came to Brooklyn for their first series of the season against the Dodgers. Sam Breadon, owner of the Cardinals, was deeply concerned that some of his players would refuse to take the field against Robinson, enough so that he made a special trip to New York to discuss the matter with Frick. The understanding of what happened next has varied somewhat, depending upon the source. At one level, there supposedly was no real threat of a strike. It was merely a lot of talk on the part of some players, but nothing beyond that. According to other accounts, Frick met with Breadon and gave the Cardinals owner the message to convey to the strike-threatening players, convincing them there would be severe repercussions for anyone who refused to play. Other versions suggested that Frick himself talked with the players who intended to strike and threatened them that they would be putting their baseball futures in jeopardy. A recent article even asserts that nothing may have happened because there had never been any real threat of a strike in the first place.[20]

In many ways the actual story is as elusive as was Bill Veeck's attempt to buy the Phillies. Other than the accounts written directly after the series in the New York press, especially the original story by Stanley Woodward in the *New York Herald Tribune* on May 9, along with stories in the *New York Times* on both May 9 and 10, there is no primary evidence other than the later recollections of Frick, Breadon, Cardinals manager Eddie Dyer, and the players. The *Herald Tribune* quoted Frick as having given a powerful speech but the NL president later claimed the story was overblown. The *Times* on May 10 quoted Frick as saying it was a dead issue, that "a mountain had been made out of a molehill, anyway."[21] The article went on to say that Breadon denied the story, that he had only come to town to help his slumping Cardinals. Dyer echoed Breadon's version.[22] Whatever occurred, it was clear that all parties involved didn't want the publicity it was receiving in the press and thus shared an interest in downplaying the story. Those desires from the parties directly involved did not stop Arthur Daley of the *Times* from praising Frick for his actions the following Tuesday in his "Sports of the Times" column. Daley concluded, based in part on the original Woodward article, that Frick had dealt the anti-Robinson movement "a sledgehammer blow from which it will never recover."[23] Essentially, in assessing the various accounts, something had unquestionably transpired when the Cardinals came to Brooklyn that caught the attention of local sportswriters and, whatever occurred, its outcome ended any threat of a strike. Further, Frick had played a role in that event, to which he would often proudly refer in later years.[24]

That role, whatever it may have been, and his approval to add Robinson to the Dodgers roster were likely instrumental in Frick joining Robinson and Rickey as the recipients of two Thomas Jefferson prizes in 1948. The awards were presented by the Council Against Intolerance in America. Robinson, for his efforts on the diamond, received an award for "the advancement of democracy during 1947." Rickey and Frick were recipients for having broken "the color barrier in American baseball." Both awards were decided by a nationwide poll of officials of 1,000 civic organizations along with editors of 500 newspapers. Rickey and Frick were ranked first in the public-service classification of the awards.[25] The honors were presented at the annual banquet in New York on April 11, where 250 witnessed Frick accepting the award.[26] Neither Rickey nor Robinson attended the event, perhaps because the baseball season had not started yet and both were still engaged in spring training in Florida. In any case, all three had received recognition for what had unquestionably been one of the most impactful events in the country in 1947. It was Frick, not Chandler, who was seen as the facilitator of Robinson integrating baseball.

As other clubs integrated, especially the Indians and Giants, and the Dodgers added other Black players, Robinson became a more accepted part of baseball. It was also inevitable that he would be treated like other players, neither singled out favorably or unfavorably due to his race. After the 1948 season, Robinson was released from his promise to Rickey to keep his emotions under control while playing. Once freed of that pledge, Robinson, known for his temper, was likely to come under the perusal of the league office, still presided over by Frick. There is no account of Robinson actually being fined for misbehavior while Frick remained NL president, with nothing at all reported in 1949 and 1950, but there was a major incident reported early in the 1951 season. Robinson claimed that some of the NL umpires were "on him" and he expected to hear from Frick about an incident with Babe Pinelli.[27] The specifics of the Pinelli incident were never explained, but two weeks later Frick weighed in on Robinson's behavior, saying that he "was tired" of his "popping off, and all that business" and that he would control the player if Brooklyn couldn't. Walter O'Malley, now majority owner of the club, said Robinson "has the full support of the Dodger organization."[28] Nothing more was published about Robinson's conflicts with umpires, suggesting that after the early-season publicity, the issue had cooled off and was resolved quietly.

Once Frick became commissioner later in 1951, the oversight of Robinson's on-field behavior came under the jurisdiction of the new NL president, Warren Giles. There was one matter, however, that the commissioner, overseeing the best interests of the game, couldn't avoid. On November 30, 1952, Robinson appeared on a New York television show called *Youth Wants to Know* and near the end of the program one teenager asked him if he thought the Yankees were "prejudiced against Negro players"? After a pause, the Dodger responded candidly: "I think the Yankee management is prejudiced. There isn't a single Negro on the team and very few in the entire Yankee farm system."[29] Unsurprisingly, the Yankees front office countered his claims and filed a complaint with Frick. The issue hit the city newspapers as the Yankees applied pressure on the commissioner to censure Robinson. Frick did speak with Robinson, asking him to "soft-pedal" such comments going forward. At the same time, he added and stressed publicly that a ballplayer "still has the right of free speech."[30] The issue passed from coverage, but it appeared that Robinson toned down his comments without tempering his views on numerous matters. Years later, Robinson claimed that Frick's support of his right of free speech was an important part of ensuring his success in integrating the game.[31]

Many years after Robinson retired from baseball, but while Frick was still commissioner, the man who had integrated the majors did offer a criticism of Frick's leadership. Robinson had published a book in 1964 titled *Baseball Has Done It*, a series of stories mostly by Black players about their experiences in baseball as minorities, in some cases having broken the color barrier on their club. Much of the theme centered on the growing civil-rights movement in the South in the early 1960s and the effort by Blacks to gain rights that were still denied them in the formerly Confederate states. The stories contained many encounters with discrimination in the South against African-American players during spring training as well as while they played for minor-league clubs in many of the cities. Near the end of the book, Robinson asserted: "Baseball, which has profited greatly both at the box office and in the quality of play from Negro participation, should stop ducking the broader issue of civil rights. ... You, Mr. Commissioner, are a general who doesn't know he has an army or is in a war."[32] In essence, baseball should have put more pressure on the South to force an end to discrimination as well as to protect its Black players. Ironically, earlier in the book, Frick had actually provided an explanation for his lack of having done so: "Baseball's function is not to lead crusades, not to settle sociological problems, not to become involved in any sort of controversial racial or religious question."[33] Their independent comments in the same book demonstrated how far apart their views were as the civil-rights movement in the South came to a head at the end of Frick's tenure.

Frick's comments in Robinson's book are in actuality a fair summary of his views and, given his comments printed in the *Defender* in 1936, seem to have been consistent throughout his baseball career. Ford Frick was never a crusader. It was not in his nature to get out in front of an issue, especially not to push his collection of magnates too far in directions they didn't want to go. At the same time, his inclination and personal beliefs tended heavily toward fairness. While his life experience never produced many interactions with African-Americans, he was not hesitant to step into a situation if he felt it fair and proper to do so. Hence, if Rickey wanted to integrate the Dodgers by adding Robinson to the 25-man roster, Frick would support it. Further, if others attempted to bring obstacles to prevent Robinson from playing, Frick would not hesitate to intervene. While he was never proactive in the integration of baseball, he played an important role in ensuring that it came about and would be maintained as Robinson's and other Black players careers continued. Thus, it is not surprising, as shown earlier in this essay, to see Robinson both praise Frick for his personal support and criticize him for not being more proactive on African-American matters in later years. While not a crusader, Frick was consistent in the way he treated Robinson and other ballplayers, with no favoritism or discrimination, but rather with equal support for their careers in baseball. In that way, Frick was an important component of Jackie's story, as Robinson himself would later recognize.

NOTES

1. John Paul Hill, "Commissioner A.B. 'Happy' Chandler and the Integration of Major League Baseball: A Reassessment," *Nine: A Journal of Baseball History and Culture*, 19, no. 1 (2000): 28-51. Hill points out that Chandler's role was not a formal one in activating Robinson.

2. Wes Wilson, email message to author, February 18, 2020. Wilson is a former archivist at DePauw University.

3. "Baseball Diners Cheer for Walker," *New York Times*, March 22, 1926: 21, references Frick and the minstrel show during the annual gathering.

4. Chris Lamb, "Baseball's Whitewash: Sportswriter Wendell Smith Exposes Major League Baseball's Big Lie," *Nine: A Journal of Baseball History and Culture*, 18, no. 1 (2009): 1-2. Lamb expands on the topic in his book *Conspiracy of Silence: Sportswriters and the Long Campaign to Desegregate Baseball* (Lincoln: University of Nebraska Press, 2012), 133-35.

5. Lamb, "Baseball's Whitewash": 7-16.

6. Ted Benson (from the *Sunday Worker*). "'League Open to Negroes' Says Frick, League Prexy," *Chicago Defender* (National edition), August 29, 1936: 13.

7. Bill Veeck with Ed Linn, *Veeck as in Wreck* (Chicago: University of Chicago Press, 1962), 171-72.

8. Jules Tygiel, *Baseball's Great Experiment* (New York: Oxford University Press, 1983), 40-41.

9. The Phillies story has certainly been the subject of considerable debate over the last two decades plus. It was started by David Jordan, Larry Gerlach, and John Rossi in "A Baseball Myth Exploded: Bill Veeck and the 1943 Sale of the Phillies," *National Pastime* (SABR: 1998): 18. Their article basically attempted to debunk the entire story. Their conclusion was partially questioned in 2006 in Jules Tygiel, "Revisiting Bill Veeck and the 1943 Phillies." *Baseball Research Journal*, (2006): 109-114. Tygiel essentially drew the same conclusion as does this paper, that there are very limited records to verify the claim. He did note that evidence showed there were indications of Veeck's idea of an integrated club during the war much earlier than his 1962 book made it public, although nothing that dated back to 1942 or 1943. In his well-researched biography of Veeck, Paul Dickson, *Bill Veeck: Baseball's Greatest Maverick* (New York: Walker & Company, 2012), argues that the Phillies story was true, devoting part of a chapter and a 10-page appendix to the issue. See pages 79-80 and 357-66. However, an article a year later again pointed out what Tygiel had claimed earlier, that no new primary evidence was presented. See Norman L. Macht and Robert D. Warrington, "The Veracity of Veeck," *Baseball Research Journal*, 42, no.2 (2013). In particular, they had a strong response to Dickson's claim that Frick never denied Veeck's allegations against him. "Frick adopted the diplomatic stance of silence, as people often do in refusing to dignify an unfounded accusation with a response." There are numerous cases during his career in baseball where Frick indeed behaved in such a fashion, choosing not to respond publicly to negative comments and thus dignify them, as I have found in my research on him.

10. National League Board of Directors Meeting Minutes, November 4, 1942, 90-91.

11. National League Board of Directors Meeting Minutes, 137.

12. *Report of Major League Steering Committee for Submission to the National and American Leagues at their Meetings in Chicago*, August 27, 1946.

13. *Joint Meeting of Major League Baseball Clubs*, Blackstone Hotel, Chicago, August 28, 1946, 13. Rickey was absent at the start, but present soon after for all the votes.

14. Roscoe McGowen, "Rickey Agrees That Club Owners Might Not Recall Anti-Negro Vote," *New York Times*, February 19, 1948: 31. In the issue the day before, Rickey had claimed the vote took place at the same meeting in April of 1945 at which Chandler was voted in as commissioner, claiming it had happened before Robinson had even played a game. In fact, Rickey had not signed Robinson until October of that year. He downplayed his Wilberforce assertion to claim he was merely trying to show how far baseball owners had progressed. in less than two years.

15. *Joint Meeting*, August 28, 1946, 1-31.

16. It may have come to a head the day before and Rickey may have been correct about a controversy and even a secret vote. On August 27 there was an unrecorded joint meeting of the owners. The minutes of the August 28 meeting twice, on pages 6 and 25, make reference to a session the previous day, implying that those in attendance on the 28th were there the day before. Further, the actual report states on its title page "For submission to National and American Leagues on 27 August, 1946." The comments refer to "meetings," unclear whether that meant the leagues met separately or that there was more than one meeting during the day on the 27th. In any case, there are no minutes recording the session(s). One can only surmise what went took place the day before, but it's clear what action items were carried over to the following day. The issue of integration, still in the original report, was definitely not brought forward. It was also suggested by Rickey that copies of the "MacPhail Report" were collected after the meetings, most likely due to the acknowledgment in the report that the reserve clause had no legal standing, not because of the comments on integration. Without minutes or surviving attendees, what took place in Chicago on August 27 will likely remain unknown.

17. Lee Lowenfish, *Branch Rickey: Baseball's Ferocious Gentleman* (Lincoln: University of Nebraska Press, 2007), 425.

18. Tygiel, *Experiment*, 103-04.

19. Tygiel, *Experiment*, 168-73.

20. See Warren Corbett, "The Strike Against Jackie Robinson: Truth or Myth?" *Baseball Research Journal* 46 (2017), no. 1. Corbett's conclusion is that Breadon overreacted, there was never a real threat, and New York sportswriters wrote about the event out of all proportion to what actually happened. Wendell Smith, Robinson's traveling partner for the 1947 season, said it "made a better newspaper story than anything else." However, much of Corbett's conclusion appears to be based on supposition and comments that came much later from some who were on the Cardinals, not actual data directly after the event. The newspaper coverage at the time still remains the best primary source as neither Frick nor Breadon kept any records of the meeting. It is clear there was some concern at the start of the series that Cardinal players would boycott the game and that Frick appeared to play a role in preventing them from doing so. It is not surprising that both Frick and Breadon downplayed the issue since it was in everyone's interest for the story to go away.

21. "Robinson Reveals Written Threats," *New York Times*, May 10, 1947: 16.

22. "Robinson Reveals Written Threats."

23. Arthur Daley, "The Passing Baseball Scene," *New York Times*, May 13, 1947: 32.

24. John P. Carvalho, *Frick,*:* Baseball's Third Commissioner* (Jefferson, North Carolina: McFarland & Company, Inc. 2016), 123-26; Ford C. Frick, *Games, Asterisks, and People* (New York: Crown Publishers, Inc.), 97-98; Jackie Robinson, *Baseball Has Done It* (Philadelphia: Lippincott, 1964), 113-14; and Buzzie Bavasi, email message to author, January 22, 2008. Bavasi, in particular, was adamant that Frick met directly with the players and threatened to remove them from baseball and keep them out for as long as he remained NL president. I had sent Bavasi an article on Frick for him to review in 2008, stating in it that whether the meeting with the Cardinals players actually occurred and who conducted it was unclear. He stated unequivocally that the meeting with Frick took place and that he was there to help arrange it. Obviously, like other sources, his comments stem from memory many years later.

25 "Major Flashes Column," *The Sporting News*, February 25, 1948: 23. "Honor Robinson, Rickey: Frick Also Cited for Breaking Color Barrier in Baseball," *New York Times*, February 16, 1948: 27.

26 "Intolerance Group Presents Awards," *New York Times*, April 12, 1948: 23.

27 "Umpires Irk Robinson," *New York Times,* April 21, 1951: 12.

28 "Dodger Office Backs Jackie; Ford Frick Explains Blast," *The Sporting News*, May 9, 1951: 2.

29 Tygiel, *Experiment*, 295.

30 "Bavasi Berates Bombers," *New York Times*, December 3, 1952: 47.

31 Jackie Robinson, *I Never Had It Made* (New York: Putnam Publishing Co., 1972), 102. Robinson added "Without that kind of support from some of the people in baseball who had power, I could not have made it, no matter how well I performed, no matter how loyal black people were."

32 Robinson, *Baseball Has Done It*, 212.

33 *Baseball Has Done It*, 109.

JACKIE ROBINSON PLAYS HIS FIRST EXHIBITION GAME FOR THE MONTREAL ROYALS

MARCH 17, 1946: BROOKLYN DODGERS 7, MONTREAL ROYALS 2, AT CITY ISLAND BALLPARK, DAYTONA BEACH, FLORIDA

by Bob Webster

On October 23, 1945, it was announced that Branch Rickey had signed Jackie Robinson to play for the Montreal Royals, the Brooklyn Dodgers' top farm team. The plan was for Robinson to play a season in Montreal to get the professional experience needed to determine if he was ready for the major leagues. In the winter of 1946, newlyweds Jack and Rachel Robinson left their home in Los Angeles for the Dodgers' spring-training camp. After being bumped off two flights to allow White passengers to have their seats, they had to take a bus from Pensacola to Jacksonville before arriving at the spring-training site. Even on that bus, the Robinsons were ordered to sit in the back.[1]

Rickey chose Daytona Beach as the Dodgers' spring-training site because it had fewer discrimination problems than other Florida cities. During a visit there in September 1945, Rickey noticed something that was different from many Southern cities – Daytona Beach had Black bus drivers, a Black middle class, and a Black political presence.[2] Rickey met with Mayor William Perry and City Manager James Titus numerous times before deciding on Daytona Beach. Titus was not at all concerned about Robinson's presence. He said, "We have a very good situation here between the races because we give the Negroes everything we give the whites. … There is no discrimination, but there is segregation."[3]

Daytona Beach, though, did not have enough fields to accommodate the hundreds of players trying out for the many teams in the organization. The Royals trained 40 miles away in Sanford, Florida, until enough players were cut and all of the teams could train in Daytona Beach.

Johnny Wright joined Robinson in spring training so Robinson would have another Black person with whom to work through this journey. Both players were sent to Sanford. The two arrived on the morning of March 4 with Wendell Smith, a writer for the *Pittsburgh Courier*, at the time the largest Black newspaper in the country, along with Billy Rowe, a *Courier* photographer. Smith had been hired by Rickey to look after Robinson and Wright.[4] As the four men stood in their street clothes and looked across the field at Sanford, they saw a couple of hundred Montreal and St. Paul players taking batting practice and shagging flies, among other spring-training activities. As soon as the players saw the four Black men, Robinson recalled, "It seemed that every one of these men stopped suddenly in his tracks and that 400 eyes were trained on Wright and me."[5]

After just the second day of practice, a White man told Black journalists that 100 or so townspeople would take matters into their own hands if Robinson and Wright were not "out of town by nightfall."[6]

The two immediately returned to Daytona Beach and trained at Kelly Field in the Black section of town. Smith and Rickey wanted to keep this incident as a secret, to avoid fueling any fires that might be stoked by reporters who did not want the two to play major-league baseball.[7]

Robinson joue le rôle de héros

"Jackie Robinson plays the role of hero," La Patrie *(Montreal), April 20, 1946.*

Daytona Beach was a better place for Robinson and Wright to stay and play baseball. The city was home to Bethune-Cookman College, founded by Mary McLeod Bethune, one of the nation's most influential Black citizens. Bethune gained the respect of President Franklin Delano Roosevelt and Eleanor Roosevelt. The first lady even appeared at a couple of fundraisers for the college. Events like this brought local Black and White residents together in a positive way.[8]

In Daytona Beach the Robinsons stayed with Joe and Duff Harris. Joe was a pharmacist and business leader in town. Wright stayed with Vernon Smith, a retired real estate agent. Smith and a couple of others involved in helping Robinson and Wright stayed at the college. The White players stayed in the Riviera Hotel.[9]

On the field, Robinson tried to impress his coaches by throwing the ball as hard as he could but hurt his arm in the process. His hitting also suffered. He said, "I could hear them shouting in the stands, and I wanted to produce so much that I was tense and over-anxious. I found myself swinging hard enough to break my back. I started swinging at bad balls and doing a lot of things I wouldn't have done under ordinary circumstances. I wanted to get a hit for them because they were pulling so hard for me."[10]

After the first day of practice, Robinson's arm was so sore he could barely lift it and had trouble sleeping that night. Royals manager Clay Hopper told Robinson to rest for a few days. At night Rachel would massage his arm, but that didn't help. Time was needed to work it out.

When Rickey heard that Robinson was taking off some time from fielding, he left City Island Ballpark, where the Dodgers played, and paid a visit to Kelly Field. He told Robinson he had to practice every day, sore arm and all. Rickey said, "Under ordinary circumstances, it would be all right, but you're not here under ordinary circumstances. You can't afford to miss a single day. They'll say you are dogging it, that you are pretending your arm is sore."[11]

Because Robinson couldn't throw across the field and the Royals already had six shortstops in camp, Robinson had agreed to play second base or wherever they need him. Because playing first base did not require having a strong throwing arm, the ballclub switched his position. Having never played first, Robinson struggled. Rickey and Hall of Famer George Sisler tutored him at first base.[12]

Montreal began its spring schedule against its organizational rival St. Paul Saints. Robinson sat out the first four games to rest his arm. Rickey waited for the right time to reveal Robinson to the baseball world.[13]

Robinson was penciled into the lineup on Sunday, March 17, as the Royals played the parent Dodgers at City Island Ballpark in downtown Daytona Beach.

Besides learning a new position, having an arm so sore that he couldn't throw, and being unable to find his hitting stroke, Robinson kept worrying about other things that morning. He kept worrying about what could go wrong – what the White spectators would yell at him, throw at him, or even the possibility that his life might be in danger. But there was excitement in the Black community that morning. In church, they prayed for Robinson and heard sermons about him. After church, the Black community paraded to the ballpark.[14]

More than 4,000 spectators filled the stands for the game, and about one-fourth were black. They filled the Jim Crow section of the ballpark, and an additional 200 or so Blacks stood beyond the right-field foul line.

Montreal did not score in the top of the first, and in the bottom of the inning, the big hit was Dixie Walker's bases-loaded triple for the Dodgers, who held a 4-0 lead after one inning.

Robinson came up to bat in the second inning. He wondered what was going to happen. He expected to hear applause from the Black section out in right field but was surprised to also hear applause from the Whites. He remembered two comments coming from the stands. One was "Come on, Black boy! You can make the grade" and "They're giving you a chance – now come on and do something about it."[15]

In his first at-bat, Robinson chased a curveball and fouled out weakly to third baseman Billy Herman. In the fourth inning, he fouled out to the catcher, Dixie Howell. Robinson put the ball in play in the sixth inning and reached on a fielder's choice. He stole second and scored on a base hit. He was removed from the game after 5½ innings to rest his arm. Brooklyn went on to win, 7-2.[16] Not a whole lot was mentioned in the newspapers about Robinson. None of the high-powered New York sportswriters mentioned the game, and while *Daytona Beach Evening News* sports editor Bernard Kahn covered the action, he did not write about Robinson until the fourth paragraph. The Associated Press started its story with Robinson, and its dispatch appeared in papers nationwide.[17]

Even though Robinson did not get a hit, he was satisfied with how the day ended, and a huge burden was lifted off his back. Even though not everyone applauded for him, he was sure now that the whole world wasn't against him. The townspeople were equally satisfied.[18]

When camp broke and the Royals returned to Montreal for the International League season, Robinson had made the team. He and Rachel were uncertain what kind of reception they would face. It turned out well. They found a place to live, and in the Royals' season opener, Robinson went 4-for-4 with a home run. He went on to lead the International League in batting average (.349) and tied for runs scored with Soup Campbell of the Baltimore Orioles (113). The Royals won the pennant with a 100-54 record and defeated the Louisville Colonels, the American Association champion, in the Little World Series.[19]

In 1988 City Island Ballpark was renamed Jackie Robinson Ballpark, and is still in use as of 2020.[20]

NOTES

1. Chris Lamb, *Blackout: The Untold Story of Jackie Robinson's First Spring Training* (Lincoln: University of Nebraska Press, 2004), 13-16.
2. Lamb, 64.
3. Lamb, 64.
4. Hall of Fame, "About Wendell Smith," baseballhall.org/discover-more/stories/wendell-smith/345.
5. Lamb, 83.
6. Lamb, 88.
7. Lamb, 88-89.
8. Lamb, 91.
9. Lamb, 92-93.
10. Lamb, 94.
11. Lamb, 95.
12. Lamb, 95.
13. Lamb, 100.
14. Lamb, 104.
15. Lamb, 106.
16. Associated Press, "Robinson Is Hitless in 3 Tries as Dodgers Wallop Royals 7–2," *Montreal Gazette*, March 18, 1946: 17.
17. Lamb, 107.
18. Lamb, 108.
19. Tabitha Marshall, *The Canadian Encyclopedia*, thecanadianencyclopedia.ca/en/article/jackie-robinson-and-the-montreal-royals.
20. Kevin Reichard, *Ballpark Digest*, ballparkdigest.com/200811291030/minor-league-baseball/visits/jackie-robinson-ballpark-daytona-cubs.

ROBINSON LEADS ROYALS ROMP IN 1946 REGULAR-SEASON DEBUT

APRIL 18, 1946: MONTREAL ROYALS 14, JERSEY CITY GIANTS 1, AT ROOSEVELT STADIUM, JERSEY CITY

by Frederick C. Bush

When Jack Roosevelt Robinson went to bat in the top of the first inning on April 18, 1946 – on a field that bore his middle name – he made history as the first Black player in Organized Baseball in the twentieth century.[1] Robinson's performance in the exhibition season had not been noteworthy, so no one expected him to be the driving force in the Montreal Royals' 14-1 rout of the Jersey City Giants. After he turned in a 4-for-5 day at the plate that included a homer, two stolen bases, four runs scored, and four RBIs, *Pittsburgh Courier* reporter Wendell Smith rhapsodized that "Jolting Jackie Robinson, the 'California Comet' looms tonight (Thursday) as the newest and most spectacular satellite to blaze across the International League baseball heavens in a decade."[2]

The excitement and joy that Smith and his fellow Black reporters and fans felt was palpable. Although Robinson was lauded from all corners, with the *New York Times* reporting that he "converted his opportunity [to make good] into a brilliant personal triumph," African-Americans knew that Robinson's accomplishment did not belong to him alone.[3] As Smith pointed out, "[t]he hopes of fourteen million Negroes [were] resting on his big broad shoulders."[4] Fellow *Courier* columnist William G. Nunn asserted, "In tearing the door from its hinges, Robinson proved to 25,000 wild-eyed fans of all hues, races and creeds that ability recognizes no color line!"[5] Indeed, Robinson's performance had been so amazing that he had "won the hearts" of all those fans.[6]

The fact that it was Opening Day normally would have provided excitement enough, but the added attraction of Robinson's debut resulted in a paid attendance of 51,872 for a venue that had a capacity of only 25,000. The result was that "[t]he park was practically filled at 1:30 P.M. and when Mayor [Frank] Hague threw out the first ball at 3 P.M. there was not an empty seat in sight."[7] Those fans fortunate enough to gain entrance applauded as Robinson, the second batter of the game, stepped to the plate. Smith observed of the crowd, "They were for him. ... They all knew how he had overcome many obstacles in the Deep South. ... And yet, through it all, he was standing at the plate as the second baseman of the Montreal Royals. ... The applause they gave so willingly was a salute of appreciation and admiration."[8] The fans' excitement waned briefly when, after working a full count, Robinson grounded out to Giants shortstop Jaime Almendro. Robinson's grounder was part of a one-two-three inning for Jersey City starter Warren Sandel, but it would be the only successful frame for the Giants hurler.

In the top of the second inning, Tom Tatum singled and Red Durrett followed with a homer for the first two Royals runs. When the third inning rolled around, the Royals went to work on Sandel again. Montreal pitcher Barney DeForge drew a leadoff walk and Marv Rackley followed with a single to set the stage for Robinson's second at-bat. This time the former Kansas City Monarch, who had ranked "number six in the Negro American League for the league's batting honors in 1945," did not disappoint.[9] He clouted Sandel's first pitch over the left-field wall

Robinson's Debut A Roaring Success

Jersey City, N. J., April 19 (U.P.)—Negro Jackie Robinson, the first of his race ever to play in modern organized baseball, was off to a sensational start today in his ambition to become in baseball what Joe Louis has been to boxing, Jesse Owens to track, Buddy Young to football and Isaac Murphy to racing.

for a three-run homer that gave the Royals a 5-0 lead. Sandel retired the next two batters but was lifted for reliever Phil Oates after he allowed Durrett's second round-tripper of the game.

Oates ended the third inning and made it through the fourth without incurring further damage, but Robinson showed another aspect to his game when he returned to the plate in the fifth. He dragged a bunt down the third-base line that he beat out handily, stole second base with ease, and advanced to third on an infield out. Robinson promptly sped halfway down the line as though he wanted to steal home. The move so unnerved Oates that he stopped in mid-windup and was called for a balk that allowed Robinson to score.

The only flaw in Robinson's spectacular debut occurred in the bottom of the fifth when he committed an error while handling his first chance at second base, a miscue that the New York Times humorously chalked up to him "proving that he was only human, after all."[10] First, shortstop Stan Breard made an error on leadoff batter Almendro's grounder. Robinson made it two Royals errors in a row when he retired Almendro at second but threw wide of first base while trying to turn the double play on Cleston Ray, a miscue that allowed Ray to take second. Ray took third on Bobby Thomson's second hit of the game and scored the Giants' lone run on Norman Jaeger's fly out.[11] Robinson atoned for that error by successfully starting the Royals' only double play of the game in the sixth inning; he handled five of his six total chances successfully with two putouts and three assists.

"A Handshake for the Century" - George Shuba congratulates Jackie Robinson after third-inning homer in his Montreal Royals debut against the Jersey City Giants at Roosevelt Stadium on April 18, 1946. © Michael Shuba. All rights reserved.

In the seventh, Robinson's third hit of the day – a solid single to right field – and second stolen base were part of another Royals onslaught that plated three runs and made the score 10-1. Hub Andrews took the mound for the Giants in the eighth inning, but he fared no better than either of his predecessors; in fact, he followed directly in Oates's footsteps. The Royals put up another three-spot in the eighth, including Robinson's fourth run of the game. Robinson reached base with his second bunt of the afternoon, again down the third-base line, and advanced to third via two infield outs. The *Baltimore Afro-American* described how

[a]gain he took advantage of the psychological factor his base-running prowess had established. As Andrews began his wind-up, Jackie stormed down the base-line toward home plate, then suddenly stopped.

The bewildered Jersey City pitcher didn't know what to do with the ball and again [home plate] Umpire Gore called Jackie across the plate.[12]

That was two pitchers, two fake steal attempts, and two balks that allowed two of Robinson's runs to score, which Wendell Smith believed to be "some kind of a record for an opening day game."[13]

Although Robinson's splashy debut was the obvious story of the day, he did not beat the Giants single-handedly. DeForge pitched masterfully. The Jersey City native scattered eight hits in a complete-game effort against his hometown team and would have thrown a shutout had it not been for the Breard and Robinson errors. Royals batters smashed 15 hits, including Durrett's two homers and three-hit performances by Tatum and Breard. Montreal was off and running in a 1946 season that would lead to an International League batting title for Robinson and a Little World Series victory for the team.

On this day, when the game ended, Robinson was mobbed by kids who had a new idol and wanted his autograph or merely to come into contact with him. Durrett "fought his way through the howling mob and finally 'saved' Robinson," telling him, "You can't possibly sign autographs for all those kids."[14] Once Robinson arrived in the visitors locker room, the scene was no different as reporters and well-wishers crowded around the star of the day. Things were so hectic and "Robinson was so excited he had to tie his necktie three or four times but he was as happy as a kid on Christmas morning."[15]

The *Jersey Journal*, hometown newspaper of the vanquished Giants, lauded Robinson and made note of the fact that the momentous occasion would not have been possible had Branch Rickey not been courageous enough to sign Robinson and had he not "stood staunchly behind [him] and permitted pre-season exhibition games to be cancelled rather than back down" and avowed that "[y]esterday, Robinson repaid him for his support."[16] The *Pittsburgh Courier's* William G. Nunn agreed, proclaiming, "But as twilight deepens over this ball park ... as the American flag waves proudly in the glooming [*sic*], we bow our heads in silent tribute to two men who opened another saga in the book which is America. ... [T]wo men with faith in God and Democracy. Thank God for a Branch Rickey and thank America for Jackie Robinson."[17]

As for Robinson himself, in the postgame locker room, he commented, "The one thing that I cared about was the way my teammates backed me up all the way. [...] There wasn't any riding out there but if there was I wouldn't have minded as long as my team was behind me. They have been swell."[18] After the postgame clamor ended, [a]s he left the park and walked out onto the street, the once brilliant sun was fading slowly in the distant western skies. ... His petite and dainty little wife greeted him warmly and kindly. 'You've had quite a day, little man,' she said sweetly. 'Yes,' he said softly and pleasantly, 'God has been good to me today!'"[19]

NOTES

1. Roosevelt Stadium was, of course, named after President Franklin Delano Roosevelt, but it seems fitting that Robinson shared the name. The International League had previous African-American players, but none since Moses Fleetwood Walker played for the Syracuse Stars in 1889 prior to Black players' exclusion from Organized Baseball due to the "gentleman's agreement" between all team owners.

2. Wendell Smith, "Jackie Hits Homer, Scores 4 Runs as Royals Win First," *Pittsburgh Courier*, April 27, 1946: 16.

3. Joseph M. Sheehan, "Montreal Winner as Robinson Stars," *New York Times*, April 19, 1946: 22.

4. Smith, "Jackie Hits Homer, Scores 4 Runs as Royals Win First."

5. William G. Nunn, "American Way Triumphs in Robinson 'Experiment,'" *Pittsburgh Courier*, April 27, 1946: 4.

6. "Jackie Robinson Hits Homer in League Debut," *Chicago Defender*, April 27, 1946: 10.

7. Sheehan.

8. Wendell Smith, "The Sports Beat," *Pittsburgh Courier*, April 27, 1946: 16.

9. "Jackie Robinson Hits Homer in League Debut."

10. Sheehan.

11. Bobby Thomson later became famous for his "Shot Heard 'Round the World" in 1951 that won the National League pennant for the Giants in their playoff series against the Dodgers.

12. "30,000 See Robinson Sparkle in Montreal Debut," *Baltimore Afro-American*, April 20, 1946: 29.

13. Smith, "Jackie Hits Homer, Scores 4 Runs as Royals Win First."

14 Smith, "The Sports Beat."

15 "'Jackie' Excited, Has Tie Trouble, Almost Loses Shirt to JC Crowd," *Montreal Gazette*, April 19, 1946: 12.

16 "The Club-House: Jackie Robinson, Despite Pressure on Him, Rose to Greatest Heights in Athletic Career at Inaugural Here," *Jersey Journal*, April 19, 1946: 13.

17 Nunn, "American Way Triumphs in Robinson 'Experiment.'"

18 "'Jackie' Excited, Has Tie Trouble, Almost Loses Shirt to JC Crowd."

19 Smith, "The Sports Beat."

JACKIE ROBINSON LEADS MONTREAL TO THRILLING 10-INNING VICTORY OVER LOUISVILLE

OCTOBER 2, 1946: MONTREAL ROYALS 6, LOUISVILLE COLONELS 5, AT DE LORIMIER STADIUM, MONTREAL

by Gary Belleville

Jackie Robinson was relieved to be back in Montreal. The Montreal Royals, a Triple-A affiliate of the Brooklyn Dodgers, had just dropped two of the first three games of the Junior World Series in Louisville under trying circumstances. While fans of the Louisville Colonels were thrilled to see their team back in the series for the third consecutive year, many were upset at having to host integrated baseball games. A vocal Louisville group, attempting to maintain their strict segregationist tradition, even demanded that the series be canceled.[1] The new baseball commissioner, Happy Chandler, made it clear to the Colonels that Jackie was going to play.[2]

Robinson was vigorously booed by most White fans from the moment he stepped out of the dugout for Game One at Parkway Field. A torrent of racist insults rained down upon him from the stands, although he was cheered by Black fans in the small Jim Crow section down the right-field line.[3] Jackie was subjected to boos and taunts every time he moved a muscle during the three games in Kentucky.[4] "If I were in his place, I would have thrown my glove on the ground and left the field and baseball altogether," admitted Colonels center fielder George Bennington during the train ride to Montreal for Game Four.[5] "Robinson is truly extraordinary."

Louisville players had been instructed by the Office of the Commissioner to refrain from using racial insults against him, and they complied with the directive, though they didn't exactly go easy on him. Colonels catcher Fred Walters attempted to injure Robinson by spiking him in Game One and Louisville pitchers weren't afraid to pitch him inside. "I remember our starting pitcher that day, Jim Wilson, knocked him down, and the fans cheered," recalled Colonels hurler Otis "Otey" Clark.[6]

Although Robinson refused to admit it at the time, the abuse in Louisville affected his play. He went 0-for-5 in Game One, the first and only time he was held hitless in five at-bats that season, and he committed an uncharacteristic fielding error in Game Two. His batting line over the first three games was a wretched 1-for-10 with three strikeouts. After watching him win the batting title and play outstanding defense all season long, his teammates knew he was capable of much more. "Robinson didn't play well down here, but wait till you see him in Montreal, where the fans are his friends," predicted his double-play partner, Al Campanis.[7]

The baseball fans in Montreal, perhaps partially in response to hearing of the indignities that he faced during spring training in Florida, had been fully behind Robinson from the beginning of the regular season.[8] Dodgers general manager Branch Rickey had surrounded Jackie with a talented group of veteran ballplayers, and they dominated the International League from wire to wire, posting a 100-54 record and finishing a whopping 18½ games ahead of the second-place Syracuse Chiefs. The Royals were an offensive juggernaut, scoring 1,019 runs and stealing 189 bases in the regular season, which left every other team in the dust.[9]

The Colonels, champions of the American Association, relied on outstanding pitching, speed, and defense to win games. Their offense was mediocre until their parent club, the Boston Red Sox, acquired 34-year-old outfielder Jim Gleeson in a trade with the Cardinals in early July.[10] When Gleeson joined the team on July 7, the Colonels were mired in third place with a 44-38 record, 6½ games behind the St. Paul Saints, Brooklyn's other Triple-A affiliate. Louisville went 48-23 (.676) for the remainder of the season and finished four games ahead of second-place Indianapolis.

Louisville cruised through the American Association playoffs, easily defeating St. Paul and Indianapolis, which earned the Colonels a five-day break before facing the Royals. Montreal knocked off the Newark Bears, led by 21-year-old Yogi Berra, in six games in the International League semifinals, and then dispatched the pugnacious Syracuse Chiefs in five games in the finals.[11]

Glen Moulder, 10-6 with a 3.25 ERA during the regular season, was the Royals' Game Four starter. The right-hander had come on in relief to save Game One by getting the dangerous Al Flair to hit a popup for the final out with a runner on base in a 7-5 Montreal victory.

Clark (11-7, 2.89 ERA), a 31-year-old right-hander making his first and only appearance in the series, took to the mound for Louisville. Surprisingly, he had faced Robinson before even though the two players had never played in the same league. While with Boston just before the start of the 1945 season, Clark had thrown batting practice to Robinson, Sam Jethroe, and Marvin Williams at Fenway Park during the bogus tryout of the three Negro League players.[12] The charade would come back to haunt the Red Sox organization for decades.

The Montreal fans, many of whom had listened to the radio broadcast of the first three games of the series, were acutely aware of Robinson's ill treatment in Louisville.[13] Many took the abuse directed at their beloved second baseman personally. The fans at De Lorimier Stadium booed lustily when the Colonels took to the field, and they proceeded to boo every single Louisville player throughout the game.[14] "I didn't approve of this kind of retaliation," Robinson said years later, "but I felt a jubilant sense of gratitude for the way Canadians expressed their feelings."[15] As a further show of support, the fans gave Jackie a rousing standing ovation.

The Colonels scored a couple of quick runs in the top of the first inning and were up 4-0 by the middle of the fifth, with three of those runs knocked in by Flair. Montreal closed the gap to 4-1 in the bottom of the fifth before Moulder ran into more trouble by walking the first three batters in the sixth inning. That caused Royals manager Clay Hopper to call for his most effective reliever, Frank Laga, to come out of the pen. Laga slammed the door by setting down the next three Colonels to escape the bases-loaded jam.[16] Dixie Howell's home run in the bottom of the sixth cut the lead to 4-2, and the teams exchanged runs in the eighth inning to make the score 5-3.

Clark, as usual, had shown excellent control in the game, walking only a single batter through the first eight innings. After he retired Campanis for the first out of the ninth inning, it appeared that the Colonels were destined to take a three-games-to-one stranglehold in the series. Pinch-hitter Herman Franks, who had an outstanding batting eye, drew a walk. After Marv Rackley hit into a fielder's choice, Robinson, 1-for-4 in the game, stepped to the plate with Montreal down to its final out. Jackie also had excellent plate discipline, and he too walked. Clark issued his third base on balls of the inning to the next batter, Tommy Tatum, to load the bases, and his evening on the hill was over. Lefty Joe Ostrowski fared no better, walking Les Burge to bring in Rackley with Montreal's fourth run, which advanced Tatum to second base and Robinson to third. The catcher Walters threw wildly to second base trying to pick off Tatum, and an alert Robinson scampered home to tie the game, 5-5. Incredibly, the Royals had scored a pair of crucial runs without registering a hit, and the game went into extra innings.

Montreal's Game One winner, Chet Kehn, threw a scoreless top of the 10th inning. In the bottom of the frame, the Royals continued to benefit from the generosity of Colonels pitchers. Ostrowski's throwing error on Howell's groundball put the potential winning run on base with nobody out. Ostrowski compounded matters by fielding Earl Naylor's sacrifice attempt and throwing late to second base, and now runners were on first and second. With righty Mel Deutsch pitching, Campanis advanced both runners with a sacrifice. Kehn followed with Montreal's third consecutive bunt, except this one was an attempt to score the catcher Howell on a squeeze play, but Walters blocked the plate and tagged Howell for out number two.

With the top of the order coming up, the Colonels were forced with a dilemma. They could pitch to the lefty Rackley, 6-for-19 to that point in the series, or the right-handed-hitting Robinson, who was only 2-for-14. Louisville chose to intentionally walk Rackley to setup a force at every base and enjoy the platoon advantage. The decision handed Robinson a chance to avenge his harsh treatment in Louisville, and it was an opportunity he did not pass up. Jackie blasted a single over shortstop Jack Albright's head to drive in Naylor with the winning run.

The victory evened the seven-game series at two wins apiece. With all remaining games set to be played in friendly De Lorimier Stadium, Jackie Robinson and the Montreal Royals had all the momentum on their side.

AUTHOR'S NOTE

The author is grateful for the research assistance provided by fellow SABR member Marcel Dugas.

SOURCES

In addition to the sources cited in the Notes, the author consulted Baseball-Reference.com and Retrosheet.org.

NOTES

1. Roger Kahn, *Rickey & Robinson: The True, Untold Story of the Integration of Baseball* (New York: Rodale Books, 2014), 217-218.

2. Commissioner Chandler claimed to have sent a message to the president of the Louisville Colonels, Bruce Dudley, telling him, "The colored boy has every right to play."

3. The attendance for Game One was 13,716. Although an estimated 20,000 African-American fans wanted to purchase tickets for the game, the Colonels refused to sell any more than the 466 tickets normally available to Black fans in the Jim Crow section. Team President Bruce Dudley said he was afraid that a large crowd of Black fans would lead to a race riot. Approximately 1,500 Black fans were turned away at the gate, many of whom watched the game from nearby rooftops and telephone poles, and atop freight cars. After much criticism, the team sold more tickets to Black fans for the next two games.

4. Marcel Dugas, *Jackie Robinson, Un Été à Montréal (A Summer in Montreal)* (Montréal: Éditions Hurtubise, 2019), Chapitre 4: Les séries (Chapter 4: The playoffs).

5. Jack Jedwab, *Jackie Robinson's Unforgettable Season of Baseball in Montreal* (Montreal: Les Éditions Images, 1996), 40. Although the quote is attributed to an unnamed Colonels player in Jedwab's book, the October 3, 1946, edition of *La Presse* newspaper includes the French translation of this quote and attributes it to George Bennington.

6. Kahn, *Rickey & Robinson*, 218.

7. William Brown, *Baseball's Fabulous Montreal Royals* (Westmount, Quebec: Robert Davies Publishing, 1996), 110.

8. Due to Florida's segregationist policies, Robinson was unable to stay in the same hotels or eat in the same restaurants as his teammates. Early in spring training, he was forced to flee Sanford after his personal safety was threatened. The Royals chose to relocate their spring training to Daytona Beach, which was less hostile to integration. Although the Royals could play integrated games in Daytona Beach, three of their road games were canceled by local authorities in a six-day period because they did not want integrated baseball games being played in their jurisdiction. On April 7 a police officer in Sanford came onto the field in the bottom of the second inning and ordered Robinson and teammate John Wright to leave. They were forced to comply. To avoid any further issues, the Royals decided to cancel four exhibition games they were to play as the team traveled north to start the regular season.

9. Montreal's 1,019 runs were 217 more than the number-two team in runs scored, the Buffalo Bisons. The Royals' 189 stolen bases more than doubled those of the Baltimore Orioles, who finished a distant second in steals with 84.

10. Jim Gleeson had five years of major-league experience under his belt, including an outstanding 1940 season with the Chicago Cubs. In 551 plate appearances that season, Gleeson posted a .313/.389/.470 slash line and 4.2 Wins Above Replacement (WAR). In the 1946 season, Gleeson hit .306 in 148 games split between Columbus and Louisville in the American Association. He also led all players in the 1946 Junior World Series with nine RBIs.

11. The Syracuse players treated Jackie Robinson worse than any other Montreal opponent in 1946. They baited him mercilessly with racist taunts whenever the two teams met.

12. Bill Nowlin, "Otey Clark," SABR BioProject, sabr.org/bioproj/person/ee62deca, accessed November 18, 2019.

13. The games in Louisville were broadcast on two radio stations: CJAD (English) and CHLP (French). It was rare to broadcast road games at the time. Even the New York Yankees only began the live broadcasting all road games on radio in 1946.

14. Dugas, *Jackie Robinson, Un Été à Montréal (A Summer in Montreal)*, Chapitre 4: Les séries (Chapter 4: The playoffs). The name "De Lorimier Stadium" is used instead of "Delorimier Stadium" to reflect the correct French name. The English press at the time anglicized the name incorrectly.

15. Brown, *Baseball's Fabulous Montreal Royals*, 110.

16. Dink Carroll, "Jackie Robinson Is Hero as Royals Edge Colonels 6-5 to Tie Up Series," *Montreal Gazette*, October 3, 1946: 16.

ROBINSON'S HEROICS PUT MONTREAL ON VERGE OF FIRST JUNIOR WORLD SERIES TITLE

OCTOBER 3, 1946: MONTREAL ROYALS 5, LOUISVILLE COLONELS 3, AT DE LORIMIER STADIUM, MONTREAL

by Gary Belleville

In December of 1945, several weeks after the signing of Jackie Robinson was announced, Branch Rickey tapped Mississippi native Clay Hopper as manager of the Montreal Royals.[1] The hiring made a lot of sense. Not only was Hopper, who had managed minor-league teams for Rickey since 1929, a trusted field general, but he was a Southerner, which would make it less likely that Robinson's White teammates would refuse to play alongside him. As it turned out, none did.

After guiding Montreal to the International League championship, Hopper had his club in a dogfight with the Louisville Colonels of the American Association for the 1946 Junior World Series. Prior to Game Five, with the series tied at two games apiece, Royals President Hector Racine announced to the crowd at De Lorimier Stadium that Hopper would be back as manager in 1947.[2] The skipper had good reason to celebrate on that day, since it was also his 44th birthday.

Hopper made the bold decision to start his staff ace, Steve Nagy, on two days' rest. The Royals left-hander had been bombed by the Colonels in his Game Three start, lasting only 2⅔ innings in a 15-6 loss. Nagy had also been battling a sore arm during the previous month, and the injury had forced him to miss his start in Game Five of the International League semifinals against Newark. His 17 regular-season wins had tied him for the league lead, and after earning two more wins in the postseason, he was looking for his 20th win of the year.

Louisville countered with 24-year-old Jim Wilson, the losing pitcher in Game One of the series. The hard-throwing right-hander pitched for the 1945 Boston Red Sox until his season was cut short when he suffered a fractured skull on a ball hit off the bat of Hank Greenberg. Although his brain surgeon suggested that he would never pitch again, Wilson proved him wrong. He began the 1946 season with the Red Sox before being sent down on May 8 to Louisville, where he posted a solid regular-season ERA of 3.02.

The Royals got to Wilson for a single run in each of the first three innings of Game Five. With one out in the bottom of the first, Robinson pulled a double down the left-field line, and the next batter, Tommy Tatum, drove him in with a solid single to center field.[3] Marv Rackley brought home another run with a fly ball in the second inning, and Dixie Howell smacked an RBI double in the third.

Nagy struggled with his control all game, but he managed to find a way out of several jams. He loaded the bases on two walks and a hit batsman in the top of the fifth inning before walking Jim Gleeson to force in a run. Fortunately for the Royals, Nagy kept the damage to a minimum by getting Al Flair to pop up to third baseman Lew Riggs to end the inning with the bases loaded. The Colonels got to Nagy in the top of the seventh inning, however, as they scored a pair of runs on an RBI single by Al Brancato and an RBI double by Gleeson to tie the game, 3-3.

Robinson led off the home half of the seventh by blasting a triple to the light tower in left-center field.[4] Although a medium-depth fly ball would have been enough to score the speedy Robinson, neither Tatum nor Les Burge could get the job done, with Wilson retiring them both on popups for the first two outs of the inning. The next batter, Riggs, a 10-year major-league veteran, slammed a clutch double to right field to score Robinson with the go-ahead run.

Nagy issued his sixth walk of the game to start the top of the eighth inning. Hopper called for Chet Kehn, the winning pitcher in Games One and Four, to relieve Nagy, and the right-hander quickly retired the side to protect the one-run lead. In addition to Kehn's assistance, Nagy also benefited from three double plays behind him, all of which involved Robinson.

The Royals added an insurance run off 37-year-old Harry Kimberlin in the eighth inning. With two out and Al Campanis on third, Robinson surprised third baseman Brancato by laying down a perfect bunt that he beat out easily for his third hit of the game. Campanis scored on the play, putting Montreal ahead by a score of 5-3.

Kehn returned to the hill for the ninth inning. With Johnny Welaj on first and Louisville down to its last out, Kehn faced the veteran slugger Gleeson. The Colonels right fielder drove the ball to right field and came within inches of tying the game, but the ball struck the top of the fence for a double, and Welaj was held up at third base. Kehn had new life, and he took advantage of his second chance by inducing Flair to ground out to end the game, giving the Royals a 3-2 series lead.

Montreal clinched the series the next night, with 43-year-old Curt Davis tossing a complete-game shutout in a 2-0 victory that gave the Royals their first Junior World Series title since they began play in 1897.[5] Robinson contributed two more hits, turned two key double plays, and helped snuff out a rally in the fourth inning by converting a hard smash that deflected off first baseman Burge into a stellar 3-4-1 putout.[6]

The 19,171 Montreal fans in attendance for Game Six celebrated wildly after the final out was made, and a scene unfolded unlike any other in Montreal sports history. The Royals retreated quickly to their clubhouse as fans descended onto the field. Refusing to leave the ballpark, fans began chanting for their heroes to emerge for a curtain call. First Hopper and then Davis returned to the field and were "chaired" around the infield on the shoulders of supporters. Still unsatisfied, the crowd began to chant Robinson's name. The ushers, wanting to appease the fans so they could close the ballpark for the season, urged Robinson to return to the field. Jackie, who was overdue to begin a barnstorming tour with the Jackie Robinson All Stars and had to hurry to catch a flight to Detroit, emerged in his street clothes and was mobbed by the adoring fans.[7] As they carried him around the infield, tears of joy streamed down Robinson's face.

He returned to the clubhouse and found that his path out of the ballpark was blocked by a couple of hundred admirers who were waiting for him in the hallway. Robinson finally made a run for it after all his teammates had left, and he managed to make his way past his devoted fans, only to be met by roughly 500 more outside. The crowd chased him for three blocks

Jackie Robinson in the Royals dugout, July 9, 1946. Photograph by Conrad Poirier.

Courtesy of Rachel Robinson and the Estate of Jackie Robinson.

before Jackie hopped into a car that whisked him off to the airport. In describing the scene, *Montreal Herald* sportswriter Sam Maltin famously wrote, "It was probably the only day in history that a black man ran from a white mob with love instead of lynching on its mind."[8]

The love was mutual. A few months later, Robinson described what was going through his mind that evening. "As my plane roared skyward and the lights of Montreal twinkled and winked in the distance, I took one last look at this great city where I had found so much happiness," he recalled. "This is the city for me. This is paradise."[9]

Rickey's "Great Experiment" had come a long way since spring training when a handful of Royals exhibition games were canceled because of segregationist policies in the South and many doubted that Robinson had the talent to make the Montreal roster.[10] Even *The Sporting News* predicted, "The waters of competition in the International League will flood far over his head."[11] Jackie made many of the naysayers look foolish. He won the batting title with a .349 average, tied for the league lead in runs scored (113), and finished second in stolen bases (40) despite missing 30 regular-season games.[12] He also had the highest fielding percentage among regular IL second basemen even though he had never played the position before.

He continued to excel in the postseason, batting .357 in the IL playoffs and .333 in the Junior World Series.

The four other African-Americans in the Dodgers' minor-league system also had successful seasons in 1946. Pitchers John Wright and Roy Partlow, who both spent a portion of the year with Montreal, saw their fortunes improve with the Trois-Rivières Royals in the Class-C Can-Am League, and Roy Campanella and Don Newcombe starred with the Nashua Dodgers of the Class-B New England League.[13] All three teams won their respective league championships. In one pivotal year, it had become apparent that the major-league color barrier would soon be broken.

SOURCES

In addition to the sources cited in the Notes, the author consulted Baseball-Reference.com and Retrosheet.org.

NOTES

1. The Montreal Royals announced the signing of Jackie Robinson at De Lorimier Stadium on October 23, 1945. It was a major news story that was widely reported across North America. Clay Hopper accepted the job as manager of the Montreal Royals in December, and so he very likely was aware at the time that he would be managing an integrated team.

2. Clay Hopper was later named Minor League Manager of the Year by *The Sporting News*.

3. Dink Carroll, "Royals Squeeze 5-3 Victory from Colonels to Lead Series 3 Games to 2," *Montreal Gazette*, October 4, 1946: 16.

4. The bottom portions of two light towers were in play at De Lorimier Stadium -- one in right-center field and the other in left-center. Both were positioned just inside the home-run fence. The lighting system was installed in 1933, approximately five years after the ballpark was shoehorned into a relatively small city block.

5. The Junior World Series was known as the Little World Series between 1904 and 1931. Although professional baseball was played in Montreal as far back as 1890, the Royals did not come into existence until 1897. They played in Montreal until 1960, winning nine pennants and three Junior World Series titles (1946, 1948, and 1953) in that time.

6. Dink Carroll, "Royals Win Little World Series for First Time in Their History," *Montreal Gazette*, October 5, 1946: 1.

7. Marcel Dugas, *Jackie Robinson, Un Été à Montréal (A Summer in Montreal)* (Montréal: Éditions Hurtubise, 2019), Chapitre 4: Les séries (Chapter 4: The playoffs).

8. John Kabfleisch, "Robinson and Montreal Were a Perfect Match," *Montreal Gazette*, October 3, 2004, montrealgazette.com/sponsored/mtl-375th/from-the-archives-robinson-and-montreal-were-a-perfect-match, accessed November 15, 2019.

9. Jackie Robinson and Wendell Smith, *Jackie Robinson: My Own Story*, (Auckland, New Zealand: Pickle Partners Publishing, 2015), International Merry-Go-Round chapter.

10. Dugas, *Jackie Robinson, Un Été à Montréal (A Summer in Montreal)*, Chapitre 1: Les débuts des Royaux (Chapter 1: The Beginning of the Royals).

11. Rick Swaine, "Jackie Robinson," SABR BioProject, sabr.org/bioproj/person/bb9e2490, accessed November 18, 2019.

12. Most of the games Robinson missed in 1946 were due to leg injuries. After Robinson had trouble eating and sleeping, a doctor recommended in late August that he take at least 10 days of rest. The team offered five. Worried that he would be accused of sitting out to protect his lead in the batting race, Jackie returned to the lineup after only three days of rest.

13. A sixth Black player, Canadian shortstop Manny McIntyre, also played in the minor leagues in 1946. McIntyre suited up for the independent Sherbrooke Canadians in the Class-C Border League. He hit .310 in 30 games with Sherbrooke.

JACKIE ROBINSON, ROYAL AT EBBETS FIELD

APRIL 10, 1947: MONTREAL ROYALS 4, BROOKLYN DODGERS 3,
AT EBBETS FIELD, BROOKLYN, NEW YORK

by Steven C. Weiner

"I hadn't even made up my mind Wednesday night. It came to me in the middle of the ball game yesterday just like that. ... Robinson is coming to the Dodgers as just a ball player." – Branch Rickey[1]

One baseball season and a spring as a Montreal Royal and Jackie Robinson was on the verge of becoming a Brooklyn Dodger. Robinson was ready for the big leagues. His performance on the field told part of the story. For the 1946 season, Robinson led the International League in batting average (.349), scored 113 runs, and stole 40 bases in 124 games.[2] His fielding average (.985) led the league's second basemen.

The Royals were dominant from the outset of the 1946 season. They opened on the road against the Jersey City Giants at Roosevelt Stadium. Robinson's debut performance – four hits, four runs batted in, two stolen bases – led the Royals' 14-1 rout. Joseph Sheehan, covering the game for the *New York Times*, noted, "Jackie Robinson converted his opportunity into a brilliant personal triumph."[3] The Royals won the league title with ease by 18½ games over the Syracuse Chiefs. A 100-54 record produced the most wins in the franchise's International League history (1928-1960).

In the playoffs, the Royals beat the Newark Bears and the Chiefs before winning the Little World Series four games to two over the American Association's Louisville Colonels, taking the last three games at Montreal's Delorimier Park.[4] The record Montreal crowd (19,171) was delirious with joy and the celebration was spontaneous after the series clincher. Robinson, who had sparked those three wins by going 6-for-14 at the plate, was mobbed by fans young and old, well after the game had ended. Sportswriter Sam Maltin wrote of the lesson of goodwill among men and the scene at hand, "the chasing of a Negro, not because of hate but because of love."[5] After the ugliness and bigotry that began with Robinson's 1946 spring-training experience in Florida, the complete acceptance that he and Rachel Robinson received in Montréal was a welcome respite. Their feelings were captured in Robinson's autobiography. "One sportswriter later commented, "For Jackie Robinson and the city of Montreal, it was love at first sight." He was right."[6]

As Opening Day 1947 fast approached, it was clear that spring training for both the Royals and Dodgers had been well orchestrated under the watchful eye of Rickey. He had a plan. He set up training camp in Havana and scheduled 13 exhibition games in Cuba and Panama between the Royals and Dodgers. Dodgers veterans would get used to having Robinson around and seeing him as an asset for a pennant drive.[7] But there was rebellion. Some Dodgers did not want Robinson on the team and the ringleaders – Hugh Casey, Bobby Bragan, Dixie Walker, and Carl Furillo – circulated a petition to that effect. Rickey got wind of the petition and became even more determined to carry out his plan, encouraging any player to quit if he could not accept a black teammate. In his autobiography, Robinson suggests that "the petition protest collapsed before it got started."[8] Indeed, Rickey knew that Robinson was ready for the big leagues. Tested against Dodgers pitching, Robinson as a Royal hit .340 in those 13 games.[9]

The mound opponents on April 10 at Ebbets Field were the Royals' Erv Palica and the Dodgers' Ralph Branca. Palica had signed with the Dodgers in 1945 as an infielder but was converted to being a pitcher. He won 15 games for the Class-B Asheville Travelers in 1946, and the 19-year-old was promoted to the Royals for the 1947 season. Although Branca was used sparingly as a 20-year-old in 1946 (3-1 in 24 games), it was his first full season in the major leagues.

The biggest crowd to watch the Dodgers all spring (14,282) greeted Robinson warmly during batting practice and saw the Royals score all their runs in the fourth inning against Branca. Robinson walked, one of six walks Branca yielded in seven innings. After Spider Jorgensen flied out, Don Lund lined a home run into the left-field stands. When Earl Naylor walked and Al Campanis homered to left-center, the Royals led 4-0. Branca could be forgiven. Both home runs would have been caught in 1946, but the left-field wall was moved 14 feet closer to home plate for the 1947 season to accommodate more seating.[10]

The Dodgers got two runs back in the bottom of the fourth inning. Walker walked and scored on Duke Snider's double to center. When Royals shortstop Lou Welaj threw a wild relay, Snider came around to score to cut the Royals' lead in half, 4-2.

Just after Robinson popped into a double play attempting to bunt in the fifth inning, Arthur Mann, an assistant to Rickey, handed out a brief announcement in the press box: "The Brooklyn Dodgers today purchased the contract of Jackie Roosevelt Robinson from the Montreal Royals."[11] The words were few, but the significance would resound beyond the game itself.

Robinson actually learned of his promotion to the Dodgers that very morning when Rickey called him into his office to tell him the news. Despite flawless defense at first base, it wasn't very surprising that he went hitless as well in his other at-bats against the Dodgers – a walk, a groundout to the pitcher, and a pop fly to the shortstop.[12] He left Rickey's office in a trance, modestly admitting later that he didn't think he was too impressive in that last game with the Royals. "But that was because, I guess, I couldn't keep my mind on the game all the time."[13]

Jack Banta relieved Palica in the seventh inning and pitched the last three innings for the Royals. Palica yielded only four hits and Banta gave up another two, but the Dodgers could score only a single run, in the seventh inning. Stan Rojek walked and Gene Hermanski doubled for the second time, scoring Rojek but leaving the Dodgers short, 4-3.[14]

What should baseball fans remember about Robinson's on-the-field performance on this day? Hy Turkin, reporting for the *New York Daily News*, reminded us of a facet of Robinson's play in the decisive fourth-inning rally. It would become his hallmark. "His cat-like movements in a long lead off the bag drew two attempted pickoff throws and a pitchout in vain. Ralph Branca, still sneaking peeks at Robbie's lead, grooved one for Don Lund and the Royal outfielder poled it into the left field stands."[15]

As for Branca, he took a meaningless loss on this day, but the 1947 season was going to be his career year statistically – 21-12, 2.67 ERA, 280 innings and a league-leading 36 starts. He well understood and appreciated that a bigger story was unfolding on the field for the Brooklyn Dodgers, the presence and play of Jackie Robinson.[16]

In his 2011 book, *A Moment In Time*, Branca wrote of facing Jackie Robinson on this day for the first time in a big-league ballpark. As Branca made his way back to the dugout at the end of an inning, their paths crossed and Robinson said, "Thanks, Ralph." Why? Robinson didn't get a hit off Branca, only a walk. Cordiality easily described their relationship this spring. Robinson must have appreciated Branca's refusal to sign a players petition in spring training suggesting that Robinson's presence on the Dodgers would be disruptive. Branca didn't know. "Whatever it was, from that day forward Jackie and I became close."[17]

The following day would be a day long anticipated by both Rickey and Robinson. First, there would be the formality of Robinson signing a Brooklyn contract. Rickey was asked directly how the Dodgers players would react to their new teammate. "We are all agreed," he said, "that Jackie is ready for the chance."[18] As for Robinson, "Just think, tomorrow I'll be with them. I'll be wearing a Brooklyn uniform."[19] Indeed on the very next day in another exhibition game, Robinson would be wearing that home white Dodgers uniform for the first time against an opponent to become all too familiar in Robinson's major-league career, the New York Yankees.[20]

SOURCES

In addition to the sources cited in the Notes, the author accessed Baseball-Reference.com for statistical information.

NOTES

1. Harold C. Burr, "Robby Makes Debut With Dodgers Today," *Brooklyn Daily Eagle*, April 11, 1947: 15.
2. Robinson finished second in stolen bases to league leader Marv Rackley (65), his Royals teammate. Robinson tied Baltimore Orioles outfielder Soup Campbell for the league lead in runs scored (113).
3. Joseph M. Sheehan, "Montreal Winner as Robinson Stars," *New York Times*, April 19, 1946: 22.
4. "Montreal Downs Louisville by 2-0," *New York Times*, October 5, 1946: 10.
5. Sam Maltin, "Fans 'Mob' Jackie in Great Tribute to Star," *Pittsburgh Courier*, October 12, 1946: 12.
6. Jackie Robinson, *I Never Had It Made* (New York: Putnam, 1972), 47.
7. Rick Swaine, "Jackie Robinson," SABR Baseball Biography Project.
8. Robinson, 56.
9. Harold C. Burr, "Robby Makes Debut with Dodgers Today," *Brooklyn Daily Eagle*, April 11, 1947: 15.
10. Louis Effrat, "Royals' Star Signs with Brooks Today," *New York Times*, April 11, 1947: 20.

11   Effrat.

12   Hy Turkin, "Robinson Bought by Dodgers; Hitless as Royals Win, 4-3," *New York Daily News*, April 11, 1947: 63.

13   Jackie Robinson, "Jackie Robinson Says," *Pittsburgh Courier*, April 19, 1947: 18.

14   Of the 12 Royals who played in this game, 11 played in the major leagues at one time or another in their baseball careers. Only David Pluss never played in the major leagues. Roy Campanella and George "Shotgun" Shuba became household names for Dodgers fans.

15   Turkin.

16   Ralph Branca with David Ritz, *A Moment in Time* (New York: Scribner, 2011), 68.

17   Ralph Branca with David Ritz, 72.

18   Effrat.

19   Robinson, *Pittsburgh Courier*.

20   Louis Effrat, "Brooks Win, 14-6, with 11-Run Fifth," *New York Times*, April 12, 1947: 12.

JACKIE ROBINSON DEBUTS FOR DODGERS AT EBBETS FIELD

APRIL 11, 1947: BROOKLYN DODGERS 14, NEW YORK YANKEES 6, AT EBBETS FIELD, BROOKLYN

by Steven C. Weiner

"The Brooklyn Dodgers today purchased the contract of Jackie Roosevelt Robinson from the Montréal Royals."[1] Arthur Mann, an assistant to Dodgers president and general manager Branch Rickey, handed out the announcement in the press box at Ebbets Field during the fifth inning of the Royals' 4-3 exhibition game victory against the Dodgers.[2] Coincidentally, Jackie Robinson, playing first base, had just popped into a double play attempting to bunt.

The words of the announcement were few and the true meaning was yet to unfold. The largest crowd (14,282) to watch the Dodgers play this spring understood the meaning of the moment and warmly greeted the appearance of Robinson for batting practice. The sentiment of Dodgers fans was clear. They remembered Dixie Walker being quoted as opposed to playing with Robinson and booed his first turn at bat.[3] Uncertainty loomed. Rumors had it that other Dodgers expressed similar sentiments. Later, during the first week of the season, Robinson expressed his own sentiments about his teammates. "I've found out that there are fellows on the club willing to help me. Eddie Stanky, a great ball player, helped me the very first day. Others have advised me and coached me since. I know by that experience that I'm not alone."[4]

Robinson actually learned of his promotion to the Dodgers that very morning when Branch Rickey called him into his office to tell him the news. Despite flawless defense at first base, it wasn't very surprising that he went hitless as well in his other at-bats against the Dodgers – a walk, a groundout to the pitcher, and a pop fly to the shortstop.[5]

He left Rickey's office in a trance, modestly admitting later that he didn't think he was too impressive in that last game with the Royals. "But that was because, I guess, I couldn't keep my mind on the game all the time. Just think, tomorrow I'll be with them. I'll be wearing a Brooklyn uniform."[6] The very next day, Robinson wore that home white Dodgers uniform for the first time after a well-orchestrated spring training.

All aspects of spring training in 1947 in Havana for the Brooklyn Dodgers, the Montréal Royals, and Jackie Robinson were under the watchful eye and control of Branch Rickey.[7] Games were played at Havana's Gran Stadium with jaunts to play in Caracas, Venezuela, the Canal Zone, and Panama. Although the Dodgers played the Yankees, Boston Braves, and a team of Cuban all-stars, most games were against Montréal with Robinson playing first base for the Royals. With the Dodgers' Eddie Stanky at second base, it was clear that first base represented the best opportunity for Robinson to play with the Dodgers in 1947. A front-page blare in *The Sporting News* suggested otherwise: "Likely to See Service Mostly as Pinch Runner."[8] Robinson was determined to succeed even if he was never really comfortable at first base.[9]

But there were things that Rickey could not control and they hit the headlines like a bombshell. On the very day that Robinson and his Royals were scheduled to play the Dodgers at Ebbets Field, Commissioner Happy Chandler took an unprecedented action against Dodgers manager Leo Durocher. Chandler construed a series of incidents involving Durocher to be "detrimental to baseball" and suspended him for the 1947 season.[10] The story became front page immediately and drew attention away from what was about to happen on the field.[11]

Jackie Robinson Goes To Brooklyn Dodgers' Team
First Negro To Enter Baseball Major League

Atlanta Daily World, April 11, 1947: 1

Clyde Sukeforth was the Dodgers' acting manager as they began a three-game exhibition series against the New York Yankees at Ebbets Field. Sukeforth selected Joe Hatten to start the first game. Hatten, a 14-game winner in 1946, would be the Opening Day starter for Dodgers in four days' time. Bill Bevens, a 16-game winner in 1946, had the starting assignment from Yankees manager Bucky Harris. Each starter pitched three innings.

As Bevens left the mound after three innings, having given up six hits, his Yankees trailed 3-1. The Dodgers scored their first two runs in the first inning on Gene Hermanski's double. For the Yankees, Johnny Lindell tripled to deep center in the second and subsequently scored their first run. The Dodgers added a run in the third inning on Robinson's first run batted in. With one out and runners on first and third, his fly to left easily scored Pete Reiser.

Left-hander Marius Russo, hoping to return to the Yankees roster from the Newark Bears, took over for Bevens in the fourth inning and safely retired the Dodgers, allowing the Yankees to tie the score in the fifth at 3-3. Then came the Dodgers fifth. Russo walked the first three batters – Stan Rojek, Carl Furillo, and Tommy Tatum. The Yankees fielding soon turned ugly when shortstop Phil Rizzuto made throwing errors on consecutive plays. Butch Woyt hit a likely double-play ball to Rizzuto, whose errant toss to Snuffy Stirnweiss at second allowed one run to score. When Robinson followed with another grounder to short, Rizzuto's wild throw into right field allowed two more runs to score. Now the Dodgers were leading 6-3 without the benefit of any hits in the inning, but they were just getting started.

After Eddie Miksis's back-to-the-pitcher force out, which would have normally ended the inning, Russo yielded consecutive run-scoring singles to Bruce Edwards and Ed Head and was done for the night. His replacement, Johnny Murphy, added to the Yankees' defensive miseries with an errant throw home on Stanky's squeeze bunt. A wave of Dodgers hits followed – Rojek's double, singles by Furillo and Tatum, and another double by Woyt. Robinson delivered his second run batted in and the 11th run of the inning by lining out to center field. The inning was mercifully over when Miksis, the 15th batter for the Dodgers, popped out to Rizzuto – 11 runs, six hits, three walks and three errors, and eventually a 14-6 win.

The remainder of the game was of little consequence offensively. The Yankees got a late-inning home run from Johnny Lindell and nine hits total for

Dodgers to Be Commended for Signing Robinson

The Brooklyn Dodgers' brief announcement that the team had purchased the contract of Jackie Robinson from the Montreal Royals has far-reaching significance.

It means that for the first time in the national pastime, a big league team will carry on its roster a member of the Negro race. It means that the barriers have finally been lifted for other Negroes to follow suit, not alone with the Dodgers, but with the rest of the National and American League teams.

And it also denotes that when Branch Rickey, president of the team, signed Robinson he had every intention and desire to give him a chance to make good as a big leaguer.

There is little doubt that Robinson is equipped, physically and mentally, as a major leaguer. A fine hitter, a speedy runner and a capable defensive player, Robinson has the ability to achieve stardom in the big time.

The Brooklyn Baseball Club is to be commended for its decision to sign Robinson.

Brooklyn Daily Eagle editorial, April 11, 1947: 10.

the game. Over the last three innings, the Dodgers faced Spud Chandler, and were held scoreless. Chandler, a 20-game winner in 1946, was the likely Yankees starter on Opening Day. Robinson didn't get any of the Dodgers' 16 hits, but he did lead them with three runs batted in.

JACKIE ROBINSON'S FIRST AT-BATS AT EBBETS FIELD AS A DODGER[12]

- First inning: flied to CF (Bevens)
- Third inning: flied to LF, RBI (Bevens)
- First inning: ground ball to SS, error, RBI (Russo)
- Fifth inning: lineout to CF, RBI (Murphy)
- Seventh inning: sacrifice bunt to P, error (S. Chandler)

How did Robinson do at first base? "On the field, he handled fifteen chances like a veteran. Two were difficult ones, but Robby did his part neatly."[13]

The Yankees returned the favor the very next day by defeating the Dodgers, 8-1, on 11 hits and solid pitching from both Allie Reynolds and Frank "Spec" Shea, who each limited the Dodgers to two hits. Of course, all eyes were on Robinson who delivered his first hit as a Dodger in addition to fielding flawlessly at first base. In the fourth inning, Robinson singled against Reynolds, scoring Pete Reiser and temporarily cutting the Yankees lead to 2-1.[14]

The Yankees also won the final game of the series, scoring four runs in the ninth inning for the 10-9 victory. Robinson, who singled in the first inning, missed a chance to be the game's hero for the Dodgers. His foul pop left the tying run stranded at second base in the ninth inning. The victory allowed the Yankees to win their spring-training series against the Dodgers five games to three. For the three games, it was clear the fans came to see Jackie Robinson. The total series attendance (79,441) set an all-time exhibition record.[15]

Spring training was now over. It was time for Opening Day at Ebbets Field. Jackie Robinson's own words in the *Pittsburgh Courier* captured his sentiments about the moment. "I know now that dreams do come true. I know because I am playing with the Brooklyn Dodgers in the big leagues."[16] Perhaps you can still hear Ebbets Field public address announcer Tex Rickards intoning, "Number 42, Jackie Robinson," for the very first time in that very first game and many games to come.

AUTHOR'S NOTE

Louis Effrat, sportswriter for the *New York Times*, reminds us that the details of an exhibition game, particularly the play-by-play accounts, can often become less interesting or important than the stories surrounding the game itself. He pulled no punches when discussing his coverage of this game, particularly the bottom of the fifth inning. "Detailed description of Brooklyn's attack and New York's defense in this frame would be pointless. Anyway, Russo and Murphy would rather forget about everything that occurred."[17] Telling his readers of Russo's walks and Rizzuto's miscues sufficed for Effrat. Dick Young was a bit more forthcoming in the *New York Daily News*.[18]

NOTES

1. Louis Effrat, "Royals' Star Signs with Brooks Today," *New York Times*, April 11, 1947: 20.
2. The 1947 Montreal Royals (International League), defending Junior World Series champions, were a very talented team. Of the 12 players whose names appear in the *New York Times* box score of the game, 11 played in the major leagues at one time or another in their baseball careers.
3. Louis Effrat, "Brooks Win, 14-6, With 11-Run Fifth," *New York Times*, April 12, 1947: 12. Effrat also reported that Dixie Walker said he had been misquoted and denied that he had voiced disapproval of Robinson.
4. Jackie Robinson, "Jackie Robinson Says," *Pittsburgh Courier*, April 19, 1947: 18.
5. Hy Turkin, "Robinson Bought by Dodgers; Hitless as Royals Win, 4-3," *New York Daily News*, April 11, 1947: 63.
6. Robinson.
7. Irv Goldfarb, "Spring Training in Havana," in Lyle Spatz, ed., *The Team That Forever Changed Baseball and America, The 1947 Brooklyn Dodgers* (Lincoln: University of Nebraska Press, 2012), 3-5.
8. Michael Gaven, "Jackie Robinson Gets Chance with Flatbush Troupe," *The Sporting News*, April 16, 1947: 1.
9. Roger Kahn, *Rickey & Robinson* (New York: Rodale Press, 2014), 236. Robinson told Kahn, "I wasn't pleased. Now, in addition to everything else, I was going to have to learn a new position."
10. "Text of the Decision by Commissioner Chandler," *New York Times*, April 10, 1947: 31.
11. Louis Effrat, "Chandler Bars Durocher for 1947 Baseball Season," *New York Times*, April 10, 1947: 1; Dan Daniel, "Chandler Rolls Up Sleeves for New Swings," *The Sporting News*, April 16, 1947: 1.
12. Dick Young, "Flock Scores 11 in 5th to Blast Yanks, 14-6, *New York Daily News*, April 12, 1947: 29.
13. Effrat, April 12, 1947.
14. Louis Effrat, "Yankees' 11 Hits Beat Dodgers, 8-1, for Series Lead," *New York Times*, April 13, 1947: 5-1.
15. Louis Effrat, "Bombers' 4 in 9th Down Brooks, 10-9," *New York Times*, April 14, 1947: 19.
16. Robinson.
17. Effrat, April 12, 1947.
18. Young.

JACKIE ROBINSON'S MAJOR-LEAGUE DEBUT

APRIL 15, 1947: BROOKLYN DODGERS 5, BOSTON BRAVES 3,
AT EBBETS FIELD, BROOKLYN

by Lyle Spatz

Jackie Robinson's major-league debut was more than just the first step in righting an historical wrong. It was a crucial event in the history of the American civil rights movement, the importance of which went far beyond the insular world of baseball.

The Dodgers signed Robinson to a major-league contract just five days before the start of the 1947 season. Baseball people, especially those in Brooklyn, were still digesting the previous day's news of manager Leo Durocher's one-year suspension (for conduct detrimental to baseball), when the story broke of Robinson's promotion from the Montreal Royals of the International League. He would be the first Black American to play in what were then designated the major leagues since catcher Moses Fleetwood Walker played for the Toledo Blue Stockings of the American Association back in 1884.

Robinson had played second base for the Royals in 1946, but on orders from the Dodgers he had been working out at first base all spring. He played the position in Brooklyn's final three exhibition games against the Yankees, and again two days later when the Dodgers opened the season at Ebbets Field against the Boston Braves. Rumors of a sellout may have discouraged some fans from attending, but whatever the reason, a crowd of only 26,623 saw Robinson's debut, including "an estimated 14,000 black fans."[1]

In his *New York Times* column the morning of the game, Arthur Daley credited the Dodgers for doing a "deft" job of paving the way for Robinson, but added, "Yet nothing can actually lighten that pressure, and Robbie realizes it full well. There is no way of disguising the fact that he is not an ordinary rookie and no amount of pretense can make it otherwise."[2]

Robinson made the game's first putout, receiving the throw from fellow rookie Spider Jorgensen on Dick Culler's ground ball to third base. Dodgers left-hander Joe Hatten started the game for Brooklyn. Hatten gave up a single and a walk in the first, but no Braves scored.

Interim manager Clyde Sukeforth had Robinson batting second, so after Eddie Stanky grounded out, the rookie first baseman stepped in against Johnny Sain for his first major league at-bat. Sain, the National League's winningest right-hander in 1946, retired him easily on a bouncer to third baseman Bob Elliott. After flying out to left fielder Danny Litwhiler in the third inning, Robinson appeared to have gotten his first big-league hit in the fifth. But shortstop Culler made an outstanding play on his ground ball and turned it into a well-executed 6-4-3 double play.

When he next batted, in the seventh, Brooklyn was trailing, 3–2. Stanky was on first, having opened the inning by drawing Sain's fifth walk of the afternoon. It was an obvious bunt situation, and Robinson laid down a beauty, pushing the ball deftly up the right side. The *Brooklyn Daily Eagle*'s Harold C. Burr wrote that Robinson had "sacrificed prettily."[3]

Boston's rookie first baseman, Earl Torgeson, fielded it, but with Robinson speeding down the line, he "made a hurried throw in an effort to get Robinson but hit him on the shoulder blade and the ball caromed into right field, allowing Jackie and the other runner to advance to second and third."[4] Pete Reiser's double scored both runners and finished Sain. Stanky scored the tying run, and Robinson scored the go-ahead run – which by game's end proved the winning run. Reiser

Robinson meets test with iron nerves

Newark Star Ledger, April 16, 1947: 55

Robinson's speed tells Dodger story

Fleet-footedness sets stage for decisive rally

Newark Star Ledger, April 16, 1947: 55.

later scored on Gene Hermanski's fly ball off reliever Mort Cooper as the Dodgers won, 5–3.

When the Dodgers took the field in the ninth inning, Robinson remained on the bench as veteran Howie Schultz took over at first base. Sukeforth had inserted Schultz as a defensive measure, but the Dodgers soon realized that Robinson needed no help. Schultz played in only one more game before Brooklyn sold him to the Phillies. Ed Stevens, the team's other first baseman, played in just five games before he was sent back to the minors.

Hal Gregg, in relief of Hatten, got the win, and Hugh Casey got the first of his league-leading 18 saves.[5] Sain bore the loss.

The popular Reiser, coming back from yet another injury, clearly had been the star of the game, and it was he, not Robinson, who was the focus of the story in the next day's *New York Times*. Roscoe McGowen's game account mentioned Robinson only in relation to his play, leaving columnist Arthur Daley to take note of his debut, which he called "quite uneventful."[6]

He wrote that Robinson "makes no effort to push himself…and already has made a strong impression," and then quoted Robinson as saying "I was nervous in the first play of my first game at Ebbets Field, but nothing has bothered me since."[7]

In retrospect, it would be easy, and fashionable, to attribute the writers' casual treatment of this history-making game to racism. It is perhaps more charitable, and accurate, to think that they handled it in this way because it took place at a time when baseball reporters believed that that's what they were: baseball reporters, men who felt their sole duty was to report what took place on the field. Red Barber and Connie Desmond, the Dodgers' radio broadcasters, did the same.

Rachel Robinson has written about this Opening Day game: "In 1947, as Jack took his place in the batter's box in Ebbets Field, and Rickey watched from the owner's box, the meaning of the moment for me seemed to transcend the winning of a ballgame. The possibility of social change seemed more concrete, and the need for it seemed more imperative. I believe that the single most important impact of Jack's presence was that it enabled white baseball fans to root for a black man, thus encouraging more whites to realize that all our destinies were inextricably linked."[8]

Robinson's first base hit came in the season's second game, on April 17 against the Braves. His first run batted in came against the New York Giants on April 18. By season's end, he had hit for a .297 batting average (with a .383 on-base percentage), with a league-leading 29 stolen bases. He scored 125 runs, and drove in 48. His 28 sacrifice hits led both leagues. Robinson was the overwhelming choice in voting for Rookie of the Year, the first player ever accorded Rookie of the Year honors, at a time before voters honored a separate rookie in each league.

SOURCES

This article is adapted from the author's "Jackie Robinson on Opening Day, 1947-1956." Joseph Dorinson, and Joram Warmund, eds. *Jackie Robinson: Race, Sports, and the American Dream* (Armonk, New York: M. E. Sharpe, 1998.)

In addition to the sources cited in the Notes, the author also consulted Baseball-Reference.com and Retrosheet.org.

Jackie Robinson's Batting and Fielding Record on Opening Day[9]

		AB	H	2B	3B	HR	BB	SB	SAC	R	RBI	PO	A	E
April 15, 1947 vs BOS	(1B)	3	0	0	0	0	0	0	1	1	0	11	0	0
April 20, 1948 at NY	(2B)	5	1	1	0	0	0	0	0	1	2	2	3	0
April 19, 1949 vs NY	(2B)	5	3	0	0	1	0	0	2	1	6	6	0	
April 18, 1950 at PHI	(2B)	4	2	1	0	0	0	0	1	0	2	1	0	
April 17, 1951 at PHI	(2B)	4	2	0	0	1	0	0	1	2	8	1	0	
April 15, 1952 at BOS	(2B)	3	1	0	0	1	0	0	0	2	3	0		
April 14, 1953 vs PIT	(3B)	3	2	0	0	0	0	0	2	0	0	2	0	
April 13, 1954 at NY	(LF)	4	1	0	0	0	0	0	0	2	0	0		
April 13, 1955 vs PIT	(3B)	4	2	1	0	0	0	0	1	1	0	3	0	
April 17, 1956 vs PHI	(LF)	3	0	0	0	0	0	1	0	1	1	4	1	
		38	14	3	0	2	1	0	2	9	7	34	23	1

NOTES

1. Jules Tygiel, *Baseball's Great Experiment: Jackie Robinson and His Legacy* (New York: Oxford University Press, 1983), 178.

2. Arthur Daley, "Play Ball!," *New York Times*, April 15, 1947: 31.

3. Harold C. Burr, "'Old' Reiser, 'New' Hernanski Stars of Dodgers' Opening Day Triumph," *Brooklyn Daily Eagle*, April 16, 1947: 19. Left fielder Hermanksi also had a run batted in.

4   Carl Rowan with Jackie Robinson, *Wait Till Next Year* (New York: Random House, 1960), 179.

5   Nobody had ever heard of "saves" in 1947, and Casey died never knowing that he had twice been the National League leader.

6   Arthur Daley, "Opening Day at Ebbets Field," *New York Times*, April 16, 1947: 32.

7   "Opening Day at Ebbets Field."

8   Rachel Robinson, with Lee Daniels, *Jackie Robinson: An Intimate Portrait* (New York: Abrams, 2014), 66.

9   Compiled from data furnished by Dr. David W. Smith of Retrosheet.

THE FIRST OF 1,518: JACKIE ROBINSON GETS HIS FIRST MAJOR-LEAGUE HIT

APRIL 17, 1947: BROOKLYN DODGERS 12, BOSTON BRAVES 6, AT EBBETS FIELD, BROOKLYN

By Kevin Larkin

During his 10-year career in the major leagues, Jackie Robinson got 1,518 hits in 1,382 games. His first safety came on April 17, 1947, against the Boston Braves at Ebbets Field in the second game of his career. Baseball's first African-American player in the twentieth century had made his debut two days earlier, on Opening Day against the Braves, and went hitless in three at-bats. The first baseman also reached on an error and scored a run.

Dodgers interim manager Clyde Sukeforth (appointed after Leo Durocher was suspended for conduct detrimental to baseball, and replaced after this game by Burt Shotton), sent veteran right-hander Kirby Higbe to the mound to face the Braves, who had finished in fourth place in 1946. Boston manager Billy Southworth's choice to start was right-hander Mort Cooper.

Leading off the game for Boston before the crowd of 10,252 at Ebbets Field was Braves shortstop Dick Culler, who grounded out to Spider Jorgensen at third base. Johnny Hopp singled but was left stranded after Bama Rowell grounded out and Bob Elliott struck out.

Brooklyn scored three times in the bottom of the first. Eddie Stanky, known for his keen eye at the plate, walked. Robinson flied out to center fielder Hopp. A single by Pete Reiser sent Stanky to third base, and he scored on a groundout by Dixie Walker that sent Reiser to second base. Gene Hermanski reached on an error by first baseman Earl Torgeson that sent Reiser across the plate with the Dodgers' second run. Brooklyn catcher Bruce Edwards singled to send Hermanski to third base, and Hermanski scored on an error by Culler.

Higbe struck out Tommy Neill leading off the second, but the next three Braves reached base. Torgeson walked, Phil Masi doubled, sending Torgeson to third, and Connie Ryan's single scored both baserunners. Ryan took second of Cooper's sacrifice, and Culler walked, but Hopp struck out swinging to end the inning with the Dodgers ahead, 3-2.

The Dodgers enjoyed another big inning in the second. Robinson got a four-pitch walk with one out. Reiser's single sent Robinson to third base and another walk, to Walker, loaded the bases with Hermanski coming to the plate. The Dodgers left fielder sent a fly ball to deep right field that scored Robinson, and a single by Edwards scored Reiser. Jorgensen drove in two runs with a double. The hit knocked Cooper out of the game; he was replaced on the mound by Andy Karl, who got Pee Wee Reese to ground out and end the inning.

In the bottom of the fourth, with Glenn Elliott now pitching for the Braves, Reiser singled, Dixie Walker walked, and with two outs, Jorgensen hit a three-run home run to put the Dodgers ahead 10-2.

Still in search of his first major-league hit, Robinson faced Elliott with one out in the fifth inning. He bunted the first pitch down the third-base line and beat it out for a single. He went to second on a groundout by Reiser but was left stranded base when Walker grounded out to Culler, the Braves shortstop. Sportswriter Dick Young called Robinson's first hit a "strong one-bounce bunt" that "took (a) twisting bounce off Elliott's bare hand as Bob charged in. When official scorer Lee Scott flashed 'H' sign on (the) scoreboard, (the) crowd cheered."[1] Harold C. Burr in the *Brooklyn Eagle* wrote that "the ball skidded away from the Braves' third baseman, but was a

Shotton Sees Robinson Hit Dodger Home Run

Milwaukee Journal, April 18, 1947: 46.

legitimate hit all the way." He added, "The negro isn't exactly wearing the ball out, but he's still under heavy pressure."2

Boston rallied in the sixth inning when Ryan followed Masi's single with a double that sent Masi to third base. Pinch-hitting for Elliott, Tommy Holmes was walked intentionally. Mike McCormick, batting for Culler, spoiled the strategy with a single scoring Masi and Ryan. Hopp doubled Holmes and McCormick home, and Brooklyn's lead was down to 10-6.

Duke Snider made his major-league debut in the Dodgers' half of the sixth. The top prospect and future Hall of Famer pinch-hit for Tommy Tatum. Facing new Boston pitcher Si Johnson, Snider led off the frame with a single to right field. He went to second on a sacrifice by Edwards and scored when Jorgensen got his sixth RBI of the game, on a double to right field. Jorgensen took third on Reese's groundout and scored when pitcher Harry Taylor singled to left field.

It was just Jorgensen's second game in the majors. Like Robinson, the third baseman had made his debut two days earlier in the Opening Day win over Boston. The year before, he was Robinson's teammate with the Montreal Royals of the International League and batted .293 with 5 home runs and 71 RBIs. The 5-foot-9-inch Jorgensen, from Folsom, California, weighed just 155 pounds, but *New York Daily News* writer Dick Young wrote that "(h)is scrawny frame is misleading."3 Young commented on the 26-year-old Jorgensen's "drawn cheeks" that "make you want to hand him a buck for meal," but added, "(S)omewhere in his bony body, he packs plenty of power."4 Jorgensen earned a late promotion to the Dodgers out of spring training and, according to the *Brooklyn Eagle*, "reported in such a hurry to the Dodgers opening day that he had to borrow a pair of baseball shoes, before he could go to third base."5

Harry Taylor's seventh inning was eventful, to say the least. It involved a single, two walks, and a wild pitch, but no runs. Sukeforth called on reliever Hugh Casey after Taylor walked Nanny Fernandez, putting runners at first and third with one out. Casey struck out Sibbi Sisti and retired Hopp on a groundout to second base. After that, the game turned relatively quiet. Only Robinson reached base for Brooklyn in the last two innings, on a walk to lead off the seventh.

Boston loaded the bases with nobody out in the eighth inning, but Casey struck out Torgeson and got Sisti to hit into a double play. Casey walked Ryan to open the ninth, but Boston could not get a rally started.

According to the *Boston Globe*, "Neither Morton Cooper nor Kirby Higbe, from whom good pitching was anticipated, survived the pounding today in a 'marathon' ballgame, in which the Durocherless Dodgers beat the Braves, 12-6."6 The Braves used 18 players, the Dodgers 14. The *Eagle's* Burr commented, "It was one of those games with pitchers wild and practically everybody except the ushers getting into one line-up or the other."7 In a separate article, Burr wrote of the Brooklyn first baseman: "The jury is still out on Jackie Robinson."8

If so, the jury was not out for much longer. Robinson picked up eight hits over his next four games and 175 in his rookie season. He batted .297 with a .383 on-base percentage and won the first-ever Rookie of the Year award.

SOURCES

In addition to the game story and box-score sources cited in the Notes, the author consulted the Baseball-Reference.com and Retrosheet.org websites.

NOTES

1. Dick Young, "Dodgers Blast Braves, 12-6, Jorgy Bats in 6," *New York Daily News*, April 18, 1947: 198.
2. Harold C. Burr, "Jorgenson[sic] Sinking Spikes Deeply Into New Dodger Third Base Job," *Brooklyn Eagle*, April 18, 1947: 15.
3. Dick Young, "Dodgers Blast Braves, 12-6, Jorgy Bats in 6."
4. Dick Young, "Jorgensen Scales only 155, but Packs Power," *New York Daily News*, April 18, 1947: 198.
5. Harold C. Burr, "Jorgenson Sinking Spikes Deeply Into New Dodger Third Base Job."
6. Melville Webb, "Jorgenson Bats In Six Runs, Dodgers Beat B's, 12 to 6," *Boston Globe*, April 18, 1947: 29.
7. Harold C. Burr, "Jorgenson Sinking Spikes Deeply Into New Dodger Third Base Job."
8. Harold C. Burr, "Braves Seeking Surplus Dodger First Baseman," *Brooklyn Eagle*, April 18, 1947: 15.

ROBINSON TALLIES FIRST CAREER HOMER AND FIRST RBI AGAINST RIVAL GIANTS

APRIL 18, 1947: NEW YORK GIANTS 10, BROOKLYN DODGERS 4, AT THE POLO GROUNDS, NEW YORK

by Brian Wright

The measurement of Jackie Robinson's success as the first major leaguer to break the color barrier was based less on statistics than on his courage, temper, and mental acuity. But the experiment conceived by Branch Rickey and performed by Robinson would have been a fruitless endeavor had Robinson not produced on the field.

In fact, according to author Jonathan Eig in his book *Opening Day*, there was no certainty early in the 1947 season that Robinson would be an everyday player.[1]

But Robinson quickly put aside any questions of his staying power. And on a Friday afternoon at the Polo Grounds, in his introduction to the famed Dodgers-Giants rivalry, Robinson recorded his first big-league home run and run batted in on one third-inning swing against Dave Koslo.

Going 2-for-4 on a day in which Brooklyn managed seven hits, Robinson accounted for half his team's scoring – the second of the four runs being a product of his speed and daring on the basepaths. In spite of these efforts, the Giants used six long balls to pull away to an easy 10-4 victory played in 2 hours and 10 minutes.

After an initial two-game series at Ebbets Field in which the Dodgers took both from the Boston Braves, Jackie Robinson played in his first major-league game beyond the confines of Flatbush. But he was not without his legion of supporters. Out on Eighth Avenue, vendors were selling "I'm for Jackie" buttons.[2]

The Polo Grounds stood on the outskirts of Harlem, a neighborhood with a heavy Black population that had risen to about 700,000 by 1947,[3] some of whom planned to attend the game to cheer their hero on.

However, this contingent of Robinson rooters had much apprehension, partly due to the volatile area Harlem had become.

"It was unclear if black Americans were on the brink of great gains or terrible troubles, but they were clearly on the brink," Eig wrote.[4]

Those tensions were amplified by a contest between the Dodgers and Giants – a cross-borough rivalry as combative as any in baseball. There was fear that the tensions that simmered throughout the local area might escalate.

Wrote Eig: "As thousands of white New Yorkers traveled to Harlem by Checker cab and train to see the games, scores of police officers – most of them white – kept careful watch to make sure fans got in and out of the neighborhood safely. … Dodger-Giant games were among the most contentious of all, dividing ethnic groups and even families. But there had never been big black crowds at a Giants game, at least not that anyone could remember. Suddenly, with the arrival of Robinson, much of black Harlem began pulling for the Dodgers."[5]

Among those concerned about what might happen was National League President Ford Frick. Despite being very accepting of Robinson's arrival to the major leagues, Frick was worried about what might take place inside and outside the ballpark.

He "suggested that it might be a fine idea if Robinson were to sprain an ankle and miss a few games," Eig wrote.[6]

With temperatures approaching 60 degrees, the paid crowd was 37,546 – a fairly large audience for a weekday afternoon. It proceeded without notable incident and certainly had its moments when the rookie performed to the best of his capabilities. But while there was relative tranquility in the stands, there was unrest within the Dodgers' hierarchy – as Robinson and the other Dodgers watched the managerial carousel continue to spin.

Burt Shotton, a soft-spoken 62-year-old grandfatherly figure, had recently been named manager. He was replacing fill-in Clyde Sukeforth, who skippered the first two games (and coincidentally was the man who first scouted Robinson in the Negro Leagues). Shotton replaced Leo Durocher, who had been suspended for a year by Commissioner Happy Chandler just before the season began over allegations of gambling associations.

For the third time in as many games, Robinson batted second and played first base. His initial turn at the plate versus Giants starter Koslo resulted in a fly out to shallow center field.

Pee Wee Reese got the Dodgers on the board with a run-scoring fly ball in the second, only to be answered by right-hand-hitting second baseman and future Dodger killer Bobby Thomson with a home run to left field, a preview of October 1951 when he did the same to give the Giants the pennant over the Dodgers.

Brooklyn had the opportunity to answer in the top of the third inning – with Robinson providing that response.

Leading off, Robinson took Koslo's first offering for a strike, high and inside. The next pitch was a little lower and a little more over the plate. He connected – a tracer that struck the left field's upper-deck scoreboard.[7]

It was the first of 137 home runs and 734 RBIs Robinson would accumulate over the course of a 10-year major-league career that stands alone in history.

"As Robinson trotted around the bases, toes turned inward, his fans stood and laughed and hollered," Eig wrote in *Opening Day*.

Jackie didn't tip his cap to acknowledge the partisan support. Greeting him at home plate was the next batter, Tommy Tatum. The photo of a White man exchanging a handshake with a Black man ran on the back page of the next day's *New York Daily News*.[8]

The round-tripper pushed the Dodgers ahead, 2-1. In retrospect, it was a milestone moment in a career unparalleled in baseball and society. But in the context of the game itself, the homer was overshadowed by an onslaught of Giants power.

Dodgers starter Vic Lombardi came into the day with a career 9-0 mark versus New York. Hopes for adding to that perfect record were hurt when he was ambushed for two more home runs in the third inning, by Bill Rigney and Johnny Mize.

Later, after Lombardi departed down 4-2, it was Ed Chandler's turn to suffer at the mercy of New York bats. With one out in the bottom of the sixth inning,

Robinson Hits First Home Run

Los Angeles Times, April 19, 1947: 6.

Willard Marshall gave the crowd in right field a souvenir. Two batters later, Thomson belted his second of the afternoon.

Robinson watched a half-dozen New York batters take the slow trot around first base, the final blast a grand slam by Rigney off Hank Behrman in the bottom of eighth to all but ensure a Giants victory.

The outcome had remained in doubt thanks to a patented Robinson-manufactured score that began with his typical intrepid baserunning. As was explained in the *New York Daily News*, "Robinson had opened the eighth with a bloop single to right, rushed to second on Marshall's well-meant but wild peg to first as Jackie took the big turn, and scored on a couple of outs."[9]

Carl Furillo soon tripled and scored on another Giants fielding miscue, as Brooklyn cut the New York lead to 6-4. However, the Dodgers' comeback efforts were squashed once Rigney connected with the bases loaded.

Robinson's successful day at bat would've been even better had more luck been on his side. A liner in the fifth inning found its way into the glove of third baseman Jack Lohrke, who fired to first base to double off Eddie Stanky.[10] But Robinson more than made up for it with solid defense. He handled without fault each of his eight chances at first base, a position he had just come to learn prior to the season.

While the disparity in the final score leaned heavily in the Giants' favor, the final standings for 1947 showed a complete reversal: The Dodgers finished 13 games better than their foes from Manhattan and would win 14 of the 22 times they played each other.

As for Robinson, who tied for the team lead in homers with 12 while also driving in 48 runs and stealing 29 bases en route to being the first-ever Rookie of the Year, his perseverance and courage are deservedly etched in history.

The *New York Age*, one of New York City's most prominent Black newspapers, foretold what the near future held in Robinson's remarkable journey.

"For Jackie, the situation becomes even more difficult. He was a guinea pig before. He is even more of one now. Every human misstep he may commit will be watched. His triumphs will be exaggerated, and his faults rendered disproportionate. However, we have confidence in his power to keep his head and watch his step so that the important victory which has been won may be extended throughout the game."[11]

SOURCES

In addition to the references cited in the Notes, the author consulted Baseball-Reference.com and Retrosheet.org.

NOTES

1. Jonathan Eig. *Opening Day: The Story of Jackie Robinson's First Season* (New York: Simon & Schuster, 2007), 62.
2. "Ottmen Win, 10-4, with Six Home Runs," *New York Times*, April 19, 1947: 18.
3. Eig, 64.
4. Eig, 64.
5. Eig, 66.
6. Eig, 63.
7. Eig, 68.
8. Eig, 69.
9. "Shotton Named Dodger Pilot; Six Giant Homers Win 10-4," *New York Daily News*, April 19, 1947: 25.
10. "Mild-Mannered Shotton Opposite of Durocher as Manager," *Brooklyn Daily Eagle*, April 19, 1947: 6.
11. "Passing the Bar," *New York Age*, April 19, 1947: 6.

JACKIE ROBINSON'S FIRST MEETING WITH BEN CHAPMAN

APRIL 22, 1947: BROOKLYN DODGERS 1, PHILADELPHIA PHILLIES 0, AT EBBETS FIELD, BROOKLYN

by Alan Cohen

Sometimes all of the elements of the story of a ballgame are not known right away. The score is known but quite often the story of the game goes far beyond the score and so it was on April 22, 1947. For the record, the Brooklyn Dodgers defeated the Philadelphia Phillies 1-0 in the opener of a three-game series at Ebbets Field. Not immediately known was the verbal abuse visited on Jackie Robinson from the Philadelphia dugout.

The story of this game, as reported in the next day's *Brooklyn Eagle* is best shown in a line attributed to winning pitcher Hal Gregg, who had thrown a one-hitter.

"It was a bad pitch (Del) Ennis hit."[1]

On a very cold April afternoon, a double by Del Ennis on a changeup with two out in the first inning was the only blemish on a stellar performance by Gregg in his first start of the season. After Ennis's double, Gregg issued an intentional pass to Ron Northey and then retired the next 20 batters in a row. That streak was broken when he hit Andy Seminick with a pitch with one out in the eighth inning.

The Phillies' pitching was almost as good. as Dutch Leonard scattered nine hits and baffled the Dodgers hitters, when it mattered, with an array of knuckleballs. He didn't allow a hit until Eddie Stanky opened the fourth inning with a single. The Dodgers' single tally, which was aided by an error, came in the eighth inning.

Brooklyn loaded the bases with none out in the sixth inning but failed to score. Singles by Stanky and Robinson and a walk to Pete Reiser loaded the bases. Leonard fielded Dixie Walker's slow roller in time to make a diving throw to force Stanky at the plate. Ron Northey in right field then grabbed a foul ball off the bat of Gene Hermanski and gunned down Robinson trying to score from third.

In 1947 the impact of Jackie Robinson was felt in virtually every game. In the eighth inning on April 22, he shined in the field, at the plate, and on the bases. In the Phillies half of the inning, Seminick was on first base with one out, Robinson made a spectacular play at first base to rob Emil Verban of a hit. Verban's hard-hit groundball was far to the right of Robinson and on its way to right field when Robinson dived for the ball, gloved it, and raced to first base to beat Verban to the bag. Philadelphia manager Ben Chapman then let Leonard hit for himself and Gregg struck out the Philadelphia pitcher for the final out of the inning.

In the Dodgers' half of the inning, Robinson singled, hitting a popup behind second base just beyond the reach of shortstop Skeeter Newsome and second baseman Verban. The next batter was Reiser. After five knuckleballs, Robinson took off for second base. Reiser swung wildly at the pitch and struck out. The ball went a short distance away from catcher Seminick. He tried to gun down Robinson at second base, but his throw went to center field and Jackie went to third base. On the play, Robinson was credited with a steal and Seminick was charged with a throwing error that allowed Robinson to advance further.

After a walk to Dixie Walker, Hermanski came to the plate. Hermanski and pitcher Leonard engaged in a classic pitcher-batter confrontation. Of the first nine pitches, six were strikes, each fouled off by Hermanski. The other three were balls. On the 10th offering of the at-bat, Hermanski found a pitch to his liking. He lined the ball to center field and when Johnny Wyrostek failed to make a shoestring catch, Robinson scored. The Dodgers threatened to extend their lead but with the bases loaded and two out, Pee Wee Reese, mired in a major batting slump, struck out to end the inning. The Dodgers shortstop, however, would have his redemption when Philadelphia came to bat in the ninth inning.

"Reese ignored the limitations of a normal infielder."
– *New York Herald Tribune*[2]

In the ninth inning with two out, Philadelphia – without the benefit of a hit – threatened to tie the game. Ennis walked and a grounder by Northey went through Robinson's legs for his first error since joining Brooklyn. The next batter, Nick Etten, sent a groundball up the middle, but Reese dashed over from his shortstop position to field the ball and, from 10 feet away, threw backhanded to Stanky at second for the force play that ended the game. The shivering 9,790 fans at the game, who endured a 45-degree afternoon, leapt to their feet to applaud the man who would be named Dodgers captain in 1950, and Robinson sprinted to Reese from his position at first to join in the celebration of Pee Wee's spectacular game-ending play.

That same day, it was announced that Dodgers President Branch Rickey had been awarded the Benny Leonard Memorial Trophy[3] by the Maccabi Association for "the year's outstanding contribution to good sportsmanship." Factoring largely in the award was Rickey's role in the signing of Robinson and the integration of major-league baseball.[4]

Robinson's two hits on April 22 brought his batting average to .444. He had a modest four-game hitting streak going. After going hitless on Opening Day, he was 8-for-18 in Brooklyn's next four games through April 22. The next evening, Robinson appeared on the radio program *Information Please*. But unbeknownst to most fans, much more was going on.

Within two weeks of the April 22 game, another story surfaced that put the great performance by Gregg in the background and brought the challenges that Robinson faced in 1947 to the forefront.

The first inkling that there was a problem was in a small piece that appeared in the *Boston Herald* on April 27 stating that the Phillies had received a letter (it did not indicate the source of the letter but it was subsequently determined that the letter came from the office of National League President Ford Frick) reminding them that "jockeying" ballplayers is all right but that profanity should be left in the locker room – particularly when Jackie Robinson is playing."[5]

That same day, Shirley Povich wrote in the *Washington Post,* "The Phillies thus far are the only club to give Jackie Robinson of the Dodgers a fierce riding from the bench, with manager Ben Chapman setting the pace."[6]

Chapman maintained that the jockeying was not malicious, saying, "We are not making a target of Robinson. Jockeying from the bench was regular long before I was born."[7] Jack Saunders of the *Pittsburgh Courier* interviewed Chapman in Philadelphia on April 29, and the Philadelphia manager admitted that prior to the series in Brooklyn, he had instructed his bench jockeys to give it to Robinson without restraint. He said he told his players to call Robinson everything and anything they wanted to. He assured him that they had his unswerving support.[8]

Chapman's comments appeared in the May 3 issue of the *Pittsburgh Courier*. Earlier, a fan who had been at the games in Brooklyn had contacted the commissioner's office. In the game on April 22, the Philadelphia manager and his players had used every measure of verbal abuse against Robinson. Fans near the dugout heard the abuse and registered complaints with the National League president, Ford Frick. That led to Frick's reprimand prior to Brooklyn's first trip to Philadelphia.

Robinson addressed and downplayed the abuse in the *Pittsburgh Courier* on May 3, saying, "[S]ome of the Phillies bench jockey's [sic] tried to get me upset last week, but it didn't really bother me."[9] Bothered or not, Robinson went into an 0-for-20 slump from April 23 to May 1.

On the evening of May 4, Walter Winchell, on his nationwide radio broadcast, broke the story. On May 5, Commissioner Happy Chandler issued a very severe warning, an order restraining the Phillies from using "vicious un-American racial remarks" against Robinson when Brooklyn visited Philadelphia in early May.[10]

The order was delivered to the Phillies' general manager, Herb Pennock, by Walter Mulbry, secretary-treasurer of the commissioner's office. According to Mulbry, "Mr. Chandler said that no favors should be granted Robinson from the bench, but there is a limit to everything and he thought that hurling racial epithets was beyond that limit."[11] A photographer had Chapman and Robinson pose together, as if there were no tensions, and the photograph appeared in the *Philadelphia Inquirer* on May 10.

In his 1972 autobiography, Robinson addressed the events of April 22, 1947, and said that the day "brought me nearer to cracking up than I ever had been."[12]

SOURCES

In addition to Baseball-Reference.com and the sources shown in the Notes, the author used:

Baumgartner, Stan. "Feller, Gregg Pitch One-Hitters, Hal Blanks Phils for Dodgers, 1-0," *Philadelphia Inquirer*, April 23, 1947: 30.

Mardo, Bill. "Gregg's 1-Hitter Stops Phils, 1-0," *Daily Worker* (New York), April 23, 1947: 10.

Woodward, Stanley. "National League Averts Strike of Cardinals Against Robinson's Presence in Baseball," *New York Herald Tribune*, May 9, 1947: 24.

Young, Dick. "Gregg Spins One Hitter, Flock Blanks Phils, 1-0," *New York Daily News*, April 23, 1947: 66.

NOTES

1. Harold C. Burr, "Gregg Barred from Hall of Fame Three Times on Single Bingle," *Brooklyn Daily Eagle*, April 23, 1947: 19.
2. Bob Cooke, "Gregg's One-Hitter Subdues Phillies for Dodgers, 1-0," *New York Herald Tribune*, April 23, 1947: 34.
3. Leonard, a former lightweight boxing champion, had died just four days earlier.
4. "Branch Rickey Honored – Will Get Leonard Trophy for Promoting Racial Tolerance," *New York Times*, April 23, 1947: 34.
5. *Boston Herald*, April 27, 1947: 54.
6. Shirley Povich, "This Morning," *Washington Post*, April 27, 1947: M12.
7. Hy Turkin, "Police Investigate Poison Pen Threats to Jackie Robinson," *New York Daily News*, May 10, 1947: 25.
8. Wendell Smith, "'Stop Race Baiting' – Chandler: Phillies Warned by Baseball Czar Over Robinson Incident," *Pittsburgh Courier*, May 10, 1947: 1, 4.
9. Jackie Robinson, "Jackie Robinson Says," *Pittsburgh Courier*, May 3, 1947: 15.
10. Smith.
11. Smith.
12. Jackie Robinson (as told to Alfred Duckett), *I Never Had It Made*, (New York, G.P. Putnam's Sons, 1972), 71.

RACIAL SLURS WON'T STOP JACKIE ROBINSON

MAY 9, 1947: PHILADELPHIA PHILLIES 6, BROOKLYN DODGERS 5 (11 INNINGS), AT SHIBE PARK, PHILADELPHIA

by Alan Cohen

Jackie has been accepted in baseball, and we of the Philadelphia organization have no objection to his playing and wish him all the luck we can. Baseball is an American game, and there are no nationalities, creeds, nor races involved. Jackie Robinson *is an American.*[1]

This quote, attributed to Philadelphia manager Ben Chapman, was made just before Brooklyn's series at Philadelphia in early May 1947 and was prompted by Chapman's verbal abuse of Robinson, in the form of bench-jockeying, during Philadelphia's visit to Brooklyn earlier in the season. It was, by far, the worst behavior of any of the teams in the league. Chapman maintained that the jockeying was not malicious, saying, "We are not making a target of Robinson. Jockeying from the bench was regular long before I was born."[2] Jack Saunders of the *Pittsburgh Courier* interviewed Chapman in Philadelphia on April 29, and the Philadelphia manager admitted that before the series in Brooklyn, he had instructed his team to give it to Robinson without restraint. He said he told his players to call Robinson everything and anything they wanted to. He assured him that they had his unswerving support.[3]

Chapman's comments appeared in the May 3 issue of the *Pittsburgh Courier*. Earlier, a fan who had been at the games in Brooklyn had contacted the commissioner's office. Criticism of Chapman's Phillies also came from Walter Winchell who commented on their antics during his May 4 radio broadcast. The next day Commissioner Happy Chandler issued an order restraining the Phillies from using "vicious un-American racial remarks" against Robinson.[4]

The order was delivered to the Phillies' general manager, Herb Pennock, by Walter Mulbry, secretary-treasurer in the commissioner's office. Mulbry said that "Mr. Chandler said that no favors should be granted Robinson from the bench, but there is a limit to everything and he thought that hurling racial epithets was beyond that limit."[5] A photographer had Chapman and Robinson pose together, as if there were no tensions, and the photograph appeared in the *Philadelphia Inquirer* on May 10.

Tensions were high in the early weeks of the season. Robinson was receiving a two-man police escort when leaving the ballpark. An article by Stanley Woodward in the *New York Herald Tribune* indicated that the Cardinals had threatened to strike rather than play against Robinson. Although Cardinals owner Sam Breadon and manager Eddie Dyer denied the claim, they spoke, per orders from National League President Ford Frick, to their ballplayers.[6] Frick said that Robinson had the full backing of the National League and that any unwarranted persecution of him would result in severe disciplinary action against the offenders.[7]

Jackie Robinson had been with the Brooklyn Dodgers for less than a month when the team visited Philadelphia to play the Phillies on May 9, 1947. He was quartered in housing apart from that of his teammates.[8] No sooner had the Dodgers arrived than it was revealed that Robinson had been on the receiving end of poison-pen letters from anonymous sources essentially implying that Robinson should get out of baseball – or else. Two of the letters, each containing a fictitious return address, were turned over to the police by Arthur Mann, assistant to Dodgers President Branch Rickey.

It was Brooklyn's first visit of the season to Philadelphia. The 22,680 fans attending the May 9 contest at Shibe Park applauded Robinson in each of his trips to the plate. They were treated to a close game with the home team winning 6-5 in 11 innings when Emil Verban doubled over the head of Pete Reiser in center field to score Andy Seminick, who had walked and gone to second on a bunt by Lee Handley, with the game-winner. The fans were also treated to Robinson's best game to date.

"There was an inning that should be embalmed in Cooperstown."
– Dick Young, May 10, 1947[9]

The Phillies jumped out to an early lead with five second-inning runs. Wildness by Dodgers starter Hal Gregg was a major factor in the big inning. Walks to Del Ennis and Seminick put runners on first and second with none out. Gregg threw Lee Handley's comebacker into right field trying for a force at second base. Ennis scored the first run of the game, and Seminick went to third base. Verban followed with a liner off the pitcher's shin that went for an infield hit, scoring Seminick. Philadelphia pitcher Oscar Judd then laid down a perfect bunt that loaded the bases. Skeeter Newsome walked to force Handley home, and Philadelphia had three runs without the benefit of a batted ball having traveled more than 60 feet.

Gregg was replaced by Ralph Branca, who poured gasoline on the fire by walking Harry Walker, forcing in Philadelphia's fourth run. Branca struck out Johnny Wyrostek for the first out of the inning, but walked Nick Etten, bringing home the fifth run. The inning came to an end when Ennis hit into a 6-4-3 double play.

The Dodgers had seven innings in which to close the gap. In the fourth, Brooklyn scored its first run. Robinson doubled to right-center, bringing the crowd to its feet, advanced to third on a fly ball by Reiser and came home on a groundball by Dixie Walker. Branca found his rhythm and retired 15 of the 16 batters he faced in innings three through seven. The score remained 5-1 until the Dodgers came to bat in the eighth inning.

Spider Jorgensen led off the eighth with an infield hit and Pee Wee Reese walked. Howie Schultz batted for Branca and hit into a double play. Eddie Stanky's hard grounder to third was handled by Handley on a great play, but Handley's throw to first was in the dirt and eluded first baseman Etten. Stanky was awarded a single and Jorgensen crossed the plate with the Dodgers' second run. Robinson's second hit of the game went to center field, and Reiser's double to left-center sent Stanky and Robinson home, making the score 5-4. Philadelphia made a pitching change, bringing in Dutch Leonard to replace Judd. Dixie Walker's single tied the score, but further damage was avoided when Leonard retired Carl Furillo on a groundball.

Hugh Casey succeeded Branca on the mound. He had not been scored upon in six of his seven outings and had two wins and four saves to show for his efforts. Casey retired the Phillies in order in the bottom of the eighth. Leonard mowed down the Dodgers in the ninth, but the Phillies mounted a threat in the home half of the inning. Lee Handley singled to right field to lead off. Emil Verban bunted toward first base and Robinson charged, grabbing the ball before it hit the ground and throwing a bullet to second baseman Ed Stanky covering first, doubling off Handley. Casey struck out Leonard to end the inning, and the game went into extra innings.

There was no scoring in the 10th, and Leonard, in his third inning of relief, put the Dodgers down in order in the 11th inning, setting up the opportunity for Philadelphia to win the game in the bottom of the inning on Verban's double.

The win went to Leonard, bringing his record to 4-1. Casey's record went to 2-1.

Robinson, who had ended April with five hitless games (0-for-18) that saw his batting average plummet from .409 to .225, was rebounding. His 2-for-5 performance on May 9 marked the fifth consecutive game in which he hit safely, and that streak eventually became 14 consecutive games. He surpassed that streak with a 21-game hitting streak from June 14 through the first game of a July 4 doubleheader. He finished the season with a .297 batting average, led the National League with 29 stolen bases, finished fifth in the MVP balloting, and easily won the Rookie of the Year Award. He played with the Dodgers through 1956, was named National League MVP in 1949, was named to six All-Star teams and entered the Hall of Fame in 1962.

Pitcher Branca, who stopped the bleeding on May 9, went on to have his best season with the Dodgers, finishing at 21-12 with a 2.67 ERA.

Schultz's pinch-hitting appearance in the eighth inning was his last at-bat with the Dodgers. The next day the Dodger first baseman was sold to the Phillies for $50,000.

The loss caused the Dodgers to drop from first to third in the standings, one game behind the Braves and Cubs, who were tied for first. But the Dodgers went on to win the National League pennant before falling to the Yankees in the World Series.

SOURCES

In addition to the sources shown in the Notes, the author used Baseball-Reference.com and the following:

Baumgartner, Stan. "Phils Beat Dodgers in 11th 6-5; 22,680 See Verban's Hit Win," *Philadelphia inquirer*, May 10, 1947: 14.

Burr, Harold C. "Flock Lose Top Spot, Rickey Wins $50,000," *Brooklyn Daily Eagle*, May 10, 1947: 6.

Brands, Edgar G. "Jackie Will Get Equal Chance, Rest Up to Him," *The Sporting News*, May 21, 1947: 4.

"'Jackie Just Another Player to Us – with No Favors,' Says Chapman," *The Sporting News*, May 7, 1947: 6.

McGowen, Roscoe. "Dodgers Beaten by Phils in 11-Inning Night Contest," *New York Times*, May 10, 1947: 16.

NOTES

1. Hy Turkin, "Police Investigate Poison Pen Threats to Jackie Robinson," *New York Daily News*, May 10, 1947: 25.
2. Turkin.
3. Wendell Smith, "'Stop Race Baiting' – Chandler: Phillies Warned by Baseball Czar Over Robinson Incident," *Pittsburgh Courier*, May 10, 1947: 1, 4.
4. Smith.
5. Smith.
6. Stanley Woodward, "Views of Sport – General Strike Conceived," *New York Herald Tribune*, May 9, 1947, reprinted in *The Sporting News*, May 21, 1947: 4.
7. "Robinson Reveals Written Threats," *New York Times*, May 10, 1947: 16.
8. "Varied Policies at Hotels Greet Robinson on Trip," *The Sporting News*, May 21, 1947: 8.
9. Dick Young, "Phils Win in Eleventh, Topple Dodgers 6-5," *New York Daily News*, May 10, 1947: 25.

ROBINSON'S BASERUNNING AND HODGES' HOMER LIFT DODGERS

JUNE 18, 1947: BROOKLYN DODGERS 5, CHICAGO CUBS 3, AT WRIGLEY FIELD, CHICAGO

by Paul Hofmann

The Wednesday afternoon game was the second of a three-game series between the Dodgers and Chicago Cubs. The series took on historical significance: It was the first time an African-American baseball player appeared in a major-league game at Chicago's Wrigley Field. The visiting Dodgers and their much-heralded rookie Jackie Robinson were making their first visit of the year to Chicago.

The fourth-place Dodgers, who won the series opener two days earlier, had yet to find their stride and were 28-25, three games behind the front-running Boston Braves. Dick Young of the *Daily News* noted that the two things the Dodgers did poorest were run the bases and hit home runs.[1] The surprising third-place Cubs were 29-23, only 1½ games off the pace.

Partly cloudy skies and afternoon temperatures in the mid- to upper 60s greeted an announced crowd of 23,313 at Wrigley Field. With little more than a gentle breeze, it was ideal weather for baseball.

Right-hander Rex Barney drew the starting assignment for the Dodgers. The 22-year-old pitcher was making his fifth start of the season and had a record of 3-2 with a 4.45 ERA. He was opposed by 31-year-old Hank Borowy. The right-handed veteran was a large part of the Cubs' early-season success. He was 7-2 with a 2.52 ERA. The two starters dominated the first 2½ innings as both teams failed to register a hit.

The Cubs scored first in the bottom of the third. First baseman Eddie Waitkus drew a leadoff walk and one out later Borowy registered the game's first hit, a double to right field that advanced Waitkus to third. Falling behind 0-and-2, Stan Hack doubled to left to drive in both Waitkus and Borowy with the game's first runs. After Don Johnson grounded out to third for the second out of the inning, Andy Pafko singled to center, scoring Hack. At the end of three innings the Cubs were leading, 3-0.

Borowy was perfect through the first four innings. However, the Dodgers began to chip away at the Cubs' lead in the top of the fifth inning. Carl Furillo drew a leadoff walk. Dixie Walker singled, advancing Furillo to second. After Spider Jorgensen bounced into a 3-6 fielder's choice that moved Furillo to third, Pee Wee Reese lined out to left field to plate Furillo and cut the Cubs' lead to 3-1.

The Dodgers tied the score in the sixth. Al Gionfriddo batted for Barney and struck out to lead off. Eddie Stanky walked and Robinson, who entered the game batting .298, followed with a single to center that sent Stanky to third. Robinson advanced to second on the throw. Left fielder Gene Hermanski singled to center to score both Stanky and Robinson, tying the score. Hermanski, who "hesitated terribly long"[2] when he attempted to advance to second on the relay throw to the plate, was thrown out by catcher Bob Scheffing. The baserunning error might have cost the Dodgers a big inning as Furillo followed with a single to right and Walker walked before Jorgensen lined out to shortstop to end the inning.

In the bottom of the inning, left-hander Joe Hatten relieved Barney. The 25-year-old was making his first relief appearance of the year after 14 starts. He entered the game with a record of 6-4 and a 3.83 ERA. After walking Johnson to start the inning, Hatten got Pafko to bounce to shortstop for a double play and struck out Phil Cavarretta looking.

With one out in the top of the seventh, Borowy tried to sneak a fastball past rookie catcher Gil Hodges. The 23-year-old Hodges, who entered the game with a .083 batting average, broke the 3-3 tie with a "370-foot smash into the ramp in left."[3] It was the first of his 370 career home runs.

After the game Branch Rickey commented on Hodges' inability to hit at the major-league level.

"He's just a baby. … [D]oesn't know what a curveball is," Rickey said.[4] Before the home run, Hodges had only one hit and had been fed a steady diet of curveballs by National League pitchers.

The Cubs threatened in their half of the seventh. Dom Dallessandro singled to left with one out and moved to second when Hatten hit Waitkus with the next pitch. Dodgers manager Burt Shotton replaced Hatten with right-hander Hugh Casey, who was 3-2 on the year with eight saves and a 3.38 ERA. Casey hit Lennie Merullo to load the bases. Cubs manager Charlie Grimm inserted Bill Nicholson as a pinch-hitter for Borowy. Nicholson popped out to Robinson in foul territory. The threat ended when Hack sent a short pop fly to left-center that was handled by Reese.

With Borowy now out of the game, Grimm turned to right-hander Emil Kush to take over on the mound and hold the game at 4-3. Kush was another early-season bright spot for the Cubs. He was 1-1 with five saves and a 2.64 ERA.

The Dodgers, on the strength of Robinson's aggressive baserunning, manufactured a run in the top of the eighth. Robinson reached on an error when Don Johnson failed to come up with his grounder to second. Hermanski sacrificed Robinson to second with a bunt that Scheffing fielded and fired to Johnson, who was covering first. Robinson "saw that third base had been left unguarded" and raced around second and headed to third.[5] Johnson "threw in the hope that somebody would show up to cover third and when the ball went hopping toward the Cubs bullpen, Robinson scored."[6] Robinson had scored from first on a sacrifice bunt!

The Cubs did not go quietly in the ninth. With one out Peanuts Lowrey singled to right. Waitkus followed with a single to center to put runners at first and second. Merullo flied out to left and the Cubs were down to their final out. With the pitcher's spot up, Grimm sent aging former All-Star Lonny Frey in to pinch-hit for Kush. After working the count full, Frey lofted a fly ball to left that Hermanski caught to end the game.

The win went to Hatten, his seventh of the year against four defeats. He went on the finish the year with a career-high 17 victories against eight defeats. Casey earned the save, his ninth of year,[7] on the way to a league-leading and career-high 18. Borowy suffered the loss, dropping his record to 7-3. The time of the game was 2 hours and 14 minutes.

The two teams went in opposite directions during the remaining part of the season. The Cubs went 40-61 the rest of the way and finished in sixth place with a record of 69-85. The Dodgers were 65-35 over their last 100 games and won the National League pennant with a record of 94-60. They lost the World Series in seven games to the New York Yankees.

Robinson continued his aggressive style of play and was amazingly consistent throughout the rest of the season. He finished the year with a .297 average, 12 home runs, 48 RBIs, and a league-leading 29 stolen bases and 28 sacrifice hits. He won the National League's Rookie of the Year award, comfortably outpolling right-handed pitcher Larry Jansen who went 21-5 for the New York Giants.

SOURCES

In addition to the sources cited in the Notes, the author consulted Baseball-Reference.com and Retrosheet.org

NOTES

1. Dick Young, "Dodgers Edge Cubs, 5-3, on Hodges' HR in 7th," *New York Daily News*, June 19, 1947: 63.
2. Young.
3. Young.
4. Young.
5. Edward Burns, "Dodgers Beat Hank Borowy and Cubs, 5-3," *Chicago Tribune*, June 19, 1947: 29.
6. Burns.
7. Saves were not a recognized statistic until 1969, but have been compiled retrospectively.

JACKIE ROBINSON STEALS HOME FOR THE FIRST TIME

JUNE 24, 1947: BROOKLYN DODGERS 4, PITTSBURGH PIRATES 2, AT FORBES FIELD, PITTSBURGH

by Steven Kuehl

On the morning of Tuesday, June 24, 1947, two titans of sport made their final preparations before doing battle that evening. Linked not only by their race, but by the last name Robinson, Sugar Ray would fight in the ring while Jackie would fight on the diamond.

Walker Smith Jr., better known as Sugar Ray Robinson, squared off against Jimmy Doyle in the first defense of his world welterweight title in front of 11,275 fans at the Arena in Cleveland. After dreaming the night before that he killed Doyle in the ring, Robinson went on to do just that after a technical knockout in the eighth round of the 15-round bout.[1] Doyle, 22, died the next day from what the county coroner determined was a cerebral hemorrhage following "blows to the jaw and face, although his head striking the ring floor may have added to the damage."[2]

Sugar Ray is widely regarded as one of the greatest boxers of all time, if not the greatest pound-for-pound boxer to ever enter a ring.[3] He competed professionally from 1940 to 1965 and was inducted into the International Boxing Hall of Fame in 1990.[4]

Some 135 miles away, in Pittsburgh, Jack Roosevelt Robinson fought a very different battle against the Pirates that evening. In front of 35,331 fans at Forbes Field, the Brooklyn Dodgers (32-26) faced off against the Pirates (22-34). The Dodgers were managed by Burt Shotton, and Billy Herman was the skipper of the Pirates. The 2-hour 41-minute game saw a pitching matchup of the Dodgers' Ralph Branca against the veteran lefty Fritz Ostermueller of the Pirates. The 21-year-old Branca came into the game with a record of 8-6 after five days' rest and Ostermueller, 39, entered with a 5-3 record after resting for six days.

This was not the first time Robinson went toe-to-toe with Ostermueller. They had met on May 17 at Forbes Field, when Ostermueller hit Robinson with a pitch in the first inning of the series' final game. The ball hit Robinson in the left arm, not in the head as history often misrepresents, and marked the fourth time that Robinson had been hit so far in the season.[5] Ostermueller faced the Dodgers five more times that season. In his autobiography, *I Never Had It Made*, Robinson remembered the death threats, the taunting, and the attempts to intimidate and injure him. But his only memory of Ostermueller was taking advantage of the pitcher's slow and deliberate windup and stealing home with the winning run.[6]

On June 24, Eddie Stanky and Al Gionfriddo led off the game for the Dodgers by grounding out and lining out, respectively, on a total of four pitches. This brought Robinson to the plate for the first time. On the ninth pitch of the at-bat, Robinson singled to center. Carl Furillo followed Robinson by grounding out. The Pirates went one-two-three to close the frame.

Each team scored a pair of runs in the second. Dixie Walker opened the inning with a long triple to left-center and Pee Wee Reese, catching a 3-and-1 pitch on the fat part of his bat, walloped the ball far over the outer left-field barrier for his eighth homer of the campaign.[7] His 400-foot blast soared clear out of the ballpark.[8] Spider Jorgensen singled to right and Ostermueller walked Gil Hodges, but he got out of the no-out situation by striking out Branca, getting Stanky to ground out, and striking out Gionfriddo. A fielding lapse by Furillo helped the Pirates tie it immediately, although both runs eventually were earned. Ralph Kiner started with a single to left and Billy Cox whacked a hit to center. When Furillo made a wild return throw, Kiner scored and Cox reached third, then scored on Elbie

> *Robinson Steals Home in Fifth With Third Tally Before 35,331 at Pittsburgh—Reese Connects With 1 On in 2d*

New York Times, June 25, 1947: 33.

Brooklyn Daily Eagle, June 25, 1947: 15.

Fletcher's single to right.[9] Branca faced five more batters but made it through the rest of the inning without any more runs scoring.

After a couple of nonproductive innings, the fifth inning started with Stanky flying out to right; Gionfriddo walked and was out at second when Robinson hit a grounder to third. Furillo belted a single to left, which advanced Robinson to third. With Walker at the plate, the Dodgers' baserunners saw their opening. Furillo casually stole an open second base. As Ostermueller began his long windup, Robinson broke for home. He slid safely under Dixie Howell's tag to give the Dodgers the lead, 3-2. The crowd applauded Robinson as he strolled to the dugout.[10] Number 42 stole home 19 times during his 10-year career playing for the Brooklyn Dodgers, good enough to tie Frankie Frisch for ninth all-time.[11]

After both teams went one-two-three in the sixth, the final Dodgers run came in the seventh after an odd break. With Gionfriddo on second and two out, Furillo swung at a third strike and tipped it. He was called out by plate umpire Bill Stewart, but a Brooklyn squawk was upheld by first-base umpire Lee Ballanfant, who ruled that the ball had lodged in Howell's pad. The Pirates, who had left the field, had to come back, and Furillo promptly slapped a single to center to bring Gionfriddo home.[12] In the Pirates' half of the inning, Branca retired the side on a total of eight pitches, allowing only a single to Ostermueller, who was erased on Culley Rikard's double-play grounder.

Both teams were hitless and left a total of two runners on base in the final two innings. The only action came when Branca walked Kiner and Cox with two outs in the bottom of the eighth. Fletcher, though, ended the rally by lining out to right. To end the game, Branca got Wally Westlake to fly out to left and then struck out Howell and Billy Sullivan, pinch-hitting for Ostermueller.

On April 15, 1947, Robinson was the Opening Day first baseman for the Dodgers, the first Black player in twentieth-century major-league baseball. The 28-year-old went on to bat .297, score 125 runs, steal 29 bases, and win the inaugural Rookie of the Year Award. He led the league in stolen bases twice: 1947 (29) and 1949 (37). Robinson represented the NL in the All-Star Game each season between 1949 and 1953, won the NL batting title and the MVP in 1949, and was elected to the Hall of Fame in 1962. His plague states, "Displayed tremendous courage and poise in 1947 when he integrated the modern major leagues in the face of intense adversity." Robinson died on October 24, 1972. His uniform number, 42, was retired by the major leagues on April 15, 1997, the 50th anniversary of his breaking baseball's color barrier.

The Dodgers won the NL title in 1947 but lost to the New York Yankees after battling through seven games in the World Series. The Dodgers drew 1,807,526 paying fans to Ebbets Field, an NL record at the time. On the road, the Dodgers drew nearly 1.9 million, also an NL record at that time. The home figures are particularly impressive considering that the Dodgers were played in a ballpark with only 34,000 seats, the league's second smallest.[13] The Dodgers' 1947 season was later dramatized in the movie *42*, which was released on April 12, 2013, and starred the late Chadwick Boseman as Robinson.

SOURCES

In addition to the sources cited in the Notes, the author consulted Baseball-almanac.com, Baseball-reference.com, and the National Baseball Hall of Fame site at baseballhall.org/hall-of-famers.

NOTES

1. boxinghalloffame.com/robinson-kos-doyle-june-24-1947/, accessed August 10, 2020.
2. "Fighter Dies," *Cincinnati Enquirer*, June 26, 1947: 16.
3. Kevin McRae, "The Top 50 Pound-for-Pound Boxers of All Time," Bleacher Report, bleacherreport.com/articles/1436191-the-top-50-pound-for-pound-boxers-of-all-time, accessed December 24, 2020.
4. ibhof.com/pages/about/inductees/modern/robinson.html, accessed December 24, 2020.
5. Bruce Markusen, "Cooperstown Confidential: What really happened with Fritz Ostermueller and Jackie Robinson," *The Hardball Times*, tht.fangraphs.com/cooperstown-confidential-what-really-happened-with-fritz-ostermueller-and-j/, accessed August 10, 2020.
6. Richard Peterson, "The Next Page / Fritz Ostermueller, Beaned by Hollywood," *Pittsburgh Post-Gazette*, post-gazette.com/opinion/Op-Ed/2014/08/03/The-Next-Page-Beaned-by-Hollywood-by-Richard-Pete-Peterson-Fritz-Ostermueller-Pirates-pitcher-unfairly-cast-as-a-racist-in-the-movie-42/stories/201408030088, accessed August 10, 2020.
7. Roscoe McGowen, "Robinson Steals Home in Fifth with Third Tally Before 35,331 at Pittsburgh – Reese Connects With 1 on in 2d," *New York Times*, June 25, 1947: 33.
8. Dick Young, "Dodgers Edge Bucs, 4-2; Robby's Steal Snaps Tie," *New York Daily News*, June 25, 1947: 59.
9. McGowen.

10 Vince Johnson, "Robinson Steals Home in Fifth," *Pittsburgh Post-Gazette*, June 25, 1947: 14.

11 espn.com/blog/sportscenter/post/_/id/61520/this-day-in-sports-jackie-robinson-steals-home-for-the-first-time, accessed August 10, 2020.

12 McGowen.

13 John Pastier, "Brooklyn Dodgers Attendance in 1947," in Lyle Spatz, ed., *The Team That Forever Changed Baseball and America* (Lincoln: University of Nebraska Press, 2012), 329.

ROOKIE ROBINSON'S HIT STREAK REACHES 20 GAMES

JULY 3, 1947: NEW YORK GIANTS 19, BROOKLYN DODGERS 2, AT EBBETS FIELD, BROOKLYN

by Mike Huber

The fireworks arrived a few days before the Fourth of July. On Wednesday, July 2, 1947, the Brooklyn Dodgers blasted the New York Giants, 11-3, in the first of a four-game series at Ebbets Field to gain sole possession of first place in the National League. The next day, the Giants exploded with five home runs, as they "reversed their one-sided defeat of the night before, but added some terrific new business that left a ladies' day crowd of 27,938 practically in a state of coma,"1 in a 19-2 shellacking of the home team. The only highlight of the day for the home team was a 2-for-4 performance at the plate by Jackie Robinson, which extended the Brooklyn rookie's hitting streak to 20 games.

Brooklyn had made a fast start to the season, winning eight of its first 10 games. The Dodgers ran into a rough stretch in May (12-14) but then won 18 of 29 in June, gaining a share of the league lead as the month expired. The Giants, meanwhile, lost seven of nine to begin its 1947 campaign. After a hot May (17-7), they split 26 games in June. Coming into this series, the Dodgers were tied with the Boston Braves atop the league, with the Giants only a half-game back. These next four games would decide who would lead the pennant race during the last three months of the season.

New York manager Mel Ott chose Dave Koslo to get the start against the Dodgers. Winner of his last two decisions, Koslo was facing the Dodgers for the fifth time, and the Giants had won two of his previous four starts against the Flock. Brooklyn's Burt Shotton countered with Hal Gregg, who had been used as both a starter and reliever the first three months of the season. Earlier in the week (June 29), Gregg had started against Koslo and the Giants at the Polo Grounds, going 7⅔ innings but getting tagged for seven runs. (Koslo did not get the decision.)

With one out in the opening inning, Buddy Kerr singled to left. Bobby Thomson followed with a homer to give the Giants a 2-0 lead they would not relinquish. An explosion of runs took place in the second inning. Twelve New York runners came to the plate and nine of them scored, "tying a league season high for one frame which had been set the night before by the Brooks."2 Sid Gordon started it with a single to right. After Jack Lohrke walked, Koslo reached on an error by first baseman Robinson, loading the bases. Buddy Blattner rolled a grounder to short, and Koslo was forced at second base as Gordon scored. Kerr then grounded to third, but Brooklyn's Spider Jorgensen couldn't get an out and everyone was safe on the fielder's choice. (Lohrke scored). Thomson worked a full count and drew a walk, again loading the bases. Shotton made a pitching change, bringing in right-hander Hank Behrman to relieve Gregg. Behrman had started the season with the Dodgers, been traded to Pittsburgh on May 3, and then "returned to Brooklyn"3 on June 14. Unfortunately for the Dodgers, he must have left his control in the bullpen; he walked Johnny Mize and Willard Marshall, with each getting a bases-loaded RBI. Walker Cooper sent Behrman's 1-and-2 offering 400 feet into the left-center-field lower stands "on a screeching line"4 for a grand slam. Four pitches later, Gordon "whacked his No. 4 against the upper left field stands,"5 ending Behrman's day on the mound. Joe Hatten became the third Brooklyn hurler of the inning, and he retired Lohrke and Koslo to end the inning.

In the third, the Giants sent only 11 batters to the plate. Blattner opened the frame with a single and scored on Thomson's one-out homer. Hatten retired Mize, but then Marshall walked and scored on Cooper's double to right. Gordon singled up the middle, plating Cooper. Then Hatten's control disappeared. With Lohrke batting, Hatten uncorked a wild pitch, allowing Gordon to advance. Then Gordon took third on a passed ball. Lohrke drew a four-pitch walk, bringing up Koslo. New York's pitcher helped his own cause with an RBI single to left. Hatten threw another wild pitch, allowing both Lohrke and Koslo to move up a base. Blattner then doubled to left, and two more runners scored, making the score 18-0.

Clyde King came in to pitch in the top of the fourth. With one down, Mize clouted his 22nd home run, a solo shot onto Bedford Avenue. According to the *Daily News*, "the pressbox boys started rushing out for the record books."[6] At the end of 3½ innings, the Giants had "carved out an incredible 19-0 bulge."[7] King then settled down, pitching the remainder of the game for Brooklyn and allowing only two more hits, both singles.

Brooklyn managed a little bit of offense in the bottom of the fourth. Carl Furillo reached on a throwing error by Giants shortstop Kerr. After Al Gionfriddo flied out, Pee Wee Reese doubled to left field. King singled, driving in Furillo to end the shutout.

In the fifth, Eddie Stanky singled up the middle. Robinson laid down a bunt and beat it out for a single. Eddie Miksis walked, loading the bases. Furillo sent a fly ball to left, bringing home Stanky, but Gionfriddo followed with a line drive double play, ending the Dodgers rally.

The score remained 19-2. In the bottom of the ninth with one out, Duke Snider reached on a bobble by second baseman Blattner. Robinson smashed a double to right, but Snider held up at third. Koslo then retired Miksis and Furillo to end the game.

Every starter, including Koslo, drove in at least one run for the Giants. Koslo went the distance for New York, picking up his eighth win. He scattered 10 hits, but "they were widely separated,"[8] as Brooklyn couldn't get more than two safeties in any one inning. According to the *Daily News*, what the Giants did "to Hal Gregg, Hank Behrman and Joe Hatten before that would make even Bela Lugosi turn his eyes away in horror."[9]

Robinson had two hits and a walk in the defeat. During his 20-game streak, he had raised his average 20 points, to .316. Robinson hit .363 during the streak (29-for-80), with a .433 on-base percentage.

With the win, the Giants moved into second place, a half-game behind the Dodgers. The Braves, losers of three straight, fell into third place. The Giants-Dodgers series concluded with a Fourth of July doubleheader, in which Brooklyn swept the New Yorkers, 16-7 and

ROBINSON'S BRILLIANT PLAYING OPENS DOOR FOR OTHER STARS

Plaindealer (Kansas City). July 4, 1947: 4

4-3. Robinson's infield single in the sixth inning of the first contest extended his streak to 21 games, but he was hitless in four trips in the second game. He had built confidence, though, and for the rest of the season he stayed consistent. Only once did he go more than two consecutive games without getting a hit. He had come six games short of tying the National League rookie hit-streak record of 27 games, set by Jimmy Williams of the 1899 Pittsburgh Pirates.[10] Williams had a great rookie season, batting .354 and leading the league with 27 triples. The American League record of 26 games was set by Chicago White Sox rookie Guy Curtright in 1943.[11] San Diego's Benito Santiago set the current major-league rookie record of 34 games in 1987. Robinson finished 1947 with a .297 average in 151 games and won the inaugural Rookie of the Year Award.

In the span of four games, 65 runs were scored at Ebbets Field between the Giants (32) and the Dodgers (33). What mattered was that the home team had won three of the four contests. Further, some bragging rights came with the series victory. Including this July 3 game, it was the sixth time in the past eight seasons that the Dodgers had been in the top spot in the National League standings on the Fourth of July. But they had only one pennant to show for it.[12]

Robinson's hitting streak was proof that he belonged in the big leagues. Interestingly, on this day, the Cleveland Indians announced the signing of infielder Larry Doby, who had been playing for the Newark Eagles of the Negro National League and now became the first black player in the American League. According to the *New York Times*, with "Robinson proving a success, both as a Brooklyn first baseman and as a gate attraction, President Bill Veeck of the Indians indicated that a wide-open scramble for Negro players was now underway."[13] Veeck said, "I don't think any man who has the ability should be barred from the majors on account of his color."[14]

SOURCES

The author wishes to thank SABR members Bill Nowlin and Lyle Spatz, as well as Cassidy Lent of the Giamatti Research Center at the National Baseball Hall of Fame and Museum, for their assistance in finding rookie hitting streak records. In addition to the sources mentioned in the Notes, the author consulted baseball-reference.com, mlb.com, retrosheet.org, and sabr.org, to include:

Tourangeau, Dixie. "Jimmy Williams," sabr.org/bioproj/person/30c2347c. Accessed August 2019.

Zminda, Don. "Guy Curtright," sabr.org/bioproj/person/5022b476. Accessed August 2019.

NOTES

1. Roscoe McGowen, "Giants Overwhelm Dodgers With Extra-Base Blows and Move to Second Place," *New York Times*, July 4, 1947: 16.
2. McGowen.
3. retrosheet.org/boxesetc/B/Pbehrm101.htm.
4. Dick Young, "Giants Massacre Flock, 19-2, on 15-Hit Barrage; Gain 2d," *New York Daily News*, July 4, 1947: 29.
5. McGowen.
6. Young.
7. Young.
8. McGowen.
9. Young.
10. "Santiago Sets Record; SF Can Win Division Today," *Galveston* (Texas) *Daily News,* September 27, 1987: 25.
11. Boston Red Sox star Nomar Garciaparra broke Curtright's AL record in 1997, when he hit safely in 30 consecutive games.
12. Brooklyn did win the National League pennant in 1947, giving the Dodgers two first-place finishes in six seasons. As in 1941, they lost the World Series to the New York Yankees.
13. "Larry Doby, Ace Negro Infielder, Signs Contract with Cleveland," *New York Times*, July 4, 1947: 16.
14. "Larry Doby, Ace Negro Infielder, Signs Contract with Cleveland."

CARDINALS BEAT DODGERS IN EXTRA INNINGS; ENOS SLAUGHTER SPIKES JACKIE ROBINSON

AUGUST 20, 1947: ST. LOUIS CARDINALS 3,
BROOKLYN DODGERS 2 (12 INNINGS),
AT EBBETS FIELD, BROOKLYN

by Thomas J. Brown Jr.

A crowd of 25,762 showed up at Ebbets Field on August 20,1947, to see the final game of the Dodgers' four-game series against the St. Louis Cardinals. Overcast skies delayed the game for 47 minutes.

After winning the first two games of the series, Brooklyn had lost the third game, 11-3. The Dodgers still had a comfortable six-game lead over the Cardinals, but fans hoped to see them extend that lead, especially after the Cardinals had shown no kindness to Jackie Robinson throughout the series.[1]

Ralph Branca started for the Dodgers. The right-hander entered the game with a 17-9 record. Branca had pitched six solid innings in his last appearance but failed to get a win when the Dodgers couldn't hold their lead after he was removed for a pinch-hitter.

Branca looked solid from the start. The Cardinals got just three baserunners through the first seven innings. Branca hit Stan Musial with a pitch in the first. Musial was stranded there when Branca got the next batter to hit a weak groundball to first.

In the second, Branca walked Whitey Kurowski but not before he brushed him back. (Kurowski claimed he had been hit by the pitch.) Branca struck out the next two Cardinals and Kurowski was left stranded.

Branca walked Kurowski again in the fifth. This time he got Marty Marion to hit into a double play to clear the bases before striking out Del Wilber for the final out.

Murry Dickson took the mound for St. Louis. Dickson entered the game with a 9-12 record after losing his last outing, a 5-3 loss to the Pittsburgh Pirates. After getting the side out in order in the first, he gave up a double to Dixie Walker in the second. Walker remained there when Dickson got the next two Brooklyn batters out with relative ease.

The Dodgers dinged Dickson for a run in the third. A two-out single by Eddie Stanky followed by a double by Jackie Robinson gave the Dodgers the lead, 1-0.

Branca and Dickson matched each other over the next four innings. As Dickson hoped for some offensive help from his teammates, Branca maintained his no-hitter and the Dodgers clung to their one-run lead. Brooklyn added an insurance run in the eighth.

Ted Wilks had come in from the bullpen after Dickson was removed for a pinch-hitter in the top half of the frame. Stanky led off with a double to left. Robinson laid down a bunt and was safe when Wilks kicked the ball as he tried to grab it.

Howie Pollet replaced Wilks. Pete Reiser grounded into a double play but pushed Stanky to third. Pollet intentionally passed pinch-hitter Carl Furillo. Walker then "drew the cheers of his large constituency by lining a single to center to score Stanky."[2]

Branca entered the ninth needing just three more outs to secure a one-hitter and his 18th win. It would be the second time he shut out the Cardinals, after having pitched a one-hitter against them on July 18. Dodgers fans were on their feet as they watched "big Branca on the hill, dominating, strong and determined."[3]

After Branca walked Red Schoendienst to lead off the ninth, he retired the next two batters on groundouts and the Cardinals' "cause looked darker than the overcast skies" in Brooklyn.[4]

Enos Slaughter stepped to the plate. After getting ahead of Slaughter 1-and 2, Branca couldn't find the plate. Slaughter walked and the Cardinals had runners at the corners. Pitching coach Ray Blades "rushed out to have a calm-down confab with the young ace. [Branca] nodded reassuringly. He was all right. But he wasn't."[5]

"[H]ome plate started jumping around on Branca"[6] and his first two pitches to Ron Northey were balls. Dodgers manager Burt Shotton determined that Branca had reached his limit and called in Hugh Casey to finish the game.

Northey banged a single to just to the right of second base. Pee Wee Reese dived in a desperate attempt to catch the ball but came up short. Schoendienst scored and Slaughter ended up on third. Chuck Diering ran for Northey.

Kurowski then "slapped a grounder of only fair speed toward third – a cinch out at first or second base."[7] Spider Jorgensen fumbled the ball and then couldn't find the handle to make the throw. By the time he did, the runners were safe and Slaughter crossed the plate with the tying run.

Brooklyn went down in order in the bottom of the ninth, and the game went into extra innings.

After Casey got the Cardinals out in order in the top of the 10th, the Dodgers had a chance to win in the bottom of the inning. But they couldn't bring a runner across the plate safely. Stanky opened with a single. He advanced on Robinson's sacrifice. Pollet intentionally walked Reiser.

With one out, Furillo sent a rocket into right field that had "Stanky heading for pay dirt. Diering charged the ball like an infielder, scooped it up and made a perfect throw to nail Stanky."[8] Stanky made his best effort to break up the play, climbing "all over the St. Loo backstop and [sending] him sprawling but [Del Wilber] held on to the ball for the big out."[9]

Casey gave up a leadoff single in the 11th but then retired the next three Cardinals. The second of the three, Enos Slaughter, hit a grounder to Robinson. Jackie hesitated for a moment to see if he might get a force out before stepping on first.

Slaughter's foot landed on Robinson's right foot, "which was not on the bag but against it. Jackie hopped around for a minute or so … but stayed in the game."[10] The Dodgers claimed that Slaughter was intentionally trying to spike Robinson. Robinson's career "came within an inch of being ended, as Red Barber and others declared.[11]

Robinson said after the game, "All I know is that I had my foot on the inside of the bag. I gave Slaughter plenty of room." Slaughter defended himself, saying, "I've never deliberately spiked anyone in my life. Anybody who does don't belong in baseball." Stanky told reporters, "Not until this year has Robinson [had] to duck a ball thrown by one of our pitchers. So you must be sure that it was no accident when Enos spiked him."[12] In his 1972 autobiography, Robinson wrote, "Slaughter deliberately went for my leg instead of the base and spiked me rather severely."[13]

Tommy Holmes of the *Brooklyn Daily Eagle* described the incident this way: "No one can read Slaughter's North Carolina mind but the crowd unanimously decided to believe that he was curious to see how Robinson would look with one leg."[14]

In their half of the 11th, the Dodgers had their second chance to reclaim victory. Bruce Edwards led off with a walk and was sacrificed to second by Eddie Miksis.

But that was as far as he got. After Reese was given an intentional walk, Shotton decided to let pitcher Casey bat instead of using a pinch-hitter. The Dodgers manager had "done the same thing in St. Louis early this season and Casey had brought him out on top."[15] His veteran reliever didn't have the same magic this afternoon and struck out.

When the Cardinals came to bat in the 12th, Kurowski was at the plate again. He sent Casey's first pitch sailing into the left-field stands, a "mean blow into the teeth of a wind,"[16] to give St. Louis a 3-2 lead.

The home run was Kurowski's 22nd of the season, a new record for him, and his third home run in three days. Roscoe McGowen of the *New York Times* wrote that Kurowski was "strictly poison to the Dodgers" in the series.[17]

The Dodgers made "one last exciting effort for the lucky fans."[18] Robinson led off the bottom of the inning with a single to center. Reiser sacrificed him to second.

Cardinals manager Eddie Dyer replaced Pollet with right-hander Red Munger to face Furillo, "who eats southpaws on the half shell."[19] Shotton countered by sending left-hander Arky Vaughan up to bat.

Before Munger could throw his first pitch, he "wheeled and threw to Marion, racing over to second base." Robinson couldn't get back fast enough and was tagged out.

Three pitches later, Vaughan grounded to Musial at first for the final out. As the teams left the field, Kurowski ran over to Slaughter to "steer him away from a fan behind the Cardinal dugout who apparently was digging in with a sharp set of spurs."[20]

The Cardinals victory split the series and they left Brooklyn in the same place, five games behind, as when they arrived. But even more importantly, they left with their "contempt for the Dodgers reestablished."[21] There had been rumors early in the season that the Cardinals would go on strike if they had to play against Robinson. The strike never materialized but hard feelings clearly still existed.

SOURCES

In addition to the sources cited in the Notes, the author used the Baseball-Reference.com and Retrosheet.org websites for box-score, player, team, and season pages, pitching and batting game logs, and other pertinent material.

NOTES

1. Cardinals outfielder Joe Medwick spiked Robinson on the left foot, leaving a bloody gash in the opening game, according to Jules Tygiel in *Baseball's Great Experiment* (New York: Oxford University Press, 1983), 202-203. Arnold Rampersad in his book *Jackie Robinson* recounts another incident, involving Cardinals pitcher Harry Brecheen. Brecheen, "rather than throw Jack out easily at first, took the ball to the baseline clearly intending to block his path with a nasty tag. Jack stopped short of Brecheen. "You better play your position as you should," [Robinson] warned: the next time he would not hesitated to knock him over.

2. Roscoe McGowen, "Kurowski's Homer Stops Brooks, 3-2," *New York Times*, August 21, 1947: 28.

3. Dick Young, "Kurowski's HR in 12th Defeats Dodgers, 3-2," *New York Daily News*, August 21, 1947: 17.

4. W. Vernon Tietjen, "Kurowski's Homer Defeats Bums in 12-Inning Thriller," *St. Louis Star and Times*, August 21, 1947: 27.

5. Young.

6. Tommy Holmes, "Dodgers May Rue Day They Let Beaten Cardinals Out of Sack," *Brooklyn Daily Eagle*, August 21, 1947: 15.

7. Tietjen.

8. McGowen.

9. Young.

10. McGowen.

11. Arnold Rampersad, *Jackie Robinson* (New York: Alfred Knopf, 1997), 184.

12. "Intentional Accident Says Stanky, Accident Says Slaughter," *The Sporting News*, August 27, 1947: 4. Although this incident received a lot of press, it was the not the only time the two players crossed paths in an adversarial way. Slaughter later told this story to Larry King: After the spiking incident on August 20, Robinson's response was simply to say, "I'll remember that." In another game, about two years later, Slaughter hit a single so sharply that it hit off the wall and he tried to stretch it into a double. Slaughter said to King: "Robinson was playing second then. I went sliding in, and Robinson took the throw from the right fielder. He made no attempt to tag me on the leg for the putout: which he could have done easily. Instead he whirled around and smacked me in the mouth with the ball in his glove. Six teeth went flying, there was blood all over me, and I later had to have gum surgery. As he walked away, Jackie said, 'I told you I'd remember.'" Richard Smith, "Jackie Robinson and a Revenge Best Served Cold," *Psychology Today*, April 3, 2018. psychologytoday.com/us/blog/joy-and-pain/201804/jackie-robinson-and-revenge-best-served-cold. Smith gives as the source Larry King and Peter Occhiogrosso, *Tell It to the King* (New York: Simon and Schuster, 1998).

13. Jackie Robinson, *I Never Had It Made* (New York: Harper Collins, 1995 edition), 67.

14. Holmes. Sportswriters disagreed as to whether the spiking was deliberate. Bill Corum of the *New York Journal-American* called it "as normal a play as anybody, whose imagination wasn't working too fast, ever saw." Bob Burnes, in the *St. Louis Globe-Democrat* argued, "If Slaughter had been trying to 'nail' Robinson, you can be sure Jackie wouldn't have been in condition to stay in the game." Slaughter's statement "I've never deliberately spiked anyone in my life. Anybody who does, don't belong in baseball," probably surprised most National Leaguers. The incident infuriated Robinson's teammates. Noting that the cut on his leg was located eight inches above the ankle on the outside of his leg, one player asserted, "How the hell could Slaughter hit him way up on the side of the leg like that unless he meant to do it?" Tygiel, 202-203.

15. Young.

16. Tietjen.

17. McGowen.

18. Young.

19. Young.

20. Holmes.

21. Holmes.

ROBINSON'S FIRST GRAND SLAM WINS IN A WALKOFF

JUNE 24, 1948: BROOKLYN DODGERS 6, PITTSBURGH PIRATES 2, AT EBBETS FIELD, BROOKLYN

by Bill Nowlin

The Dodgers hosted the Pittsburgh Pirates for a Thursday afternoon doubleheader at Ebbets Field, with the Pirates only one game behind the Boston Braves in the National League standings. They'd been in third place for most of the season, but had tied for first for one day, June 16. The second game was a makeup for a rainout on the 22nd. The Dodgers were in sixth place, 7½ games back. They hadn't seen the first division since May 15. Two right-handers opposed each other as starting pitchers: Harry Taylor for Brooklyn and Bob Chesnes for Pittsburgh. Taylor had been 10-5 in 1947, his official rookie year.[1] Chesnes, a rookie, was undefeated and riding a three-game win streak.[2]

After five innings the Pirates held a 2-0 lead and Taylor was out of the game, replaced by pinch-hitter Marv Rackley in the bottom of the fifth. The runs had come on a third-inning single by third baseman Frankie Gustine and a fifth-inning triple by center fielder Johnny Hopp. He drove in Chesnes, who had walked.

Left-hander Paul Minner threw three scoreless innings for Leo Durocher's Dodgers.[3] After seven innings, the score remained 2-0. But Brooklyn tied it in the bottom of the eighth. The two runs scored on what the *Pittsburgh Press* characterized as "one hit and some shoddy fielding."[4] Chesnes walked pinch-hitter Bruce Edwards and second baseman Billy Cox, with groundout in between.[5] First baseman Jackie Robinson singled to shallow left, loading the bases. (The *Press* put "single" in quotation marks; the ball had tipped off Hopp's glove.)[6] Carl Furillo lifted a fly ball to his Pirates counterpart in center field. Edwards tagged up and scored – and so did Cox, when second baseman Danny Murtaugh committed an error. Chesnes intentionally walked Pee Wee Reese, and got Gene Hermanski to ground out and end the inning.

In the ninth, reliever Willie Ramsdell set down the Pirates in order.

Chesnes walked the leadoff batter in the bottom of the ninth, catcher Gil Hodges.[7] Tommy Brown, who had come into the game to play third base, sacrificed Hodges to second. Pirates manager Billy Meyer turned to his bullpen and summoned Mel Queen. Preston Ward pinch-hit for Ramsdell, and Queen walked him intentionally, setting up a potential double play. Then he got Dick Whitman to foul out to third base. But he walked Cox on four pitches, loading the bases and bringing up Robinson, the Rookie of the Year in 1947.

Robinson watched two pitches go by, a strike and then a ball. He swung at the third pitch and hit a grand slam to win the game, "a drive that went deep into the left-field stands."[8] The *Times* added, "The customers went a bit off their trolleys when they saw the ball going into the stands, and Jackie wasn't unhappy about it, either. 'It's the first time in my life that I ever hit a grand-slam homer anywhere.'"[9]

It was Robinson's third home run of the season. With four runs batted in, he now had 27.

As in the eighth inning, the Dodgers' runs all scored on one base hit. Vince Johnson of the *Pittsburgh Post-Gazette* grumbled a bit about the grand slam: "A single would have done just as well," Tell that to the 24,745 fans from Flatbush.[10]

Ramsdell, of course, got the win. Chesnes bore the defeat. The time of game was 2:49.

Dodgers Defeat Pirates, 6-2, 8-6, As Robinson Drives Home 6 Runs

Jack's Grand-Slam Homer in Ninth Wins Opener—Barney Takes Nightcap Though He Loses Control After 6-Inning No-Hitter

New York Times, June 25, 1948: 30.

The Bums saw their team sweep the Pirates. And they saw more hitting from Robinson in the second game.

The Associated Press game story declared, "Jackie Robinson went on a batting rampage today, banging out seven hits including six in a row."[11] He had two doubles and two singles in the second game, called on account of darkness after 7½ innings; the Dodgers outscored the Pirates, 8-6, and leapfrogged the Phillies into fifth place. Robinson was 4-for-4, was the lead runner in a first-inning double steal after singling Arky Vaughan home with the first run of the game and moving to second when Furillo was hit by a pitch. Robinson scored three runs, and drove in a pair. The late-June steal was his first stolen base of the year. He'd reported to spring training 25 pounds overweight.[12]

In the doubleheader, Robinson was 7-for-9 with six RBIs and four runs scored. The "ebony clouter" boosted his batting average from .280 to .306.[13]

At the end of his sophomore season, Robinson had driven in 85 runs to the 48 RBIs he had in 1947. His batting average was one point lower, at .296. He hit 12 homers in 1947 and 12 in 1948. He scored 108 runs, 17 fewer than the 125 he had scored the year before. He'd led the league with 29 stolen bases in 1947; in 1948, he stole 22. In 1949 he was named the National League's Most Valuable Player.

Of Robinson's 137 career home runs, nine were hit in the ninth inning and six were hit in extra innings. Fifty were hit with two outs. Seventy-seven of them were hit at Ebbets Field. Jackie Robinson hit only one other grand slam in his career. It came precisely two years later – on June 24, 1950. It was also hit late in an Ebbets Field game, against the same Pittsburgh Pirates team, this time off Vic Lombardi. The Dodgers won that game, 21-12.

SOURCES

In addition to the sources cited in the Notes, the author consulted Baseball-Reference.com and Retrosheet.org. Thanks to Gregory Wolf for assistance.

NOTES

1. He had appeared in four games without a start or a decision late in 1946. His 10-5 record in 1947 was accompanied by a 3.11 earned-run average. He had a very good 2.82 ERA before the June 24 game, but a record of 1-3.

2. Chesnes finished the 1948 season with a 14-6 (3.57 ERA) record. His only other two years in the majors saw him go 7-13 (5.88) in 1949 and 3-3 in just nine appearances in 1950 (5.54 ERA).

3. Minner had appeared in four major-league games as a reliever, three in 1946 and just one to this point in 1948. Most of his career was spent with the Cubs (1950-56). The 1948 season was his best for ERA; he was 4-3 with a 2.44 ERA. In 1952, he won 14 games for the Cubs.

4. Lester J. Biederman, "Pirates Right Back Where They Started," *Pittsburgh Press*, June 25, 1948: 30.

5. Cox had started the game playing third base, but moved to second in the top of the eighth.

6. Biederman. The *Post-Gazette*'s Vince Johnson, though, acknowledged that Hopp had only gotten to the ball "after a hard run." Vince Johnson, "Robinson's Batting Big Factor in Bums' Double Triumph," *Pittsburgh Post-Gazette*, June 25, 1948: 20.

7. Hodges had caught in 24 of his 28 games in his first season, 1947. In 1948 he caught in 38 games and played first base in 96. By 1949, he was the Dodgers' full-time first baseman (and an All-Star for seven seasons in succession).

8. Roscoe McGowen, "Dodgers Defeat Pirates, 6-2, 8-6, As Robinson Drives Home 6 Runs," *New York Times*, June 25,1948: 30.

9. McGowen.

10. The *New York Times* reported attendance of 28,835. The *Post-Gazette* had the lower figure. The *Brooklyn Daily Eagle* counted 10 more attendees than the *Times*: 28,825.

11. Associated Press, "Jackie Robinson on Spree as Dodgers Top Bucs Twice," *Standard-Speaker* (Hazleton, Pennsylvania), June 25, 1948: 29.

12. Jackie Robinson, *I Never Had It Made* (New York: Ecco, 1995), 71.

13. The phrase was used by James J. Murphy, "Lip Smiles Again as Dodgers Come Alive Against Bucs," *Brooklyn Daily Eagle*, June 25, 1948: 16.

JACKIE ROBINSON HITS REVERSE NATURAL CYCLE AS DODGERS BEAT CARDINALS

AUGUST 29, 1948: BROOKLYN DODGERS 12, ST. LOUIS CARDINALS 7, AT SPORTSMAN'S PARK III, ST. LOUIS

by Michael Huber

On August 29, 1948, before a season record crowd of 33,826 at Sportsman's Park, the Brooklyn Dodgers and the St. Louis Cardinals played in a "furiously fought doubleheader"[1] that had postseason implications. In the first game, Brooklyn second baseman Jackie Robinson hit for the cycle,[2] leading the Dodgers to a victory over the St. Louis Cardinals. The Dodgers also captured the second game of the twin bill, 6-4, putting them briefly atop the National League. Robinson's cycle was the 137th in the major leagues.[3]

The first game of the doubleheader featured 19 runs, 29 hits, and 6 errors, but it took just 2 hours and 32 minutes to play, even though 91 batters came up to the plate. Brooklyn sent Paul Minner, with a 1-1 record, up against St. Louis's Harry Brecheen, who had entered the game with a 15-5 mark.

The game started as a "free-hitting affair,"[4] as both Jackie Robinson and Bruce Edwards sent Brecheen offerings into the bleachers for home runs. Billy Cox led off the game for Brooklyn and singled to center. Robinson, swinging at a 3-and-2 pitch, brought Cox home with a line-drive home run into the left-field seats, his 10th round-tripper of the season. Pee Wee Reese reached on an error by Cardinals shortstop Marty Marion, and then, with a one-strike count, Edwards launched a two-run shot. Four batters, four Dodgers runs, and St. Louis manager Eddie Dyer strode to the mound and pulled Brecheen. Ted Wilks relieved and retired the next three Brooklyn batters. In the bottom of the inning, George Shuba replaced Edwards in left field.[5]

Robinson led off the top of the third with a triple to right field. He trotted home when Reese tripled to left field. Shuba singled and the score was now 6-0. Robinson came up for the third time in the top of the fourth. After Cox grounded out to third baseman Erv Dusak, Robinson stroked a line-drive double to left.

With Reese batting, Jackie stole third base and then came home on Reese's line out to center. Robinson's stolen base was his 17th of the season. It was also the second time he had "pilfered third base"[6] in the season.

Stan Musial put the Cardinals on the board with a solo home run in the bottom of the fourth inning, making the score 7-1. In the top of the fifth, however, Brooklyn's Roy Campanella doubled and Gene Hermanski hit a two-run line-drive home run, adding two more tallies for the Dodgers.

The St. Louis bats came to life from the sixth through the eighth, scoring six runs. In the bottom of the sixth, Enos Slaughter reached base on Robinson's error. Red Schoendienst walked, and Nippy Jones singled to left field. Slaughter scored easily, and when Gil Hodges fumbled the relay from Shuba in left, Schoendienst scored and Jones scampered to second base. Del Rice lined out to Robinson at second, but then, with Bill Baker pinch-hitting for pitcher Red Munger, Minner uncorked a wild pitch and Jones motored to third. Jones then scored when Baker smashed a double to left. Hank Behrman relieved and finished the game for Brooklyn. He gave up two runs in the seventh and one in the eighth. Brooklyn added solo runs in the seventh, eighth, and ninth frames. Dodgers starter Minner lasted 5⅓ innings to pick up the victory. The final score was 12-7.

The Cardinals used six pitchers in the game. After relieving Brecheen, Wilks gave way to Al Brazle in the third inning. Munger came on in the sixth, Gerry Staley started the seventh inning, and Jim Hearn pitched the ninth. Only Munger was not touched for a Brooklyn run.

Roscoe McGowen of the *New York Times* wrote that "Robinson came up with the 'hat trick,' following his homer with a triple, double, and, after flying out [in the sixth], a single."[7] The phrase "hitting for the cycle" was not in use at this time. When Robinson came up in the eighth, he drove a ball to center field for his fourth hit, a single. He came up again in the top of the ninth and flied out to left. Robinson's line for the game was six at-bats, four hits, three runs scored, two runs batted in, and a stolen base. Reese had a 2-for-5 game with three RBIs, and Campanella went 2-for-4 with an intentional walk and an RBI.

The Dodgers scored in seven of nine innings. Brooklyn started the day in third place, two games behind the Boston Braves and a half-game behind the Cardinals. The Dodgers won the second game too, 6-4, with Robinson collecting two more hits. For the day, Robinson had 6 hits in 10 at-bats, scored four runs, and drove in a pair. His batting average rose during the day from .293 to .300, and his slugging percentage jumped from .438 to .456.

After their sweep and Boston's doubleheader loss to the Pittsburgh Pirates, the Dodgers were tied with the Braves for first place; the Cardinals remained 1½ games back. With about 30 games left to play, the chase for the National League pennant was close.[8] The Cardinals had used nine pitchers in the doubleheader. The Dodgers and Cardinals played another doubleheader the next day, the 30th (the Dodgers swept again), and the day after, August 31, the Dodgers played the Chicago Cubs in yet another doubleheader (the Dodgers lost both games).

Robinson's cycle on the 29th was the third and last of the 1948 season. Joe DiMaggio had one on May 20 against the Chicago White Sox at Comiskey Park (his second career cycle), and Pittsburgh's Wally Westlake had one on July 30 against the Dodgers at Ebbets Field. All three 1948 cycles occurred in away games for the batters. On June 14, 1949, Wally Westlake hit for the cycle again, so his two cycles "sandwiched" Robinson's.

SOURCES

In addition to the sources mentioned in the notes, the author consulted baseball-reference.com, mlb.com, and retrosheet.org.

NOTES

1 Roscoe McGowen, "Dodgers Take Two From Cardinals and Gain Lead in Pennant Race," *New York Times*, August 30, 1948.

2 There are 24 possible combinations of hitting for the cycle. When a batter hits the single first double, triple, and home run in order, he has completed a "natural cycle." When he hits a home run, triple, double, and single in order, he has achieved a "reverse natural cycle."

3 retrosheet.org/cycles_chron.htm.

4 McGowen.

5 Edwards started the second game as well, but was again pulled by manager Burt Shotton in favor of Shuba, this time in the eighth inning.

6 McGowen.

7 McGowen.

8 The Dodgers faded in September, finishing the 1948 season in third place.

JACKIE ROBINSON HAS THREE HITS WITH A HOME RUN ON OPENING DAY

APRIL 19, 1949: BROOKLYN DODGERS 10, NEW YORK GIANTS 3, AT EBBETS FIELD, BROOKLYN

by Nathan Bierma

The bleachers at Ebbets Field were filled two hours before the first pitch. The game was a sellout by noon, and many of the estimated 10,000 fans who were turned away continued to line the streets around the park. Young boys tumbled over a gate near the corner of McKeever Place and Montgomery; most were thwarted, but "here and there," the *Brooklyn Daily Eagle* reported, "a cop seemed to look the other way, infected by the holiday spirit which ruled."[1]

First in line when the gates opened was Carrie Koschnick, 62, an Opening Day regular who had left her Brooklyn home at 5 A.M..[2] Also in attendance were Margaret Truman, daughter of President Harry Truman. New York City Mayor William O'Dwyer would arrive midway through the game after taking part in Opening Day ceremonies at Yankee Stadium.[3] The Fourteenth Regiment Band led a parade out to the center-field flagpole for the national anthem,[4] with the Giants and Dodgers marching in columns behind them.[5] The sole somber moment was the dedication of the seat of Shorty Laurice, the late founder of the Dodgers' ragtag pep band, the Sym-Phony.[6] His seat in Section 8 would be left vacant for the afternoon, the lone empty seat in the packed park. The crowd numbered 34,530, surging past the Ebbets Field attendance record from 1941 by over 3,000.[7]

Jackie Robinson Off To Fast Start

Daily Advocate (Stamford, Connecticut), April 20, 1949: 27.

Dodgers fans were feeling more than just the perennial optimism of spring; they were sensing the strange new burden of expectations. After reaching the World Series in 1947 (when they fell to the Yankees in seven games), the Dodgers slipped to third place in '48 thanks to injuries and the midseason ouster of manager Leo Durocher, who joined the Giants. Now many expected the Dodgers to return to form, and not just in Brooklyn; a survey by *The Sporting News* found that 46 percent of baseball writers picked the Dodgers to win the pennant in 1949, compared with 33 percent who thought the Boston Braves would repeat in the National League.[8]

Dodgers president Branch Rickey was preaching caution,[9] but conceded on the night before Opening Day, "This is the best team coming back from spring training I have ever been associated with."[10] Rickey's bold social experiment of desegregation was set to pay its biggest on-field dividend yet. Jackie Robinson was established as the starting second baseman and cleanup hitter, Roy Campanella was starting his second season behind the plate, and pitcher Don Newcombe would soon be called up from Montreal.[11] The first three African Americans in the National League would all play for the Dodgers,[12] and they would all help make the team a contender.

Robinson, entering his third season, was now expected not just to contribute but to help carry the offense. The two-year moratorium Rickey had given Robinson on responding to racial hostility had expired, but while Robinson would be more vocal in 1949, he still wanted his bat to speak the loudest. "More than revenge, I wanted to be Jackie Robinson," Robinson recalled of his mindset entering the '49 season. "When I reported to spring training I was right on target, weightwise, in excellent condition, and my morale was high."[13] Rickey had brought in Hall of Famer

George Sisler to work with Robinson in the offseason; Sisler had Robinson hit off a tee for hours at a time, and helped him to sit back in his stance.[14] Robinson responded by hitting .521 in spring training. "Sisler showed me how to stop lunging," Robinson said. "I'll never stop being grateful to him."[15]

Once the opening game started, the Giants punctured the crowd's festive mood almost immediately. After taking the opening pitch for a strike, leadoff hitter Bill Rigney hit the second pitch from Dodgers starter Joe Hatten over the left-field fence. Rigney, who had lost his starting job to rookie Bob Hofman in spring training but was back in the lineup thanks to Hofman's sore finger,[16] tied a record for the earliest home run in Opening Day history.[17]

Carl Furillo tied the game for the Dodgers with a home run off Larry Jansen to lead off the bottom of the second, but the Giants took the lead again in the fourth on a single by Buddy Kerr that scored two runs. (The rally was quelled when Rigney, the first-inning hero, hit a single to right and had a head of steam on his way to second. He didn't notice that Kerr was holding at second and nearly ran into him before being picked off first.)[18]

Jackie Robinson led off the bottom of the fourth with the Dodgers down 3-1, still looking for his first hit of the season after grounding out in the first. Robinson swung at the 2-and-2 pitch and lifted it into the left-field seats to bring the home crowd to its feet. Four batters later, Campanella came to the plate with runners at the corners and the Dodgers still down by one. He swung at the first pitch and hit a deep line drive that cleared the wall before curling around the foul pole.[19] The Dodgers took the lead, 5-3.

Robinson got a two-out single in the fifth but was stranded. Billy Cox tripled and came home on a wild pitch in the sixth to make it 6-3. Then Robinson dazzled the sellout crowd in the top of the seventh with his defense. When Johnny Mize hit a grounder that deflected off first baseman Gil Hodges' hand, Robinson swooped in, grabbed the ball and fired to first, where Hatten was alertly covering, to end the inning.[20]

The Dodgers would pour it on with another four-run rally in the seventh. They were facing reliever Hank Behrman, whom the Dodgers sold to the Giants in the offseason. Pee Wee Reese led off with a single and Robinson added a single to center. Robinson reached third on a Cox single that scored Reese, and came home on a wild pitch to Hodges to make it 8-3.

After Hodges singled to put runners at the corners, Campanella hit his loudest blast of the day, a fly ball to deep center field. It looked like his second round trip of the day, but the wind suddenly held it up. Bobby Thomson slipped and fell making the adjustment, and the ball hit the ground.[21] Two runners scored and Campanella made it to third on the error. Hatten, for whom Dodgers manager Burt Shotton was about to pinch-hit in the fifth before Campanella homered,[22] held the Giants hitless the rest of the way and the Dodgers won 10-3.

"It makes it easy on a manager," Shotton joked afterward about his team's three (nearly four) home runs. "All I had to do was ask 'em to hit a home run and they up and did it."[23]

"The Dodgers did, indeed, perform magnificently in the brilliant glare of a Flatbush sun as they weathered a first-inning Giant homer and then steam-rollered right over the so-called pulverizing Polo Grounders," wrote the *New York Times*. "So far as the vast majority in a record inaugural gathering of 34,530 were concerned they could toss the remaining games of the 1949 National League schedule right out of a window and start the world series at Ebbets Field tomorrow."[24]

"The Dodgers look to be on their way," the *Brooklyn Daily Eagle* allowed. "Baseballs, like footballs, take funny bounces, and there are still 153 games to go. But for one day, anyway, the Flock[25] had the gleam of champions in their batting eyes."[26]

Among the Dodgers' brightest stars on Opening Day was Robinson. He led the Dodgers with three hits, finishing 3-for-5 with one RBI and two runs scored. In the field he had six putouts and six assists. "Robinson's spectacular opener," wrote Lyle Spatz, "set the stage for what would be his greatest season, one that culminated in his winning the league's Most Valuable Player award."[27]

SOURCES

In addition to the sources mentioned in the Notes, the author consulted Baseball-Reference.com and Retrosheet.org.

NOTES

1. "Ebbets Field Jammed in Real Holiday Style," *Brooklyn Daily Eagle*, April 19, 1949: 3.
2. "Ebbets Field Jammed in Real Holiday Style."
3. "Ebbets Field Jammed in Real Holiday Style."
4. John Drebinger, "Dodgers Rout Giants With Pair of Four Run Innings Before 34,530," *New York Times*, April 20, 1949: 34.
5. Arthur Daley, "Battle of the Boroughs," *New York Times*, April 20, 1949: 34.
6. Harold Burr, "Dodgers Call on Hatten to Oppose Giants," *Brooklyn Daily Eagle*, April 19, 1949: 1.

7. Lyle Spatz, "Jackie Robinson on Opening Day, 1947-1956," in Joseph Dorinson and Joram Warmund, eds., *Jackie Robinson: Race, Sports, and the American Dream* (London: Routledge, 1998), 136.

8. Lyle Spatz, 136.

9. So many prognosticators are throwing their opinions around that the Dodgers are going to win the National League pennant that President Branch Rickey is frightened lest this ball club gets a big head and blows the works," wrote Harold Burr. "Burr Sees Dodgers Copping N.L. Duke," *Brooklyn Daily Eagle*, April 17, 1949: 23.

10. "Knot-Holers Hail '49 Dodgers as 'Champs,'," *Brooklyn Daily Eagle*, April 19, 1949: 3.

11. Tommy Holmes, "Red Barber's Pet and Other Rookies," *Brooklyn Daily Eagle*, March 10, 1949: 27.

12. Larry Doby broke the American League color line with the Indians in July of 1947, followed by Hank Thompson with the St. Louis Browns later that month. Monte Irvin and Hank Thompson would debut together for the Giants in July of 1949. No other major league team would integrate before the decade was out.

13. Jackie Robinson and Alfred Duckett, *I Never Had It Made: An Autobiography of Jackie Robinson (As Told to Alfred Duckett)* (New York: HarperCollins, 1995), 79.

14. Arnold Rampersad, *Jackie Robinson: A Biography* (New York: Alfred A. Knopf, 1997), 208.

15. Rampersad, 208.

16. Drebinger, "Dodgers Rout Giants."

17. Herman O. Krabbenhoft, *Leadoff Batters of Major League Baseball: Complete Statistics, 1900-2005* (Jefferson, North Carolina: McFarland, 2006), 343. Rigney was the second visiting leadoff batter to hit a home run on the second pitch of the season, joining Charlie Jamieson of Cleveland, who homered on Opening Day in St. Louis in 1925. A first-pitch Opening Day home run by a visiting batter would not occur until Gary Thomasson of the Giants achieved the feat against Don Sutton in Los Angeles in 1977: at least five more players have done it since then. Krabbenhoft, 343.

18. Daley, "Battle of the Boroughs."

19. Daley, "Battle of the Boroughs."

20. Daley, "Battle of the Boroughs."

21. Daley, "Battle of the Boroughs."

22. Harold Burr, "Dodgers Swipe Giants' Thunder," *Brooklyn Daily Eagle*, April 20, 1949: 27.

23. Burr, "Dodgers Swipe Giants' Thunder."

24. Drebinger, "Dodgers Rout Giants."

25. This nickname referred to the Dodgers' previous name, the Robins.

26. Burr, "Dodgers Swipe Giants' Thunder."

27. Spatz, "Jackie Robinson on Opening Day," 137.

JACKIE GETS CAREER-HIGH SIX RBIs IN DODGERS' LAMBASTING OF CARDINALS

MAY 21, 1949: BROOKLYN DODGERS 15, ST. LOUIS CARDINALS 6,
AT SPORTSMAN'S PARK, ST. LOUIS

by Richard Cuicchi

Brooklyn Dodgers President Branch Rickey took a calculated gamble in the historic signing of Jackie Robinson in 1946, eventually enabling the integration of major-league baseball. Robinson didn't disappoint the Dodgers. He was voted the game's first-ever Rookie of the Year in 1947. Other spectacular seasons followed. Baseball fans soon grew to like his energetic, aggressive style of play that helped propel the Dodgers into a perennial power.

Robinson emerged as the best player on the team in 1948, leading the Dodgers in runs, hits, doubles, and RBIs. He finished second in home runs, slugging percentage, and stolen bases. The Dodgers grew accustomed to his heroics, so there was little surprise when he became the best player in the league in 1949. Perhaps with an element of bias, Rickey declared him "the best since Cobb."[1]

The game on May 21, 1949, before 13,320 fans at Sportsman's Park was one of his best. He set a career high for RBIs in one game with six.

After hitting just .188 in April, Robinson had raised his batting average by more than 100 points – to .298 – when the Dodgers squared off against the Cardinals. The Dodgers held third place in the National League while the Cardinals were in seventh, but the two teams would be neck-and-neck for first place throughout most of the season.

Right-hander Ralph Branca got the starting nod for Burt Shotton's Dodgers. The 23-year-old had won all six of his previous, including five in which he pitched nine or more innings. The Cardinals countered with Jim Hearn, who was winless in three previous starts.

After the Dodgers scored a run in the top of the first inning, the Cardinals jumped on Branca in the bottom half, sending nine batters to the plate and scoring three runs on four hits and two walks. Enos Slaughter and Eddie Kazak supplied the run-scoring hits. Branca didn't last past the second inning. He took himself out of the game, afterward, saying, "My arm felt fine but I just couldn't get anything on the ball."[2]

The Cardinals sent only nine batters to the plate over the next three innings. The Dodgers took a 4-3 lead in the fourth inning on Robinson's two-run double and Gil Hodges' single that scored Robinson. Branca was off the hook.

The Dodgers added to their lead in the fifth when they manufactured a run on Pee Wee Reese's walk and stolen base, a bunt single by Dick Whitman, and Robinson's groundout to second base.

The Cardinals pulled to within a run at 5-4 in the sixth inning on Hal Rice's double, scoring Rocky Nelson, who had tripled. But in the next inning, Robinson and Hodges combined again to get back-to-back run-scoring hits that made the score 7-4. The Cardinals could have prevented the run on Robinson's hit if outfielder Ron Northey had thrown to the correct base and kept Robinson from advancing into scoring position.

Cardinals rookie sensation Kazak kept the game close with a two-run home run in the eighth. It would have tied the game had Northey thrown to the right base in the prior inning.

The Cardinals had veteran Howard Pollet warming up in the bullpen, since he had a good record of success against the Dodgers. However, with his

Los Angeles Times, May 22, 1949: A9.

Four days earlier, Robinson attempted to steal home during a Cubs game in Chicago on May 17, 1949

team trailing, manager Eddie Dyer instead chose Ken Johnson to start the ninth inning.[3]

The Dodgers put the game out of reach, unloading eight more runs by sending 12 batters to the plate. While fans jeered the hapless St. Louis pitchers, Robinson ripped a double to account for two more runs, while Carl Furillo hit a run-scoring single. Inexperienced Ray Yochim, the Cardinals' fifth hurler, who replaced Johnson, didn't produce different results. He yielded a two-run single to Eddie Miksis, followed by Reese's three-run home run.

The Dodgers battered Cardinals pitchers for 16 hits, with every starting position player getting in on the action. Reese led the team with four hits, followed by Robinson's three. It was the second time in the 1949 season that Brooklyn scored eight runs in an inning, the other being against the Giants at the Polo Grounds on April 28.

Robinson continued his torrid hitting during the rest of May, ending with a slash line of .431/.480/.741, with 6 home runs and 34 RBIs. Arguably, it was the best single month of his career.

For the rest of the season, he reached base at a fantastic rate and finished the season with a .432 on-base percentage, tied with Ralph Kiner and second only to Stan Musial's .438. He had a streak of 35 consecutive games getting on base that started on May 24. He posted another streak of 27 games as well as four additional stretches of at least 10 games.

The Dodgers' home ballpark, Ebbets Field, hosted the 1949 All-Star Game. Robinson, Don Newcombe, and Roy Campanella became the first Black National League players chosen for the annual classic. (Larry Doby from the Indians, the American League's first Black player, was named to the junior league's All-Star squad that same year.) Only Ted Williams received more votes than Robinson on the All-Star rosters.[4]

The Dodgers were never more than four games out of first place the entire season. Except for one day, they held the lead from June 7 to July 23. The Cardinals then overtook the Dodgers, and the pennant winner was decided in the final days. With the Cardinals losing eight of their last 14 games, the Dodgers eventually recaptured first place on September 29 and won their second pennant in three years. Oddly, the Cardinals were the only team against which the Dodgers had a losing record that season. Brooklyn lost the World Series to the Yankees in five games.

Robinson capped his spectacular season by beating out Musial for the National League MVP Award. Third-place finisher Enos Slaughter declared, "Without Robinson, [Brooklyn] would be in the second division."[5] Robinson led the league in batting average (.342) and stolen bases (37), while posting 16 home runs and driving in a career-best 124 runs, much better than his 162-game average of 86. His final slash line was a phenomenal .342/.432/.528.

SOURCES

In addition to the sources cited in the Notes, the author consulted Baseball-Reference.com and the following:

Burr, Harold. "Dodgers Pummel Cards by 16-5, Exploding 8 Runs in Last Inning," *Brooklyn Daily Eagle*, May 22, 1949: 24.

NOTES

1. Harold Burr, "Brooks Bill Jackie as Big Show of N.L.," *The Sporting News*, June 8, 1949: 20.
2. Roscoe McGowen, "Dodgers Get 8 Runs in Ninth and Overwhelm Cards, 15-5," *New York Times*, May 22, 1949: 5, 1.
3. Bob Broeg, "Dodgers Rout Cards, 15-6; Robinson Drives in 6 Runs," *St. Louis Post-Dispatch*, May 22, 1949: 5, 1.
4. "Williams, Jackie Top Record Vote," *The Sporting News*, July 13, 1949: 2.
5. Arnold Rampersad, *Jackie Robinson: A Biography* (New York: Alfred A Knopf, 1997), 216.

JACKIE ROBINSON RIPS TWO HOME RUNS VS. PITTSBURGH

MAY 24, 1949: BROOKLYN DODGERS 6, PITTSBURGH PIRATES 1, AT FORBES FIELD, PITTSBURGH

by Blake W. Sherry

It was not an ideal night for a ballgame. There were no warm-up drills, after a rainstorm delayed the start of the uncovering of the field until 8:20 P.M.[1] Once the game started, however, Jackie Robinson wasted no time in making an impact on this damp evening game at Pittsburgh's Forbes Field. Robinson homered in his first two at-bats as the Brooklyn Dodgers defeated the Pittsburgh Pirates, 6-1, before a crowd of 29,625.[2] The storm also grounded the plane that Dodgers general manager Branch Rickey was taking to Pittsburgh and kept him from getting to the game.[3]

Earlier in the week, on May 20, newly promoted Don Newcombe made his major-league debut in a relief appearance for the Dodgers. Along with Robinson and Roy Campanella, his arrival distinguished the Dodgers as the only team to have three African-American players active.[4] In his first season, Newcombe went 17-8 with a 3.17 ERA on his way to winning the National League Rookie of the Year Award.

The starting pitcher for the Pirates was Bob Chesnes, a right-hander who had led the Bucs staff the previous season with 14 wins against 6 losses. Starting for the Dodgers was another right-hander, All-Star Ralph Branca, who had also won 14 games the previous season. Branca was the NL's starting pitcher in the previous year's All-Star Game.

Like the Dodgers, the Pirates had the day off before this game. While the season was barely over a month old, one of the local writers bemoaned the fact that the Pirates had already lost eight one-run games. He declared that there had been much joy watching the team take batting practice on Monday knowing that at least they could not lose an offday by a single run.[5]

Chesnes got two quick outs with his first five pitches. Pee Wee Reese flied out to center field and Johnny Hopp grounded out to second. However, slugger Duke Snider followed with a line single to right, and Robinson pounded his first home run of the game, a drive to deep left field. As it turned out, it was all the runs the Dodgers would need.

After a three-up, three-down inning in the second, the Dodgers were back to the top of their batting order in the third. In a near-replica of the first inning, a fly out and groundout by Reese and Hopp, brought Snider to plate again with two out. This time Snider drove a double to center. Then Robinson hit his second home run to deep left field in as many at-bats. Both home runs landed in the visitors bullpen.[6]

The Dodgers added to their lead in the fifth. A leadoff double by Reese and a groundout by Hopp to second base moved Reese to third. Snider's third straight hit scored Reese, giving the Dodgers a 5-0 lead. Robinson then came to the plate looking for a third straight homer. It was not to be: Chesnes hit Robinson with the third pitch of the at-bat.

The Bucs avoided being shut out in the bottom of the seventh thanks to a single by Stan Rojek, a walk to Ed Fitz Gerald, and a run-scoring single to right by Marv Rackley.

In the top of the ninth, after Snider collected his fourth hit of the game, Robinson got his third hit, a sharp single to left, moving Snider to second base. Spider Jorgensen closed out the scoring for the Dodgers with a line-drive single scoring Snider. It was Jorgensen's third hit of the game. The third, fourth, and fifth hitters in the Dodgers lineup accounted for

Robinson Belts 2 Homers As Branca Wins Seventh

Atlanta Constitution, May 25, 1949: 9.

10 of the team's 13 hits and drove in all six runs, five of them with two outs.

Only Robinson's groundout to short in the seventh kept him from a 4-for-4 game. He drove in four runs as part of his productive 3-for-4 night with two home runs, a single, and a hit-by-pitch. His 32 RBIs led the league at the time.[7]

Weeks later Robinson was named a starter on the National League All-Star team for the first of six consecutive seasons. He was touted as "the greatest one-man show in the National League" by a Dodgers beat reporter in *The Sporting News*. Dodgers GM Branch Rickey claimed he was "the best since Cobb."[8] Robinson won his only Most Valuable Player Award after finishing the 1949 season with a league-leading .342 batting average, 16 home runs, and 124 runs batted in. He also led the league with 37 stolen bases and 17 sacrifices. Statistically, 1949 was one of Jackie's finest years.

Robinson's two-home-run performance against the Pirates was his first. He did it seven more times in his career, including twice in 1953 and 1954. He also hit a home run in each game of a doubleheader on August 3, 1952, against the Chicago Cubs. His last two-homer game came in his final season, 1956, at the age of 37. He finished his career with 137 regular-season home runs.

While Robinson's two home runs were the story of the day, Ralph Branca deserved some kudos as well. Branca went the distance for Dodgers, scattering nine hits and raising his season record to 7-0. He also was named to the NL All-Star team for the third consecutive season. The 23-year-old Branca finished the season 13-5 with a 4.39 ERA. His .722 winning percentage led the National League.

The Dodgers gained ground on both teams they were chasing. Both the New York Giants and the Boston Braves lost that day, putting Brooklyn just two games back. They won again the following afternoon at Forbes Field and beat Boston on Friday. The modest three-game win streak allowed them to pull even with the Braves for the league lead.

Two weeks later, in the June 8, 1949, issue of *The Sporting News*, it was announced that Branch Rickey "had been singled out in special honor" by the Harlem YMCA in New York City for his efforts in integrating baseball.[9] Robinson had taken on the role of youth director for the organization as a way of giving back to the community. In his role, he worked with at-risk children to improve their minds and not just their bodies.[10] Not surprisingly, juvenile involvement with the Harlem YMCA quickly doubled. Robinson's association with the Harlem YMCA lasted the rest of his life.[11]

Robinson's autobiography, *I Never Had It Made*, said 1949 was a year when Rickey had told him that he no longer had to turn a cheek to taunts and heckling. And it was a season in which there was a "tremendous improvement in the closeness of the Dodger team. Racial tensions had almost completely dissipated, and the team cared most about acquiring talented players" like Campanella and Newcombe.[12] The Dodgers went on to win the National League pennant by one game over the Cardinals.

The Dodgers lost the World Series to the crosstown rival New York Yankees in five games. In the only game the Dodgers won, by a 1-0 score, Robinson scored from third on a single by Gil Hodges. Robinson had been bluffing stealing home, and the losing pitcher, Vic Raschi, was highly complimentary. "I had just never seen anything like him before," Raschi said, "a human being who could go from a standing start to full speed in one step. He did something to me that almost never happened: He broke my concentration and I paid more attention to him than to Hodges. He beat me more than Hodges."[13]

SOURCES

In addition to the sources included in the Notes, the author consulted Baseball-Reference.com and Retrosheet.org.

NOTES

1. Jack Hernon, "Werlin' Willie Opposes Rex Barney Wednesday," *Pittsburgh Post-Gazette*, May 25, 1949: 18.
2. Chester I. Smith, "Pirates Host Dodgers Again After Losing First Game, 6-1," *Pittsburgh Press*, May 25, 1949: 32.
3. Hernon: 18.
4. Harold Burr, "Newcombe Tagged New Dodger Dandy," *The Sporting News*, June 1, 1949: 11.
5. Vince Johnson, "Once Over Lightly, *Pittsburgh Post-Gazette*, May 24, 1949: 15.
6. Jack Hernon, "Branca, Robinson Rout Pirates, 6-1," *Pittsburgh Post-Gazette*, May 25, 1949: 18.
7. Lester Biederman, "The Scoreboard," *Pittsburgh Press*, May 25, 1949: 32.
8. Harold Burr, "Brooks Bill Jackie as Big Show of N.L.," *The Sporting News*, June 8, 1949: 20.
9. Oscar Ruhl, "From the Ruhl Book," *The Sporting News*, June 8, 1949: 20.
10. William C. Kashatus, *Jackie & Campy* (Lincoln: University of Nebraska Press, 2014), 123.
11. Arnold Rampersad, *Jackie Robinson: A Biography* (New York: Random House, 1997), 204.
12. Jackie Robinson, *I Never Had It Made* (New York: Putnam, 1972), 86.
13. David Halberstam, *The Summer of '49* (New York: William Morrow and Company, Inc. 1989), 258.

A "WEIRD AFFAIR" AND SLUGFEST IN FLATBUSH

JUNE 24, 1950: BROOKLYN DODGERS 21, PITTSBURGH PIRATES 12,
AT EBBETS FIELD, BROOKLYN

by Glen Sparks

The Dodgers and Pirates broke off what *New York Daily News* sportswriter Dick Young called their "weird affair"[1] at just before midnight on June 24, 1950. Brooklyn led, 19-12. A report from the Associated Press boasted, "The crowd of 22,010 was treated to one of the wildest games in Ebbets Field history."[2] And it wasn't over.

Umpires suspended the action with one out in the bottom of the eighth inning. According to the New York state Sunday baseball law, play could not continue – no matter how exciting – after 11:59 P.M. Saturday. When the game picked up on August 1, Brooklyn hitters ripped a few more line drives. One of baseball's brawniest teams won, 21-12. The Dodgers collected 25 hits, including eight for extra bases. Jackie Robinson, Carl Furillo, and Roy Campanella knocked four hits apiece.

The three-game series began on June 23. Brooklyn scored eight times in the seventh inning and won, 15-3. Duke Snider drove home four runs and led a 19-hit attack. Furillo smacked a home run "into the center-field bleachers – that used to be more or less unprofaned ground."[3] Brooklyn upped its record to 34-22 and led the pennant chase by one game over the Phillies. Pittsburgh dropped to 21-38 and looked up from seventh place, 14½ games from the top.

Young gave Brooklyn batters only so much credit. He wrote that "the Pirate pitching may have had some small part in the one-sidedness of the tilt. Buc bowlers make the good old American game look like cricket, inasmuch as a team may remain at bat against them all night."[4]

Harold C. Burr from the *Brooklyn Eagle* noted that one "sarcastic" fan yelled "Fore!" after Furillo's long blast. That fan, according to Burr, "has been rooting for the return of the old-fashioned pitchers' battle for years." Were the baseballs of 1950 livelier than ones from past seasons? According to Burr, "The manufacturers claim that their baseballs are turned out on the same old machines and that perhaps some of 'em are wound tighter than others." Also, of note, Burr wrote, "Baseball is a perverse game where a famine follows hard after a feast. It's just possible the Flock would like to recall some of those 15 runs tonight."[5]

In the second game, the Dodgers' 24-year-old right-hander Ralph Branca faced 28-year-old lefty Cliff Chambers. Both pitchers took early showers. Pittsburgh scored four runs in the opening frame. Branca, already a three-time All-Star, began by walking Stan Rojek and Ted Beard. Ralph Kiner singled to load the bases. Pittsburgh went ahead, 1-0, when Gus Bell grounded out and Rojek raced home. Danny Murtaugh popped out, and first baseman Dale Coogan ripped a pitch deep into the right-field stands. Coogan, playing his first and only big-league season, never hit another home run.

Branca's day ended after catcher Earl Turner homered to start the second inning. His replacement, the often wild-armed right-hander Rex Barney, retired Pittsburgh in order.

Brooklyn scored its first run in the second inning. Furillo led off with a line-drive single to center field, advanced to second on a Campanella base hit, and made it to third after Pee Wee Reese's grounder forced Campanella at second. Barney drew a walk, which loaded the bases. Chambers also walked Billy Cox, bringing Furillo home.

Dodgers hitters knocked out Chambers in the third. Furillo lined a two-run double that scored Snider and Robinson after both players singled. Gil Hodges, the next batter, doubled Furillo home. Chambers gave way to Murry Dickson, a reliever known as "Tom Edison Jr." "because," according to his SABR biography, "he was always experimenting on the mound."[6]

Dickson, though, could not figure out a way to put down the Brooklyn rally. Campanella greeted him with an RBI single. Reese followed by knocking a base hit into right field. After Barney struck out, Cox singled to fill the bases once again. Pirates manager Billy Meyer pulled Dickson for Mel Queen. Snider greeted the new pitcher with a two-run double, making the score 8-5.

Strong hitting – weak pitching? – kept this game suspenseful. Barney, in the last year of a once-promising career, battled his control once again and walked Turner to lead off the fourth. He got Johnny Hopp, pinch-hitting for Queen, to ground into a double play but issued free passes to Rojek and Beard. Kiner stepped to the plate. The Pirates outfielder had slammed a career-high 54 home runs in 1949 and led the NL in homers for a fourth straight season. Against Barney, Kiner hit his 16th round-tripper of 1950 "into the upper deck in deepest left center,"[7] tying the game, 8-8.

Enter a new reliever for the Pirates, Frank Papish. The left-hander appeared in just four games in 1950 and just once after this contest. With one out, Hodges, the big first baseman and former Marine, blasted a solo home run, one of his 32 round-trippers in 1950.

Brooklyn manager Burt Shotton called on Dan Bankhead in the fifth. Baseball's first African American pitcher, a former member of the Birmingham Black Barons and Memphis Red Sox, Bankhead found himself in quick trouble. The right-hander gave up a two-run double to Nanny Fernandez, along with the lead. Pittsburgh took a 10-9 advantage.

Bankhead began the sixth by walking Beard and Kiner. Dodgers pitchers had now given up 10 bases on balls. Shotton, surely tiring of the gifts, asked Preacher Roe, usually a starter, to end this rally. Wally Westlake, though, greeted Roe with a run-scoring double. Two batters later, Coogan added a run-scoring fly ball. The Pirates now led 12-9. It wasn't enough.

The Dodgers pushed across five runs in the sixth. Bill Werle gave up all of them. Robinson and Furillo singled to open the frame. After Hodges flied out, Campanella and Reese followed with RBI hits. Preacher Roe, a woeful hitter, "laid down a poor bunt to the left of the mound."[8] Werle grabbed the ball and that's when, Young wrote, "the screwiness started."[9] Werle threw wildly to third base while trying to force out Campanella, and the ball sailed into left field. The Brooklyn catcher and Reese easily scored. Kiner threw to the plate, wildly like Werle did. Roe, rounding second, "was waved all the way home on a unique four-base bunt." The Dodgers moved ahead, 14-12.

Roe held the Bucs scoreless over his next two innings. In the bottom of the eighth, Brooklyn added seven more runs. Vic Lombardi, a 5-foot-7-inch left-hander, endured the agony. The former Dodger (1945-47) walked Reese and, after Roe grounded out, gave up a triple to Billy Cox. Jim Russell walked, and Snider singled to fill the bases.

Robinson, with three hits already, stepped to the plate. Exactly two years earlier, he hit a grand slam in the ninth inning to beat the Pirates at Ebbets Field, 6-2. On this day, he boasted a .358 batting average and a robust .447 on-base percentage. The first African American major leaguer of the twentieth century was the reigning National League Most Valuable Player. He topped the circuit in 1949 with a .342 batting average and 37 stolen bases. He also drove home 124 runs and scored 122. The former football and basketball star at UCLA and infielder for the Kansas City Monarchs slammed a pitch "deep into the left-field seats."[10] Pittsburgh sportswriter Charles J. Doyle called that blast "the most sensational moment of the battle."[11]

Furillo singled, and Hodges came to bat. That's when the clocked ticked to 11:59. Young, in his lead the following day, wrote, "Running out of time before the Bucs ran out of pitchers, Brooklyn last night scored 19 runs but still didn't have a victory, for sure." In the following paragraph, he added, "You can bet the 22,010 fans who sat through the dizzy doings will be talking about it right up to the date of resumption."[12] Doyle called the game up to that point a "sensational affair."[13] Brief rain showers, one in the second inning and another in the third, had stopped the action, though just briefly. Those delays, Young estimated, "added up to only 19 minutes."[14]

By time play resumed, the Dodgers had slipped to fourth place with a 51-40 record. The Phillies, a team with talented young players like Robin Roberts and Richie Ashburn and labeled the Whiz Kids, had moved into first. The Pirates, meanwhile, had dropped into last place, with a 34-60 mark, 22½ games behind their cross-state rival.

More than one month after the game's opening pitch, Campanella drove a one-out double to right field that scored Furillo and Hodges. Reese and Roe grounded out to end the inning. Young wrote, "Brooklyn batters, too accustomed to the extravagance of their own pitchers, weren't satisfied to coast on the seven-run bulge they enjoyed last night."[15] Even so, he added, "They needn't have bothered" to tack on those extra runs. "The game was in good hands, Preacher's left."[16] Roe quickly retired the Pirates in the top of the ninth. Thus ended what the *Pittsburgh Press* back in June, nearly echoing the words of Young, had called "a weird conflict."[17]

SOURCES

In addition to the sources cited in the Notes, the author accessed Retrosheet.org, Baseball-Reference.com, and SABR.org.

NOTES

1. Dick Young, "Dodgers Lead Bucs, 19-12; Suspend at Midnight," *New York Daily News*, June 25, 1950: 421.
2. Associated Press, "Dodgers Leads Bucs, 19-12, as Law Halts Tiff," *Rochester* (New York) *Democrat and Chronicle*, June 25, 1950: 60.
3. Harold C. Burr, "Dodgers Take Turns on Alternate Days of Going from Ridiculous to Sublime," *Brooklyn Eagle*, June 24, 1950: 6.
4. Young, "Dodgers Soak Pirates, 15-3, on 19 Hits, 3 HR," *New York Daily News*, June 24, 1950: 162
5. Burr.
6. Murry Dickson SABR bio, sabr.org/bioproj/person/1bb26f23.
7. Young, "Dodgers Lead Bucs, 19-12; Suspend at Midnight."
8. Young, "Dodgers Lead Bucs, 19-12; Suspend at Midnight."
9. Young, "Dodgers Lead Bucs, 19-12; Suspend at Midnight."
10. Charles J. Doyle, "Bucs Trail, 19-12, as Curfew Stops Game," *Pittsburgh Sun-Telegraph*, June 25, 1950: 31.
11. Doyle.
12. Young, "Dodgers Lead Bucs, 19-12; Suspend at Midnight."
13. Doyle.
14. Young, "Dodgers Lead Bucs, 19-12; Suspend at Midnight."
15. Young, "Flock Cops Buc Encore 21-12, Then Wins, 3-1," *New York Daily News*, August 2, 1950: 194.
16. Young, "Flock Cops Buc Encore 21-12, Then Wins, 3-1."
17. Les Biederman, "Curfew Halts Battle in the 8th Inning; Kiner Clouts No. 16," *Pittsburgh Press*, June 25, 1950: 39.

JACKIE'S PERFECT DAY SENDS DODGERS ON WIN STREAK

JULY 21, 1951: BROOKLYN DODGERS 3, ST. LOUIS CARDINALS 2, AT EBBETS FIELD, BROOKLYN

by Richard Cuicchi

The Brooklyn Dodgers were driving toward another pennant in the summer of 1951, with Jackie Robinson leading the way. He had a .356 batting average and .453 on-base percentage on the morning of July 21.

Brooklyn hosted the St. Louis Cardinals that afternoon at Ebbets Field. The Dodgers had moved into first place on May 13 and hoped to avoid their fate from a year earlier when Brooklyn was two games back of the Phillies for the league lead with two games left at the end of the season. Two Dodgers wins would have forced a tiebreaker playoff, but Philly's Whiz Kids managed to hang on, winning one of the last two games. The season's results provided strong impetus for the Dodgers to make a comeback in 1951.

In his fifth season since breaking the color barrier in major-league baseball in 1947, Robinson was part of a potent Dodgers offense that included Roy Campanella, Gil Hodges, Duke Snider, Pee Wee Reese, and Carl Furillo. But he still found himself the target of hostility from the opposition.

Early in the season, Robinson became embroiled in a public war of words with Giants manager Leo Durocher. The friction between them stemmed from a situation in 1948 when Durocher, then the Dodgers manager, humiliated his young star for being overweight coming into spring training. While they sparred through the press, their feuding also spilled onto the playing field. In one game, Durocher instructed his Giants pitcher to knock down Dodgers batters. Robinson, in turn, intentionally bunted toward Giants pitchers so that he could bump them while racing down the basepath. The bickering between the two fiery, headstrong men continued through the end of the regular season. At one point Durocher's wife, actress Laraine Day, got into the act, referring to Robinson and his teammates as "a bunch of sissies." Robinson denied that he hated Durocher, who had backed Jackie's entry into baseball. Robinson said of his feelings toward Durocher, "I just don't like to be called big-headed and I don't care to be knocked down."[1]

Despite all the distractions, Robinson still posted outstanding numbers. He had won the batting championship in his MVP season of 1949 and now in 1951 was in a race with the Cardinals' Stan Musial for another crown. Musial was batting .370 for the Cardinals, who were in third place, nine games behind the Dodgers.

A pregame ceremony held by the Dodgers commemorated the 75th anniversary of the National League. Dazzy Vance, a former Brooklyn pitching star, threw batting practice to several of the current Dodgers sluggers, none of whom could tag him with a hit out of the park.

Newcombe, the National League's Rookie of the Year in 1949, started for the Dodgers. He was one of the hottest pitchers in the league, having posted six straight wins for manager Chuck Dressen. His record coming into the game was 12-4. He was opposed by right-handed pitcher Gerry Staley, who also had 12 wins but nine losses.

Furillo got the scoring started for Brooklyn in the bottom of the first when he hit Staley's third pitch for his 11th home run of the season. Robinson singled for his first hit of the game later in the inning.

In the bottom of the third, Snider doubled with two outs, and Robinson drove him in with his second single of the game. When Hodges' pop-fly single bounced off the tip of shortstop Solly Hemus's glove in left-center, Robinson daringly tried to score from first base. However, he was tagged out at the plate by catcher Del Rice on a throw from Wally Westlake.[2] Robinson didn't slide on the play at home and wound up falling after he crossed the plate. His skinned knee had to be bandaged by the trainer before he could resume his position at second base.

Newcombe gave up hits in his first three innings but remained in control. He appeared headed for trouble in the top of the fourth, when the Cardinals led off with two singles. However, he recovered by striking out the next three batters to end the Cardinals' spurt.

Robinson added his third single off Staley in the sixth frame, but the score remained 2-0 through the seventh inning as both Newcombe and Staley battled hard to contain their opposition. Staley was lifted for a pinch-hitter in the seventh and Al Brazle continued to hold the Dodgers in the bottom of the inning.

Some of Newcombe's luck ran out in the eighth. After walking Musial, he gave up a game-tying home run to Hal Rice.

In the bottom of the eighth, the Dodgers were unsuccessful in manufacturing a run. Reese singled, but the inning was ended when he was thrown out trying to steal second with Robinson at the plate.

Robinson led off the bottom of the ninth with his fourth single, off Tom Poholsky, the third Cardinals hurler. After trying a sacrifice bunt, Hodges singled, advancing Robinson to third, and took second on an errant throw from outfielder Hal Rice. Campanella was intentionally walked to load the bases. Harry Brecheen was brought in to face .216 hitter Wayne Terwilliger, who pinch-hit for Don Thompson. With no outs and the infield pulled in for a play at the plate, Terwilliger responded with a walk-off single, scoring Robinson, to win the game, 3-2.

Newcombe recorded his seventh straight win, as he yielded 10 hits. He allowed the leadoff batter to reach base in six of the nine innings. But the 6-foot-4, 240-pound hurler struck out nine to extend his National League-leading total to 93. Newcombe finished the season with 20 wins and topped the league with 164 strikeouts. Poholsky took his third loss of the year against the Dodgers.

Robinson's perfect day at the plate gained him 8 percentage points on his batting average, after which he trailed league-leader Musial .364 to .370. Musial wound up winning his fifth title, .355, to Robinson's third-place finish at .338.

The Dodgers' win was their eighth straight against St Louis and the 10th of their 12 games against each other for the season. They led the second-place Giants by 7½ games. The victory was the second of what would eventually be 10 straight and part of an overall string of 19 wins in 23 games. The Dodgers had good reason to believe they would march on to win the pennant.

Yet the baseball gods turned against the Dodgers, as they faltered at the end of the season, posting a 27-24 record after August 11 (when they held the 13-game lead). Durocher and his Giants turned the tables on the Dodgers, beginning their own 16-game winning streak on August 12 and finishing the season with 39 wins and 8 losses. The regular season ended in a tie. In a best-of-three tiebreaker series, Bobby Thomson hit his historic walk-off "Shot Heard Round the World" home run in Game Three, and the Giants won their first pennant since 1937.

Despite any ill feelings Robinson still harbored for Durocher, he was one of the few Dodgers who congratulated the Giants on their victory. In his book *Nice Guys Finish Last*, Durocher said, "I knew Jackie was bleeding inside. I knew he'd rather have been congratulating anybody in the world but me. And still Jackie had come in smiling."[3]

The 1951 season was the third straight in which the NL race came down to the last few games of the season, and the Robinson-led Dodgers were involved in each of them. Robinson was spectacular during those three seasons, posting an average slash line of .336/.428/.519.

SOURCES

In addition to the sources cited in the Notes, the author consulted Baseball-Reference.com and the following:

Broeg, Bob. "Cards Lose in Ninth to Bums, 3-2," *St. Louis Post-Dispatch*, June 22, 1951: 4,1.

NOTES

1 Arnold Rampersad, *Jackie Robinson: A Biography* (New York: Alfred A. Knopf, 1997), 235-238.

2 Roscoe McGowen, "Brooks Top Cards in Ninth, Newcombe Taking 13th, 3-2," *New York Times*, July 22, 1951: 5, 1.

3 Leo Durocher and Ed Linn, *Nice Guys Finish Last* (New York: Simon and Schuster, 1975), 16.

JACKIE ROBINSON SAVES THE DAY AND THE SEASON

SEPTEMBER 30, 1951: BROOKLYN DODGERS 9,
PHILADELPHIA PHILLIES 8 (14 INNINGS),
AT SHIBE PARK, PHILADELPHIA

by C. Paul Rogers III

Sunday, September 30 was supposed to be the last day of the most memorable 1951 National League season. The New York Giants, 13 ½ games behind the Brooklyn Dodgers on August 26, had come roaring back to tie the Dodgers for the lead heading into that last day. They were playing the Braves in Boston in an early start time, which meant the Dodgers were scoreboard watching as their game against the Phillies in Philadelphia began. The crucial game drew a record Shibe Park crowd of 31,755 with many thousands coming down from Brooklyn to cheer on their Bums.[1]

The Dodgers started Preacher Roe, who with a gaudy 22-3 record had to instill confidence in the Brooklyns. The disappointing fifth-place Phillies, coming off their Cinderella Whiz Kids season the year before, started Bubba Church. Bubba possessed one of the best curve balls in the league and his 15 wins were second most on the club.

Church escaped a first-inning one-out first and third jam by serving up a double-play grounder to Jackie Robinson. On the other side, Preacher surprisingly didn't have it as the Phillies showed by chasing him with a four-run second. A solo home run by Tommy Brown, a run-scoring double by Eddie Pellagrini and a two-run infield single by Richie Ashburn were the big blows. The Dodgers plated a run in the top of the third on Pee Wee Reese's run-scoring triple to right, but the Phillies came back in the bottom half with two more runs. Church, an excellent-hitting pitcher who batted .256 for the year, singled sharply to right to plate the two runs off reliever Ralph Branca.

It looked bleak for the Dodgers, down 6-1 in the fourth, with the scoreboard showing the Giants leading the Braves 3-1 late in the game. They managed a second run in that inning on a triple by Roy Campanella and an infield error to make it 6-2. After Clyde King, another Dodger reliever, held the Phillies scoreless in their fourth, the resilient Dodgers put together their first real rally of the game, scoring three runs to close the score to 6-5. Robinson's one-out triple was the key hit and chased Church from the game.

But it looked like the Phillies' day when, in the bottom half of the inning, Granny Hamner followed Bill Nicholson's single to right with what looked like a similar shot to the same field. But as right-fielder Carl Furillo went to field the ball it took a bad hop and bounced over his head for a run-scoring triple. It was the fourth triple in five innings. Pellagrini drove in Hamner with a single to left and the Phillies again had some breathing room, 8-5.

Then, with the score the same in the bottom of the sixth with Carl Erskine of the Dodgers pitching to Willie Jones, the scoreboard posted that the Giants had defeated the Braves, 3-2. It was now win or go home for the winter for the Dodgers.[2]

Clem Labine and Erskine managed to keep the Phillies from extending their lead and Karl Drews, in relief of Church, held the Dodgers at bay until the eighth inning. But with one out Drews gave up consecutive singles to Gil Hodges, who beat out a grounder to shortstop, and Billy Cox, who blooped a ball just inside the right-field foul line.[3] Rube Walker batted

**Jackie Hero of Philly Story
—Durocher Praises Giants**
Home Run Clout
Brings Victory
In 14th Frame

Brooklyn Daily Eagle, October 1, 1951: 14.

for Erskine and on an 0-2 pitch doubled deep to left to drive in two runs and bring the score to 8-7.[4]

Phillies manager Eddie Sawyer showed that he was pulling out all the stops by bringing in ace Robin Roberts to pitch to Furillo. It was something of a surprise move because Roberts had pitched eight innings the day before in a 5-0 loss to the Dodgers. Furillo, however, singled to left to score pinch-runner Don Thompson with the tying run before Roberts could get out of the inning.

Dodgers manager Charlie Dressen was also leaving it all out there and brought his ace Don Newcombe in to pitch the bottom of the eighth. Newcombe had also pitched the day before, tossing a seven-hit shutout against Philly. The two 20-game winners quelled any further scoring as the game went into extra innings with both still on the mound. At one point, Roberts retired 10 Dodgers in a row, while Newcombe was almost as effective.

The Phillies almost got to Newcombe in the 11th, however, when Newk issued a two-out walk to Hamner. Andy Seminick then laced a shot to left-center that looked like it was ticketed for two bases. Running with two outs, Hamner would have scored easily to end the game, but Andy Pafko in left made a running, game-saving catch to keep the Dodgers alive.[5]

In the bottom of the 12th the Phillies mounted a serious threat when Roberts, hitting for himself, led off with a walk. Pellagrini bunted and both runners were safe when Roberts beat the throw to second. Ashburn hit a two-hopper to Hodges; his only play was at first so the runners advanced to second and third with one out. A run would win it for the Phillies and end the Dodgers season.

Brooklyn intentionally walked Willie Jones to load the bases and set up a force at any base. Del Ennis was next and worked the count to two and two before taking a called strike three for the second out. That brought up Eddie Waitkus who smashed a low liner to the right side of second base. Jackie Robinson, playing second, dove for the ball, reaching across his body with his glove hand inches above the ground. He landed hard with the ball in his glove and immediately rolled over and weakly tossed the ball towards second base, like he was attempting to get a force out there, before collapsing on the infield.

Roberts, running from third base, watched the ball all the way and was certain that Robinson had trapped it and that he was scoring the winning run.[6] But umpire Lon Warneke lifted his right hand and called Waitkus out to end the inning, so the game continued despite vociferous protests from the Phillies bench.[7] Robinson apparently knocked the wind out of himself on the play and lay on the infield for several minutes before walking gingerly to the dugout.[8]

Neither team scored in the 13th inning, although the Phillies again threatened. After Newcombe tired and walked two in the bottom half with two outs, Bud Podbielan relieved and retired Pellagrini on a flyball to Duke Snider in center to end the inning.

Roberts continued to sail along and in the top of the 14th quickly retired Reese and Snider on harmless foul pop ups. The smooth sailing stopped abruptly with the next batter, Jackie Robinson, who was still in the game after his hard dive. With the count one and one, Robinson got hold of a high fastball and sent it far into the left-field stands for a solo home run and a 9-8 Brooklyn lead. Campanella doubled to left but Roberts bore down to retire Pafko on a groundout to short to end the inning.

The tension continued in the bottom of the inning as Ashburn led off against Podbielan with a line drive single just over Reese's outstretched glove at shortstop.[9] Jones immediately sacrificed Ashburn to second to bring up Ennis, the Phils' clean-up batter. He worked the count full before popping up to Hodges at first for the second out. Waitkus was next but could not deliver, flying out to Pafko in left to end the drama and the game.

The Dodgers of course went on to lose a dramatic three-game playoff for the pennant to the New York Giants on Bobby Thomson's famous "Shot Heard 'Round the World" off Ralph Branca.[10] But without Robinson's spectacular catch in the bottom of the 12th, there would have been no playoff and Bobby Thomson would be remembered as a solid player who is the only major leaguer born in Scotland rather than as the architect of the most dramatic home run in baseball history.

But did Jackie Robinson really catch Waitkus's liner in the 12th? The Phillies to a man thought he trapped the ball. Russ Meyer was so vocal from the Phillies bench that he was almost ejected.[11] Roberts believed that Robinson's wild toss of the ball from a prone position towards second showed that Jackie thought he had trapped the ball and was desperately trying for a force out at second.

That off-season Roberts saw Robinson at a winter banquet. He said to Robinson, "Jackie, you didn't catch that ball that Waitkus hit."

Roberts recalled that Robinson grinned at him and said, "What did the umpire say?"[12]

SOURCES

In addition to the sources cited in the Notes, the author accessed Baseball-Reference.com and Retrosheet.org for box score/play-by-play information.

NOTES

1. Roscoe McGowen, "Brooks beat Phils in Fourteenth, 9-8," *New York Times,* October 1, 1951: 26.
2. Roscoe McGowen.
3. Roscoe McGowen.
4. Roscoe McGowen.
5. Roscoe McGowen.
6. Robin Roberts and C. Paul Rogers III, *My Life in Baseball* (Chicago: Triumph Books, 2003), 104.
7. Carl Lundquist, "Drama in Philadelphia: Jackie's Forgotten Day," *The National Pastime* No. 26 (1997): 4.
8. Frederick G. Lieb, *The Philadelphia Phillies* (New York: A. S. Barnes & Co., 1953), 234. Another account had Robinson jamming his shoulder. McGowen, 26.
9. Lieb, 234.
10. We would also be missing from our history Russ Hodges' wonderful description of Thomson's home run: "The Giants win the pennant! the Giants win the pennant! the Giants win the pennant! . . . "
11. Lundquist, 4.
12. Roberts and Rogers, 105.

PLAYOFF FOR NL PENNANT KNOTTED AT ONE GAME APIECE

OCTOBER 2, 1951: BROOKLYN DODGERS 10, NEW YORK GIANTS 0, AT THE POLO GROUNDS, NEW YORK

by Alan Cohen

"Dressen first saw this boy in Boston in 1944 when a group of boys came to Braves Field for a tryout. Charlie liked him then and the club (Brooklyn) signed him."
– Brooklyn scout John "Red" Corriden, speaking about Clem Labine, October 2, 1951[1]

He would ultimately become known as the man with the rubber arm but, on this day Clem Labine was a relatively unknown rookie whom manager Chuck Dressen of the Dodgers had chosen to save the Dodgers from elimination in their best-of-three playoff with the New York Giants for the National League pennant. Labine had been called up from St. Paul in July, and his Dodgers contract called for a stipend of $5,000 per year. The hopes of the Dodgers were being pinned on a man who would be paid $38.50 for that day's work.[2] Labine pitched a six-hit shutout as the Dodgers won, 10-0, to force a decisive third game at the Polo Grounds.

The second game was played at the home of the Giants, the Polo Grounds, and the fans hoped to see their heroes win the National League pennant. Overcast skies and threatening weather conditions kept the crowd down to 38,609.

Labine shared the spotlight with Jackie Robinson, whose first four appearances in New York had been as a member of the Kansas City Monarchs in 1945. Robinson's first-inning homer, on the first pitch to him after a leadoff single by Pee Wee Reese and Duke Snider's strikeout, gave the Dodgers a 2-0 lead before the Giants had an opportunity to bat. The homer barely made it over the 315-foot sign in left field. It came off the Giants starter, Sheldon "Available" Jones, whose career was on a downward spiral at the relatively young age of 29. Going into the game, his record for the 1951 season was 6-10, after a combined 44-36 record over the prior three seasons. His major claim to fame was having led the National League in hit batsmen for two consecutive years (1948-1949).

In the top of the third inning, the day's brouhaha (what's a Dodgers-Giants game without a good argument?) took place. A one-out walk to Snider and a single by Robinson put runners on first and second and occasioned a visit by Giants manager Leo Durocher to the mound to remove Jones from the game. The new Giants pitcher was George Spencer. After Andy Pafko popped out, Gil Hodges hit a grounder back toward Spencer. Spencer's throw to Whitey Lockman at first base hit Hodges and bounded about 10 feet away. Snider rounded third and raced toward home but Lockman retrieved the ball and gunned out the Duke at home, catcher Wes Westrum applying the tag. Dodgers coach Cookie Lavagetto and manager Dressen got into a heated exchange with umpire Larry Goetz after Snider was ruled out, Goetz saying that he never touched home plate. After the game Dressen noted that "Snider did a hook side and one of his feet touched the base, but the other didn't. Goetz looked at the wrong leg – the one off the base."[3]

The Giants mounted threats in three consecutive innings against Labine but came up empty. In the second inning with one out, the Giants threatened as Bobby Thomson doubled and Willie Mays had an infield hit. They were left stranded.

Dodgers Tie for Pennant on Robinson's Homer In 14th After Giants Win; Playoffs Begin Today

Jackie Also Saves Game With Diving Catch in 12th

Washington Post, October 3, 1951: A9.

Jackie

An inning later, the Giants loaded the bases on an error by Reese, a single by Don Mueller, and a walk to Whitey Lockman. With two out and the count full, Labine got Thomson lunging after a wide curve for a strikeout to end the inning. In the fourth inning, with two out, Spencer and Eddie Stanky singled. Al Dark's liner was snatched by Billy Cox at third, and that threat died. After that, the Giants had little in the way of offense, and not a runner got past first base.

In the top of the fifth inning, the Dodgers extended their lead to 3-0 when Snider's double was followed by an RBI single by Robinson, giving Jackie three hits and three RBIs – and the game was only in the fifth inning.

In the top of the sixth inning, the umpires ordered the lights turned on as dark clouds assembled in the skies above the ballpark in Harlem, and the Dodgers broke the game open with three runs. Hodges led off the inning with a homer, his 40th of the season. Cox then hit a liner that third baseman Thomson knocked down. Bobby's throw to first base was wild and Cox wound up at second on the error. A fly out by Rube Walker advanced Cox to third, bringing up Labine. Dressen ordered a suicide squeeze. Spencer's pitch went wide of the plate and Labine could not reach it with his bat. The Giants had Cox in a rundown between third and home. The ball eventually wound up in the glove of Spencer and when he attempted the tag, Cox jarred the ball loose and scampered home with the Dodgers' fifth run. Labine then walked, and Carl Furillo lined out for the second out of the inning. The rains then came and suspended play for 41 minutes. After the game resumed, Reese singled off Spencer, advancing Labine to third base. Clem scored on a single by Snider to make the score 6-0.

After sending up a pinch-hitter, Bill Rigney, for Spencer in the bottom of the sixth, the Giants brought in Al Corwin to pitch and his first throw in the seventh inning was hit over the left-field wall by Andy Pafko, his 30th of the season, bringing the score to 7-0. Hodges drew a walk and after Cox lined out to left field, Walker singled to center field. Mays misplayed the ball and Hodges scored from first base. Walker wound up on second. The error by Mays was the fifth by the Giants in the game. Three of the Dodgers runs to that point were unearned.

In the bottom of the seventh inning, Robinson topped off his great day with a fielding gem. He raced from his second-base position to the other side of the bag to grab a soft liner. In the same inning, two late-arriving pigeons positioned themselves in the Dodgers infield so as to get an up-close view of Jackie Robinson. Robinson chased them away, but they came back some time later (they were not on the field when the Dodgers were at bat) and positioned themselves near Gil Hodges. They helped themselves to a meal, on the sod behind Hodges, doubtless knowing of the fielding wizardry of the Dodgers first baseman.[4]

The Dodgers completed the scoring with two ninth-inning runs. With two out, Cox walked and came home on Walker's homer, "the longest home run I ever hit in my life," he said.[5] It was Rube's third hit of the game. He had proved to be more than an adequate replacement for Roy Campanella, who sat out the game with a bad leg.

The Dodgers win snapped a Giant win streak of eight games. They had won the last seven games on the schedule and won the first playoff game before succumbing to Labine and Robinson.

"The magic number is down to one."
 – Ralph Branca, October 2, 1951[6]

The Dodgers, if they could win Game Three of the playoff the following day, would head to Yankee Stadium for the first game of the World Series. Robinson had first appeared at Yankee Stadium on June 17, 1945, in a 3-1 Kansas City Monarchs win over the Philadelphia Stars. In that game his seventh-inning single ignited a rally that accounted for all of his team's runs.[7] He next appeared there on August 12, 1945, going 2-for-3 and doubling in a run in the seventh inning when the Monarchs defeated the New York Black Yankees, 4-1.[8]

Robinson's first appearances in Brooklyn had also been in 1945, with the Monarchs on June 22 and August 15 at Dexter Park against the Bushwicks. In June he went 3-for-4 with a pair of doubles and an RBI, accounting for all of his team's runs in a 4-3 loss to the Bushwicks.[9] In August he went 2-for-5 in a 9-3 win.[10] By the end of August, Robinson was back in Brooklyn for his first meeting with Branch Rickey.[11] In October he was back at the Dodgers offices to sign his first contract with the Dodgers.

Robinson's 3-for-5 against the Giants brought his average for the season to .337. The next day he went 1-for-2 to bring his batting average for the full 1951 season to .338. His first-inning homer was his 19th and last of the season. It was his third consecutive season over .300. He continued to hit over .300 through 1954.

PERSPECTIVES ON 42

As for Bobby Thomson, who struck out against Labine with the bases loaded in the bottom of the third inning, tomorrow would be another day.

The next day, at the Polo Grounds, the Giants won, 5-4, and advanced to the World Series.

SOURCES

In addition to Baseball-Reference.com and the sources cited in the Notes, the author used:

Drebinger, John. "Dodgers Win, Tie Play-Offs as Labine Halts Giants, 10-0," *New York Times*, October 3, 1951: 1, 42.

Haley, Martin J. "Bums Bounce Back, Even Playoff on Labine's 6-Hitter and Four Homers," *St. Louis Globe Democrat*, October 3, 1951: 3C.

Holbrook, Bob. "Rookie Labine Stuns Baseball World," *Boston Globe*, October 3, 1951: 1.

Rennie, Rud. "Dodgers Trounce Giants, 10-0, and Tie Play-Offs as Labine Pinches Six-Hitter," *New York Herald Tribune*, October 3, 1951: 1, 29.

Siler, Tom. "Rookie Labine Saved Brooks for Day, Now It's Up to Big Guys, Maglie or Newcombe," *Knoxville* (Tennessee) *News Sentinel*, October 3, 1951: 20.

Smith, Red. "Views of Sport," *New York Herald Tribune*, October 3, 1951: 29.

Talbot, Gayle (Associated Press). "Dodgers Maul Giants, 10-0, Knot Playoff," *Wilmington* (Delaware) *Morning News*, October 3, 1951, 1, 28.

Young, Dick. "Labine Trips Giants 10-0 on 6 Hits: Flock Ties Playoff, Blasts Four Homers," *New York Daily News*, October 3, 1951: 90, 93-94.

NOTES

1. Roscoe McGowen, "Rookie Pitcher's Brilliant Performance Hailed by Jubilant Brooklyn Team," *New York Times*, October 3, 1951: 42.
2. Lester J. Biederman, "Desperate Move Saves Dodgers: Rookie Labine Starts, Blanks Giants, 10-0," *Pittsburgh Press*, October 3, 1951: 33.
3. Will Grimsley (Associated Press), "Dodgers Jubilant Over Playoff Win," *Wilmington* (Delaware) *Morning News*, October 3, 1951: 28.
4. Chester L. Smith, "The Village Smithy: NL Winner Due for Rough Time," *Pittsburgh Press*, October 3, 1951: 33.
5. McGowen.
6. McGowen.
7. "Paige Sparkles as K.C. Tops Philly," *Pittsburgh Courier*, June 23, 1945: 16.
8. "Satchel Paige Slips Black Yankees 4 to 1 Defeat: Monarchs Win Before 19,000 Fans," *New York Amsterdam News*, August 18, 1945: 8-B.
9. "Martin Bombers in Doubleheader with Bushwicks," *Brooklyn Eagle*, June 23, 1945: 6.
10. "Monarchs Show Bushwicks Some Stylish Tricks," *Brooklyn Eagle*, August 16, 1945: 14.
11. "Rickey Admits Calling in Jackie Robinson," *Pittsburgh Courier*, September 1, 1945: 16.

A WET ALL-STAR GAME AT SHIBE

JULY 8, 1952: NATIONAL LEAGUE 3, AMERICAN LEAGUE 2,
AT SHIBE PARK, PHILADELPHIA

by Paul E. Doutrich

On July 8, 1952, it rained all morning in Philadelphia. It rained the previous night and more rain was predicted for the afternoon. It was not a day for baseball. Commissioner Ford Frick had a dilemma. The 1952 All-Star Game was scheduled for that day. Since the inaugural contest in 1933, no All-Star Game had been canceled for any reason. Fans, media, and sponsors anxiously awaited the 1952 game. And of course, 52 of baseball's best players had assembled in the city. With the rain slowing by late morning, Frick decided that the game would be played.

Because of the weather there was no pregame hitting or fielding. Instead, warming up was limited to stretching in the dugout and a few minutes of catch before the game. Finally, 19 minutes after the scheduled start time, 32,785 patrons watched the American League's leadoff hitter, Dom DiMaggio, step up to the plate. DiMaggio had played in the previous three All-Star Games but this one was different. His brother Joe, who had retired after the 1951 season, was not on the squad. Neither was his Red Sox sidekick, Ted Williams. He was in the Marines flying jet fighter planes in Korea.

On the mound for the National League was hometown favorite Curt Simmons. As a steady drizzle continued to fall, DiMaggio patiently worked the Phillies ace for a walk. Simmons fared better with the next three hitters. He struck out Yankees outfielder Hank Bauer and Cleveland's Dale Mitchell and then got Al Rosen, the Indians third baseman, to roll one to his Phillies teammate Granny Hamner at short.

The American League manager, Casey Stengel, penciled in one of his Yankees hurlers, Vic Raschi, to start the game. For Stengel there was a little extra pressure that came with the 1952 game. He had been the losing manager in the two previous All-Star Games. No manager had ever lost three in a row. Raschi started well, getting New York Giants first baseman Whitey Lockman on a pop to Phil Rizzuto at shortstop. Jackie Robinson followed Lockman. Robinson had three hits in the seven official times he had faced Raschi. This time he smacked Raschi's first pitch to him into the left-field upper deck. Already down a run, Raschi recovered impressively, striking out the National League's batting-average leader, Stan Musial, and home-run leader, Hank Sauer.

The second inning went well for both pitchers. Simmons sandwiched a strikeout of the White Sox first baseman Eddie Robinson between a line out off the bat of catcher Yogi Berra and second baseman Bobby Avila's groundout to Hamner at shortstop. In the bottom half of the inning, catcher Roy Campanella led off for the National League. Campy had been the league's Most Valuable Player the previous season but a series of minor injuries slowed him in 1952. Three times he had been hurt on collisions at the plate, the worst of which kept him out of the starting lineup for 10 days and required a cast on his left thumb. Campanella played through his injuries as much as possible but his hitting had suffered a bit. Facing Raschi, Campanella popped out to third. Veteran Cardinals outfielder Enos Slaughter then struck out and Bobby Thomson flied out to Bauer.

In the third, DiMaggio briefly added a bit of life to the American League attack. Despite some control problems, Simmons continued to mow through opposition hitters. Rizzuto opened the frame with a foul pop to third. Gil McDougald *pinch-hit for Raschi*. Playing in his first All-Star Game, McDougald grounded out to third. DiMaggio followed with his team's first hit off Simmons, a slicing double into right field. With a runner in scoring position, Hank Bauer fouled out to Campanella, ending the threat.

Bob Lemon, the Cleveland ace, took over for Raschi in the bottom of the third. Leadoff hitter Granny Hamner flied out to Hank Bauer in right field. Stengel then made a surprise maneuver. He attempted to replace Dale Mitchell in left field with Chicago's

Minnie Miñoso.[1] Immediately NL manager Leo Durocher challenged the move. He contended that except for pitchers, starting players in All-Star Games were required to play three full innings. Stengel later explained that he made the move because Mitchell had a bad leg and Casey was concerned that he might further aggravate it playing on the rain-soaked outfield. According to the *Philadelphia Inquirer*, Home-plate umpire Al Barlick upheld Durocher's argument.[2] Mitchell returned to left field and Miñoso to the bench. In the bottom of the inning, Durocher sent Pee Wee Reese up to pinch-hit for Simmons. Reese was playing in his eighth All-Star Game and still looking for his first All-Star base hit. He did not get it this time; he flied to left, pushing his hitless streak to 13. Lockman followed Reese and lifted one that center fielder DiMaggio easily hauled in.

The rain began to fall harder as the game entered the fourth inning. Small puddles were forming in the outfield. The infield, which had been dry until the tarp was removed just before the first pitch, was getting muddy and slippery.

The Cubs' Bob Rush, who took over for Simmons, got into trouble immediately. Now that Dale Mitchell's required playing time was over, Miñoso was sent in to hit for him, and rapped a double into right field. Al Rosen followed with a walk after watching a string of low, outside pitches miss the plate. Yogi Berra stepped into the batter's box. With his team down a run, many expected him to be bunting. Instead Stengel chose to play for a big inning and let his catcher swing away. The strategy failed. Berra popped one to short right field. The next batter, Eddie Robinson, made up for Berra's failure. He sizzled a pitch a couple of steps to the right of Jackie Robinson at second. Normally Jackie would have gobbled the ball up but wading through the infield mud, he slipped and the ball skipped under his glove. Miñoso scored easily. Jackie was part of the American League's second run as well. Bobby Avila bounced a Rush pitch up the middle. Slow getting to the ball, Robinson was able to knock it down but couldn't make a play, and Rosen scored. Phil Rizzuto came to the plate with runners on first and second, two runs in, and one out. Swinging at an inside fastball, he knocked a sharp groundball to his counterpart at shortstop. Hamner handled the ball cleanly and tossed it to second. Robinson got to the ball to force Avila with no problem, but on his double-play pivot he slipped off the bag and made an awkward throw, pulling Lockman at first off the bag a bit. Whitey was able to recover in time to easily get Rizzuto, who was merely jogging down the line. After the game Stengel defended Rizzuto's apparent sloth to critical reporters: "Couldn't you see it? … He slipped and fell on his hands."[3]

Now with his team down a run, Jackie Robinson came to the plate hoping to atone for his costly error. He did not. Instead he popped to third. Lemon then plunked Stan Musial, putting the tying run on base. Hank Sauer did more than tie the game. He launched a rocket onto what Philadelphia fans sometimes referred to as Foxxville, the left-field pavilion where numerous Jimmie Foxx blasts had landed. The National League now led, 3-2. The home run was especially rewarding for Sauer. Two years earlier, All-Star team manager Burt Shotton had attempted to keep Sauer out of the starting lineup even though fans voted for him to start. Satisfied with his revenge, after the game Sauer said: "I wonder how Shotton feels now."[4]

Lemon's problems didn't end with Sauer's shot. Campanella walked, Slaughter doubled, and after Thompson popped to third, Hamner was intentionally walked, loading the bases. Next up was pitcher Rush. Most expected to see a pinch-hitter but Durocher surprised them. Rush did not. He punched one to third for the final out.

Lemon was scheduled to lead off the American League fifth but after the previous inning's problems and with a crew of heavy hitters on the bench, a pinch-hitter seemed appropriate. Instead Casey let his pitcher hit. Lemon had started his major-league career as a power-hitting third baseman, so Stengel had confidence with him at the plate. After the game Stengel explained: "I wasn't going to use one of my big hitters. … I might need 'em later. Besides, Lemon's a pretty good hitter."[5] Lemon grounded out to second. Bauer followed with a single off Rush's glove. Then, in another surprising move, Bauer attempted to steal second. Campanella cut him down easily for the final out.

Though he had allowed Lemon to hit in the top of the inning, Stengel pulled him in the bottom of the inning. Little (5-feet-6½, 139 pounds) Bobby Shantz, another hometown favorite, was sent out to face the heart of the National League lineup. Mixing a sharp curveball with a fastball, Shantz used 13 pitches to strike out the three hitters he faced. Asked after the game if he regretted not having a chance to duplicate or better Carl Hubbell's strikeout feat in the 1934 game, Shantz replied, "No, I was just thinking how awful it would be to get knocked out in the next inning."[6]

Shantz didn't get his chance to better Hubbell. Before he could throw another pitch, the game was halted. Fifty-six minutes later, the umpires deemed the field unplayable and so ended the shortest and wettest All-Star Game ever played, with the National League a 3-2 winner.

SOURCES

In addition to the sources cited in the Notes, the author also consulted Baseball-Reference.com, Retrosheet.com, the *New York Times,* and the *St. Louis Post Dispatch.*

NOTES

1. Joe Trimble, "NL Stars Defeat AL in Rain, 3-2," *New York Daily News,* July 9, 1952: 21.
2. Hank Littlehales, "A's Southpaw Fans Side on 13 Pitches," *Philadelphia Inquirer,* July 9, 1952: 45.
3. Gene Ward, "Stengel 'Waited' Too Long," *New York Daily News,* July 9, 1952: 21.
4. "Sauer Recalls Shotton's Snub," *Chicago Tribune,* July 9, 1952: 41.
5. Ward.
6. Littlehales.

JACKIE AND DODGERS END SLUMP IN HOME-RUN BARRAGE

SEPTEMBER 15, 1952: BROOKLYN DODGERS 11, CINCINNATI REDS 5, AT EBBETS FIELD, BROOKLYN

by Gregory H. Wolf

Jackie Robinson and the Brooklyn Dodgers were slumping as they prepared to wrap up the season series with the sixth-place Cincinnati Reds (64-79) in Flatbush. Skipper Chuck Dressen's squad still possessed the best record (89-53) in the big leagues and held a comfortable three-game lead over the New York Giants in the pennant race, but 'Dem Bums had lost 13 of their last 21 games. The 33-year-old Robinson, the heart and soul of the team's high-scoring offense, had managed just 11 hits in his last 51 at-bats, dropping his batting average to .302. Never one to panic, Dressen knew the team needed to turn things around with the red-hot Giants (winners of 11 of their last 15 contests) on their tail.

It was a dreadful Monday afternoon in Brooklyn with weather more conducive to football than baseball. The skies were gloomy, and a light drizzle fell, which ultimately forced the ballpark lights on by the second inning. Temperatures dropped into the 50s. On Ladies Day, the sparse crowd of 2,612 paid spectators, plus 1,642 women and 100 knotholers, was "chilled and dampened," noted the *Brooklyn Eagle*.[1]

Toeing the rubber for the Dodgers was 25-year-old right-hander Carl Erskine, who had enjoyed a breakout season as a swingman in '51, winning 16 games. Used almost exclusively as a starter in '52, Erskine had pitched well (12-6, 2.78 ERA), but had suffered from elbow pain in the last weeks. Brooklyn sportswriter Dave Anderson reported that the pitcher had his right elbow "sprayed … with ethyl chloride before and during the game" to deaden the pain.[2] Whether from discomfort or the inclement playing conditions, Erskine was erratic in the opening frame, loading the bases with one out on a single and two walks. His third walk, to Jim Greengrass, forced in the game's first run. It appeared as if Erskine might not make it through the first inning, but two consecutive punchouts defused the threat.

The Reds had one of baseball's greatest hitters on their team, but he was their manager, Rogers Hornsby, the club's third skipper of the season. The Dodgers knew the Raj's choice for starting pitcher very well. Right-hander Bud Podbielan had been a mop-up artist for the Dodgers the previous three years and had been reduced to pitching primarily batting practice until the club traded him to the Reds two months earlier. Shut out by Herm Wehmeier on six hits the day before to suffer just their fifth loss in 21 games against the Reds in '52, the Dodgers took their whacks against their former teammate. Carl Furillo led off with a single, Duke Snider lined another with one out, then Jackie Robinson blasted one into the left-corner seats for his first home run in 17 games to give the Dodgers a 3-1 lead.[3]

The game's next four runs were all leadoff solo home runs off the starting pitchers. Two were from Snider, who connected in the third for what sportswriter Dick Young of the *Daily News* described as a "tremendous poke" that soared beyond the flagpole on the left side of the scoreboard.[4] In the fifth he launched his 19th round-tripper of the season "high over the right-field screen."[5] Between the Duke's shots were Gil Hodges' fourth-inning bomb into the left-field seats. It was his 31st home run and 100th RBI of the season, Hodges becoming the first Brooklyn player to knock in 100 or more runs in four consecutive seasons. The

Robinson and Snider Blast 2 Homers Apiece in Slugfest

News and Courier (Charleston, South Carolina), September 16, 1952: 10.

Reds' light-hitting Bobby Adams joined the home-run parade in the fifth.[6]

Leading 6-2, the Dodgers were poised to tack on some more runs in the sixth. They loaded the bags with singles by Billy Cox and Furillo and a walk to Pee Wee Reese, all off Bubba Church, the Reds' third reliever of the game. But Church registered his third strikeout of the frame, fanning Snider, to end the threat.

Erskine was back on the mound in the bottom of the seventh, but was laboring. He yielded a leadoff single to Johnny Temple, then issued a season-high sixth walk two batters later to Willard Marshall. After retiring Ted Kluszewski for the second out, Erskine stared down rookie Jim Greengrass, who had connected off the Dodgers' Johnny Rutherford in the previous game for a grand slam, his first major-league home run. Greengrass parked Erskine's offering in the lower left-center stands for a three-run home run. With one swing, the game was suddenly close.

But the Dodgers wasted little time in padding their 6-5 lead. Robinson, who would finish the season with a big-league-best .440 on-base-percentage, coaxed a walk from Church to lead off the seventh. After Andy Pafko singled, Roy Campanella blasted one to deep left field. Racing back, Joe Adcock "got his glove-top on the drive, couldn't hold on," wrote Dick Young, and Robinson scored.[7] It was his 100th run of the season. Rubber-armed reliever Frank Smith replaced Church and intentionally walked Hodges despite the righty-righty matchup; then again, Hodges at the time ranked third in home runs and second in RBIs in the NL. Cox hit a tailor-made double-play grounder to Roy McMillan. The "flashy shortstop," opined Young, used poor judgment and instead of taking the DP, threw home.[8] The toss pulled catcher Hobie Landrith off the plate and Pafko scored (unearned) to make it 8-5. George Shuba, pinch-hitting for Erskine, added another run on a fly out. McMillan would become one of the best shortstops of the 1950s, but his tough inning continued. According to Dick Young, he collided with third baseman Bobby Adams on Furillo's routine double-play grounder; Adams held onto the ball and tossed to second to erase Cox while Hodges scored the Dodgers' fourth run of the inning.

The Dodgers tallied their 11th and final run in the eighth on Jackie Robinson's solo shot off reliever Joe Nuxhall. It was Jackie's 19th round-tripper of the season, matching his career-best from the previous season. It was also the third of eight times that he hit two home runs in a game.

In an era when relievers were often failed starters, Dressen had a unique weapon: Joe Black. The 28-year-old right-hander was a trail-blazing rookie in 1952, but had loads of experience. He established his reputation with the Negro League Baltimore Elite Giants, where he was a teammate of Campanella's. Making his 51st appearance of the season, second only to knuckleballer Hoyt Wilhelm of the Giants, Black retired all six batters he faced to end the game in 2 hours and 43 minutes. It was the 38th time Black finished a ballgame, breaking the Dodgers' team record of 37 set by Hugh Casey in 1947. (Black was ultimately named NL Rookie of the Year and finished third in the NL MVP voting, just 18 points behind winner Hank Sauer and three points behind Robin Roberts in one of the closest three-way ballots in baseball history.)

The Dodgers' big bats were the story of the game. They tied a team record with five home runs (achieved many times). Their "resurgence came at a most timely and critical point of the year," noted Anderson.[9] The team went on to win six of the final 11 games (one was a tie) to capture its third pennant in six years. And for the third time since 1947 "Dem Bums" played their archrivals, the New York Yankees. They succumbed yet again, this time in agonizing fashion, losing Games Six and Seven at Ebbets Field.

Jackie Robinson ended his slump in dramatic fashion with this game. Given a few days off down the stretch with the Dodgers' pennant in hand, Robinson went 11-for-26 in his final 10 games while slugging .769. He finished the season with 19 home runs, 75 RBIs, and a .308 batting average. By one modern metric that was not used in his time, Robinson was the most valuable offensive player in the major leagues by leading baseball in Offensive WAR (7.9) and WAR for position player (8.5).[10]

SOURCES

In addition to the sources cited in the Notes, the author accessed Retrosheet.org, Baseball-Reference.com, SABR.org, and *The Sporting News* archive via Paper of Record.

McGowen, Roscoe. "Brooklyn Victor on 5 Homers, 11-5," *New York Times*, September 16, 1952.

Smith, Lou. "Brooklyn Trims Redlegs, Hold Edge," *Cincinnati Enquirer*, September 16, 1952: 21

NOTES

1. Dave Anderson, "Dodgers Low in Majors on Miscue Totem Pole," *Brooklyn Eagle*, September 16, 1952: 15.
2. Anderson, "Dodgers Low in Majors on Miscue Totem Pole."

3 Home run location from Dick Young, "Flock Clips Reds, 11-5; 5 HRs Hold 3-Up Lead," (New York) *Daily News*, September 16, 1952: 58.

4 Young.

5 Dave Anderson, "'Please, Lord, Let There Be No Miracle This Year,'" *Brooklyn Eagle*, September 16, 1952: 15.

6 Adams entered the game with just 22 home runs in 2,411 at-bats.

7 Young.

8 Young.

9 Anderson, "'Please, Lord, Let There Be No Miracle This Year.'"

10 WAR, an acronym for Wins Above Replacement, is according to Fangraphs, "an attempt by the sabermetric baseball community to summarize a player's total contributions to their team in one statistic." It represents the number of wins a player provided compared with a replacement player. See Steve Slowinski, "What is WAR," Fangraphs, February 10, 2010. library.fangraphs.com/misc/war/.

ROBINSON, ERSKINE LEAD DODGERS TO VICTORY

SEPTEMBER 20, 1952: BROOKLYN DODGERS 1, BOSTON BRAVES 0,
AT BRAVES FIELD, BOSTON

by Glen Sparks

Jackie Robinson's potent bat and Carl Erskine's sore right arm led the Dodgers to a 1-0 win in 10 innings against the Boston Braves on September 20, 1952. Brooklyn took a five-game lead in the National League pennant chase with seven games to play.

Erskine, "who has been complaining about his pitching elbow for the past two weeks,"[1] hurled his fourth shutout of the season in front of 6,038 fans at Braves Field. He gave up just three hits, walked two, and struck out seven. Robinson collected four straight hits – half the Brooklyn total – including the game winner. The *Brooklyn Eagle*'s Harold C. Burr wrote that "Robinson took over the Dodger attack this afternoon."[2]

This was the second of a three-game series between the teams. Brooklyn scored twice in the eighth inning and took the opener, 4-2. Roy Campanella smacked a double against starter Max Surkont to lead off the frame and advanced to third on Gil Hodges' sacrifice. Carl Furillo popped out, and Rocky Nelson reached on an intentional walk. With Bobby Morgan at bat, Surkont unfurled an ill-timed wild pitch that allowed Campanella to rumble home and give Brooklyn the lead. Morgan subsequently worked a walk to put runners on first and second. Pee Wee Reese singled Nelson home to provide the Dodgers with an insurance run. Joe Black pitched a scoreless ninth and notched a save. Jim Hughes earned the win in relief of starter Preacher Roe.

Brooklyn lifted its won-lost record to 92-54 as it pushed toward a pennant. The Dodgers were trying to get back to the World Series for the first time since 1949. They fell two games short in 1950 against the Whiz Kids of Philadelphia. The following year, in one of the most epic collapses in baseball history, Brooklyn blew a 13½-game lead against their archrivals, the New York Giants. Bobby Thomson hit his famous, and pennant-winning, shot heard 'round the world home run off Ralph Branca in the third game of a playoff series at the Polo Grounds. In the spring of 1952, Robinson said to reporters, "I think every player on the team will be putting out a little more this year because he feels that we let the fans down in bad finishes the two previous years."[3]

This was Robinson's sixth season in Brooklyn. The 1949 Most Valuable Player in the National League put together a big year in 1951 with his .338 batting average, 19 home runs, and 88 RBIs. He stole 25 bases and scored 106 runs. Robinson entered the game against the Braves with a .301 mark and a .433 on-base percentage.

The Dodgers were a hard-hitting bunch. They had led the National League in scoring for the past three years and were tops again in 1952. Erskine was the team's best starting pitcher. The right-hander from Anderson, Indiana, entered the game against Boston with a 13-6 won-lost record and a 2.91 ERA despite missing some action due to that sore arm. The 25-year-old of slight frame (5-feet-10, 165 pounds) liked to throw big-breaking overhand curveballs.

"Oisk," as Brooklyn fans called Erskine, had faced Boston three times thus far in 1952 and was 2-0 with a no-decision. The Braves were struggling and entered the day in seventh place with a 63-83 mark. Manager Charlie Grimm, who took over for Tommy Holmes on May 31, sent Warren Spahn to the mound. A four-time 20-game winner, Spahn was 14-17 in 1952. The left-hander from Buffalo, New York, had lost all four decisions against Brooklyn.

Robinson recorded his first hit in the fourth inning, a single to left field with one out. He was thrown out at second base by Sid Gordon trying to stretch the base hit into a double. Campanella ended the frame by striking out.

With two outs in the sixth, Robinson ripped a double but was left stranded. Spahn gave Campy a free pass, and Andy Pafko lifted an inning-ending fly ball to Sam Jethroe in center field. Erskine, meanwhile, was humming along. He had given up just one hit, a bunt single to Jack Daniels, in the third.

Erskine "ran into his only sweat of the game" in the seventh inning.[4] Jethroe led off the frame by slicing a single to left and advanced to second base on Logan's sacrifice. Eddie Mathews flied out to Furillo in right field, but Cooper and Gordon walked to load the bases. According to Dick Young in the *Daily News*, "Erskine was pitching to both sluggers carefully and just missing the outside corner."[5] Oisk went to 3-and-2 on Earl Torgeson and then hurled a fastball that headed for the outside corner. Umpire Bill Jackson gave the borderline call to Erskine, which infuriated Torgeson. "Well, you should have heard what Torgeson bawled," Young wrote. "He charged at the rookie ump like a madman. He screamed. He elbowed the ump."[6] He also remained in the game, much to Furillo's surprise. "Torgy overstepped his bounds in the argument," Furillo said. "He should have been put out of the game."[7]

Robinson knocked his third straight hit, and second single, with one out in the top of the eighth. Campanella, though, hit into an inning-ending double play. The game remained scoreless going into the ninth. Both pitchers retired the opposition in order in that late frame. The duel headed into extra innings.

Billy Cox led off Brooklyn's half of the 10th inning by singling to left field. He made it to second after Erskine put down a sacrifice bunt. Spahn walked Furillo to set up a possible game-ending double play. Reese followed by hitting a line drive straight to Daniels in right field. Robinson stepped to the plate. The second baseman lined a single to left field, scoring Cox for the game's only run. Pafko flied out to Sam Jethroe in center field to end the frame. Erskine allowed a one-out single to Sid Gordon in the bottom of the 10th but got Torgeson to hit into a game-ending double play.

According to the *Boston Globe*, "Robinson smashed all four hits viciously."[8] It was his first four-hit game of the season. He had 15 three-hit games. Robinson told reporters, "It was exceptional for me to hit Spahn that way. I've never hit him very hard and very few have, for that matter. That's the first time all season I have hit four balls well in the same game."[9]

Clif Keane wrote that Erskine pitched a "grand game" and that "there must have been some confusion over which arm bothered him."[10] Dick Young decided that "Erskine's sore arm isn't as sore as it's cracked up to be."[11] The pitcher improved his won-lost record to 14-6 and dropped his ERA to 2.77. Just a few months earlier, on June 19 against the Cubs, Erskine threw the first of his two career no-hitters. "This was by far his best game since his no-hitter," wrote Young.[12] Just 10 days earlier, he wrote, "Erskine was scratching himself off as useless for the remainder of Brooklyn's pennant drive."[13]

Brooklyn manager Chuck Dressen said, "Who says Erskine has a sore arm? He was throwing bullets out there today. Man, he had something." The Dodgers beat Spahn and the Braves on Dressen's 58th birthday. "That was my real birthday present," the skipper said. "This victory means more to me than all the presents I received."[14]

The Dodgers made a habit out of beating the Braves in 1952. The teams played 18 games, and Brooklyn won 16 of them. According to Young, "They say, in some slightly prejudiced headquarters, that Brooklyn beats the Humpty-dumpty teams." But the Dodgers were now 5-0 against Spahn. "And, he's no humpty."[15]

Brooklyn won the next day, 8-2, and swept the series. Campanella, Furillo, and Black all drove home two runs. Robinson collected two more base hits and walked twice. Brooklyn ended the year 96-57 and earned its third pennant in six years. Robinson batted .308 with 19 home runs and 75 RBIs. He stole 24 bases and scored 104 runs. The All-Star, though, could not bring a championship to the borough. The Yankees knocked off the Dodgers in a seven-game World Series. Robinson batted just .174 (4-for-23) against New York pitching. He hit a home run and scored four times. The Yankees won two games by two runs and another by one run. "We came so close," Robinson said. "We had so many opportunities."[16]

SOURCES

In addition to the sources cited in the Notes, the author accessed Retrosheet.org, Baseball-Reference.com, and SABR.org.

NOTES

1. Associated Press, "Dodgers Near Flag; Lead Giants by 5 with 7 Games Left," *Binghamton* (New York) *Press and Sun-Bulletin,* September 21, 1952: 39.
2. Harold C. Burr, "Dodgers Win in 10th, 1-0, Lead by 5," *Brooklyn Eagle*, September 21, 1952: 24.
3. Roscoe McGowen, "Brooks 'To Put Out a Little More This Year,' Says Jackie," *The Sporting News*, February 20, 1952: 11.
4. Dick Young, "Dodgers Shade Braves, 1-0 in 10; Erskine Gives 3 Hits," *New York Daily News*, September 21, 1952: 325.
5. Young.
6. Young.
7. Bob Holbrook, "Erskine 'Better Than in No-Hit Win,'" *Boston Globe,* September 21, 1952: 58.

8 Clif Keane, "Dodgers Stretch Lead to Five Games," *Boston Globe*, September 21, 1952. 58.
9 Holbrook.
10 Keane.
11 Young.
12 Young.
13 Young.
14 Holbrook.
15 Young.
16 Will Grimsley (Associated Press), "'They Didn't Miss Joe DiMaggio – Mantle Killed Us,' Says Robby," *Elmira* (New York) *Advertiser*, October 8, 1952.

JOE BLACK AND TREMENDOUS DEFENSE BEAT YANKEES IN GAME ONE OF 1952 WORLD SERIES

OCTOBER 1, 1952: BROOKLYN DODGERS 4, NEW YORK YANKEES 2, AT EBBETS FIELD, BROOKLYN

by Brian M. Frank

Harold C. Burr gave a tepid review of the Dodgers pitching staff that headed into the 1952 World Series. "Some are pitchers with good arms, some with sore arms, some with tired arms, and some with no arms at all," he wrote. "But it's by this motley corps that the Dodgers must rise or fall with in the World Series."[1]

On paper, Brooklyn's pitchers didn't match up well with the well-seasoned New York Yankees staff, particularly when it came to postseason experience. Dodgers starters had only two career World Series wins. Preacher Roe had one and Ralph Branca, who wouldn't even pitch, had the other. On the other hand, the Yankees' top three pitchers had won 10 games in the fall classic. Their Game One starter, Allie Reynolds, had four wins, while Vic Raschi and Ed Lopat had each won three.

Manager Chuck Dressen's solution to his team's pitching conundrum for Game One was to start a rookie right-hander who had been used as a reliever for most of the season. Joe Black was one of Brooklyn's best pitchers all year, going 15-4 with a 2.15 ERA in 56 games, 54 of which were in relief. Black's two starts came in his final two appearances of the season. Dressen's logic was that if he threw Black in the first game, he'd have the option of using him in relief or starting him again, depending on how the Series unfolded. "If that guy pitches the way he has pitched all season, our chance is as good as theirs," Dressen said the day before the opener.[2]

The young hurler seemed unfazed by his starting assignment against a team attempting to win its fourth consecutive World Series, and its first since Joe DiMaggio retired. "These aren't the same Yankees I first saw when they had DiMaggio, (Tommy) Henrich, and (Charlie) Keller," Black said. "They're wearing the same letters on their shirts, but I don't believe they frighten anybody." He added, "They're a good ballclub – hope nobody thinks I'm knocking them – but the Dodgers seem to me to be a pretty good ballclub, too."[3]

A huge crowd of 34,861 saw Brooklyn open the scoring in the second inning. Jackie Robinson hit one of Reynolds' sliders "in a long white loop which rode with a tailwind into the delighted laps of the distant patrons. They lifted hats, threshed arms, windmill fashion, clasped hands in congratulations or shook fists encouragingly at their hero, who circled the bases at a sedate trot."[4] It was Robinson's first home run in World Series play.

The Yankees answered right back in the top of the third when Gil McDougald led off by hitting one just over the left-field wall. The ball cleared the fence so narrowly that Dodgers left fielder Andy Pafko argued that a fan in the front row had reached over and interfered. His protest came to no avail and the game was tied. Black rebounded from the homer by striking out the next three batters.

The top of the fourth inning was rather eventful, even though the Yankees failed to score. Phil Rizzuto led off with a single. Mickey Mantle bunted up the third-base line and beat Black's throw to first. Yogi Berra hit a groundball to first baseman Gil Hodges, who threw to Pee Wee Reese at second for the force. Mantle's hard slide into second successfully broke up the double play but injured Reese in the process. The Dodgers shortstop was able to stay in the game with a thigh bruise. Joe Collins then hit a fly ball to right fielder Carl Furillo, who "fired the blurred white spec (sic) to the plate" as Rizzuto reversed course and scampered back to third, just beating catcher Roy Campanella's throw.[5] Black was then able to get Irv Noren to ground out to Robinson to end the inning.

Brooklyn's defense was sensational in the fifth inning. After McDougald led off with a walk, Billy

Martin looped a single into left. Pafko charged it and fired to third. Billy Cox took the throw and slapped the tag on McDougald for the first out of the inning. McDougald later claimed Cox missed him. "He hasn't tagged me yet," the Yankees third baseman said after the game.[6] Pafko's tremendous throw stood out on the play, as did Cox's play on the receiving end. "The tag that Cox made after Pafko's great throw on Martin's single in the fifth inning was one of the great plays of the game," Robinson said. "Billy had to come down fast with that tag to get McDougald, and if he hadn't made it that might have been a big inning for the Yankees. They'd have had men on second and third and nobody out."[7] Reynolds grounded harmlessly to Reese for the second out. Pafko then made his second great play in three batters, a "sliding, sitting catch of Hank Bauer's difficult Texas Leaguer" to end the inning.[8]

Collins just missed hitting a two-run home run in the top of the sixth when his deep drive "curved foul by inches."[9] In the bottom of that frame, Duke Snider, who'd already doubled earlier in the game, came up with Reese on base. He sent "the little white ball arching against the blue sky past snapping flags and billowing bunting" over the scoreboard and onto Bedford Avenue, to give the Dodgers a 3-1 lead.[10]

The top of the seventh provided more eye-popping defense from Cox. Black walked Noren to lead off the inning as the Brooklyn bullpen began warming. McDougald hit a groundball to Cox, who made a great stop when it took a bad hop and turned it into an around-the-horn double play. The next batter, Martin, hit a sharp grounder down the third-base line; Cox made a "breath-taking backhand stop" and threw it to first for the out.[11] "You writers call him the best fielding third baseman around," Reese said after the game. "Listen, he's the best fielder, period. I don't care whether he's playing third, second, or shortstop, he's the best fielder in the major leagues no matter where he plays."[12]

Gene Woodling, who didn't start because of a pulled thigh muscle, helped produce another run for the Yankees when he pinch-hit in the eighth inning. Woodling hit a ball off the center-field wall and was able to go into third standing up with a triple. He scored on Bauer's fly ball to cut the Dodgers lead to one at 3-2.

Reese got the run back in the bottom of the eighth. The Dodgers shortstop lined a ball into the left-field seats to put Brooklyn ahead 4-2 and finish the scoring for the day. Black retired the side in order in the ninth, striking out Noren looking to finish the game and give the Dodgers a one-game-to-none lead in the series.

After the game, both managers raved about Brooklyn's amazing glove work. "That fellow at third (Cox) did pretty good in a game that had plenty of good fielding, I'd say," Yankees manager Casey Stengel remarked. "He came up with a couple of nice ones on McDougald and Martin in the seventh."[13] An exuberant Dressen exclaimed, "How about that defensive play of ours? Ever since I've managed this club everybody has talked about how great the hitters are, but nobody said anything about their fielding, which rates with any team in history, if you ask me." He added, "The throw and sliding catch Pafko made. Furillo's throw and Cox's tag on Pafko's throw and those two plays of his in the seventh – going to his left for the double play and spinning around to his right for the third out, they don't come any better than that."[14]

In his complete game, Black allowed two runs on six hits and two walks, while striking out six. He became the first African-American pitcher to win a World Series game. Campanella noted that Black was effective even though he didn't have his best stuff. Black admitted that despite his confidence the day before the game, he felt the pressure of pitching on the big stage. "I was nervous before the game and I stayed nervous," he said. "I've been faster and my control wasn't too sharp but I felt stronger as I went along."[15] Even without his best stuff, the Yankees were impressed with the Dodgers hurler. "You have to hit against him to believe how good he really is," Rizzuto said.[16]

Dressen's strategy of using his recently converted reliever to start Game One had seemingly paid off, with Brooklyn grabbing an early Series lead and his best pitcher ready to pitch again in whatever role his manager asked. "Black will be there tomorrow if I need him," the Dodgers manager said. "He's ready to pitch all the time or any time."[17]

SOURCES

In addition to the sources cited in the Notes, the author consulted Baseball-Reference.com and Retrosheet.org.

NOTES

1. Harold C. Burr, "Pilot Dressen to Play Hunches with Twirlers," *Brooklyn Eagle*, September 29, 1952: 11.

2. Roscoe McGowen, "Joe Black Unawed by Yankee Legend," *New York Times*, October 1, 1952: 41.

3. McGowen.

PERSPECTIVES ON 42

4. Jimmy Powers, "The Powerhouse," *New York Daily News*, October 2, 1952: 78.
5. Dick Young, "Black, 3 HRs Bash Yanks in 1st, 4-2, Robby, Duke, Reese Circuit for Flock," *New York Daily News*, October 2, 1952: 76.
6. James P. Dawson, "Stengel Praises Dodgers' Power and Pitching but His Yankees Blame Umpire," *New York Times*, October 2, 1952: 37.
7. Roscoe McGowen, "Brooklyn's Defensive Stars Get Big Share of Credit for Victory in Opener," *New York Times*, October 2, 1952: 36.
8. Tommy Holmes, "Erskine Faces Raschi on Hill, Woodling Gets Outfield Call from Yankees," *Brooklyn Eagle*, October 2, 1952: 18.
9. Harold C. Burr, "Sniders's Homer May Set Series Pattern/Reynolds Struck Out Duke Three Times in Series of 1949," *Brooklyn Eagle*, October 2, 1952: 17.
10. Young: 76.
11. Burr, "Snider's Homer May Set Series Pattern."
12. Dave Anderson, "Black Hurling Workhorse," *Brooklyn Eagle*, October 2, 1952: 18.
13. Dawson.
14. Dave Anderson, "Dressen Puts Black on Relief, Joe Available for Emergency Work Today," *Brooklyn Eagle*, October 2, 1952: 18.
15. Anderson.
16. Anderson.
17. Roscoe McGowen, "Brooklyn's Defensive Stars Get Big Share of Credit for Victory in Opener." Black started two more games in the Series, but never pitched in relief. He took the loss in Game Four, even though he allowed only one run on three hits and five walks over seven innings. He also took the loss in Game Seven, when he allowed three runs in 5⅓ innings.

ROBINSON'S BIG DAY HELPS DODGERS COMPLETE HOME SWEEP OF CARDINALS

SEPTEMBER 1, 1953: BROOKLYN DODGERS 12, ST. LOUIS CARDINALS 5,
AT EBBETS FIELD, BROOKLYN

by Mark Simon

The 1953 Dodgers enjoyed so much success against the St. Louis Cardinals that it has stood the test of time. It was impressive dominance by a great team against a pretty good team that struggled mightily at Ebbets Field.

The Ladies Day game between the Dodgers and Cardinals on September 1 was the last of 11 that the two teams played in Brooklyn in 1953. The Dodgers had won the first 10, including all three started by that day's Cardinals starter, second-year man Joe Presko.

Stan Musial did his best to get the Cardinals off to a good start in the first inning, homering off Dodgers starter Preacher Roe, who entered the game having won his last eight decisions.

The lead didn't last long. Jackie Robinson had been left at the plate when Duke Snider was caught stealing to end the first inning. In the second, Robinson doubled, went to third on a lineout to right field by Roy Campanella, and scored on a double by Gil Hodges to tie the game, 1-1.

Presko escaped further damage in the second but ran into trouble in the third. Robinson's two-out single brought home Pee Wee Reese from second base and was the first of four straight hits for the home team. Robinson scored on Hodges' single, and Campanella went home on a single by Carl Furillo. Presko was done after 2⅔ innings, having allowed four runs.

Cardinals relievers fared no better. After Snider grounded out to produce a run, Robinson followed with a single that scored Reese. Robinson advanced a base on the throw home, but the play at second was close. When it didn't go the Cardinals' way, their shortstop, Solly Hemus, and manager Eddie Stanky (a former Robinson teammate) were ejected for arguing with umpire Hal Dixon.[1] Hemus was so upset that he threw a baseball into the stands in frustration.[2] His team trailed 6-1 through four innings.

The remainder of the game was one of Cardinals home runs and Dodgers counterpunches (the boxing term a tribute to St. Louis native Sonny Liston, who the newspapers noted was making his pro debut the next day).[3]

Harry Elliott and Rip Repulski cut into the Dodgers' lead with fifth-inning solo homers. The Dodgers rebounded with three runs in the sixth. Snider drove in Reese with a double, then scored on a single by Robinson, who came home on Furillo's double to make it 9-3.

Steve Bilko's home run in the seventh was countered by three more Dodger runs in the bottom of the inning, with Reese, Campanella, and Hodges each driving in a run. Robinson made his only out of the game, striking out against reliever Cliff Chambers.

The Cardinals had one more home run in them. Bilko hit it off Roe with two outs in the ninth inning to account for the final score. The Dodgers won, 12-5. It was their sixth straight win and reduced their magic number to clinch the pennant to 13. The win was emblematic of how things went at Ebbets Field for the two teams that season. The Dodgers outscored the Cardinals 109-36 in the 11 matchups there.

Robinson finished 4-for-5 with three RBIs and three runs scored. He had two four-hit games in 1953, the other having come nine days earlier, in the second game of a doubleheader against the Pirates on August 23. It was also the 11th game in a 16-game span for Robinson in which he hit .468 with 29 hits, 16 runs batted in, and 16 runs scored.

This game also featured an odd statistical occurrence. The Dodgers had 25 at-bats with runners in scoring position. The Cardinals had none. It is the only game in the Retrosheet database (spanning 1933 to August 2019) in which one team had that many such at-bats and the other team had none.[4]

The consolation for the Cardinals was that their five home runs gave them a franchise-best 120 for the year. Their previous record was 119, set in 1940.[5] The Cardinals finished the season 0-11 at Ebbets Field but 83-60 everywhere else. Their final record of 83-71 was good for third in the NL.

The Dodgers' home winning streak against the Cardinals spanned 12 games, ending on May 14, 1954, with a 10-1 Cardinals win. The Dodgers have not had a longer home winning streak against a team since then, although they did win a dozen straight at home versus the Phillies (1958-59) and the Reds (2006-2009).

SOURCES

In addition to the endnotes listed below, the author used box scores at Baseball-Reference.com and Retrosheet.org.

NOTES

1. Martin J. Haley, "Cardinals Blast Five Home Runs, But Bums Grab 12-5 Victory," *St. Louis Globe-Democrat,* September 2, 1953: 18.
2. Joseph M. Sheehan, "Roe Victor, 12-5 For 9th Straight," *New York Times,* September 2, 1953: 29.
3. Charles Gould, "Durando, Sandy to Tangle Tonight," *St. Louis Globe-Democrat,* September 2, 1953: 18.
4. [4] Research by David Smith, Retrosheet.org, August 17, 2019.
5. [5] Haley.

JACKIE ROBINSON STEALS HOME VS PITTSBURGH

APRIL 23, 1954: BROOKLYN DODGERS 6, PITTSBURGH PIRATES 5,
AT FORBES FIELD, PITTSBURGH

by Blake W. Sherry

It was a season when Jackie Robinson was supposed to be slowing down. He was 35 and some critics already considered Robinson to be one of the "aging" veterans. But on this day, the small crowd of 10,574 at Forbes Field saw a thrilling 13-inning game in which Robinson doubled home the winning run and stole three bases, including home. Nearly all the fans were still there at 12:42 A.M. when the game was finally decided, 6-5 in favor of the Brooklyn Dodgers over the Pittsburgh Pirates.[1]

The season started with several reports of Robinson slowing down due to aging knees.[2] In 1953 he had been pushed into playing left field to make room for Junior Gilliam at second base. This year's push came from the sparkling play of Sandy Amoros, who hit a robust .421 in spring training. But Robinson helped put some of that aging talk to rest by finishing spring training with 16 hits in his last 26 at-bats, and 12 RBIs over the last eight games.[3] Still, the newspapers wrote about Robinson's age, including a prediction that he would retire at the end of the season.[4] Jackie, on the other hand, was not talking retirement. He talked of leading the league in hitting, winning another MVP award, and of his goal of passing Ty Cobb's major-league record of 21 steals of home.[5] Jackie had stolen home 16 times.

Just five games into the season, however, the narrative started to change. After A 4-for-4 game against Philadelphia, which included a double and a home run, the *New York Post* proclaimed, "He ain't what he used to be, that's for sure, but Jackie Robinson can still make the wheels go 'round and 'round on occasion."[6]

Robinson's Hit In 13th Gives Dodgers 6-5 Win

Hartford Courant, April 24, 1954: 11.

The starters on Friday evening, April 23, were fourth-year right-hander Bob Friend for the Pirates and reliable right-hander Russ Meyer for the Dodgers. The previous year, Meyer had won 15 games for Dodgers, finishing behind only 20-game winner Carl Erksine for the team lead in victories.

Robinson grounded out to second in the first inning. A solo home run by Gil Hodges to lead off the second got the Dodgers on the board first. In Robinson's second at-bat, he led off the top of the fourth with a single to left field. After moving to second on Hodges' single, he was left stranded when Roy Campanella grounded into a double play.

The Pirates tied the score in the bottom of the fourth on an RBI single by Toby Atwell. But the Dodgers came right back in the fifth with a run on a sacrifice fly by Jim Gilliam scoring Carl Furillo. Furillo had doubled to lead off the inning and took third on Meyer's sacrifice.

Brooklyn added another run in the sixth. After Duke Snider grounded out to start the inning, walks to Robinson, Hodges, and Amoros loaded the bases. Campanella popped out to third, bringing up Furillo. On a 2-and-0 count, the Dodgers pulled off one of the most exciting plays in baseball, a triple steal, with Robinson stealing home "easily."[7] Adding to the excitement of the triple steal was the report that just before the theft, Pirates general manager (and former Dodgers GM) Branch Rickey had predicted it. Watching the threatening move by Robinson, according to *The Sporting News,* Rickey said, "He's got him" (referring to Pirates pitcher Bob Friend). "He knows he can make it. He's coming on the next pitch."[8] And off he went! It was Robinson's first stolen base of the season, and the 17th steal of home in his career.

It was Robinson's first steal of home since May 18, 1952, against the Chicago Cubs. He was called out on his only attempt to steal home in 1953, on July 16 versus St. Louis.[9] The steal of home against the Pirates was Robinson's only successful steal of home in 1954. He tried to steal home once more, on June 17 against the Milwaukee Braves, but was out. In his career, Jackie attempted to steal home five times at Forbes Field, more than at any other opposing ballpark.

After the triple steal, Friend walked Furillo intentionally to load the bases again. Meyer popped out to short and the threat ended, leaving the Dodgers up 3-1.

Having walked eight batters and given up five hits, Friend left the game after the Dodgers' seventh. In the bottom of the inning, the Pirates tied the game at 3-3. Hal Rice led off with a double, moved to third on Curt Roberts' single, and scored on Preston Ward's pinch-hit single. Ward's hit moved Roberts moved to third, and he scored on Sid Gordon's pinch-hit sacrifice fly to right off new Dodgers pitcher Jim Hughes.

The Dodgers quickly untied the score. Johnny Hetki entered the game as the new Pirates pitcher in the eighth inning. A single, an error by newly inserted shortstop Dick Cole, and a walk loaded the bases., and Gilliam's two-run single restored the Dodgers' two-run lead.

The Pirates got one run back in the eighth. The Dodgers threatened in ninth. Robinson singled to center field, stole second as Hodges struck out, then stole third. It was to no avail. After Don Thompson walked, Campanella struck out swinging and Furillo grounded out. Robinson was left stranded at third.

The missed opportunity looked big, but the Dodgers got some luck to keep the game going. The Bucs tied it again at 5-5 with a run in the ninth on a walk to Bob Skinner and Frank Thomas's RBI double to left. If Thomas's drive had carried an inch or two more, it would have been a walk-off home run. Instead, the ball hit the barbed wire on the top of the fence and dropped back into the field of play.[10]

The Dodgers took the lead for good in the top of the 13th inning. None other than Jackie Robinson again played the role of hero, ripping a go-ahead double off Bob Purkey. But the Pirates didn't go quietly. Leadoff batter Dick Cole singled in the bottom of the inning, but two fly outs and a grounder ended the game. Bob Milliken pitched the final four extra frames for the winners, giving up only two hits and no walks.

Including four games at the end of the 1953 season, it was the sixth straight Brooklyn win over the Pirates. The next day, Saturday, the Dodgers ran the streak to seven with a 3-0 win. On Sunday the Pirates defeated Newcombe, 9-3, in game one of a doubleheader before losing the second game, 4-2. At that point, dating back to the 1952 season, the Dodgers had taken 43 of 49 contests against the lowly Bucs.[11]

The Dodgers' 1954 season was not what the club had hoped it to be. They failed to defend their pennant and finished in second place to the New York Giants by five games. For the veteran Robinson, it was his sixth and final All-Star season. He hit .311 with 15 homers and 59 RBIs and stole just four more bases during the season. Tensions with the front office were also beginning to wear on him.[12]

The Dodgers series marked only the second week in the big leagues for the Pirates' first African-American player, second baseman Curt Roberts. The Pirates had been one of eight major-league teams that had still not integrated at the end of the 1953 season.[13] Roberts fielded brilliantly and hit successfully in 10 of his first 12 games.[14]

SOURCES

In addition to the sources included in the Notes, the author consulted Baseball-Reference.com and Retrosheet.org.

NOTES

1. Jack Hernon, "Robinson's Double Decides Contest," *Pittsburgh Post-Gazette,* April 24, 1954: 12.
2. Harold Rosenthal, "Jackie Best Bet, but His Knees Creak," *The Sporting News*, April 7, 1954: 3.
3. Roscoe McGowen, "Dodgers in Dither – What to Do with a Handy Guy Like Sandy?" *The Sporting News*, April 21, 1954: 10.
4. Oscar Ruhl, "From the Ruhl Book," *The Sporting News*, April 7, 1954: 18.
5. Arnold Rampersad, *Jackie Robinson: A Biography* (New York: Random House, 1997), 267.
6. Rampersad, 268.
7. Hernon, "Robinson's Double Decides Contest": 12.
8. "B.R. Calls Turn on Jackie's Steal of Home Against Bucs," *The Sporting News*, May 5, 1954: 18.
9. Shane Tourtellotte, 'And That Ain't All, He Stole Home!' *Hardball Times*, March 2, 2012.
10. Lester Biederman, "Dodger Star Steals Home, Then Doubles for 13th Inning Win," *Pittsburgh Press*, April 24, 1954: 6.
11. Jack Hernon, "Bucs End Dodger Mastery, 9-3, Then Lose 4-2," *Pittsburgh Post-Gazette*, April 26, 1954: 18.
12. Jackie Robinson, *I Never Had It Made* (New York: Putnam, 1972), 116-118.
13. Bill Madden, *1954* (Philadelphia: Da Capo Press, 2014), 5.
14. Lester Biederman, "Pirates' Roberts Proves He's Here to Stay," *Pittsburgh Press*, April 21, 1954: 31.

JACKIE ROBINSON STEALS HOME: THE CALL, THE MEANING

SEPTEMBER 28, 1955: NEW YORK YANKEES 6, BROOKLYN DODGERS 5,
WORLD SERIES GAME ONE, YANKEE STADIUM, NEW YORK

by Steven C. Weiner

"I saw Robinson coming in. I didn't move because I had to stay to make the call on the pitch first. That's why I stayed crouched over. I saw it perfectly. Yogi put the ball at the back of the plate and Robinson slid across the plate into the glove. I'm satisfied I made the call right."

– Umpire Bill Summers[1]

When the Dodgers lost to the Yankees in Game One of the 1955 World Series, there was an eerie sameness to the outcome. In the two decades leading to the 1955 season, they had lost the World Series five times to their archrival – 1941, 1947, 1949, 1952, and 1953. Only in 1952 did they manage to win the first game.[2] But there was something different about the 1955 season and this Game One.

If you were a kid who lived in the New York City area in the early 1950s, you were marked as a fan of the Yankees, Giants, or Dodgers, baseball cards and all. Celebrations of World Series titles became commonplace for faithful Yankees fans. Giants fans reveled in the 1954 World Series sweep over the Cleveland Indians, their first title since 1933. For long-suffering fans of the Brooklyn Dodgers, it was always "Wait 'til Next Year," a euphemism for baseball seasons gone awry.[3]

What was different in 1955? The season turned into a "no contest" National League title for the Dodgers. On April 16, four days into the season, they were all alone in first place, where they remained for the rest of the season. The Dodgers won their first 10 games

Robby's Theft of Home Biggest Thrill of Game

Springfield Union, September 29, 1955: 40

and on May 10 were 22-2, 9½ games ahead of the Giants. Their first-place lead grew to 17 games in early September and they finished the season 13½ games ahead of the second-place Milwaukee Braves.

However for Jackie Robinson, the regular season was the worst statistically of his career. The 36-year-old Robinson's competitive instincts were as sharp as ever, but his physical skills were diminishing. He knew that his peak years as an athlete were behind him.[4] Knee and ankle ailments, perhaps a result of the wear and tear of his multisport playing days at UCLA, forced Robinson to miss playing time in the middle of the season.[5] He played in the fewest games (105) of his career, and his season-ending batting average (.256) had never been that low. His streak of six consecutive All-Star Game appearances was broken.

Both teams started their All-Star pitcher in Game One, Whitey Ford (18-7, 2.63 ERA) for the Yankees and Don Newcombe (20-5, 3.20 ERA) for the Dodgers. Although he was a 20-game winner, Newcombe had won only two games in the last two months of the season. Neither pitcher had yet earned a World Series game victory in this rivalry. Newcombe lost twice to the Yankees in 1949 when the Yankees won the World Series in five games. Ford lost Game Four of the 1953 World Series to the Dodgers, but pitched a solid seven innings to a no-decision in the decisive Game Six won by the Yankees for the title.

The teams matched long balls in the second inning when Carl Furillo hit a solo home run off Ford just before Jackie Robinson tripled and Don Zimmer singled for a 2-0 Dodgers lead. In the bottom of the inning, Elston Howard hit a two-run homer off Newcombe to knot the score, but not for long. Duke Snider led off the third inning with another solo home run. Both home runs were memorable. For Howard, it was his first at-bat in a World Series. Snider hadn't hit a home run since Labor Day and with this one, he became the first National League player with as many as six World Series homers.[6]

As the game moved to the middle innings, Joe Collins took offensive control for the Yankees with a solo home run off Newcombe to lead off the fourth and a two-run homer in the sixth, scoring Yogi Berra ahead of him for a 6-3 Yankee lead.

It was now time for baserunning to set the tone for this World Series. It was a marker that captured the intensity of the rivalry and the competitiveness of its combatants, including Robinson. With two outs in the sixth, Billy Martin tripled to deep left field off Newcombe. Manager Walter Alston's confidence in Newk was shaken, and Don Bessent replaced him on the mound. Martin was the last batter Newcombe faced in this World Series.

Martin tried to steal home off Bessent, but was tagged out by Roy Campanella, later to be named the National League's Most Valuable Player. The fiery Martin took a few steps toward Campanella, but decided instead to retreat to the Yankees dugout. He later said he thought he had been tagged on the throat. After the game in the company of the press, Campanella replied, "Tell that little so-and-so that I missed. I tried to put the ball in his mouth." Undoubtedly, Campy knew that Martin had labeled him as "spike shy" before the World Series started.[7]

The Dodgers came to bat in the eighth inning still trailing by three runs. Furillo opened by bouncing a single over second base against Ford. With one out, Robinson grounded through third baseman Gil McDougald's legs. The error put Robinson on second and Furillo on third. Zimmer's sacrifice fly to center fielder Irv Noren scored Furillo and advanced Robinson to third. In typical fashion, he danced off the base to disturb Ford. When Robinson darted toward home, Berra, crouched behind the plate, moved forward to receive Ford's pitch and apply the tag. The safe call by umpire Bill Summers was immediate. The protestations by the Yankees catcher were to no avail.[8] The Yankees held their 6-5 lead and won Game One.

For years to come, Yogi would insist that Robinson was out. Dale Berra wrote, "As he always told me, if you get beat, accept it and move ahead. But Jackie, he would say to his dying day, was out."[9] The heartfelt tribute expressed by Rachel Robinson, Jackie's widow, on the passing of Yogi Berra in 2015 seals the sense of timelessness that this single baseball moment holds. Over the years, she and Yogi would often greet each other with a humorous exchange – "He was out/He was safe."[10]

What did this steal of home say about baseball strategy? Trailing by two runs, Robinson well understood that his steal was not the best baseball strategy, but "whether it was because of my stealing home or not, the team had a new fire."[11] Second-guessing was immediate. Fred Haney, deposed manager of the Pirates, and Chuck Dressen, manager of the Senators, differed in their appraisal when interviewed on Bill Stern's radio show after the game. "Haney called it a 'stupid' move, while Dressen upheld it as a move that had an upsetting influence on the Yankees."[12] But broadcaster Harry Caray captured it best: "Perhaps never in the history of the World Series has one man played such a unique role as has Jackie Robinson this year … through the inspiration of his own play … his own daring and imagination."[13]

Robinson started the first six games of the Series at third base with a weak batting average of .182, four hits, and one dramatic steal of home. He did not play in Game Seven when Elston Howard's groundout, Pee Wee Reese to Gil Hodges, in the ninth brought the Brooklyn Dodgers their first and only World Series title.[14] But "42" was right in the middle of the mob scene just off the pitcher's mound.[15] Robinson wrote, "It was one of the greatest thrills of my life to be finally on a World Series winner."[16] There is no doubt that Jackie Robinson always understood the meaning of the moment, standing up to all he had to endure since 1947, stealing home in Game One of the 1955 World Series, and celebrating a championship with his teammates right in the middle of the diamond.

AUTHOR'S NOTE

The steal of home, arguably baseball's most exciting play, and the home run are the only plays in baseball on which one player single-handedly changes the score. There is no better example than Jackie Robinson's steal of home in Game One of the 1955 World Series. Robinson stole home on 19 other occasions in his 10-year career, 1947-1956.[17] His name became synonymous with the play.

However, the baseball record book looks no differently at a single runner stealing home or a double-steal play in which one runner steals home. Players see it differently. The San Francisco Giants' Aaron Rowand thought back to one of his successful attempts to steal home. "Oh, yeah," he said finally. "Off a double steal. It wasn't a Jackie Robinson."[18]

SOURCES

The author accessed Baseball-Reference.com for box scores/play-by-play information (baseball-reference.com/boxes/NYA/NYA195509280.shtml) and other data, as well as Retrosheet.org (retrosheet.org/boxesetc/1955/B09280NYA1955.htm). Baseball Almanac (baseball-almanac.com/recbooks/rb_stbah.shtml) notes that "Stealing home plate is NOT an officially recorded statistic so research into this unusual feat is still considered on-going."

NOTES

1. Ed Pollock, "Kellert Blundered – Not Ump," *Baseball Digest*, November-December 1955: 47.
2. On October 1, 1952, Joe Black beat Allie Reynolds, 4-2, in the first game of the 1952 World Series, powered by home runs by Jackie Robinson, Duke Snider, and Pee Wee Reese.
3. Paul Dickson, *The Dickson Baseball Dictionary, 3rd Edition* (New York: W.W. Norton & Company, 2009), 918. "A Willard Mullin cartoon (*New York World-Telegram*, August 9, 1939) depicted a character in a Dodgers uniform claiming that his theme song was 'Wait 'Till Next Year: A Torch Ballad in One Flat' with words and music by The Dodgers."
4. Jackie Robinson, *I Never Had It Made* (New York: Putnam, 1972), 118.
5. Mary Kay Linge, *Jackie Robinson, A Biography* (Westport, Connecticut: Greenwood Press, 2007), 106.
6. Frederick G. Lieb, "Collins' Two Homer Clouts Send Yanks Off in Front," *The Sporting News*, October 12, 1955: 20.
7. *The Sporting News*, October 12, 1955: 21.
8. "Jackie Robinson Steals Home," MLB.com, accessed August 9, 2019, mlb.com/video/robinson-steals-home/c-9336883.
9. Dale Berra, *My Dad, Yogi* (New York: Hachette Books, 2019), 48.
10. Rachel Robinson, "Rachel Robinson & JRF on the Passing of Yogi Berra," The Jackie Robinson Foundation, accessed August 17, 2019, jackierobinson.org/press/rachel-robinson-on-the-passing-of-yogi-berra/.
11. Robinson, 120.
12. "Haney Raps Jackie's Theft, but Dressen Calls It Smart," *The Sporting News*, October 12, 1955: 21.
13. Arnold Rampersad, *Jackie Robinson* (New York: Ballantine Books, 1997), 285.
14. Steven C. Weiner, "October 4, 1955: Brooklyn Dodgers win first World Series as 'Next Year' finally arrives," SABR Games Project.
15. "1955 World Series Dodgers Win," YouTube, accessed August 15, 2019, youtu.be/1Li5QM_cxPg.
16. Robinson, 120.
17. Shane Tourtellote, "And That Ain't All, He Stole Home," *The Hardball Times*, March 2, 2012, accessed August 21, 2019, tht.fangraphs.com/and-that-aint-all-he-stole-home/.
18. Bruce Schoenfeld, "Stealing Home," *Sports Illustrated*, August 16, 2010, accessed August 21, 2019, si.com/vault/2010/08/16/105972601/stealing-home.

BROOKLYN DODGERS WIN NL PENNANT ON FINAL DAY OF SEASON

SEPTEMBER 30, 1956: BROOKLYN DODGERS 8, PITTSBURGH PIRATES 6, AT EBBETS FIELD, BROOKLYN

by Thomas J. Brown Jr.

The reigning World Series champion Brooklyn Dodgers finally made a push to the National League pennant late in the 1956 season. After being 1 ½ games out of first place following a doubleheader split September 7, the Dodgers charged forward and held a one-game lead on September 30.

Brooklyn had swept the Pirates in a doubleheader on September 29, 6-2 and 3-1. Sal Maglie won the first game. Clem Labine, usually the team's relief ace, started the second game and went the whole way.1 The second-place Milwaukee Braves, meanwhile, lost 2-1 to the St. Louis Cardinals. Now, it was coming down to the final game of the season. Could Brooklyn win the game and the pennant? A Dodgers loss against Pittsburgh and a Braves win against St. Louis would force a playoff.

Don Newcombe took the mound for Brooklyn against Vern Law. Newcombe brought a 26-7 record into the game. Law, meanwhile, was trying to avoid his 16th loss for the Pirates, who occupied seventh place in the eight-team NL, 26 games out of first.

Newcombe retired the side in order in the top of the first inning The Dodgers jumped on Law in the bottom of the frame. Law walked leadoff batter Jim Gilliam and gave up a single to Pee Wee Reese that sent Gilliam to third. Duke Snider now stepped to the plate. He sent the first pitch from Law over the Ebbets Field outfield wall for his league-leading 42nd home run of the season. Law got the next two batters out, but gave up a single to Gil Hodges. Pirates manager Bobby Bragan had seen enough, although the score was still just 3-0. He replaced Law with Roy Face, who got the third out.

Newcombe kept the Pirates in check in the second inning but faltered in the third. He gave up a single to leadoff batter Jack Shepard and walked Dick Cole. After throwing a wild pitch that allowed Shepard and Cole to advance, Roberto Clemente stroked a two-run single. The score was now 3-2.

In the bottom of the third, Bob Purkey came on in relief for Pittsburgh. Reese grounded out to start the frame; Snider followed up by flying out to center field. Jackie Robinson then hit his 10th home run of the season. It was the 137th homer of his career and also his last.[2]

Newcombe did not have one of his better days on the mound and allowed six earned runs. After giving up the two runs in the third, he held the Pirates to one hit in each of the fourth, fifth, and sixth innings. The Pirates failed to score each time, although they got a runner to third when Lee Walls tripled with one out in the fourth.

Ron Kline took over the pitching duties for the Pirates in the fifth inning. He gave up a leadoff double to Newcombe, who went to third on Gilliam's grounder to first. Newcombe scored when Reese hit a sacrifice fly to left field. Snider followed with his second home run of the game and 43rd of the season. Robinson struck out, and the inning ended with the Dodgers leading 6-2. They padded that lead in the sixth when Sandy Amorós hit a leadoff home run.

The Pirates, down 7-2, scored three runs off Newcombe in the seventh inning. Dick Groat led off with a double to right field. Consecutive singles by Bill Mazeroski and Shepard loaded the bases. Newcombe got two outs and nearly wiggled out of the threat, but Bill Virdon brought home three runs with a double to center field. The Dodgers lead had been to cut to 7-5.

Bob Friend took the mound for the Pirates and held the Dodgers scoreless in the seventh inning. Walls homered off Newcombe in the top of the eighth, cutting the Pirates' deficit to a single run at 7-6 and knocking the Brooklyn starter out of the game. Dodgers manager Walter Alston summoned second-year right-hander Don Bessent from the bullpen.

Bessent had saved eight games in 37 relief appearances on the season. Labine was unavailable after the previous day's work in his third start of the season.[3] Bessent gave up a hit to Groat, and third baseman Robinson made an error on pinch-hitter Gene Freese's grounder. Jack Shepard flew out and Dale Long struck out to end the threat. Amorós gave the Dodgers a little cushion when he led off the bottom of the eighth with his second solo home run of the game.

Clemente opened the ninth with a single off Bessent. Virdon, though, hit into a double play, and Hank Foiles struck out to end the game. The Dodgers were 8-6 victors.

The Braves beat the Cardinals 4-2, but it didn't matter. Brooklyn had won its second straight pennant. Once again, the Dodgers would face the New York Yankees in the World Series. Brooklyn fans looked forward to seeing their "Bums" celebrate in October one more time.

SOURCES

In addition to the sources cited in the Notes, the author also used the Baseball-Reference.com, Baseball-Almanac.com, and Retrosheet.org websites for box-score, player, team, and season pages, pitching and batting game logs, and other pertinent material.

NOTES

1. Bryan Soderholm, "Baseball Historical Insight: Last Day 60 Years Ago, September 30, 1956," brysholm.blogspot.com, September 30, 2016.

2. Soderholm. This was Robinson's final regular-season homer; he retired after the 1956 season. He also homered once in the World Series.

3. Soderholm.

LABINE HURLS EXTRA-INNING SHUTOUT TO FORCE GAME SEVEN

OCTOBER 9, 1956: BROOKLYN DODGERS 1, NEW YORK YANKEES 0 (10 INNINGS),
AT EBBETS FIELD, BROOKLYN
GAME SIX OF THE WORLD SERIES

by Brian M. Frank

The Brooklyn Dodgers had fallen behind in the 1956 World Series in historic fashion. In Game Five, their hitters came up empty as Yankees hurler Don Larsen threw the first World Series perfect game. Larsen's performance put the defending world champion Dodgers' backs to the wall, trailing in the series three games to two.

Faced with the prospect of elimination, Dodgers manager Walter Alston made an unlikely choice for a Game Six starter in Clem Labine. Labine had pitched in a franchise-record 62 games during the regular season, going 10-6 with a 3.35 ERA; however only three of his 62 appearances had been starts. The veteran right-hander had also pitched in eight World Series games in his career, all in relief. In the 1956 World Series, he'd thrown two innings out of the bullpen in Game Three, allowing one unearned run, and he'd also warmed up in the bullpen behind Sal Maglie during Larsen's Game Five masterpiece. "I had Labine up in the ninth inning," Alston said, "but only with the idea that I'd bring him in if we tied the score. Labine didn't throw hard in his warm-up because he knew he'd have time if we did tie it."[1]

Yankees manager Casey Stengel tapped Bob Turley to try to close out the Series and give the Yankees their seventh championship in the last 10 seasons. After a solid season in 1955, fastballer Turley struggled through the 1956 season, going 8-4 with a 5.05 ERA. He'd pitched in three games in the 1955 World Series, including a rough start in Game Three at Ebbets Field, lasting only 1⅓ innings, allowing four earned runs. But he'd performed better in the postseason in 1956, working in relief in Games One and Two, and striking out three of the four batters he faced. Even with Turley's recent success, Stengel took no chances. He had Johnny Kucks warming up before Turley threw his first pitch. Kucks wouldn't be needed, as Turley was brilliant.

A beautiful blue sky greeted the 33,224 fans on hand at Ebbets Field. The cloudless sky and stiff breeze blowing out to right made it a tough afternoon for outfielders, especially Yankees left fielder Enos Slaughter.

Jim Gilliam hit a high fly ball in the third inning that Slaughter lost in the sun. "Gilliam's ball went up in the sun and stayed there," Slaughter said. "I waited for it to come out, but it never did. Sometimes you can play those balls from the side and catch a sight of them when they come out of the sun. This one didn't come out."[2] The ball dropped for a hit, but Slaughter picked up the ball and fired it to second to beat a sliding Gilliam for the second out of the inning.

There were some tense moments in the sixth inning as "Turley's control which was uniformly good all day, momentarily faltered" and the wind and sun played havoc with some popups that would have been routine under normal conditions.[3] Turley walked Gilliam to start the inning, and with one out he walked Duke Snider. Jackie Robinson hit a high popup "into short left, whipping around in the tricky currents as Slaughter and shortstop Gil McDougald drifted uncertainly underneath."[4] The next batter, Gil Hodges, also hit a high popup to the left side of the infield. This time, third baseman Andy Carey and McDougald both staggered under it "in the bright glare" before Billy Martin raced all the way over from second base to make the grab for the final out of the inning.[5]

Labine and Turley continued to dominate as the game remained scoreless. The Yankees threatened in the eighth inning when they put two runners on with one out. Cleanup hitter Yogi Berra stepped to the plate. "I threw him a curve that broke inside," Labine said of the pitch he managed to get Berra out on. "He swung at it, the first pitch, and the Duke came in and got it on the fly in left center."[6] Labine induced Slaughter to ground out to Gilliam to end the inning.

The weather affected play once again in the bottom of the eighth, when Labine hit a ball to left that Slaughter stopped running for because it seemed certain to go foul. "But the strong crosswinds picked up the pill and swept it back. The ball plunked between Slaughter and the railing, no more than a foot fair, then bounced up above the low, white[-]painted bar, and was grabbed by a fan for a ground-rule double."[7] Turley fanned Gilliam for his 11th strikeout of the afternoon. He then retired Pee Wee Reese on a fly ball for the second out. Stengel ordered Snider intentionally walked, and the strategy paid off when Robinson popped out to end the inning.

As the game moved to extra innings, it was only the second time in World Series history that a game had been scoreless through nine innings, and the first since 1913. To compound matters for the Brooklyn faithful, the Dodgers hadn't scored in 18 innings.

The Dodgers finally broke through in the 10th. Gilliam drew a four-pitch walk. Reese then sacrificed Brooklyn's speedy leadoff hitter to second. With the winning run in scoring position, Stengel used the same strategy that had been successful in the eighth inning. He ordered Turley to intentionally walk Snider and pitch to Robinson with runners at first and second with two down. "He is their longest hitter," Stengel said of Snider. "If he got one into the wind, he'd have won the game. I figured Robinson would be hitting into the wind while anything Snider pulled would be helped by the wind."[8]

This time, Robinson made the Yankees pay. He drove a 1-and-1 pitch to left field, where Slaughter had been struggling to chase down fly balls all afternoon. Slaughter initially took a step in and then "leaped awkwardly but couldn't touch it" as the ball sailed over his head and bounced off the base of the wall, while Gilliam raced home to score the winning run.[9] "I thought when Jackie hit the ball, I might have a chance to catch it," Slaughter said. "But that ball took off, it rose suddenly and hit the base of the wall. I had no chance."[10]

"That was the same pitch Turley got me on in the eighth inning," Robinson said of Turley's side-arm fastball.[11] In the eighth Robinson popped it up to end the inning, but in the 10th he drove it to left to end the game. "I thought that ball would take off. I knew I'd hit it pretty good," Robinson said of his game-winning hit.[12]

"It was a perfect – well almost perfect – pitch," Turley said. "It was fast, it was low, it was in the strike zone. I thought it was tight enough, too, but I guess the ball came in just an inch or so off the spot I wanted. I can't find fault with that pitch, though. I'd try it again if I had to."[13]

The dramatic victory forced the Series to a deciding seventh game and put the Dodgers within one win of a second consecutive world championship. Brooklyn overcame an incredible performance by Turley, who set a Yankees World Series record by striking out 11. In a 143-pitch performance, Turley allowed just four hits, "one legit, two misjudged, and another lost in the air."[14] Stengel proclaimed, "That's the best game he's pitched all year."[15]

But Labine matched Turley pitch for pitch, allowing seven hits and two walks while striking out five over 10 shutout innings. Catcher Roy Campanella said it was the best game Labine had hurled over a prolonged outing. "He's done some amazing things coming in from the bullpen," the Dodgers catcher said, "but he's never been strong over a long route. Curve balls and sinkers; sinkers and curve balls. They killed them."[16] The hero at the plate, Jackie Robinson, said, "I'm awfully happy to have a part in getting that victory for Clem. He has done a wonderful job for us all year. No one deserved to win more."[17]

"It was the longest game I've pitched in the majors," Labine said, "the greatest one, I'd say, and certainly the most important."[18] He also acknowledged the day's other hero, exclaiming, "I never thought they'd ever find that run for me today. When Jackie hit that ball, I could have kissed him."[19]

SOURCES

In addition to the sources cited in the Notes, the author consulted Baseball-Reference.com and Retrosheet.org.

NOTES

1. Roscoe McGowen, "Maglie Discloses Every Bomber Hit Was Made Off a Breaking Pitch," *New York Times*, October 9, 1956: 56.
2. Joe Trimble, "I Never Had a Chance to Catch Drive: Enos," *New York Daily News*, October 10, 1956: 95.
3. John Drebinger, "Dodgers Defeat Yanks in 10th, 1-0, and Even Series," *New York Times*, October 10, 1956: 64.
4. Dick Young, "All Even! Dodgers Win, 1-0, in 10th," *New York Daily News*, October 10, 1956: 96.
5. Drebinger.

6 Roscoe McGowen, "Robinson's Appraisal of Bomber Hurler's Speed Questioned by Team-Mates," *New York Times*, October 10, 1956: 64.

7 Young: 97.

8 Trimble: 101.

9 Young: 94.

10 Louis Effrat, "Turley Is Cheered by Return of Confidence Despite His Defeat by Dodgers," *New York Times*, October 10, 1956: 65.

11 Dana Mozley, "2-Iron Shot Felt Good," *New York Daily News*, October 10, 1956: 95.

12 McGowen, "Robinson's Appraisal of Bomber Hurler's Speed Questioned by Team-Mates."

13 Effrat.

14 Young: 94.

15 Trimble: 95.

16 Mozley.

17 Mozley.

18 Mozley.

19 Mozley.

Another attempted steal.

Courtesy of the National Baseball Hall of Fame Library.

SAYONARA JACKIE ROBINSON:

HOW AN AMERICAN HERO FINISHED HIS CAREER IN JAPAN

by Robert K. Fitts

There was a saying in Japan during the late 1950s: Kamisama, Hotokesama, Inaosama (God, Buddha, Inao). The 19-year-old Kazuhisa Inao was out there on the mound. The kid wasn't that big, at least not by American standards – about 5-foot-9, 185 pounds. But he was strong – and fast. Stories claimed that his strength came from hauling nets on his father's fishing boat from the time he was a young boy. Only a year earlier, he had been pitching for his high school and now had just completed his rookie season with the Nishitetsu Lions, winning 21 games and posting a league-leading 1.06 ERA.

Jackie Robinson strode to the plate, his familiar blue cap covering a head speckled with gray. At 38 he was thicker and moved slower than he had during his prime. But he was still the star, the reason many of the 12,000 Japanese fans had come out to Fukuoka Stadium on this cloudy Saturday in mid-November of 1956.

It was the final game of a long tour of Japan and an even longer, grueling season. The Dodgers had played 183 games since April; 154 during the regular season, 7 in the World Series, 3 in Hawaii, and another 19 in Japan. All season they had battled the Milwaukee Brewers and Cincinnati Reds, winning the pennant by a single game on the last day of the season. For the second consecutive season and the sixth time in the past 10 years, the Dodgers had faced the Yankees in the World Series. The series went to seven games, ending with a 9-0 Yankees victory in the finale.

The morning after the devasting loss, the Dodgers straggled into Idlewild Airport in Jamaica, Queens, to begin a four-week tour of Japan. The subdued party of 60 consisted of club officials, players, family members, and an umpire. Although participation was voluntary, most of the team's top players had decided to take advantage of the $3,000 bonus that came with the all-expenses-paid trip.[1]

After a one-day stopover in Los Angeles, the Dodgers spent five days in Hawaii, attending banquets, sightseeing, sunbathing on Waikiki Beach, and playing three games against local semipro teams, before bordering an overnight flight for Japan on October 17. They arrived in Tokyo at 3:25 P.M. the following day, five hours behind schedule after mechanical trouble forced a seemingly endless stopover on Wake Island. "Man, we're beat," Robinson complained as he left the plane. "We were on the plane, off the plane, on the plane, off the plane." "We are all very tired," Duke Snider added, "but we're glad to be here. If we have a chance to shower and clean up, we'll feel much better."[2]

Japanese dignitaries and 40 kimono-clad actresses bearing bouquets of flowers welcomed the Dodgers as a crowd of fans waved from the airport's

Early 1950s Japanese publication. Author's collection.

spectator ramp. During a brief press conference, Walter O'Malley proclaimed that "his players would play their best … and hoped that the visit would contribute to Japanese-American friendship." "We hope to give the Japanese fans some thrills," said Robinson.[3]

Despite the delay and relentless drizzle, thousands of flag-waving fans lined the 12-mile route from Haneda Airport to downtown Tokyo, where the Dodgers stopped by the Yomiuri newspaper headquarters before checking into the Imperial Hotel. A few hours later, they were out again. Yomiuri hosted a welcoming banquet at the Chinzanso Restaurant followed by "a giddy round of parties." Many players staggered beck to the hotel in the wee hours of the morning.[4]

Exhausted from the trip and the late night, the players struggled to get out of bed the next morning for a game against the Yomiuri Giants at Korakuen Stadium. The opening ceremonies began at 1 P.M. with the two teams parading onto the field in parallel lines behind a pair of young women clad in fashionable business suits. Each woman held a large sign topped with balloons, bearing the team's name in Japanese. The players lined up on the foul line for introductions before Matsutaro Shoriki, the owner of the Yomiuri newspaper and father of professional baseball in Japan, threw out the first pitch.

The Giants jumped out to a quick 3-0 lead, but Brooklyn battled back to take the lead in the fourth on five hits, including homers by Robinson and Gil Hodges. But that would be all for Brooklyn as relief pitcher Takumi Otomo stifled the Dodgers on 10 strikeouts. Homers by Kazuhiko Sakazaki and Tetsuharu Kawakami in the eighth gave Yomiuri the upset victory. Since the major-league tours began in 1908, the game was just the third defeat by a Japanese team against 139 wins. (The other losses came in 1921 and 1950.) After the loss, manager Walt Alston made no excuses, "They just beat us. They hit and we didn't." "We'll snap out of it," predicted Robinson. Pee Wee Reese agreed, "We don't expect to lose any more. But," he added, "we didn't expect to lose this one either."[5]

As predicted, the Dodgers bounced back the next day, winning 7-1 behind Roy Campanella's two home runs.[6] But the next afternoon, 45,000 fans watched the All-Japan team – a conglomeration of the top Japanese professionals – send Dodger ace Don Newcombe to the showers after just 17 pitches as the Japanese scored four in the first en route to an easy 6-1 victory.[7]

The Dodgers' malaise continued in Game Four against the Yomiuri Giants. Twenty-year-old Sho Horiuchi shut out the visitors for six innings before the Giants ace Takehiko Bessho took over with another two scoreless innings. Meanwhile Carl Erskine dominated the Giants, scattering just three hits. In the top of the ninth, Duke Snider homered off Bessho to salvage a 1-0 victory.[8] "The Dodgers' 'old men' are tired," noted Bob Bowie of the *Pacific Stars and Stripes*. "Pee Wee Reese and Jackie Robinson and Gil Hodges and Duke Snider and Roy Campanella are so weary it's an effort for them to put one foot before another. It's been a long season and they are anxious to get back home and relax before heading for spring training in February."[9]

Indeed, the "Boys of Summer" were aging. The core of the team had been together nearly a decade. The starting lineup averaged 32 years old with Robinson and Reese both 37. Their weariness showed on the playing field. After four games, the team was hitting just .227 against Japanese pitching. Robinson was batting a respectable .250 but had not yet thrilled the fans with a stolen base while Reese, at .091, was stuck in a rut.

Both management and fans knew it was time to consider changes. The team had plenty of young talent. At the top of the list were power hitters Don Demeter, who hit 41 home runs in 1956 for the Texas League Fort Worth Cats, and his teammate first baseman Jim Gentile who hit 40. Outfielder Gino Cimoli had ridden Brooklyn's bench in 1956 and was now ready for a more substantial role. Smooth-fielding Bob Lillis from the Triple-A affiliate in St. Paul seemed to be Reese's heir at shortstop while his teammate Bert Hamric would fight for a role in team's crowded outfield. On the mound, knuckleballer Fred Kipp had just won 20 games for the Montreal Royals and looked ready to join Brooklyn's rotation. The tour of Japan was an ideal chance try out these players. As the tour progressed, Alston moved the prospects into the starting lineups.

In Game Five, held in Sendai, Alston gave Kipp the start and backed him up with Gentile at first, Demeter in center and Cimoli in left. For seven innings Kipp baffled the Japanese with his knuckleball – a pitch rarely used in the Japanese leagues, while the hurler's fellow rookies racked up five hits during an easy 8-0 win.[10]

Another rookie, future Hall of Famer Don Drysdale, started Game Six in Mita, a small city about 60 miles northeast of Tokyo. For seven innings the promising young pitcher dominated the Japanese, before the Japanese erupted for three runs in the bottom of the eighth inning, breaking a streak of 29 straight shutout innings by Dodger pitching. With the scored tied, 3-3, after nine innings, the Dodgers requested that they end the game in a tie so that the team could catch their scheduled train back to Tokyo.[11] Although it was not a win, the *Pacific Stars and Stripes* called the result "a moral victory for Japanese baseball."[12] After six contests, the National League champions were 3-2-1 – the worst record of any visiting American professional squad.

Criticism came from both sides of Pacific. The Associated Press reported that "most Japanese fans have been disappointed in the caliber of ball played so far by the Brooklyns."[13] "The Dodgers are known for their fighting spirit," noted radio quiz-show host Ko Fujiwara, "but they have shown little spirit in the games here thus far."[14] Masao Yuasa, the former manager of the Mainichi Orions, complained, "They are even weaker than was rumored … and we are very disappointed to say the least. It would not be an overstatement to say that we no longer have anything to learn from the Dodgers."[15]

The US media picked up these criticisms, reprinting the stories in large and small newspapers across the country. "Japanese Baseball Expert Hints Brooks Are Bums," screamed a headline in New York's *Daily News* on October 23.[16] Three days later, a *Daily News* headline noted, "Bums 'Too Dignified, Say Japanese Hosts." The accompanying article explained that some Japanese experts believed that the Dodgers were "too quiet and dignified on the playing field … and … were acting like they were all trying to win good conduct medals" rather than playing hard-nosed baseball.[17]

Despite the team's poor start, about 150,000 spectators attended the first five games while hundreds of thousands more, if not millions, watched the games on television or listened to them on the radio.[18] All of the sports dailies and many of the mainstream newspapers covered each game in detail – often including exclusive interviews and pictorial spreads of the players.

Many features focused on Jackie Robinson – revered in Japan for both his aggressive style of play as well as his historic role in integrating the major leagues. "Japanese fans want to see Robinson steal bases and steal home," noted Tetsu Yamaguchi of the *Pacific Stars and Stripes*.[19] Robinson appeared on the covers of magazines and in full-page newspaper pictorials. A shot of an airborne Robinson as he turned a double play dominated the cover of a 16-by-11-inch, eight-page booklet on the Dodgers tour inserted into the October 19 issue of the Yomiuri newspaper. At the ballparks, he often "received the biggest ovation when he was introduced during the pre-game ceremonies."[20]

Even in Japan, Robinson was more than just a ballplayer. Prior to the trip, a governmental official told him, "Your own presence in Japan will make a contribution [to international diplomacy], the value of which cannot be estimated."[21] During the tour, Jackie met with officials and diplomats and even spoke about race relations in the United States at Tokyo's American School. "I hope," he told the audience, "people will look back at the success in baseball [integration] and realize that what can happen in baseball can happen anywhere."[22]

Perhaps sparked by the ongoing criticism, perhaps finally rested, the Dodgers began winning in late October as the rookies led the way. On October 27 in Kofu, Gentile hit two home runs and Demeter and Cimoli each hit one out during a 12-1 romp over an all-star squad of players drawn from the Tokyo-area professional teams. The following day Gentile went 5-for-5 with another home run as the Dodgers beat All-Japan 6-3 in Utsunomiya. On October 31 Kipp pitched two-hit ball and Gentile and Demeter each homered to pace Brooklyn to a 4-2 win over All-Japan. During these games the players began showing a little fighting spirit. Somehow, they learned the Japanese word "mekura," meaning "blind," and began shouting it at the umpire after questionable calls.[23]

On the evening of October 31, the team arrived in Hiroshima. The next morning the Dodgers visited the Peace Park and in a solemn ceremony before the start of the 2 P.M. game, presented a bronze plaque reading: "We dedicate this visit in memory of those baseball fans and others who died by atomic action on Aug. 6, 1945. May their souls rest in peace and with God's help and man's resolution peace will prevail forever, amen."[24]

The emotion from the morning boiled over during the game against the Kansai All Stars. In the bottom of the third inning with the Japanese already up 1-0 and one out and a runner on second, future Hall of Fame umpire Jocko Conlon called Kohei Sugiyama safe at first on what looked to be a groundout. Incensed, Jackie Robinson walked over to first to protest the call. "Everybody knew Jocko had missed the play because he was in back of the plate and couldn't see clearly," Robinson explained.25 Conlon, of course, did not reverse his decision so Robinson persisted, eventually arguing "so loud and so long" that Conlon tossed him from the game. "I never told him how to play ball," Conlon said after the game, "and he, or anybody else, can't tell me how to run a ball game."²⁶ Kansai would pad its lead to 4-1 before Brooklyn tied the game in the sixth on Roy Campanella's three-run homer and went ahead in the seventh on a steal of home by Gilliam and another home run by Gentile.²⁷

After the Dodgers won 14-0 on November 2, the Japanese squads rebounded. On the 4th the Dodgers and the All-Japan team entered the eighth inning knotted 7-7 before Brooklyn erupted for another seven to win 14-7. The following day, Japanese aces Takehiko Bessho and Masaichi Kaneda held the Dodgers to just one run for eight innings as the hosts entered the ninth winning 2-1. The Dodgers rallied in the ninth as Snider led off with a 480-foot home run to tie the game. Two outs later with the bases loaded, Robinson tried to steal the lead with a surprise two-out squeeze play. But Jackie missed the bunt and Demeter was tagged out on his way to the plate. In the bottom of the inning, Tetsuharu Kawakami, the hero of the opening game, came through again with a bases-loaded single to win the game.²⁸

After a day of rain, the Dodgers squeaked out a 3-2 win over the All-Japan squad in Nagoya. Gil Hodges, however, stole the headlines. Alston started the normally staid first baseman in left field and to keep himself amused Hodges "pantomimed the action after almost every play for five innings. He mimicked the pitcher and the ball's flight through the air, the catcher and the umpire. When a Dodger errored, Hodges glowered and pointed his finger. He made his legs quiver, shook his fist, stamped on the ground, swung his arms, frowned and smiled in the fleeting instant between pitches." The fans loved it, cheering him so loudly as he left the game in the eighth inning that "(y)ou would have thought it was Babe Ruth leaving."²⁹

During the game, Jackie Robinson entertained a special guest. Twenty-three-year-old Shigeyuki Ishikawa had been writing fan letters to the Dodgers for five years in an effort to improve his English. The team's front office read and responded to each of his 24 "adoring letters and notes of advice." Robinson invited the Nagoya native to sit with the team during the game even through spectators were usually barred from the dugout. "We've got to get him in or it will destroy his confidence in us," argued Robinson. "Baseball is built on guys like him."³⁰

Robinson was enjoying Japan and the Japanese people. Rachel Robinson told her husband's biographer Arnold Rampersad, "What was unusual about Jack in Japan was that he tried new things eagerly, which was not always the case at home. There he was, dressing up in kimonos, trying gamely to eat all kinds of unfamiliar food. We had a lot of fun watching the geisha girls try to make him comfortable, because he literally could not sit down with his legs out, his leg muscles were so tight and large. But he tried; he was in high spirits most of the time. I think he saw the tour of Japan as a culmination of his Dodger career, especially after the World Series victory the year before. I think he knew the end was in sight.³¹

The Dodgers and All-Japan met again on November 8 at Shizuoka, a small town at the foot of Mount Fuji, where 22 years earlier, 17-year-old Eiji Sawamura no-hit Babe Ruth and the All-Americans for five innings before losing 1-0 on Lou Gehrig's seventh-inning home run. Once again, the Japanese team thrilled the fans of Shizuoka, this time breaking a 2-2 tie in the bottom of the ninth for a walk-off victory.³² With their fourth loss, criticism of the Dodgers' performance continued. An International News Service article headlined, "Fans Debate Reasons for Dodger Losses" asked, "Are Japanese baseball teams improving, major leaguers getting careless or the Brooklyn Dodgers just getting old?"³³

A day later, the Dodgers returned to Tokyo for a rematch with their hosts the Yomiuri Giants. Once again the game was tight. With the score tied, 2-2, Gilliam led off the bottom of the 11th with a single and two outs later stood on second base as Robinson strode to the plate. Robinson had not hit well during the tour. He had started slowly, hitting just .214 (3-for-14) after the sixth game, but he had improved to .278 (10-for-36) with just one home run and no stolen bases at the start of the game against the Giants. So far that night, he had walked and scored a run but otherwise had been hitless in three at-bats.

On the mound Takehiko Bessho stared in for the sign. Bessho had been one of Japan's top pitchers since his debut as a 19-year-old in 1942. Unlike many Japanese pitchers, who nibbled at the corners of the plate with pinpoint control, Bessho was aggressive, coming straight after hitters with a blazing fastball and biting curve.

Catcher Shigeru Fujio flashed the sign for an intentional walk. Bessho shook his head. The catcher trotted out to the mound to explain that the order came from manager Shigeru Mizuhara. Bessho refused, sending Fujio running to the dugout to relay the pitcher's message. After "a hurried conference with the manager, the catcher dashed back to the mound." Bessho still refused. A reluctant Fujio moved back behind the plate.³⁴

Jackie jumped on Bessho's first pitch, pounding it foul "far over the left-field stands." On the next offering, he "drove a hot grounder through the pitcher's box," bringing Gilliam home to win the game.[35] The win seemed to energize both the Dodgers and Robinson. They won the next two games easily, 8-2 and 10-2, as Jackie went 2-for-5 with two runs and two RBIs. After the game in Tokyo on November 12, the Dodgers flew to the southern city of Fukuoka to make up a game that had been rained out on October 30.

Fittingly, the final meeting of the 19-game series was tight. Kazuhisa Inao and Kipp dueled for eight innings, each surrendering one run. The score remained tied as Duke Snider led off the top of the 11th with a groundball to first, which the usually sure-handed Tokuji Iida muffed, allowing Snyder to advance to third base.

Robinson strode to the plate – unknowingly for the last time in his professional career – and readied himself for Kazuhisa Inao's pitch. Jackie swung, grounding a single between third and short to score Snider and give the Dodgers the lead. After two outs and a walk, Don Demeter singled and Robinson crossed home plate for the final time. Immediately after the 3-1 victory, the Dodgers flew back to Tokyo and after a day of rest, returned to the United States. Within a month, Robinson decided to leave baseball.

Back in the United States, Robinson praised the Japanese as ballplayers and hosts. He told reporters that he was "dead tired" but he "enjoyed every minute of the trip." "The All-Japan team would do quite well in the Pacific Coast League. … (T)hey have good control pitching and they know how to pitch." The Japanese people "did everything pleasantly and went all out to make things comfortable and pleasant for us."[36]

"I know I gave it all I had over there," he told *The Sporting News*. "And I think that goes for every Dodger player. We lost more games than the Yankees, but if our record in Japan suffers by comparison with theirs, I think the credit should go to the Japanese for their big improvement in all-round play and baseball techniques. I looked at some pretty good pitching over there. In fact, it amazed me."[37]

Jackie's brief visit to the Land of the Rising Sun left a lasting impression. United States ambassador John M. Allison thanked him for "what you have done while in this country," noting that his "magnificent sportsmanship" helped strengthen the ties "between the people of Japan and the people of America."[38]

NOTES

1. "All Dodgers' O'Malley Gets Is Ride," *New York Daily News*, October 13, 1956: 36.
2. Associated Press, "Bums Arrive in Tokyo," *Herald-News* (Passaic, New Jersey), October 18, 1956: 46.
3. "Japanese Fans Defy Rain to Hail Dodgers," *New York Daily News*, October 19, 1956: 155.
4. Vin Scully, "The Dodgers in Japan," *Sport*, April 1957: 92; Bob Bowie, "Actresses, Flowers, Cheers Welcome Tourists to Tokyo," *The Sporting News*, October 24, 1956: 9.
5. SP3 Mel Derrick, "Alston Explains 'They Hit, and We Didn't,'" *Pacific Stars and Stripes*, October 20, 1956: 23.
6. Bob Bowie, "Dodgers Belt Central Loop Stars 7-1," *Pacific Stars and Stripes*, October 21, 1956: 23; *Japan Times*, October 21, 1956.
7. Bob Bowie, "All-Stars Rout Brooks 6-1," *Pacific Stars and Stripes*, October 22, 1956: 23-24.
8. United Press, "Brooks Nip Giants 1-0 on Snider's Home Run," *Pacific Stars and Stripes*, October 24, 1956: 24.
9. Associated Press, "Sportscaster Disagrees with Yuasa, Japanese 'Can Learn from Brooks,'" *Pacific Stars and Stripes*, October 24, 1956: 22.
10. "Brooks Whitewash All-Kanto Nine, 8-0," *Japan Times*, October 25, 1956: 8.
11. Associated Press, "Kanto All-Stars Tie Dodgers 3-3," *Pacific Stars and Stripes*, October 27, 1956: 24.
12. "Kanto All-Stars Tie Dodgers 3-3."
13. Associated Press, "Japanese Can Learn from Bums," *Hawaii Tribune-Herald* (Hilo, Hawaii), October 23, 1956: 7.
14. United Press, "Dodgers' Good Behavior Mystifies Japanese Fan," *Honolulu Advertiser*, October 26, 1956: 14.
15. United Press, "Banzais Changed to Brickbats for Dodgers on Japanese Tour," *New York Times*, October 23, 1956: 42.
16. United Press, "Japanese Baseball Expert Hints Brooks Are Bums," *New York Daily News*, October 23, 1956: 124.
17. United Press, "Bums 'Too Dignified,' Say Japanese Hosts," *New York Daily News*, October 26, 1956: 125.
18. Bob Bowie, "Gates Spin as Bums Battle for Wins in Japan," *The Sporting News*, October 31, 1956: 7.
19. Bob Bowie, "Japan's Big Welcome to Make Dodgers Feel Like Champions," *The Sporting News*, October 17, 1956: 13.
20. Pfc. Frank Morgan, "Booklyn Tops All-Japan Stars 6-3," *Pacific Stars and Stripes*, October 29, 1956: 24.
21. Arnold Rampersad, *Jackie Robinson* (New York: Alfred Knopf, 1997), 300-301.
22. "Robinson Predicts Dixie Gains," *Pacific Stars and Stripes*, November 18, 1956: 16.
23. Associated Press, "Japan's Pitchers Surprise Brooks," *Pacific Stars and Stripes*, October 30, 1956: 19.
24. Associated Press, "Dodgers to Dedicate Game to Bomb Victims," *Pacific Stars and Stripes*, October 29, 1956: 24.
25. "Dodgers vs. Kansai All Stars at Hiroshima Stadium, Hiroshima – November 1, 1956. walteromalley.com/en/dodger-history/international-relations/1956-Summary_November-1-1956. Retrieved October 25, 2020.
26. "Jackie Drops Verbal Bomb at Hiroshima – Gets Thumb," *The Sporting News*, November 14, 1956: 4.

27 "Dodgers vs. Kansai All Stars at Hiroshima Stadium, Hiroshima – November 1, 1956. walteromalley.com/en/dodger-history/international-relations/1956-Summary_November-1-1956. Retrieved October 25, 2020; United Press, "Dodgers Top Kansai, 10-6; Robby Chased," *New York Daily News*, November 2, 1956: 175.

28 Associated Press, "Bums Win 14-7 Before 60,000," *Honolulu Star-Bulletin*, November 3, 1956: 11; Associated Press, "Labine of Dodgers Loses in Japan, 3-2," *New York Times*, November 5, 1956: 44.

29 Associated Press, "Hodges Delights Fans with Baseball Performance," *Pacific Stars and Stripes*, November 8, 1956: 22.

30 Associated Press, "No. One Japan Brooklyn Fan Sits in Dugout," *Hawaii Tribune-Herald*, November 7, 1956: 7.

31 Rampersad, 301.

32 United Press, "Dodgers Downed by Japanese, 3-2," *New York Times*, November 9, 1956: 37.

33 International News Service, "Fans Debate Reasons for Dodger Losses," *Pacific Stars and Stripes*, November 8, 1956: 19.

34 Associated Press, "Dodgers Win in Eleventh by 5-4 as Tokyo Hurler Shakes Off Sign," *New York Times*, November 10, 1956: 22.

35 United Press, "Dodgers Edge Tokyo Giants 5-4," *Pacific Stars and Stripes*, November 10, 1956: 24.

36 Kenny Haina, Dodgers Tired on Japan Trip, Alston Lauds Isle Player," *Honolulu Advertiser*, November 17, 1956: 11.

37 Jack McDonald, "Bums Back Tired, but Glowing Over Reception in Japan," *The Sporting News*, November 28, 1956: 9.

38 Allison quoted in Rampersad, 301.

JACKIE ROBINSON CALLS IT QUITS

by Robert Nash

In October 1956, the Brooklyn Dodgers faced the New York Yankees in the World Series for the sixth time in Jackie Robinson's 10 years as a major leaguer. After splitting the first four games, the Dodgers were victims of Don Larsen's historic perfect game and fell behind three games to two. In Game Six, both teams failed to score through the first nine innings. In the bottom of the 10th inning, Robinson singled to left field to drive in the game's only run. No one knew it at the time, but that dramatic game-winning hit turned out to be the last hit of Robinson's storied major-league career.

There would be no such heroics in Game Seven. Robinson did, however, provide the Ebbets Field faithful with one last bit of excitement. With the Dodgers behind 9-0, Robinson came to the plate in the bottom of the ninth inning with two outs and Duke Snider on first base. In his last major-league at-bat, Robinson struck out, but Yankees catcher Yogi Berra was unable to hang onto the third strike. An unrelenting competitor to the very end, Robinson hustled down to first base in a futile attempt to beat Berra's throw for the final out of the Series.

Robinson and his Dodgers teammates had little time to dwell on their disappointing World Series loss. They left immediately for a monthlong exhibition tour of Japan, where they compiled a 14-4-1 record against tough Japanese competition. Japanese baseball fans got to experience the full range of Robinson's baseball talents. Midway through the tour, his competitive fires still unquenched, these included the spectacle of a third-inning ejection for too strenuously disputing an umpire's call.[1]

Less than a month after the Dodgers returned from Japan, on December 13, 1956, came the stunning news that Jackie Robinson had been traded. Even worse in the eyes of Brooklyn's supporters, he had been dealt to the Dodgers' crosstown adversaries, the New York Giants. In exchange for the player who had been such a significant contributor in the most successful decade in franchise history, the Dodgers received a much-traveled left-handed pitcher, Dick Littlefield, and a reported $30,000 in cash. Littlefield was coming off a 4-4 season for the Giants, his seventh team in seven years. One dismayed Dodger fan, undoubtedly echoing the views of many of her fellow fans, said, "I'm shocked to the core. This is like selling the Brooklyn-Battery Tunnel. Jackie Robinson is a synonym for the Dodgers. They can't do this to us."[2]

In his introduction to the 1995 edition of Robinson's autobiography *I Never Had It Made*, fellow Hall of Famer Hank Aaron observed: "…after all the things he'd done for the Dodgers, after everything he had suffered, they found it necessary to trade a man of his stature, a man who *was* the Dodgers. I thought at the time: Stan Musial was never traded; Ted Williams was never traded. We're talking about someone who was very special, who should have always had a place with the Dodgers. It should have been understood that this man started with the Dodgers and that he would end up with the Dodgers. Certain people you never trade, and Jackie Robinson should never have been traded."[3]

Rachel Robinson, Jackie's widow, confessed years later that when she learned of the trade, "I was angry that the Dodgers would trade him to the enemy Giants. I felt they should have had enough of a sense of history and enough appreciation for what he did to retire him with honors instead of selling him off to the Giants."[4]

Although unexpected, rumors involving a Robinson trade had circulated for years. He himself generated such talk as early as his fourth season. Following an August 1950 game in which he had been removed from the lineup after making an error, a frustrated Robinson remarked that it would not surprise him if he were traded: "After all, as ball players go, I'm pretty old at 31 and it wouldn't be any shock to me."[5] Dodgers President Branch Rickey firmly denied any such plans, but trade rumors continued to crop up for the remainder of Robinson's career.

During spring training 1955, Robinson expressed his frustration with manager Walter Alston over his playing time and uncertainty about his playing position for the coming season. The previous Dodgers manager, Chuck Dressen, who was then skippering the Washington Senators, created a fuss when he suggested that it looked as though the Dodgers wanted to trade Robinson.[6]

His ultimate trade to the Giants was even foreseen earlier in the 1956 season when it was suggested that "trade winds are blowing in odd directions. ... baseball breezes may blow Jackie Robinson into the Polo Grounds."[7]

Robinson had not been consulted beforehand about his trade. While he was undoubtedly disappointed by the news, he was probably not as shocked as baseball fans and members of the news media. He had few illusions, if any, about professional baseball as a business. He would later say, "After you've reached your peak, there's no sentiment in baseball. You start slipping, and pretty soon they're moving you around like a used car. You have no control over what happens to you."[8]

On the same evening that Robinson learned about the deal, he received a phone call from the Giants owner, Horace Stoneham who wanted to get his new acquisition's thoughts about joining the team. Robinson said he would be happy to play for the Giants, but that he was considering retirement and needed several weeks before giving Stoneham an answer.

For their part, the Giants were very excited about the prospect of having Robinson on their ballclub. Stoneham called him "the greatest competitor I've ever seen in baseball."[9] Not only did they value his potential role as a team leader, but even at age 38, they felt, he could still be a key contributor on the field. They hoped he could fill in for their young first baseman, Bill White, who had been called into service with the US Army. Willie Mays, the Giants' star center fielder, was reportedly thrilled that Robinson would be joining the team, saying it "was the best thing that could have happened to the Giants."[10] Team executives also knew that the Dodgers star and longtime Giants nemesis would be a big box-office draw.

There was much speculation among baseball fans and the press that Robinson would retire rather than accept a trade to the Giants. At a public appearance in December, however, he declared that "as long as I had to be traded, I'm glad it was to the Giants."[11] What no one knew outside of Robinson's family and a few close associates was that he had already decided to retire *before* he learned of the trade.

Several years earlier, keenly aware of the inevitable decline of his athletic skills, Robinson had asked his financial adviser and close friend Martin Stone to seek out post-baseball-career opportunities. Those efforts bore fruit when Robinson was approached in early December by William Black, owner of Chock Full o'Nuts, a large chain of New York City coffee shops. Black wanted him for a full-time executive position as vice president for personnel relations. In an untimely confluence of events, Robinson had agreed to a contract with Black only to learn on the very same day that he had been traded to the Giants.

Much of the subsequent controversy surrounding his retirement would have been avoided if Robinson had informed the Dodgers and Giants of his decision to retire at the time of the trade. Two years earlier, however, he had signed a contract with *Look* magazine giving it the exclusive rights to the story of his retirement. The principled Robinson felt both contractually and morally bound to keep his retirement a secret until the article was published.

The story was to appear in the January 22, 1957, issue of *Look*, which was scheduled to hit newsstands around the first week of January. Plans called for him to hold a press conference that would coincide with the release of the article. But subscribers received their copies of the magazine a couple of days early, and the news leaked out ahead of time. Much of the baseball establishment and news media reacted negatively, feeling they had been deliberately deceived.

In a brief article titled "Why I'm Quitting Baseball," Robinson laid out his reasons for retiring, and explained the unusual circumstances surrounding the timing. "There shouldn't be any mystery about my reasons," he said. "I'm 38 years old, with a family to support, I've got to think of my future and our security. At my age, a man doesn't have much future in baseball – and very little security. It's as simple as that." He went on to say, "I'm through with baseball because I know that, in a matter of time, baseball would have been through with me."[12]

Robinson anticipated the potential outcry over his misleading public statements. He wrote, "Some people may now feel I haven't been honest with them these past few weeks when they've asked me about my plans. I've always played fair with my newspaper friends, and I think they'll understand why this one time I couldn't give them the whole story as soon as I knew it."[13]

Despite widespread assumptions to the contrary, Robinson also made it clear that his decision was not due to an unwillingness to play for the rival Giants. He had already decided to retire before he learned of the trade. It was equally evident, however, that he would not have welcomed a trade to *any* team. "I had just been able to avoid what I dreaded most in baseball," he commented: "the moment when they would start moving me around."[14]

Besides the weeks-long secrecy leading up to his announcement, many were also bothered by the fact that Robinson had sold his story instead of providing it to the newspapers. The selling of a retirement story, however, was not without precedent. Several years earlier, in April 1954, Ted Williams had declared "This Is My Last Year" in a three-part series that appeared in the *Saturday Evening Post*.[15] Williams, who would turn 36 before the end of that season, commented, "I can't think of a ballplayer I ever saw who looked as if he belonged in a major-league uniform after the age of thirty-six … excepting pitchers, who work only once a week when they're that old."[16] Of course, not only did Williams not retire after the 1954 season, but he continued to play for six more years before finally ending his Hall of Fame career. Williams's example held out hope that Robinson might yet reconsider his decision to retire.

If Robinson was seriously entertaining any second thoughts about retiring, however, they were quickly dismissed when Buzzie Bavasi, the Dodgers vice president, suggested in the press that Robinson's apparent retirement was merely a ploy to get more money out of the Giants. An angry Robinson responded, "There isn't a chance in the world I'll ever put on a baseball uniform again,"[17] and also that he "wouldn't play baseball again for a million dollars."[18]

Nevertheless, the Giants worked hard to get him to reconsider in hopes that he might consent to play for one more year. Black informed the Giants that he was willing to delay Robinson's new position for a year. Robinson though, quickly made it clear that his decision to retire was final. On January 14, 1957, in a letter written on a Chock Full o' Nuts letterhead, Robinson formally announced his retirement. He thanked Horace Stoneham and vice president Chub Feeney, and reiterated that his retirement was not due to his trade to the Giants. "From all I have heard from people who have worked with you," he wrote, "it would have been a pleasure to have been in your organization."[19]

Robinson's retirement became official after his letter was forwarded to the office of the National League president, Warren Giles. As a result, his December trade to the Giants was rescinded, meaning that he would retire as a member of the Dodgers. His frequent statements that his trade to the Giants was not a factor in his retirement appear to have been sincere. Nevertheless, he said that he was "glad I quit baseball before I was traded, and I bet I'm not the only one. I'm sure the true Brooklyn fans – the ones I really care about – will be tickled to death that they'll never have to see me playing for another club."[20]

The fact that baseball was not the sole priority in Robinson's life was lost in the commotion surrounding his retirement. On the same day he dramatically broke the major leagues' color line on April 15, 1947, he told a reporter, "Give me five years of this and that will be enough."[21] Later that same year, after completing his historic first season, he was already hinting about retirement, saying, "I've been in sports for a long time and I'm getting a little tired of it."[22]

Although Robinson would go on to play for nine more seasons, he frequently spoke about hanging up his uniform. One month after Joe DiMaggio retired at age 36 in December 1951, citing injuries and declining skills, Robinson was asked if he might ultimately retire in the same way. "Well, for one thing," he responded, "I don't think I'll ever last as long as Joe did because those early years in football and other sports (at UCLA and in semipro leagues) took too much out of me. One thing for sure, though, I won't try to hang on a minute longer than I feel I'm helping the club."[23] In a magazine article published two years before his retirement, he even made the surprising confession that he had never wanted to be a baseball player.[24]

It is revealing that in Robinson's autobiography *I Never Had It Made*, published shortly before his death in 1972 at age 53, the greater part of the book is devoted to his life outside of the game that made him famous. An indication that he had important activities in mind beyond the baseball diamond was demonstrated just five days before his trade to the Giants. On December 8, 1956, he was presented with the Spingarn Medal, awarded annually by the NAACP "for the highest achievement of an American Negro." The first sports figure to receive the award, Robinson was recognized for his "achievements in business and in public appearances in the interest of race relations."[25] In the following year, the Spingarn Medal was bestowed on Martin Luther King Jr.

It should not be too surprising that Robinson's departure from baseball ended in such a tumultuous manner. His outspoken manner generated controversy both on and off the field throughout his career. At least some of his troubles were undoubtedly the result of racial bias within the press and baseball's executive offices. One writer, for example, has contrasted Robinson's negative treatment with that of Cleveland's longtime star pitcher Bob Feller, who retired shortly before Robinson.[26] Feller was similarly free with his opinions, and not averse to challenging the powers in major-league baseball.

On the other hand, Robinson certainly provided fuel for his critics. Leo Durocher, manager of both the Dodgers and Giants, and himself no stranger to controversy, once commented that "Mr. Rickey might not have been willing to say that Jackie had the ability to make a bad situation worse, but I don't think he would have said that Jackie ever went out of his way to make it any better either."[27] Robinson himself provided some validation for that opinion: "When I agreed to become the first Negro in Organized Baseball, I also didn't realize that distinction would get me into so many public arguments and controversies. Ever since I've been with the Dodgers, I have been in the middle of all kinds of beefs on the sports pages. Rachel says it's my own fault. She says I'm too willing to sound off with an opinion when a sportswriter is looking for a story, and she's probably right. It's hard for me to say, 'No comment.'"[28]

Ultimately, Jackie Robinson delivered this fitting interpretation of the controversial ending to his baseball career: "Some of the writers damned me for having held out on the story. Others felt it was my right. Personally, I felt that Bavasi and some of the writers resented the fact that I had outsmarted baseball before baseball had outsmarted me. The way I figured it, I was even with baseball and baseball with me. The game had done much for me, and I had done much for it."[29]

SOURCES

In addition to the sources cited in the Notes, the author consulted Baseball-Reference.com.

NOTES

1. "Dodgers Triumph in Hiroshima," *New York Times*, November 2, 1956: 33.
2. "Brooklyn's Fans Rocked by Trade," *New York Times*, December 14, 1956: 46.
3. Hank Aaron, "Introduction," in Jackie Robinson, *I Never Had It Made* (Hopewell, New Jersey: Ecco Press, 1995), xvii.
4. Ross Newhan, "Rachel Robinson," *Los Angeles Times*, March 31, 1997, latimes.com/archives/la-xpm-1997-03-31-ss-43970-story.html (accessed October 17, 2020).
5. "Rickey Makes a Denial – Dodgers' Head Says He Has No Idea of Trading Robinson," *New York Times*, August 17, 1950: 32.
6. "'Tsk, Tsk,' Says Chuck to Smokey Stew," *The Sporting News*, April 20, 1955: 24.
7. "Trade of Robinson to Giants Possible," *New York Times*, June 7, 1956: 38.
8. Jackie Robinson, "Why I'm Quitting Baseball," *Look*, January 22, 1957: 91.
9. Jimmy Burns, "He's Greatest Competitor of All – Stoneham," *The Sporting News*, December 19, 1956: 3.
10. "'Jackie Will Help Me,' Says Willie, Signing Giant Contract for 35 Gees," *The Sporting News*, January 9, 1957: 8.
11. "Jackie Beams Over Giants at Kids' Party in Stamford," *The Sporting News*, January 2, 1957: 26.
12. "Why I'm Quitting Baseball": 91.
13. "Why I'm Quitting Baseball": 91.
14. "Why I'm Quitting Baseball": 92.
15. Ted Williams, "This Is My Last Year," *Saturday Evening Post*, Part One, April 10, 1954: 17-19, 90-94; Part Two, April 17, 1954: 24-25, 147-150; Conclusion, April 24, 1954: 31, 155-158.
16. "This Is My Last Year," *Saturday Evening Post*, Part One, April 10, 1954: 17.
17. Dick Young, "Robby Nixes Giants' Bid to Lure Him Back to '57," *New York Daily News*, January 8, 1957: 47.
18. Gordon S. White Jr., "Robinson, Incensed by Remarks of Bavasi, Is Adamant on Decision to Retire," *New York Times*, January 7, 1957: 31.
19. "Robinson Applies for Retirement," *New York Times*, January 15, 1957: 47.
20. "Why I'm Quitting Baseball": 92.
21. Ward Morehouse, "Debut 'Just Another Game' to Jackie," *The Sporting News*, April 23, 1947: 3.
22. "Jackie Robinson Planning 3 More Years on Diamond," *New York Times*, October 26, 1947: S5.
23. John Drebinger, "Robinson Becomes Best Paid Dodger – Signs for Reported $40,000," *New York Times*, January 10, 1952: 38.
24. Jackie Robinson, "A Kentucky Colonel Kept Me in Baseball," *Look*, February 8, 1955: 90.
25. "Gold Medal Given to Jackie Robinson," *New York Times*, December 9, 1956: 50.
26. Ron Briley, "Do Not Go Gently into That Good Night: Race, the Baseball Establishment, and the Retirements of Bob Feller and Jackie Robinson," in Joseph Dorinson and Joram Warmund, eds., *Jackie Robinson: Race, Sports, and the American Dream* (Armonk, New York: M.E. Sharpe, 1998), 194.
27. Leo Durocher, *Nice Guys Finish Last*, (New York: Simon & Schuster, 1975), 212.
28. Jackie Robinson, "Your Temper Can Ruin Us!," *Look*, February 22, 1955: 78.
29. Robinson, *I Never Had It Made*, 122.

JACKIE ROBINSON, ALL-STAR

by Mark S. Sternman

A star among stars, Jackie Robinson had an excellent batting record in six career All-Star appearances. The influx of Robinson and other African-American stalwarts for the National League helped reverse the course of the series. Prior to integration, the American League won nine of the first 13 contests. Surprisingly, Robinson played in neither the 1947 nor 1948 midsummer classics although he finished in the top 15 of the MVP voting both years. The AL took both games to up its mark to 11-4. Robinson's teams won four of the six games in which he played as the quicker-to-integrate National League dominated the All-Star Game from 1950 to 1987.

The top vote-getter among National Leaguers,[1] Robinson immediately made an impact on the 1949 game, the first to feature African-Americans, which started off poorly for the senior circuit when the American League plated four runs against Warren Spahn. Robinson helped get the NL back in the game. Starting at second and batting second, he doubled off Mel Parnell in his first plate appearance and scored on Stan Musial's homer. In the third, Robinson helped tie the score at 4-4 when he walked. Musial "and Robinson put on a beautiful hit-and-run play, Musial's ground ball going through the vacant shortstop spot for a single, and Robinson scorching the base paths as he fairly flew into third."[2] He scored as Ralph Kiner hit into a double play. Robinson reached on a fielder's choice in the sixth and tallied his third run of the day on a two-run homer by Kiner that cut the AL lead to 8-7. The National League got no closer and lost 11-7. Robinson's three runs scored tied the NL standard that Frankie Frisch set in 1934 and still remains through 2019. (Besides Robinson, the other African-American players in the 1949 game included fellow Dodgers Roy Campanella and Don Newcombe, plus Larry Doby of the Cleveland Indians.)

Robinson hit cleanup for the NL in 1950 and scored the game's first run in the top of the second. After he singled, Enos Slaughter smacked an RBI triple. Robinson played the first 10 innings of the extra-inning affair before Brooklyn manager Burt Shotton pinch-hit for him with Johnny Wyrostek. After the game, Shotton said, "I didn't want [Robinson] to hit into a

Jackie Robinson's 1949 Bowman card #50 - his MVP year.

double play, and Wyrostek, who hits .320, was a better bet, that's all. ... Jackie is slowed up by a leg injury."[3] Red Schoendienst's homer in the 14th inning gave the NL a 4-3 win.

Again placed in the cleanup slot in 1951, Robinson played a key role in the game's latter stages to ensure that the NL would win consecutive games for the first time in the history of the series. With the NL up 4-3 in the sixth, Robinson walked and scored on Gil Hodges' homer. With runners on the corners, including the speedy Richie Ashburn on third and the NL now up 6-3 in the seventh, Robinson had a two-out bunt single that drove in an insurance run. Robinson had another infield hit in the ninth as the NL romped, 8-3. Commenting after the game, "Robinson said he was completely surprised by the type of pitching dished out by the AL's five pitchers. 'They told me this American League was a fast ball league,' he shouted above the dressing room din. 'I never saw so many curves, screwballs, and changes of pace in my life.'"[4]

In 1952 Robinson moved back up to second in the batting order. Robinson "crashed [Vic] Raschi's first pitch into the second deck of the left field stands, about three rows deep."[5] Robinson's only All-Star homer gave the NL a 1-0 lead. The NL would eventually triumph 3-2 in a game called on account of rain after five innings.

Robinson made the 1953 team as a reserve and pinch-hit in the game. His seventh-inning popup proved inconsequential in the 5-1 NL win.

Robinson reprised his outfield role but started and batted seventh in his 1954 All-Star finale. As with the first game he played in the series, Robinson's NL team trailed 4-0, this time through three innings. By the time Robinson batted in the fourth, the NL had cut the lead to 4-2. Facing Sandy Consuegra with Ted Kluszewski on second and Ray Jablonski on first, Robinson, "though playing on creaky knees,"[6] "walloped a double to center"[7] to score both and tie the game. Don Mueller's pinch-hit double scored Robinson with the go-ahead run. (Willie Mays replaced Robinson in the outfield the next inning) in a game the AL would win, 11-9.

Mays and Robinson also both appear on the list of most runs scored as All-Stars:

Runs Scored (Career)	R	PA	R/PA	Debut Age
1. Willie Mays	20	82	.24	23
2. Stan Musial	11	72	.15	22
3. Ted Williams	10	57	.18	21
4. Rod Carew	8	48	.17	21
5. Hank Aaron	7	72	.10	21
Joe DiMaggio	7	43	.16	21
Nellie Fox	7	41	.17	23
Al Kaline	7	40	.18	20
Joe Morgan	7	31	.23	22
Steve Garvey	7	30	.23	25
Jackie Robinson	7	20	.35	30

Robinson has the highest percentage of runs scored per plate appearance of those who scored the most All-Star Game runs. He doubtless would have placed even higher on the career list had baseball apartheid not forced him to wait until the age of 30 to play in an All-Star Game.

Jackie Robinson's performance as an All-Star represents a microcosm of his career. Although through no fault of his own he got off to a late start, Robinson excelled individually and led his teams to more victories than defeats once he finally had a chance to confront competitors of all colors.

NOTES

1 "Williams, Jackie Top Record Vote of Fans," *The Sporting News*, July 13, 1949: 2.

2 Roger Birtwell, "Brissie Great in Relief Role," *Boston Globe*, July 12, 1949: 34.

3 "Schoendienst Homer First of Year as Righthander," *Boston Globe*, July 12, 1950: 10. An alternative theory has Shotton selecting a left-handed batter to face the right-handed pitcher Allie Reynolds. Oscar Ruhl, "All-Star Glints," *The Sporting News*, July 19, 1950: 34.

4 "National Leaguers Praise Garver; 'He's Great,' Say Musial, Robinson," *Boston Globe*, July 11, 1951: 8.

5 Gene Mack Jr., "Robinson, Sauer Homers Give N.L. Third Straight, 3-2," *Boston Globe*, July 9, 1952: 16.

6 Frederick G. Lieb. "A.L. Stars Hurdle 13th – Win Hump on Hitting," *The Sporting News*, July 21, 1954: 8.

7 Rud Rennie, "Rosen Hits 2 Homers, Bats In 5 Runs," *Boston Globe*, July 14, 1954: 8.

JACKIE ROBINSON AND THE WORLD SERIES

by Steven C. Weiner

"No sporting event so decisively enthralls the national consciousness as baseball's annual October pageant.... There is something heroic about the pitched combat of two teams that are at once survivors and winners, meeting to decide the world championship."
– Donald Honig[1]

Even though the nature of postseason baseball has changed dramatically over the past 50 years, the essence of the World Series is as it was 100 years ago, a best-of-seven playoff to determine a champion.[2] Over six months of toil in the regular season and now the early rounds of the postseason are boiled down to a final week of intensity like no other competition. Every pitch, every play is under scrutiny and presents an opportunity for heroes, goats, joy, and agony, all at the same time.

The Bronx Bombers versus Dem Bums.[3] The Yankees and Dodgers have met more times in the World Series than any other pairing in postseason history.[4] Perhaps no World Series rivalry better captures the nature of the combat. Its history is punctuated by riveting games, indelible moments, and striking individual performances, both joyous and painful, that have become a part of baseball history. We remember when the wait finally ended for the Brooklyn Dodgers in 1955, winning their first and only World Series title.[5] Don Larsen's Game Five pitching performance the following year against the Dodgers stands as the only perfect game in World Series history.[6] Dodger fans also sympathetically remember Gil Hodges' 0-for-21 batting slump in the 1952 World Series. In the midst of losing another World Series to the Yankees, they sent him all manner of cards, letters, best wishes, batting tips, prayers, and condolences. "My warmest memory in baseball." said Hodges years later. "What I'll never forget is the way fans rallied around rather than dig a ditch for me."[7]

One of those moments of timeless memory belongs to Jackie Robinson, a daring steal of home in Game One of the 1955 World Series against the Yankees. The Dodgers were batting in the eighth inning, trailing by two runs. Robinson danced off third to disturb Yankee pitcher Whitey Ford and finally darted toward home. Yogi Berra applied the tag but the safe call by umpire Bill Summers was immediate.[8] The call and the meaning of that play are discussed in another essay in this book. And there are many more memorable plays dotting the Dodgers versus Yankees World Series rivalry of the 1940s and 1950s.[9]

In his 10 seasons with the Dodgers, 1947 through 1956, Jackie Robinson played in six World Series, all against the Yankees. There was no better time for baseball fans of all ages in the New York City area.[10] What did Jackie Robinson accomplish on the World Series stage and what did it mean to him?

1947 – YANKEES, DODGERS RESUME WORLD SERIES RIVALRY

Their first meeting, in the 1941 World Series, was now a distant but still agonizing memory for Dodger fans. With two outs in the ninth inning of Game Four and the Dodgers leading 4-3, the Yankees' Tommy Henrich swung and missed on a full count. The ball eluded Dodgers catcher Mickey Owen and the Yankees rallied to win that game and the 1941 World Series the following day.

The 1947 World Series meant several firsts for baseball. Robinson and pitcher Dan Bankhead[11] were the first African-Americans to play in a World Series, which was being televised for the first time, although only in the Eastern part of the United States. Two weeks before the Series, Robinson was named Rookie of the Year by *The Sporting News* and its editor J.G. Taylor Spink on the basis of "stark baseball values ... his hitting, his running, his defensive play, his team value."[12] Spink wrote, "The sociological experiment that Robinson represented, the trail blazing he did, the barriers he broke down did not enter into the decision."[13]

Robinson seemed more than ready for his first World Series and displayed no outward sign of the jitters. "Gosh," he said with a smile, "it can't be any more nerve-wracking than that St. Louis series. After that, nothing can seem too important."[14] The contempt from various members of opposing teams for Robinson's role in integrating baseball has been well chronicled. The spiking of Robinson at first base, intentional or otherwise, by the Cardinals' Enos Slaughter on August 20, 1947, at Ebbets Field is just one such example.[15]

In Game One[16] at Yankee Stadium, the Dodgers struck first and Robinson was at the center. In the first inning, he drew a one-out walk. "Then the agile Negro started prancing back and forth off first base and a wave of expectancy swept through the stands."[17] With Frank Shea pitching, Robinson stole second. Moments later he was tagged out between second and third on Pete Reiser's tap to the mound. Robinson, though, prolonged the rundown sufficiently to allow Reiser to advance to second and subsequently score on Dixie Walker's single. The first run in the first inning in his first World Series was to some extent of Robinson's doing, as unrecognizable as it might appear in the box score. It was just the beginning.

The Dodgers would go on to lose the game and, eventually, the Series in seven games, but not before there was another highlight-reel moment to remember. There were two outs in the ninth inning of Game Four and the Yankees' Bill Bevens was pitching a no-hitter even though he had yielded 10 walks. Pinch-hitter Cookie Lavagetto's double ended that bid and tied the World Series at two games apiece.[18]

1949 – YANKEES WIN THE FIRST OF FIVE CONSECUTIVE WORLD SERIES TITLES

It was a banner year for Jackie Robinson even without a World Series title. Robinson, teammates Roy Campanella and Don Newcombe and the Indians' Larry Doby became the first African-Americans to play in an All-Star Game and the setting was perfect: Ebbets Field. The American League won 11-7 with Robinson contributing a first-inning double and scoring three runs.

In November Robinson was named the National League Most Valuable Player by the Baseball Writers Association of America. He received 12 first-place votes from the 24-member panel, beating out Stan Musial and Enos Slaughter, who finished second and third, respectively, in the voting. It was another first for baseball as integration on the playing field continued, and it was truly deserved. Robinson led the league in batting (.342) and stolen bases (37) and finished second in RBIs (124). What was his reaction? "Well, what do you know," Jack piped modestly. "I ought to sleep well tonight. This is the nicest thing that could have happened to me."[19] The World Series wasn't so kind.

After losing to Allie Reynolds and the Yankees 1-0 in Game One, Preacher Roe returned the favor in Game Two and shut out the Yankees 1-0, thanks to Jackie Robinson and Gil Hodges. In the second inning, Robinson doubled off Vic Raschi. In typical fashion, Robinson feinted and danced off second base, thoroughly distracting Raschi, who said later, "Robinson had broken my concentration. I was pitching more to Robinson than I was to Hodges and as a result I threw one up into Gil's power and he got the base hit that beat me."[20] That was Jackie Robinson on the basepaths. The series was tied 1-1 but the Yankees won the next three games, all at Ebbets Field, and the World Series title. Although he walked four times, Robinson managed only three hits and didn't steal a base.

1952 – FACING THE YANKEES AGAIN

The prior two seasons had been agonizing for Brooklyn fans. National League pennant races were decided on the last day of the season and the Dodgers came out on the losing end both times as described in detail by SABR authors.[21] Now it was time for another "subway series."[22] Author Samuel G. Freedman once put it in simple terms: "Subway series is a synonym for civil war."[23]

It was another banner regular season for Robinson, an All-Star for the fourth consecutive season, In addition to his .308 batting average, he led the major leagues in on-base percentage (.440), having walked 106 times and gotten plunked by the baseball another 14 times. Robinson was excited for another shot at the Yankees. "The main thing is to beat the Yankees," he admitted. "But I'd like to come through with one really good World Series, and I know I'm not going to have many more opportunities."[24]

The Yankees frustrated Robinson. After his opening-game homer, the Yankees' strategy was to pitch him around the knees, mostly with curveballs. It worked. He got only three other hits, one a bunt, one a blooper, and one a lined single.[25] The teams traded victories over the first six games but the decisive defensive play of the series ironically came in Game Seven[26] at the expense of Robinson.

Robinson came to bat against Bob Kuzava in the bottom of the seventh inning with two outs and the bases loaded. The Dodgers trailed, 4-2. On a 2-and-2 count, Robinson skied a pop fly just to the right of the pitcher's mound. Second baseman Billy Martin came running in at full speed to make a shoe-top catch. Or as Yankees manager Casey Stengel described it in his inimitable way, "My feller at first (Joe Collins) is asleep and my feller behind the bat – I don't know what he's doin'…. If that 130-pound kid don't make the catch we blow the World Series."[27] And so they won their fourth consecutive World Series.

1953 – "IF WE DON'T WIN IT THIS YEAR, WE'LL NEVER WIN IT."[28]

It was a banner season for the Dodgers. In first place since late June, they pulled away to win the National League crown by 13 games over the Milwaukee Braves. They led the major leagues with 208 home runs and the National League in many offensive categories, including batting average (.285). The lineup was stacked with .300 hitters: Gil Hodges (.302), Roy Campanella (.312), Jackie Robinson (.329), Duke Snider (.336), and Carl Furillo (.344). Furillo won the NL batting crown and Campy was named league Most Valuable Player. Throw in Pee Wee Reese and you have Brooklyn's 1953 All-Star Game contingent. It was time for another shot at the Yankees.

The Yankees won the first two games and the Dodgers took the next two. In the pivotal Game Five at Ebbets Field, Dodgers rookie pitcher Johnny Podres made his inauspicious World Series debut and never made it out of the third inning, losing 11-7. Podres would have to wait two years for redemption. When Billy Martin's record-setting 12th hit of the Series scored Hank Bauer in the bottom of the ninth inning of Game Six, the Yankees were World Series champions for the fifth consecutive time.

Jackie Robinson had his best offensive showing in this World Series, batting .320, including a double, a single, and a steal of third base in Game Six, but he readily shook off any congratulations. "Fine, if we had won, but what good when we lost?"[29] The front page of the day's final edition of the *Brooklyn Eagle*, draped with a black streamer, expressed the sentiment of Dodgers fans everywhere. The message tucked in the corner read "Please omit the flowers."[30]

1955 – FINALLY!

Wait 'til Next Year? The 1955 World Series title meant that next year was finally here. The phrase became a euphemism for a baseball season gone awry and nowhere did it receive greater play than in the 1940s and 1950s with the Brooklyn Dodgers and their long-suffering fans.[31]

For Robinson, the regular season was the worst statistically of his career. He played in the fewest games of his career (105) and hit for the lowest batting average (.256). His streak of six consecutive All-Star Game appearances was broken. The 36-year-old Robinson's competitive instincts were as sharp as ever but his physical skills were diminishing. He knew that his peak years as an athlete were behind him.[32] Knee and ankle ailments forced him to miss playing time in the middle of the season.

With two outs in the eighth inning of Game One and the Dodgers trailing the Yankees by two runs, Robinson's steal of home was probably not the best baseball strategy. He well understood that, but "whether it was because of my stealing home or not, the team had a new fire."[33] They lost the game as well as Game Two at Yankee Stadium. The Series shifted to Ebbets Field for the next three games and fans had to hope that there would not be a repeat of what happened in the 1949 World Series. In 1955, they would have to win only two games for the title.

Game Three was entrusted to Johnny Podres to start for the Dodgers, and he delivered a complete-game victory. The Dodgers could certainly celebrate key performances throughout their lineup in Game Three. Jackie Robinson's outstanding play covered the gamut: a single, a double, two runs scored, opportunistic baserunning in the seventh inning, and seven assists playing the hot corner. They swept the next two games at home before the Yankees tied the series at three games apiece at Yankee Stadium.

The stage was set for the classic Game Seven, of which much has been written.[34] Jackie Robinson remained on the bench, having injured his heel in an earlier game. Podres' stellar pitching, Sandy Amoros's great catch leading to a double play in the sixth inning, and the final out, Pee Wee Reese to Gil Hodges, on Elston Howard's groundball are vivid memories sealing the first and only World Series title for the Brooklyn Dodgers.

Robinson once said, "It kills me to lose. If I'm a troublemaker – and I don't think that my temper makes me one – then it's only because I can't stand losing. That's the way I am about winning. All I ever wanted to do was finish first."[35] When the wait finally ended for the Brooklyn Dodgers, "42" was right in the middle of the mob scene just off the pitcher's mound, celebrating the moment he well understood.[36] "It was one of the greatest thrills of my life to be finally on a world series winner."[37]

1956 – THE LAST ONE

The Yankees were in first place virtually the entire season, winning the American League crown by nine games over the Cleveland Indians. Meanwhile, the Dodgers won four of their last five games, including

Sal Maglie's no-hitter against the Philadelphia Phillies, to edge the Milwaukee Braves by one game.

When the Series opened at Ebbets Field, the Dodgers' bats were hot for two games, starting off with Jackie Robinson's second-inning home run in Game One. In the first two games, they scored 19 runs to take a 2-0 lead into Yankee Stadium for the next three games. And then the bats went cold. Six runs in the last five games.[38]

Of course, 1956 will be forever remembered for Don Larsen's perfect Game Five, the first in World Series history, but Yankees pitchers threw complete games for the remainder of the Series: Whitey Ford, Tom Sturdivant, Larsen, Bob Turley, and Johnny Kucks. Jackie Robinson was the hero in Game Six as Turley and Clem Labine dueled in a scoreless game. With two outs in the bottom of the 10th and Jim Gilliam on second, Turley intentionally walked Duke Snider to pitch to Robinson. Imagine what Jackie was thinking. Jackie's walk-off line drive single to left scored Gilliam and tied the Series at three wins each.

Unfortunately for the Dodgers, Kucks limited the Dodgers to three hits in Game Seven, pitching against an ineffective Don Newcombe, and the Yankees won easily, 9-0. The game ended with Kucks striking out Robinson in what turned out to be the last at-bat of his major-league career. Robinson bemoaned the drubbing: "I didn't mind so much that they beat us, but I hated to be beaten that way. I'd rather it had been close and that we had had a chance."[39]

Oh yes, the Dodgers and Yankees would meet again in the World Series after 1956, but it would not be the same. It became transcontinental.

Jackie Robinson and the World Series

A look at Jackie Robinson's batting line for those six World Series can tell us only part of the story (Table 1). Six stolen bases in the same number of attempts provides a hint of speed and daring. For his 10-year career, Robinson stole 197 bases but was caught stealing 76 times. His ability to draw walks with minimal strikeouts is remarkable and foreign to today's game. Over those 10 years, Robinson walked 740 times and struck out only 291 times. However we might analyze his World Series numbers, even the most cynical of baseball sabermetricians would have to admit there was more to the man than the numbers.

George Will once wrote, "Jackie Robinson was an alloy of fire and ice, a fierce competitor in 1947 who had to leash his pride and smother his resentment, channeling his passion into baseball performance."[40] All he ever wanted to do was finish first and that he did.

WS	AB	R	H	2B	3B	HR	RBI	SB	CS	BB	SO	BA
1947	27	3	7	2	0	0	3	2	0	2	4	.259
1949	16	2	3	1	0	0	2	0	0	4	2	.188
1952	23	4	4	0	0	1	2	2	0	7	5	.174
1953	25	3	8	3	0	0	2	1	0	1	0	.320
1955	22	5	4	1	1	0	1	1	0	2	1	.182
1956	24	5	6	1	0	1	2	0	0	5	2	.250
Totals	137	22	32	7	1	2	12	6	0	21	14	.234

Table 1. Jackie Robinson's batting line in six World Series

AUTHOR'S NOTE

I first saw Jackie Robinson play at Ebbets Field in 1951, thanks to my father and Uncle Joe.[41] Subsequent returns to Brooklyn and visits to the Polo Grounds and Yankee Stadium in the 1950s were joyous occasions. The opportunity to read what others have written about Jackie Robinson, the significance of his presence in the lineup, and his performance on the field have brought those memories back to life. For that I am grateful to many.

SOURCES

The author accessed Baseball-Reference.com statistical information about Jackie Robinson, box scores/play-by-play information for regular season and World Series games and other data.

NOTES

1. Donald Honig, *The October Heroes* (New York: Simon and Schuster, 1979), 13.
2. With the introduction of divisional play in each league in 1969, four teams qualified for postseason play. When each league expanded to three divisions in 1995, eight teams qualified for postseason play. The first wild-card games in 2012 introduced an additional team in each league to the postseason.
3. Bronx Bombers is "a nickname for the New York Yankees that first became popular in the 1930s when heavyweight boxing champion Joe Louis was known as the Brown Bomber." (Paul Dickson, *The Dickson Baseball Dictionary, 3rd Edition* [New York: W.W. Norton & Company, 2009], 137.) Dem Bums is a "traditional affectionate nickname for the Brooklyn Dodgers established and characterized by a bewhiskered, cigar-chomping cartoon tramp drawn by Willard Mullins." (Dickson, 250.)
4. In 1981 the Dodgers and Yankees met for the 11th time in World Series history. Through the 2019 season, the Yankees and Giants have met seven times in the World Series and the Yankees and Cardinals have met five times.
5. Steven C. Weiner, "October 4, 1955: Brooklyn Dodgers win first World Series as 'Next Year' finally arrives," SABR Baseball Games Project.
6. Charles F. Faber, "October 8, 1956: Don Larsen throws a perfect game in the World Series," SABR Baseball Games Project.
7. Tom Clavin and Danny Peary, *Gil Hodges* (New York: New American Library, 2012), 145.
8. "Jackie Robinson Steals Home," MLB.com, accessed August 9, 2019, mlb.com/video/robinson-steals-home/c-9336883.
9. Two other memorable plays culled from a long list: (1) Brooklyn's Al Gionfriddo robbed the Yankees' Joe DiMaggio

of a three-run home run (Game Six in 1947); (2) The Series-saving catch by Brooklyn's Sandy Amoros off Yogi Berra (Game Seven in 1955).

10 During 1947-1956, at least one New York team played in every World Series with the exception of 1948, when the Cleveland Indians beat the Boston Braves. The New York Giants played in the 1951 World Series against the Yankees and in the 1954 World Series against the Indians.

11 Dan Bankhead pinch-ran for Bobby Bragan and scored on Pee Wee Reese's single in the sixth inning of Game Six; it was the only World Series appearance of his career.

12 Associated Press, "Robinson 'Rookie of Year,'" *New York Times*, September 13, 1947: 15.

13 Associated Press.

14 Arthur Daley, "Sports of the Times," *New York Times*, October 1, 1947: 35.

15 Joseph Wancho, "Enos Slaughter," SABR Baseball Biography Project, sabr.org/bioproj/person/fd6550d9. "With the score tied at two in the top of the 11th inning, Stan Musial was on first base. Slaughter hit a Hugh Casey offering to first base, which was fielded by Jackie Robinson, who looked to second, thought better of it, and ran to first base to record the out. As Robinson turned toward the field of play to ensure that Musial did not take off for third base, Slaughter was coming hard down the line and spiked Robinson's right ankle, causing Robinson to clutch his ankle in tremendous pain. He was able to remain in the game after receiving treatment. Slaughter's action was viewed more as dirty than aggressive. Robinson was rightly upset, but commented little about the incident other than to say, 'All I know is that I had my foot on the inside of the bag. I gave Slaughter plenty of room.' Slaughter maintained that he had never spiked another player in his life. Unfortunately for Slaughter, because of this incident and rumors of a boycott against Robinson, there were racial undertones directed at him."

16 Thomas J. Brown Jr., "September 30, 1947: Yankees score 5 in 5th inning to beat Dodgers in World Series," SABR Baseball Games Project.

17 John Drebinger, "Yanks' 5 in Fifth Beat Dodgers 5-3, in Series Opener," *New York Times*, October 1, 1947: 34.

18 "Lavagetto's Walk-Off Double," YouTube, accessed March 28, 2020, youtu.be/oWjpOAy5zCM.

19 Arnold Rampersad, *Jackie Robinson* (New York: Ballantine Books, 1997), 217.

20 Mary Kay Linge, *Jackie Robinson, A Biography* (Westport, Connecticut: Greenwood Press, 2007), 79.

21 C. Paul Rogers III, "October 1, 1950: Dick Sisler's 10th-inning home run clinches Phillies' pennant on the last day of the season," SABR Baseball Games Project; Scott Ferkovich, "October 3, 1951: The Giants win the pennant!" SABR Baseball Games Project.

22 Dickson, 839: "A World Series in which the opposing clubs could travel between their home fields by using the New York City subway system."

23 Samuel G. Freedman, "2 Cities in Combat: It's in New York, Met Charm Stirs Hearts," *New York Times*, October 19, 1986: 50.

24 Rampersad, 249.

25 Franklin Lewis, "Highlights – and Low Spots," *Baseball Digest*, November 1952: 35.

26 Stew Thornley, "October 7, 1952: Billy Martin Saves the Series," SABR Baseball Games Project.

27 Arthur Daley, "Martin Made Key Play: Stengel, *Baseball Digest*, November 1952: 37.

28 Jackie Robinson from Rampersad, 259.

29 Roscoe McGowen, "Vanquished Praise Martin of Victors," *New York Times*, October 6, 1953: 36.

30 *New York Times*, October 6, 1953: 36.

31 Dickson, 918: "A Willard Mullin cartoon (*New York World-Telegram*, August 9, 1939) depicted a character in a Dodgers uniform claiming that his theme song was 'Wait 'Till Next Year: A Torch Ballad in One Flat' with words and music by The Dodgers."

32 Jackie Robinson, *I Never Had It Made* (New York: Putnam, 1972), 118.

33 Robinson, 120.

34 Weiner.

35 David Plaut, *Speaking of Baseball* (Philadelphia: Running Press, 1993), 369.

36 "1955 World Series Dodgers Win," YouTube, accessed August 15, 2019, youtu.be/1Li5QM_cxPg.

37 Robinson, 120.

38 The Dodgers set several dubious batting records for a seven-game World Series including lowest club batting average (.195) and fewest base hits (42). *New York Times*, October 11, 1956: 54.

39 Roscoe McGowen, "Brooklyn's Pilot Praises Bombers," *New York Times*, October 1, 1956: 55.

40 George F. Will, *Bunts* (New York: Scribner, 1998), 88.

41 Steven C. Weiner, "June 3, 1951: Don Newcombe strikes out 12 Cubs in Sunday opener at Ebbets Field," SABR Baseball Games Project; Steven C. Weiner, "June 3, 1951: Preacher Roe, Gene Hermanski lead Dodgers to sweep of Cubs," SABR Baseball Games Project.

JACKIE ROBINSON'S STEALS OF HOME

by Bill Nowlin

Jackie Robinson was fast on the basepaths, and he enjoyed "disruptive baserunning" as well – trying to distract the opposing pitcher any way he could. His older brother, Mack, was a sprinter who broke the Olympic record in the 200-meter race at the 1936 Olympics (but still finished behind Jesse Owens). Jack was a speedster himself – "Jackrabbit Jack" – who excelled at Southern California track events as well as broken-field running in football.[1]

Biographer Arnold Rampersad recounts a baseball game in which Jackie stole second, third, and then home for Pasadena Junior College.[2] Indeed, Rampersad cites *Pasadena Post* sportswriter Rube Samuelsen as writing that "in almost every game" he had stolen second, third, and home at least once, adding, "It's practically a habit."[3] At UCLA at least once, he was cited for a "sensational steal of home."[4]

In major-league baseball, Jackie Robinson stole home 19 times in the regular season and once in the World Series. He was caught stealing home 12 times.

He had baserunning smarts. He was a crafty baserunner. One of Robinson's more startling moves was the time on Opening Day 1955 when he intentionally allowed himself to be hit by a batted ball in a game the Dodgers were leading, 1-0. The bases were loaded with one out. Robinson had been on second base. He allowed himself to be struck by an infield grounder off the bat of Roy Campanella. That resulted, of course, in Robinson being ruled out. But it also prevented what would almost certainly have been a double play, and it left the bases still loaded, Campy on first.[5]

MINOR-LEAGUE YEAR – WITH THE MONTREAL ROYALS IN 1946

The Dodgers executive who signed Jackie Robinson, Branch Rickey, was well aware of Robinson's talent at distraction on the basepaths. During the spring of 1946, Rickey had told Robinson, "Jackie, we scouted you for a long time. So I know what you can do, and I want you to do it. I want you to run those bases like lightning. I want you to worry the daylights out of those pitchers. Don't be afraid to take a chance, to try to steal that extra base. Sure, sometimes you'll get caught but just remember this: I prefer the daring player to one who is afraid to take a chance. Just remember the best base runners get caught, even Ty Cobb. Just go out there and run like the devil."[6]

In his very first game with the Montreal Royals, on April 18, 1946, Robinson bunted for a base hit in the fifth inning, stole second base, took third on a daring play on a grounder, and then began hopping around on third base and feinting breaks for home. He drew three throws from relief pitcher Phil Oates and finally induced Oates to balk when he stopped his motion without completing the throw to the plate. It wasn't a steal of home, but Robinson scored on the balk.[7] And then he did it again in the eighth – he was balked home again for another run thanks to his distracting behavior on the basepaths.[8]

A longtime Montreal Royals rooter wrote to *The Sporting News*: "I don't think there's a smarter player in the International League. … The real trouble starts when he gets on base. Then the boys start throwing the ball around trying to get him. He seems to have the knack of sensing what the pitcher is going to do, like Cobb used to."[9]

Jackie Robinson slides to home plate in an attempt to avoid the tag during a game between the New York Giants and Brooklyn Dodgers game at Ebbets Field on May 13, 1956. Catcher is Ray Katt. Batter is Clem Labine. It was one of the times he didn't make it.

He'd been booed badly in Baltimore his first visit there but had won the fans over with his play, so much so that Carl Rowan told of a "late-season night when he stole home in a close game and the Baltimore fans gave him a thunderous standing ovation."[10]

That fall, during the Little World Series against Louisville, the Colonels won two of the first three games and then the series moved to Montreal. On October 2, the Royals were down by two runs in Game Four, but Louisville pitchers had walked the bases loaded. Louisville lefty Joe Ostrowski walked in one run. Robinson was on third and faked a couple of breaks to the plate. Seeing that the other runners were taking lengthy leads, and figuring Robinson was indeed only faking, the catcher came up firing – and threw to second base, hoping to pick off the runner there. The ball bounced into center field and Robinson took his time trotting home.[11] The game was tied, and the Royals won it in the 10th.

MAJOR-LEAGUE CAREER – WITH THE BROOKLYN DODGERS, 1947-1956

JUNE 24, 1947

Jackie Robinson's first major-league steal of home plate came in Pittsburgh on June 24, 1947. Several teams were contending for first place in the National League, and the Dodgers had just reached second place, one game behind the Boston Braves. The last-place Pirates hosted the June 24 game at Forbes Field. Each team had scored twice in the second inning and the game was a 2-2 tie heading into the fifth. With one out, the Pirates' Fritz Ostermueller walked Al Gionfriddo, but Gionfriddo was forced out at second base when Robinson grounded to the third baseman. Robinson went first to third when Carl Furillo singled to left field. On a 2-and-0 count, Furillo stole second base. On the very next pitch, Robinson stole home, beating Ostermueller's throw "by an eyelash."[12] It proved to be the winning run in a 4-2 Dodgers victory. Robinson had "streaked for the plate and made it with a long slide under Dixie Howell's tag."[13] Roscoe McGowen of the *New York Times* suggested that Ostermueller had "learned … that it is unwise to wind up with Jackie Robinson on third base."[14]

JULY 19, 1947

Robinson didn't wait long during this Saturday afternoon game at Ebbets Field. The Cardinals had scored twice in the top of the first, but the Dodgers evened the score quickly. Howie Pollet started for St. Louis. Eddie Stanky walked and Robinson doubled him to third. A foul out to the catcher was followed by Carl Furillo's fly ball to right field, Robinson tagging up and taking third while Stanky scored. After a four-pitch walk put Dixie Walker on first, with the count 2-and-1 on Pee Wee Reese, Walker and Robinson executed a double steal, Cardinals catcher Del Rice firing the ball to Red Schoendienst at second base and then Robinson just beating the "rather high" return throw from Schoendienst to the plate.[15] Robinson's run tied the game. The Cards ultimately won, 7-5.

JULY 26, 1947 – CAUGHT STEALING

At Forbes Field on July 26, Robinson hit a two-run homer his second time up against Preacher Roe. In the top of the sixth, the Dodgers still held a 3-0 lead. Robinson walked to lead off the inning. With one out, he scampered to third on Furillo's single. With Dixie Walker batting and the count 1-and-2, Furillo and Robinson tried to get another run in on a double steal. Walker lunged at the pitch and struck out. The throw went to second, but quickly back home and caught Robinson in a rundown, the play going 2-4-5-1 with Roe tagging him out.

AUGUST 29, 1947

Robinson stole home a third time in 1947. It was at home, at Ebbets Field. The fourth-place New York Giants were the visiting team. The Dodgers held a solid 7½-game lead over the pack. The score was tied 1-1 after 5½. Dave Koslo had started for the Giants, but the Dodgers got to him for two runs in the bottom of the sixth. Robinson singled to center off reliever Joe Beggs, making it 5-1. He took second on the throw to the plate, then advanced to third on Pete Reiser's fly to center field. With Furillo at the plate, Robinson stole home on the very first pitch. Three pitches later, Furillo grounded out, pitcher to first base. Brooklyn won the game, 6-3. Reiser had set the National League record for steals of home in a season, with seven in 1946. Ty Cobb has the major-league record with eight in 1912. More recently, Rod Carew also had seven, for the 1969 Twins.

In September, *Time* magazine declared of Robinson, "He dances and prances off base, keeping the enemy infield upset and off balance, and worrying the pitcher."[16]

JULY 4, 1948

As if stealing home three times in 1947 wasn't impressive enough, Robinson did it five times in 1948 and five more times in 1949. His first was on the Fourth of July, his 57th game of the season. The Giants were at Ebbets and after six innings held an 8-3 lead. With two out and nobody on in the bottom of the seventh, Reese singled and so did Robinson. Gene Hermanski doubled, scoring Reese and putting Robinson on third. Andy Hansen replaced Giants starter Ray Poat. On Poat's very first pitch, both Robinson and Hermanski took off. Robinson stole home as Hermanski broke for third. Giants catcher Walker Cooper, "alert to the fact that he couldn't nail Robinson, made a perfect throw to third base which would have gotten Gene Hermanski, on the other end of the double steal, but Sid Gordon stood still a few feet from the bag and let the ball go into left field."[17] Hermanski came around to score on Gordon's error. Robinson singled twice more in the game, scoring just the once. Reiser's two-run single in the bottom of the ninth gave the Dodgers four runs in the inning, enough to edge the Giants, 13-12.

JULY 21, 1948 (1) – CAUGHT STEALING

Robinson attempted three steals of home in a five-day stretch. The first two times, he was thrown out. At Wrigley Field in the first game of a doubleheader, the Dodgers had a comfortable 7-3 ninth-inning lead over the Cubs when Robinson tripled, driving in two runs and making in 9-3. He must have thought he had a shot at the plate. With two outs and a 1-and-1 count, he tried to steal home off Cliff Chambers. The *Brooklyn Daily Eagle* wrote, "Robinson sought to give the big crowd of 40,280 paid admissions one last thrill and attempted to steal home in the ninth inning of the nightcap, but he went skidding away from the plate and McCullough put the ball on him in transit."[18]

JULY 23, 1948 – CAUGHT STEALING

In Pittsburgh for a Friday night game at Forbes Field, Marv Rackley tripled in the top of the fifth to add a run and take a 2-0 lead over the Pirates. Robinson bunted Rackley in for their third run. With two outs, he stole second, taking third base on a throwing error by the catcher. He figured to take one more, stealing home against Mel Queen. It didn't work. He was cut down at home, "barely nipped at the plate to end the inning."[19] The Dodgers got their fourth run on a seventh-inning leadoff home run by third baseman Tommy Brown, and won the game, 4-3.

JULY 25, 1948 (1)

Still at Forbes Field, the two teams played two on Sunday. It was another game when one run made a difference. The Dodgers were down 5-3 after seven innings. They scored once and had runners on first and second when the Pirates brought in Kirby Higbe to pitch to Robinson. On a 2-and-2 count, a wild pitch saw both baserunners advance. On the next pitch, Higbe hit Robinson. Hermanski then doubled, scoring two, giving the Dodgers a 6-5 lead. Higbe threw two balls to George Shuba. Then Robinson made his move and stole home. Shuba then grounded out, but the Dodgers led, 7-5, and when the Pirates scored once more in the bottom of the ninth, it still left them short by one. It was only Robinson's fifth steal of the year, and the second one of home. This one proved to be the winning run of the game.

AUGUST 4, 1948

In the top of the first inning, the Cubs went down one-two-three. Marv Rackley tripled leading off Brooklyn's first. Robinson walked. Hermanski grounded out, Rackley scoring and Robinson taking second. On another groundout, to first base unassisted, Robinson reached third. With Reese at bat and one strike on him, Robinson stole home. "Bob Scheffing, the catcher, had the ball in plenty of time but Frank Dascoli, the plate umpire, said he didn't put the tag on the sliding runner, a decision that had the Cubs jumping and roaring around the plate until Russ Meyer, the Chicago starting pitcher, was chased out of the game."[20] Cubs manager Charlie Grimm replaced Meyer with Dutch McCall. Reese lined out to second base. The Dodgers saw the Cubs score four times, but added single runs in the seventh, eighth, and ninth and won the game.

AUGUST 22, 1948

This was a game in which the Dodgers ran freely on the basepaths, stealing eight bases against the visiting Boston Braves. Five of the thefts came in the bottom of the fifth. There had been two stolen bases, one run had come in, but there were two outs. An intentional walk to Reese loaded the bases. Billy Cox was at the plate, facing Braves starter Bill Voiselle. The Dodgers pulled off a triple steal. Robinson stole home. Hermanski stole third (his third stolen base of the game), and Reese stole second. It wasn't as though Voiselle didn't know Robinson might steal. Clif Keane of the *Boston Globe* wrote, "Voiselle faked him back to the bag a couple of times then went into a swaying motion while Robinson jumped up and down along the base path. Suddenly Jackie set sail for the plate. Voiselle completed a short windup and fired the ball high to [Bill] Salkeld. The catcher shoved his right foot across the plate while he completed catching the pitch, and it looked as though Robinson's sliding right foot had been blocked off. However, Umpire Jocko Conlan called Robinson safe, while Salkeld's gripe lasted only a few seconds."[21] A few pitches later, Cox grounded out. The Braves won the game, 4-3, on Clint Conatser's two-run homer in the top of the eighth.

SEPTEMBER 3, 1948 (2) – CAUGHT STEALING

Robinson was caught stealing home once more, on September 3. It was a home game, the second of two in a Friday doubleheader against the Giants. Brooklyn lost the first game, 7-5; Robinson was 2-for-4 with an RBI. In the first inning of the second game, he hit a one-out single off starter Andy Hansen. He took second on Hermanski's single, and then third base when Snider grounded into a 1-6 force play at second base. Snider on first, Robinson on third. He'd successfully stolen home off Hansen back on July 4. Reese was at the plate. He fouled off a couple of pitches. On the fifth pitch of the at-bat, Robinson broke for the plate. He was out.

SEPTEMBER 28, 1948

Robinson's last steal of the season was also against the Braves, the next time they came to Brooklyn. This time Robinson stole against Warren Spahn. The Dodgers had a slim 5-4 lead at midgame. In the bottom of the fifth, Robinson doubled in Eddie Miksis, who had doubled before him. Reese hit a ball deep enough to center field that Robinson was able to tag up and take third. First-pitch swinging, Reiser grounded back to the pitcher. Robinson had to hold, and Spahn threw to first base for the second out. On the first pitch to Furillo, Robinson stole home. The Braves came back with three runs in the top of the eighth, and the game went into extra innings. either team scored in the 10th, 11th, or 12th. Leading off the bottom of the 13th, Robinson homered, winning the game. It was Robinson's fifth steal of home for the season, and the 14th for the Dodgers as a team.[22]

MAY 17, 1949 – CAUGHT STEALING

The first time Robinson tried to steal home in 1949, he got caught. After seven innings, the Dodgers held a 1-0 lead over the Chicago Cubs. With two outs and Duke Snider on first, and Cubs starter Monk Dubiel still on the mound, Robinson tripled to right field. Gil Hodges came to bat. On the first pitch, Robinson raced for the plate but was "speared at the plate by an eyelash."[23] The game went into extra innings, and Robinson's fleetness of foot paid off in the top of the 11th. Leading off, he doubled to left on the first pitch to him. Hodges was up next. First-pitch bunting, he hit the ball back to the pitcher, while Robinson scored all the way from second base on the throw to first base to retire Hodges. Brooklyn scored six runs in the inning, holding off the Cubs, who scored three.

JUNE 2, 1949

"Robinson made his first steal of home in the sixth to the extreme mortification of Harry, the Cat." So wrote Burr in the *Brooklyn Daily Eagle*.[24] The Cardinals were in from St. Louis. They took a 1-0 lead in the first inning. Robinson led off the bottom of the second and reached on an error by Cardinals third baseman Eddie Kazak. Harry "The Cat" Brecheen was pitching for St. Louis, with Joe Garagiola catching. Robinson stole second. Gil Hodges popped up to third and Snider struck out, but Roy Campanella singled to center and Robinson scored. It was 3-1, Dodgers, in the sixth. Robinson led off with a single to left. Hodges sacrificed him to second. He took third on Snider's groundout to first, unassisted. Campanella took the first two pitches for balls. On the third pitch, Robinson stole home, making it 4-1. The Cards scored three runs in the top of the ninth off Dodgers starter Don Newcombe, tying the game, took it into extra innings, and won in the 14th inning, 7-4.

JULY 16, 1949

Cincinnati was visiting Brooklyn. The Reds scored once in the top of the second on catcher Walker Cooper's home run. In the bottom of the second, Robinson led off and drew a walk. Hodges singled to right, and Robinson took third. After a strikeout, Hodges stole second base. Billy Cox drew a walk, loading the bases. Roy Campanella was up. Strike one. On the next pitch, the three baserunners pulled off a triple steal. Robinson scored, tying the game. It was the only run they got that inning. A photograph in the *Brooklyn Daily Eagle* shows Robinson sliding across the plate with catcher Cooper having to bend over to his left to catch the ball, a couple of feet from the plate.[25] Robinson scored three runs in the game, one on a 10th-inning solo home run, but Cooper had hit another homer (a two-run homer) in the top of the 10th, and the Reds won the game, 7-6.

JULY 18, 1949

The Cubs came to town and played a Monday game. Robinson stole home again. Joe Hatten shut out the Cubs with a five-hit complete game. The only run the Dodgers turned out to need was provided by a Gil Hodges fly ball in the first. But insurance runs are always important. In the sixth, Robinson led off with a base on balls off Cubs starter Bob Rush. "If there is anything rival moundsmen dread, it is having Jackie on first," wrote the *New York Times*'s Effrat. "Rush was no exception. Obviously upset, the right-hander could not prevent Robinson's steal of second, even with a pitchout. And when [catcher] Mickey Owen's throw was wild, Jackie continued to third."[26] Burr of the *Daily Eagle* talked about how the "Ebony Eagle … kept dancing off the bag until Rush just let him go" – at which point Owen's throw "skidded into center field."[27] The next batter grounded out short to first, but Robinson was unable to run home. With Furillo at the plate, on a 1-and-1 count, Robinson "twice … went dashing down the line toward the plate, and on the third start he kept going."[28] He stole home and made it 2-0, Dodgers. He slid across the plate "unnecessarily as Rush's throw went over Owen's – and Robinson's – head."[29] Brooklyn added a third run in the bottom of the eighth when Robinson tripled in Gene Hermanski.

AUGUST 9, 1949

Carl Erskine held the Phillies to three hits in an 8-1 win for the Dodgers at Shibe Park. Jackie Robinson's first-inning sacrifice fly brought in the first Dodgers run. Campanella doubled in the second run, in the second inning. After four innings, it was 5-0 and Phillies starter Robin Roberts was gone. In the top of the fifth, Robinson tripled with two outs. Hermanski walked, and then two executed a double steal. "Robinson came in standing up and turned his left ankle slightly" but stayed in the game.[30] His steal of home was the first of three runs scored before the inning was done.

AUGUST 14, 1949 – CAUGHT STEALING

Five days later, the Dodgers were back home and hosting the Boston Braves. It was 3-1, Brooklyn, after 4½. Johnny Sain was pitching for the Braves. Robinson singled to right field, then wasted no time in stealing second on the first pitch to Hermanski. The catcher's throw went astray, so he scampered on to third base. Hermanski hit a foul popup to third base. Hodges was hit by Sain's pitch. There were runners on first and third. On a 1-and-0 pitch to Billy Cox, Robinson tried to steal home. The throw went 2-4-2 (Del Crandall to Eddie Stanky to Crandall), and Robinson was out at the plate.[31] The game ended a 7-2 win for the Dodgers.

SEPTEMBER 20, 1949

Brooklyn was in second place, just 1½ games behind the St. Louis Cardinals. They were playing a Tuesday afternoon game at Wrigley Field. The Dodgers scored three runs in the top of the sixth. In the eighth, with Brooklyn's Jack Banta working on what became a five-hit shutout, they added two final runs. Bob Muncrief was pitching in relief. With one out, Furillo singled to left and Robinson singled to center, sending Furillo to third. Hodges grounded out, pitcher to first base, while Robinson ran all the way from first to third on the play. On a 1-and-1 count, Robinson stole home. The throw appeared to be a bit off, judging from the photograph in the September 21 *New York Times*. Catcher Mickey Owen thought he got Robinson, though, and "pushed the umpire [Art Gore] so violently that Gore went down. [Manager Frankie] Frisch joined in the turbulent scene around the plate and he, too, was chased."[32] Gore was off-balance "and it took only a slight body contact to bowl him over."[33] Nonetheless, he went down. Bob Scheffing replaced Mickey Owen as catcher. Robinson's steal was the final run in the game; the Dodgers won, 5-0. It was, matching his 1948 total, his fifth steal of home on the season. His 37 stolen bases led the majors in 1949, but the 16 times he was caught stealing led the National League.

A NOTE FROM THE 1949 WORLD SERIES

Yankees pitcher Vic Raschi lost Game Two to the Dodgers, 1-0. Robinson doubled, leading off the top of the second. He tagged up and took third on a foul popup. After one more out, Gil Hodges singled to score Robinson with what proved to be the lone run of the game. Raschi attributed a lack of concentration to being distracted by Robinson on third: "I was pitching more to Robinson than I was to Hodges and as a result I threw one up into Gil's power and he got the base hit that beat me."[34] The Yankees nonetheless won the Series.

JUNE 19, 1950 (1) – CAUGHT STEALING

Robinson scored the first run of the game on Furillo's second-inning homer. By the end of the second, the Dodgers held a 5-0 lead over the Giants. It was 8-4 after 5½. After Kirby Higbe struck out both Duke Snider and Gene Hermanski, Robinson hit an infield single to the first baseman. Then he tried to steal himself a run. He began by stealing second and taking third on the catcher's throwing error. Furillo was batting, with a 2-and-1 count, and Robinson broke for home. "He got a good jump and almost made it," declared the *Daily Eagle*, "But Kirby Higbe, the pitcher of the moment, got the ball in fast, low and over the plate., in perfect position for Wally [sic] Westrum to make the tag."[35] He was erased at the plate.

JULY 2, 1950

The Phillies hosted a Sunday doubleheader on July 2, the Phils' Russ Meyer against Ralph Branca in the first game. Hermanski hit a solo homer off Meyer in the first, but the Phillies had scored four runs after their first three innings. In the top of the fourth, Robinson led off with a double. Furillo grounded out, second to first, and Robinson took third. After Campanella lined out to third, he watched Meyer throw three pitches to Gil Hodges, then took off for home on the fourth pitch. He was safe, the second time he'd stolen home off Meyer.[36] Though the Dodgers tied it up in the sixth, Bill Nicholson's two-run homer in the eighth won the game, 6-4. The second game ran for 10 innings and ended in an 8-8 tie due to a Sunday curfew. Robinson stole only 12 bases in 1950, less than a third of the total he had stolen in 1949.

MAY 2, 1951 – CAUGHT STEALING

Pete Castiglione of the Pirates hit the first pitch of the game for a home run off Don Newcombe. The Dodgers went down one-two-three in the first. Murry Dickson was pitching for Pittsburgh. Robinson led off the bottom of the second, beating out a single to third base. With one out, Campanella grounded a single into right field, and Robinson ran first to third. On a 3-and-1 strike to Pee Wee Reese, Robinson tried to steal home on what might have looked like a double steal. Campy, though, was just trying to draw a throw to second, so that Robinson could make it home. Pirates catcher Clyde McCullough fired the ball to second baseman Monty Basgall, who promptly returned the throw, wanting to cut down the run at the plate more than to secure an out at second. His alertness worked and Robinson was out. His hand looks to have been about six inches from reaching the plate when McCullough placed the tag on him.[37] Campanella was not credited with a steal of second but advanced there on the throw back to the plate. The Pirates won, 4-3. Had the call been closer, there might have been a ready excuse for a quick ejection of Robinson. At the time, he was not in good graces with the umpiring staff.[38]

SEPTEMBER 26, 1951

The Dodgers embarrassed the Boston Braves with a 15-5 beatdown at Braves Field, Don Newcombe extending his season mark to 19-9. When it came to the top of the eighth, Robinson had scored twice and his two-run single made the score 12-3, Dodgers. Then Campanella singled off incoming relief pitcher Lew Burdette, putting Brooklyn baserunners on first and third with one out. With Andy Pafko at the plate, Robinson stole home, just barely beating the throw to catcher Ebba St. Claire, who was unable to hold onto the ball. Wayne Terwilliger took Robinson's place in the field when the Braves came to bat. Braves manager Tommy Holmes didn't mention Robinson in particular but griped that the Dodgers were trying to rub it in by running up the score. Robinson himself said, "I was playing baseball. I had a chance to steal home and I did. I've tried to steal home a couple of other times this year and failed. I may have a new way. Anyway, today, I kept going down and down, and before I knew it, I was home."[39]

MAY 18, 1952

Brooklyn trailed 1-0, Preacher Roe pitching against the visiting Cubs, as the Dodgers came up to bat in the bottom of the fourth. A leadoff walk, a single, and Robinson being hit by a pitch loaded the bases with nobody out. Willie Ramsdell walked Pafko, forcing in a run. A Gil Hodges grounder to shortstop resulted in a force out at second, but a run scored and Robinson took third base. Dick Williams grounded out, third to first, Robinson holding at third but Hodges taking second. Rube Walker was walked intentionally. On 3-and-1 pitch to Preacher Roe, Robinson and Hodges pulled off a double steal, while Walker stayed put on first base. A dramatic photograph in the *New York Times* shows Robinson's cap flying off as his right foot reaches the plate just under catcher John Pramesa's glove.[40] On the next pitch, Roe singled, boosting the score to 4-1. Walker hit a two-run homer later in the game, and Roe drove in another run. Brooklyn won, 7-2.

JULY 16, 1953 – CAUGHT STEALING

The only year in which Robinson failed to steal home at least once was 1953. He tried it only once; it was the second time he tried to steal against Cliff Chambers. Both times he was unsuccessful. It was Gil Hodges's first-inning grand slam that deservedly earned all the headlines. The Dodgers held a 7-1 lead after six innings, then saw the Cardinals score once in the top of the seventh. Chambers was the fourth Cardinals pitcher, brought in to pitch the bottom of the seventh inning. He got Reese and Snider for the first two outs, keeping the ball in the infield. Robinson lined a triple to right field. Hodges was hitting, with the count 0-and-1, when Robinson tried in vain to steal the plate. He had stolen second base in the fifth inning, one of five steals the Dodgers made in the course of the game. He was 17-for-21 in stolen base attempts in 1953.

APRIL 23, 1954

In 1954 Robinson attempted only 10 steals all season long. He succeeded seven times. Three of those seven came in this one game. They were his first steals of the year. It was a Friday night game at Forbes Field, Pittsburgh. It was Dodgers 2, Pirates 1 after five innings. The top of the sixth began with a groundout and then a walk to Robinson, followed by two more walks. A popup to the third baseman was the second out. On a 2-and-0 count, all three baserunners stole the base ahead of them, Robinson stealing home on pitcher Bob Friend. In the top of the ninth, it was Dodgers 5, Pirates 4. Robinson singled, then stole second, and then stole third on the very next pitch. No Dodger scored, and the Pirates tied it in the bottom of the ninth. In the top of the 13th, Robinson drove in the decisive run when he doubled in Jim Gilliam. The Pirates were unable to score and thus lost the game. Afterward, Pee Wee Reese marveled, "Look at that Robinson. Tape in his knees, on his feet, on his elbows." To Robinson, he said, "You'd probably fall apart if it weren't for that tape." "'But I'm playing, Mr. Captain,' Jackie grinned back. 'I'm playing." He added, "Pellagrini came in to hold me on, then he went back. When he did, I got the extra two yards. That's all I needed."[41]

JUNE 17, 1954 – CAUGHT STEALING

Robinson's only other attempt to steal home in 1954 came against the Milwaukee Braves in Brooklyn on June 17. It came early in the game, in the bottom of the second inning, the Braves up 1-0. He was caught easily, still standing up, by catcher Del Crandall, ending the inning. A photograph in the next day's *New York Times* shows the moment.[42] Robinson was 4-for-4, every hit an extra-base hit. He later hit two solo home runs and a second double in the game, but the Braves prevailed, 6-4.

AUGUST 28, 1955 – CAUGHT STEALING

It was more than 14 months later before Robinson tried to steal home again. In the bottom of the second of a scoreless game against the visiting Cardinals, he hit an infield single to third base. The Cardinals' Larry Jackson picked him off first base – but the throw went wild, and Robinson ran all the way to third base. Perhaps feeling he had built up a head of steam, he tried to steal home on the very next pitch, but fell short. The Dodgers won the game, though, 6-1.

AUGUST 29, 1955

The very next day, the same two teams faced off in a Monday afternoon game. The Dodgers led, 2-1, entering the bottom of the sixth. Furillo singled in one run. Sandy Amoros drew a bases-loaded walk to drive in another. Robinson advanced to third base on the walk to Amoros. Reliever Paul LaPalme was brought in, and he might have been close to walking Johnny Podres. On a 3-and-1 count, Robinson stole home, Gil Hodges stole third, and Amoros stole second. Hodges tried to keep coming but was tagged out when the shortstop returned the catcher's throw. Inning over, but the score was 5-1, Dodgers. They won, 10-4.

SEPTEMBER 28, 1955 – WORLD SERIES

Jackie Robinson stole six bases in World Series play. In his very first Series, in 1947, he stole second base in Game One and also in Game Three. In the 1952 World Series, he stole second base in Game Three and third base in Game Five. He stole third base in Game Six of the 1953 Series. His only other stolen base was in Game One of the 1955 Series, on September 28. He was up against a Hall of Fame battery – Whitey Ford on the Yankee Stadium mound and Yogi Berra behind the plate. Robinson had tripled and scored his first time up, in the second inning. After seven innings, though, the Yankees held a 6-3 lead. (Interestingly, the Yankees' Billy Martin had been thrown out trying to steal home in the sixth inning.) In the top of the eighth, with one out and a runner on first, Robinson reached on an error, taking second base on the play. A sacrifice fly scored Furillo from third and was deep enough for

Robinson to tag up and take third. The score now 6-4, he decided to try to give the Dodgers another run. With pinch-hitter Frank Kellert at the plate, he stole home. Kellert then singled, but that was no means guaranteed, and, besides, a steal of home is tremendously exciting. It was the last run scored in the game and the final score stood Yankees 6, Dodgers 5.

Both Robinson and manager Walter Alston agreed that Robinson had stolen on his own account. "It's easier to get one run than two," Robinson said, "and when they give me the run, I'm certainly going to take it. The only ridiculous thing about that play was the Yankees' squawking about me being called safe. There wasn't any question about it. I was over the plate before Berra got the ball on me."[43] Berra disagreed, and "protested vehemently."[44] He certainly bumped umpire Bill Summers in the process of protest, but Summers wisely refrained from any reprimand.

The Associated Press quoted Ford: "He didn't catch me by surprise at all. I had my eye on him from the start. Frankly, I didn't think he'd try it, with his team two runs behind. But once he started I took my time and threw a low fast one in what I thought was plenty of time. I think we got him."[45] Berra said he had gone out to the mound and warned Ford of the possibility of an attempted steal, with Robinson on third, but "I reminded him Brooklyn was two runs behind and I said I didn't think Robinson would try to steal home. … Sure, we were surprised. It was a dumb play with his team two runs behind, but it worked and so it was a good one."[46]

Plate umpire Summers called Robinson safe. A sequence of photos in the *Los Angeles Times* gives the impression the ball might have been there in time. "I was safe," Robinson said. "No doubt in my mind at all. I could see the plate when I slid in. Yogi was back of the plate. I suppose Yogi figured he had me or he wouldn't have raised such a fuss. In my opinion it wasn't close. Probably in Yogi's it was."[47] Berra never changed his mind; there was, of course, no replay in those days, but to the end of his days Berra believed that Robinson had been tagged out. The historical record shows a successful steal of home, but the play could not have been much closer.[48]

In Game Three, with the score tied 2-2 in the bottom of the second, Yankees pitcher Bob Turley got one out, then Robinson singled. He danced around so much on first base faking moves to second and was said to have flustered Turley so much that Turley's pitch hit Sandy Amoros. Johnny Podres beat out a bunt, loading the bases and advancing Robinson to third. Junior Gilliam was up and took three balls as Robinson kept dancing off third. "The more Robinson danced, the more irritated Turley became. He threw four straight balls to Gilliam, forcing in a run. … A creaking old man [Jackie Robinson] had danced [Yankees manager Casey Stengel's] pitcher out of the game."[49]

APRIL 25, 1956

In the seventh game of the young season, Jackie Robinson stole home for the 19th time. The game was at the Polo Grounds, against the New York Giants. Carl Erskine pitched a 7-2 complete game for the Dodgers. Robinson produced the first run on the game, doubling in the second inning and then moving to third base on a groundout. It was a straight steal of home off pitcher Jim Hearn and catcher Wes Westrum. Once more, a photograph captured the moment of Robinson "up to his old tricks."[50]

MAY 13, 1956 – CAUGHT STEALING

In his 20th game of 1956, Robinson tried one more time. Hoyt Wilhelm was pitching for the Giants. The Dodgers had a 6-4 lead in the bottom of the eighth inning. With one out, Robinson singled. Sandy Amoros doubled. Carl Furillo was intentionally walked, loading the bases. The three tried a triple steal, and two of them succeeded, but the lead man – Robinson – was tagged out at the plate. The *New York Times*'s photo caption said it had been an attempted squeeze. Two pitches later, Clem Labine struck out. The Dodgers won the game by the 6-4 score.

NOTES

1   One instance is recounted in Carl Rowan with Jackie Robinson, *Wait Till Next Year* (New York: Random House, 1960), 40, 41.

2   Arnold Rampersad, *Jackie Robinson: A Biography* (New York: Ballantine Books, 1997), 42.

3   Rube Samuelsen, *Pasadena Post*, July 10, 1937. See Rampersad, 44. Carl Rowan writes that Robinson stole 25 bases in 24 games; see also Rowan with Robinson, *Wait Till Next Year*, 39.

4   *California Daily Bruin*, March 11, 1940. See Rampersad, 74.

5   See "Robinson Can Still Do It All," *New York Post*, April 14, 1955.

6   Rowan with Robinson, *Wait Till Next Year*, 149-150.

7   Rowan with Robinson, *Wait Till Next Year*, 153-4.

8   "30,000 See Robinson Sparkle in Montreal Debut," *Baltimore Afro-American*, April 20, 1946: 29.

9   "Vet, Analyzing Robinson, Asserts Jackie Can't Miss," *The Sporting News*, September 11, 1946: 4. Ty Cobb holds the major-league record for career steals of home, with 54 successful steals (1905-28).

10 Rowan with Robinson, *Wait Till Next Year*, 163. See also Jackie Robinson, *I Never Had It Made* (New York: Ecco, 1994), 49.

11. Rowan with Robinson, *Wait Till Next Year*, 8, 9.
12. United Press, "Dodgers Cop 4-2 Victory from Bucs," *Daily Notes* (Canonsburg, Pennsylvania), June 25, 1947: 8.
13. Harold C. Burr, "Speed on Basepaths Gives Dodgers Well-Earned Verdict Over Bucs," *Brooklyn Daily Eagle*, June 25, 1947: 15.
14. Roscoe McGowen, "Robinson Steals Home in First with Third Tally Before 35,331 at Pittsburgh," *New York Times*, June 25, 1947: 33.
15. Roscoe McGowen, "14 Hits Trip Brooks," *New York Times*, July 20, 1947: S1.
16. *Time*, September 22, 1947.
17. Roscoe McGowen, "Dodgers Count Four Times in 9th to Overcome Giants; 37 Players in Action," *New York Times*, July 5, 1948: 10.
18. Harold C. Burr, "Dodger Flag Chase Sets League Ablaze," *Brooklyn Daily Eagle*, July 22, 1948: 17.
19. Roscoe McGowen, "Brooks Turn Back Pirates by 4 to 3," *New York Times*, July 24, 1948: 10.
20. Tommy Holmes, "Dodgers Enjoy Fruits of Victory," *Brooklyn Daily Eagle*, August 5, 1948: 16. Edward Burns of the *Chicago Tribune* characterized the Cubs' reaction as "hysterical protests of [Dascoli's] decision." See Edward Burns, "Cubs Lose to Dodgers in 9th, 5 to 4," *Chicago Tribune*, August 5, 1948: B3. The *New York Times* account said the argument lasted 10 minutes. See Louis Effrat, "Dodgers Set Back Cubs by 5 to 4 on Single by Edwards in the Ninth," *New York Times*, August 5, 1948: 26.
21. Clif Keane, "Conatser Homer Beats Dodgers, 4-3; Bums Steal 8 Bases, 5 in 5th," *Boston Globe*, August 23, 1948: 1.
22. Roscoe McGowen, "Brooks Overcome Flag Winners, 9-8," *New York Times*, September 29, 1948: 39.
23. Edward Burns, "Cubs Lose 8-5, in 11th; Boston Beats Sox, 4-3," *Chicago Tribune*, May 18, 1949: B1.
24. Harold C. Burr, "Musial Murder Inc. to Dodger Hurlers," *Brooklyn Daily Eagle*, June 3, 1949: 16.
25. See the *Brooklyn Daily Eagle*, July 17, 1949: 22.
26. Louis Effrat, "Hatten of Dodgers Blanks Cubs Before 25,595," *New York Times*, July 19, 1949: 12.
27. Harold C. Burr, "Robinson's Prancing on Bases Ruins Cubs," *Brooklyn Daily Eagle*, July 19, 1949: 13.
28. Burr, "Robinson's Prancing on Bases Ruins Cubs."
29. Effrat, "Hatten of Dodgers Blanks Cubs Before 25,595."
30. Roscoe McGowen, "Erskine of Brooks Scores 8-1 Victory," *New York Times*, August 10, 1949: 28.
31. On page 21 of the August 15, 1949, edition of the *New York Times*, there is a photograph of Robinson being tagged out at the plate.
32. Roscoe McGowen, "Banta Downs Cubs with 5-Hitter, 5-0," *New York Times*, August 21, 1949: 42.
33. "Robinson's Steal Starts Rhubarb," *Brooklyn Daily Eagle*, September 21, 1949: 25.
34. Donald Honig, *Baseball Between the Lines* (New York: Coward, McCann & Geoghegan, 1976), 173.
35. Tommy Holmes, "Happy Dodger Days Here Again!" *Brooklyn Daily Eagle*, June 20, 1950: 13.
36. On page A3 of the July 3, 1950, *Chicago Tribune*, one can see a photograph of Robinson sliding in with plenty of room to spare.
37. See photograph on page 37 of the May 3, 1951, *New York Times*.
38. Harold C. Burr, "Frick, O'Malley Clash on Robby's Conduct," *Brooklyn Daily Eagle*, May 3, 1951: 22.
39. Hy Hurwitz, "Holmes Charges Dodgers 'Rubbed It In,'" *Boston Globe*, September 27, 1951: 6. A photograph accompanying the article shows the action.
40. "The Count was 3 and 1, The Bases Were Loaded – And Jackie Stole Home," *New York Times*, May 19, 1952: 21.
41. Dave Anderson, "'Infielder' Robinson One-Man Hurricane," *Brooklyn Daily Eagle*, April 24, 1954: 8. He added that he didn't try to steal home in the ninth because he couldn't get as good a jump off left-handed reliever Joe Page.
42. See page 28 with the lead caption, "It Doesn't Pay to Steal."
43. Roscoe McGowen, "Brooks Disappointed, Not Discouraged by Defeat and Showing of Newcombe," *New York Times*, September 29, 1955: 40.
44. John Drebinger, "Yankees Win First," *New York Times*, September 29, 1955: 1.
45. Associated Press, "Jackie Certain He Was Safe at Home," *Los Angeles Times*, September 29, 1955: C1.
46. "Berra Takes Blame for Steal," *Boston Globe*, September 9, 1955: 14.
47. "Berra Takes Blame for Steal."
48. Summers was in the proper position for the pitch, but not in an ideal one to make a call. Had there been multiple cameras recording the moment, one could not predict an ultimate ruling. See the steal, and some other Game One highlights at: youtube.com/watch?v=k4EUXTbbsAg.
49. Rowan with Robinson, *Wait Till Next Year*, 271.
50. The photograph accompanies John Drebinger's article on page 40 of the April 26, 1956, *New York Times*.

ANALYZING JACKIE ROBINSON AS A SECOND BASEMAN

by Mike Huber

Second base. It might not have the pizzazz of shortstop. It also might not have the glamour of third base, which is known as the "hot corner." Fans don't normally expect the same power numbers from a second baseman that they see in others who play the infield, like the stereotypical slugger who plays first base. And yet second base is called the keystone position.

Over the past century many second sackers have put up great offensive numbers. Twenty second basemen are enshrined in the National Baseball Hall of Fame.[1] In an attempt to determine the greatest-ever offensive force from a second baseman, let's list these Hall of Famers in approximately the chronological order in which they appeared in the major leagues. They all have played second base for most, if not all, of their careers. With the exception of Jackie Robinson, who was not permitted to play in the big leagues until he was 28 years old, and Joe Gordon, who missed two seasons during World War II, all the players listed had relatively long careers.[2]

Player	From	To	G	HR	RBI	BA	OBP	SLG	OPS	WAR
Bid McPhee	1882	1899	2138	53	1072	0.272	0.355	0.373	0.728	52.5
Nap Lajoie	1896	1916	2480	82	1599	0.338	0.380	0.466	0.846	107.3
Johnny Evers	1902	1929	1784	12	536	0.270	0.356	0.334	0.690	47.7
Eddie Collins	1906	1930	2826	47	1299	0.333	0.424	0.429	0.853	123.9
Rogers Hornsby	1915	1937	2259	301	1584	0.358	0.434	0.577	1.010	127.1
Frankie Frisch	1919	1937	2311	105	1244	0.316	0.369	0.432	0.801	70.8
Charlie Gehringer	1924	1942	2323	184	1427	0.320	0.404	0.480	0.884	83.8
Tony Lazzeri	1926	1939	1740	178	1194	0.292	0.380	0.467	0.846	47.3
Billy Herman	1931	1947	1922	47	839	0.304	0.367	0.407	0.774	56.0
Bobby Doerr	1937	1951	1865	223	1247	0.288	0.362	0.461	0.823	51.1
Joe Gordon	1938	1950	1566	253	975	0.268	0.357	0.466	0.822	55.7
Red Schoendienst	1945	1963	2216	84	773	0.289	0.337	0.387	0.724	44.2
Jackie Robinson	1947	1956	1382	137	734	0.311	0.409	0.474	0.883	61.7
Nellie Fox	1947	1965	2367	35	790	0.288	0.348	0.363	0.710	49.5
Bill Mazeroski	1956	1972	2163	138	853	0.260	0.299	0.367	0.667	36.5
Joe Morgan	1963	1984	2649	268	1133	0.271	0.392	0.427	0.819	100.5
Ryne Sandberg	1981	1997	2164	282	1061	0.285	0.344	0.452	0.795	68.0
Roberto Alomar	1988	2004	2379	210	1134	0.300	0.371	0.443	0.814	67.0
Craig Biggio	1988	2007	2850	291	1175	0.281	0.363	0.433	0.796	65.5

From this chart we can see that Robinson did indeed have the fewest number of games played. While Rogers Hornsby might be acknowledged as the greatest offensive second baseman to play the game, given that his Wins Above Replacement (WAR) value is higher than the others, we should recognize that it is difficult to compare players from different eras, especially given that some did not play in all of their potentially prime years.

That leads to the question: Who was the greatest second baseman of the late 1940s to mid-1950s, when Jackie Robinson played?

Jack Roosevelt Robinson debuted for the Brooklyn Dodgers on April 15, 1947, and he was immediately an everyday player. An everyday player who played first base. What?!?

Robinson had played second base for the Kansas City Monarchs as part of the Negro Leagues. In 1945, he batted .414 for the Monarchs. Signed by Branch Rickey, Robinson joined the Montreal Royals, the top farm team in the Brooklyn organization, in 1946. That season he led the International League by batting .349 and stealing 40 bases, all the while playing second base. When Robinson was called up to the Dodgers, he did not disappoint, leading the National League in 1947 with 29 stolen bases while posting a solid .297 batting average. The Brooklyn first baseman earned Rookie of the Year honors, winning the award over New York Giants pitcher Larry Jansen and Yankees hurler Spec Shea.

The 1946 Dodgers had featured a solid leadoff batter in Eddie Stanky. The 31-year-old Stanky led the National League in both 1945 and 1946 in walks, with 148 and 137, respectively. Combined with his .273 batting average in 1946, he had the knack of getting aboard and scoring runs. His on-base percentage was tops in the league that year (.436), so manager Burt Shotton penciled in Stanky to lead off in 1947 as well, in order for him to get on base and be moved along by the strong-hitting Robinson and perhaps driven in by Bruce Edwards, Carl Furillo, or Dixie Walker, all of whom had at least 80 RBIs in that season.

Jackie

Since Stanky was a fixture at second base, Robinson played first. However, in 1948, Stanky was dealt to the Boston Braves during spring training. This meant that Robinson slid over to second base for the 1948 campaign, and over the course of his next nine seasons, Robinson played 748 games (starting 740 of them) at second base. More on this later.

Jackie Robinson, of course, was the first Black ballplayer to play major-league baseball in the twentieth century. No one knows what numbers Robinson would have put up had he been allowed to begin playing baseball at the age of 21 or so, like so many of the others now enshrined in Cooperstown. More than likely, though, his professional baseball career would have been affected by the war.

From our table above, we see that Robinson is one of five Hall of Fame second basemen who played during the mid-1940s to mid-1950s. Let's trim the table to focus on Robinson's playing era.

Using the WAR statistic, which is a nonstandardized measure that attempts to indicate how many more wins a player would provide for his team in lieu of a replacement player, we can compare the best players who played second base during Robinson's time in the majors.

While there is no clear-cut or consistent formula to compute the WAR number, there is some sense of uniformity. Some websites calculate the statistic differently. Using baseball-reference.com/leaders/, second baseman Rogers Hornsby ranks 12th in the all-time list with a WAR of 127.1. To put this number in perspective, the leader in this category is Babe Ruth with a WAR of 182.5. Robinson's career WAR value (61.7) ranks 169th all-time.

Back to our era, which took place after World War II. How do Jackie Robinson, Bobby Doerr, Joe Gordon, Red Schoendienst, and Nellie Fox stack up against one another? Can we go beyond using WAR for comparison? For the sake of comparison, Billy Herman is not included, since he ended his career the season before Robinson started at second base. Likewise, Bill Mazeroski is not included, as he was a rookie in Robinson's final playing season.

According to baseball-reference.com/leaders/WAR_career.shtml, WAR has a scale for a single season: 8+ indicates MVP quality, 5+ indicates All-Star quality, 2+ indicates a starter, and 0-2 indicates a reserve. Any number less than 0 indicates a replacement player. Further, WAR can be calculated as a total player number (offense and defense) or separately for offense and defense.

If we search for all second basemen[3] who played from 1948 through 1956 who had an Offensive WAR (oWAR) of at least 4.0 (not quite All-Star quality), we obtain the following table (bold entries designate league leaders):

Rk	Player	oWAR	Year	Tm	G	H	HR	RBI	BA	OBP	SLG	OPS
1	Jackie Robinson	8.3	1949	BRO	156	203	16	124	0.342	0.432	0.528	0.960
2	Jackie Robinson	8.1	1951	BRO	153	185	19	88	0.338	0.429	0.527	0.957
3	Jackie Robinson	7.8	1952	BRO	149	157	19	75	0.308	0.440	0.465	0.904
4	Eddie Stanky	6.9	1950	NYG	152	158	8	51	0.300	0.460	0.412	0.872
5	Bobby Avila	6.7	1954	CLE	143	189	15	67	0.341	0.402	0.477	0.880
6	Jackie Robinson	6.5	1950	BRO	144	170	14	81	0.328	0.423	0.500	0.923
7	Red Schoendienst	6.1	1953	STL	146	193	15	79	0.342	0.405	0.502	0.907
8	Bobby Avila	5.3	1952	CLE	150	179	7	45	0.300	0.371	0.415	0.787
9	Eddie Stanky	5	1949	BSN	138	144	1	42	0.285	0.417	0.358	0.775
10	Joe Gordon	4.8	1948	CLE	144	154	32	124	0.280	0.371	0.507	0.879
11	Jackie Robinson	4.8	1948	BRO	147	170	12	85	0.296	0.367	0.453	0.820
12	Eddie Stanky	4.7	1951	NYG	145	127	14	43	0.247	0.401	0.369	0.770
13	Cass Michaels	4.7	1949	CHW	154	173	6	83	0.308	0.417	0.421	0.837
14	Red Schoendienst	4.6	1952	STL	152	188	7	67	0.303	0.347	0.424	0.772
15	Bobby Doerr	4.4	1948	BOS	140	150	27	111	0.285	0.386	0.505	0.891
16	Bobby Doerr	4.3	1949	BOS	139	167	18	109	0.309	0.393	0.497	0.890
17	Jerry Priddy	4.3	1948	SLB	151	166	8	79	0.296	0.391	0.443	0.834
18	Bobby Avila	4.2	1951	CLE	141	165	10	58	0.304	0.374	0.410	0.783
19	Jim Gilliam	4.1	1956	BRO	153	178	6	43	0.300	0.399	0.396	0.794
20	Nellie Fox	4.1	1954	CHW	155	201	2	47	0.319	0.372	0.391	0.763
21	Nellie Fox	4.1	1951	CHW	147	189	4	55	0.313	0.372	0.425	0.798

Robinson is clearly the offensive leader. He put up six consecutive seasons in the top 10 list in oWAR during his career, from 1948 through 1953 (although he played only nine games at second base in 1953), and five of those times put him into the top 11 spots during this period. His 1952 oWAR mark of 7.8 led all major leaguers, not just second basemen, but as can be seen, it was only his third-best seasonal performance. He owns the top three spots in this table for all second basemen with his 1949, 1951, and 1952 performance, and he has four of the top five oWAR numbers. This also confirms Baseball-Reference's ratings, as Robinson was the 1949 National League Most Valuable Player.

In his 1949 MVP season, Robinson led all National League batters with a .342 batting average. His 37 stolen bases led every player in the majors (as did the 16 times he was caught stealing).[4] He had 17 sacrifice hits to pace the NL. His on-base percentage in 1952 (.440) was tops in the majors, justifying his replacement of Stanky in the lineup. By 1952, Robinson was batting in either the third or fourth position in the batting order. Robinson had six seasons in the top 10 in the National League Adjusted Batting Wins (consecutively, from 1949 to 1954). In three of those seasons, he placed in the top 10 of all major leaguers (1949, 1951, and 1952). Recall that Adjusted Batting Wins refers to a "set of formulas developed by Gary Gillette, Pete Palmer, and others that estimates a player's total contributions to a team's wins with his bat."5 A value of 0 is an average performance, less than 0 is worse than average, and greater than 0 is better than average.

We see that many of the top-21 players in oWAR in the table above are indeed Hall of Famers, but none reached Robinson's level.

DEFENSE

Robinson was a definite force with a bat, and once he got on base, he was a threat to score. What about his defense? Throughout baseball history, two qualities seem to have defined excellence at second-base defense: avoidance of errors and participation in double plays. Robinson's plaque in Cooperstown claims that he "led second basemen in double plays four times."6 However, some of the more recent measures seem to converge to a single point of agreement: The number of assists per game by a second baseman is of utmost importance in determining fielding skill. These numbers can be inflated in light of such matters as the first baseman's range and the propensity of the pitching staff to induce groundballs.

In comparing offensive statistics of all second basemen in both the American League and National League from 1948 through 1956, we make some discoveries. First, Robinson did not start playing second base for the Dodgers until his second season (1948), when he played 116 games at second and 30 games back at first. (He also played six games at third base.) He then played all of his games from 1949 through 1952 at the keystone position (596 games). In 1953 the 34-year-old added the outfield to his repertoire (76 total games). In fact, after 1952, Jackie played only 36 games at second (in five seasons). As a result, in 10 seasons in the National League, Robinson played 748 games (with 740 starts) at second, which comes to 55.24 percent. Amazingly, he started in all but 10 of his 1,354 total games over that 10-season stretch.

Robinson was a six-time All-Star, and he received votes for the league's Most Valuable Player award in all but two seasons, claiming the honor in 1949. In 1953 he was voted in as a reserve All-Star outfielder and appeared as a pinch-hitter. The next season, he was the starting left fielder in the senior circuit's lineup.

By comparison, Joe Gordon played all but two games in his career at second. He won the AL MVP Award in 1942 and was a nine-time All-Star. Bobby Doerr played all of his games at second and was a nine-time All-Star. Nellie Fox played all but eight games in his career at second. (And those eight were in his final season.) He won the AL MVP award in 1959 and was a 15-time All-Star (including twice each season from 1959 to 1961). Red Schoendienst played 1,834 games at second (89.7 percent of his total games) and was a 10-time All-Star.

What to do? How do we normalize the data for equal comparisons? The table below provides a Defensive WAR value for second basemen between 1948 and 1952 (bold entries designate league leaders).

Rk	Player	dWAR	Year	Tm	G
1	Jerry Priddy	2.7	1950	DET	157
2	Jackie Robinson	2.4	1951	BRO	153
3	Joe Gordon	2.3	1948	CLE	144
4	Billy Martin	2.2	1952	NYY	109
5	Eddie Stanky	2.1	1950	NYG	152
6	Joe Gordon	2.1	1949	CLE	148
7	Jackie Robinson	1.8	1949	BRO	156
8	Bobby Doerr	1.8	1949	BOS	139
9	Eddie Stanky	1.7	1951	NYG	145
10	Red Schoendienst	1.7	1949	STL	151
11	Nellie Fox	1.6	1952	CHW	152
12	Red Schoendienst	1.6	1952	STL	152
13	Jackie Robinson	1.6	1950	BRO	144
14	Jerry Coleman	1.6	1949	NYY	128
15	Snuffy Stirnweiss	1.5	1948	NYY	141

From 1949 to 1952, there were 15 instances in which a second baseman had a Defensive Wins Above Replacement (dWAR) value of at least 1.5. (Robinson also comes in at 16th with a 1.4 mark in 1952.) Baseball-Reference concedes that the "replacement level on defense is the league average."7

Robinson had a .983 fielding percentage in 748 games at second base, making 68 total errors but turning 607 double plays. There is a statistic known as WAR Fielding Runs (Rfield). The following table lists seasons for second basemen when an Rfield value of at least 6 was attained.

Jackie

Rk	Player	Rfield	Year	Tm
1	Jerry Priddy	20	1950	DET
2	Jackie Robinson	16	1951	BRO
3	Joe Gordon	16	1948	CLE
4	Billy Martin	15	1952	NYY
5	Eddie Stanky	14	1950	NYG
6	Joe Gordon	14	1949	CLE
7	Bobby Doerr	11	1949	BOS
8	Eddie Stanky	10	1951	NYG
9	Jackie Robinson	10	1949	BRO
10	Jackie Robinson	10	1950	BRO
11	Nellie Fox	8	1952	CHW
12	Snuffy Stirnweiss	8	1948	NYY
13	Nellie Fox	7	1951	CHW
14	Pete Suder	7	1948	PHA
15	Jackie Robinson	6	1952	BRO
16	Bobby Avila	6	1951	CLE
17	Cass Michaels	6	1949	CHW
18	Bobby Doerr	6	1948	BOS

Fielding runs (Rfield) above average are relative to the positional average. Therefore, a +10 second baseman is 10 runs better than the average second baseman. The best during Robinson's four seasons at second belongs to Detroit Tigers second baseman Jerry Priddy, with a value of +20 in 1950. But that was only one season. Only 18 times did a player score above 5, and Robinson had four of them (including the second-highest mark of 16 in 1951).

In 1951 Robinson led the National League in putouts (390) and assists (435) by a second baseman.

Three times (1948, 1950, and 1951) he led all second basemen in fielding percentage.

Final note: A useful statistic in comparing the fielding of position players is the Total Zone Fielding Runs, which characterizes the number of runs above or below average the player was worth based on the number of plays made. Unfortunately, this statistic is available for second baseman only after 1953, the season when Robinson stopped his second-base duties.

It is safe to say that Robinson was the best second baseman in the majors, both offensively and defensively, during his playing days at the keystone position. His manager moved Robinson around the diamond and into the outfield, probably because he was a great athlete, but one thing is certain: Jackie Robinson deserved to be enshrined into the Hall of Fame based on his statistics.

NOTES

1. The website at the Hall of Fame claims that 21 second basemen have been enshrined, but they show only 20 when directed to the page of second basemen.
2. Our list does not include Frank Grant, who played for the Cuban Giants, and, according to the Baseball Hall of Fame, was "perhaps the best of the African-American players who played in organized baseball in the 1880s, before the color line was drawn." See baseballhall.org/hall-of-famers/grant-frank.
3. The search restricts players who played at least 50 percent of their games in that season at second base.
4. Interestingly, Robinson stole 88 bases in his first three seasons but was caught 41 times. Over his next seven seasons, he stole 109 bases but was caught just 35 times.
5. See baseball-reference.com/leaders/abWins_top_ten.shtml.
6. See baseballhall.org/hall-of-famers/robinson-jackie.
7. See baseball-reference.com/leaders/WAR_def_top_ten.shtml.

JACKIE ROBINSON AND OWNERS

by Andy McCue

Jack Roosevelt Robinson was not a man to be owned.

Yet, professional baseball's rules ensured that he would have contractual relations with the owners of the team he played for. And his position as team leader and cultural flashpoint ensured that the relations would be more than purely contractual.

The two owners of Robinson's team, the Brooklyn Dodgers, were very different men and Robinson had very different relationships with them. One was a mentor and supporter. The other clashed repeatedly with Robinson when Jackie strayed beyond the role of complacent athlete.

Branch Rickey was a vastly complicated man – an innovator, an intellectual in a visceral game, a moralist who knew how to navigate the gray areas of life and baseball's rules. One of those gray areas was the sport's attitude toward allowing African-American players into Organized Baseball. Commissioners, such as Kenesaw M. Landis, said it was very possible. The reality was that it did not happen until Rickey's moral streak and his desire to find the best players and win came together.

The Rickey-Robinson relationship began on a warm day in August 1945. Rickey's scouts had assured him of the player's baseball skills. Now Rickey wanted to see if Robinson had the courage and self-control to handle what the first Black player would endure. After three hours of probing, personal questions, and role-playing confrontations, Robinson left the office with the promise of a contract with the Dodgers' top minor-league club – the Montreal Royals.

Rickey's support would be steady over the next five years. He helped stifle a clubhouse revolt before Robinson was promoted to the Dodgers in 1947. He stood with him in racist confrontations with the Philadelphia Phillies and St. Louis Cardinals. He insisted Robinson would play in Southern exhibition games, notably in Atlanta in 1949. That season, he freed Robinson from a promise made in that August 1945 meeting. Robinson would no longer have to turn the other cheek.

Robinson's loyalty to Rickey was strong. "I found myself admiring him, glad to be around him, and

Jackie Robinson and Walter O'Malley in 1956.

ready to do whatever he wanted me to do," he said in a 1948 autobiography.[1]

But Branch Rickey also had his patronizing side, a character trait not limited to his relations with African-Americans. In February of 1947, anticipating Robinson's promotion, he arranged a dinner with prominent Blacks, many of them professionals, at a YMCA in Brooklyn.[2] "The one enemy most likely to ruin that success – is the Negro people themselves," he chided his audience. "You'll strut. You'll wear badges. You'll hold Jackie Robinson Days ... and Jackie Robinson Nights. You'll get drunk. You'll fight. You'll be arrested. You'll wine and dine the player until he is fat and futile. You'll symbolize his importance into a national comedy." As Rickey's assistant Arthur Mann, who was present, wrote, "It was a sharp slap against every Negro face in the room."[3]

In 1947, when Cleveland Indians owner Bill Veeck signed Larry Doby to be the first Black player in the American League, Rickey counseled Veeck to "control the boy."[4] Rickey felt controlling Robinson's, or Doby's, reaction to the inevitable racist incidents was necessary to integration's success. It was at the root of Rickey's efforts in his first interview with Robinson to take the temperature of his ability to control his temper.

Following Rickey's advice was not always easy for Robinson. In his rookie season he that was mercilessly race-baited by Philadelphia Phillies manager Ben Chapman. When a backlash ensued, Chapman sought to defuse the situation by asking Robinson to take a picture together. "Having my picture taken with this man was one of the most difficult things I had to make myself do," Robinson said.[5]

Regrets also sprouted after Rickey pressured Robinson to testify at a 1949 hearing of the House Un-American Activities Committee. The hearing sprang from singer Paul Robeson's statement that African-Americans would not go to war to defend a country which had "oppressed us for generations against a country which in one generation has raised our people to the full dignity of mankind."[6] In his testimony, Robinson declined to criticize Robeson directly, but did argue that Blacks would support the US. In later years, he tempered his testimony, saying he stood by it but was much more sympathetic to Robeson and his position.[7]

These incidents had little impact on the pair's relationship. "After I left the game, after I had nothing left to offer Mr. Rickey in his business life, he continued to remain close to me, to be concerned about how I was doing," Robinson said.[8] Rickey appeared, and appeared pleased, at Robinson's induction into baseball's Hall of Fame.[9] "I happen to think Mr. Rickey is a great man with a big heart as well as a big mind. … I shall always speak out with the utmost praise for this man."[10]

And that was part of the problem between Robinson and Walter O'Malley. O'Malley and Rickey had been partners owning the Dodgers since 1944. As such, O'Malley could have vetoed the Robinson signing, and did not. In 1950 it became clear that O'Malley and the other partners were not willing to extend Rickey's generous contract as president and general manager. Rickey decided he had to get out and triggered a clause in their partnership that gave O'Malley the first right to buy him out. O'Malley's offer was low, and Rickey found an outside buyer whom O'Malley was forced to match – at a much higher level than he wanted. O'Malley was left with control of the team and a resentment at how much it had cost.[11] In the early 1950s, Dodgers employees who used Rickey's name were fined a dollar.[12]

"I never had any real troubles with the Dodger management until Mr. Rickey left; after that trouble of one kind or another became routine," Robinson said. "O'Malley had a burning dislike for Rickey people, and I certainly was one."[13]

The day-to-day problems revolved around O'Malley's desire for ballplayers to avoid controversy. Robinson regularly called attention to segregated hotels on Dodgers road trips. To O'Malley, this was the undesirable "causing a scene."[14] When Robinson was notified of a fine for umpire-baiting that he considered unjust, he approached O'Malley, who offered to help if Robinson didn't say anything to reporters. But Robinson was sitting with a reporter when another Dodgers official approached their table and started discussing the incident. The reporter soon printed the story of the dispute and O'Malley assumed Robinson had violated his promise.[15] Roger Kahn reported that O'Malley called Robinson a "shameless publicity seeker."[16]

In the end, O'Malley would accuse Robinson of being a "prima donna" for missing spring-training exhibition games because of minor injuries.[17] Rae Robinson, Jackie's wife, exploded at that. "Bringing Jack into Organized Baseball was not the greatest thing Mr. Rickey did for him. In my opinion, it was this: Having brought Jack in, he stuck by him to the very end. He understood Jack. He never listened to the ugly little rumors like those you have mentioned to us today. If there was something wrong, he would go to Jack and ask him about it. He would talk to Jack and they would get to the heart of it like men with a mutual respect for the abilities and feelings of each other.[18]

In the end, Robinson believed, "O'Malley's attitude toward me was viciously antagonistic."[19] And, he added, "I was not O'Malley's kind of Negro."[20]

Despite Robinson's perception, O'Malley was not constantly opposed. He extended the desire to avoid controversy to his own actions. There was a public flap when a woman on a television show asked Robinson if he thought the Yankees, who had no Black players, discriminated. Robinson said yes and O'Malley defended his right to say so.[21] When Ford Frick singled out Robinson in the midst of a Giants-Dodgers beanball war. O'Malley again publicly rose to Robinson's defense.[22]

The contractual relationship ended in further recriminations. After the 1956 season, Robinson decided it was time to retire. He had been approached by the Chock Full o' Nuts coffee chain and on December 10 agreed to be a vice president. But he was bound by a previous contract with *Look* magazine, which had bought exclusive rights to the story of his retirement for $50,000. *Look*, a weekly, couldn't publish the story until January 8. That delay seemed fine until Buzzie Bavasi, the club's general manager, called two days after the Chock Full o' Nuts contract to tell Robinson he'd been traded to the Giants. Because of the *Look* contract, Robinson felt he couldn't alert Bavasi to his retirement. The trade story generated anguish among many Dodgers fans. Bavasi and O'Malley were roundly criticized even though the latter had been on a two-month around-the-world cruise until a few days before Bavasi made the trade.

Still feeling bound by the *Look* contract, Robinson made the appropriate remarks about his anticipation about joining the Giants and let the Dodgers executives take the heat. On January 5, 1957, *Look* began advertising their story. Then the critical spotlight shifted to Robinson for his refusal to be up-front. Bavasi and Robinson had some cutting remarks to make about each other.[23] As for O'Malley, it remained a relationship "of conflict and mutual distrust."[24]

When the Urban League of Los Angeles gave O'Malley a plaque honoring his "enlightened leadership" in integration, Robinson called it "preposterous" and gave full credit to Rickey.[25] When the NAACP's Pasadena chapter honored Robinson in 1959, O'Malley pointedly did not attend.[26]

Robinson's attitude mellowed somewhat over the years, mostly because Rachel Robinson developed a strong relationship with both O'Malley and his wife.[27] In 1964 he told *Los Angeles Times* columnist Sid Ziff, "It was because of my love and admiration for (Rickey) that I had my difficulty with Mr. O'Malley. That is the only thing that caused the resentment. I'm glad our relations have been ironed out."[28]

Despite this resolution, some of the feelings clearly remained. Robinson's public reconciliation with the Dodgers would have to wait until 1972, when a dying Robinson joined Sandy Koufax and Roy Campanella as the Dodgers retired their uniform numbers, the first time the team had given that honor.[29] Significantly, it was not Walter O'Malley, but his son, Peter, who reached out to both Jackie and Rachel and convinced them of the organization's commitment to racial equality and to repairing their relationship with Robinson.[30]

NOTES

1. Jackie Robinson, as told to Wendell Smith. *Jackie Robinson: My Own Story* (New York: Avon Publishers, 1948), 26.
2. Lee Lowenfish, *Branch Rickey: Baseball's Ferocious Gentleman* (Lincoln: University of Nebraska Press, 2007), 416-7.
3. Arthur Mann, *The Jackie Robinson Story* (New York: Grosset & Dunlap, 1951), 162-3.
4. Jackie Robinson (Charles Dexter, ed.), *Baseball Has Done It* (Philadelphia: J.B. Lippincott, 1964), 58.
5. Jackie Robinson, as told to Alfred Duckett, *I Never Had it Made* (New York: G.P. Putnam's, 1972), 75.
6. Arnold Rampersad, *Jackie Robinson: A Biography* (New York: Alfred A. Knopf, 1997), 211-6.
7. Robinson and Duckett, 98.
8. Robinson and Duckett, 269.
9. Robinson and Duckett, 270.
10. Carl T. Rowan with Jackie Robinson, *Wait Till Next Year: The Life Story of Jackie Robinson* (New York: Random House, 1960), 259.
11. Andy McCue, *Mover and Shaker: Walter O'Malley, the Dodgers and Baseball's Westward Expansion* (Lincoln: University of Nebraska Press, 2014), 74-83.
12. McCue, 85.
13. Rowan with Robinson, 256, 259.
14. Sam Lacy, *Fighting for Fairness: The Life Story of Hall of Fame Sportswriter Sam Lacy* (Centreville, Maryland: Tidewater Publishing, 1998), 121.
15. Rowan with Robinson, 259-60; Robinson and Duckett, 128-9.
16. *Los Angeles Times*, January 8, 1997.
17. Rowan with Robinson, 257.
18. Robinson and Duckett, 112.
19. Robinson and Duckett, 105.
20. Rowan with Robinson, 261.
21. *The Sporting News*, December 10, 1952: 3.
22. *The Sporting News*, May 9, 1951: 2; *New York Times*, May 2, 3, 1951.
23. McCue, 94-5.
24. Rowan with Robinson, 255.
25. *Newark Star-Ledger*, May 9, 1958.
26. *Los Angeles Times*, December 14, 1959.
27. Robinson and Dexter, 160.
28. *Los Angeles Times*, March 22, 1964.
29. *Los Angeles Times*, June 5, 1972.
30. *The Sporting News*, July 1, 1972: 24; *The Sporting News*'s March 31, 1997, Jackie Robinson Fiftieth Anniversary commemorative section: 2.

MANAGING HISTORY: JACKIE ROBINSON AND MANAGERS

by Joe Cox

In reviewing the career of Jackie Robinson in hindsight, one advantage is that everything seems as if it was a certainty. Robinson was one of the great players in the history of the sport, an innovator who was soon dubbed "Ty Cobb in Technicolor."[1] His Dodgers were an annual contender for the pennant, and Robinson became a fixture on those teams.

The future of Robinson looking forward was far less certain. He played out his career under a bevy of managers, and his interactions and appreciation (or lack thereof) for each is instructive as regards his personality and preferences in the days when the future of baseball's "great experiment" was far from settled.

Unfortunately for the historians, Robinson apparently rarely had much to say about his earliest managers. He infamously hit .097 in his last (partial) season at UCLA and had played only a few months with the Kansas City Monarchs when Branch Rickey signed him for Brooklyn. Likely, Jackie Robinson's determinedly negative view of the Negro Leagues impacted any potential lessons he may have drawn in his few months with the Monarchs.[2]

On the other hand, the pairing of Robinson and Montreal manager Clay Hopper in 1946 was an auspicious one. Robinson would write years later that he "had been briefed about Hopper. What I had heard about him wasn't encouraging. A native of Mississippi, he owned a plantation there, and I had been told he was anti-black."[3] Hopper's heritage was an open fact, and his reluctance to be the manager of an African American player was virtually certain. When he asked Dodgers GM Branch Rickey not to make him manage Robinson, the Mahatma supposedly offered, "You can manage correctly or be unemployed."[4]

The legendary story about Hopper, as recounted by Rickey and subsequently by Robinson is that Rickey and Hopper were watching spring training together when Rickey praised a play by Robinson as "superhuman." Hopper then asked Rickey, "Do you really think a n----r's a human being?" For his part, Rickey later explained, "I saw that this Mississippi-born man was sincere, that he meant what he said; that his attitude of regarding the Negro as subhuman was part of his heritage; that here was a man who had practically nursed race prejudice at his mother's breast. So I decided to ignore the question."[5]

Robinson's season in Montreal provided all the evidence that Hopper needed as to his humanity and, indeed, near super-humanity. Robinson recounted himself that at the end of the season, Hopper approached him, offered a handshake, and exclaimed, "You're a great ballplayer and a fine gentleman. It's been wonderful having you on the team."[6] On another occasion, Robinson wrote of Hopper approaching him in September 1946 and telling him, "I'd sure like to have you back on the Royals next spring."[7] But of course Robinson's 1947 season would be spent in Brooklyn.

The initial plan was for the legendary Leo Durocher to manager Robinson. Durocher had managed the Dodgers since 1939, and there was no reason to expect that he wouldn't manage Brooklyn in 1947. During spring training Durocher himself went to work on changing the chemistry of the Dodgers clubhouse. Hearing rumors of a potential petition against Robinson making the Dodgers team, Durocher called a meeting of the rest of the team and advised, "I don't care if the guy is yellow or black, or if he has stripes like a [expletive] zebra. I'm the manager of this team, and I say he plays."[8] Durocher also offered to make sure of the trade of any players who disagreed.[9] However, a few weeks later, it would be Durocher and not Robinson who would be on the sidelines.

Durocher was suspended just before the season by Commissioner Happy Chandler for "conduct detrimental to baseball," much of it likely centering on ties to organized gambling.[10] The move so confounded Rickey and the Dodgers that Robinson's first big-league manager was longtime coach Clyde Sukeforth, who skippered the first two games of the 1947 season. Sukeforth would later recall, "I remember writing out the lineup card, didn't think anything special of it. I just wanted to follow what Mr. Rickey and Durocher wanted."[11]

Sukeforth's interaction with Robinson was much more significant than his two games as a manager. As the scout who brought Robinson into contact with Rickey, he was one of the first principal characters in the "great experiment." He also helped Robinson greatly as a coach, to the extent that Robinson named Sukeforth as the person who had helped him most during his career in a publicity questionnaire that Robinson completed for the National League before the 1948 season.[12]

For his part, Sukeforth always professed surprise that Robinson gave him significant credit for his improvement as a player. Shortly before Robinson's death in 1972, the two met at an event honoring Robinson at Mama Leone's restaurant in New York. Sukeforth was called upon to speak and he downplayed his role in Robinson's rise, only for Robinson to follow up a few days later by writing him, noting, "While there has not been enough said of your significant contribution in the Rickey-Robinson experiment, I consider your role, next to Mr. Rickey's and my wife's – yes, bigger than any other persons with whom I came in contact."[13]

After Sukeforth's two-game interim stint, veteran manger Burt Shotton took over as the Dodgers skipper. Shotton had last managed a major-league team in 1934, and his grandfatherly approach earned him the semi-mocking sobriquet of "Kindly Old Burt Shotton." Along with Connie Mack, Shotton was one of the last two managers to wear street clothes rather than a uniform. His unassuming style was immediately impressed on the 1947 Dodgers, as he met with the team shortly before his first game and told them, "You fellas can win the pennant in spite of me. Don't be afraid of me as a manager. I cannot possibly hurt you."[14]

When his star rookie hit a lengthy early slump, Shotton simply continued putting Robinson's name on the lineup card. Years later, Robinson wrote of Shotton, "He gave me all the opportunities possible. … When I broke in I had a particularly bad streak, but he handled me so wisely that I didn't lose heart."[15] One biographer wrote of Shotton that he "was never given to extreme highs or lows. He kept a balanced perspective, which unfortunately was at times misinterpreted by reporters and fans as aloofness."[16]

Shotton led the Dodgers through 1947, and returned to the helm in mid-1948, leading the team in a second run through the end of the 1950 season. The *Saturday Evening Post* noted, "[Robinson's] rise to big-league stardom has come almost entirely under the managership of wise old Burt Shotton. This may be a coincidence, but seasoned students of the game do not think so. In their opinion, Shotton did a better job than Durocher or almost anyone else could have done in bringing Robinson through the dangerous period when he was the only Negro player in the major leagues."[17]

For his part, Robinson later noted that Shotton "was quick" and his only issue with the older skipper was that "he almost never came out of the dugout."[18] In fact, because he didn't wear a uniform, Shotton couldn't come out of the dugout. The major-league rules prohibited him from doing so. But Robinson's preference for a manager who would "[go] out on the field to fight the team's battles"[19] would require another protagonist.

In between Shotton's two stints in Brooklyn, Robinson finally got a chance to play for Durocher, who returned from his suspension for the 1948 season, only to find Robinson wildly out of shape in spring training. When Durocher saw Robinson's condition, he exploded, "What in the world happened to you? You look like an old woman. Look at all that fat around your midsection. Why, you can't even bend over!"[20] Durocher soon promised the media, "Robinson will shag flies until his tongue hangs out."[21]

Durocher lasted only until the All-Star break, when he left the 35-37 Dodgers to jump to the archrival Giants. Robinson had rounded into shape and was hitting .295 at the time of Durocher's departure. Still, from that point on, Robinson and Durocher were rivals. Durocher would bench-jockey Robinson, and the player would respond by alleging that Durocher wore his wife Laraine Day's perfume.[22] Day herself joined the feud, penning a letter insisting that Alvin Dark was a better second baseman than Robinson.[23]

For his part, Robinson didn't seem to hold a grudge. He ranked Durocher his second favorite manager to play under, stating, "[I]f you have a winning team nobody is better than Durocher. … But with a losing team, Durocher would lose his composure."[24]

On the other hand, Charlie Dressen was Robinson's favorite manager. "Dressen was steady day in and day out, win or lose," wrote Robinson.[25] Dressen took over after Shotton's second turn, and managed the Dodgers from 1951 to 1953. In his three seasons, Dressen led the Dodgers to a playoff for the NL pennant in 1951 and then back-to-back pennants in the following two seasons.

Dressen was not necessarily an easy manager to play under. Bill James wrote, "Dressen just couldn't resist telling you, pretty much on a daily basis, how smart he was. Walker Cooper once said that Charlie

Dressen wrote a book on managing; on every page it just said, 'I.' ... Charlie was one of the few managers in baseball history who truly believed that he was the key to his team's success."[26] James's comments aside, Dressen knew who made the Dodgers go. During spring training, he told the media, "I am counting on Robinson to be the most valuable player in the National League next year."[27]

Robinson delivered frequently during Dressen's three seasons, and he held the skipper in highest regard. He wrote, "During the years I knew him as manager we players gave him one hundred percent effort. ... He is the ball player's best friend because he fights for the player's rights."[28]

Fighting for his rights was often on Robinson's mind during Dressen's tenure. Whether because he was no longer under Rickey's request for restrained behavior or simply because he had become a veteran star in baseball, Robinson was often in the thick of the fray with umpires,[29] and Dressen's presence with him in those battles apparently weighed heavily in Robinson's regard.

When Dressen couldn't beat the Yankees in the 1952 or 1953 World Series and then wouldn't sign another one-year contract with the Dodgers, the team moved on to Walter Alston. By this point, Robinson was on the back side of his big-league career, shuffling between multiple positions and seeing decline in his production. He frankly did not care for Alston.

Interestingly, in his own *Baseball Has Done It*, Robinson discusses his first three major-league managers (Shotton, Durocher, Dressen), and then pointedly does not discuss Alston in any way. A few years earlier in *Wait Till Next Year*, Robinson had spoken his piece. He wrote about an incident at Wrigley Field in 1954 when a call went against Duke Snider on a long drive that went over the wall but was erroneously ruled a double by umpire Bill Stewart. Robinson charged onto the field in protest of the call. His manager did not. Robinson later wrote, "Alston stood at third base, hands on hips, staring at me as if to say: All right, Robinson, all the fans see you. Cut out the grandstand tactics and retire to the dugout."[30]

Once in the dugout, Robinson continued to express his feelings. "If that guy didn't stand out there at third base like a damned wooden Indian," he said in regard to Alston, "you know, this club might go somewhere. ... What the hell kind of manager is that?"[31]

This wasn't their first conflict, although it was the most public. Robinson recalled Alston approaching him soon after being hired, with hopes that Robinson would "put out for him the way I had for Charlie Dressen." Nonplussed by the request, Robinson later noted, "I wondered why Alston should have any doubt about my putting out for him. ... Yet I soon found out that Alston could not get over the notion that, because of my high regard for Dressen, I had to resent him."[32]

An uneasy truce persisted between Robinson and Alston, and Robinson played out the last three years of his career, including winning the 1955 World Series. Alston stayed with the Dodgers much longer than Robinson and won three more World Series titles in Los Angeles. Alston made the transition from a playing career that included one big-league at-bat to winning 2,040 games as a manager and earning a spot in the Baseball Hall of Fame.

Meanwhile, once Robinson retired, many wondered if he would ever manage. But even in 1964, Robinson wrote, "I used to have managerial ambitions. I don't now."[33] He did go on to note, "Americans must learn ... that many Negroes are qualified through experience for managing."[34]

At Robinson's final public appearance, for the 1972 World Series, mere weeks before his death, he told the crowd, "I am extremely proud and pleased to be here this afternoon, but must admit I'm gonna be tremendously more pleased and more proud when I look at that third base coaching line one day and see a black face managing in baseball."[35] In his final appearance, Robinson was again being a trailblazer and while he didn't live to see Frank Robinson earn that honor or Cito Gaston become the first African American manager to win a World Series, he helped to jump-start those journeys.

NOTES

1. Arnold Rampersad, *Jackie Robinson: A Biography* (New York: Alfred A. Knopf, 1997), 185.
2. An example of Robinson's issues with the Negro Leagues can be found at Rampersad, 116.
3. Jackie Robinson, *I Never Had It Made* (New York: HarperCollins, 1995), 42.
4. Red Barber and Robert Creamer, *Rhubarb in the Catbird Seat* (Lincoln: University of Nebraska Press, 1997), 274.
5. The entire incident is chronicled at Robinson, 48, but also at many other sources.
6. Robinson, 52.
7. Jackie Robinson, *Baseball Has Done It* (Brooklyn: IG Publishing, 2005), 54.
8. Jules Tygiel, *Baseball's Great Experiment: Jackie Robinson and His Legacy* (New York: Oxford University Press, 1997), 170.
9. Tygiel, 170.
10. Rampersad, 166.

11 C.E. Lincoln: "A Conversation with Clyde Sukeforth," *Baseball Research Journal*, 16 (1987): 73.

12 The questionnaire is included in the Jackie Robinson Papers at the National Baseball Hall of Fame and Museum.

13 Joe Cox, *A Fine Team Man: Jackie Robinson and the Lives He Touched* (Guilford, Connecticut: Lyons Press, 2019), 131. The original copy of Robinson's letter is in the Jackie Robinson Papers at the National Baseball Hall of Fame and Museum.

14 Peter Golenbock, *Bums: An Oral History of the Brooklyn Dodgers* (New York: G.P. Putnam's Sons, 1984), 169.

15 Robinson, *Baseball Has Done It*, 77.

16 David Gough, *Burt Shotton, Dodgers Manager: A Baseball Biography* (Jefferson, North Carolina: McFarland, 1994), 58.

17 Roger Butterfield, "Brooklyn's Gentleman Bum," *Saturday Evening Post*, August 20, 1949.

18 Carl T. Rowan with Jackie Robinson, *Wait Till Next Year: The Story of Jackie Robinson* (New York: Random House, 1960), 264.

19 Rowan with Robinson, 264.

20 Lee Lowenfish, *Branch Rickey: Baseball's Ferocious Gentleman* (Lincoln: University of Nebraska Press, 2009), 448.

21 Lowenfish, 448.

22 Rampersad, 236.

23 The note was included in the *New York Daily News*, June 19, 1950.

24 Rowan with Robinson, 263.

25 Rowan with Robinson, 263.

26 Bill James, *The Bill James Guide to Baseball Managers From 1870 to Today* (New York: Scribner, 1997), 187.

27 Rampersad, 233.

28 Robinson, *Baseball Has Done It*, 78.

29 Rampersad, 246 and 249 includes details of two such umpire feuds for Robinson.

30 Rowan with Robinson, 265.

31 Rowan with Robinson, 266.

32 Rowan with Robinson, 262-63.

33 Robinson, *Baseball Has Done It*, 78.

34 Robinson, *Baseball Has Done It*, 78.

35 A transcript of Robinson's comments is included in the Jackie Robinson papers at the National Baseball Hall of Fame.

JACKIE ROBINSON'S FAITH SUSTAINED HIM DURING UNRELENTING TURMOIL

by Chris Lamb

Brooklyn Dodgers President Branch Rickey and Jackie Robinson, the shortstop of the Kansas City Monarchs of the Negro American League, first met the morning of August 28, 1945, in Rickey's fourth-floor office at 215 Montague Street in Brooklyn, New York. Clyde Sukeforth, a Brooklyn scout, told Robinson that Rickey was interested in signing the ballplayer for a Black team he was organizing, the Brooklyn Brown Dodgers.

Rickey's interest in a Black team, however, was a smokescreen to hide his intention of ending the national pastime's color barrier by identifying talented players in Black baseball. His scouts recommended Robinson and other ballplayers for the Brooklyn Dodgers organization.[1] Rickey had examined every part of Robinson's life, including his time at UCLA, where he had been a four-sport athlete; in the US Army, where he had been court-martialed for protesting after he had been sent to back of a bus; and with the Monarchs in the Negro leagues.[2]

Rickey was impressed with Robinson's athleticism but was worried about reports of the ballplayer's temper and whether he could control it in response to what would be an unceasing amount of physical and emotional abuse from fans and players on opposing teams. If Robinson lost his temper, it would give his critics reason to confirm their belief that Blacks should not be allowed in the game.

"I'm looking for a ballplayer with the guts not to fight back," Rickey told Robinson.

Rickey wanted to find out for himself how Robinson would respond to such indignities. He decided to test Robinson. Rickey took off his sport coat and transformed himself into a bigoted White clerk refusing Robinson a room in a Whites-only hotel; a White waiter in a restaurant denying Robinson service and calling him "boy"; and an opposing ballplayer who, as Robinson later remember, criticized "my race, my parents, in language that was almost unendurable." And finally, Rickey was a foul-mouthed basestealer sliding hard into Robinson with his metal spikes high in the air. Rickey then swung his fist at Robinson's head, calling him a racist epithet.[3]

Rickey then opened a book published in the 1920s, Giovanni Papini's *Life of Christ*, and read Jesus' words from the Sermon on the Mountain in the Gospel of Matthew: "You have heard that it hath been said, an eye for an eye, and a tooth for a tooth: But I say unto you, That ye resist not evil; but whosoever shall smite thee on thy right cheek, turn to him the other also."

Robinson knew the Gospel and knew what was required of him.

"I have two cheeks, Mr. Rickey. Is that it?" he replied.[4]

The meeting between the two Methodists, Rickey and Robinson, ultimately transformed baseball and America itself.

"Robinson's a Methodist. I'm a Methodist. God's a Methodist," Rickey says. "You can't go wrong." The exchange is included in *42*, the movie starring Chadwick Boseman, as Robinson, and Harrison Ford as Rickey.

What is often overlooked in books, articles, documentaries, and movies about Robinson's life is that it is also a religious story. His faith in God, as he often said, carried him through the pain and anguish of integrating the major leagues.

Michael Long and I wrote about Robinson and his faith in the 2017 book *Jackie Robinson: A Spiritual Biography*, which was published by Westminster John Knox Press.[5]

The book begins with Robinson's birth on January 31, 1919. As Jackie's mother, Mallie, held her newborn son, she looked at her husband, Jerry, her brother, and her brother-in-law trying to make "sugar teats" – lard and sugar wrapped in cheesecloth to resemble nipples that would ease the baby's assimilation into the world.

Mallie slowly shook her head as she watched the hapless men spill most of the lard on the floor and then whispered a blessing to Jackie. "Bless you, my boy," she said. "For you to survive all this, God will have to keep his eye on you."[6]

Shortly after Jackie's birth, Jerry Robinson hopped a train with another woman. Mallie found herself alone to support five children in rural Cairo, Georgia, in the hostile South, where Blacks had few opportunities, if any, to improve their standing, and any Black who confronted racial injustice ran the risk of ending up in jail, beaten, or lynched.[7]

In May 1920, Rachel moved her family to Pasadena, California, where she repeatedly told Jackie and his four siblings that God would take care of them.[8] Jackie, however, did not yet have his mother's faith or the strength to turn the other cheek. The Robinsons were the only Black family living on Pepper Street and their White neighbors made no effort to welcome them. When Jackie was 8, a girl who lived across Pepper Street from the Robinsons, called him a nigger. Jackie yelled back at her that she was "nothing but a cracker." The girl's father came outside the house and threw a rock at Jackie, who returned fire with a rock of his own.[9]

As a teenager, Jackie refused to go with his mother to Scott Methodist Church. He belonged to a neighborhood gang, the Pepper Street Gang, which consisted not of violent boys and men as the word conjures up today but of boys who shoplifted from local grocers and got into fights with other teens.[10]

The boys' petty crimes got them in trouble with the police. This increased Mallie's concern about her son. She expressed his worries to the Rev. Karl Downs, the young minister at Scott Methodist. Downs found Robinson on a Pasadena street corner, told him to come see him, and persuaded him to come to church.[11]

Arnold Rampersad wrote in his biography of Robinson that Downs, who was just seven years older, became a good friend and a father figure to Robinson. His impact on Robinson was particularly significant when it came to shaping the young man's religion. Rampersad said that Downs became the channel through which religious faith "finally flowed into Jack's consciousness and was finally accepted there, if on revised terms, as he reached manhood," Rampersad said. "Faith in God then began to register in him as both a mysterious force, beyond his comprehension, and a pragmatic way to negotiate the world."[12]

At Downs's request, Robinson began teaching Sunday school – even on the mornings after football games he played at Pasadena Junior College and then at UCLA. "On Sunday mornings, when I woke up sore and aching because of a football game the day before, I yearned to just stay in bed. But no matter how terrible I felt, I had to get up."[13]

Robinson made a habit of praying beside his bed before going to sleep. Robinson learned that exercising faith was not just about praying. Downs instilled in Robinson the pride in being a Black man in a White-dominated world and in standing up to social injustice in a world where there was so much racial injustice. Robinson carried himself with pride. He wore White shirts that showed off his dark skin.[14]

Rachel Isum, who was three years behind Robinson at UCLA, was attracted to Robinson's handsome looks but also to his self-confidence. Robinson and Isum, who were both Methodists, began dating and remained a couple until his death in 1972.

Robinson's faith gave him strength during his court-martial in the Army in 1944. He was drafted in March 1942, three months after Japan bombed Pearl Harbor, bringing the United States into World War II. Robinson, like most, if not every other Black soldier, faced racial discrimination in the Army. Bases were largely segregated but segregation was prohibited on military buses.

While stationed at Fort Hood in Texas, a bus driver ordered Robinson to the back of a bus. Robinson knew he didn't have to move and did not move. An argument followed. The base assistant provost conducted an inquiry, interviewing the bus driver, White passengers, and White MPs, but ignoring Robinson. Robinson, who felt he was not given the respect demanded of an officer, interrupted the questioning. He was accused of not showing proper respect to a commandeering officer. If found guilty, he could be sentenced to a military prison. As Robinson sat in shackles in the courtroom, he relied on his faith in God, remembering his mother's words. "You are a child of God, made in God's image. Because God is there, nothing can go wrong with you," she had told him. "You can allow yourself to take risks because you just know that the Lord will not allow you to sink so far that you can't swim."[15]

Robinson was acquitted of all charges.

By the time of the acquittal, Robinson's battalion had left for Europe, where it fought in the bloody Battle of the Bulge. By confronting racial discrimination at Fort Hood, he was prevented from going abroad where he might have been injured or killed. Robinson was discharged and began playing in the segregated Negro leagues, where he was playing when Branch Rickey was searching for the right player to break baseball's color barrier.

By confronting racial discrimination in the Army, he would be available to confront racial discrimination in baseball.

Robinson did not like playing in Negro leagues. He did not like the catch-as-catch-all playing schedule or the constant traveling where they might play games in two different cities on the same day and couldn't stay in Whites-only hotels or eat in Whites-only restaurants.

He did not drink alcohol or chase women as many of his teammates did. Robinson openly scorned his whiskey-drinking and promiscuous teammates, once tossing a glass of scotch into a burning fireplace to demonstrate the lethality of liquor. He stunned his teammates by telling them he was waiting until marriage to have sex. "His sense of self was tightly wound around core values of dignity and self-esteem, and he believed in God and the Bible," Rampersad wrote about Robinson. "Absurdly or not, he drew a line in the dirt between himself and sin, and tried not to cross it."[16]

As influential as Karl Downs was in Robinson's life, no one had a more profound impact on Robinson than Rickey. Rickey too owed his strong sense of faith to his mother, Emily, who taught him stories from the Bible. Rickey biographer Lee Lowenfish said Emily Rickey's stories from Scripture reinforced in her son "the belief that there was a right way and a wrong way to life."[17] This meant that God came first to Rickey, whose religious devotion was such that he didn't attend baseball games on Sundays.

Rickey and Robinson forever changed baseball and society on October 23, 1945, when the Montreal Royals, the Triple-A team in the Brooklyn organization, announced it had signed Robinson. Robinson knew that much of White America would judge all Blacks by how well he played and how well he comported himself. If he failed in either way, his failure reflected badly on all Blacks.

Robinson's first test came when Jackie and Rachel, having just married, left Southern California for the Deep South, where Jackie would try to win a spot on the Montreal roster during spring training in Florida. The Robinson were bumped from two planes and replaced by White passengers. Shortly after they boarded a bus near Pensacola, a bus driver, calling Jackie "boy," ordered the newlyweds to the back of the bus. Jackie turned his cheek both times.[18]

Robinson was chased out of Sanford, Florida, by the Ku Klux Klan. A number of cities refused to allow the integrated Montreal team to play. Robinson struggled with his hitting and he injured his throwing arm. Robinson played his first game of the spring in Daytona Beach on Sunday, March 17.[19]

Black ministers gave sermons about Robinson that morning and asked their parishioners to pray for him. When services ended, Blacks, in their Sunday clothes, walked to the ballpark.[20]

What happened in Daytona Beach repeated itself elsewhere in cities where Robinson played. "I know how wonderful it felt on a number of occasions, when a Negro minister approached me at the ball club and said, 'You know, I cut my sermon short today so the people could get out of church early and get to the ball park to root for you,'" Robinson said. "My minister friends tell me that when the average minister cuts down his sermon, he is making one of the greatest sacrifices known to man." Robinson credited Black ministers for his success. "I owe so much to the Negro ministers, and it is a debt I never intend to forget."[21]

Robinson played the 1946 season with the Montreal Royals and was then promoted to the Dodgers the following spring. He knew that if he succeeded in the major leagues, he would change the way a lot of Whites thought about Blacks. If he succeeded, it would mean that other Blacks would get opportunities that were now closed to them. If he could overcome racial discrimination, then others could, too.[22]

No athlete ever faced either the pressure or abuse that Robinson did when he took the field for the first time in a Brooklyn uniform on April 15, 1947. Robinson clearly understood the stakes at play. Robinson knew Rickey could only do so much and that his own success depended on his own ability, but also on luck and fate. "His religion had taught him that the line between confidence and Satanic pride is a fine one; and chance – a twisted ankle, a turned knee – might yet intervene to reassert the inscrutable ways of Providence," Rampersad wrote. "The drama would unfold; he would be both spectator and the man at the plate; God would decide the outcome."[23]

Robinson believed that God was on his side.[24]

Robinson did not merely endure in the face of constant death threats, opposing pitchers throwing at him, baserunners spiking him, or fans screaming the ugliest of racial epithets; he thrived. His faith formed in him an indomitable spirit. Robinson promised Rickey he would respond to his detractors by turning the other cheek, and he did.

"In observing that trust," Rickey said, "he has had an almost Christ-like taste of turning the other cheek."[25]

Robinson continued with his nightly ritual of praying, once telling a reporter about his faith in God and his nightly ritual of kneeling at his bedside. "It's the best way to get closer to God," Robinson said, and then the second baseman added with a smile, "and a hard-hit groundball."

After Robinson retired from baseball, he wrote newspaper columns for the *New York Post* and the *Amsterdam News* in New York. Many of the columns are collected in the book *Beyond Home Plate,* which is edited by Michael Long. In one column, Robinson compared his own experience with "turning the other cheek" with the nonviolent confrontation of the civil-rights movement espoused by his friend, Martin Luther King Jr. "I can testify to the fact that it was a lot harder to turn the other cheek and refuse to fight back than it would have been to exercise a normal reaction," Robinson wrote. "But it works, because sooner or later it brings a sense of shame to those who attack you. And that sense of shame is often the beginning of progress."[26]

NOTES

1. Lee Lowenfish, *Branch Rickey: Baseball's Ferocious Gentleman* (Lincoln: University of Nebraska Press, 2007), 373-374. Arnold Rampersad, *Jackie Robinson: A Biography* (New York: Alfred A. Knopf, 1997), 125-126.
2. Lowenfish, 368-369.
3. Rampersad, 127.
4. Lowenfish, 375-376; Rampersad, 127.
5. Michael Long and Chris Lamb, *Jackie Robinson: A Spiritual Biography* (Louisville: Westminster John Knox Press, 2017).
6. Long and Lamb, 13.
7. Long and Lamb, 18.
8. Long and Lamb, 18.
9. Rampersad, 24.
10. Long and Lamb, 23-24.
11. Long and Lamb, 25.
12. Rampersad, 53.
13. Jackie Robinson and Alfred Duckett, *I Never Had It Made* (Hopewell, New Jersey: Ecco Press, 1972), 8.
14. Long and Lamb, 34-36.
15. Rampersad, 102-111.
16. Rampersad, 118.
17. Lowenfish, 17.
18. Chris Lamb, *Blackout: The Untold Story of Jackie Robinson's First Spring Training* (Lincoln: University of Nebraska Press, 2012), 5-14.
19. Lamb, *Blackout*, 87-89, 94-95, 103, 135, 140.
20. Lamb, *Blackout*, 104, 105.
21. Long and Lamb, 75.
22. Long and Lamb, 84.
23. Rampersad, 168.
24. Long and Lamb, 85.
25. Wendell Smith, "Sports Beat," *Pittsburgh Courier*, February 28, 1948. Quoted in Long and Lamb, 98.
26. Chris Lamb, "Jackie Robinson: Faith in Himself and in God," *Wall Street Journal*, April 11, 2013.

JACKIE ROBINSON AND THE DECLINE OF THE NEGRO LEAGUES

by Nathan Bierma

Jackie Robinson's breakthrough with the Brooklyn Dodgers was a triumph for the integration of baseball and a death sentence for the Negro Leagues. Once the barrier to entry for the top Black ballplayers finally and justly fell, the leagues that used to be the only place to see them play struggled to survive.

The ambivalence of cheering integration but lamenting the fate of once-thriving Black-only institutions was growing in the mid-twentieth century. "The gradual yet perceptible trend toward integration would prompt a reexamination of the support and need for black organizations and enterprises," wrote Neil Lanctot.[1] A study published in 1947 identified the "dilemma of the Negro business man who as a Negro disapproves of racial segregation but as a business man has a vested interest in segregation because it creates a convenient market for his goods and services."[2]

As 1947 dawned, Negro League owners, enjoying steady attendance and presuming that looming integration was "likely to proceed slowly," did not yet fear the worst.[3] They soon suffered two serious blows related to their two biggest stars, neither of whom was Jackie Robinson. In January Josh Gibson died of a stroke at age 35. In the early weeks of the season, fellow superstar Satchel Paige was often absent from the Kansas City Monarchs, opting for an increase in more lucrative exhibition appearances. "The absence of Paige and Gibson during the season's crucial early months seriously affected the box office appeal of black baseball."[4]

But it was Robinson's debut with the Brooklyn Dodgers on April 15, 1947, that was clearly a watershed moment in the history of baseball – both its all-Black and previously all-White versions – as well as American history as a whole. The dam erected in the name of racial segregation was loudly cracked and poised to burst, releasing a new torrent of Black talent into what were then considered the major leagues.

Robinson and Branch Rickey were the courageous protagonists of the integration story, but neither was poised to champion the cause of the continuation of the Negro Leagues. Robinson had played one season in Kansas City in 1945 and had quickly soured on the experience. He was surprised by the lack of formal contracts, the lack of consistency and professionalism in umpiring and scorekeeping, the poor quality of buses and accommodations, and the drinking and late-night partying of his teammates.[5] The disaffection was mostly mutual. "He did not fit in very well," wrote Donn Rogosin. "He was not a popular player in Kansas City."[6] Robinson later voiced his scathing critiques in a 1948 article for *Ebony* titled "What's Wrong with Negro Baseball," in which he scolded owners "to place more emphasis on the character and morals of the men they select" and less on "worrying so much about heavy schedules and getting in as many games as they can, regardless of the caliber of ball that is played."[7] Back in 1945, before Rickey came calling, Robinson declared his intentions to retire from baseball altogether.[8]

Rickey was no fan of the Negro Leagues either. He, too, disparaged Negro League owners as unprofessional and lamented their lack of centralized leadership. He gave this as rationale to found his own franchise, the Brooklyn Brown Dodgers, in an upstart all-Black United States League, though this was likely primarily conceived to give cover to his scouts to start watching Black players.[9] He then sparred with the Monarchs over the terms of Robinson's acquisition.[10] "There is no Negro league as such, as far as I am concerned," Rickey said, adding that the Negro Leagues "have no right to expect organized baseball to respect them."[11]

Thus the fate of the Negro Leagues was far from Robinson's and Rickey's minds in 1947. Nor did it appear to give pause to Black fans, who flocked to Ebbets Field and Dodgers road games at the expense of the teams they used to frequent. "The overall attendance decline in black baseball in 1947 was startling," Lanctot wrote."[12] Negro Leagues executive Frank Forbes said that while he expected a dip in attendance, "frankly we were not prepared for what we were to experience."[13] The very things that made Robinson's debut season such a seismic success – his play putting him in contention for Rookie of the Year honors and his team's trip to the World Series – captivated Black fans and Black sportswriters all season long.[14] Unlike Negro League teams, the Dodgers enjoyed prominent coverage in mainstream newspapers and on the radio, keeping them constantly on the minds of Black fans.[15]

So while integration did proceed slowly when measured by the number of Black players, the intrigue of the effort and the exploits of Robinson had an outsize impact. "With only three of sixteen teams employing a total of five black players in 1947, major league baseball was still far from integrated," Lanctot wrote. "Yet already many fans had permanently turned away from black baseball, which seemed increasingly less relevant and meaningful when juxtaposed against the enormous appeal of Jackie Robinson excelling in interracial competition."[16]

As the 1948 season dawned, the Negro Leagues' "still decentralized control ... limited the likelihood that [they] would assertively address the new challenges with substantial improvement or innovation."[17] Owners appealed to Black fans to return out of loyalty. They cut player salaries to limit their losses. They pursued minor-league affiliations with major-league clubs, but found few takers.[18] They sought more revenue from the sale of players to major-league clubs, but lacked leverage to get fair value, and relinquishing their top talent further devalued their product.[19]

In the midst of a tumultuous offseason, Negro Leagues owners reeled from the added impact of Robinson's *Ebony* broadside in early 1948. "Robinson is where he is today because of organized colored baseball," Newark Eagles owner Effa Manley – now the only woman enshrined in the National Baseball Hall of Fame – blasted back. "[A]n apology is due the race which nurtured him – yes, the team and league which developed him."[20] It was a terrible time to spar with Robinson, who had just soared to stratospheric levels of superstardom.

Robinson's critique "contained more than a grain of truth," Lanctot observed. But it showed "little sympathy for the previous decades of struggle to establish the industry and largely failed to acknowledge the impact of inadequate financing and revenue. ... Evaluated in this context, black baseball had achieved a great deal despite substantial odds, a fact Robinson chose to ignore."[21]

One can now wonder if some combination of forces – centralized leadership among Negro Leagues owners, more favorable representation from Robinson and Rickey, minor-league affiliations and fair player sales from major-league owners, and sustained fan attention – could have saved the Negro Leagues, or if an institution defined by segregation was inherently obsolete once the color barrier was broken. But each of these factors did its damage, and the result was irreversible.

After another season of crushing losses in 1948, the Negro National League was forced to fold. Manley put her Eagles up for sale.[22] "[T]he golden era has passed," Birmingham Black Barons owner Tom Hayes declared. "Teams that are to survive must retrench and proceed with caution."[23] In the ensuing decade, remaining franchises cobbled together rosters, schedules, and crowds – some would even enlist White players – but they were shells of their former selves. "We'd get 300 people in a game," Buck Leonard lamented. "We couldn't even draw flies."[24] The Negro American League folded in 1960.[25]

For decades, the memory of the Negro Leagues faded, before being revived at the end of the twentieth century by researchers and ambassadors. The Negro Leagues' rightful place in history was finally recognized by Major League Baseball in December 2020 when Commissioner Rob Manfred gave what he called "long overdue recognition" by retroactively conferring major-league status on seven Negro Leagues between 1920 and 1948.

"Negro League players ... never looked to Major League Baseball to validate them," said Negro Leagues Baseball Museum president Bob Kendrick. "But for fans and for historical sake, this is significant. ... [I]t does give additional credence to how significant the Negro Leagues were, both on and off the field."[26]

NOTES

1. Neal Lanctot, *Negro League Baseball: The Rise and Ruin of a Black Institution* (Philadelphia: University of Pennsylvania Press, 2004), 306.
2. Quoted in Lanctot, 302.
3. Lanctot, 299.
4. Lanctot, 310.
5. Arnold Rampersad, *Jackie Robinson: A Biography* (New York: Alfred A. Knopf, 1997), 115.
6. Donn Rogosin, *Invisible Men: Life in Baseball's Negro Leagues* (New York: Atheneum, 1983), 203. The view that Robinson was not a true ambassador of Black baseball would temper enthusiasm within the Negro Leagues that he was the player chosen to break the color barrier.
7. Lanctot, 332.
8. Rampersad, 124.
9. Rampersad, 123.
10. Rampersad, 130.
11. Rampersad, 131.
12. Lanctot, 317.

13 Lanctot, 317.

14 Lanctot, 316. Robinson won the inaugural award, which at the time spanned both the American and National Leagues, signifying that he not only broke the color barrier, but did so with dominance.

15 Lanctot, 316.

16 Lanctot, 317. Joining Robinson in the majors that year were Larry Doby with the Cleveland Indians, Hank Thompson and Willard Brown with the St. Louis Browns, and Dan Bankhead, also with the Dodgers.

17 Lanctot, 321.

18 Lanctot, 335. Only Alex Pompez, owner of the New York Cuban Stars, was able to secure such an affiliation, with Horace Stoneham and the New York Giants.

19 Lanctot, 336.

20 Lanctot, 334.

21 Lanctot, 333.

22 Lanctot, 338.

23 Lanctot, 342.

24 Rampersad, 132.

25 Leslie Heaphy, *The Negro Leagues: 1869-1960* (Jefferson, North Carolina: McFarland & Co., 2003), 224.

26 Anthony Castrovince, "MLB Adds Negro Leagues to Official Records," MLB.com, December 16, 2020. Accessed at mlb.com/news/negro-leagues-given-major-league-status-for-baseball-records-stats.

JACKIE ROBINSON AND CIVIL RIGHTS: FROM 1947 UNTIL HIS DEATH

BY LESLIE HEAPHY

I know that you realize that in the tasks that lie ahead all freedom-loving Americans will want to share in achieving a society in which no man is penalized or favored solely because of his race, color, religion or national origin.

– Jackie Robinson[1]

Historians and sportswriters have presented various views of Jackie Robinson and his civil-rights efforts. Some have characterized him as simply following along, while others have argued that he was much more aggressive than he has been given credit for being. The story of Branch Rickey looking for a player willing to keep quiet and not react to fans' taunts, insults, and more has contributed to the more passive view. So many books and articles have only examined his baseball achievements and not his off-the-field activities. In more recent years, Michael Long and others have started to explore Robinson's career after he retired from the Dodgers. Looking at Robinson's jobs, writings, and personal interactions provide a new look at his importance to the civil-rights movement while he played and after he retired. The picture created is more complicated than simply the passive or aggressive views suggested by others.

Robinson made his debut for the Brooklyn Dodgers on April 15, 1947, and made an immediate impact. Though hitless in the game, he reached on an error and scored the go-ahead run as the Dodgers beat the Boston Braves. Stepping onto the field that long-ago April day thrust Robinson into the spotlight and marked his name in the history books forever. His place was cemented not just as a ballplayer, but also in the history of civil rights. The experiment that Rickey and Robinson started proved to be a success and changed more than the face of baseball; it changed America. Robinson's play affected the game and the fans in the stands.

Robinson's success opened the door for others to follow. During his 10-year career, Robinson, rather than marching or protesting, let his play do most of his talking. When he retired after his last game on October 10, 1956, Robinson's primary efforts shifted from the field to writing, speaking, marching, and working to bring about further changes that would give Blacks in America first-class citizenship. In a speech Robinson gave in June 1964, he acknowledged that he was fortunate enough in life to earn many advantages. But he also said that no Black person had made it in America until even the least privileged Black American had made it.

Every day Robinson took the field, he was making a stand for civil rights, for changing views about what Blacks were able to do. Roy Campanella, Don Newcombe, Willie Mays, Hank Aaron, and Ernie Banks are all examples of players whose careers were made possible in part because of Robinson's career. Though everyone acknowledged that Robinson was not the best player in the Negro Leagues at the time, he was the right choice to integrate and push civil

Jackie Robinson at the August 28, 1963, Civil Rights March on Washington, D.C.

Courtesy of Rachel Robinson and the Estate of Jackie Robinson.

rights forward in America's national pastime. Buck O'Neil said, "Yet when you look back, what people didn't realize, and still don't, was that we got the ball rolling on integration in our whole society."[2] Rickey signing Robinson happened before Brown v. Board of Education and Rosa Parks. Martin Luther King Jr. was still in college as were many other recognized leaders of the movement. Robinson's position as the first to integrate the White majors in the twentieth century, coupled with his success on the field is only a part of his legacy. His baseball accomplishments made his post-baseball life possible. Robinson used his celebrity status to continue what he started in April 1947. He believed he had a responsibility to use his voice to stand up for change, to fight for rights for all. In his first column for the *New York Amsterdam News*, in January 1962, Robinson wrote about the obligation he felt to speak out because of who he was.[3]

Robinson was called to testify before the House Un-American Activities Committee on July 18, 1949, because the committee wanted him to denounce Paul Robeson. He was called to speak out against Robeson for comments attributed to Robeson by the press during a trip to Paris. Robinson went but made some important statements about the voice and role of Black people in America. Robinson began by saying that even if Robeson made comments against the United States, no single Black could speak for all the millions living in America. Robinson declared that Blacks were angry before the Communist Party grew and would continue to be agitated until Jim Crow no longer existed in America. Unfortunately for Robeson, the committee did not really hear what Robinson was saying about American issues with race, but Robinson spoke out clearly on the inequalities that were a part of American history. A few years later, Robeson sent an open letter to Jackie encouraging him to continue speaking out against oppression and wrongs.[4]

Robinson seemed to live out what Robeson wanted him to do, speak and write against injustices. Robinson became vice president for a major retail industry, wrote for the *New York Post* and the *New York Amsterdam News*, served on the board for the NAACP, led fundraising efforts for various civil-rights efforts, and started his own company. He used each of these opportunities to call out racism by his actions and words. In addition, Robinson was also a prolific letter writer, sending hundreds of letters and telegrams to politicians, celebrities, business leaders, and community leaders, challenging them and praising them when he thought that was necessary. While we know today that Robinson used a ghostwriter for some of his columns, his voice is still loud and clear.

After retiring from baseball, Robinson took on the role of vice president for personnel at Chock Full O' Nuts (1957-1963), becoming the first African American to hold such a position at a large American corporation. Much of his job involved listening to concerns and complaints from employees. For Robinson the job was a chance to encourage and promote Black workers as well as be a role model in the business world. While working for the coffee company, Robinson lent his name to a column appearing in the *New York Post* that was mostly ghostwritten. He found himself in an early controversy that cost the company some customers after he called out a group of citizens from the Glendale-Ridgewood area of Queens for their "bigotry." The issue at question was overcrowding of schools. William Black, the head of Chock Full O' Nuts, came out in support of Robinson, and the company actually gained more customers for that stance.[5] He used his position in the company to also send letters to politicians such as President Eisenhower. A May 13, 1958, letter on the company letterhead chastised the president for urging Black Americans to be patient in the face of continued discrimination. These are examples of Robinson's statements made on numerous occasions that he would not be silent in the face of things he believed to be wrong.[6]

Robinson also wrote to Richard Nixon in 1957 and thanked him for some of his public remarks, showing early support that would continue for the Republican politician from California. Robinson actually served for a few months in 1960 on Nixon's election campaign. This support caused some to question Robinson's commitment to civil rights, but Robinson felt Nixon had a longer record of support than other candidates had. His 1957 letter ended with the following admonition reminding Nixon that the work was far from done. Robinson wrote, "I know that you realize that in the tasks that lie ahead all freedom-loving Americans will want to share in achieving a society in which no man is penalized or favored solely because of his race, color, religion or national origin."[7] Later that same year, Robinson again praised Nixon for his actions aimed at improving the world, focusing on his current actions rather than his record.[8]

Believing that actions counted most, Robinson withdrew his support for Nixon in the 1968 presidential election. In a January 1969 letter to Nixon, Robinson explained why he and other Black Americans did not support his election. Robinson said, "I must respectfully say I am very much concerned over what I consider a lack of understanding in White America of the desires and ambitions of most Black Americans." He went on to say that if changes were not made, the confrontations between the two races would get worse. Nixon responded by thanking Robinson for his letter but also asking for his help in healing divisions within the country.[9]

Robinson wrote continually to politicians and other civic leaders and urged them to do better or challenged them when he disagreed. His letters to John F. Kennedy are a perfect example of this approach. One of his letters to Senator Kennedy in 1959 asked whether Blacks should be happy with what had been accomplished or more focused on what issues still needed to be addressed throughout the country. A February 1961 letter stated, "While I am very happy over your obviously fine start as our President, my concern over Civil Rights and my vigorous opposition to your election is one of sincerity."[10] He hoped that his fears were wrong and that Kennedy would provide the right leadership. Later Kennedy gave a speech on civil rights, and Robinson praised him publicly for his words. Robinson sent Kennedy a telegram thanking him for being a strong leader. Kennedy's 1963 speech called on America to finally fulfill its original promise to all its citizens. Robinson's column was published just as news came out about the assassination of Medgar Evers, so he called on people to keep up the pressure, to not give in. He wanted Evers' death to not have been in vain.[11]

Robert Kennedy also received much attention from Robinson. Robinson continually called upon the younger Kennedy to not just talk but to act in his role as US attorney general. The former ballplayer said Black America was tired of good words and needed to see real change. This is why he supported Nixon over Kennedy for president, believing Nixon to be the sincerer candidate. Robinson wrote to Robert Kennedy shortly after his brother sent protection for the Freedom Riders in 1961, praising such decisive action and hoping that it would continue.[12]

Letters and telegrams were also sent regularly to Hubert Humphrey, Barry Goldwater, Lyndon Johnson, and Nelson Rockefeller, calling on them to do more in their political roles. Robinson campaigned for Rockefeller when the New York Republican ran for president in 1964. At the same time, Robinson made clear his dislike of Barry Goldwater's candidacy. Goldwater responded to some of Robinson's public criticism in a letter that acknowledged that Robinson's remarks held more importance than others because of his fame as a former Brooklyn Dodger. People listened to what Robinson wrote and said. Robinson responded to Goldwater's invitation to meet to talk about civil rights, telling him he thought it was too late and that what Goldwater needed to do was share his views on civil rights publicly and not in private conversations.[13]

Malcolm X, Martin Luther King Jr., and NAACP president Roy Wilkins corresponded with Robinson as well as being frequent topics in some of his news columns. Robinson and King developed a strong friendship through shared goals and beliefs, while Malcolm X and Robinson disagreed on tactics that should be used to bring about change. Wilkins and Robinson had a relationship that waffled between support and criticism. Robinson joined the NAACP board in 1957 believing in their work, but resigned in 1963 after criticizing Wilkins' leadership and lack of desire to recruit new and younger leaders to the cause.

When King gave his famous "I Have a Dream" speech in 1963, Robinson and his children were there in support. King called Robinson "... a pilgrim that walked in the lonesome byways toward the high road of Freedom. He was a sit-inner before sit-ins, a freedom rider before freedom rides."[14] At a 1962 Southern Christian Leadership Conference dinner, Robinson praised King as a great man. Following his own words to others, Robinson also acted to help King with his name and his time. He and his wife, Rachel, hosted jazz concerts at their home in Connecticut to help raise bail money to be used for protesters arrested at marches. A June 1963 concert featured the music of Duke Ellington, Dizzy Gillespie, Billy Taylor, and Dave Brubeck. These concerts eventually became an annual event with the proceeds going to the Jackie Robinson Foundation for scholarships. Upon his election to the National Baseball Hall of Fame, Robinson donated proceeds from a dinner to honor him to the SCLC voter registration drive. Robinson sent a telegram to President Johnson after Bloody Sunday asking for him to call for an end to the violence before it could get any worse. In October 1958 and April 1959, Robinson and King served together as honorary chairs for the Youth March for Integrated Schools, which was held in Washington.[15]

King did not escape criticism or challenges from Robinson. In 1960 King received a letter from Robinson questioning some fundraising practices and more importantly asking about supposed comments from SCLC leadership that criticized the NAACP. King assured Robinson in early June that was not something he permitted at any meetings where he was present. He also told Robinson, "I absolutely agree with you that we cannot afford any division at this time and we cannot afford any conflict. And I can assure you that as long as I am President of SCLC, it will not be a party to any development of disunity."[16] Robinson and King realized that any progress toward civil rights would happen more quickly with united voices from the African American community. This was often why so many groups invited Robinson to be present or asked if he would lend his name to their efforts.

In his role as fundraising chair for the NAACP Freedom Fund Campaign beginning in 1957, Robinson traveled all over the country. He visited local chapters to help them in their efforts to raise funds. In January alone, he made trips to nine cities. Robinson's trips made such an impact that he was invited back to Boston to attend a dinner in his honor. The proceeds from the dinner, hosted by the New England Bowling Association, were donated to the Freedom Fund.[17]

Invites came regularly for Robinson to speak at all kinds of events, especially those concerning race-related issues. Robinson responded to as many as he could because he felt this was a responsibility that came with the fortune he had in his life. For example, in February 1958 he spoke in Mississippi at a rally for the state's NAACP branches. The title of his talk was "Patience, Pride and Progress." Robinson urged those attending to not lose hope but to keep pushing for change and to end discrimination. He gave speeches for a number of Elks organizations over the years, generally focusing on their efforts to give out scholarships to minority students and to help in efforts supporting school desegregation. Robinson also gave suggestions to groups for other speakers who he thought would help them in their civil-rights efforts. One of those suggestions was boxer Floyd Patterson after Patterson took a stand against segregated seating at his fights in Florida.[18]

Robinson's work and support of the NAACP was extensive. Not only did he serve on the board and chair various campaigns, he corresponded regularly with Executive Secretary Roy Wilkins. Robinson treated Wilkins as he did all other leaders, both in praise and challenge when he felt the right effort was not happening. When Robinson took a stand over a White restaurant group in Harlem in 1962, Wilkins and the NAACP came out in support of Robinson's stance. Robinson condemned the anti-Semitic words of a small group of Black protestors chanting outside the steakhouse. Wilkins agreed with Robinson's column in the *New York Amsterdam News* and said progress is led by those who treat everyone fairly and not just those like them. Later in 1967 Robinson wrote letters criticizing Wilkins' leadership of the NAACP, stating he was unhappy with the lack of progress and asking for new membership to move the organization forward. Robinson again said, "I don't intend to remain silent when I see things I believe to be wrong."[19]

While Robinson wrote extensively to public leaders, he also contributed two regular newspaper columns to the *New York Post* and the *Amsterdam News*. He was listed as the editor for *Our Sports* for its five issues in 1953. Robinson was certainly not the writer of many of his columns, but his name was attached and he would not have lent his voice to topics he did not agree with. Alfred Duckett was the likely ghostwriter of his *Post* columns in 1959 and 1960. Robinson was let go from the *Post* and had a column in the *Amsterdam News* from 1962 to 1968. Researcher Raymond McCaffrey studied all 330 *News* columns that Robinson wrote. He determined that 285 were unique to the *Amsterdam News*, making them an important resource to understanding Robinson's full importance to civil rights. Of the articles, 310 dealt specifically with civil rights and 68 with sports and civil rights.[20]

Robinson used his columns to speak on a range of issues. Sometimes the columns were personal and reflected on his playing days, but most dealt with issues of the day. In 1959, for example, he spoke out about the prejudice within the Boston Red Sox organization. He related how he, Sam Jethroe, and Marvin Williams were invited to a tryout in 1945 and nothing ever came of it. Another 1960 *Post* article called out a *Sports Illustrated* writer for an article titled "The Private World of the Negro Ballplayer." Robinson wrote, "In many respects I found this article unbelievable, insulting and degrading, both to Negro ballplayers and to the intelligence of *Sports Illustrated*'s readers."[21] Robinson believed the writer was contributing, as many did, to stereotypes about African American athletes. The writer talked about Black ballplayers living in their own world and having their own language, one that no White player could enter. His point was that they had something of their own and did not need the majors, which was not true.[22]

Speaking about the lack of a Black manager in the major leagues, Robinson challenged Bill Veeck after he became part-owner of the Chicago White Sox. Veeck laid out in an article what he saw as the different characteristics needed for a Black manager to make it. Robinson took Veeck to task for giving in to society and not pushing to hire a Black manager. He wrote, "What is important, however, is the fact that a man like Bill Veeck should find it necessary to retreat from the hard-won standard in baseball today that a man's abilities are what count, not his color or his 'temperament' when it comes to considering a man for management responsibility."[23]

As to his possible election to the National Baseball Hall of Fame in 1962, Robinson made it clear that he would not beg. He did not want to be elected simply because he was the first Black in the majors but also should not be denied because he spoke out for his own rights and those of others who had no voice. After his election, Robinson wrote about what his selection meant, and said, "These men elected me in spite of the fact that they knew and know now that Jackie Robinson would always say and do only the things in which he believed."[24] A 1963 *Amsterdam News* column built on this idea as he praised former teammate Roy Campanella for speaking out against discrimination but showed disappointment that Willie Mays and Maury Wills were not more vocal. Again, Robinson felt they all had a duty to use their voices to right wrongs against those to whom no one listened.

Robinson did not limit his columns to chastising baseball for not doing enough. A number of his stories challenged the discriminatory practices of the PGA. When Charlie Sifford was finally allowed to play in PGA tournaments in 1960, he credited Robinson's columns for helping to get his application accepted. Sifford's acceptance did not immediately open membership at all clubs to African Americans, just as Robinson's play with the Dodgers did not throw open the doors of the majors.[25]

Robinson also wrote about current leaders from Truman to Nixon, apartheid in South Africa, sit-ins, Black power, the Vietnam War and much more. Robinson supported the US presence in Vietnam and disagreed with King on this issue. He was not a fan of Malcolm X and his calls for all-Black movements and the division he believed was caused by the more militant actions of the Black Muslims and Black Panthers. Robinson believed Malcom X and his followers needed to take responsibility for creating an atmosphere that pushed for division and even, at times, violence. At the same time, Robinson also supported Cassius Clay's turn to Islam, saying that was the beauty and right of the individual in America. Instead of supporting Malcolm X, Robinson seemed to favor the ideas of Adam Clayton Powell, who described Black Power as people taking charge of their own futures and not relying on others.[26]

To help create a future for Black Americans that did not rely on White America, Robinson also created a number of businesses. He started his own construction company and bank to give Blacks a position of strength to push for further change. Economic independence would give the Black community a stronger voice. This is why Robinson encouraged people to boycott businesses that did not employ African Americans in their advertisements. He was building off earlier campaigns supported by Newark Eagles owner Effa Manley and others, to not buy where you could not work. In 1970 Robinson and partners created the Jackie Robinson Construction Corporation. Even more significantly, Robinson co-founded the Freedom National Bank in Harlem in 1964. The bank survived until 1990, when it finally closed its doors. From the moment the bank was founded, it struggled against both the White banking industry and even the Black community. The hurdles and expectations were a difficult balancing act, but Robinson believed the good the bank could do outweighed the struggles. After Robinson's death in 1972, his widow, Rachel, took over the Construction Corporation and continued to build low-income housing. Then, with their children, she created the Jackie Robinson Foundation to continue his legacy by providing educational support to hundreds of students so they could continue their education and build their self-reliance.[27]

Robinson received a wide array of awards during his lifetime and after his death. Two in particular stand out in recognizing his influence on civil rights in America. In 1956 Robinson became the first athlete to receive the Spingarn Medal, given by the NAACP since 1914. Robinson believed the award showed that his work and efforts transcended the baseball diamond. The second award was the NAACP Annual Merit Award, presented in 1947 to honor his work in integrating baseball.[28]

Jack Roosevelt Robinson contributed greatly to the civil-rights movement, both on and off the baseball diamond. Much has been written about his integration of America's national pastime, but far less attention has been paid to his various contributions after he retired. Robinson used his name and position to write to leaders and challenge them to be better. He wrote columns to reach a larger audience and helped raise money for many different causes. He spoke out whenever he saw something he felt was wrong and encouraged others to do the same. Robinson lived with the belief that the work would not finish until every person was treated equally and fairly. One of Robinson's most often repeated quotes is "A life is not important except in the impact it has on other lives."[29] Those words truly express what he believed and how he tried to live his life. A final statement from a 1967 Robinson column captures his view of civil-rights activity. "It is the duty and responsibility of each and every one of us to refuse to accept the faintest sign or token of prejudice. It does not matter whether it is directed against us or against others. Racial prejudice is not only a vicious disease, it is contagious."[30]

NOTES

1. Letter to Richard Nixon, March 19, 1957, in Michael G. Long, ed., *First Class Citizenship: The Civil Rights Letters of Jackie Robinson* (New York: Times Books, 2007), 27.

2. Larry Hogan, *Shades of Glory, The Negro Leagues and the Story of African American Baseball* (Washington: National Geographic, 2006), 377.

3. Raymond McCaffrey, "From Baseball Icon to Crusading Columnist," *Journalism History* 46:3, 185-207.

4. Eric Nusbaum, "The Story Behind Jackie Robinson's Moving Testimony before the House Un-American Activities Committee, https://time.com/5808543/jackie-robinson-huac/, March 24, 2020; "Negroes Won't Fight Soviets, Robeson Says," *Washington Post*, April 21, 1949: 3; Peter Dreier, "Half a Century before Colin Kaepernick, Jackie Robinson Said, 'I Cannot Stand and Sing the Anthem,'" *The Nation*, https://www.thenation.com/article/archive/huac-jackie-robinson-paul-robeson/, July 18, 2019; H. Heft, "Jackie Robinson Chides Robeson," *Washington Post*, July 19, 1949: 2.

5. Todd Brauckmiller Jr., "Jackie Robinson: An Unexpected Hero of Business and Civil Rights," STMU History Media, St. Mary's University of San Antonio, stmuhistorymedia.org/Jackie-robinson.

6. Letter from Jackie Robinson to President Dwight D. Eisenhower; White House Central Files Box 731; File: OF-142-A-3; Dwight D. Eisenhower Library; National Archives and Records Administration, https://www.archives.gov/historical-docs/todays-doc/index.html?dod-date=513.

7. Letter from Jackie Robinson to Richard Nixon, March 4, 1957, BA MSS 102 Series IV Box 1 Folder 5, Jackie Robinson Papers 1934-2001, Library of Congress, copy from Jackie Robinson Papers, National Baseball Hall of Fame, Cooperstown, New York.

8. Long, *First-Class Citizenship*, 38.

9. Long, *First-Class Citizenship*, 290-292.

10. Long, *First-Class Citizenship*, 125.

11. Long, *First-Class Citizenship*, 171-172.

12. Long, *First-Class Citizenship*, 126, 129.

13. Long, *First-Class Citizenship*, 198-199.

14. Mike Bertha, "Martin Luther King Jr. and Jackie Robinson: Friends and Civil Rights Icons," https://www.mlb.com/cut4/mlk-jr-and-jackie-robinson-were-good-friends-c162102154, January 18, 2016.

15. Martin B. Cassidy, "Beyond the Dream: Remembering King's Visit to Stamford," https://www.stamfordadvocate.com/news/article/Beyond-the-dream-Remembering-King-s-visit-to-4795988.php, September 7, 2013.

16. Letter from Martin Luther King Jr. to Jackie Robinson, June 19, 1960, MLKP-MBU, Martin Luther King Jr. Papers, 1954-1968, Boston University.

17. Tour lists, BA MSS 102 Series IV Box 1 Folder 1, Jackie Robinson Papers 1934-2001, Library of Congress, copy from JR Papers, National Baseball Hall of Fame, Cooperstown, New York.

18. Letter to Robinson, January 22, 1958, and Letter to Roy Wilkins, March 15, 1961.

19. Letter from Robinson to Roy Wilkins, February 15, 1967, and Robinson correspondence and columns, BA MSS 102 Series IV Box 1 Folder 3, Jackie Robinson Papers 1934-2001, Library of Congress, copy from JR Papers, National Baseball Hall of Fame, Cooperstown, New York.

20. McCaffrey.

21. Michael G. Long, ed., *Beyond Home Plate: Jackie Robinson on Life after Baseball* (Syracuse, New York: Syracuse University Press, 2013), 17.

22. "The Private World of the Negro Ball Player," *Sports Illustrated*, March 21, 1960, https://vault.si.com/vault/1960/03/21/the-private-world-of-the-negro-ballplayer.

23. Long, *Beyond Home Plate*, 21.

24. Long, *Beyond Home Plate*, 25.

25. Long, *Beyond Home Plate*, 36-41.

26. Long, *Beyond Home Plate*, 86-97; Jackie Robinson, "Egg-Throwing and Dr. King," *New York Amsterdam News*, July 13, 1963: 11.

27. "Freedom National Bank in Harlem Prepares to Open," *New York Times*, December 19, 1964: 37; Roger Wilkins, "Rachel Robinson: the Survivor," https://archive.nytimes.com/www.nytimes.com/library/magazine/millennium/m5/album-robinson.html; Reggie Wade, "Jackie Robinson Was the 'Jackie Robinson' of Banking in Harlem," https://finance.yahoo.com/news/jackie-robinson-was-the-jackie-robinson-of-banking-in-harlem-192114397.html, February 20, 2019; "As Black-owned Harlem Bank Dies, So Does a Symbol," *Baltimore Sun*, November 14, 1990, https://www.baltimoresun.com/news/bs-xpm-1990-11-14-1990318052-story.html.

28. H.L. Moon, "News from NAACP, Jackie Robinson Named 41st Spingarn Medalist" (New York, June 14, 1956), Reproduced from the Collections of the Manuscript Division, Library of Congress.

29. Quotes, https://www.jackierobinson.com/quotes/.

30. *New York Amsterdam News*, January 28, 1967: 15.

THE BLACK KNIGHT: A POLITICAL PORTRAIT OF JACKIE ROBINSON

by Steven K. Wisensale

On July 18, 1949, Jackie Robinson appeared before the House Un-American Activities Committee (HUAC) to testify against Paul Robeson, another prominent Black man who was accused of being a member of the Communist Party. It marked a turning point in the lives of both men. For Robinson, it meant being catapulted into the political arena, where he would remain until his death 23 years later. For Robeson, an internationally known opera star, the first African-American to ever play *Othello* on stage, and one who had walked a picket line outside Yankee Stadium to protest segregated baseball, it meant the end of his brilliant singing career.

Robinson's impact on Robeson's career in 1949 illustrates the complexity of his life during a crucial period in American history. Both were African-American men who had reached the pinnacle of their respective careers in a society dominated by Whites. But opera was not baseball and thus Robinson found himself in a much more influential position to integrate a segregated society. After all, it was Robinson who came alone and arrived before the others. He came before Campanella and Newcombe, before Doby and Miñoso, and before Mays and Aaron. He came before Banks, Clemente, Gibson, Brock, Stargell, and all the other greats. He came before Rosa Parks and James Meredith, before Martin Luther King Jr. and Malcolm X, and before the Little Rock Nine, bus boycotts, freedom riders, and the March on Washington.

When baseball desegregated itself in 1947, the first major American institution to do so voluntarily, Jackie Robinson was penciled into the lineup for what was to become a whole new ballgame. He stood at home plate years before an executive order desegregated the US military, before the Supreme Court integrated public schools, and before Congress enacted the Civil Rights Act of 1964 and the Voting Rights Act of 1965.

Writing in *Take Time for Paradise*, Bart Giamatti emphasized the importance of an integrated game. "Late, late as it was, the arrival of Jack Roosevelt Robinson was an extraordinary moment in American history. For the first time a Black American was on America's most privileged version of a level field."[1] Martin Luther King Jr. put it more succinctly during a meeting with Don Newcombe. "You will never know how easy it was for me because of Jackie Robinson," he said.[2]

The year 1997 marked the 50th anniversary of Jackie Robinson breaking major-league baseball's racial barrier. Although remembered primarily for his athletic skills, both at UCLA and in a Dodgers uniform, Robinson always appeared to be someone on a much broader and more important mission in life. "He used his athletics as a political forum," said his widow, Rachel, in an interview with Peter Golenbock. "He never wanted to run for office but he always wanted to influence people's thinking."[3] Perhaps that explains why Mrs. Robinson always emphasized that Jackie was a civil-rights activist first and a ballplayer second.

Yet, despite numerous books and articles on Robinson the ballplayer published between 1947 and 1997, few drew attention to his role as a political activist. Consequently, only a small minority of Americans were aware of his battles with the military (he was court-martialed), his appearance before the House Un-American Activities Committee to testify against Paul Robeson, his involvement with Martin Luther King Jr., Roy Wilkins, and Thurgood Marshall during the Civil Rights Movement, and the role he played in several presidential campaigns.

The purpose here, therefore, is to paint a political portrait of Jackie Robinson. What were his major political views and which individuals (in baseball and out) were most influential in shaping them? To capture his political portrait, we will focus on three significant episodes of his life: the Paul Robeson affair; his involvement in the Civil Rights Movement; and his role in presidential campaigns.

THE PAUL ROBESON AFFAIR

The signing of Jackie Robinson in 1945 is legendary. Scouted while a member of the Kansas City Monarchs, Robinson spent the 1946 season in Montreal before joining the Dodgers in 1947. For

Jackie

Rickey, Robinson was a jewel. He neither smoked nor drank and, like Rickey, he was born and raised in a strict Methodist home. He attended a major university (UCLA) and participated in four sports, both with and against White athletes. He was combative, proud, and courageous. On the field, he excelled. Promising Rickey that he would "turn the other cheek" at least initially when targeted by opponents who slung racial slurs and insults at him, Robinson devoted all of his energy to baseball in 1947. After his first season, *The Sporting News* named him Rookie of the Year – the first time the award was given to any player. His record spoke for itself: 42 successful bunts (14 for hits, 28 sacrifices), 29 stolen bases, 12 home runs, and a .297 batting average. J.G. Taylor Spink, publisher of *The Sporting News*, commented on his accomplishments: "Robinson was rated solely as a freshman player – on his hitting, his running, his defensive play, his team value."[4] For 10 seasons, from 1947 to 1956, he led the Dodgers to six National League pennants and one World Series championship.

It can be argued, however, that 1949 was the most significant year of Robinson's life – both on the field and off. On his way to his first and only MVP award, he led the league in hitting (.342) and stolen bases (37), hit 16 home runs, and collected 124 RBIs as the Dodgers won the pennant by one game over the St. Louis Cardinals. It was also the year in which he became the first Black to participate in the All-Star Game.

Also, in June of 1949, Paul Robeson returned to the United States after completing a European tour. Robeson, the first Black to ever play Othello on stage in the United States, had become a major critic of America's segregationist policies. Born in Princeton, New Jersey, in 1898, he was Phi Beta Kappa and the valedictorian of his graduating class at Rutgers. A few years later he received a law degree from Columbia University. On the athletic field, he was equally impressive, earning 15 varsity letters and twice being named an All-American in football. Unable to find a job in a predominantly White world, he chose instead to pursue a musical career, focusing primarily on opera.

By the mid-1940s, Robeson's concerts became a combination of songs and political messages, as he frequently spoke out on the plight of America's Blacks. "The Ballad of Joe Hill," a song about a union organizer, replaced famous arias. Before a packed audience at the Bolshoi Theater in Moscow, he announced that he had changed the original words of "Ol' Man River" to mean "we must fight to the death for peace and freedom."[5] And as the years passed, he became more closely associated with the American Communist Party. However, it was a statement he made before an audience in Paris that drew the attention of the US government and changed Robeson's life forever: "It is unthinkable that American Negroes would go to war on behalf of those who have oppressed us for generations against the Soviet Union which in one generation has lifted our people to full human dignity."[6]

It was the early years of the Cold War and an emerging concern that the Communist Party was making inroads among America's Blacks bordered on paranoia. Robeson was confronted regularly with protesters at his concerts and twice, in Peekskill, New York, his performances sparked riots. In Harlem's Red Rooster Restaurant, Dodgers pitcher Don Newcombe refused to shake his hand.[7] Meanwhile, the House Un-American Activities Committee continued its assault against "disloyal" Americans. In early July 1949, it opened its "Hearings Regarding Communist Infiltration of Minority Groups." Soon after the hearings concluded, Robeson was stripped of his passport by the FBI and, consequently, performance contracts were either canceled or never initiated, driving him into obscurity. For more than four decades, he was the only two-time All-American to not be inducted into the College Football Hall of Fame. He was finally admitted posthumously in 1995. His passport was reactivated in 1958 following a US Supreme Court ruling that his due-process rights had been violated.[8]

If life is a chess game, then Jackie Robinson's role in the summer of 1949 was to checkmate Paul Robeson. In early July, Representative John S. Wood, Democrat of Georgia and chairman of the House Un-American Activities Committee, contacted Robinson and invited him to appear before his committee "to give lie to" Robeson's statements.[9] It is not surprising that Robinson was selected to testify. According to Alvin Stokes, a Black investigator for the committee, it was imperative to get someone of Robinson's stature to discredit Robeson.[10]

Robinson was clearly confronted with a dilemma. On one hand, if he testified, he might be little more than a Black pawn in a White man's chess game that pitted Black against Black. If he did not testify, however, Robeson's statement might be upheld as a view representative of all Blacks, a view Robinson and millions of other Blacks vehemently disagreed with. Despite advice from his wife to not testify, he was ultimately won over by the more persuasive views of Branch Rickey, who apparently decided that a public appearance of this nature was a necessity. Assisted by Lester Granger of the Urban League, a Black civil-rights organization, Robinson wrestled vigorously with the content of his statement. "It must be placating, so that the white race will not be alienated," he said. "And of course it must be strong enough so that it won't lose the colored audience either."[11] He found himself suspended in what the writer Carl Rowan referred to as "a patriot's purgatory."[12] On July 18, 1949, just six days after he played in his first All-Star Game, he presented his prepared statement before the House Un-American Activities Committee.

In essence, Robinson's appearance before HUAC was a checked swing. He lunged after Robeson's Paris statement and dismissed it as "silly" before pulling back his bat and attacking Jim Crow and American racism in general. Years later and shortly before his death in 1972, he reflected on his 1949 testimony: "I have grown wiser and closer to the painful truth about America's destructiveness. And, I do have an increased respect for Paul Robeson who sacrificed himself, his career, and the wealth and confidence he once enjoyed because, I believe, he was sincerely trying to help his people."[13] After all, it was Paul Robeson who picketed Yankee Stadium in the 1940s demanding that baseball be integrated.[14] But Robeson clearly paid a price for his activism. With his career shattered, his income dropped from $100,000 in 1947 to $6,000 in 1952. In his later years, he lived a reclusive life in poverty with his sister and died from a stroke in Philadelphia on January 23, 1976.[15]

THE CIVIL RIGHTS MOVEMENT

A year after his appearance before the House Un-American Activities Committee, *The Jackie Robinson Story* opened at movie theaters nationwide. Jackie played himself in the film. Ruby Dee played Rachel. Years later, he would lament that the film was made much too soon.[16] Indeed it was! For Robinson's overall contributions to society went far beyond his display of outstanding athletic skills. Over the next two decades, he actively participated in the Civil Rights Movement and three presidential campaigns. He cultivated close friendships with Martin Luther King Jr., Thurgood Marshall, Nelson Rockefeller, and Jesse Jackson, while he feuded openly with Adam Clayton Powell, Malcolm X, and William F. Buckley. He wrote a regular syndicated column on political issues, hosted a radio show, appeared on *Meet the Press*, coordinated jazz concerts at his home to raise funds for civil-rights causes, served as a corporate executive, was named to the directorship of a major bank, and was appointed to numerous boards and commissions in both the private and public sectors.

Throughout the 1950s and the early '60s, a dormant America, most of which was satisfied with the status quo, was rudely awakened by sit-ins, freedom rides, and mass marches – all in support of racial equality. Soon, the unfamiliar became the familiar. There was Birmingham and Little Rock, Greensboro and Selma. There was Emmett Till and Medgar Evers, James Meredith and Schwerner, Chaney, and Goodman. While Congress passed the Civil Rights Act of 1964 and the Voting Rights Act of 1965, the nation was stunned by urban riots and the assassinations of four of its most prominent leaders: John Kennedy, Malcolm X, Martin Luther King Jr., and Robert Kennedy. Still to come was the pain and agony of the Vietnam War.

Through it all, Jackie Robinson immersed himself in the cause, clarified his political views, fortified his basic principles, and acted upon his most cherished beliefs. When he retired from baseball after the 1956 season, after refusing a trade to the New York Giants, he immediately entered the business world as a vice president of personnel for Chock Full O' Nuts, a New York City restaurant chain. Under the tutelage of owner William Black, he not only learned how to manage employees in the private sector (a skill he would later apply to other business ventures), but he was given the opportunity to continue his quest for racial equality nationwide. Permitted to use Chock Full O' Nuts stationery to express his views, he lobbied key political figures and advocated strongly for Black capitalism.[17]

In 1957 Robinson was named chairman of the NAACP Freedom Fund Drive, which required him to travel the country to recruit new members and raise funds for the civil-rights organization. In April of that year, he was a guest on NBC's *Meet the Press,* discussing two topics in particular: civil rights ("we're moving too slow") and baseball's reserve clause (he supported it). However, by 1972 Robinson changed his mind on the reserve clause. He, Hank Greenberg, Jim Brosnan, and Bill Veeck were the only people affiliated with major-league baseball to support Curt Flood's quest to end the reserve clause by appealing to the Supreme Court. Fearing reprisals, perhaps, no active player at the time spoke out in favor of Flood.[18]

By 1959, Robinson found another outlet for expressing his views. Writing a syndicated column three days a week, he explored a variety of topics that ranged from a lynching in Mississippi to substandard housing in Harlem. In one column, he announced he was politically independent, but he was being wooed by both parties.[19] In another column, he accused the Boston Red Sox of racism because they failed to bring Pumpsie Green (their only black player with major-league skills at the time) north after spring training.[20] But his political interests would broaden and include other topics.[21]

Although he had met Dr. Martin Luther King Jr. as early as 1955 (after King's home was firebombed), it was not until the early 1960s that Robinson developed a close working relationship with the civil-rights leader and accompanied him on numerous speaking tours. However, when King openly opposed the Vietnam War and attempted to blend the peace movement with the Civil Rights Movement, Robinson retreated. "Isn't it unfair for you to place all the burden of blame on America and none on the communist forces we are fighting?" he asked King in a public letter.[22] Similarly, Robinson also had a public conflict with Muhammad Ali when the heavyweight boxing champion declared himself a conscientious objector and openly opposed the war.[23] Eventually, however, after his son Jackie Jr. returned from the war wounded, Robinson began to view US intervention in Vietnam differently. He became particularly concerned about the disproportionate number of poor Blacks being dispatched to the war zone.

Relentless, Robinson's assault on racism continued. In 1968 he was one of the leading organizers of the effort to block South Africa's participation in the Olympics because of its continuing practice of apartheid. In 1970 he testified before the Senate Small Business Subcommittee and criticized what he termed the Nixon administration's anemic efforts to support Black capitalism. And shortly before his death in 1972, he attacked professional baseball for its reluctance to hire Black managers, coaches, and front-office personnel. But unlike many professional athletes who have found the transition from the playing field to mainstream society difficult, Robinson appeared to thrive on it and always reminded people of the evils of racism.

THE PRESIDENTIAL CAMPAIGNS

Robinson's involvement in the civil-rights struggles led him naturally toward the political arena. As more Blacks demanded greater power, their votes increased in value. Not surprisingly, politicians in both parties aggressively sought out well-respected role models who could deliver Black votes. Jackie Robinson, in particular, was viewed as a prize catch for any aspiring political candidate. By 1959, however, he still maintained his political neutrality, though he was actively recruited by both parties. A year later, things changed.

The presidential election year of 1960 proved to be pivotal for the nation. Aware of its significance, Robinson sought the presidential candidate who he thought most clearly understood the racial issue and best represented the cause of civil rights. He initially chose Hubert Humphrey, a liberal Democrat. "I had campaigned for Senator Humphrey in the Democratic primaries because I had a strong admiration for his civil rights background as mayor of Minneapolis and as a U.S. Senator. I had heard him publicly vow to be the living example of a man who would rather be right morally than to achieve the presidency."[24] His choice of Humphrey, however, would be short-lived. After losing the West Virginia primary, the Minnesota senator ended his quest for the presidency, leaving Robinson to choose between Richard Nixon and John F. Kennedy in the general election.

Later in 1960, Robinson traveled to Washington and met with both candidates. "Finally, I didn't think it was much of a choice, but I was impressed with the Nixon record on rights," he wrote years later. "And, when I sat with him in his office in Washington, he certainly said all the right things."[25] Also, he got the impression later that Nixon would appoint a Black person to his Cabinet if elected. On the other hand, he found Kennedy to be courteous, awkward, and uncomfortable in his presence. "My very first reaction to the Senator was one of doubt because he couldn't or wouldn't look me straight in the eye. My second reaction, much more substantial, was that this was a man who had served in the Senate and wanted to be president, but who knew little or nothing about Black problems and sensibilities. I was appalled that he was so ignorant of our situation and be bidding for the highest office in the land."[26]

According to Harvey Frommer's account in *Rickey and Robinson: The Men Who Broke Baseball's Color Barrier* (1982), Robinson was also upset that Kennedy had offered him money for his support. Clearly, Robinson did not find it easy supporting the Republican Party, but his reasoning appeared to be sound. If Blacks did not play an active role in both parties, he argued, they would eventually be ignored by Republicans on the one hand and taken for granted by Democrats on the other. Such a combination, he emphasized, would leave Blacks both powerless and vulnerable. His reasoning would be tested in 1964.

Still licking their wounds from a devastating loss of the White House in 1960, the Republicans' reaction was consistent with that of a party out of power and uncertain of its mission. It nominated an extremist for president. In August of 1964 at the Cow Palace in San Francisco, Senator Barry Goldwater of Arizona accepted his party's nomination and promptly delivered his "extremism in the pursuit of liberty is no vice" speech. Robinson, who worked the floor in support of Governor Nelson Rockefeller of New York, was shocked when the delegates booed his candidate loudly before a national TV audience. "As I watched this steamroller operation in San Francisco, I had a better understanding of how it must have felt to be a Jew in Hitler's Germany," he wrote in his 1972 autobiography. He referred to Goldwater as "anti-Negro, anti-Jewish, and anti-Catholic" and predicted that he would be defeated soundly in November, which was indeed the case, as Lyndon Johnson won the presidency in a landslide. Consequently, Robinson's greatest fear, that the Republican Party would become a party of "Whites only," was becoming a reality.

In 1966 Rockefeller appointed Robinson to be a special assistant for community relations in New York state. Two years later, he resigned, just a few days after his party nominated Richard Nixon for president. Distraught over a report that the South "had a veto" over the party's nomination for vice president, he announced his resignation from Rockefeller's staff and prepared to campaign for Democratic candidate Hubert Humphrey again. In a front-page article in the *New York Times*, he expressed his feelings in baseball terms: "I don't know of anything that hurt me more than the nomination of Richard Nixon and the rejection of Governor Rockefeller. It made me feel like I felt when Bobby Thomson hit a home run to beat us out of the pennant in 1951."[27]

By 1971, Robinson's disillusionment with White politics had even penetrated his relationship with Rockefeller. He became dismayed over the governor's cuts in education and welfare and his implementation of a one-year residency requirement to qualify for welfare. "He seems to have made a sharp right turn away from the stand of the man who once fought the Old Guard Establishment so courageously," Robinson wrote in 1972.[28]

So after years of fighting for civil rights and campaigning for presidential candidates, the Black Knight from Brooklyn with the pigeon-toed gait and graying hair found himself stranded on second – "far out at the edge of the ordered world at rocky second – the farthest point from home. Whoever remains out there is said to 'die' on base," wrote Bart Giamatti. "Home is finally beyond reach in a hostile world full of quirks and tricks, and hostile folk. There are no dragons in baseball, only shortstops, but they can emerge from nowhere and cut one down."[29] For Robinson, the shortstops came in the form of John Kennedy, Barry Goldwater, Richard Nixon, and even Nelson Rockefeller.

In the numerous books and articles written about Robinson over the years, one may conclude that he learned three important lessons that could be passed on to succeeding generations: First and foremost, he learned and believed that people can change for the better. A Jim Crow Army was integrated, reluctant Dodgers teammates accepted him, and Malcolm X overcame a life of drugs and crime. Second, he learned the importance of mentors and role models in shaping one's life. The three most important teachers in his life, other than his wife, Rachel, were Branch Rickey, William Black, and Nelson Rockefeller. And third, he learned that one should never be satisfied with the status quo. Most importantly, he learned the power of questions. "Why can't I sit in the front of the bus?" he asked in 1944 on a military base in Texas. "Why don't the Yankees have more Black ballplayers?" he asked in 1953. "Why doesn't John Kennedy know more about the plight of Black people?" he asked in 1960. "And how can the Republicans ever hope to recruit Black voters after rejecting Rockefeller?" he asked in 1964 and again in 1968.

As years have passed, new insights into Robinson's life and legacy have appeared in books and film. Arnold Rampersad's *Jackie Robinson* is considered by many to be the definitive biography of the trailblazer's life.[30] In *Jackie Robinson: An Intimate Portrait*, Rachel Robinson provides her perspective on Jackie's life both on and off the field.[31] On the 60th anniversary of Robinson's breaking the color barrier, Michael Long published *First Class Citizenship: The Civil Rights Letters of Jackie Robinson,* which captures Jackie's passion for social justice through a rich trove of letters to major political figures and civil-rights activists that were penned between 1946 and 1972.[32] In *After Jackie – Pride, Prejudice, and Baseball's Forgotten Heroes: An Oral History,* Carl Fusman traces Robinson's enormous legacy by interviewing famous athletes, politicians, celebrities, and activists who came after him but who explain how he opened a path for them.[33] And in Lisa D. Alexander's *When Baseball Isn't White, Straight and Male: The Media and Difference in the National Pastime*, we are warned about major-league baseball's tendency to whitewash Robinson's legacy by either outright ignoring or playing down his social activism.[34] Retiring his number on April 15, 1997, for example, was a nice gesture, but not good enough. In 2016 Ken Burns helped set the record straight with his four-hour documentary, *Jackie Robinson*, which aired on PBS and focused almost entirely on Robinson's commitment to social justice and equal rights.[35]

When Robinson appeared at Riverfront Stadium in Cincinnati on October 15, 1972, it was, for him, the bottom of the ninth, as he was battling diabetes and partial blindness. Rachel guided him to the microphone for a brief pregame ceremony. It was minutes before the start of the second game of the World Series when he was presented a special award by Commissioner Bowie Kuhn commemorating the 25th anniversary of breaking baseball's color barrier. But in accepting the honor, Jackie seized the opportunity to steal one more base one last time. A polite and gracious thank you was not good enough. "I'd like to see a Black manager," he said while millions watched on national TV. "I'd like to see the day when a Black man is coaching third base," he emphasized.[36]

It was to be the last public appearance of Robinson's life. Nine days later, he succumbed to a heart attack at his home in Stamford, Connecticut. Rev. Jesse Jackson delivered the eulogy at the Riverside Church in Manhattan. "He was the Black Knight in a chess game," shouted Jackson. "He was checking the King's bigotry and the Queen's indifference. He turned a stumbling block into a steppingstone ... and his body, his mind, his mission cannot be held down by a grave." Robinson was interred at Cypress Hill Cemetery in Brooklyn. Serving as pallbearers were former teammates Pee Wee Reese, Ralph Branca, and Don Newcombe, basketball great Bill Russell, and future Hall of Famers Monte Irvin and Larry Doby, among others. Engraved on his gravestone was his own quote: "A life is not important except in the impact it has on other lives."[37]

And, indeed, Robinson continues to impact the lives of others. In 1973, just one year after his death, Rachel created the Jackie Robinson Foundation, which provides multiyear scholarships for minority students who are admitted to leading U.S. colleges and universities. According to its website, the foundation has graduated over 1,500 alumni, maintained close to a 100 percent graduation rate, and provided over $70 million in financial assistance and extensive support services to scholarship recipients. In 2017 the foundation was instrumental in the creation of the Jackie Robinson Museum, which was scheduled to open in 2020 at One Hudson Square in New York City.[38]

SOURCES

This chapter is drawn from the author's article in Peter M. Rutkoff, ed., *The Cooperstown Symposium on Baseball and American Culture, 1997* (Jackie Robinson) (Jefferson, North Carolina: McFarland, 2000). Used by permission of McFarland & Company, Inc.,

NOTES

1. Bart Giamatti, *Take Time for Paradise: Americans and Their Games* (New York: Harcourt, Brace and Jovanovich, 1989), 64.

2. Peter Golenbock, *Bums* (New York: Pocket Books), 280.

3. Golenbock, 178.

4. Michael Delnagro, "It's the 40th Anniversary of Robinson's Historic Debut," *Sunday Observer–Dispatch* (Utica, New York), April 5, 1987: 4b.

5. Edwin Hoyt, *Paul Robeson: The American Othello* (New York: World Publishing Company, 1967), 176.

6. Eric Nussbaum, "The Story Behind Jackie Robinson's Moving Testimony Before the House Un-American Activities Committee," *Time*, March 24, 2020.

7. Hoyt, 161. Two additional sources on the Paul Robeson affair are Martin Duberman's *Paul Robeson*, published by Knopf in 1988, and Kenneth O'Reilly's *Racial Matters: The FBI's Secret File on Black America*, published by the Free Press in 1973.

8. Paul Robeson appeared before the House Un-American Activities Committee on June 12, 1956, to discuss the reinstatement of his passport. His testimony can be accessed at historymatters.gmu.edu/d/6440/. In 1958 the Supreme Court ruled that Robeson's due-process rights had been violated and his passport was reactivated.

9. Ronald Smith, "The Paul Robeson-Jackie Robinson Saga and a Political Collision," *Journal of Sports History*, 1979: 5-27.

10. *Pittsburgh Courier*, July 16, 1949: 2. According to Eric Nussbaum's account (*Time*, March 24, 2020, see Note 6), Alvin Stokes believed that if Blacks acted preemptively and testified before HUAC they would clear their names from future scrutiny. He also believed Robinson's testimony would benefit the Dodgers franchise.

11. Bill Roeder, *Jackie Robinson* (New York: A.S Barnes and Company, 1950), 154.

12. Carl Rowan, *Wait Till Next Year* (New York Random House, 1960), 201.

13. Jackie Robinson, *I Never Had It Made* (New York: G.P. Putnam and Sons, 1972), 98. A short video on Robinson's testimony can be accessed at youtube.com/watch?v=KN9dPSRtyLQ.

14. Ronald Smith. Another source for the actions of the House Un-American Activities Committee is Eric Bentley's *Thirty Years of Treason: Excerpts from Hearings before the House Un-American Activities Committee, 1928-1968*, published by Viking Press in 1968. An audio recording of Paul Robeson's June 12, 1956, appearance before HUAC can be accessed at youtube.com/watch?v=kmFjjaFNHK0.

15. Alden Whitman, "Paul Robeson Dead at 77; Singer, Actor and Activist," *New York Times*, January 24, 1976.

16. Jackie Robinson, *I Never Had It Made*. An interesting exercise would be to view *The Jackie Robinson Story* (1950) and compare it to *42*, the 2013 film that focuses on Robinson's first season with the Dodgers. The latter is more raw in its language and less restrained in the portrayal of racism, compared with the 1950 sanitized version. Neither film, however, captures Robinson's political activism that emerges later in his career.

17. Robinson's letter to President John F. Kennedy on February 9, 1961, just a few weeks after the inauguration of the new president, illustrates his political savvy as well as his passion for social change. The letter can be accessed at archives.gov/files/education/lessons/jackie-robinson/images/letter-1961-01.jpg. Note the use of the Chock Full O' Nuts letterhead that he used frequently.

18. Robinson appeared on *Meet the Press* on April 14, 1957. A transcript and audiotape of Robinson's interview can be accessed at loc.gov/collections/jackie-robinson-baseball/articles-and-essays/baseball-the-color-line-and-jackie-robinson/meet-the-press.

19. *New York Post*, May 8, 1959: 92.

20. *New York Post*, May 27, 1959: 96.

21. Robinson's columns that appeared in the *New York Post* and the *Pittsburgh Courier* were ghostwritten by Wendell Smith, who had traveled with him during his rookie season. Smith also was the ghostwriter for Robinson's first book, *My Own Story*. In 1972 Smith died one month after Jackie Robinson's passing. The last story he wrote was Robinson's obituary.

22. Jackie Robinson, *I Never Had It Made*, 224.

23. Although there is little in the literature about the relationship between Ali and Robinson, a flavor of their conflict is captured in two video clips. The first covers Robinson's reaction to Ali's protest against the Vietnam War. It can be accessed at bing.com/videos/search?q=Relationship+between+Jackie+Robinson+and+Muhammad-+Ali&docid=608009722375245459&mid=EEDA926C939DC73B52AEEE-DA926C939DC73B52AE&view=detail&FORM=VIRE. The second clip includes the conflict between Malcolm X and Robinson as well as Robinson's reaction to Ali's stance on the Vietnam War. It can be accessed at bing.com/videos/search?q=Jackie+Robinson+quotes+on+Muhammad+Ali&docid=608055047092113230&mid=E7497E0592 1E897BDC11E7497E05921E897BDC11&view=detail&FORM=VIRE.

24. Jackie Robinson, *I Never Had It Made*, 148.

25. Jackie Robinson, *I Never Had It Made*, 148.

26. Jackie Robinson, *I Never Had It Made*, 149.

27. *New York Times*, August 12, 1968: 1. Jon Meacham, "Jackie Robinson's Inner Struggle." *New York Times*, July 20, 2020. Historian Jon Meacham reflects on Robinson's autobiography, *I Never Had It Made*, placing it in historical context with respect to the contemporary relationship between the Republican Party and African-Americans.

28. Jackie Robinson, *I Never Had It Made*, 220.

29. Giamatti, 93.

30. Arnold Rampersad, *Jackie Robinson* (New York: Alfred A. Knopf, Inc. 1997).

31. Rachel Robinson, *Jackie Robinson: An Intimate Portrait* (New York: Henry N. Abrams Inc., 1996).

32. Michael Long, *First Class Citizenship: The Civil Rights Letters of Jackie Robinson* (New York: Macmillan, 2007).

33. Carl Fusman, *After Jackie – Pride, Prejudice, and Baseball's Forgotten Heroes: An Oral History* (New York: ESPN Books, 2007).

34. Lisa D. Alexander, *When Baseball Isn't White, Straight and Male: The Media and Difference in the National Pastime* (Lincoln: University of Nebraska Press, 2013). Not widely known, and certainly not included in any major-league baseball tributes to Jackie Robinson is a statement he made in 1972 in his autobiography that resonates in the US political climate in the post-Obama years: "I cannot stand and sing the anthem. I cannot salute the flag; I know that I am a Black man in a white world. In 1972, in 1947, at my birth in 1919, I know that I never had it made." The "I never had it made" statement is captured in an impassioned speech he gave at a civil-rights rally in St. Augustine, Florida, on June 16, 1964. The video can be accessed at abcnews.go.com/Archives/video/jackie-robinson-delivers-passionate-speech-1964-civil-rights-60752464.

35. Ken Burns, Sarah Burns, and David McMahon, *Jackie Robinson*, a two-part, four-hour documentary on Jackie Robinson with a special focus on his social activism. A two-minute video preview of the film can be accessed at latimes.com/86469443-132.html.

36. Jackie Robinson, October 15, 1972. This appearance and statement by Robinson before the start of the second game of the 1972 World Series at Riverfront Stadium in Cincinnati was the last public appearance of his life.

37. Eulogy delivered by Rev. Jesse Jackson at Robinson's funeral on October 27, 1972, at Riverside Church in Manhattan.

38. More information about the Jackie Robinson Foundation can be accessed at jackierobinson.org/. Additional information about the Jackie Robinson Museum can be accessed at jackierobinsonmuseum.org/.

JACKIE ROBINSON, REPUBLICAN

by Jeff English

Nelson Rockefeller (R – NY) and Jackie Robinson.

Between 1960 and 1968, Jackie Robinson was widely regarded as the most famous Black Republican in the country. Following his announced retirement from baseball in January 1957, and in remarkably short fashion, he dived head-first into the world of corporate America and the civil-rights movement, with equal gusto. He spent the next three years polishing old skills and developing new ones while demonstrating a knack for fundraising on behalf of the National Association for the Advancement of Colored People. Splitting his time as a vice president at the Chock Full o' Nuts restaurant chain in New York, and as an active member of the NAACP, he maintained a relentless travel schedule that carried him from one side of the country to the other. By the time he began hosting a radio show and publishing a nationally syndicated newspaper column in 1959, his reach had grown extensive. Thus, when the time came for the nation to turn its eyes to the 1960 race to succeed Republican Dwight D. Eisenhower as president, Robinson's political support was deemed a valuable commodity.

Prior to his retirement from baseball, Robinson's political involvement was minimal, occasionally taking the form of soliciting funds for socially conscious projects such as repairs for a community center.[1] When he was hired in the spring of 1959 by the *New York Post* to write the newspaper column, editor James Wechsler described Robinson as, "an intelligent, independent, and articulate human being who follows no party line."[2] In one of his first columns for the *Post*, Robinson explained to his readers his approach to political participation:

> I guess you'd call me an Independent, since I've never identified myself with one party or another in politics. As a Negro, I've been wooed by the Democrats with the memory of Franklin D. Roosevelt and the New Deal, and cultivated by the Republicans with the memory of Abraham Lincoln and the Civil War. But, like more and more people nowadays, I always decide my vote by taking as careful a look as I can at the actual candidates and issues themselves, no matter what the party label or the ancestral ghost.[3]

Robinson was in fact registered as an independent dating at least as far back as his decision to buy a home in Stamford, Connecticut, in 1956.[4] Although his time as an operative and influence in American politics lasted from his retirement in 1957 until his untimely death in October 1972, it was during the period from 1960 through 1968 that he exerted his greatest impact. Robinson often lent his considerable support nationwide to Republican and Democratic candidates alike, at all levels of government, who opposed Jim Crow and desired equality for all Americans. He held a sincere desire for a robust two-party system, honest and open debate, and for the success of neither party to hinge on a maintenance of the status quo. But set against the backdrop of a rapidly changing American political landscape, Robinson somehow became not only the most prominent Black Republican in America but also one of the party's sharpest and most damning critics, often at the same time. In a 2019 assessment of what he deemed a kind of "radical legacy," author David Naze described Robinson's political identity as manifesting itself "in his attempt to publicly articulate his critical insights regarding the contemporary American racial landscape, a version that runs counter to the neat, obedient version to which most Americans have become accustomed."[5] In its proper context, Jackie Robinson's political life, like so much else about the man, defies convenient labels.

Although the news was leaked beforehand, the January 22, 1957, issue of *Look* magazine published an exclusive Robinson-penned essay announcing his retirement from baseball. In the essay, he told readers he had accepted an offer from William Black, founder and owner of the Chock Full o' Nuts restaurant chain in New York, to become the company's vice president for personnel. He described his excitement over the prospect of spending more time with his family. And he offered no regrets, crediting his time in baseball for opportunities ranging from meeting Branch Rickey and breaking the game's color line, to his 1949 testimony before the House Un-American Activities Committee rebuking entertainer Paul Robeson's purported statement that Black Americans were unwilling to fight in a war against the Soviet Union. Robinson's position at Chock Full o' Nuts included a March starting date, and made him the first Black US vice president of a national corporation.

On January 6, 1957, at the behest of Roy Wilkins, executive secretary of the NAACP, Robinson assumed the role of national chairman for the organization's 1957 Freedom Fund drive with the stated goal of raising one million dollars.[6] In his 1972 autobiography, *I Never Had it Made,* Robinson credits his new boss for encouraging his involvement, writing that Black "approved wholeheartedly of my participation, and if it didn't interfere with my work at Chock, I was free to use company time to travel, work, and speak for the NAACP."[7] On Sunday, April 14, Robinson appeared on NBC's *Meet the Press* and fielded questions about the Freedom Fund drive and baseball's reserve clause. In response to a question concerning people claiming the NAACP was moving too fast, Robinson responded, "I think if we go back and check our record, the Negro has proven beyond a doubt that we have been more than patient in seeking our rights as American citizens."[8] On June 8, 1957, Connecticut's Democratic

Jackie Robinson at the White House, with U.S. President Dwight D. Eisenhower and comedian Joe E. Brown on November 5, 1957.

Governor Abraham Ribicoff appointed Robinson to a newly created three-man board of parole as part of a broader effort to reform the state's prison system. Biographer Arnold Rampersad has written that by the time the 48th Annual NAACP Convention was held in Detroit, in June, Robinson had been transformed by his experience working for the organization. "I sometimes find it hard to remember what my life was like just a brief year ago," he told the convention crowd on June 30.[9]

On September 4, 1957, Arkansas's Democratic Governor Orval Faubus, in opposition to the federally mandated desegregation of public schools, utilized the Arkansas National Guard to block nine African American students from integrating Little Rock Central High School. Six days later, Eisenhower drew Robinson's ire when he preached "patience" on integration in an address to a group of Rhode Island Republicans.[10] In a pointed September 13 response to the president, Robinson wondered to whom Eisenhower was referring when he urged patience, while drawing attention to the fact that the events in Little Rock were useful "material" for America's enemies abroad.[11] When on September 24 Eisenhower finally ordered the deployment of the Army's 101st Airborne Division to quell the harassment and violence, Robinson, who was often just as quick to offer praise as he was criticism, responded the following day with a letter congratulating the president on the "positive position" he took.[12]

The stick-and-carrot criticism and praise of Eisenhower over the crisis in Little Rock was emblematic of an approach that, with few exceptions,

Robinson maintained throughout his political life. Disagreements were seldom personal, and he often reserved his harshest criticism for those on whom he placed his highest expectations. For Robinson, personal relationships usually trumped party, and if he believed a candidate or elected official was right or wrong, particularly on matters pertaining to civil rights and American security, he had few qualms in saying so.

The year 1957 was a transformative one for Jackie Robinson. In his role as national chairman for the NAACP's Freedom Fund drive, he achieved the organization's million-dollar fundraising goal while also attracting a record number of life memberships.[13] Recognition of his success came on January 6, 1958, when he was selected as one of three new members to the organization's board of directors.[14] Twelve days later, and not for the last time, he issued a denial to the press that he planned to seek political office himself, stating, "There is just not one kernel of truth to any such report. I have a job to do; but not in affiliation with a political party."[15] Robinson immersed himself in his work, and continued to maintain a relentless travel schedule that included an NAACP-sponsored speaking tour through the South in February. In the fall, he led 10,000 students on an October 25 march to the Lincoln Memorial in protest of the violence endured by African American children attempting integration in the South. When the Eisenhower administration refused a request to meet with some of the youth marchers, a thoroughly displeased Robinson asked, "How can you support these people when they treat you this way?"[16] In one of his most publicly overt statements to date, he told a reporter that he had never considered himself a Democrat until October 25.[17]

Whereas professional baseball had a reserve clause, no such thing existed in politics and when Robinson turned his attention to the coming 1960 race to succeed Eisenhower, he was essentially a free agent. In January 1959 he began hosting an interview show on a small New York-based radio station, where his guests included such political luminaries as Governor Abraham Ribicoff of Connecticut, New York City Mayor Robert Wagner, and Eleanor Roosevelt. On May 25, 1959, he attended the Harlem YMCA Century Club Dinner to honor Elston Howard of the New York Yankees, and professional football player Jim Brown of the Cleveland Browns.[18] The keynote speaker at the event was Democratic Senator Hubert Humphrey of Minnesota. The senator's progressive bona fides on issues of race dated back to his time as mayor of Minneapolis, when he helped procure enactment of the first municipal Fair Employment Practices Act in the United States.[19] And his rousing, 10-minute speech demanding adoption of a civil-rights plank in the Democratic Party platform at the national convention in 1948 made him a hero to many progressives.[20] In his autobiography, Robinson recounts having strongly admired Humphrey, calling him "a man who would rather be right morally than achieve the Presidency."[21] When 1959 drew to a close, Robinson had found his candidate in Humphrey. But perhaps because he was not entirely convinced of the senator's overall electability, he kept a watchful eye on another expected contender to succeed Eisenhower: Vice President Richard Nixon.

By all accounts, Robinson was rather charmed by Richard Nixon at their first meeting, in Chicago in 1952. Introduced by Harrison McCall, president of the California Republican Assembly, Nixon recounted to Robinson in granular detail an unusual play Robinson was involved in during a 1939 football contest between UCLA and the University of Oregon. Recalling the introduction years later, McCall noted that "while Robinson had undoubtedly met a lot of notables in his career, nevertheless (McCall) was sure there was one person he would never forget."[22] In fact, Robinson and Nixon had struck up a friendship of sorts, and corresponded multiple times in the following years. By 1960, Robinson had come to view Nixon's civil-rights rhetoric as notably more forward-leaning than the administration as a whole. Robinson was particularly drawn to the vice president's penchant for framing America's racial divide in international terms, noting that Nixon had "returned from a trip around the world, and he came back saying that America would lose the confidence and trust of the darker nations if she didn't clear her own backyard of racial prejudice. Mr. Nixon made those statements for the television cameras and other media for all the world to hear."[23] Robinson, himself a staunch anti-communist, often employed similar arguments in his many speeches advocating for the benefits of equality.

The front-runner for the Democratic Party's nomination heading into the Wisconsin primary was Senator John F. Kennedy of Massachusetts. For a host of reasons, Robinson vehemently opposed his candidacy. He resented Kennedy's decision to vote against the 1957 Civil Rights Act, which he considered a naked political attempt on the senator's part to court Southern Democratic votes for an eventual Oval Office run. He was also particularly dismayed at the

Massachusetts senator for having previously hosted segregationist Alabama Governor John Patterson and Sam Englehardt, president of the Alabama White Citizens Councils, to a June breakfast at his home in Georgetown. Commenting on the meeting, Robinson wrote, "Would you have me support a Kennedy who met with one of the worst segregationists in private, and then this man, the Governor of Alabama, comes out with strong support of Senator Kennedy?"[24] But the Massachusetts senator won the Wisconsin primary by a comfortable margin over Hubert Humphrey. Better financed than his rival from Minnesota, Kennedy all but wrapped up the nomination with a commanding victory in the West Virginia primary on May 10. With Humphrey's path no longer viable, Robinson turned his attention and support to the Nixon campaign.

During the Republican National Convention in Chicago in July 1960, Robinson applauded both an effort by Nixon to insert an aggressive civil-rights plank into the party's platform that explicitly supported the Supreme Court's Brown v. Board of Education decision, and his selection of progressive running mate Henry Cabot Lodge. In September Robinson was granted a leave of absence from Chock Full o' Nuts to campaign full-time for Nixon. Like most everything he involved himself with, Robinson threw himself head-first into his support for the Republican candidate.

On October 19 Dr. Martin Luther King Jr. was one of 52 people arrested in downtown Atlanta for holding a sit-in at the lunch counters in the Magnolia Room of Rich's department store. As author Steven Levingston has written, "Neither Kennedy nor Nixon wanted to risk alienating white Southern voters just weeks before the election by speaking out on behalf of King and the protesters."[25] Robinson, a close friend and frequent collaborator of King's, desperately urged Nixon to issue a show of support for the jailed civil-rights leader, even providing the campaign with the phone number to the jail where his friend was being held.[26] After a direct confrontation with Nixon on the matter, Robinson emerged with tears in his eyes to say, "He thinks calling Martin would be 'grandstanding.' Nixon doesn't deserve to win."[27]

For his part, John Kennedy found a way. On October 26 he placed a phone call to the governor of Georgia, Ernest Vandiver, to advocate for King's release in a move Levingston describes as "so delicate that Kennedy told few, if any, of his advisors about his efforts."[28] The next day, under pressure from several close aides, he agreed to reach out to Coretta Scott King in order to express consternation over her husband's predicament. In a call that lasted less than 90 seconds, Kennedy conveyed his concern over Dr. King's confinement, and concluded by telling her, "If there is anything I can do to help, please feel free to call me."[29] The following day, on a $2,000 bond, her husband was released from the maximum-security state prison in Reidsville, where he had been recently transferred. Hours later at Peachtree-Dekalb Airport, a newly free Dr. King paid Kennedy a high compliment when he told gathered reporters, "For him to be that courageous shows that he is really acting upon principle and not expediency."[30] King's father, a lifelong Republican and a Nixon backer, rescinded his endorsement while declaring, "I've got a suitcase full of votes, and I'm going to take them to Mr. Kennedy and dump them in his lap."[31]

In the historically close 1960 race between Kennedy and Nixon, few can doubt that Kennedy's intervention in King's arrest aided his winning cause. In a race ultimately decided by fewer than 120,000 votes and two-tenths of a percentage point, the Democrats gained a seven-point swing among Black voters over their totals from four years earlier, and in several of the largest metropolitan areas, increased Black voter turnout proved decisive.[32]

While many of Robinson's closest friends and family members were still struggling to understand his avid support for candidate Nixon, Robinson kept a skeptical eye trained on the words and deeds emanating from the new administration.[33] Although he remained a consistent critic, in a manner commensurate with his critiques of the Eisenhower administration, when he found something to applaud, he applauded loudly. Robinson lauded Attorney General Robert F. Kennedy's May 6, 1961, Law Day address at the University of Georgia in a letter, telling him, "I find it a pleasure to be proven wrong. May you continue to give your demonstrated leadership, which is so necessary at this time."[34] Likewise, when President Kennedy delivered his televised Report to the American People on Civil Rights, on June 11, 1963, where he laid out his administration's intention to pursue legislation that ultimately comprised significant portions of the 1964 Civil Rights Act, Robinson telegraphed the White House to declare the address "not the speech of a politician. It was the pronouncement of a stateman."[35]

On September 9, 1962, two African-American churches in southwest Georgia were set ablaze in a racially motivated act of hatred. Robinson had only recently spoken at a voter registration drive in the area, and quickly traveled south to visit the sites. Telling reporters, "It really makes you want to cry deep down in your heart," he agreed, at the behest of Dr. King, to chair a drive to raise funds to rebuild both churches. Robinson himself contributed $100, and reached out to other prominent African Americans such as Archie Moore and Floyd Patterson to solicit their support. In no time at all, donations began to arrive from the likes of William Black and Nelson Rockefeller, New York's progressive Republican governor, who gave $10,000.

Nelson Rockefeller occupied a prominent position on the Republican Party's left flank, particularly where civil rights were concerned. His great-grandparents were involved in the Underground Railroad, Rockefeller money had long flowed to Black higher education, he held an endorsement from the National Urban League, and he carried a third of New York's overall African American vote to get elected governor in 1958. Robinson campaigned with Rockefeller in Harlem on behalf of the Nixon campaign in October 1960 and the governor later confided to Robinson his effort to persuade Nixon to intercede on Dr. King's behalf, late in the campaign.[36]

Robinson spent a great deal of time in the fall of 1962 campaigning on behalf of candidates running in a host of state and local elections, which included multiple telethons for Richard Nixon's failed race for California governor.[37] He reserved his greatest effort for Nelson Rockefeller's bid for re-election as New York's governor. He attended multiple receptions and conducted campaign walks with the governor throughout Harlem and Brooklyn to generate support in African American communities.[38] In November, Rockefeller comfortably defeated Democrat Robert M. Morgenthau by over 9 percentage points while also acquiring a dedicated ally in Jackie Robinson.[39]

President John F. Kennedy was assassinated in Dallas on November 22, 1963. Although Robinson had often been highly critical of the administration, he called the fallen president "a noble man," in a December 7 column in the *New York Amsterdam News*. But in just a few short paragraphs, he quickly turned from sorrowful American to pragmatic politico, citing his own support for Rockefeller before asking his readers, "(W)here will the Negro stand?" if Lyndon Johnson and Barry Goldwater emerged as their party's standard-bearers.[40] As he looked to 1964, Robinson now viewed Rockefeller as the only man who offered a way forward for Black participation in the Republican Party.

On January 31, 1964, Robinson announced his resignation from Chock Full O' Nuts, effective February 28. Four days later, Governor Nelson Rockefeller announced Robinson's hire as one of six deputy directors for his presidential campaign team, calling him a "constructive competitor" with "the drive of a winner."[41] Rockefeller's chief rival for the nomination was Arizona Senator Barry Goldwater, whose brand of states-rights conservatism found few takers among Black Republicans. Author Leah Wright Rigueur wrote in *The Loneliness of the Black Republican* that Goldwater's detractors frequently cited the senator's tendency to "vote with the southern political bloc 67 percent of the time, his popularity with southern segregationists, and his vote against the 1964 Civil Rights Act."[42] For his part, Robinson thought Goldwater a bigot, insisting that any leader in the Black community who supported the conservative senator would be ostracized, since "(t)he Negro is not going to tolerate any Uncle Toms in 1964."[43]

Goldwater secured the nomination at the party's national convention held July 13-16, 1964, at the Cow Palace in Daly City, California, just south of San Francisco. Robinson attended as a special delegate for Rockefeller, but with only 15 delegates and 28 alternates, African Americans comprised less than one percent of the total convention body.[44] The convention was marred by violence and numerous displays of racial intolerance. In his description of the scene in a column in August, Robinson told his readers, "I would say that I now believe I know how it felt to be a Jew in Hitler's Germany."[45] Robinson's response was to co-found the National Negro Republican Assembly, an organization "characterized by a demand that the party recognize and address racial equality, integrate the mainstream machine, promote black advancement, and champion liberal and moderate Republican philosophies."[46] On August 14, Robinson wrote a letter to Democratic vice presidential candidate Hubert Humphrey volunteering his services for the ticket, an effort he believed necessary to "save the country."[47]

Lyndon Johnson won 44 states and cleared 60 percent of the popular vote in a landslide win over Goldwater. He did so with a full 94 percent of the Black vote, as Goldwater managed victories in just six states, most of which had not gone Republican since Reconstruction. While the Arizona senator had failed to win the presidency, his campaign would serve as a template of sorts in the coming years for Republican outreach to white Southern voters long the provenance of the Democratic Party. For his part, Robinson's defection made him the brunt of some criticism on the right, particularly from noted conservative columnist William F. Buckley.[48] Nevertheless, Robinson remained hopeful. If he could help Rockefeller get re-elected in 1966, it would place the governor in good standing to once again pursue the Republican nomination in 1968 and perhaps rescue the party from the most extreme elements.

On February 7, 1966, Rockefeller hired Robinson to serve as a special assistant to the governor for community affairs. In media reports announcing the hiring, Robinson described his anticipated duties as "bringing the remarkable Rockefeller record to the attention of minority groups throughout the state."[49] That same month, he declined an offer from New York Mayor John Lindsay to serve on a commission on athletics, calling himself a "Rockefeller Republican" and the 1966 elections "(t)he most important in the history of the Negro people."[50]

When the campaign got underway, Robinson worked tirelessly, describing, the "day to day, almost around the clock" effort as one of the "most rewarding experiences" of his life.[51] His efforts paid off on Election Day when Rockefeller defeated Democrat Frank D. O'Connor by a margin of nearly 400,000 votes. Robinson biographer Arnold Rampersad has called Robinson's involvement the "crowning moment of his career as a political operative."[52] Robinson also took heart in the victory of moderate Massachusetts Republican Edward Brooke, the first African American elected to the United States Senate by popular vote. He hoped the victories of Rockefeller and Brooke were evidence that the Republican Party could remain a viable option for Black voter participation. Nevertheless, he remained wary, noting rising conservative star Ronald Reagan's election as governor in California by remarking, "In my book, Ronald Reagan is as bad news for minority people as Governor Rockefeller is good news."[53]

While Robinson certainly had ambitious plans for Nelson Rockefeller in 1968, the first half of the year began on a somber note when his son, Jack Jr., was arrested on drug-possession charges in early March. Jack Jr. had enlisted in the US Army in March 1964, and earned a Purple Heart when he was wounded in an ambush in Vietnam on November 19, 1965. Honorably discharged the next year, he found life difficult in his return home. In a response to reporters' questions before posting bail for his son, Robinson gloomily remarked, "He fought in Vietnam and was wounded. I've had more effect on other people's kids than on my own."[54] On April 4 tragedy struck not only the Robinson family, but also the rest of the nation when the Rev. Martin Luther King Jr. was assassinated in Memphis, Tennessee. For Robinson, it was a tremendous personal loss, as he considered King a dear friend, mentor, and ally. Calling it "the most disturbing and distressing thing we've had to face in a long time," he expressed grave concerns over the prospect of violent repercussions.[55]

President Lyndon Johnson, mired in a seemingly unwinnable war in Vietnam, shocked the nation when on March 31 he announced he would not seek another term in November. On April 5 his vice president and expected contender Hubert Humphrey wrote Robinson to offer his condolences for Dr. King's passing and to solicit support for his campaign. Robinson responded the following month that while he considered the vice president "one of the best qualified men" he knew, he would only offer an endorsement if Nelson Rockefeller failed to capture the Republican nomination.[56] On June 23 Robinson invited Black newspaper publishers and editors to his home in Stamford, Connecticut, to preach African American support for Rockefeller against Richard Nixon. In the ensuing years following his loss in the 1962 California governor's race, Nixon had worked tirelessly raising money and campaigning on behalf of the Republican Party in dozens of races across the country. By 1968 there was a sense among many Republicans that he had earned another opportunity to claim the nomination. But Robinson considered Nixon's failure to denounce Goldwater four years earlier as a personal betrayal, and, reading the tea leaves, saw clearly that a Nixon candidacy would no doubt benefit from Goldwater's supporters.

The 1968 Republican National Convention was held in Miami Beach, Florida, August 5-8. Robinson, still partially recovering from a small heart attack suffered in June, did not attend. With little drama, Nixon secured the nomination while selecting Maryland Governor Spiro T. Agnew as his running mate. The selection of Agnew only served to further infuriate Robinson, as reports had surfaced that Nixon had allowed segregationist Southern Senator Strom Thurmond veto power over his selection.[57] On August 11, appearing on the NBC television program *Searchlight*, Robinson announced that he was resigning from Governor Rockefeller's staff to campaign full-time for the Democratic nominee. He accused Nixon of "prostituting himself to the bigots in the south" and declared, "I'm a black man first, an American second, and then I will support a political party-third."[58] On October 7 Robinson made an appearance with Democratic Governor Richard Hughes in Newark, New Jersey, and accused Nixon of competing for the same votes as segregationist Alabama Governor George Wallace, running as an independent. In the closing weeks of the contest, Robinson campaigned relentlessly throughout the Midwest.

On November 5, 1968, Richard Nixon defeated Hubert Humphrey by more than half a million votes to become America's 37th president. His election was the continuation of a seismic shift in American politics as the Republican Southern strategy," which sought to appeal to the racial grievances of White Southerners finally culminated in Ronald Reagan's election as president in 1980. For Robinson, the 1968 campaign served as a bookend of sorts. His sharp turn against the Republican Party, his deteriorating health, and a number of significant personal setbacks rendered him largely a nonfactor politically for the remainder of his life. In 1970 he offered his support to Democrat Charles Rangel, who managed a primary defeat of longtime Robinson rival Adam Clayton Powell Jr. for the opportunity to represent New York's 18th Congressional District in Harlem. Robinson died on October 24, 1972, just two weeks before Richard Nixon won re-election in a landslide over Democrat George McGovern.

The story of Jackie Robinson's political odyssey is not only his story. It is also the story of an America undergoing a series of rapid-fire changes amid a seismic shift in its political tectonics. Any assessment of his political life practically demands that it be filtered through his extensive work in the civil-rights movement. He reserved his endorsements for candidates he sincerely believed counted the best interests of Black America, and by extension, all of America, high among their priorities. Although he held a reputation as a Republican, he did not wield party affiliation as a disqualifier. He was willing to work with anyone who was willing to work with him for the benefit of the country, and for his people. Modern-day attempts to frame Robinson's politics in ultra-contemporary terms miss the point entirely. Robinson's brand of politics, as well as the goals it aimed to achieve, were almost entirely relationship-based, from his early friendship with Nixon to his enduring professional and personal friendship with Nelson Rockefeller. If Robinson were still alive today, it seems an almost certainty that he would still be working tirelessly for racial equality. Whether or not he would find today's Republican Party the ideal vehicle for that work is highly questionable.

In a very real sense, Jackie Robinson never endorsed Nixon or Rockefeller because he was a Republican. Rather, it is more accurate to say that Robinson was a Republican because he endorsed Nixon and Rockefeller.

SOURCES

In addition to the sources cited in the Notes, the author consulted the following:

Books

Tygiel, Jules. *Extra Bases: Reflections on Jackie Robinson, Race, and Baseball History* (Lincoln: University of Nebraska Press, 2002)

Articles

Farrington, Joshua D. "Evicted from the Party: Black Republicans and the 1964 Election," *Journal of Arizona History* 61, no. 1 (2020): 127-148.

Khan, Abraham. "Jackie Robinson, Civic Republicanism, and Black Political Culture," *Sports and Identity* (2013): 83-105.

Rutkoff, Peter M. "Introduction – Jackie Robinson: Baseball, Brooklyn, and Beyond," in Peter M. Rutkoff, ed., *The Cooperstown Symposium on Baseball and American Culture, 1997 (Jackie Robinson)* (Jefferson, North Carolina: McFarland, 2015), 3.

Wisensale, Steven. "The Black Knight: A Political Portrait of Jackie Robinson." In Peter M. Rutkoff, ed., *The Cooperstown Symposium on Baseball and American Culture, 1997 (Jackie Robinson)* (Jefferson, North Carolina: McFarland, 2015), 189.

NOTES

1. "Political Vacuum," *Hartford Courant*, February 3, 1953: 10.
2. Michael Long, *Beyond Home Plate* (Syracuse: Syracuse University Press, 2013), xxiii.
3. Long, *Beyond Home Plate*, 127.
4. William F. Buckley, "Robinson's GOP Bolt Is Nothing Original," *Tennessean* (Nashville), August 19, 1969: 12; Arnold Rampersad, *Jackie Robinson* (New York: Ballantine, 1997), 340.
5. David Naze. *Reclaiming 42: Public Memory and the Reframing of Jackie Robinson's Radical Legacy* (Lincoln: University of Nebraska Press, 2019), 75.
6. "Jackie Robinson Heads '57 Drive of Freedom Fund," *Boston Globe*, January 7, 1957: 13.
7. Jackie Robinson, *I Never Had It Made* (New York: Harper Collins, 1995), 126.
8. Library of Congress, https://www.loc.gov/collections/jackie-robinson-baseball/articles-and-essays/baseball-the-color-line-and-jackie-robinson/meet-the-press, accessed January 14, 2021.
9. Rampersad, 319.
10. "Eisenhower Asks Patience in Integration," *Newport* (Rhode Island) *Daily News*, September 10, 1957: 1.
11. Michael Long, *First Class Citizenship: The Civil Rights Letters of Jackie Robinson* (New York: Henry Holt and Company, 2007), 40.
12. Long, *First Class Citizenship*, 41.
13. Long, *First Class Citizenship*, 315.
14. "18 Elected to NASCP???? NAACP? Nat'l Board," *Black Dispatch* (Oklahoma City), January 17, 1958: 3.
15. "No Politics for Jackie," *Star Tribune* (Minneapolis) February 1, 1958: 9.

16. "Randolph: DC March a Success," *New York Age*, November 1, 1958: 35.
17. Rampersad, *Jackie Robinson*, 336.
18. "Sports Achievers," *Press and Sun-Bulletin* (Binghamton, New York), May 26, 1959: 30.
19. Rampersad, *Jackie Robinson*, 341.
20. "Humphrey Sparks Convention," *Minneapolis Star*, July 15, 1948: 7.
21. Robinson, *I Never Had it Made*, 136.
22. Long, *First Class Citizenship*, 26.
23. Robinson, *I Never Had it Made*, 135.
24. Steven Levingston, *Kennedy and King: The President, the Pastor, and the Battle Over Civil Rights* (New York: Hachette Books, 2017), 4.
25. Levingston, *Kennedy and King*, 75.
26. Rampersad, *Jackie Robinson*, 351.
27. Rampersad, *Jackie Robinson*, 351.
28. Levingston, *Kennedy and King*, 87.
29. Levingston, *Kennedy and King*, 88.
30. Levingston, *Kennedy and King*, 91.
31. Joshua D. Farrington, *Black Republicans and the Transformation of the GOP* (Philadelphia: University of Pennsylvania Press, 2016), 111.
32. "Kennedy Reported Winning Bulk of Negro Vote in Big Key Cities," *Minneapolis Star*, November 4, 1960: 3.
33. Long, *First Class Citizenship*, 128.
34. Long, *First Class Citizenship*, 127.
35. Long, *First Class Citizenship*, 172.
36. Rampersad, *Jackie Robinson*, 353.
37. "Tonight, on Channel 11," *Valley Times Today* (North Hollywood, California), November 3, 1962: 19.
38. Rampersad, *Jackie Robinson*, 369.
39. Our Campaigns, https://www.ourcampaigns.com/ContainerHistory.html?ContainerID=258, Accessed January 17, 2021.
40. Long, *Beyond Home Plate*, 141.
41. "Robinson Named Rockefeller Aide," *The Record* (Hackensack, New Jersey), February 5, 1964, 10.
42. Leah Wright Rigueur, *The Loneliness of the Black Republican* (Princeton: Princeton University Press, 2015), 48.
43. Leah M. Wright, "Conscience of a Black Conservative: The 1964 Election and the Rise of the National Negro Republican Assembly," *Federal History*. 1 (2009): 33.
44. Wright, "Conscience": 35.
45. *Indianapolis Recorder*, July 25, 1964: 2.
46. Wright, "Conscience": 34.
47. Long, *First Class Citizenship*, 203.
48. William F. Buckley, "Baseball, Politics Aren't the Same," *Arizona Republic* (Phoenix), November 5, 1965: 6.
49. "Rocky Hires Jackie," *New York Daily News*, February 8, 1966: 34.
50. "Robinson Rejected Post," *Ithaca Journal*, February 10, 1966: 14.
51. Rampersad, *Jackie Robinson*, 409.
52. Rampersad, *Jackie Robinson*, 409.
53. Rampersad, *Jackie Robinson*, 409.
54. Rampersad, *Jackie Robinson*, 423.
55. "Robinson Comments," *Quad-City Times* (Davenport, Iowa), April 5, 1968: 4.
56. Long, *First Class Citizenship*, 277.
57. "Jackie Robinson Quits Rocky and Slides to Dems," *New York Daily News*, August 12, 1968: 3.
58. "Jackie Robinson Quits Republicans," *News-Palladium* (St. Joseph, Michigan), August 12, 1968: 7.

JOURNEY TO JUSTICE

THE CONVERGING PATHS OF JACK ROOSEVELT ROBINSON
AND DR. MARTIN LUTHER KING JR.

by Bryan Steverson

"Justice too long delayed is justice denied" was the phrase used by Dr. Martin Luther King Jr. in his 1963 "Letter from Birmingham Jail."[1] King and Jackie Robinson both devoted their lives to a timely march to justice. Delay was unacceptable and they proceeded accordingly. It was Robinson, along with his wife, Rachel, and their children, Jack Jr., Sharon, and David, who joined King as platform guests in the 1963 March on Washington. The two leaders had also appeared together earlier, in September 1962, when Robinson spoke to the Southern Christian Leadership Council's annual Freedom Dinner in Birmingham, Alabama.[2] Robinson had become concerned about King's welfare. On June 15, 1963, he sent a telegram to President John F. Kennedy stating, "The world cannot afford to lose Martin Luther King Jr." King at the time was in Mississippi for the funeral of recently slain civil-rights leader Medgar Evers.[3]

When King and other protesters were imprisoned, Robinson had hosted a jazz fundraiser to obtain the needed bail money. Soon after the "Bloody Sunday" tragedy at the Edmund Pettus Bridge in Selma, Alabama, on March 7, 1965, Robinson sent a telegram to President Lyndon Johnson demanding that he take action against the violence inflicted on protesters. These actions led to the passage in 1965 of the Voting Rights Bill.[4] King was there when the president signed the legislation.

The careers of Robinson and King became intertwined in the history of the United States. King was born a minister's son into a middle-class family in Atlanta in 1929. Ten years earlier, Robinson was born into a struggling sharecropper family more than 200 miles to the south in Cairo, Georgia. Their two careers would cross in the 1950s, and civil rights and the nation's history would forever be changed.

Both men were college educated. King graduated from Morehouse College and earned his Ph.D. at Boston University. Robinson attended UCLA and was one semester short of graduating when he withdrew based upon a lack of perceived opportunities for Blacks. They stood side-by-side in 1957 when receiving honorary doctorates from Howard University.[5] King and Robinson came from religious homes and both practiced their faith. King's first job was as pastor of Dexter Avenue Baptist Church in Montgomery, Alabama.[6] While Robinson attended Pasadena Junior College and UCLA, Pastor Karl Downs enlisted him to teach a class on Sunday mornings at the Scott Methodist Church. Even after punishing football games on Saturdays, Robinson, who yearned to sleep late, found the motivation to get up and teach.[7] One became a man of the cloth and the other a world-famous athlete. Their commonality in faith and the pursuit of racial justice would unite them in a lasting and significant bond.

King was awarded the Nobel Peace Prize in 1964. Robinson became the first Black inducted into the National Baseball Hall of Fame, in 1962. Both were awarded the Presidential Medal of Freedom and a Congressional Gold Medal for their service to the nation and the world. They were freedom fighters putting their lives at risk for the good of the oppressed.

Robinson and King were change agents. When asked to name the most important Americans of the twentieth century, Pulitzer Prize-winning historian Doris Kearns Goodwin named King, Eleanor Roosevelt, and Robinson.[8] The author reiterated these names and added Franklin Delano Roosevelt to the list in subsequent responses.[9]

As a Nobel laureate, King's accomplishments have been documented. Like Goodwin, Pulitzer Prize-winning journalist David Halberstam thought highly of Robinson.[10] He would state, "He was history's man. Nothing less. Though he came to the nation disguised as a mere baseball player, he was, arguably, the single most important American of the first post-war decade." Legendary sportscaster Howard Cosell said, "And when people ask me, "Who was the greatest all-around athlete this nation has ever produced? I say Jackie Robinson, also the greatest all-around man."[11] Others have agreed with Robinson's significant role in history, including President Barack Obama, who said, "You think about what Jackie Robinson ended up meaning not just to baseball but to the entire society. I would not be sitting here if it weren't for him."[12]

On July 6, 1944, US Army Second Lieutenant Robinson boarded a bus at Camp Hood, Texas. Noticing the wife of a fellow Black lieutenant, Virginia Jones, sitting by herself near the front, Robinson sat down beside her. Mrs. Jones was a light-skinned Black and could be mistaken for being white. She was the wife of fellow Lieutenant Gordon Jones, who like Robinson was a member of the 761st Tank Battalion.[13] The bus driver, thinking Robinson, a Black man, was sitting next to Jones, a white woman, ordered Robinson to move to the back of the bus. Robinson refused to give up his seat and an ugly incident ensued. After a military trial, Robinson was found to be not guilty of all charges.[14]

Similarly, 11 years later, in December 1955, it was seamstress Rosa Parks who refused to give up her seat on a Montgomery, Alabama, bus, leading to a boycott and effectively launching the civil-rights movement. "The boycott mirrored almost exactly (Robinson's) own single most dangerous act of protest against Jim Crow – in July 1944 ... at Camp Hood in Texas." King was president of the Montgomery Improvement Association, which brought attention to the bus boycott.[15]

The two civil-rights icons had known of each other for some time. In 1949 the Brooklyn Dodgers, on their way north from spring training, scheduled an exhibition game in Atlanta. Roy Campanella, another Black man on the team, and Robinson had received a threatening telegram from the wizard of the Atlanta Ku Klux Klan. It read, "If you come to Atlanta, we'll kill you. We'll shoot you out on the field." Branch Rickey, the Brooklyn general manager, sought out King, who told him, "Definitely see that Campanella and Robinson come to Atlanta to play." Upon arriving in Atlanta, the two players went to King's home for dinner. They stayed with him most of the trip. King, who faced similar threats himself, told them, "Don't worry about these threats. You carry on just as you've been doing. That's the greatest thing for our country."[16]

In January 1956 in Chicago, Robinson attacked Georgia's governor, Marvin Griffin, for attempting to withdraw Georgia Tech from playing in the 1956 Sugar Bowl against a racially integrated University of Pittsburgh football team. Robinson called on other Southerners to assert: "[T]his is not what we want, that we don't share this belief."[17] As Georgia natives, actions like these by Robinson and King proved meaningful.

The civil-rights sit-in campaigns began at a Woolworth lunch counter in Greensboro, North Carolina, on February 1, 1960. Four Black students from nearby North Carolina A&T College sat down at the all-white counter but were refused service for nearly an hour. King referred to their action as an "electrifying movement of Negro students [that] shattered the placid surface of campuses and communities across the South."[18]

Earlier, in October 1959, after delivering a speech to 1,700 NAACP supporters in Greenville, South Carolina, Robinson had arrived at the airport for his flight back to New York. Bypassing the labeled "Colored Lounge," he and supporters sat in the main lounge reserved for whites. They were asked to move to the colored lounge. Robinson and his followers refused. After some unrest, these early sit-inners were allowed to stay.[19]

After Robinson's election to the Hall of Fame was announced, King played a key role in organizing a testimonial dinner on July 20, 1962, at the Waldorf-Astoria Hotel. King's action was a source of pride to Robinson. Funds were raised for the civil-rights cause.[20]

In August and September of 1962, two Black churches in Georgia involved in voter registration, Shady Grove Baptist and Mount Olive Baptist, were destroyed by arson. Soon thereafter, King phoned his friend Robinson and asked him to serve as national fundraising chairman to rebuild the churches. Robinson agreed and money was raised to rebuild the churches.[21]

The synergy of King and Robinson surfaces in the perspectives of those who knew them.

King himself said of Robinson, "[H]e underwent the trauma and the humiliation and the loneliness which comes with being a pilgrim walking the lonesome byways toward the high road of freedom. He was a sit-inner before sit-ins, a freedom rider before freedom rides."[22]

Author Roger Kahn wrote, "I think it is reasonable to suggest that without Jackie Robinson, Martin

Luther King would have lived out his days delivering eloquent sermons in an obscure Baptist church in Georgia."²³

Don Newcombe of the Brooklyn Dodgers was the first major-league pitcher to win all three awards for excellence: the Rookie of the Year, Most Valuable Player, and Cy Young Awards. He remembered, "Martin (i.e., King) said to me a month before he died at my home at my dinner table. He said, Don, you and Roy and Jackie will never know how easy you made it for me to do my job."²⁴

Robinson likewise supported King and stated, *"Let there be no doubt in any man's mind where I stand on the subject of Dr. Martin Luther King Jr. If ever a man was placed on this earth by divine force to help solve the doubts and ease the hurts and dispel the fears of mortal man, I believe that man is Dr. King."*²⁵

Bringing the two leaders together, the philosopher and author Cornell West said, "More even than either Abraham Lincoln and the Civil War, or Martin Luther King Jr. and the Civil Rights movement, Jackie Robinson graphically symbolized and personified the challenge to the vicious legacy and ideology of white supremacy in American history."²⁶ A responsive Robinson called King "the greatest leader of the twentieth century."²⁷

Robinson and King did not agree on every issue. Their major disagreement involved the Vietnam War. King was an early opponent of the war and Robinson initially was a supporter. Robinson's son, 19-year-old Jackie Jr., was wounded in an ambush in the war on November 19, 1965, and awarded a Purple Heart.²⁸ Although Robinson could be openly critical at times of other civil-rights leaders, "Martin Luther King Jr. was Robinson's favorite civil rights leader of all time."²⁹

Perhaps the ultimate compliment from King to Robinson was when the civil-rights leader said, "Jackie Robinson made it possible for me in the first place. Without him, I would never have been able to do what I did."³⁰ Likewise, in an interview with Dr. King, host Larry King introduced him as "the founder of the civil-rights movement." The host was corrected by Dr. King, who said, "The founder of the civil-rights movement was Jackie Robinson."³¹

Both Robinson and King had strong and intelligent women at their side. Rachel Isum Robinson and Coretta Scott King continued the journeys of their husbands. These two Black men, from different backgrounds, separated by a decade in age, became friends in the struggle for justice. In so doing, the synergy of their efforts changed America.

NOTES

[1] Ali B. Ali-Dinar, Ph.D., page editor, "Letter from a Birmingham Jail [King Jr.]," April 16, 1963, African Studies Center, University of Pennsylvania.

[2] Franck C. Girardot, "Baseball Great Jackie Robinson Joined MLK at March on Washington," *Pasadena Star-News*, August 24, 2013.

[3] Victoria Taylor, "Jackie Robinson to JFK in 1963 Telegram: Rev. King Needs More Protection in Miss.," *New York Daily News*, April 13, 2013.

[4] Amanda Scurlock, "Jackie Robinson and King Became Friends Through Civil Rights," *Los Angeles Sentinel*, January 11, 2017.

[5] Photo caption of Jackie Robinson and Martin Luther King Jr. receiving honorary degrees from Howard University in 1957, with photo courtesy of the National Museum of American History.

[6] "Martin Luther King Jr. as Pastor," *Religion & Ethics Newsweekly*, January 13, 2006, pbs.org.

[7] Michael G. Long and Chris Lamb, *Jackie Robinson, A Spiritual Biography* (Louisville: Westminster John Knox Press, 2017), 32.

[8] Doris Kearns Goodwin, interview on C-Span2, November 6, 2005.

[9] Chrysler Hall in the Norfolk Forum, Tuesday April 30, 2013; Bijou Theater, Knoxville, Tennessee, April 25, 2017.

[10] John R.M. Wilson, *Jackie Robinson and the American Dilemma* (New York: Longman, 2020), Introduction, xiv.

[11] Henry Metcalfe, *A Game for All Races, An Illustrated History of the Negro Leagues* (New York: MetroBooks, 2000), 127.

[12] "Charles Barkley Interviews Obama About LeBron, Obamacare & Black Men," TNT, February 16, 2014, video rebroadcast on CNN.

[13] Arnold Rampersad, *Jackie Robinson, A Biography* (New York: Alfred A. Knopf, Inc., 1997), 100.

[14] Eric Metaxas, *7 Men, and the Secret of Their Greatness* (Nashville: Thomas Nelson Publishers, 2013), 120-122.

[15] "Montgomery Bus Boycott," Martin Luther King, Jr. Research and Education Institute, Stanford, University.

[16] Peter Golenbock, *Bums, an Oral History of the Brooklyn Dodgers* (Mineola, New York: Dover Publishing, Inc., 1984), 222, 224.

[17] Rampersad, 287-289.

[18] "Sit-Ins," Martin Luther King, Jr. Research and Education Institute, Stanford University.

[19] Long and Lamb, 116.

[20] Rampersad, 364.

[21] Rampersad, 367-368.

[22] Chris Lamb, "Spring Training," *American Legacy*, Spring 2007: 14-20.

[23] Roger Kahn, *October Men* (New York: Harvest Edition, 2004), 11.

[24] Don Newcombe, *Hank Aaron, Chasing the Dream*, 1995 TBS Productions, Turner Home Entertainment, VHS.

[25] *"Jackie Robinson," New York Amsterdam News, July 1, 1967.*

[26] Jackie Robinson, *I Never Had It Made, The Autobiography of Jackie Robinson* (Hopewell, New Jeresy: Ecco Press, 1995), Foreword, ix-x.

[27] Wilson, 178.

[28] Rampersad, 402.

[29] *New York Amsterdam News*, April 13, 1968: 21.

[30] Joseph Dorinson, "Hank Greenberg, Joe DiMaggio, and Jackie Robinson: Race, Identity, and Ethnic Power," in Joseph Dorinson and Joram Warmund, eds., *Jackie Robinson, Race, Sports, and the American Dream* (Armonk, New York: M.E. Sharpe, Inc., 1989), 112.

[31] Bob Nightengale, "Contracts Need Good Home," *USA Today Sports Weekly*, August 31-September 6, 2016: 20.

JACKIE'S LAST STAND: JACKIE ROBINSON'S LAST PUBLIC APPEARANCE AND HIS APPEAL FOR THE INTEGRATION OF MAJOR-LEAGUE BASEBALL MANAGEMENT

by Richard J. Puerzer

On the afternoon of Sunday, October 15, 1972, Jackie Robinson stood on the field of Cincinnati's Riverfront Stadium in the brilliant afternoon sunshine. Game Two of the World Series between the Oakland A's and the Cincinnati Reds was to be played that day, and in a pregame ceremony, Robinson was being recognized on the 25th anniversary of his joining the Brooklyn Dodgers, ending the insidious segregation existent in the modern era of major-league baseball. Although Robinson's entry into the majors was and remains the most important cultural event in the history of baseball, major-league baseball entered the 1972 season with nary a plan to commemorate the event. It was not until 1997, 25 more years later, that Jackie Robinson Day was established with an annual celebration of Robinson and his achievements. However, during the 1972 season, pressure built to formally recognize Robinson. Finally, at the very end of the season, before Game Two of the World Series, the baseball establishment did the right thing and properly recognized one of its greatest and most impactful players. Although Robinson's presence at the World Series was significant in and of itself, it was of greater importance and magnitude because this moment would prove to be Jackie's last stand. Robinson took the opportunity to criticize major-league baseball for not yet having hired a Black manager or providing post-playing-career opportunities for Black players. In retrospect, the event was also quite poignant as it was Jackie Robinson's last public appearance before his death.

Jackie Robinson had a prickly relationship with baseball following his career as a player. His retirement was the initial cause of this contentiousness. After the 1956 season, Robinson was 37 years old and had played 10 seasons with the Brooklyn Dodgers, leaving his body aching and unable to perform as he had a few years before. He was looking for an opportunity that would allow for him to move on from earning a living by playing baseball and to still support his growing family. However, it was clear that opportunity would most likely not come from baseball, as no Black men were working in baseball management at that time. Toward the end of his career, he also had a turbulent relationship with Dodgers management, including manager Walter Alston, general manager Buzzie Bavasi, and, especially since the departure of Branch Rickey from the Dodgers organization, with owner Walter O'Malley.

As a result of both the erosion of his baseball skills and his sour relationship with the Dodgers, Robinson began looking for business opportunities. After the 1956 season those opportunities presented themselves in two ways. First, Robinson signed an agreement with *Look* magazine giving the magazine the exclusive rights to the story of his retirement. Additionally, Robinson was approached by the president of the Chock Full o' Nuts company about taking an executive position at the company. With these opportunities before him, Jackie Robinson chose to retire from baseball. Unbeknownst to him, in December of 1956 while he was determining his future career path, the Brooklyn Dodgers negotiated a trade to send Robinson to the New York Giants. Initially, in order to keep the *Look* story exclusive, Robinson indicated that he might join the Giants and continue playing. However, the *Look* story was leaked to the public and Dodgers general manager Bavasi became annoyed with Robinson for not telling him of his plans to retire. Robinson was in turn angry with the Dodgers after they insinuated that he was claiming that he was retiring as a ploy to get a better playing contract. The ire on both sides resulted in a quiet feud between the Dodgers and Robinson that would last for nearly the rest of his life.

Toward the end of his playing career, there had been discussion of Robinson possibly taking a management position in the Dodgers organization, perhaps taking the manager's position in Montreal, where he had begun his career in the Dodgers system. However, Robinson felt that his contentious relationship with Walter O'Malley made that very unlikely.[1] Additionally, he knew that he and all Black players faced blatant racism if they sought management positions in baseball. In his 1972 autobiography *I Never Had It Made*, Robinson stated that as he approached retirement from the playing field, he felt that there were "many capable black athletes in the game who could contribute greatly as managers or in other positions of responsibility but it just isn't happening."[2]

Even before he retired, Robinson was indirectly lobbying for Black players to move into coaching positions after their playing days were done. Robinson was the named editor of *Our Sports*, a monthly sports magazine aimed for the Black audience which had its first issue in May 1953. In the debut issue of the magazine, Milton Gross wrote an article titled, "Will a Negro Ever Become Manager in the Big Leagues?"[3] In the article, Satchel Paige and Roy Campanella are confidently described as having already been assured coaching jobs after their retirement from the playing field. Monte Irvin is also identified as having managerial potential. Likewise, Oscar Charleston and Winfield Welch, both former Negro League managers, are named as potential major-league managers. Curiously, the article plays down the prospects of Robinson himself managing, although it does project that his approach would be comparable to that of Leo Durocher. None of these well-qualified Black men mentioned in the article went on to manage in the major leagues.

After Robinson dismissed the thought that he himself would get a job in the baseball establishment, he continued to lobby for the desegregation of baseball management for others. In a 1962 newspaper article he is quoted as criticizing the American League for being slow to integrate its teams, but also commented on the absence of Blacks in management positions. Robinson declared, "The most serious problems [*sic*] facing Negro ballplayers today is the off-the-field baseball jobs." He went on to say, "[T]here's little place in the baseball world for a retired Negro ballplayer."[4] In his book *Baseball Has Done It*, published in 1964, Robinson pointed out that the Dodgers employed only one African-American, in a rather menial job, and that most clubs employed no African-Americans in their offices. He went on to state, "Without belaboring this point I know that many Negroes are qualified as private secretaries, road secretaries, statisticians, press agents, head scouts, farm supervisors, coaches, and managers," and "that any experienced player with leadership qualities can pilot a ball club to victory, no matter what the color of his skin."[5] Later, in 1968, in an article titled "There Are No Rickeys Today," he took Larry McPhail, the Yankees' general manager, to task for offering the excuse "that it is difficult to find qualified Negroes with the right educational background for front office jobs." Robinson retorted that "The clubs spend all kinds of money, time, and effort scouting for talent. Yet, they find it "difficult" to look right over their noses to discover quite a few articulate, intelligent players who could fit quite ably into administration."[6] Robinson generally remained at a distance from major-league baseball after his retirement and watched as many Black players retired from baseball with no opportunities to stay in the industry.

Over the years, Jackie Robinson's health suffered severely. By 1972, he was suffering from diabetes as well as advanced heart disease caused by blockages in his arteries and hypertension. He was also losing his eyesight, due in part to strokes that had caused ruptures of blood vessels in his eyes.[7] Twenty-five years after he debuted with the Brooklyn Dodgers, although he was only 53 years old, Jackie Robinson was an old man.

Compared with the response that Jackie Robinson and his accomplishments rightfully receive today, the attention he was given in 1972 by the baseball establishment was quite underwhelming. The first recognition he received from was a June 4 ceremony held by the Los Angeles Dodgers as a part of their Old-Timers Day. Initially Robinson declined to take part in the event. However, the ownership of the Dodgers had now been passed on to Walter O'Malley's son Peter, who took a diplomatic approach to Robinson. Peter O'Malley also called upon Robinson's former teammate Don Newcombe, a Dodgers employee, who successfully persuaded Robinson to attend.[8] Before the event, Robinson met with Peter O'Malley and discussed with him his concerns regarding the lack of post-playing careers in Organized Baseball for Black players. Robinson later reported that he was heartened that O'Malley "felt Frank Robinson has tremendous ability and that the club also recognizes the talents of Maury Wills and Jim Gilliam."[9] Still, Robinson remained pessimistic, stating prophetically, "I don't think we'll see a Black manager in my lifetime. I don't think that's the Black man's loss as such, but baseball's loss and America's loss."[10]

Given our perspective today, it is surprising that the event held by the Dodgers was not focused upon Robinson. The day was actually billed as Casey Stengel Day at Dodger Stadium, with Stengel being recognized and managing one of the teams of old-timers. In a separate pregame ceremony, Robinson and his former teammates Roy Campanella and Sandy Koufax received equal billing as their numbers retired by the Dodgers. Although the retirement of all three players' numbers was certainly appropriate, the ceremony really had nothing specific to do with the anniversary of Robinson making it to the majors and recognizing what he had to endure once he got there. That anniversary was not celebrated until after the season, during the World Series.

Joe Black, Robinson's former Dodgers teammate, was working as a representative of the commissioner's office in the early 1970s and had been advocating for some time that baseball "do something, anything" to recognize Robinson.[11] Commissioner Bowie Kuhn eventually agreed to honor Robinson, but again Robinson was reluctant to take part, once again citing his dissatisfaction with the plight of Black players in gaining management positions in baseball after retirement. Kuhn in his autobiography asserts that he was able to convince Robinson to take part during a lunch meeting at which Kuhn made his case that he was lobbying baseball's owners to hire more Black former players.[12] Another angle that major-league baseball took to entice Robinson was to also make the event a tribute to Robinson's son Jackie Jr., who had died earlier that summer, and to support and make donations to Daytop, the drug-rehabilitation center where Jackie Jr. had been treated.[13] Ultimately, Robinson agreed to take part in a ceremony at which he would be honored before Game Two of the World Series and would throw out the ceremonial first pitch.

Video of the on-field ceremony captures the brief but powerful event.[14] Robinson is joined on the turf of Cincinnati's Riverfront Stadium by his family: wife Rachel, daughter Sharon, and son David. Additionally, Commissioner Kuhn, National League President Charles Feeney, Dodgers President Peter O'Malley, commissioner's public-relations director Joe Reichler, former teammates Joe Black and Pee Wee Reese, and Larry Doby, who also debuted in the majors 25 years before, all joined Robinson on the field. Former Dodgers radio announcer Red Barber was the master of ceremonies. After everyone assembled on the field, Barber introduced the baseball dignitaries along with the Robinson family. He then introduced Kuhn, who came to the microphone. Kuhn congratulated Robinson, and then read a statement from President Richard Nixon commending Robinson both for his pioneering baseball career and for his work championing the fight against drug abuse, especially with the youth of America. After reading Nixon's statement, Kuhn called Robinson, who was escorted by his wife, Rachel, to the microphone. Kuhn once again congratulated Robinson and presented him with a small trophy. Robinson then delivered a brief speech to the crowd at the ballpark and the national television audience, estimated at 60 million, who tuned in this Sunday afternoon.[15]

Jackie Robinson led his remarks by expressing humility, stating, "I was just really a spoke in the wheel of the success we had some 25 years ago." He then thanked Pee Wee Reese for attending the event and also expressed that "it would have been a real pleasure if Mr. Rickey could have been here today." Robinson then stated that he was thankful that his family was with him for the day, and thanked "baseball for the tremendous opportunities it has presented to me and also for this thrilling afternoon." Then Robinson, for the last time publicly, took the opportunity to reprimand baseball and express his conviction that baseball should be doing more to continue the progress of racial equality that he had started more than 25 years ago. Robinson eloquently and purposefully declared, "I am extremely proud and pleased to be here this afternoon, but must admit that I am going to be tremendously more pleased and more proud when I look at that third-base coaching line one day and see a Black face managing in baseball. Thank you very much."

After the on-field ceremony, Robinson was escorted off the field to the stands where he would make the ceremonial first pitch. As he made his way across the diamond, Dick Williams, the Oakland A's manager and Robinson's former Dodgers teammate, came up to and effusively shook hands with Robinson and kissed his wife, Rachel. Moments later, Cincinnati Reds second baseman Joe Morgan respectfully approached Robinson and shook hands. Robinson then made his way to the stands, and was handed a ball by Bowie Kuhn. Despite his failing eyesight, Robinson looked strong as he threw the ceremonial first pitch to Reds catcher Johnny Bench. The game was then played, with the A's winning, 2-1, on their way to winning the Series.

On October 24, 1972, just nine days after the celebratory event, Jackie Robinson died in his home of a heart attack. His appearance at the World Series provided Robinson, for the last time, with a platform to remind baseball and America what he had accomplished, and what he had spent most of his life championing. It would be more than two years before Frank Robinson was hired to be the player-manager of the Cleveland Indians for the 1975 season. More than two decades later, in 1997, acting Commissioner Bud Selig announced that Jackie Robinson would be celebrated annually across baseball each April 15, now named Jackie Robinson Day.

NOTES

1. Arnold Rampersad, *Jackie Robinson: A Biography* (New York: Alfred A. Knopf, 1997), 299.
2. Jackie Robinson and Alfred Duckett, *I Never Had It Made* (New York: Putnam, 1972), 118.
3. Milton Gross, "Will a Negro Ever Become Manager in the Big Leagues?" *Our Sports*, Vol 1 No 2, May 1953: 7, 58-61.
4. "Jackie Calls American League Shortsighted," *New York Amsterdam News*, July 14, 1962: 30.
5. Jackie Robinson, *Baseball Has Done It* (Brooklyn, New York: Ig Publishing, 2005), 211-212.
6. Jackie Robinson, "No More Rickeys," *New York Amsterdam News*, February 24, 1968: 17.
7. Rampersad, 444.
8. Rampersad, 456.
9. Bob Hunter, "Dodgers and Ex-Star Robinson Bury Hatchet at Stengel Day," *The Sporting News*, June 24, 1972: 9.
10. Ross Newhan, "No Black Manager in Jackie's Time," *The Sporting News*, July 1, 1972: 24.
11. Dick Young, "An Impatient Man in a Slow-Moving World," *New York Daily News*, October 25, 1972: 55.
12. Bowie Kuhn, *Hardball: The Education of a Baseball Commissioner* (New York: Times Books, 1987), 113-114. There are numerous reasons to be skeptical of Kuhn's assertion, including the fact that he states that the meeting took place on June 20, 1972, just three days after the death of Robinson's son, Jackie Jr. Kuhn also claims that when Robinson made his on-field plea for a Black manager in major-league baseball, he credited Kuhn with supporting the cause. Video of the event show that Robinson did not mention Kuhn at all with regard to the topic.
13. Young. Daytop received the donations of a station wagon from the Chrysler Corporation and a double-decker bus from Greyhound.
14. A nine-minute video clip of the pregame ceremony is available on YouTube: youtube.com/watch?v=Pdg0WApbYjI.
15. Rampersad, 459.

"THE NECESSITIES"
AL CAMPANIS'S MOMENT OF TRUTH

by Warren Corbett

April 6, 1987, was a slow news day. President Reagan spoke to the Canadian Parliament, hardly a reason to stop the presses. Republican former quarterback Jack Kemp announced his candidacy to succeed Reagan in 1988. The Dow Jones Industrial Average topped 2,400 for the first time. It was Opening Day for 16 of the 26 major-league teams.

With no headlines screaming for attention that Monday, producers of the ABC News program *Nightline* turned away from their usual topics, the latest controversies in national and world politics, to commemorate the 40th anniversary of a heroic moment: Jackie Robinson's major-league debut. *Nightline* anchorman Ted Koppel later said he expected a feel-good half-hour of "rather bland if warm clichés about one of the great men in baseball."[1]

But nothing in Jackie Robinson's short life was bland. Nearly 15 years after his death, he could still stir up a storm. This time the tempest sank one of his former teammates, Dodgers general manager Al Campanis.

Campanis had played shortstop beside second baseman Robinson on the 1946 Montreal Royals, in the pioneer's first season in White baseball. "Al Campanis was a good guy," Robinson once said. "He was very good on integration when it counted."[2] The two were close enough that Robinson was a guest for show-and-tell in the classroom of Campanis's son Jimmy.

On *Nightline*, Koppel, anchoring the program in Washington, introduced a taped interview with Rachel Robinson, who said her husband had been frustrated by the way baseball cast aside its African-American players and resisted hiring Black men as managers or front-office executives.

In his last visit to a ballpark, when he threw out the first ball for Game Two of the 1972 World Series, Jackie Robinson had said, "I am extremely proud and pleased but I will be more pleased when I can look over there and see a Black manager."[3] By 1987, Frank Robinson, Larry Doby, and Maury Wills had managed in the majors, and Bill Lucas of the Braves had served as the first Black general manager (although he didn't hold the title), but at the time there were no African-Americans in either job.

Koppel turned to his live guests: Roger Kahn, author of *The Boys of Summer* and a friend of Robinson's, spoke from a New York studio, and Campanis sat alone under a spotlight behind home plate in the Houston Astrodome, where the Dodgers had played their opening game that night.

Just before *Nightline* went on the air, Koppel had told Kahn, "I grew up in England and I don't know much about baseball, so you may have to carry this show."[4] The anchorman was an international affairs specialist, but he was well briefed by his staff and was one of the premier interviewers who ever sat before a live television camera. First, he lobbed a few softballs, inviting Kahn and Campanis to reminisce about Robinson, then he threw a high, hard one.

Koppel: *Mr. Campanis, it's a legitimate question for you. You were a friend of Jackie Robinson, but it's a tough question for you. You're still in baseball. Why is it that there are no Black managers, no Black general managers, no Black owners?*

Campanis: *Well, Mr. Koppel, there have been some Black managers, but I really can't answer that question directly. The only thing I can say is that you have to pay your dues when you become a manager. Generally you have to go to the minor leagues. There's not very much pay involved, and some of the better-known Black players have been able to get into other fields and make a pretty good living in that way.*

Koppel: *You know that that's a lot of baloney. There are a lot of great Black players, great Black baseball men, who would dearly love to be in managerial positions. ... Is there still that much prejudice in baseball today?*

Campanis: *No, I don't believe it's prejudice. I truly believe that they may not have some of the, uh, necessities, uh, to be, uh, let's say, a field manager or perhaps a general manager.*

Koppel: *Do you really believe that?*

Campanis: *Well, I don't say that all of them, but they certainly are short. How many quarterbacks do you have, how many pitchers do you have that are Black?*

Koppel: *Yeah, but I gotta tell you, that sounds like the same sort of garbage we were hearing 40 years ago about players.*

Campanis: *No, it's not garbage, Mr. Koppel. ... Why are Black men or Black people not good swimmers? Because they don't have the buoyancy.*

Koppel: *It may just be because they don't have access to all the country clubs and the pools.*

During a commercial break, producer Rick Kaplan remembered, "Ted was trying to help him. I've never seen Ted off-air try to bring the guy back and say, 'Al, are you hearing yourself? Do you hear what you're saying? Are you sure you don't want to rethink that?'"[5] When the interview resumed, Koppel bent over backward to let his guest repair the damage.

Koppel: *From everything I can understand, you're a very decent man and a highly respected man in baseball. ... I'd like to give you another chance to dig yourself out, 'cause I think you need it.*

Campanis: *Well, let me just say this, Mr. Koppel. How many executives do you have on a high echelon in your business, in TV? How many Black anchormen do you have?*

Koppel: *You're exactly right. Fortunately there are a few Black anchormen. But if you want me to tell you why there aren't many Black executives, I'm not gonna tell you it's because the Blacks are not intelligent enough. I'm gonna tell you it is that whites have been running the establishment of broadcasting, just as they have been running the establishment of baseball, for too long and seem to be reluctant to give up power. I mean, that's what it finally boils down to, isn't it?*

Campanis: *Well, we have scouts in our organization who are Black and they're very capable people. I have never said that Blacks are not intelligent. I think many of them are highly intelligent. But they may not have the desire to be in the front office. I know that they have wanted to manage and some of them have managed. But they're outstanding athletes, very God-gifted, and they're very wonderful people. And that's all I can tell you about it.*

After some comments from Kahn, Koppel went back to Campanis and reminded him that it had been 40 years since Robinson first played in the majors.

Koppel: *It seems so strange that we are able to see integration on the field and not be able to visualize it in the managerial suite. And in all fairness, Mr. Campanis, you're right – not be able to visualize it in the executive ranks of the networks and some of the major newspapers. You're right, we've all been much too slow. What reasons do you attribute that to, Mr. Campanis?*

Campanis: *I think that Jackie Robinson probably did more for the acceptance of a Black athlete than anyone that I have seen or known. But what you gotta realize is that when you had the problems from the Civil War, it becomes a thing that doesn't happen overnight. I think Jackie did a tremendous job in making the Black athlete acceptable in the areas in which that had never occurred before, namely playing professional, major-league baseball. And if you look back and think about the fact that it took so long for an athlete, you've got to realize that it's also going to take a little while for executives and managers.*

Koppel: *How many generations is this going to take, do you think?*

Campanis: *I don't have a crystal ball, Mr. Koppel, but I can only tell you that I think we are progressing very well in the game of baseball. We have not stopped the Black man from becoming an executive. They also have to have the desire, just as Jackie Robinson had the desire to become an outstanding ballplayer.*

Roger Kahn, interjecting: *I can't imagine that there is no Black that has the desire to be a major-league general manager. There's a Don King in boxing who seems to be a pretty good entrepreneur. There has never been a Black owner of a major-league baseball team. I don't know why. In a business where about a third of the ballplayers are Black, perhaps a little more, it's about time we had a Black president of a team.*

Koppel: *Just as a matter of curiosity, Mr. Campanis, what is the percentage of Black ballplayers, for example, in your franchise?*

Campanis: *I would say, I think Roger mentioned that about a third of the players are Black, and that might be a pretty good number. And deservedly so, because they are outstanding athletes. They are gifted with great musculature and various other things. They're fleet of foot. And this is why there are a lot of Black major league ballplayers. Now as far as having the background to become club presidents, or presidents of a bank, I don't know. But I do know, when I look at a Black ballplayer, I am looking at him physically and whether he has the mental approach to play in the big leagues.*

(The interview, transcribed from YouTube, has been edited for clarity and to eliminate redundancy and irrelevant comments.)

Right after the program, Dodgers broadcaster Vin Scully, who hadn't seen it, found his former roomie "pale and shaking." "I think I fucked up," Campanis told him.[6] The next day he issued a public apology, saying "my statements have been misconstrued" and adding, "This is the saddest moment of my entire career."

The reaction was brutal. Rachel Robinson was "appalled." Henry Aaron said baseball couldn't eliminate racial prejudice "because you still have people like Campanis with his beliefs."[7]

"He just said what a lot of baseball people have been thinking for years," observed Frank Robinson, the first Black manager in the majors. "I'm glad it's finally out in the open, so we can address it."[8]

Those who knew Campanis stepped up to defend him. "I don't believe he has a prejudiced bone in his body," the Black former pitcher Don Newcombe said. Another Black former Dodger, Maury Wills, went to Campanis's home, picked up a ringing telephone, and said, "This is Maury Wills, a friend of Al Campanis." Campanis's son George remembered his father whipping him because he spoke the "N" word, "the only time my dad took a belt to me."[9]

Dodgers owner Peter O'Malley at first issued his own apology and said Campanis would not lose his job. Two days later, facing the raging bonfire of criticism, O'Malley forced him to resign. "I told Al I didn't have any choice," O'Malley said later, "and he understood."[10]

Trying to explain himself, Campanis told the *Los Angeles Times's* Jim Murray that he hadn't meant what he said or said what he meant: "When I said Blacks lacked the 'necessities' to be managers or general managers, I meant the necessary experience, not things like inherent intelligence or native ability."[11] "Necessities" may have been a slip of the tongue, but he had rambled on in the same vein and worse.

A rumor circulated that Campanis had been drunk. Not so, said writer Bud Furillo, who had been sitting near him in the Astrodome press box that evening: "He was drinking Coca-Cola."[12] Fred Claire, the Dodgers executive who succeeded him as GM, believed the 70-year-old Campanis was worn out at the end of a long day.[13]

Campanis's apologists charged that Koppel had ambushed him, but some acquaintances thought the interview sounded like typical Campanis – the manner of speaking, not the message. "He had a way of mangling the language," *Los Angeles Times* writer Mark Heisler recalled. "As much as I liked the guy, he would go off the point and say something weird so often, people actually wondered if he was senile, or just pretending to be that way to confuse them."[14] The *New York Times's* George Vecsey said Campanis's convoluted conversations left listeners guessing what he was talking about: "He was a perfect example of why most of us should be cautious about appearing on live radio or television."[15]

For years afterward, Tommy Lasorda repeated, "They hung an innocent man."[16] But nothing Campanis or his friends said mattered. He had written the first line of his obituary.

The backlash reverberated throughout baseball. Commissioner Peter Ueberroth hired an outspoken critic, the African-American sociologist Harry Edwards, as a consultant on minority hiring. And Edwards enlisted Campanis to assist him. "It wasn't a simple case of Al being a bigot," Edwards said, "to say he was just a bigot is simply wrong – people are more complex than that. To a certain extent, it was the culture Al was involved with. To a certain extent, it was a comfort with that culture."[17]

Ueberroth's initiative generated headlines, but little change. Two years later the National League installed a Black former player, Bill White, as its president, but White acknowledged that he made scant progress in persuading teams to add minorities to their executive ranks.[18]

In 47 years in baseball, Campanis had built a reputation as one of the game's great teachers and scouts. Born on the Greek island of Kos, he and his mother immigrated to New York when he was a child. He grew up speaking Greek with his family and Spanish with his neighbors, and learned French while playing in Montreal. He played football and baseball at New York University and earned a master's degree.

He got into seven games at second base for the Dodgers in a wartime major-league trial and spent the rest of his seven-year playing career in the minors. He managed in the Dodgers farm system, then did everything for the franchise except laundry: scout, instructor, spring-training coordinator, director of scouting, and banquet-circuit raconteur before he was promoted to GM after the death of Fresco Thompson in 1968. He devised the 20-to-80 grading system for players that became a scouting standard.

His book *The Dodgers' Way to Play Baseball*, published in 1954, was translated into at least four languages and became a standard text for youth coaches. The teaching bible was borrowed from his revered mentor, Branch Rickey. Fourteen tapes of Rickey's spring training lectures were among his prized possessions. He hung three photographs on his office wall: Robinson, Roberto Clemente, and Sandy Koufax. A Black man, a Puerto Rican, and a Jew.

When Los Angeles won its first pennant on Campanis's watch as GM in 1974, first baseman Steve Garvey was chosen the National League's most valuable player with Dodgers reliever Mike Marshall finishing third and center fielder Jimmy Wynn fifth in the sportswriters' voting. Marshall became the first relief pitcher to win the Cy Young Award. But columnist Jim Murray said the MVP was Campanis, who had drafted Garvey and the rest of the infield, and traded for Marshall, Wynn, starting pitcher Andy Messersmith, and others.[19]

Those few minutes on television wiped out all that he had achieved. He was never able to rehabilitate his reputation. The only baseball job he could find was as general manager of an independent-league team, the Palm Springs Suns. He wrote an autobiography, but no publisher would touch it. The Dodgers didn't shun him; O'Malley invited him to ballgames, and he visited his successor, Fred Claire, in his old office to talk baseball. He was a ghost haunting Dodger Stadium, "a forlorn and increasingly frail figure at ballparks and owners meetings, vainly seeking a job in the game," Ross Newhan wrote.[20]

His son Jim had played six years in the majors with Los Angeles, Kansas City, and Pittsburgh, where he was briefly a teammate of Clemente. His grandson Jimmy was drafted by Seattle in the third round in 1998 and topped out in Double A. Jimmy was the model for illustrations in his grandfather's instruction book for children, *Play Ball with Roger the Dodger*.[21]

Several years after the disastrous interview, Campanis heard that Ted Koppel was in Los Angeles. They met amiably for coffee. "I think there are a lot of genuine bigots in this country," Koppel said. "… I don't think Al was one of them."[22]

After suffering several strokes, Campanis died of coronary artery disease at 81 on June 21, 1998, Father's Day. "He didn't get a raw deal," Harry Edwards said, "he got the deal he ordered up, but he was one of the most honorable men in the whole process and he handled it with class, with conscientiousness and with courage."[23]

This story is adapted from the author's biography of Campanis for SABR's BioProject.

NOTES

1. William Weinbaum, "The Legacy of Al Campanis," espn.com, April 1, 2012. espn.com/espn/otl/story/_/id/7751398/how-al-campanis-controversial-racial-remarks-cost-career-highlighted-mlb-hiring-practices, accessed August 2, 2019.
2. Roger Kahn, *A Season in the Sun* (New York: Harper & Row, 1977), 39-40.
3. "To Thine Own Self Be True," *The Sporting News*, November 11, 1972: 14.
4. Bill Dwyre, "Kahn Sadly Recalls the Night of the Campanis Incident," *Los Angeles Times*, June 22, 1998: C8.
5. Weinbaum, "The Legacy."
6. Steve Springer, "The Nightline that Rocked Baseball," *Los Angeles Times*, April 6, 1997: C9.
7. "Some Answers No One Expected," *New York Times*, April 8, 1987: B10.
8. Peter Gammons, "The Campanis Affair," *Sports Illustrated*, April 20, 1987, si.com/vault/1987/04/20/106777673/scorecard, accessed August 2, 2019.
9. Ross Newhan, "A Lifetime Destroyed by His Own Words," *Los Angeles Times*, June 22, 1998: C1, C8.
10. Newhan, "Campanis, Ex-Dodger Official, Dies," *Los Angeles Times*, June 22, 1998: A17.
11. Jim Murray, "The Bitter Lesson for Campanis: Just Say 'No, Thanks,'" *Los Angeles Times*, July 2, 1987: III-5.
12. Steve Delsohn, *True Blue* (New York: William Morrow, 2001), 180.
13. Fred Claire with Steve Springer, *My 30 Years in Dodger Blue* (New York: Sports Publishing, 2004), 65.
14. Delsohn, *True Blue*, 182
15. George Vecsey, "Sports of the *Times*," *New York Times*, August 23, 1998: S2.
16. Springer, "The Nightline."
17. Weinbaum, "The Legacy."
18. Warren Corbett, "Bill White," SABR BioProject.
19. Murray, "The Dial-a-Pennant Man," *Los Angeles Times*, September 29, 1974: III-1.
20. Newhan, "Campanis, Ex-Dodger Official, Dies."
21. Jim Campanis Jr., *Born into Baseball* (South Orange, New Jersey: Summer Game Books, 2016), 15.
22. Delsohn, *True Blue*, 183.
23. Weinbaum, "The Legacy."

OF MEMORY AND MYSTERY GUESTS: JACKIE ROBINSON, SOUPY SALES, AND *WHAT'S MY LINE?*

by David Krell

Memory is a tricky thing.

Soupy Sales, a popular children's TV show host in the 1960s and 1970s, discovered this immutable concept when he met Jackie Robinson during an episode of *What's My Line?* The show's premise: Four panelists deducing the job or "line" of a guest, through "yes or no" questions. These guests were everyday people with everyday jobs. But each episode also had a famous "mystery guest" segment requiring the panelists to be blindfolded as they attempted to discover his or her identity.

Robinson appeared on the November 20, 1969, broadcast; *What's My Line?* ran from 1950 to 1967 on CBS and from 1968 to 1975 in first-run syndication. John Daly hosted the CBS incarnation; Wally Bruner and Larry Blyden were the hosts in the syndicated version.

After the panel of Sales, Joanna Barnes, Arlene Francis, and Bert Convy failed to figure the Hall of Famer's identity, they removed their blindfolds. Then Sales offered his memory of seeing Robinson play college football: "You want to know something? One of the big thrills of my life and I get a big kick out of telling people this. It was in 1944 and I was in the Navy and I went to the Coliseum on Saturday afternoon. And UCLA in their backfield at the time had Jackie Robinson, Bob Waterfield, and Kenny Washington. You played USC that day and whipped them good. He was an All-American football player before he was a baseball player."[1]

It wasn't true. Robinson corrected Sales – he did play with Washington at UCLA, but in 1939. Here's what might have happened to cause Sales's confusion.

UCLA played USC at the Coliseum in the last game of the 1944 season. It was a blowout: final score 40-13. But the Trojans were victorious in the November 25 contest, not the Bruins; USC secured an undefeated record and later won the Rose Bowl against the University of Tennessee Volunteers. Sales was right about Waterfield being the UCLA quarterback, though.

It's possible that Sales talked with UCLA fans who reminisced about Robinson and Washington. In turn, he fixed them in his mind as playing in that game and subconsciously changed the winning team from USC to UCLA.

Robinson played semipro football in 1944 with the Los Angeles Bulldogs of the Pacific Coast Professional Football League. If Sales went to the November 26 game at Los Angeles's Wrigley Field, he would have seen the San Diego Bombers thrash the Bulldogs. But Robinson was on the field for only one play before an ankle injury sent him to the LA bench.[2] In this paradigm, one can presume that Sales talked

Publicity photo of Jackie Robinson as an ABC broadcaster for Major League Championship Baseball. Jackie Robinson's TV credits include being an ABC color commentator for MLB games in 1965. In addition to the appearance on What's My Line?*, Robinson also made the went on talk shows to be interviewed by Merv Griffin, Dick Cavett, and David Frost.*

Courtesy of Rachel Robinson and the Estate of Jackie Robinson.

with Bulldogs fans who mentioned Robinson and his exploits at UCLA. But it requires the supposition that Sales confused the two stadiums.

Sales going to both games on the last weekend in November and mixing the facts together is another possibility.

After correcting Sales, Robinson and Bruner had a brief conversation about the baseball icon's involvement with the Freedom National Bank in Harlem, which focused on minority customers. Bruner then gave an effusive declaration of Robinson's impact on baseball and the ex-ballplayer responded by acknowledging the import of Brooklyn Dodgers general manager Branch Rickey in signing Robinson to break baseball's color line in 1947.

This was not Robinson's first presence on *What's My Line?* The Brooklyn Dodgers legend appeared on the August 16, 1950, show. Often, viewers saw great ballplayers in the 1950s be the "mystery guest" trying to stump the panel: Roy Campanella, Phil Rizzuto, Yogi Berra, Mickey Mantle, Sal Maglie, Ted Williams, Willie Mays, and the 1956 Cincinnati Reds are some members of the post-World War II baseball pantheon who graced the stage. Rickey appeared on a 1959 episode; his conversation with Daly included boosting the Continental League, of which he was president. The CL never launched, but it led to expansion: Los Angeles Angels, Washington Senators (second incarnation), New York Mets, Houston Colt .45s (renamed Astros in 1965).

Two days after he was elected to the Hall of Fame, Satchel Paige – Robinson's teammate from the 1945 Kansas City Monarchs in the Negro Leagues – appeared on the February 11, 1971, episode. Although Robinson – who had been inducted in 1962 – notched a year with the Monarchs on his résumé, Paige was the first true Negro Leagues star to be acknowledged with an enshrinement at Cooperstown.

There was controversy because Paige did not meet the requirement of playing in the major leagues for 10 years. But it was an unfair fiat because Black players were not allowed to join the ranks of major leaguers.

Commissioner Bowie Kuhn said, "Technically, you'd have to say he's not in the Hall of Fame."[3] Fans, scholars, ballplayers, and executives differed from Kuhn's blunt assessment, of course.

Sales served in the Navy from 1944 to 1946 on the *USS Randall* and left with the rank of seaman first class. He saw action during the invasion of Okinawa.[4] Though primarily known for his comic antics, usually slapstick, Sales made a dramatic turn in a 1964 episode of *Route 66*.[5] He played a carefree millionaire with an unusual fixation: helping sick women. But when women learned his inclination, they tried to gain his love – and potentially marriage – by faking illnesses including being wheelchair-bound. Sales's trademark pie-in-the-face gag gives the episode comic relief; A scene in the dining room of the Ponce de Leon Hotel in St. Augustine, Florida, becomes a pie-throwing free-for-all.

Sales died in 2009. He was 83.

Robinson died in 1972; diabetes and heart problems led to his premature death. But the episode of *What's My Line?* and interviews on *The Mike Douglas Show*, *The Dick Cavett Show*, and *The David Frost Show* in the late 1960s and early 1970s comprise a time capsule of a slowly deteriorating, gray-haired man who not only understood his significance in sports and society, but also showed terrific humility in recounting the times when he ran the basepaths with the speed of Mercury and the determination of Zeus.

NOTES

1 *What's My Line?*, Syndicated, November 20, 1969.

2 "Bombers Ramble Over Bulldogs Here, 41-14," *Los Angeles Times*, November 27, 1944: 20.

3 Joseph Durso, "Paige Is First Star of Old Negro Leagues to Be Selected for Hall of Fame," *New York Times*, February 10, 1971: 52.

4 Supman, Milton, S1C, Navy – Together We Served website, navy.togetherweserved.com/usn/servlet/tws.webapp. WebApps?cmd=ShadowBoxProfile&type=Person&ID=497615 accessed November 27, 2020.

5 Ganzer, Alvin, dir. *Route 66*. Season 4, episode 19, "This Is Going to Hurt Me More Than It Hurts You." Aired February 14, 1964, on CBS.

JACKIE ROBINSON AND JOURNAL SQUARE

by David Krell

"Heroes get remembered. But legends never die." So says an apparition of Babe Ruth in *The Sandlot*.

Statues affirm their permanence. Capturing a ballplayer's essence creates a bond with passersby who stop to absorb the player's importance to the game and admire the sculptor's handiwork framing a moment. Ruth's likeness adorns Oriole Park as a reminder of the Sultan of Swat's Baltimore roots; Comerica Park boasts statues of six legendary Tigers; and Bob Feller's statue at Progressive Field represents pride for Clevelanders. Two statues of Ted Williams stand outside Fenway Park.

But it will be challenging to find a player with more statues than Jackie Robinson.

At the Rose Bowl in Pasadena, California, Robinson's football career at UCLA enjoys prominence through a statue of the four-sport varsity athlete in a running pose carrying a football.1 When visitors enter the foyer at the National Baseball Hall of Fame and Museum in Cooperstown, New York, three statues greet them – Lou Gehrig, Roberto Clemente, and Robinson. At Brooklyn's MCU Park, a statue of Pee Wee Reese with an arm around Jackie Robinson commemorates a moment in Cincinnati when the Kentucky-born shortstop showed the crowd – only 100 miles from his hometown of Louisville – that he accepted Robinson as his teammate and friend.

Dodger Stadium's Robinson statue shows the legend as he's sliding into a base. Jackie Robinson Ballpark in Daytona Beach, Florida, has a statue marking the location of the Hall of Famer's first spring-training game, in 1946. Near Olympic Park in Montreal, a statue of Robinson giving a baseball to two young boys in Montreal highlights his connection to the city – he played for the Montreal Royals in 1946 season after a year with the Kansas City Monarchs in the Negro Leagues.

Another statue of Number 42 stands in Jersey City, the metropolis owning the distinction of being the location of Robinson's first official game in what was then known as "Organized Baseball." On April 18, 1946, the Royals played the Jersey City Giants at Roosevelt Stadium; Robinson went 4-for-5 with a three-run homer and four RBIs. He proved to be a highly significant factor in the Royals' championship season that ended with a victory over the Louisville Colonels in the Little World Series.

Roosevelt Stadium has been gone since the mid-1980s, when it was demolished for a housing complex of townhouses, condominiums, and rental apartments. Robinson's nexus to Jersey City inspired the power brokers and decision makers to erect a statue commemorating the icon who won the 1947 Rookie of the Year Award, batted .311 in a 10-year major-league career, played on six National League pennant winners and one World Series championship squad, and changed baseball history as the first Black player in the twentieth century. On February 25, 1998, the statue sculpted by Susan Wagner was unveiled. "When (people) drive down the Boulevard, when they see Jackie Robinson reaching for the stars, then all of us want to claim him for our own," praised Mayor Bret Schundler.[2]

Wagner's statue weighs 2,500 pounds and cost $155,000. It stands next to the Journal Square station of the Port Authority Trans-Hudson (PATH) train system.[3] For a basis, Wagner got an assist from Robinson's widow, Rachel. "She sent me five photographs," said the sculptor. "I chose it because it showed a victory. I love sculpting and what he represented. I always admire people like that and to know what he went through, and persevered is amazing."[4]

Viewing the Jersey City statue through the paradigm of legendary architect Jean Labatut offers an expanded perspective of its meaning as a work of art, not just a depiction of a great ballplayer with historical, civic, and geographical significance. Labatut's 1952 essay, "Monuments and Memorials," outlines the impact that sculptors, architects, and artists may have on the culture through their depictions: "Memorials and monuments, landmarks and signposts for remembrance and for warning, are an integral part of the physical, intellectual, emotional, and spiritual human trail. There always will be memorials to express not only what has happened but also our aspirations, to show the journey already accomplished and to point forward in some definite direction. There always will be monuments giving precise information as to place and time. Both are inevitable footprints of an era."[5]

Indeed, Robinson's presence in Journal Square conveys the basic information about the game on April 18, 1946, and how it marked the first step toward integrating major-league baseball. But Wagner's work doesn't merely honor historical noteworthiness. It is, as Labatut theorizes, a symbol of aspiration. Robinson represented hope that baseball – and, in turn, America – could live up to its moniker as the Land of Opportunity. A quarter-century after he made his major-league debut in 1947, the national pastime still had not done so in Robinson's opinion. Before Game Two of the 1972 A's-Reds World Series, he told the crowd at Riverfront Stadium in Cincinnati that he wanted to see a Black manager. That didn't happen until Frank Robinson managed the Cleveland Indians in 1975.

Labatut also emphasizes art as education. "Words, customs, methods of reasoning, and techniques may vary, but art is the easiest channel for common understanding; through the arts we can become easily acquainted with other times and other peoples and with other people in our own time," explains the architect.[6]

Wagner's statue of Robinson jumping with arms outstretched is a dynamic representation of Robinson's athleticism. It evokes not only a moment but also a bygone era when Roosevelt Stadium was in its prime. An Art Deco project of the Works Progress Administration during the Great Depression in the 1940s, the ballpark underlined Jersey City's importance as a cultural, economic, and political force. When the Jersey City Giants left after the 1950 season, there were occasional sparks of life for the edifice. But the subsequent baseball tenants didn't last too long.[7]

Robinson's quote adorns the statue: "A life is not important except in the impact it has on other lives." Neither is art. In Robinson's case, the works of Wagner and her fellow sculptors affect, educate, and inspire those who want to know more about an American icon who withstood ignorance, championed tolerance, and transformed baseball.

NOTES

1. Robinson lettered in football, baseball, basketball, and track and field.
2. Michael Y. Park, "Robinson Statue Is Unveiled," *Jersey Journal* (Jersey City), February 26, 1998: 1.
3. Park. The statue is 14 feet high. The poundage is broken down as follows: "quarter inch thick bronze, 1,500 lbs. of bronze reinforced with 1,000 lbs. of stainless steel armature and mounting plate." Roz Hamlett, "Jackie Robinson Tribute at Journal Square: And Here's to You, Mr. Robinson," Port Authority of New York & New Jersey website, portfolio.panynj.gov/2017/02/07/jackie-robinson-tribute-at-journal-square-and-heres-to-you-mr-robinson/, February 7, 2017.
4. Susan Wagner, telephone interview with writer, February 11, 2020.
5. Jean Labatut, "Monuments and Memorials," in Talbot Hamlin, ed., *Forms and Functions of Twentieth-Century Architecture*, Volume 3 (New York: Columbia University Press, 1952), 521.
6. Labatut, 523.
7. Roosevelt Stadium was home to the Jersey City Jerseys in 1960-1961; Jersey City Indians in 1977; and Jersey City A's in 1978.

NOT AN EASY TALE TO TELL: JACKIE ROBINSON ON STAGE AND SCREEN

by Ralph Carhart

Jackie Robinson was one of the most complicated men to ever play the game, and so it is no surprise that fictional representations of him largely fail to fully capture this nuanced hero. His is a story that defies a simplistic three-act structure. Still, this has not stopped many from attempting to do so. It is possible that no single figure from baseball history has commanded as much screen (and stage) time as he. The "character" of Robinson can be found everywhere, from made-for-TV fare to big-screen blockbusters; from a Broadway musical to one-man shows touring local schools. His integration of the Dodgers is a historic moment that is not limited to the opus of baseball, but has extended into the whole American mythos. One could say that the quiet narrator of this tale is the woman to whom he entrusted his heart and legacy, his wife, Rachel Robinson.

The first attempt to produce a film that told the story of Robinson's rookie season was in the works before his historic freshman campaign was even over. In October 1947, Robinson signed a contract with producer Jack Goldberg for $14,500 for a picture called *Courage*, with Robinson tapped to play himself. The movie was never made and Robinson sued the wayward producer, creating a protracted legal battle that was decided in Jackie's favor by the Brooklyn Supreme Court in 1954.[1]

Having learned his lesson, Robinson knew he needed someone with more experience than himself to represent his business interests. He enlisted the services of lawyer Martin Stone. Understanding the tremendous potential value of a Hollywood deal, Stone immediately secured the rights to the book *My Own Story*, which Jackie had written with the considerable assistance of *Pittsburgh Courier* sportswriter Wendell Smith. By releasing Jackie from that deal, which was heavily lopsided in favor of the publisher, he now had the freedom to shop the story around to whomever he pleased.[2]

Stone, with screenwriter Lawrence Taylor, spent two nearly-fruitless years looking for a producer. The biggest obstacle to finding a buyer was a predictable one. The major studios were hesitant to release a motion picture in which the hero was a Black man. They didn't think it would sell in the "heartland." One studio proposed a doctored version of the story, rewritten to make it more palatable to White America. This incarnation had a blatantly pandering subplot, which claimed that Jackie owed all his athletic prowess to a fictional White coach who taught him everything he knew. They passed on this insulting adaptation and continued to look for takers.[3]

When UK-based Eagle-Lion Films approached Stone with the intent to purchase the rights to the Robinson story, he knew he would be working with a smaller company than the picture deserved. However, producer William J. Heineman's enthusiasm for the project, after so much ambivalence and tinkering from the big studios, convinced Stone and Robinson to give Eagle-Lion a chance. Jackie was promised $30,000 (nearly $10,000 more than his 1949 Dodgers salary), paid in two equal amounts before and after filming, as well as 15 percent of the profits from the film. Additionally, another 5 percent of the box office was to be donated to the National League players' fund.[4]

What neither Stone nor Robinson knew was just how bleak Eagle-Lion's financial situation was. The company was nearly bankrupt, and struggling to find anyone who was willing to give them money to make a film. Heineman's solution was novel. Rather than locating a small number of large-scale investors, he approached the very employees of Eagle-Lion and asked *them* to become backers of the project. The outpouring was instantaneous and effusive, and not just from the wealthier men who sat in the boardroom. Secretaries, switchboard operators, publicists, and assistants all gave money to the cause, ranging in amounts from $50 to several thousand dollars. By the time he was done, Heineman had collected $300,000. Certainly not an exorbitant amount to make a film, modest even by the standards of the day, but it was enough.[5]

Director Alfred E. Green was tapped to steer the film. Saddled with an inexperienced lead actor, a shoestring budget, and a razor-thin shooting schedule,

Green started out with a number of challenges. He mitigated these, in part, by making a film that was at least visually captivating. He chose close-up angles that put the viewer in the thick of the action. He modeled much of the pace on the popular newsreel-style that moviegoers were used to seeing before the feature picture.[6]

Of the multitude of portrayals of Robinson, it is this very first that may have ultimately been the most evocative, a curiosity since, as was the plan for *Courage*, the star of the film was Jackie, himself. Part of the reason the movie was shooting on such a tight schedule was that Rachel was expecting, and Jackie refused to leave for California until the baby arrived. Sharon Robinson was born on January 13, 1950, and a month later Jackie and his son, Jackie Jr., flew to Hollywood.

It was a challenging situation for the normally unflappable Robinson. He had learned to ignore the outside distractions thrown at him on the diamond – he had been training for that his whole life. Being an actor was another matter entirely. Two weeks after he arrived in California, he called Rachel and asked her to join him for the remainder of the shoot. Rachel and their baby flew to Los Angeles, which offered her the rare treat of being picked up by a limousine every morning and taken to the film lot. There, she and newborn Sharon became favorites among the cast and crew.[7]

The actor who was most drawn to Sharon was, fittingly, Ruby Dee, who had been cast to play Rachel. Dee was a well-known name after her star turn in the title role of the American Negro Theater production of *Anna Lucasta*. Even before *The Jackie Robinson Story*, she was familiar with the particular challenges of working with a professional athlete. In 1948 she starred on the silver screen opposite another sports legend, Joe Louis, in *The Fight Never Ends*. Dee was pregnant herself while filming *Story*, and she got to know Rachel over the final days of shooting.

The early chemistry between Dee and Jackie had been lacking, in large part because Robinson felt awkward about the intimacy of the scenes between them. It wasn't until Rachel was on the set that he began to relax. Dee realized what a powerful presence Rachel was, and how much her famous husband needed the

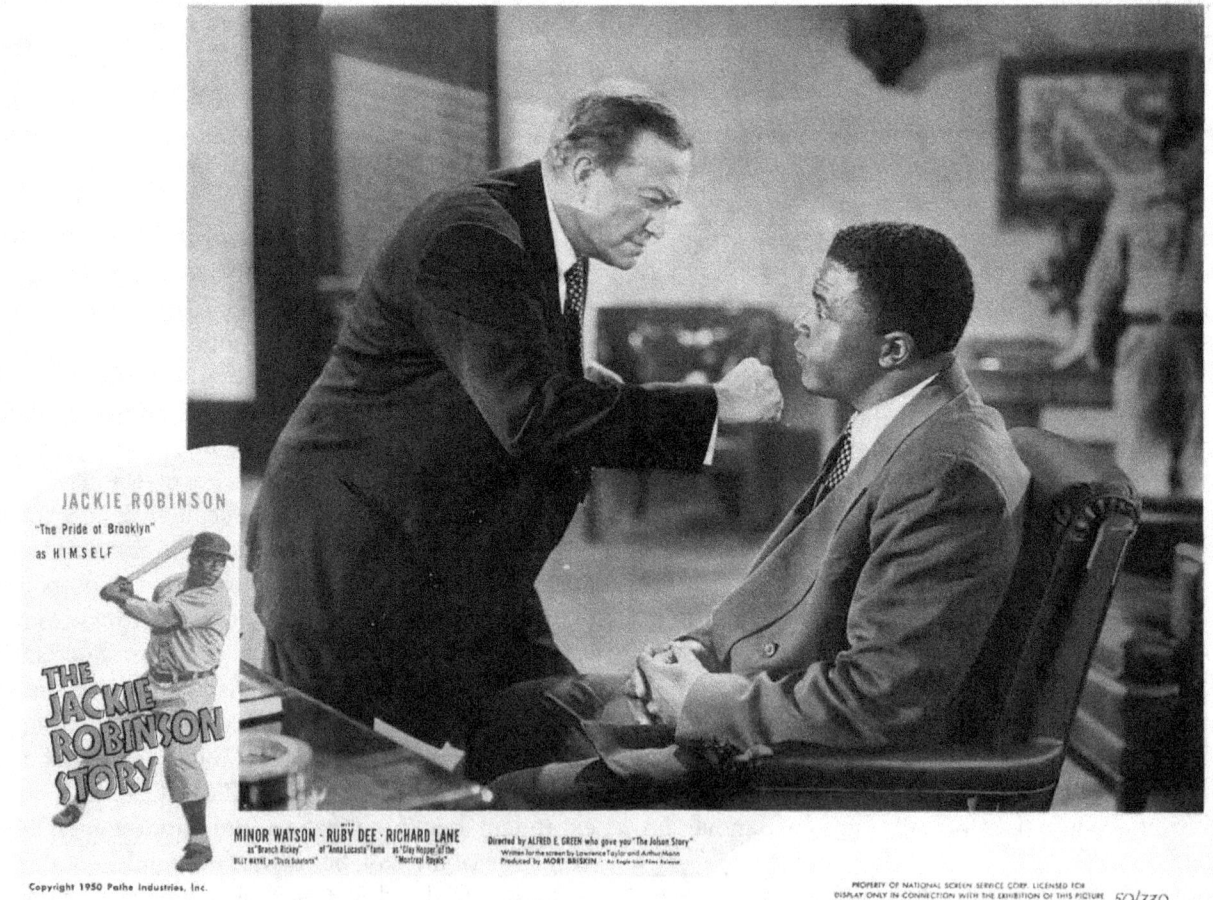

Courtesy of Rachel Robinson and the Estate of Jackie Robinson.

A lobby card promoting *The Jackie Robinson Story* (1950).

stability and approval she provided. This epiphany led to one of Dee's greatest regrets about the picture. She had listened to the advice of her director, Green, and had portrayed Rachel as a passive observer of the real-life Jackie Robinson story. In truth, she was one of the main motivators.[8] Now, Rachel was providing Jackie the inspiration to approach his acting with the same vigor with which he approached the game.

Other than Robinson, Dee was the only "name" in *The Jackie Robinson Story*. Loaded with the responsibility of carrying the picture, Robinson does not disappoint. There are certainly moments that come across as stilted, though even those have the believability of a young, inexperienced ballplayer faced with an unimaginable journey. The script does fall into the predictable tropes of biopics – a simplistic view of its subject as well as the individuals who stand in his way. There is no mention of Robinson's troubled past as a youth, nor of the complicated reality of Rickey's signing Robinson away from the Kansas City Monarchs, who appear in the film as the fictional Black Panthers. Perhaps most egregiously, the Rachel character is not only passive but woefully underutilized. Still, it is Robinson's story, and he gives it to us with a believable truth.

The New York City premiere took place at the Astor Theatre, an old Broadway house on 45th Street that had been converted to a movie theater in 1925. The event was one of the most elaborate and costly of its kind, with elite seating for the film approaching $100. Guests included Cab Calloway, Adam Clayton Powell, Gil Hodges, Brooklyn Borough President John Cashmore and New York City Mayor William O'Dwyer. A huge Brooklyn banner was raised over the theater, as Times Square became Flatbush for a day. Eagle-Lion pledged all proceeds from the night to Youth United, a charity dedicated to addressing juvenile delinquency.[9]

The Jackie Robinson Story opened to mixed, but mostly positive, criticism. Robinson received nearly universal praise for his heartfelt portrayal, and there were many who saw the film for the bigger picture it represented. As one critic succinctly put it, "Judged entirely on its merits as screen entertainment, it certainly cannot be rated among the best pictures of the year, but judged as a goodwill winner for our American way of life it deserves an Academy Award."[10]

The film turned out to be a modest commercial success. The fears that kept larger production companies away from the project, that middle America would not take to the film, proved to be unfounded.

The movie made history in the state of Utah when six different theaters in Salt Lake City had screenings at the same time, a first.[11] It played to long lines in small towns and big cities across the country, although, curiously, it also struggled at the box office in cities like Baltimore, Boston, and even Brooklyn.[12] In the end, the employees of Eagle-Lion Films made roughly five times their original investment.

Despite that success, *The Jackie Robinson Story* was the only fictionalization of Robinson ever filmed during his lifetime. While he made frequent television appearances both during and after his baseball career, Hollywood, and a big-budget telling of his tale, remained elusive. When he died on October 24, 1972, at the age of 53, the nation mourned the loss of a giant. Keenly aware that they were now responsible for shepherding his legacy, the Robinson family took a collective moratorium on the telling of his tale. It was not until 1981 that the next large-scale representation of Robinson was proposed, and this time it was a whole new medium.

It was announced in September 1980, that producers were negotiating with the Robinsons to bring his story to Broadway in the unlikely form of a musical. Director Martin Charnin had scored his first Broadway hit in 1977 with *Annie*, his homage to the comic strip *Little Orphan Annie*, which initially appeared in the *New York Daily News* in 1924. A longtime theatre veteran, Charnin made his Broadway acting debut as the character Big Deal in the original 1957 production of *West Side Story*. By the early 1960s he had shifted the focus of his career from being on stage to working behind the scenes, as a lyricist, where he toiled for two decades. After the overwhelming success of *Annie*, the genesis for his next directorial exercise happened in a New York minute. While sitting in the office of his business manager, David Cogan, Charnin struck up a conversation with another of Cogan's clients, famed film critic Joel Siegel. During the course of the chat, Siegel, a history buff, suggested that the Robinson story would make an interesting musical. Within a month, the two were at work, with Siegel writing the book and Charnin the lyrics. Robert Brush was hired to do the music.[13] The three men called their Robinson script *The First*.

The team persuaded producer Michael Harvey to back the project. Harvey, a relative lightweight who had never produced a Broadway show that had run for more than a month, enlisted the additional help of Zev Bufman, a theatre legend, and Neil Bogart, the founder of Casablanca Records. Bufman had just come off a hugely successful string of revivals, including updated productions of *Peter Pan*, *West Side Story*, *Oklahoma*, and *Brigadoon*. As the Robinson project was being developed, he was actively mounting a production of Lillian Hellman's *The Little Foxes*, starring his creative partner of many years, Elizabeth Taylor, in her Broadway debut.[14]

The initially announced production team for *The First* was impressive, with David Mitchell designing sets, Theoni Aldredge on costumes, and Peter Gennaro serving as choreographer, each of them Tony Award winners. The original ambitious timeline was delayed by a theatre shortage. *The First* was on the waiting list for two different venues, the Lunt-Fontanne and the Martin Beck, but the first had an unexpected hit on its hands in the Duke Ellington-based revue *Sophisticated Ladies*, while the latter was still hosting Bufman's *The Little Foxes*.[15] The entire project was put in a holding pattern while they waited for an appropriate house to become available. The delay cost them their original design team.

When it was announced in August that *The Little Foxes* was closing after the Labor Day weekend, the entire production went into overdrive. With the exception of costume designer Carrie Robbins, a two-time Tony nominee, the new design team was not nearly as accomplished as its predecessors. Still, they set to work creating the world of Ebbets Field on the stage of the Martin Beck in short order. Rachel Robinson, who had given her permission for the re-creation of Jackie's story, joined the team under the title of creative consultant, immediately lending gravitas to the project.

Many names had been suggested to play the coveted role of Robinson, including, briefly, Michael Jackson.[16] The producers decided the better (cheaper) route was to go with an unknown, and they considered many during the extended delay. With only two weeks remaining before rehearsals were scheduled to begin, they ultimately cast a newly minted Yale graduate who had never appeared in a professional play in his life, David Alan Grier. A decade after *The First*, Grier gained fame as a cast member of the television show *In Living Color*. In 1981 he was still a green, recent grad who was suddenly thrust into the spotlight of Broadway.

His castmates included Lonette McKee as Rachel and Darren McGavin as Branch Rickey.[17] McKee had come to the public consciousness just five years earlier with her harrowing portrayal of the drug-addicted Sister Williams in the film *Sparkle*. McGavin was a longtime fixture of stage and screen. He had made his Broadway debut in 1953, and is best known as the profanity-slinging father in the now iconic holiday film, *A Christmas Story*. Curiously, both would also later appear in baseball movies. McKee starred as the love interest of Richard Pryor in *Brewster's Millions* and McGavin played gambler Gus Sands in *The Natural*.

When the cast assembled for the first rehearsal on August 26, Rachel was in attendance. She told the gathered press that she didn't consider the play to be a "baseball show," as the themes were larger than just a game. "The show will carry the message that where there's opportunity, there's hope." Also present was Red Barber, whose gentle Southern cadence served as the voice of the Dodgers during the early days of Jackie's career. With the story of *The First* concentrating on the years 1946 and '47, Barber would be "appearing in the musical, in the form of a prerecorded voiceover. He also recorded television ads promoting the show.[18]

Rehearsals were going smoothly until mid-October, when McGavin withdrew from the show right before previews were scheduled to begin. As the script evolved in the rehearsal room, a frequent occurrence with new productions, it became clear to the writers that the real heart of the story was the relationship between Jackie and Rachel. The casualty of this realization was the importance of Rickey. As he witnessed his role trimmed from a starring to a supporting one, McGavin bowed out of the production[19] and was replaced by David Huddleston, a veteran actor who would ultimately perform in over 150 films and television shows, but whose Broadway résumé was relatively thin at the time.

After 33 preview performances, the show opened on November 17, 1981. There was plenty of baseball royalty on hand for the premiere, including Rachel, Barber, Duke Snider, Larry Doby, Ralph Branca, and Leo Durocher (a characterization of whom appeared in the show). Audience reaction was reported as enthusiastic, a perception that was likely aided by how friendly a large percentage of them were to the subject. The critics were not as kind. Jay Sharbutt reported that the show had "about as much passion, fire and complexity as your average TV movie."[20] In the *New York Times*, Frank Rich opined that the show was "written with all the flavor of a civics class chalk talk."[21] Sports columnist Dick Young was particularly aggrieved by the end of the first act, in which the Brooklyn faithful, who in reality had been largely supportive of Jackie, rained racial epithets down on Robinson, right down to a watermelon being hurled on to the stage.[22]

There were some bright spots. Grier was almost universally lauded for his characterization of Robinson. Rich claimed that Grier gave audiences an "impassioned, strong-voiced and tough-minded Jackie Robinson – not an impression, but a real performance." The portrayal earned Grier a Theatre World Award, as well as a Tony nomination. The production elements of the show were also praised, with both Marc B. Weiss and David Chapman earning Drama Desk nominations for their designs of lights and sets, respectively. Despite the harsh criticism, Siegel (for the book) and Charnin (for direction) also got Tony nominations, though the show ultimately won none of Broadway's biggest prizes. *The First* closed on December 13, less than a month after it opened, after only 31 performances.[23]

Purveyors of theatre remained undaunted by the financial failure of *The First*. It was not long before an onslaught of Robinson-themed scripts started making their way to stages. However, the difference in these subsequent attempts to cram Robinson's complicated, nuanced tale onto the confines of a stage was a calculated shift in the intended audience. Beginning with New York City-based Theatreworks/USA's 1984 production of *Play to Win*, another musical, producers realized that the simplified moral message of baseball's integration, that good can overcome evil with perseverance and bravery, was perfect fodder for children's theatre. Where Broadway critics lambasted the one-dimensional aspect of *The First*'s portrayals of the likes of Leo Durocher and Branch Rickey, archetypes are standard fare for school-age drama.

Play to Win was particularly memorable, making it all the way to Off-Broadway's Promenade Theatre in a 1989 production that the *New York Times* called a "joyous and very smart celebration."[24] With book and lyrics by Carles Cleveland & James de Jongh, and music by Jimi Foster, the show had the advantage of being created by Black artists, as opposed to the entirely White design team that was responsible *The First*. This more personal understanding of race led to some clever and thoughtful choices with the show. While Robinson was portrayed by a Black actor, the remaining four actors (who all played multiple roles, including the narrator character of Satchel Paige), were both Black and White. The race of their characters changed throughout the play, signaled by a black or white baseball cap, which the actors would switch depending on whom they were playing.[25] The show won the 1984 AUDELCO Award for best writing of a new show by Black authors for the noncommercial theatre.

Since *Play to Win*, the Robinson story has proved to be a reliable one for the educational theatre circuit, and continues to be so to this day. Additional titles include *Jackie Robinson Steals Home* by Peter Manos; another musical, developed by Mad River Theater Works, entitled *Everybody's Hero*; and *Jackie and Me*, based on the book by Dan Gutman, in which a kid discovers he can travel through time via his baseball card collection. Just before a global pandemic closed down theatres in 2020, Toby's Dinner & Show in Columbia, Maryland, presented *Most Valuable Player: The Jackie Robinson Story*.

One other "adult" playscript of note is the curious *Mr. Rickey Calls a Meeting*, written by Edward Schmidt and originally produced in 1989. The story is driven by the titular character bringing together Jackie, Joe Louis, "Bojangles" Robinson, and Paul Robeson for a conversation about how to get the Black community behind the coming announcement of Jackie's signing. *Meeting* is singular in that it does not shy away from how Jackie's arrival doomed the Negro Leagues, a topic largely ignored in other fictionalizations of the integration story. *Variety* gave the Old Globe production in San Diego high marks in 1992. The *New York Times* panned the 1994 version at the George Street Playhouse, lamenting that "[a] catalogue of conflicts is uncorked, integration versus elitism, the practical versus the principled, the divisiveness of those with a common cause. ... All that ought to add up to more than just words."[26]

Jackie Robinson (the fictional character) made his small-screen debut in the form of a story that, for the first time, was not centered on baseball. *The Court Martial of Jackie Robinson* instead chose to focus on the circumstances that brought Jackie to serve in the US Army, and the events that led to his honorable discharge in 1944. While Jackie's most celebrated accomplishment is given mention in an intertitle epilogue, the whole of the action takes place before Robinson ever sets foot in Branch Rickey's Brooklyn office. The made-for-TV movie was directed by television veteran Larry Peerce from a script written by four different scribes. It premiered on October 15, 1990, on TNT, the cable network controlled by Ted Turner, then the owner of the Atlanta Braves.

The cast featured Andre Braugher as Jackie and Kasi Lemmons as Rachel. Daniel Stern appeared in the film as Capt. William Cline, the defense attorney assigned to the case. Additional historical figures included veteran character actor J.A. Preston as scribe Wendell Smith and Stan Shaw as Joe Louis. The heavyweight champion, who was stationed alongside Robinson at Fort Riley in Kansas, had played an active role in Robinson attending Officer Candidate School,[27] still a rarity at the time despite that particular color line having been broken four decades earlier. Shaw had previously appeared as a character very loosely based on Robinson (in that he was the first to make the majors) in the 1976 comedy about the Negro Leagues, *The Bingo Long Traveling All-Stars and Motor Kings*.

Perhaps the most touching, and meaningful, performance in the film came from Ruby Dee. After portraying Rachel in *The Jackie Robinson Story* 40 years earlier, Dee returned in *The Court Martial*, this time as Jackie's mother, Mallie. This clever bit of casting gave Dee an opportunity to address her greatest regret from the first picture, her timid performance of Rachel. In a pivotal scene, as Jackie laments his separation from his beloved, Mallie delivers a fiery speech in which she berates her son for his antiquated thinking, declaring, "Oh, I understand, all right. You're being a man, and you're saying, oh Rae, you can't do this, and don't do that. Well, Rae's not the sort of woman that'll take that." Her vindication is palpable.

The Court Martial attempted to avoid the seemingly eternal fate of the Robinson story, a simplistic division between good and evil, in the fictional character of Brooklyn scout Ed Higgins, played by noted actor Bruce Dern. Higgins spends the picture spouting racial epithets before ultimately being the willing bird dog sent by the Dodgers to enlist Robinson. Still, the villains in the film, enlisted racists who targeted Robinson because he refused to move to the back of a desegregated military bus, suffered from "an element of exaggeration [that] is almost unavoidable, but certainly in this instance, unnecessary," in the words of *New York Times* critic John O'Connor. Despite this flaw, critics roundly agreed that *The Court Martial* had an effective message, one that "the film captures [in] the heart of the story: the emotional lynching of black men in America. Here is an unblinking indictment."[28]

The next screenplay to feature Robinson was a work that would have marked an unprecedented collection of talent for a Jackie biopic, including writer/director Spike Lee and Hollywood superstar Denzel Washington. After the two worked together on the 1992 picture *Malcom X*, Lee wrote a screenplay based on Robinson's autobiography *I Never Had it Made*. His intention was for Washington to play the title role, but the 42-year-old actor begged off from the project, stating he was too old for the part. Absent Washington, Lee was unable to find the necessary financing to make the picture, despite the enthusiastic support of Rachel. After years of trying, the project was eventually shelved.[29]

Lee's script was, in many ways, similar to the earlier incarnations, with quite a few of the iconic moments from his story replayed. Lee, however, seemed to recognize the obstacles to giving us a new perspective, using the clever device of framing the film with a late-night viewing of *The Jackie Robinson Story* in the Robinsons' home in Stamford in 1972.[30] With that largely sanitized and simplified version of the story as a preface, Lee tells his tale.

Lee's film, simply named *Jackie Robinson*, would have diverged from *Story* in the way it portrays a much more holistic view of Jackie's life. Previous fictionalizations idealized Robinson by highlighting the solitary nature of his struggle. Lee's film would have been the first to show that after Jackie opened the door, others walked through. Don Newcombe and Joe Black are both characters, and both have significant moments. Satchel Paige has a tragic scene, drunkenly opining that it should have been he, "the greatest pitcher who ever lived," who had broken the color line.[31] Most powerful is the representation of Roy Campanella, whose noncombative personality became a source of frustration for Jackie. Their famous rift, as well as their reconciliation, are dramatized.[32]

The film also would have been the first to explore Jackie's post-playing career, including his business ventures and his political activism. It is in this final point that *Jackie Robinson* would have humanized its subject in a way that had previously never been portrayed. Despite the deserved social canonization of Robinson, he was not perfect. His support of Richard Nixon in the 1960 presidential campaign, as well as his fall from grace with the more "militant" (Lee's word)[33] arm of the civil-rights movement, are both put under the microscope in the script. Also given prominent attention is his complicated relationship with his son Jackie Jr., whose stirring speech in front of Congress about drug use in the military is re-created near the conclusion of the film.[34] The scene is a fascinating callback to Jackie's HUAC testimony, the dramatization of which served as the final moment in the deeply anti-Communist *Story*. Alas, Lee's multilayered vision was never realized.

It would once again be the small screen that would serve as the venue for the next representation of

Jackie, in the HBO film *Soul of the Game*. Released in 1996, the movie was the first of its kind in that it made Robinson a supporting character. Set during a highly fictionalized version of the Kansas City Monarchs' 1945 season, the film's main character is really Satchel Paige, portrayed by Delroy Lindo. In *Soul of the Game*, Lindo's Paige is a multifaceted version of the Ageless One, vying for the attention of the scouts sent by the Dodgers in his last gasp attempt to make the major leagues.

Much of the action of *Soul* centers on the relationship between Paige, his longtime foil Josh Gibson (Mykelti Williamson) and a rookie Robinson, this time embodied by Blair Underwood, at the time a fast-rising star of television's *L.A. Law*. Virtually all of the interactions between the three men are fictionalized for the sake of creating the ultimate, predictable, dramatic tension when it is Robinson who is selected by Rickey (portrayed by Edward Herrmann). Lindo's arrogant but fragile Paige is shattered when the serious, argumentative Robinson is promoted over himself.

Unfortunately, Paige may be the only multidimensional character in the film. Gibson is reduced to a caricature, devouring all within his reach and battling imaginary demons sans clothing. Robinson is portrayed with such a rigid moral code that he is nearly unlikable. In an early scene, a serious Jackie refuses to clear the diamond so that Paige can re-create his famous routine of striking out the batter with no fielders behind him. Later, Robinson comes to blows with fellow Monarch Jesse Williams, after Williams called the college-educated, former Army officer a house "servant" (my adaptation of the actual term) to team owner J.L. Wilkinson. Rachel Robinson was not pleased with the liberties taken with Jackie's story.[35]

Historical inaccuracies such as Paige and Gibson starring in the 1945 East-West All-Star Game (neither even appeared; Paige refused to play because of a salary dispute and Gibson had been suspended from the league because of his erratic behavior), and the claim that Gibson hit 972 home runs can almost be forgiven. After all, director Kevin Rodney Sullivan was not tasked with making a documentary. Still, the fact that the relationship between these three iconic figures, the story at the supposed heart of the film, is a complete fabrication makes the entire effort ring hollow.

There are a few aspects of the movie that should be commended. Not many films have a cast that includes characterizations of Happy Chandler, Willie Mays, Cum Posey, Gus Greenlee, Ella Fitzgerald, Fiorello La Guardia, and "Bojangles" Robinson. True, this would have been a stronger point in the picture's favor had any of them been more fully realized, but it's still a fun bunch to see appearing on screen together. Much more culturally significant, however, is the fact that *Soul* marked the first time a Black auteur had helmed a Robinson film. It is perhaps the insight provided by Sullivan's own experiences that account for this largely fictional film's greatest factual contributions to the dramatization of Jackie's story.

Soul is the first movie to address two of the oft-ignored truths about integration, neither of which is particularly flattering to Rickey. The first is the raiding of the Monarchs roster without compensation by the Dodgers. In a few effective lines, both Rickey's contempt for the ownership of the Negro Leagues, as well as Wilkinson's (portrayed by R. Lee Ermy) indignation at the eventual ruination of his business, are conveyed. The other usually ignored kernel is the fact that ultimately Rickey's hand was forced by progressive New York Mayor LaGuardia, who was prepared to announce that the local major-league teams were going to be required to integrate. Not wanting LaGuardia to steal his thunder, Rickey quickly pulled the trigger on signing Robinson.

Undeterred by the disappointing critical response to *Soul*, others, including Robert Redford (who longed to portray Rickey), tried to mount a big-screen version of the Robinson story but all were blocked by the familiar refrain of funding issues. It took until 2013 for a big-budget (in this case, $40 million) major-motion-picture biopic of Jackie Robinson to hit movie theaters. *42: The True Story of An American Legend*, produced by Legendary Pictures and distributed by behemoth Warner Bros., marked the first time Tinsel Town finally pulled out all the stops to tell the Robinson tale.

Rachel was again brought on to consult, and Redford was swapped out for the equally estimable Harrison Ford, who turned in one of his finest performances as the complex Rickey. A mixture of laconic charm, occasional bluster, and a fair amount of eyebrows, Ford does a brilliant job of embodying the Mahatma. Jackie was portrayed by relative newcomer Chadwick Boseman, who went on to superstardom as T'Challa, the Black Panther, in the eponymous blockbuster Marvel Studios hit. In addition to his superhero persona, Jackie would mark the first of three true-life American groundbreakers that Boseman played in a five-year span, including James Brown in *Get on Up* (2014) and Thurgood Marshall in *Marshall* (2017).

After so many failed attempts to get a film made, Rachel initially looked at *42* with apprehension. She arranged a meeting with the film's star at which she asked him, in Boseman's words, "Who are you, and why do you get to play my husband?" His answer satisfied her, and the two quickly became close. She remained a presence on set throughout filming, as was former Dodgers pitcher Ralph Branca. Both lent their experiences with Robinson to the studious actor, who worked hard to please Jackie's most ardent admirer.[36] Boseman's performance was almost universally appreciated by critics, if seen as occasionally lacking Jackie's fire.[37] When Boseman tragically died of colon cancer in 2020, at the age of 43, it was his performances in *Black Panther* and *42* that were most often cited in his memorials.

Written and directed by Brian Helgeland, *42* is beautifully presented, with lush sepia tone camera filters aiding in the nostalgic presentation of the story. Like Lee's script, Helgeland leans heavily on *I Never Had it Made*. However, rather than taking a complete look at Robinson's career, *42* mirrors the *The Jackie Robinson Story*. The focus is on the narrow window between his recruitment by the Dodgers and the completion of his rookie year. As such, the script feels like a collection of familiar tales about Robinson that do little to further our appreciation of the man as a whole. Still, the film would gross nearly $97 million, and had the distinction of the highest opening-weekend box office for a baseball picture in history.[38]

42 was released to coincide with Jackie Robinson day, April 15, when the major leagues celebrate his historic achievement, including all players donning his now universally retired number 42, for one game only. Warner Bros. was sure to cross-promote their picture with the assistance of the Los Angeles Dodgers, who brought the production company on as a sponsor for their Robinson festivities. Harrison Ford was on hand, as was Kelley Jakle, great-granddaughter of Branch Rickey, who had a small role in the film.[39] Also in attendance was Rachel Robinson, who had been a part of more Jackie fictionalizations than anyone else. She was complimentary of the film, satisfied that it gave a realistic portrayal of the culture that she and Jackie had to face. She privately told director Helgeland that her favorite parts were when her character, played by Nicole Beharie, and Robinson kissed.[40]

It is with that simple, sweet critique that one understands that the many fictionalizations of Robinson have served an important role in ways both public and, for Rachel, very personal. They have kept the myth of Jackie at the forefront of the American consciousness, even as they have largely sanitized some of the more complex racial and social issues that are integral to his tale. Perhaps it is a story that is simply too big to be told by the constraints of fiction. This premise led to Jackie's return to television in 2016 with the four-hour documentary by acclaimed filmmaker Ken Burns, arguably the most exhaustive look at his life ever captured on film.

But it is the fictional representations that have afforded Rachel, who served as an adviser and inspiration for so many of them, a rare opportunity. Perhaps that is why, among the numerous other accomplishments of her life, she has shepherded Jackie's tale with such devotion. Each new portrayal is not only an opportunity to spread his story to a wider audience, it also offers her the chance to have her husband's spirit revived in the flesh and blood, alive again on stages and screens, ready to make history and to give her one more kiss.

This treatise barely skims the surface of the pop culture phenomenon of Jackie Robinson on stage and screen. It quickly became apparent in the writing that it was too much for a single chapter to contain.

SABR plans a full volume on the subject, with the working title Not an Easy Tale to Tell: Jackie Robinson on Page, Stage, and Screen. *This book will add written fiction to the mix, including children's books, a pair of espionage thrillers, and a comic book series. We take a much deeper look at the artistic desire to explore Jackie's tale, and what he has come to mean as a symbol in American culture.* Not an Easy Tale to Tell *is due to be published in Spring 2022, just in time to celebrate the 75th anniversary of Jackie's integration of the Dodgers.*

NOTES

1. "Jackie Wins Law Suit For Sum of $14,500." *Alabama Tribune* (Montgomery), January 15, 1954: 7.
2. Ron Briley, *The Baseball Film in Postwar America: A Critical Study, 1948-1962* (Jefferson, North Carolina: McFarland, 2011), 62.
3. Arnold Rampersad, *Jackie Robinson: A Biography*. (New York: Ballantine Books, 1997), 224.
4. Hal Erickson, *The Baseball Filmography, 1915-2001* (Jefferson, North Carolina: McFarland, 2002), 244.
5. "Robinson Film to Hit Screen," *Spokesman-Review* (Spokane, Washington), May 14, 1950: 63.
6. Erickson. *The Baseball Filmography*, 244.
7. Rachel Robinson, *Jackie Robinson: An Intimate Portrait* (New York: Abrams), 113.
8. Rampersad, *Jackie Robinson: A Biography*, 225.

9. Jane Corby, "Screenings," *Brooklyn Daily Eagle*, May 14, 1950: 29.

10. Jimmie Fidler, "News & Views of Hollywood," *Valley Times* (Hollywood, California), May 30, 1950: 5.

11. "'Jackie Robinson Story' Set in Six S.L. Theaters," *Desert News* (Salt Lake City, Utah), August 23, 1950: 22.

12. Rampersad, *Jackie Robinson: A Biography*, 226.

13. Carol Lawson, "Charnin's Idea for Broadway's 'The First' Came in Seconds," *Star Tribune* (Minneapolis), February 8, 1981: 120.

14. Christine Arnold, "Bufman's Biggest Production: The Whole World is his Stage," *Miami Herald*, June 14, 1981: 209.

15. Liz Smith, "Moving, Shaking and Tucking In," *New York Daily News*, March 15, 1981: 107.

16. "Jackie Robinson Story to B'way?" *New York Daily News,* September 10, 1980: 414.

17. Harry Huan, "Broadway Melody," *New York Daily News*, August 14, 1981: 454.

18. "Show to Rekindle Spirit of Jackie Robinson," *Millville* (New Jersey) *Daily,* August 29, 1981: 8.

19. Liz Smith, "Springfield Making New Album," *Fort Worth-Star Telegram*, October 17, 1981: 23.

20. Jay Sharbutt (Associated Press), "Jackie Robinson Show on Broadway: 'No Hit,'" *Santa Cruz* (California) *Sentinel*, November 18, 1981: 25.

21. "Detroiter Scores Broadway Points," *Detroit Free Press*, November 19, 1981: 41.

22. Dick Young, "Opening Night Audience Likes 'The First,'" *Gettysburg Times*, November 20, 1981: 13.

23. Internet Broadway Database page for *The First*. https://www.ibdb.com/broadway-production/the-first-4145#People. Accessed July 19, 2020.

24. D.J.R. Bruckner, "'Play to Win,' a Musical About the Integration of Baseball," *New York Times,* July 21, 1989: C3.

25. Bruckner, "Play to Win": C3.

26. Alvin Klein, "The Stuff of Legends," *New York Times*, December 11, 1994: 13.

27. T. Anthony Bell, "Soldier-Champ: Joe Louis Sacrificed Much for His Country." US Army website, February 28, 2014. https://www.army.mil/article/121005/soldier_champ_joe_louis_sacrificed_much_for_his_country.

28. John O'Connor, "2 Cable Movies of Substance," *New York Times*, October 15, 1990: C17.

29. Marshall Fine and Georgette Gouveia, "Rediscovering Jackie," *Journal News* (White Plains, New York), March 2, 1997: 2C.

30. Spike Lee, *Jackie Robinson* (Unpublished film script, 5th Draft, 1996), 2.

31. Lee, *Jackie Robinson,* 39.

32. Lee, *Jackie Robinson*, 129.

33. Lee, *Jackie Robinson*, 136.

34. Lee, *Jackie Robinson*, 143.

35. Lee, *Jackie Robinson*, 143.

36. Steven Zeitchik, "Rachel Robinson, Jackie's Widow, Says '42' Hits Home," *Times* (Streator, Illinois), April 10, 2013: 19.

37. Richard Roeper, "Admirable, Overdue '42' Doesn't Quite Knock It Out of the Park," *Herald-Palladium* (St. Joseph, Michigan), April 12, 2013: B4.

38. Grady Smith, "Box Office Report: '42' Knocks It Out of the Park with $27.3 Million," *Entertainment Weekly,* April 14, 2013.

39. Daniel Miller, "Jackie Robinson Film '42' Promotes Ties with Dodgers." *Los Angeles Times*, April 9, 2013: 17.

40. Zeitchik, "Rachel Robinson, Jackie's Widow."

REACHING THE NEXT GENERATION: JACKIE ROBINSON'S STORY IN CHILDREN'S AND YOUNG ADULT LITERATURE

by Mary E. Corey

"A life is not important except in the impact it has on other lives"
— Jack Robinson

As people and events recede into the mists of the past, people and events that have resonated in our own times become as remote to the next generation as ancient history is to ours, and our task is to find ways to keep alive those parts of the past that we value. But keeping the past alive is a tricky proposition as the historic record becomes a crowded avenue with all sorts of important people and events pushing and shoving to keep their place in our collective memories.

Children's and young adult literature and films have a unique place in the process of deciding who, what, how, and whether we remember the past. Through picture books, graphic media that looks a lot like what we of a certain age used to call comic books (remember Classic Comics, boys and girls?), and chapter books, parents, librarians, and teachers make choices about what their kids read and watch long before they can choose for themselves.

Courtesy Penguin Random House.

What do we want children's and young adult literature to bring into our kids' universes? Well, we want them to learn something. We want them to feel something. We want them to travel with people they will never meet to worlds they may never visit. We want them to enjoy these adventures. We want them to find worthy heroines and heroes. We want them to see things through the eyes of other people. And we want to show them what we value through the choices we offer them early in their lives. This is especially important in the case of the earliest books for children, picture books, and the pictures in books used as illustrations. Far from being strictly the domain of the youngest emerging readers, picture books and illustrations can be wonderful portals into that most permanent memory-maker, visual imagery. Kadir Nelson's *We Are the Ship, The Story of Negro League Baseball*,[1] is an apt example of a picture book for all ages. But because they are such potent transmitters of long-lasting imagery, they can also be a minefield for the same reason. The imagery of Disney characters is an apt example of this.

In the case of films for children, we've seen how many of Disney's visual portrayals of native people and other cultures have come under intense scrutiny. "[W]ho can deny the fact that Disney provides many young children in the United States with their first glimpse of the larger world, some of their first ideas about people and cultures in the Middle East (*Aladdin*), Africa (*The Lion King, Tarzan*), India (*The Jungle Book*), China (*Mulan*), as well as Native American (*Pocahontas, Peter Pan*) and African American culture (*Dumbo, The Lion King*)?"[2] I'd add to this list *Song of the South*.

A recent critic offered a summary of some of these problems. For example,

In Disney's 1941 film, *Dumbo*, the leader of a pack of crows is named Jim Crow. The poor and seemingly uneducated crows use slang and black vernacular while calling each other 'brotha.' That portrayal drew scrutiny for stereotypical depiction of African-Americans. 'I'd be done see'n about everything, when I see an elephant fly,' the jive-talking crows sing. *Song of the South*, a 1946 Disney musical about post-Civil War Georgia, came under intense criticism from black civil-rights leaders for its depiction of African-Americans. They said the Uncle Remus collection of black folklore stories was based on racial caricatures.[3]

As a result, the film has not been released since.

Indeed, these kinds of concerns have a long history that reflect our country's uncomfortable racial past. Imagery, common to 19th century and early 20th century popular magazines such as *Leslie's Weekly* cover art, "Baseball at Possumville," and *Harper's Weekly*, "Baseball at Blackville," and lithographs by Currier and Ives prints found on postcards and calendars, "A Foul Tip" and "A Baseball Hit," demeaned and ridiculed African American players by portraying them as inept buffoons, in large part justifying in the public's mind their exclusion from the White leagues.

For an in-depth exploration of the Jim Crow past that produced the Negro Leagues, a stroll through Ferris State University's Museum of Jim Crow is a painful but necessary confrontation with White supremacy, the same White supremacy that made Jackie Robinson's courage remarkable.[4]

What we don't want to do is bore them to tears. Parson Weems, the early pedant who famously used public admiration of George Washington as a vehicle to teach moral rectitude to children, may have been okay in his day, but I doubt it. Even the most avid young student of history can't help but think the "cherry tree" story is more than a little fishy. No, we don't want to feed them a diet of plaster saints to admire and ignore.

In the case of telling Jackie Robinson's story, there is the complexity of how best to explain the adversity he faced. By singling out Robinson's story as a life worth remembering, we can't help but run directly into the wall that Jim Crow built. Smart kids are going to want to know why he couldn't play in the major leagues. By extension, they may follow up with questions about why the major leagues were closed to African American players in the first place. After all, how could Jackie be chosen if there weren't equally capable choices from which to choose. And where did those other baseball players play? Were there other ballclubs just for them? Suddenly a universe of interest has opened up. So, glossing over the racism and Jim Crow laws of his times closes down all these promising avenues of interest for students. Fully calling out the racism of the time, however, runs the risk of opening up a painful past and raising uncomfortable conversations about the present. But as we now see, not confronting this painful past is not an option. How and how much and at what age we do the confronting are the questions that children's and young adult literature have been asking and answering. How well has that been done and what new directions are being taken?

One other area worth noting, especially if these books are used in classrooms (and they should be) is assessing the actual prior knowledge and world views of teachers and students. Teaching about Jackie Robinson as a stand-alone figure can result in missing the valuable context from which to understand his role in both baseball and civil rights. As I was reading the sampling of children's and young adult literature about him, I was struck that mention of the Negro Leagues, with some notable exceptions discussed below, was given minimal attention. Really, how do you explain why his story is worthy, if you don't explain why his entry into major-league baseball was extraordinary? Add to that, the muddled status of co-hero given to Branch Rickey also becomes problematic. If you asked Effa Manley, co-owner and business manager of the Newark Eagles, if Rickey was a hero, you would get a resounding "No!" The push for White baseball to open its doors to Black players was advocated by everyone in the Black community, including Effa Manley. But the often underhanded way that Rickey and other owners robbed the Negro League teams of players without honoring contracts or paying for their services can be seen as leading directly to the demise of the Negro Leagues. This was not an expected or happy outcome. So while integrating White baseball was the goal, losing everything to do it was not.

While the story is one of an exceptional man, it can and should be a portal to understanding the world he came from so students can appreciate that although Jackie was exceptional because of his place in a historic moment, he was one of hundreds of exceptional players – any one of whom could have taken his place. When asked about Negro League players worthy of induction into the National Baseball Hall of Fame,

Effa Manley said, "I could name a hundred, but I'd settle for thirty!"[5] We also need to show the injustice of the system. Even the youngest students understand the concept of fairness and will respond to the idea that opportunity is a door that should have been open to those who didn't qualify as exceptional, but were as talented as, and sometimes more talented than, any of the White players on major-league teams. That was the source of Troy's frustration in August Wilson's play *Fences*. A former Negro League player, Troy was outraged at Jackie Robinson's entry into major-league baseball. "Times have changed," his wife tells him. "You just come along too early." His response: "There ought not never had been no time called too early!" He recalls someone who played right field for the Yankees. "Man batting .269. What kind of sense that make? I was hitting .432 with 37 home runs!" When his wife says, "Folks had to wait for Jackie Robinson," he explodes. "I done seen a hundred niggers play baseball better than Jackie Robinson. Hell, I know some teams Jackie Robinson couldn't make! ... Don't care what color you were. Come telling me I come along too early. If you could play ... then they ought to have let you play."[6] Any and all of the books for children and young adults open opportunities for parents or teachers to introduce the concept of injustice, an opportunity that should be taken.

To begin evaluating how Jackie Robinson is represented in children's and young adult literature, I selected a representative sampling of the many, many books available about him. For this, I turned to widely respected publishers and authors. They ranged from the most basic, *My Little Golden Book About Jackie Robinson*,[7] published in 2018, to Step into Reading's *Jackie Robinson and the Story of All-Black Baseball*,[8] and Penguin's Young Readers, Level 3, *Jackie Robinson, He Led the Way*.[9] Chapter books included Scholastic Press's books by Sharon Robinson, *The Hero Two Doors Down*[10] and *Child of the Dream*.[11] Two that take a very different path are Lee and Low's *Baseball Saved Us*[12] by Ken Mochizuki, illustrated by Dom Lee, and Bette Bao Lord's classic, from HarperCollins Press, *In the Year of the Boar and Jackie Robinson*.[13] I also reviewed the picture books *Dad, Jackie, and Me*,[14] by Myron Uhlberg, illustrated by Colin Bootman, and Sharon Robinson's *Promises to Keep*.[15]

The criteria I used to evaluate all of the materials included the quality of the writing, age appropriateness, contextual background for Jackie's story, factual integrity, and more ephemeral qualities: Was it interesting? Was the story told in such a way that it was likely to engage young readers? For this last quality, besides my own judgment, I turned to reviews on a variety of booksellers' websites for other readers', teachers', and students' comments and recommendations.

As schools strive for a more inclusive curriculum, teaching Jackie Robinson's story offers multiple opportunities to weave Black history into the American story. It, of course, lends itself to inclusion in Black History Month lessons. And it's also a story that can coordinate with the major leagues' Jackie Robinson Day every April 15, the anniversary of his first game with the Brooklyn Dodgers on April 15, 1947. But the baseball season is a long one stretching from opening days in April to the frosty evenings of late October, so for teachers his story can be integrated at nearly any point in the year's curriculum, especially when they put his story in the context of American history itself. Baseball's season is a long one, and its history is equally long. The back story of Jackie Robinson's story is the great swath of American history from Reconstruction to the civil-rights movement of the early 1960s and beyond.

For teachers, a good place to refresh their own background on this lengthy timeframe is the teacher edition of *Before Jackie: The Negro Leagues, Civil Rights, and the American Dream*.[16] In it, teachers will find clear connections between the people and events of the Reconstruction Era and first half of the twentieth century that impacted directly on the history of baseball and the America that produced both the Negro Leagues and Jackie Robinson. Another plus is that it also provides teaching suggestions that cover this era. Equally helpful would be the student edition of this same title. For older students looking for background material, two are recommended: *Black Diamond: The Story of the Negro Baseball Leagues,* by Patricia C. McKissack and Fredrick McKissack Jr., and *Jackie Robinson and the Story of All-Black Baseball,* by Jim O'Connor with illustrations by Jim Butcher.[17] *Black Diamond* is a chapter book recommended for students in grades 3-7. *Jackie Robinson* is on Step 5 of Random House's Step into Reading series. All but the most advanced readers in grade 3 will find *Black Diamond* daunting, so a more reasonable recommendation would be for students in grades 5-7. Both books are very nicely illustrated and make good use of vintage photographs. Of all the documentaries available for background information on the Negro Leagues, one of the best is *Life in the Negro Leagues, There Was Always Sun Shining Someplace, 1981*, 59 minutes; available in its entirety with captions on YouTube, youtube.com/watch?v=C21elBvoyQo.[18]

An overview of the reviews of parents, educators, evaluators like *School Library Journal* and the Center for Children's Books showed that they cared about the quality of the books they selected for their children and students. Comments referenced readability, accuracy of information, historical context, the quality of the illustrations, and the interest levels of their children and students. One of the burdens carried by all of the books was the real possibility that the selection may be the only book about Jackie Robinson that a child or student may read. As might be expected, professional reviewers were more exacting about their recommendations, whereas parents and teachers remarked more often about how their own child or class responded to a particular selection. I was glad to see that each of the selections offered some of the necessary historical context for appreciating Jackie Robinson's story and how often parents' reviews commented on the quality of the historical context given. To be sure, *My Little Golden Book About Jackie Robinson* doesn't offer the same detail that books for older children contained, but it doesn't shy away from the racial segregation that shaped Jackie's life. Indeed, it is illustrated with a two-page picture of passengers on a segregated bus. Jackie stands with his back to the reader at the front of the aisle. Looking down the row of seats the reader sees the averted and suspicious eyes of the White passengers and the large signs denoting "Only Colored Passengers." In this way, even the youngest readers will have the opportunity to begin processing this part of our past.

Apt comparisons between professional reviews, educators' reviews, and a parent's review[19] is illustrated in the reviews of the books *Step into Reading, Jackie Robinson* and *Stealing Home: The Story of Jackie Robinson.* The *School Library Journal* reviewer, Tom Hurlburt of Rio Rancho Public Library, for *Step Into Reading, Jackie Robinson,* was put off, writing that "a more indicative title for this book might be The Story of All-Black Baseball and Jackie Robinson ..." and criticizing the writing style as choppy and unimaginative, the illustrations as unremarkable.

The *Bulletin*, from the Center for Children's Books, an "educational research center whose mission is to facilitate the creation and dissemination of exemplary and progressive research and scholarship related to youth-focused resources, literature, and librarianship,"[20] was pleased that the book had "the story of the rise and fall of black baseball and some of its star players and managers." Mr. Hurlburt is, however, a tough guy to impress. In his review of *Stealing Home: The Story of Jackie Robinson,* he starts: "Still another biography of the black baseball pioneer." Ho hum, I guess! He then complains that the "standard black-and-white photographs, many of which are found in the plethora of juvenile Robinson biographies that abound, are included. ..."

A parent's review of *Stealing Home*, however, spoke to the illusive quality of interest. She was excited that her third-grade "reluctant" reader really enjoyed it. And she further commented that she was "pleased with its coverage of the history of segregated America – adding to its inspirational qualities." As to the comment regarding the repetition of photographs in juvenile biographies, the fact that there are many books with the "standard black-and-white photographs" actually enhances the chances that readers will see these photographs no matter which of the books they choose. Happily, one of the positive aspects of nearly all of the books, including *My Little Golden Book About Jackie Robinson*, was their inclusion of Jackie's "after baseball" story and his work as an advocate for civil rights.

Many of the reviews emphasized that both parents and teachers were looking to evaluate the educational impact of their selections. One five-star reviewer sent me back to reread *The Magic Treehouse, Play Ball Jackie Robinson*. For this parent, the book's best feature was its readability for her son with dyslexia. At second glance, it's clear why she was so enthusiastic. The print is large and clear and the sentences are relatively short, neither of which detracts from the engaging writing style. There is nothing on the flyleaf or inside that says the book was written with students with dyslexia in mind, but it seems that, intentional or not, it's hitting that mark.

Two books told the story of Jackie Robinson through the eyes of youngsters dealing with handicaps. Myron Uhlberg's *Dad, Jackie, and Me*, tells the author's story. Uhlberg's dad was deaf and felt a personal connection to Jackie Robinson because of his own experience with prejudice. The main event was going to Ebbets Field to watch Jackie play. Through conversations between father and son we learn that when the father was in a residential school for deaf students, "it was considered a waste of time to teach deaf kids to play sports." One of the criticisms of the book from a parent was that the real "meat" of the story is in the afterword. As this reviewer writes, "In the story itself, we're told that 'The Giants hated Jackie Robinson,' but no detail is given." The afterword explains that the author's father told him to watch for all the unfair treatment Robinson would get but it's left out of the story's narrative proper. Much of what would explain why Robinson was the butt of this kind of prejudice is simply not part of the main story. That's a shame, since the afterword is one of the best features of the book. Because it is a designated picture book, I gave special attention to the illustrations. I think most people would find them vivid and engaging. The inside covers front and back are filled with replicas of newspaper clippings and the team picture of the 1947 Dodgers. The inside pages use to good advantage the space of its 9½-by-11 format to re-create in deep reds, blues, and greens the Brooklyn neighborhood of 1947 and Ebbets Field on game day.

In Bette Bao Lord's classic chapter book *In the Year of the Boar and Jackie Robinson*, 8-year-old Shirley Temple Wong is a recent Chinese immigrant to Brooklyn and knows little to no English. She takes the name Shirley Temple as her American name and adopts the Brooklyn Dodgers as her home team and Jackie Robinson as her special hero. By listening to the games on the radio, she learns English and eventually becomes at home with her neighbors, her new friends at school, and being what she considered herself to be, "a real American." Fully the first half of the book follows Shirley's experiences as an immigrant learning the ways of her new Brooklyn neighborhood. It isn't until she is invited to play stickball and, through a series of fortuitous events, actually scores a run by stealing home, that the story segues into her devotion to baseball and Jackie Robinson. The other kids start calling her Jackie Robinson, which occasions her teacher to teach her whole class Jackie Robinson's story and why his story was uniquely American. Of all the books, this one, perhaps more than the others, conveys the spirit of baseball as more than just a game. For Shirley it was a way to *be* American. For young readers, they get to view the immigrant experience through the eyes of someone their own age. Along the way they will have the extra added attraction of learning about Shirley's Chinese culture as well.

Baseball Saved Us, by Ken Mochizuki, illustrated by Dom Lee, offers another avenue into baseball's role in our often painful past as it tells the story of a Japanese American boy in an internment camp during World War II. Although this picture book doesn't address Jackie Robinson, it does address another chapter in our history of discrimination. *Publishers Weekly* praised its "stylish prose and stirring illustrations." And a chorus of teachers have praised it. One teacher said she "used it with [her] 6th graders. They were able to relate the text to the current societal issues facing us today." Another related that she "was eager to read this book because in my early years of teaching I worked with a wonderful man who, as a child, was in one of these internment camps with his family. This story sounded so much like the ones he told of his time in the camps that I felt he could have written it. The illustrations are very well done and will show young children that it was definitely not summer camp."[21] Thus, we find baseball, again, a dynamic catalyst for teaching students about the past in ways they can relate to and understand.

Sharon Robinson's works are in a class by themselves. By bringing her own personal perspective to Jackie Robinson's story, she enriches our understanding of not only Jackie's public journey, but that of his family life. *Promises to Keep, How Jackie Robinson Changed America, The Hero Two Doors Down, Jackie's Nine, Values to Live By, Jackie Robinson: American Hero,* and her latest, *Child of the Dream* work together to show her father as more than the icon celebrated on April 15. In each she adds depth and dimension to his story, his sorrows, trials, values he lived by, and accomplishments in the face of ridicule and worse from people who were still dedicated to a segregated society. In addition to being his daughter, Sharon Robinson brings professional expertise to her writings about her father.

According to her website, "Sharon Robinson is an author and educational consultant for Major League Baseball. As founder and consultant, Sharon, MLB, and Scholastic co-manage Breaking Barriers: In Sports, In Life, a baseball-themed national character-education curriculum designed to empower students to face obstacles in their lives. The program includes a national essay contest for students in grades 4-9 and throughout MLB's RBI program. Each year thousands of students write an essay about how they used the values demonstrated by Jackie Robinson to overcome their challenges. Essay winners are celebrated in their schools and in major-league ballparks. Since 1997 the program has reached over 34 million students and 4.6 million educators in the continental United States, Canada, and Puerto Rico."[22]

Promises to Keep is unique as a picture book, as it situates her father in a wide historic timeframe. It begins by tracing the black and white world of Jim Crow and the important Black leaders who moved mountains toward civil rights that made his achievement possible, men and women like Ida B. Wells, W.E.B. DuBois, Zora Neale Hurston, and Langston Hughes. Because of these pioneers, when Jackie Robinson was born in 1919 the world was already beginning with glacier-like speed to change. Robinson makes good use of both vintage newspaper and magazine photographs and news clippings as well as personal ephemera like family photographs, love letters between her mom and dad, and family photographs from his baseball career and civil rights events. Two of its best features are the chapters "A Civil Rights Champion" and "Jackie Robinson's Legacy." In these two chapters the reader travels with Jackie as a civil-rights leader and into the future. His work with all of the leaders of the modern civil-rights movement rounds out the fullness of his legacy, leaving that legacy to be carried on after his death in 1972. This picture book stands out because of the richness of its narrative and the scope of the history it covers as it positions Jackie Robinson in the events of the twentieth century. In captivating words and pictures, Robinson chronicles the life of her legendary father. Tracy Bell of the Durham Public Schools, writing for *School Library Journal,* agrees: "She weaves historical events into the story of one of baseball's greatest players, revealing how they shaped his life. Her text, combined with numerous black-and-white archival and family photographs, reproductions of newspaper headlines, magazine pages, and letters, illustrates Jackie Robinson's journey from childhood to the moment that he integrated major-league baseball to his life as a businessman and civil-rights spokesperson. In addition to personal details, this intimate biographical sketch and authentic glimpse into the life of a great African American provides information on the post-Civil War world, race relations, and the struggle for civil rights."

The Hero Two Doors Down is based on a true story. In 1948, 8-year-old Steven Satlow learns that his new neighbor in his all-Jewish Brooklyn neighborhood is none other than Jackie Robinson, his hero. Booklist calls it "a charming tale" that offers "good fodder for discussion about prejudice, discrimination, friendship, and family." *School Library Journal* calls it "a home run." One parent wasn't as enthusiastic. Her complaint? Too much history! "The story of what happens with the people gets weighed down with a lot of drag about historic detail that doesn't help move the plot along. So I thought I'd read it and tell my son the story. I couldn't get through it. The author uses too many historical facts in the places where she is supposed to be building suspense. And it just takes too long to get to the satisfying parts of the story." The rest of the reviews, however, echoed the praise from this fourth-grade teacher: "This is a well-written story that's perfect for 2020. I am a fourth-grade teacher, and I was looking for a new read-aloud. This book just made the top of the list. I read it in one sitting. I loved the themes of friendship, respect, and acceptance. Such a perfect, feel-good book for our society. I can't wait to read it to my students."

Sharon Robinson's latest, *Child of the Dream,* focuses on the events of 1963, the year she turned 13 and the year she became fully aware of the civil-rights work of her parents. The personal triumphs of her own coming of age set against the worldly events, in particular the March on Washington, makes this a compelling book sure to interest middle-school students. *Kirkus Reviews* deems it "a lovingly honest memoir of a racial – and social activist – past that really hasn't passed." Robinson's civil-rights activism has often been overshadowed by his baseball career. *Child of the Dream* will go a long way toward balancing how we view the entirety of his life's work.

So, what's the verdict? How is Jackie Robinson's memory being kept alive in children's and young adult literature? From the sampling of children's and young adult literature available today, the legacy of Jackie Robinson is in good hands. His story has been embraced by parents and educators looking for stories that vibrate with life. The fact of the discrimination he faced has led to conversations about discrimination in a variety of settings other than baseball: the discrimination felt by people with hearing loss, the discrimination of the Japanese internment camps, the discrimination felt by recent immigrants. All find something in Jackie's story that intersects with their own, making Jackie's story universal. His "after-baseball" story of civil-rights activism opens pathways for today's students to see their own way forward as the next generation of Americans to strive for the American dream. If there is criticism, it would be that with the notable exceptions discussed above, the books don't do as much with the "before" story. Much more attention to the national stain of Jim Crow would only make it clearer why Jackie's story is exceptional. But because all of the books have to grapple to some extent with the "why" of racial discrimination to explain Jackie's achievements, it forces students, parents, and teachers to grapple with the same issues.

As popular interest in the Negro Leagues and African American history and life continues to grow as evidenced by movies like *42* and *The Green Book*, the yearly April commemoration of Jackie Robinson's entry in major-league baseball, and the growing literature about him all will do their part to keep his legacy alive and resonating with future generations yet to come.

NOTES

1. Kadir Nelson, *We Are the Ship, The Story of Negro League Baseball*, (New York: Little, Brown Books for Young Readers, 2008).

2. John Murnane, "Reversing the 'Disneyfication' Process," *World History Connected*, Vol. 5, No. 1, University of Illinois Press, worldhistoryconnected.press.uillinois.edu/8.1/murnane.html.

3. Russell Contreras (Associated Press), "A look at Minorities in Previous Disney Productions," AP News, November 29, 2017. apnews.com/article/38a447209d5e4b06ba17d8c642a0b207.

4. ferris.edu/jimcrow/.

5. James Overmyer, *Queen of the Negro Leagues: Effa Manley and the Newark Eagles* (Lanham, Maryland: Scarecrow Press, 1998). Bob Luke, *The Most Famous Woman in Baseball, Effa Manley and the Negro Leagues* (Washington: Potomac Books, Inc., 2011).

6. August Wilson, *Fences* (New York: Plume,1986). I'm not suggesting using *Fences* with young students, just that it's the clearest example I am aware of of a character expressing their outrage at the injustice of the system.

7. Frank Berrios and Betsy Bauer, illus., *My Little Golden Book About Jackie Robinson* (New York: Golden Books, 2018).

8. Jim O'Connor and Jim Butcher, illus., *Jackie Robinson and the Story of All-Black Baseball* (New York: Random House Step Into Reading, 1989).

9. April Jones Prince and Robert Casilla, *Jackie Robinson, He Led the Way* (New York: Penguin Young Readers, 2008).

10. Sharon Robinson, *The Hero Two Doors Down* (New York: Scholastic Press, 2016).

11. Sharon Robinson, *Child of the Dream* (New York: Scholastic Press, 2020).

12. Ken Mochizuki and Dom Lee, illus., *Baseball Saved Us* (New York: Lee & Low Books, 2009).

13. Bette Bao Lord, *In the Year of the Boar and Jackie Robinson* (New York: HarperCollins, 1984).

14. Myron Uhlberg and Colin Bootman, illus., *Dad, Jackie, and Me* (Atlanta: Peachtree Publishers, 2005).

15. Sharon Robinson, *Promises to Keep* (New York: Scholastic Press, 2004).

16. Mary Corey and Mark Harnischfeger, *Before Jackie, The Negro Leagues, Civil Rights, and the American Dream*, Teacher Edition (Ithaca, New York: Paramount Market Publishing, 2014).

17. Patricia C. McKissack and Fredrick McKissack Jr., *Black Diamond: The Story of the Negro Baseball Leagues*, (New York: Scholastic Press, 1998). See also Jim O'Connor and Jim Butcher.

18. *There Was Always Sun Shining Someplace, Life in the Negro Baseball Leagues*, Craig Davidson, director, narrated by James Earl Jones, 1984.

19. All referenced reviews can be found on the Amazon website for each of the books mentioned. Professional reviews cite the journal that published the review but many are from readers identified only by a first name. The two most common professional reviews are available in print and on the websites of *School Library Journal*, slj.com/, and *The Bulletin of the Center for Children's Books*, bccb.ischool.illinois.edu. Kirkus Reviews are also published on Amazon and can also be found in print and on their website at kirkusreviews.com/. Professional reviews from these reviewers can also be found on the website of Barnes & Noble, with no substantive deviation from those published on Amazon. For the sake of convenience, I stayed with Amazon for reviews.

20. *The Bulletin of the Center for Children's Books*.

21. Review of *Baseball Saved Us,* smile.amazon.com/Baseball-Saved-Us-Ken-Mochizuki/dp/1880000199/ref=cm_cr_arp_d_product_top?ie=UTF8.

22. sharonrobinsonink.com/about-sharon-robinson.

THE JACKIE ROBINSON FOUNDATION:

A Legacy of Excellence and Impact

by Mark Harnischfeger

After two years at UCLA, I decided to leave. I was convinced that no amount of education would help a black man get a job.
— Jackie Robinson[1]

Three decades after he left college, the Jackie Robinson Foundation was established to encourage, promote, and fund higher education for African American students. The cultural, economic, and political landscapes of America were changing, and Jackie Robinson had played a pivotal role.

The year was 1940 and in America, 44 years after the United States Supreme Court launched an era of legalized segregation in its *Plessey v. Ferguson* decision, Jack Robinson knew that it was going to take more than education to advance the cause of African Americans. Throughout the country, in the North, South, East, and West, African Americans could not stay at the same hotels as Whites, eat in the same restaurants, or even drink from the same water fountains. It was a time when Robinson's older brother, Mack, second only to Jesse Owens in the 200-meter event in the 1936 Berlin Olympics, returned home only to wear his Olympic jacket to his street-sweeping job. And where Jack, a five-sport athlete at UCLA, was described by the *Los Angeles Times* as carrying a football "like it was a watermelon and the guy who owned it was after him with a shotgun."[2] It was a time when schools and neighborhoods were segregated, in some places by law, in others by unwritten codes and traditions.

April 15, 1947, was a day unlike any other. For the first time in the twentieth century, a Black man played on a White major-league baseball team. And although much of America's focus that day was on the now-broken color line of professional baseball, the true impact of that event crossed much greater lines. The late author and former *New York Post* and *New York Daily News* editor, Pete Hamill, experienced that impact and described it years later: "The great accomplishment of Robinson in 1947 was not so much that he integrated baseball, but that he integrated those stands. Which is to say he started to integrate his country, our country. And so when Robinson jittered off second base, upsetting the enemy pitcher, the number 42 sending signals of possible amazement, we *all* roared. Whites and blacks roaring for Robinson."[3]

"The right of every American to first-class citizenship is the most important issue of our time. ... If I had to choose between baseball's Hall of Fame and first-class citizenship for all of my people, I would choose first-class citizenship time and again."
-- Jack Robinson[4]

Jackie Robinson and young fan, Stephen Rozansky in 1951 at the Hall of Fame Game in Cooperstown. Inspiring youth remains a goal of today's Jackie Robinson Foundation.

Jackie

His baseball career behind him, his passion for equal rights for all still burning brightly, Robinson embarked on a journey of political and social activism. With his wife, Rachel, at his side, herself a social activist with a fire and commitment to rival that of her husband, the couple reflected Jack's assertion that "life is not a spectator sport." Throughout the 1960s, he conferred with Dr. Martin Luther King Jr. and other civil-rights leaders and was an established presence in the movement, as the host or special guest at numerous gatherings and fundraising events.

In January 1963 Jack co-founded the Freedom National Bank in New York City to address discrimination in mortgage applications by Black people and to encourage Black entrepreneurship. It went on to become the largest Black-owned and -operated bank in New York state.[5] In June of that year, he and Rachel hosted a jazz concert at their home in Connecticut to raise bail money for jailed civil-rights activists, an event that raised funds for social and education programs until 2001. Jack's passing in October 1972 cut short his commitment to "full citizenship" for African Americans, but Rachel was undeterred.

That December, less than two months after his death, she took over the presidency of the Jackie Robinson Construction Corporation, renamed it the Jackie Robinson Development Corporation, and oversaw the company's focus on providing housing for those with low to moderate incomes.[6] In May of 1973, with the assistance of several others and a gift of corporate sponsorship, she founded the Jackie Robinson Foundation (JRF), with a mission to honor his life and legacy and to continue his vision for advancement and equal opportunity, specifically the growth toward "full citizenship" that defined her husband's life work.

The JRF was founded to not only address the financial needs of minority students who aspired to attend college but to also guide them through the process of higher education. Rachel Robinson and the co-founders of the foundation recognized an achievement gap for minority students when it came to the pursuit of higher education. Years of economic and social discrimination had left many deserving students of color frequently unable to take advantage of these opportunities to the same extent as their White counterparts. If full equality was ever to be achieved, educational opportunity was deemed to be a key component. However, the founders astutely realized that opportunity – admission to a college or university – was but the first step toward achieving academic success. Unequal access to educational opportunity had meant a historical inequality in the kinds of experience that would contribute to the development of the kinds of skills needed to not only survive in the higher-education environment, but to thrive. Consequently, JRF provides an extensive curriculum for its "JRF Scholars," titled "42 Strategies for Success," focused not only on active support to achieve academic success but on the development and enrichment of character, responsibility, and citizenship. A sampling of curriculum topics – Navigating Campus Resources, Time Management, Money Matters 101, Health and Wellness, How to Interview, Résumé Writing, Social Etiquette, Career Discernment – reveals the broad scope of information that is provided and the skill development that is expected. Attention is also paid to professional dress and behavior. And as JRF board chairman Gregg Gonsalves emphatically states: "We make sure every scholar passes."[7]

Good citizenship is introduced and developed as all scholars must participate in community service, helping to instill a sense of sense of belonging to something greater than oneself and a pay-it-forward mentality. This commitment is described by Ashley Kyalawzi, a 2018 graduate as a JRF scholar: "Jackie's legacy challenges each and every one of us actively to do what we can with whatever resources we have, big or small, and to use our own voices to really lift up other people in tough times."[8]

And finally, the curriculum includes extensive exposure to Black success. Reginald Livingston, Class of 1996, described the environment he walked into at one of the foundation's annual weekend conferences: "Here are actual doctors we can talk to, actual lawyers we can talk to."[9] Years later, there is still a sense of wonder and amazement in his voice as he describes the experience. Jermain Robertson, '17, echoes that wonder: "To be able to walk into the room with so (many) people who are striving to be excellent, (to be) literally drowning in Black excellence."[10] The exposure to role models of success and the ensuing advice, mentoring, and networking opportunities serve to excite and further motivate JRF scholars, and they can begin to see what is possible. As stated by JRF's CEO and president, Della Britton Baiza, education is the initial goal, "[B]ut what's more, JRF scholars become self-actualized, they go on to become leaders in their field and in the community."[11]

The first step, as is the initial step in most social endeavors, is financial and it begins with the awarding of a scholarship. JRF advances higher-education opportunities by providing generous multiyear scholarship awards to deserving minority students. The JRF scholarship is awarded to outstanding high-school graduates who plan to earn a bachelor's degree from an accredited four-year college or university. The selection process is a national one and the JFR Scholars who are selected receive a grant of up to $28,000 over four years to assist with the cost of the college of their choice, complementing the financial aid they receive from the college. In addition, they are enrolled in the foundation's comprehensive mentoring program, 42 Strategies for Success.

To again emphasize, 42 Strategies at its core is an experiential, hands-on program of support and encouragement. JRF staff, volunteer Scholar Advisory Committee members, corporate and university partners, community leaders, JRF alumni, and volunteer staff that comprise the Scholar Advisory Committee combine to provide academic, professional, and practical life mentoring to JRF Scholars on an individualized, year-round basis. JRF sponsors and institutional partners offer valuable career opportunities to JRF Scholars, providing internships, permanent employment and exposure to a rich network of professionals. The JRF staff works on a customized basis with corporations, community leaders, government agencies, and other employers to identify "good fit" job opportunities and to prepare JRF Scholars to become leaders in a global economy. In recent years JRF scholars have received over 275 internships and full-time jobs at companies like General Electric, Nike, Coca-Cola, Boeing, Bloomberg, Unilever, and the United Health Foundation.[12] Noteworthy examples of scholar opportunity include Jermaine Medley, '17, who after interning at Boeing accepted an offer as a structural engineer, and Chelsea Miller, '18, who spent a semester interning at the White House, learning about the criminal justice system.[13]

The mentoring program consists of a number of specific components, all designed to help support not only ongoing academic success but to prepare for a rewarding career. In addition to the scholarship award, funding is also provided for students to attend JRF's annual four-day Mentoring and Leadership Conference, a key component of the foundation's curriculum.

Originally called the Scholars' Networking Weekend, the first such conference took place at the Robinson home in 1983. It has expanded to an annual four-day event held in New York City each spring, hosted for all JRF Scholars. It is held in conjunction with JRF's annual alumni reunion, providing the opportunity for important mentor and networking interaction between scholars and alumni. Students participate in workshops focused on career exploration, leadership development and practical life skills. They will network with corporate executives, dozens of community leaders, and government officials. This engagement is further enhanced through cultural, recreational, and community service outings. At the 2019 weekend, scholars participated in the Rise Against Hunger Project and listened to Lauren Underwood trace her path from a JRF Scholar at the University of Michigan to an advisory role at the White House to her current position as a congresswoman from Illinois.[14]

The Mentoring and Leadership Conference is a highlight of JRF's year-round mentoring efforts and culminates in scholars attending the foundation's annual Robie Awards Dinner, an event that pays tribute to individuals who embody the humanitarian ideals of Jackie Robinson, while also serving as a fundraiser for the JRF. The first recipients of the award, in spring 1979, were Arthur Ashe and Ralph Ward, the latter the chairman of the board of Chesebrough-Pond Inc. (now part of Unilever), the first corporate sponsor of JRF from its very inception in 1973. In 1989 Ward established the Ralph E. Ward Achievement Award, which he gave annually to recognize the graduating JRF Scholar with the highest cumulative grade-point average. The Robie Awards have since gone on to recognize many of the most celebrated names in business, politics, education, media, sports, and the arts. Recipients have included Henry Aaron, Clive Davis, J.W. Marriott, George Lucas, Bishop Desmond Tutu, Michael Jordan, Stevie Wonder, Robert Manfred, and Maverick Carter, all of whom have in some way contributed to the promotion of social justice and human dignity and shared their success with underserved communities.

The four-day MLC conference is not a standalone event, as smaller, regional gatherings and events are held throughout the year. These events include webinars and on-site workshops focused on the development of effective study habits, practical life skills, strong character traits and leadership. Program topics include public speaking, time management, conflict resolution, personal financial management, professional and personal etiquette, and strategies to address stress and social challenges. JRF Scholars are afforded opportunities to practice and hone these skills through networking, participating in public events, engagement in national and local media, and other ambassadorial platforms facilitated by JRF. A primary example of this is the Point/Counterpoint activity that is included in the conference, in which teams of students engage in active debate. For those participating as well for those watching, it's an opportunity to engage and to model critical thinking, an important focus of the 42 Strategies.

JRF Scholars are required to perform community service throughout their JRF experience and they are held accountable for it, an important character trait of focus and emphasis throughout the curriculum. Students must document the specifics of their work and keep all accounts on file with JRF staff. In addition to establishing their accountability, students gain practical skills that enhance their self-confidence and self-esteem and in turn impact the lives of the many others who benefit from their community-based projects. JRF Scholars contribute over 4,500 hours of community service annually.[15] The vast majority of this service is of the grass-roots level, delivered locally within their home communities. Internet videos abound with displays of JRF Scholars sitting in elementary-school classrooms and working with young children. Others can be seen painting gymnasiums and restoring playgrounds. As is the case when reaching out to help others, the scholars always note that they are receiving as much as or more than they're providing. It's a lesson they carry with them in their subsequent careers.

Opportunities for JRF Scholars became international in 2008 with the establishment of the Rachel Robinson International Fellowship. Established to promote and support international service and study opportunities, it chooses students by a competitive process among JRF Scholars who apply, and they may use the grant for a variety of initiatives. Eligible examples include financial support for a study-abroad program, an international volunteer or philanthropic effort, or in conjunction with an approved internship or course of study abroad. To date, over 77 scholars have participated in more than 39 countries.[16] Examples include Jermaine Medley, '17, who built bathrooms in a rural village in Bolivia; Cinneah El-Amin, '16, who traveled to both Sao Paulo, Brazil, and Cape Town, South Africa, to explore the evolution of cities in the twenty-first century;[17] and Riley Jones IV, '16, who taught financial literacy to a rural village in Panama.[18] And in conjunction with the Me to We Foundation, JRF is engaging in a groundbreaking project called Project Tanzania, in which the entire graduating class of 2021will journey to that African country to volunteer in local Masai tribe communities. Part adventure, part giving back, it will be one more way that JRF scholars are realizing Rachel Robinson's vision in making an impact on lives around the world.[19]

In addition to the addition of international opportunity, JRF has expanded to include graduate education. The Extra Innings Fellowship was established to help highly motivated JRF Scholars fund the cost of advanced professional or graduate training. Through Extra Innings fellowships, JRF seeks to promote the study of a broad range of topics and disciplines that address communities in need both across the country and around the world. Extra Innings fellows receive multiyear gifts of up to $10,000 per year depending on need.

As of 2019, JRF has disbursed over $85 million in grants and direct program support to 1,500 students who have attended over 260 colleges and universities.[20] With the support of JRF's support and program curriculum, JRF Scholars have consistently achieved a 98 percent college graduation rate. JRF alumni are leaders in their communities and across a broad range of professional fields, true ambassadors of Jackie Robinson's legacy of service and humanitarianism.

The year 2019 marked the 100th anniversary of Jackie Robinson's birth and JRF was set to culminate a yearlong schedule of special events with a significant expansion of its mission of education and the Robinson legacy. The foundation had been preparing for the anniversary year by initiating two major additions to its programming. Project IMPACT was launched in 2018, a digital online service that could offer the 42 Strategies to a larger population of college students. And ground had been broken on April 27, 2017, on the foundation's crowning project, the Jackie Robinson Museum. Located in Lower Manhattan's burgeoning cultural district, just a few blocks from the World Trade Center and Freedom Tower, it will occupy the first two floors of the 16-story Hudson Square tower. It was initially scheduled to open in December 2019 as a way to culminate the yearlong celebration. Various delays, first in funding and construction and most recently the Covid virus pandemic, postponed the opening until sometime in 2021. In the absence of personal visitation, virtual experiences opened and are available at https://jrlegacy.org. Educational programming for elementary and middle-school students is offered and podcasts, specifically targeted toward teachers and parents, are also available. The general public has a number of options as well. Once the museum opened, Jackie Robinson's athletic career and his social impact was to be chronicled through artifacts, state-of-the-art exhibits, film, and other media, with an emphasis on interactive programming. In addition, the museum planned to partner with public schools to enrich curriculum, further functioning as a catalyst for social change. With a mission to "Educate, Inspire and Challenge, this physical tribute to Jackie Robinson will serve as a destination for those seeking innovative, educational programming and a venue for vibrant dialogue on critical social issues."[21] Its location is destined to become a dynamic venue for lectures, concerts, and receptions, all designed to provide a forum for interaction, dialogue, and debate.

*****

On the field and off, throughout his athletic career and his decades of subsequent public service and social activism, Jackie Robinson was a profile in courage. And on April 15, 1997, during a celebration honoring the 50th anniversary of his first regular-season game with the Brooklyn Dodgers, his widow, Rachel Robinson, took a moment to remember. Waiting with their daughter, Sharon, and son, Jesse, to be introduced to a sold-out crowd at Shea Stadium in New York City, Mike Lupica, a sportswriter covering the event for MLB.com, turned to her and asked what she most remembered best about her husband. "My husband was good," she replied, "and he was brave."[22]

Fast forward 23 years to April 15, 2020, and ballparks across the United States are dark. Within the midst of a growing viral pandemic, a wave of uncertainty and fear began to grow as well. Americans were being asked to be brave and for their behavior to make a difference in their communities. Robinson would be the captain of both of those teams. His life and his legacy are embodied in the mission of the Jackie Robinson Foundation, offering students the opportunity to practice his words carved on his gravestone: "A life is not important except in the impact it has on other lives." Years after leaving college with a view of the futility of education for African American advancement, the foundation in his name provides a beacon of promise and hope through education that he felt was unrealistic in his own time. The Jackie Robinson Foundation serves to honor the ideal that one life can make a difference and the life of Jackie Robinson is that example: A pretty good baseball player who embraced and embodied ideals well beyond the confines of a sport and devoted his life to making a difference.

To contact the Jackie Robinson Foundation and learn more about its work, visit https://jackierobinson.org.

NOTES

1. Jackie Robinson, *I Never Had It Made* (New York: HarperCollins, 1995), 11.
2. Paul Zimmerman, "Jackie Robinson: Big Threat on U.C.L.A. Football Eleven," *Los Angeles Times*, August 27, 1939: A15.
3. https:/www./brooklyndodgermemories.com/pete-hamill-on-ebbets-field-t900.html.
4. https:/www.thejackierobinsonproject42.weebly.com/leadership.html.
5. https://jackierobinson.org
6. https://youtube.com/watch?v=MKZNcCbQ-4s.
7. https://www.youtube.com/watch?v=NOmOsh-Aryk.
8. https://www.youtube.com/watch?v=NOmOsh-Aryk.
9. https://www.youtube.com/watch?v=NOmOsh-Aryk.
10. https://www.youtube.com/watch?v=NOmOsh-Aryk.
11. https://www.jackierobinson.org/our-programs/jrf-effect.
12. https://www.jackierobinson.org/about/sponsors.
13. https://www.youtube.com/watch?v=xfQGj5h6tzk.
14. https://jackierobinson.org.
15. https://www.jackierobinson.org/our-programs/jrf-effect.
16. https://www.youtube.com/watch?v=NOmOsh-Aryk.
17. https://www.youtube.com/watch?v=NOmOsh-Aryk.
18. https://www.youtube.com/watch?v=MKZNcCbQ-4s.
19. https://www.jackierobinson.org/category/rrif/?page=1.
20. https://www.jackierobinson.org/museum.
21. https://www.jackierobinson.org/museum.
22. Mike Lupica, "The Consummate Captain of Braveness," MLB.com, April 14, 2020. https://www.mlb.com/news/jackie-robinson-braveness-still-holds-true.

Brooklyn Dodgers Jackie Robinson batting in game in Chicago Wrigley Field, c. 1948.

Courtesy of the National Baseball Hall of Fame Library.

CONTRIBUTORS

JACK ANDERSON is an Urban Planning graduate of Concordia and McGill Universities in Montreal, and has worked in the construction supply manufacturing business for 40 years. He has written articles for local and regional historical societies and is a lifelong baseball aficionado, having grown up a fan of first the Montreal Royals, and then the Montreal Expos. He is an active member of SABR in Quebec, and has a longtime franchise, the Montreal Royals, in the Diamond Mind Historical Baseball simulation league, the Hall of Fame league. He and his wife, Maureen, expect to complete their pilgrimage to every major-league park within the next two years, and then intend to start on the minor-league parks. The Andersons live in Montreal.

GARY BELLEVILLE is a retired information technology professional living in Victoria, British Columbia. He has written articles for SABR's *Baseball Research Journal,* the Games Project, and the Baseball Biography Project, in addition to contributing to several SABR books. Gary grew up in Ottawa, Ontario, and graduated from the University of Waterloo with a Bachelor of Mathematics (Computer Science) degree. He patiently awaits the return of his beloved Montreal Expos.

NATHAN BIERMA is president of SABR Southern Michigan. He lives in Grand Rapids, Michigan. His writing has appeared in the *Chicago Tribune, Chicago Sports Review,* and the *Detroit Free Press,* and in SABR's recent books on the greatest games at Wrigley Field and Comiskey Park. He is the author of *The Eclectic Encyclopedia of English: Language at Its Most Enigmatic, Ephemeral, and Egregious.* His website is www.nathanbierma.com.

DAVE BOHMER, a Cleveland native, remains an avid fan of his hometown team. He taught baseball history for over a decade at DePauw University, his alma mater, where he became interested in Ford Frick after learning he was also an alum. He has been a SABR member since 2007.

CÉSAR BRIOSO is a digital producer and former baseball editor for *USA Today Sports*. In more than 30 years as a sports journalist, he also has written for the *Miami Herald* and the *South Florida Sun-Sentinel*. He is author of *Havana Hardball: Spring Training, Jackie Robinson and the Cuban League,* and *Last Seasons in Havana: The Castro Revolution and the End of Professional Baseball in Cuba,* winner of the 2020 SABR Baseball Research Award.

THOMAS J. BROWN JR. is a lifelong Mets fan who became a Durham Bulls fan after moving to North Carolina in the early 1980s. He was a national board-certified high-school science teacher for 34 years. Tom still volunteers with ELL students, serving as a mentor to those students while they are in school as well as after graduation. He is also a resource for ELL teachers in the local school system. Tom has been a member of SABR since 1995 after learning about the organization during a visit to Cooperstown on his honeymoon. He became active in the organization after his retirement and has written numerous biographies and game stories, mostly about the New York Mets. Tom also enjoys traveling as much as possible with his wife and has visited major-league and minor-league baseball parks across the country on their trips. He loves to cook, making the meals for his family as well as writing about the recipes that he cooks on his blog, Cooking and My Family.

DR. JOHN J. BURBRIDGE JR. is currently professor emeritus at Elon University, where he was both a dean and professor. He is also an adjunct at York College of Pennsylvania. While at Elon he introduced and taught *Baseball and Statistics*. He has authored several SABR publications and presented at SABR Conventions, NINE, and the Seymour meetings. He is a lifelong New York Giants baseball fan. The greatest Giants-Dodgers game he attended was a 1-0 Giants victory in Jersey City in 1956. Yes, the Dodgers did play in Jersey City in 1956 and 1957. John can be reached at burbridg@elon.edu.

FREDERICK C. "RICK" BUSH has written articles for numerous SABR books as well as for the Biography and Games Project websites. Together with Bill Nowlin, he has co-edited three SABR books about the Negro Leagues: *Bittersweet Goodbye* (1948 Birmingham Black Barons and Homestead Grays), *The Newark Eagles Take Flight* (1946 Newark team), and *Pride of Smoketown* (1935 Pittsburgh Crawfords). Rick and Bill are currently collaborating on two additional SABR volumes, about the 1942 Kansas City Monarchs (for 2021) and the 1920 Chicago American Giants (for 2022). Rick lives with his wife, Michelle, their three sons – Michael, Andrew, and Daniel – and their border collie mix, Bailey, in Cypress, Texas, northwest of Houston. Rick has been an educator for over 25 years and is in his 17th year of teaching English at Wharton County Junior College's satellite campus in Sugar Land.

RALPH CARHART is the head of the Society for American Baseball Research's 19th Century Baseball Gravemarker Project. He is the recipient of the SABR Nineteenth Century Committee's 2015 Chairman's Award and the Baseball Reliquary's 2019 Hilda Award. His historical interests include baseball's pioneer days, the Negro Leagues, the Hall of Fame, Brooklyn, and Cuba. He is the creator of The Hall Ball, an epic photo essay featuring pictures of (almost) all of the members of the Hall of Fame, living and deceased. His story was featured in the *New York Times* and on the *CBS Evening News*. His book *The Hall Ball: One Fan's Journey to Unite Cooperstown Immortals with a Single Baseball*, was published by McFarland & Company in June 2020. Inspired by working on this volume in your hands, he is currently editing a new book for SABR on Jackie Robinson on page, stage, and screen, tentatively titled *Not an Easy Tale to Tell*. www.thehallball.com

JOSHUA M. CASPER is a journalist and author from Brooklyn, New York. A graduate of Hofstra University, he has returned to his passion, documenting the cross-section of history, culture, and sport. Mr. Casper, once a marketing and communication consultant, is published in the United States and abroad, writing about topics ranging from Prince of Wales to the Canyon of Heroes and, of course, Jackie Robinson. He is a passionate fan of the New York Mets and a SABR member, and his work can be found at https://joshuamcasper.wordpress.com.

ALAN COHEN has been a SABR member since 2010. He serves as vice president-treasurer of the Connecticut Smoky Joe Wood Chapter, is datacaster (MiLB First Pitch stringer) for the Hartford Yard Goats, the Double-A affiliate of the Colorado Rockies, and has been serving as head of SABR's fact-checking committee since December 13, 2020. His biographies, game stories, and essays have appeared in more than 50 SABR publications. Since his first *Baseball Research Journal* article appeared in 2013, Alan has continued to expand his research into the Hearst Sandlot Classic (1946-1965) from which 88 players advanced to the major leagues. He has four children and eight grandchildren and resides in Connecticut with his wife, Frances, their cats, Morty, Ava, and Zoe, and their dog, Buddy.

WARREN CORBETT is the author of *The Wizard of Waxahachie: Paul Richards and the End of Baseball as We Knew It*, as well as more than 100 SABR biographies and articles. He lives at Pawleys Island, South Carolina.

MARY E. COREY is an associate professor of American history and social studies education emerita at the State University of New York, Brockport. Her work combines scholarly interests in women's history and civil-rights history. She has published numerous articles and presented her research at the Organization of American Historians Annual Conferences, Researching New York Annual Conferences, the Annual Conferences of the Association for the Study of African American Life and History, and the Jerry Malloy Negro Leagues Conferences. Recent publications include the co-authored Faculty and Student editions of *Before Jackie: The Negro Leagues, Civil Rights, and the American Dream*. Individually, *United States History, Parts I and II*, for the National Center for Migrant Education. Her latest is *The Political Life and Times of Matilda Joslyn Gage*.

JOE COX has written or contributed to 10 sports books. His most recent solo offering, *A Fine Team Man: Jackie Robinson and the Lives He Touched*, was published by Lyons Press in 2019. Joe practices law and lives near Bowling Green, Kentucky, where he's looking forward to being able to return to rooting on the Class-A Bowling Green Hot Rods.

RICHARD CUICCHI joined SABR in 1983 and is an active member of the Schott-Pelican Chapter. Since his retirement as an information technology executive, Richard has authored *Family Ties: A Comprehensive Collection of Facts and Trivia about Baseball's Relatives*. He has contributed to numerous SABR BioProject and Games publications. He does freelance writing and blogging about a variety of baseball topics on his website, TheTenthInning.com. Richard lives in New Orleans with his wife, Mary.

PAUL E. DOUTRICH is professor emeritus at York College of Pennsylvania, where he taught American history for 30 years. He now lives in Brewster, Massachusetts. Among the courses he taught was a one entitled "Baseball History." He has written scholarly articles and contributed to several anthologies about the Revolutionary era, and has written a book about Jacksonian America. He has also curated several museum exhibits. His recent scholarship has focused on baseball history. He has contributed numerous manuscripts to various SABR publications and is the author of *The Cardinals and the Yankees, 1926: A Classical Season and St. Louis in Seven*.

PETER DREIER is the E.P. Clapp Distinguished Professor of Politics and founding chair of the Urban & Environmental Policy Department at Occidental College. He has written or coauthored five books, including *The 100 Greatest Americans of the 20th Century: A Social Justice Hall of Fame* (Nation Books), *Place Matters: Metropolitics for the 21st Century* (University Press of Kansas), and *We Own the Future: Democratic Socialism, American Style* (The New Press). His next book, coauthored with Robert Elias, *Baseball Rebels: The Reformers and Radicals Who Shook Up the Game and Changed America*, will be published in 2022. He writes for the *Los Angeles Times*, *American Prospect*, *The Nation*, *Talking Points Memo*, and other publications, mostly about politics but occasionally about baseball. *He has written profiles of pitchers Sam Nahem and Joe Black for the SABR Biography Project.*

ERIC ENDERS is a freelance writer, editor, and former research librarian at the National Baseball Hall of Fame Library in Cooperstown. He is the author of a dozen books, including *Ballparks: A Journey Through the Fields of the Past, Present, and Future* and *Mexican-American Baseball in El Paso*. His writing on baseball has also appeared in the *New York Times*, MLB's World Series programs, and numerous SABR publications. A native of El Paso, Texas, he was inducted into the El Paso Baseball Hall of Fame in 2016.

JEFF ENGLISH is a graduate of Florida State University and a lifelong Chicago Cubs fan. He lives in Tallahassee, Florida, with his lovely wife, Allison, and their twin boys, Elliott and Oscar. He has contributed to multiple SABR books including *Mustaches and Mayhem: 1972-74 Oakland A's*, *The 1986 Boston Red Sox: There Was More Than Game Six*, and *A Pennant for the Twin Cities: The 1965 Minnesota Twins*.

A former archaeologist with a Ph.D. from Brown University, **ROB FITTS** left academia behind to follow his passion – Japanese Baseball. He is an award-winning author and speaker, and his articles have appeared in numerous magazines and websites. He is the author of seven books on Japanese baseball: *The Pioneers of Japanese American Baseball* (2021); *Issei Baseball: The Story of the First Japanese American Ballplayers* (2020); *An Illustrated Introduction to Japanese Baseball Cards* (2020); *Mashi: The Unfulfilled Baseball Dreams of Masanori Murakami, the First Japanese Major Leaguer* (2015); *Banzai Babe Ruth: Baseball, Espionage, & Assassination During the 1934 Tour of Japan* (2012); *Wally Yonamine: The Man Who Changed Japanese Baseball* (2008); and *Remembering Japanese Baseball: An Oral History of the Game* (2005). Fitts is the founder of the Society for American Baseball Research's Asian Baseball Committee. His honors include SABR's 2013 Seymour Medal for Best Baseball Book of 2012; the 2019 McFarland-SABR Baseball Research Award; the 2012 Doug Pappas Award; and the 2006 *Sporting News*-SABR Research Award. He has also been a finalist for the Casey Award for best baseball book of the year in both 2012 and 2020, and a silver medalist at the Independent Publish Book Awards. You can learn more about Rob's books and current projects at www.RobFitts.com.

BRIAN FRANK is passionate about documenting the history of major- and minor-league baseball. He is the creator of the website The Herd Chronicles (www.herdchronicles.com), which is dedicated to preserving the history of the Buffalo Bisons and professional baseball in Buffalo. His articles can also be read on the official website of the Bisons. He was an assistant editor of the book *The Seasons of Buffalo Baseball, 1857-2020*, and he's a frequent contributor to SABR publications. Brian and his wife, Jenny, enjoy traveling around the country in their camper to major- and minor-league ballparks and taking an annual trip to Europe. Brian was a history major at Canisius College, where he earned a bachelor of arts. He also received a Juris Doctor from the University at Buffalo School of Law.

VINCE GUERRIERI likes to think of himself as a sportswriter who's gone straight. He's spent more than 20 years in newspapers, and has bylines in publications like *Smithsonian*, *Mental Floss*, *Popular Mechanics*, *Deadspin*, and the *Hardball Times*. He's the author of two books on sports history.

MARK HARNISCHFEGER is a longtime Pittsburgh Pirates fan who resides in Rochester, New York. As the published author of two books and several related articles about Negro League baseball and civil rights, he has presented at numerous national and regional conferences and events. He holds a master's degree in education from the SUNY College at Brockport with certifications in Social Studies (5-12) and Inclusive Education (7-12.) He has taught in the Rochester City School District and several surrounding districts after a three-decade career in community mental health, and currently works in admissions at the University of Tampa.

LESLIE HEAPHY is an associate professor of history at Kent State University at Stark. She is the author and/or editor of a number of books, book chapters, and articles on the Negro Leagues, women's baseball, and the New York Mets. She is currently serving as SABR's vice president and as a board member for the IWBC (International Women's Baseball Center).

PAUL HOFMANN, a SABR member since 2002, is the associate vice president for international affairs at Sacramento State University and a frequent contributor to SABR publications. Paul is a native of Detroit and a lifelong Tigers fan. He currently resides in Folsom, California.

MIKE HUBER is professor of mathematics at Muhlenberg College in Allentown, Pennsylvania. Part of his research involves studying rare events in baseball, to include games in which a batter hits for the cycle. Mike joined SABR in 1996, and he enjoys writing for SABR's Games Project. One of his first articles on hitting for the cycle for the Games Project described Jackie Robinson's reverse natural cycle against the Cardinals, and that article is included in this book. Since then, he has chronicled more than 120 games involving the rare cycle.

DAVID KRELL is the chair of SABR's Elysian Fields Chapter in Northern New Jersey and the Spring Training Research Committee. He wrote *1962: Baseball and America in the Time of JFK* and *Our Bums: The Brooklyn Dodgers in History, Memory and Popular Culture*. SABR twice granted him honorable mention for the Ron Gabriel Award. Additionally, David edited the anthologies *The New York Mets in Popular Culture* and *The New York Yankees in Popular Culture*. He often contributes to SABR's Games Project, Biography Project, and Ballparks Project in addition to speaking at SABR conferences and the Cooperstown Symposium on Baseball and American Culture.

A lifelong Tigers fan, **STEVEN KUEHL** was born in Michigan's Upper Peninsula, but now resides in Wisconsin with his wife, Kathleen, and son, Connor. A regulatory analyst at Acuity Insurance, he has been published in the *Baseball Research Journal* and has also worked on a number of SABR publications, most recently including *Harvey's Wallbangers: The 1982 Milwaukee Brewers* and *Kansas City Royals: A Royal Tradition*.

CHRIS LAMB is chair of the journalism and public-relations department at Indiana University-Indianapolis. He is the author of 11 books, including *Blackout: The Untold Story of Jackie Robinson's First Spring Training*; *Conspiracy of Silence: Sportswriters and the Long Campaign to Desegregate Baseball*; *Jackie Robinson: A Spiritual Biography*; and, most recently, *Sports Journalism: A History of Glory, Fame, and Technology*.

For over 20 years, **KEVIN LARKIN** patrolled the highways and byways of the roads in his home town of Great Barrington, Massachusetts. When not at work keeping the citizens of his hometown safe, inevitably Larkin was listening to a baseball game on the radio. He has been going to baseball games since he was five years old. His baseball life is the only thing he loves more than his children and grandchildren. One day while he was browsing through the local bookstore, the owner of the bookstore asked him if he was interested in writing a book about baseball. Larkin's first effort was *Baseball in the Bay State: A History of Baseball in Massachusetts*. He then took quite an interest in the history of the game, authoring a book on one of his heroes, Lou Gehrig, called *Gehrig: Game by Game*, a look at every game the Iron Horse played during his major-league career. He has since written three more books on the sport and has two more due out. He also writes and fact-checks for SABR, an experience he considers the best decision he has ever made. According to Larkin, writing about baseball is a great way to keep the memory of the sport alive and he will continue to delve into sports history with more to come.

BOB LEMOINE is a librarian and adjunct professor in New Hampshire. A lifelong Red Sox fan, Bob has contributed to several SABR projects and was co-editor of two SABR books: *Boston's First Nine: the 1871-75 Boston Red Stockings*, and *The Glorious Beaneaters of the 1890s*.

LARRY LESTER is co-founder of the Negro Leagues Baseball Museum and serves as chairman of SABR's Negro League Research Committee. Since 1998 he has chaired the annual Jerry Malloy Negro League Conference, the only scholarly symposium devoted exclusively to Black Baseball. Lester is the recipient of SABR's Bob Davids Award (2017) and Henry Chadwick Award (2016). He is a listed contributor to more than 215 books on sports history. Lester has authored or edited 12 books. They are available on Amazon at https://tinyurl.com/ycbv67n3. Lester lives in Raytown, Missouri.

LEN LEVIN is a longtime newspaper editor in New England, now retired. He lives in Providence with his wife, Linda, and an overachieving orange cat. He now (Len, not the cat) is the grammarian for the Rhode Island Supreme Court and edits its decisions. He also copyedits many SABR books, including this one. He is just down the interstate from Fenway Park, where he has spent many happy hours.

ANDY MCCUE is the author of *Mover and Shaker: Walter O'Malley, the Dodgers and Baseball's Westward Expansion*, winner of the Seymour Medal as the best book of baseball history or biography for 2014. He is a former president of SABR and a winner of the Bob Davids Award. His next book, *Mis-Management 101: Integration, Expansion, and the Growing Irrelevance of the American League*, is due out in 2022.

ROBERT NASH, a SABR member since 1992, is a retired special collections librarian and professor emeritus at the University of Nebraska at Omaha. He was a contributor to *Kansas City Royals: A Royal Tradition* (SABR, 2019) and *Rosenblatt Stadium: Essays and Memories of Omaha's Historic Ballpark, 1948-2012* (McFarland, 2020).

BILL NOWLIN wishes the Red Sox had signed Jackie Robinson when they could have back in 1945. Born in Boston that very year, he has been a Red Sox fan since he can remember. He has been active with SABR since helping host the Boston convention in 2002 and on the board of directors since 2004. As a volunteer with SABR, he has helped edit several dozen books and over 1,000 research articles.

RICHARD J. PUERZER is an associate professor and chairperson of the Department of Engineering at Hofstra University. His writings on baseball have appeared in: *Bittersweet Goodbye: The Black Barons, The Grays, and the 1948 Negro League World Series; Pride of Smoketown: The 1935 Pittsburgh Crawfords;* and *The Negro Leagues Were Major Leagues,* and the journals: *Black Ball; Nine: A Journal of Baseball History and Culture; The National Pastime; The Cooperstown Symposium on Baseball and American Culture* proceedings; *Zisk;* and *Spitball*.

CARL RIECHERS retired from United Parcel Service in 2012 after 35 years of service. With more free time, he became a SABR member that same year. Born and raised in the suburbs of St. Louis, he became a big fan of the Cardinals. He and his wife, Janet, have three children and he is the proud grandpa of two.

PAUL ROGERS is a law professor at the Dedman School of Law at Southern Methodist University, where he served as dean for nine years. In addition, he has served as SMU's faculty athletic representative for 34 years. He has co-authored four baseball books, including two with his boyhood hero Robin Roberts, who had great admiration for Jackie Robinson from their battles in the late 1940s and the 1950s. Rogers has also co-edited two SABR team histories: *The Team That Time Won't Forget – the 1951 New York Giants* and *The Whiz Kids Take the Pennant – the 1950*

Philadelphia Phillies – as well as frequently contributing to the SABR BioProject and Games project. He is the president of the Ernie Banks-Bobby Bragan DFW SABR Chapter.

BLAKE W. SHERRY is a lifelong Pittsburgh Pirates fan who resides in Dublin, Ohio. A retired chief operations officer of a public retirement system, he has been a member of SABR since 1997. He co-leads the Hank Gowdy SABR Chapter in Central Ohio, and currently runs that chapter's quarterly baseball book club. He contributed to several previous SABR books, including *Moments of Joy and Heartbreak: 66 Significant Episodes in the History of the Pittsburgh Pirates*.

MARK SIMON is a senior research analyst and content coordinator for Sports Info Solutions. He previously worked as a sportswriter at the *Trenton Times* and then for nearly 16 years as a researcher for ESPN Stats & Information (including a long stint as the head researcher for *Baseball Tonight*). He has previously contributed to SABR books on the 1964 Cardinals, 1969 Mets, 1986 Mets, and the greatest games in Expos history. He considers January 31, the birthdate of Jackie Robinson, Nolan Ryan, and Ernie Banks (among many), as the best baseball birthday of all time.

WAYNE SOINI co-authored *Judge Fuchs and the Boston Braves, 1923-35* with Robert S. Fuchs, (McFarland & Co., 1998). He also contributed to the recent SABR book *The Babe* (SABR, 2019). Soini is a longtime member of and occasional speaker at meetings of the Boston Braves Historical Association. McFarland has accepted, for publication in 2021, Soini's biography of Boston-born radio legend Norman Corwin, entitled *Norman Corwin: His Early Life and Radio Career, 1910-1950*. Soini, who holds a master's degree in history from the University of Massachusetts Boston and a Juris Doctor from Suffolk University, recently retired after working over 30 years for labor unions.

GLEN SPARKS has contributed to several SABR books and is completing a biography of Hall of Fame shortstop Pee Wee Reese for McFarland & Co. He has a journalism degree from the University of Missouri.

LYLE SPATZ has been a SABR member since 1973. He was the chairman of SABR's Records Committee from 1991 through 2016.

MARC STEINER is a lifelong baseball fan who resides in Renton, Washington. He is a senior director of sales in the wine and spirits industry and has been a member of the Northwest Chapter of SABR for almost two years. His primary baseball interests are the Negro Leagues, the Brooklyn/Los Angeles Dodgers, and the Seattle Mariners. He also is president of the Pony Baseball League in Renton and is also actively involved in coaching youth baseball in his local community.

MARK S. STERNMAN had the good fortune to attend the 1999 All-Star Game at Fenway Park and to profile Jackie Robinson's predecessor Bonnie Serrell for a forthcoming SABR book on the 1942 Kansas City Monarchs. A fan of the New York Yankees who grew up in New York before settling in Boston, Sternman dedicates this article to his father, who stayed in the Empire State and as a child rooted for Robinson and his Brooklyn Dodgers.

BRYAN STEVERSON is a baseball fan dating back to the Class-B Piedmont League of the late 1940s. He is the author of three books: *Amazing Baseball Heroes, Inspirational Negro League Stories* (2011); *Baseball, A Special Gift from God* (2014); and *Baseball's Brotherhood Team* (2018), and has contributed to other edited works on the game. He is a 1964 engineering graduate from Virginia Tech with postgraduate studies at the University of Minnesota and Cal. Poly in Pomona. A retired chief metallurgist in a Fortune 500 Corporation, Bryan and his wife, Barbara, have five children and nine grandchildren. They currently reside in Venice, Florida, spring-training home of the Atlanta Braves.

RICK SWAINE is a baseball historian and longtime SABR member. Born and raised In Miami and a graduate of Florida State University, he is a retired CPA who resides in the Tallahassee area and is a collector of vintage baseball cards and memorabilia. He still coaches and plays in adult baseball leagues and tournaments. Rick specializes in writing about baseball's unsung heroes. He has authored four full-length books on baseball history and a historical fiction, *Do It for Chappie: The Ray Chapman Tragedy*. He is a contributor to *The National Pastime*, the *Baseball Research Journal*, BioProject, and several other SABR publications, and is currently working on a book about the integration of the minor leagues.

PERSPECTIVES ON 42

BOB WEBSTER grew up in northwest Indiana and has been a Cubs fan since 1963. Now living in Portland, Oregon, Bob spends his time working on baseball research and writing and is a contributor to quite a few SABR projects. He worked as a stats stringer on the MLB Gameday app for three years, is a member of the Pacific Northwest Chapter of SABR, and is on the board of directors of the Old-Timers Baseball Association of Portland.

STEVEN C. WEINER, a SABR member since 2015, is a retired chemical engineer and a lifelong baseball fan starting with the Brooklyn Dodgers of the 1950s. During his undergraduate years at Rutgers University, Steven worked in the sports information office and broadcast baseball and basketball play-by-play on WRSU radio. Steven obtained his doctoral degree in engineering and applied science from Yale University and has been a contributor to the technical literature on hydrogen and fuel cell safety. Steven currently serves as assignments editor for the SABR Games Project with essay contributions in four SABR books, *Moments of Joy and Heartbreak*; *Met-rospectives*; *The Base Ball Palace of the World: Comiskey Park*; and *Baseball's Biggest Blowout Games*. He volunteers as an in-classroom and virtual teacher at local schools.

STEVEN K. WISENSALE is professor emeritus of public policy at the University of Connecticut, where he taught a very popular course, "Baseball and Society: Politics, Economics, Race, and Gender." In 2017 he went to Japan as a Fulbright scholar and taught another baseball course, "Baseball Diplomacy in Japan-U.S. Relations." A longtime member of SABR, Steve has been both a frequent attendee and an occasional presenter at the Cooperstown Symposium on Baseball and American Culture. An avid Orioles fan, he resides in Essex, Connecticut, with his wife, Nan, and their two dogs, Song and Blue Moon, both of whom have been invited to the 2021 Arizona Fall League.

GREGORY H. WOLF was born in Pittsburgh but now resides in the Chicagoland area with his wife, Margaret, and daughter, Gabriela. A professor of German studies and holder of the Dennis and Jean Bauman Endowed Chair in the Humanities at North Central College in Naperville, Illinois, he has edited a dozen books for SABR. He is currently working on projects about Shibe Park in Philadelphia and Ebbets Field in Brooklyn. Since January 2017 he has been co-director of SABR's BioProject, which you can follow on Facebook and Twitter.

BRIAN WRIGHT has authored two books on the New York Mets: *Mets in 10s: Best and Worst of an Amazin' History*, which was released in April 2018 from The History Press, and *The New York Mets All-Time All-Stars*, which came out in February 2020 from Lyons Press. He currently serves as a historian for Metsmerized Online, contributing weekly features on notable Mets moments and players. He was managing editor for *Met-rospectives*, a publication from the Society for American Baseball Research chronicling the greatest games in franchise history, and has contributed to other books, including the most memorable moments at Wrigley Field, Comiskey Park, and for the San Diego Padres.

WILLIAM A. YOUNG is professor emeritus of religious studies at Westminster College in Fulton, Missouri. He is the author of several books on the world's religions and, in retirement, two books on the history of baseball: *John Tortes "Chief" Meyers: A Baseball Biography* (McFarland, 2012) and *J.L. Wilkinson and the Kansas City Monarchs: Trailblazers in Black Baseball* (McFarland, 2016). For the second book he received a SABR Research Award in 2018. He is a SABR member and resides, with his wife, Sue, in Columbia, Missouri.

SABR Books on the Negro Leagues and Black Baseball

From Rube to Robinson: SABR's Best Articles on Black Baseball

From Rube to Robinson brings together the best Negro League baseball scholarship that the Society of American Baseball Research (SABR) has ever produced, culled from its journals, Biography Project, and award-winning essays. The book includes a star-studded list of scholars and historians, from the late Jerry Malloy and Jules Tygiel, to award winners Larry Lester, Geri Strecker, and Jeremy Beer, and a host of other talented writers. The essays cover topics ranging over nearly a century, from 1866 and the earliest known Black baseball championship, to 1962 and the end of the Negro American League.

Edited by John Graf; Associate Editors Duke Goldman and Larry Lester
$24.95 paperback (ISBN 978-1-970159-41-7)
$9.99 ebook (ISBN 978-1-970159-40-0)
8.5"X11", 220 pages

Pride of Smoketown: The 1935 Pittsburgh Crawfords

The 1935 Pittsburgh Crawfords team, one of the dominant teams in Negro League history, is often compared to the legendary 1927 "Murderer's Row" New York Yankees. The squad from "Smoketown"—a nickname that the *Pittsburgh Courier* often applied to the metropolis better-known as "Steel City"—boasted four Hall-of-Fame players in outfielder James "Cool Papa" Bell, first baseman/manager Oscar Charleston, catcher Josh Gibson, and third baseman William "Judy" Johnson. This volume contains exhaustively-researched articles about the players, front office personnel, Greenlee Field, and the exciting games and history of the team that were written and edited by 25 SABR members. The inclusion of historical photos about every subject in the book helps to shine a spotlight on the 1935 Pittsburgh Crawfords, who truly were the Pride of Smoketown.

Edited by Frederick C. Bush and Bill Nowlin
$29.95 paperback (ISBN 978-1-970159-25-7)
$9.99 ebook (ISBN 978-1-970159-24-0)
8.5"X11", 340 pages, over 60 photos

The Newark Eagles Take Flight: The Story of the 1946 Negro League Champions

The Newark Eagles won only one Negro National League pennant during the franchise's 15-year tenure in the Garden State, but the 1946 squad that ran away with the NNL and then triumphed over the Kansas City Monarchs in a seven-game World Series was a team for the ages. The returning WWII veterans composed a veritable "Who's Who in the Negro Leagues" and included Leon Day, Larry Doby, Monte Irvin, and Max Manning, as well as numerous role players. Four of the Eagles' stars—Day, Doby, Irvin, and player/manager Raleigh "Biz" Mackey, as well as co-owner Effa Manley—have been enshrined in the National Baseball Hall of Fame in Cooperstown. In addition to biographies of the players, co-owners, and P.A. announcer, there are also articles about Newark's Ruppert Stadium, Leon Day's Opening Day no-hitter, a sensational midseason game, the season's two East-West All-Star Games, and the 1946 Negro League World Series between the Eagles and the renowned Kansas City Monarchs.

Edited by Frederick C. Bush and Bill Nowlin
$24.95 paperback (ISBN 978-1-970159-07-3)
$9.99 ebook (ISBN 978-1-970159-06-6)
8.5"X11", 228 pages, over 60 photos

Bittersweet Goodbye: The Black Barons, The Grays, and the 1948 Negro League World Series

This book was inspired by the last Negro League World Series ever played and presents biographies of the players on the two contending teams in 1948—the Birmingham Black Barons and the Homestead Grays—as well as the managers, the owners, and articles on the ballparks the teams called home. Also included are articles that recap the season's two East-West All-Star Games, the Negro National League and Negro American League playoff series, and the World Series itself. Additional context is provided in essays about the effects of baseball's integration on the Negro Leagues, the exodus of Negro League players to Canada, and the signing away of top Negro League players, specifically Willie Mays. Many of the players' lives and careers have been presented to a much greater extent than previously possible.

Edited by Frederick C. Bush and Bill Nowlin
$21.95 paperback (ISBN 978-1-943816-55-2)
$9.99 ebook (ISBN 978-1-943816-54-5)
8.5"X11", 442 pages, over 100 photos and images

Friends of SABR

You can become a Friend of SABR by giving as little as $10 per month or by making a one-time gift of $1,000 or more. When you do so, you will be inducted into a community of passionate baseball fans dedicated to supporting SABR's work.

Friends of SABR receive the following benefits:
- ✓ Annual Friends of SABR Commemorative Lapel Pin
- ✓ Recognition in This Week in SABR, SABR.org, and the SABR Annual Report
- ✓ Access to the SABR Annual Convention VIP donor event
- ✓ Invitations to exclusive Friends of SABR events

SABR On-Deck Circle - $10/month, $30/month, $50/month

Get in the SABR On-Deck Circle, and help SABR become the essential community for the world of baseball. Your support will build capacity around all things SABR, including publications, website content, podcast development, and community growth.

A monthly gift is deducted from your bank account or charged to a credit card until you tell us to stop. No more email, mail, or phone reminders.

  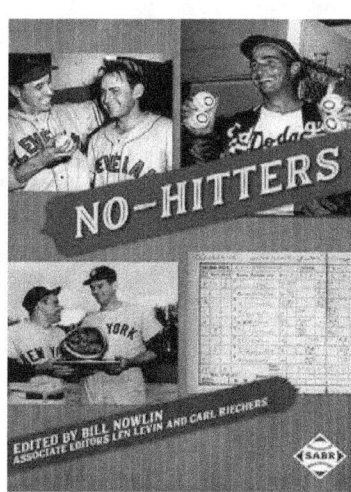

Join the SABR On-Deck Circle

Payment Info: _____ Visa _____ Mastercard

Name on Card: _____

Card #: _____

Exp. Date: _____ Security Code: _____

Signature: _____

○ $10/month

○ $30/month

○ $50/month

○ Other amount _____

Go to sabr.org/donate to make your gift online

Society for American Baseball Research
Cronkite School at ASU
555 N. Central Ave. #416, Phoenix, AZ 85004
602.496.1460 (phone)
SABR.org

Become a SABR member today!

If you're interested in baseball — writing about it, reading about it, talking about it — there's a place for you in the Society for American Baseball Research.

SABR memberships are available on annual, multi-year, or monthly subscription basis. Annual and monthly subscription memberships auto-renew for your convenience. Young Professional memberships are for ages 30 and under. Senior memberships are for ages 65 and older. Student memberships are available to currently enrolled middle/high school or full-time college/university students. Monthly subscription members receive SABR publications electronically and are eligible for SABR event discounts after 12 months.

Here's a list of some of the key benefits you'll receive as a SABR member:

- Receive two editions (spring and fall) of the *Baseball Research Journal*, our flagship publication
- Receive expanded e-book edition of *The National Pastime*, our annual convention journal
- 8-10 new e-books published by the SABR Digital Library, all FREE to members
- "This Week in SABR" e-newsletter, sent to members every Friday
- Join dozens of research committees, from Statistical Analysis to Women in Baseball.
- Join one of 70+ regional chapters in the U.S., Canada, Latin America, and abroad
- Participate in online discussion groups
- Ask and answer baseball research questions on the SABR-L e-mail listserv
- Complete archives of *The Sporting News* dating back to 1886 and other research resources
- Promote your research in "This Week in SABR"
- Diamond Dollars Case Competition
- Yoseloff Scholarships

- Discounts on SABR national conferences, including the SABR National Convention, the SABR Analytics Conference, Jerry Malloy Negro League Conference, Frederick Ivor-Campbell 19th Century Conference, and the Arizona Fall League Experience
- Publish your research in peer-reviewed SABR journals
- Collaborate with SABR researchers and experts
- Contribute to Baseball Biography Project or the SABR Games Project
- List your new book in the SABR Bookshelf
- Lead a SABR research committee or chapter
- Networking opportunities at SABR Analytics Conference
- Meet baseball authors and historians at SABR events and chapter meetings
- 50% discounts on paperback versions of SABR e-books
- Discounts with other partners in the baseball community
- SABR research awards

We hope you'll join the most passionate international community of baseball fans at SABR! Check us out online at SABR.org/join.

SABR MEMBERSHIP FORM

	Standard	Senior	Young Pro.	Student
Annual:	❑ $65	❑ $45	❑ $45	❑ $25
3 Year:	❑ $175	❑ $129	❑ $129	
5 Year:	❑ $249			
Monthly:	❑ $6.95	❑ $4.95	❑ $4.95	

(International members wishing to be mailed the Baseball Research Journal should add $10/yr for Canada/Mexico or $19/yr for overseas locations.)

Participate in Our Donor Program!
Support the preservation of baseball research. Designate your gift toward:
❑ General Fund ❑ Endowment Fund ❑ Research Resources ❑ _____
❑ I want to maximize the impact of my gift; do not send any donor premiums
❑ I would like this gift to remain anonymous.

Note: Any donation not designated will be placed in the General Fund.
SABR is a 501 (c) (3) not-for-profit organization & donations are tax-deductible to the extent allowed by law.

Name _____

E-mail* _____

Address _____

City _____ ST _____ ZIP _____

Phone _____ Birthday _____

* Your e-mail address on file ensures you will receive the most recent SABR news.

Dues $ _____
Donation $ _____
Amount Enclosed $ _____

Do you work for a matching grant corporation? Call (602) 496-1460 for details.

If you wish to pay by credit card, please contact the SABR office at (602) 496-1460 or sign up securely online at SABR.org/join. We accept Visa, Mastercard & Discover.

Do you wish to receive the *Baseball Research Journal* electronically? ❑ Yes ❑ No
Our e-books are available in PDF, Kindle, or EPUB (iBooks, iPad, Nook) formats.

Mail to: SABR, Cronkite School at ASU, 555 N. Central Ave. #416, Phoenix, AZ 85004

www.ingramcontent.com/pod-product-compliance
Lightning Source LLC
Chambersburg PA
CBHW081343070526
44578CB00005B/706